FINANCIAL ACCOUNTING

Principles and Issues

Second Canadian Edition

MICHAEL H. GRANOF
University of Texas

PHILIP W. BELL
Boston University

ROBERT C. MAHER
University of New Brunswick

Prentice Hall Canada Inc.
Scarborough, Ontario

To my students, past, present and future.

Canadian Cataloguing in Publication Data

Granof, Michael H.
        Financial accounting : principles and issues

2nd Canadian ed.
Includes index
ISBN 0-13-349911-1

I. Accounting. I. Bell, Philip W.
II. Maher, Robert C. (Robert Christopher), 1951-
III. Title.

HF5635.G724 1996   657   C95-931330-3

Prentice-Hall, Inc., Englewood Cliffs, New Jersey
Prentice-Hall International (UK) Limited, London
Prentice-Hall of Australia, Pty. Limited, Sydney
Prentice-Hall of Hispanoamericana, S.A., Mexico City
Prentice-Hall of India Private Limited, New Delhi
Prentice-Hall of Japan, Inc., Tokyo
Simon & Schuster Asia Private Limited, Singapore
Editora Prentice-Hall do Brasil, Ltda., Rio de Janeiro

ISBN 0-13-349911-1

ACQUISITIONS EDITOR: Pat Ferrier
DEVELOPMENTAL EDITOR: Dawn du Quesnay
COPY EDITOR: James Leahy
PRODUCTION EDITOR: Lisa Berland
PRODUCTION COORDINATOR: Sharon Houston
COVER DESIGN: Matthews Communications•Design
COVER IMAGE: G & V Chapman/The Image Bank
PAGE LAYOUT: Valerie Bateman/ArtPlus Limited

Original English Language edition published by Prentice-Hall, Inc., Englewood Cliffs, New Jersey Copyright © 1991

1 2 3 4 5 CC   00 99 98 97 96

Printed and bound in the United States

We welcome readers' comments, which can be sent by e-mail to
collegeinfo_pubcanada@prenhall.com

Contents

2

The Accounting Equation and the Three Fundamental Financial Statements 33

3

The Accounting Cycle   81

4

Accruing Revenues and Expenses   129

5 Measuring and Reporting Revenues   191

6 Valuation of Assets; Cash and Marketable Securities   231

7 Receivables and Payables   273

8 Inventories and Cost of Goods Sold   321

9 Long-Lived Assets and the Allocation of Their Costs 365

10 Liabilities and Related Expenses 419

11

Transactions between a Firm and Its Owners 477

12

Special Problems of Measuring and Reporting Dividends and Earnings 515

13 Intercorporate Investments and Earnings 555

14 Statement of Changes in Financial Position   607

15

Accounting for Changes in Prices   655

16

Financial Reporting and Analysis in Perspective   711

Appendix   751

Glossary   761

Index   777

Preface to the Second Canadian Edition

Financial Accounting: Principles and Issues, Second Canadian Edition, continues to place the emphasis on the user, rather than the preparer, of financial accounting information. This approach reflects our belief that a primary objective of a first course in accounting should be to enable students to ask the right questions, not necessarily to answer them. Our aim is to have the students understand that there is often more than one right way to report a financial transaction. Although we emphasize a user approach, it is important that the students understand the procedural aspects of the accounting cycle. This text will provide students with a solid grounding in both the accounting cycle and the principles of financial accounting as it is practiced today. In addition, however, we strive to assure readers that after studying the text they will be aware of some of the fundamental issues that face the accounting profession.

The text is designed to be used in an introductory course in accounting, at either the undergraduate or graduate level. The text has been successfully used in both one- and two-term introduction to financial accounting courses. In addition, because of the conceptual nature of the problems, it is well suited to students enrolled in professional accounting programs. The text has two principal audiences, those who will continue to study accounting and those who will take no additional courses in financial accounting. For the latter, the primary purpose of the text is to provide them with the necessary tools to interpret financial reports in their future roles as managers, investors, or other users of financial accounting information. We want these students to know how to derive the maximum amount of information from the financial statements and, at the same time, to be somewhat skeptical and able to make relevant enquiries about that information—how it was shaped and what its limitations might be. For those who will continue to study accounting, we hope that, in addition to teaching the basics of the discipline, this text will instill an attitude of challenging the status quo, responding creatively to changes in business practices and advancing our profession.

Features

The most distinctive feature of our text relative to competitors is its focus not only on the currently accepted accounting principles but on alternative possibilities as well. The text focuses primarily on the historical cost model and standards established by the Accounting Standards Board. However, when the historical cost model produces information that may not be the most relevant to the users, we look to other possible models to see if they might provide for better financial reporting. Moreover, we intentionally seek to convey a sense of accounting's controversies. There are many situations in which an answer is not clear, and we see this as an example of the profession's dynamism, richness, and intellectual vibrancy. To us, they are a positive feature of our profession, and one to which even students in a first course in accounting should be exposed. If a student is able to understand the controversy in a given situation, chances are the student will have a better grasp of the basic principles. In addition, reference to these controversies will help the student to understand that many of the problems in accounting are related—they are timing problems of one sort or another.

There is much to be said for restricting a first course in accounting to current practices and underlying theories. Many students have difficulty grasping even a single method of accounting for a complex economic event. Why then confuse them with one or more options? Our response is that for many students—particularly the more intellectually curious students—the extra effort that is required is more than offset by the numerous benefits. We can list the advantages:

- Seeing present practices in a context of possible alternatives prevents simple mechanistic acceptance of them and deepens one's understanding of them. It also leads to a recognition of the inherent inadequacies of present practice.
- Financial statements intended to facilitate one type of decision may be inappropriate for others. Managers must be aware of the statements' shortcomings and be able to compensate accordingly.
- Companies have considerable discretion over amounts reported in their financial statements. Analysts or other users of accounting information may have to adjust these statements to make the information comparable.
- Current accounting conventions are only as fixed as the membership on the present rule-making bodies. Managers and investors need the skills to evaluate the impact of proposed changes in accounting principles.

New to This Edition

The changes to the Canadian second edition are designed to build on the strengths of the first edition. Modifications have been made to sharpen the focus on the user, rather than the preparer, of financial accounting information. Specific changes are as follows:

- The introduction of the debit/credit terminology has been moved from the second chapter to the third chapter. This delay allows the student to focus more on the fundamentals of the accounting equation prior to the introduction of the debit/credit terminology. It is critically important that the student be able to grasp the impact of economic transactions and events on the accounting equation before learning the rules of debit and credit.

- An expanded discussion of debit/credit terminology in Chapter 3. This expanded discussion is intended to convince the students that there is nothing magical, no ultimate truth, when it comes to debits and credits. The use of debits and credits is governed by a set of rules, arbitrarily created. Taking away some of the mystique makes the recording process easier to understand.

- Chapter 5 has been extensively reworked to reduce the necessity of understanding complicated journal entries. The alternative points of revenue recognition are now explained by showing the impact on the income statement accounts (revenue, expense, net income) rather than by journal entry illustration. This allows the student to focus on what is most important, the impact on income of selecting among alternative revenue recognition points.

- Chapter 9, Long-Lived Assets and the Allocation of Their Costs, has been modified to reflect the new wording of the Capital Assets section of the *CICA Handbook*. The individual terms of *amortization, depreciation* and *depletion* have been changed to *amortization*. This change has also been made throughout the text. Although this change is being implemented only slowly in practice, the use of the new terminology in this text will help it become more widely accepted.

- A section on the preparation of statement of changes in financial position using the indirect method has been added to Chapter 14. This reflects the fact that the majority of companies in Canada report their statement of changes in financial position using the indirect basis.

- The problem material has been updated, where appropriate. Additional basic problem material has been added, especially in the earlier, more procedural chapters. The bulk of the problem material continues to focus on the issues raised rather than the record-keeping details. Many problems continue to be based on information from actual Canadian and U.S. company annual reports.

Organization

The text follows a logical sequence for a first course in financial accounting. The first five chapters are dedicated to the accounting cycle, showing how financial transactions or economic events are initially captured in the accounting system through to the results being reported in the periodic financial statements. Included in this examination of the accounting cycle is the description of accrual accounting, including a discussion of the issue of revenue and expense recognition. Although these chapters focus on introducing the student to the recording process, the effect of alternative accounting practices on income is displayed as early as the first chapter. This is done to show the student, right from the beginning, that accounting is necessarily based on estimates and assumptions and there is often no one right answer.

The next eight chapters focus on specific asset and liability accounts and their related expenses and revenues, as well as the owners' equity accounts. In these chapters, the current practices for the recording of transactions and economic events are discussed. In addition, alternative treatments are referred to where there are weaknesses uncovered in the present historical cost model. The Balance Sheet and Income Statement of Sun Ice Limited, a Canadian-based manufacturer of active wear, are introduced in Chapter Seven. The numbers from these statements are used to illustrate various financial ratios, which are introduced in Chapter Seven and subsequent chapters.

The final three chapters wrap up the introduction to financial accounting. Chapter 14 provides additional details for the preparation of the statement of changes in financial position, which was introduced in the first chapter. Chapter 15 provides a comprehensive discussion of accounting for changes in prices. This alternative accounting model is presented as a partial solution to some of the problems with the historical cost model that were identified in earlier chapters. The final chapter on financial statement analysis is intended to pull together the various financial ratios that were introduced in previous chapters and explain more fully how financial statements may be used to evaluate investment and credit decisions.

The text includes a glossary with definitions of the major accounting terms introduced in the text. We trust students will find it a useful reference and study aid.

Supplements

There are several supplements available to users of the text:

Solutions Manual: Contains complete solutions for all problem material.

Test Item File: Contains 800 questions on the text material. Available in computerized format as well.

Study Guide: Outlines key points presented in the text and provides additional illustrations, exercises and problems, less issue-oriented than the text, designed to provide additional practice in the fundamental accounting concepts. Many students will find it helpful, particularly for grasping the basics of the accounting cycle and the analysis and recording of specific economic events and transactions.

The Financial Post

Contemporary Views: The *Financial Post* and Prentice Hall Canada have joined together in an exclusive arrangement to produce a student edition of the *Financial Post*, tailored to students of accounting. Through this program, the core subject matter provided in the text is supplemented by a collection of specially chosen, time-sensitive articles from one of Canada's most distinguished business newspapers. these articles demonstrate the vital, ongoing connection between what is learned in the classroom and what is happening in Canada and the world around us, and are updated annually. This is a free supplement that comes shrinkwrapped to the text.

Robert C. Maher
1996

Acknowledgements to the Second Canadian Edition

I would like to thank the following individuals who reviewed the manuscript and provided many excellent comments, clarifications, and suggestions, many of which have been included in the text:

Martyne Boutot, CGA Canada; Judy Cumby, Memorial University; Ronald A. Davidson, Simon Fraser University; Ian Hutchinson, Mount Allison University; Shu-Lun Wong, Memorial University of Newfoundland; Shelley Donald; Christine Watt of Curtis, Diefenbacher;

I have learned much through the use of the first edition of this text. My students have shown me, by their comments and responses, where refinements were necessary. Many instructors who have used the first edition have also provided me with valuable feedback. To all of these users, I am deeply indebted.

I would again like to acknowledge the Canadian Institute of Chartered Accountants for the many references made to the *CICA Handbook*. The Bank of Montreal has once again kindly given permission to reproduce one of their promissory notes.

The editorial and production staff at Prentice Hall Canada, particularly Lisa Berland and Dawn du Quesnay, deserve much credit for keeping writing and production on schedule. Special thanks to Mike Ryan for his continued strong support of the book.

It would not be possible to write this book without the strong support of my employer and my family. The Faculty of Administration at the University of New Brunswick provides the opportunity and a supportive environment. Elin, Alexandra, and Tory Anne deserve most of the credit for the completion of this book. They give me the incentive to write and patiently understand the time that it takes away from them.

Robert C. Maher
Fredericton , New Brunswick
1996

1

Accounting: A Dynamic Discipline

Accounting involves the collection, summarization, and reporting of financial data. It is a dynamic discipline, one in which new principles and procedures are constantly evolving. In our modern society, it is exceedingly difficult to carry out even routine activities without at least a rudimentary knowledge of accounting.

This text is directed primarily at current and future managers and investors who will use accounting in their professional or business endeavours. Its aim is to provide such readers with the knowledge and skills to take full advantage of accounting reports, to make them aware not only of the wealth of information that financial reports contain but also of the limitations. Perhaps, too, the managers and investors we address will be sufficiently stimulated by the issues discussed in this text to consider accountancy as a career.

We live in an information age. To communicate information about business, we must use the language of business—accounting. This chapter will define accounting, distinguishing between financial and management accounting; examine the framework for financial reporting; introduce the accounting rule-making processes; and discuss the structure of the accounting profession in Canada.

After studying this chapter, you will be able to

- Distinguish between financial and management accounting
- Understand the principal qualities of accounting information

- Understand why the same economic event may be reported differently under the rules of accounting
- Describe the purpose of each of the three principal financial statements
- Describe the accounting standard-setting process in Canada and internationally
- Describe the three primary functions of public accountants
- Identify the major professional accounting organizations in Canada

WHAT IS ACCOUNTING?

Accounting is concerned with describing economic events, with measuring resources, and with determining periodic changes in those resources. Accounting measurements are almost always expressed in monetary units and pertain to economic organizations such as businesses, governments, or individuals. Accounting is a service function. It provides information that fulfills several broad objectives:

1. *Allocating the scarce resources of our society.* Under any form of economy, be it capitalism or socialism, decisions as to where capital should be invested are made on the basis of information contained in financial statements. In a free-enterprise system, private investors make determinations as to the shares of companies they purchase largely on the basis of data contained in periodic financial reports. Bankers and other suppliers of funds study financial reports before making loan decisions. Government departments use them in deciding whom to tax and whom to subsidize. The decisions of labour unions as to how much of a wage increase to seek are strongly influenced by reports of profit or loss.

2. *Managing and directing the resources within an organization.* Managers of profit and nonprofit entities alike rely upon accounting information to assure that they maintain effective control over both their human and material resources and that they allocate such resources to the products, subunits, or functions in which they can be most productive.

3. *Reporting on the custodianship of resources under the command of individuals or organizations.* Individuals, acting either as investors or merely as citizens, entrust resources to professional managers and government officials. They expect the managers and officials to provide them with periodic reports by which their performance can be evaluated.

Focus on Future

Accounting focuses on the *measurement* and *communication* of a wide range of financial data. Accountants provide the information required to make decisions as to where to allocate financial resources and how to control them effectively. Periodically, as the management process is being carried out, accountants "report the score"—they provide information by which the results of prior decisions can be evaluated.

Viewed from a slightly different perspective, accounting aims to enable managers, investors, creditors, and other users of financial statements to predict the future earning power of an enterprise. Decisions made today can affect only the future, not the past. Those who seek information from financial statements are primarily concerned with how well the enterprise will perform in the years to come rather than in years gone by. Will the enterprise be able to satisfy its obligation to those to whom it is indebted? Will it be able to meet the wage demands of its employees? Will it be able to provide adequate returns to its owners?

What will occur in the future, however, can partly be predicted by what has taken place in the past. One of the indicators of future earnings, for example, is past earnings. Accounting, in reporting on events of the past, facilitates decisions that will affect the future.

Financial versus Management Accounting

A distinction is commonly made between financial accounting and management accounting. *Financial accounting* focuses on providing information for parties external to the organization—actual and potential owners and lenders, creditors, labour unions, suppliers, financial analysts, economists, trade associations, and the public.

Management accounting is directed at insiders—directors, managers, and employees of the organization. It provides the information needed to establish the objectives of the organization, to develop the strategies and plans to fulfill those objectives, to administer and control the day-to-day activities of the organization, and to evaluate the success of the organization in fulfilling its objectives. When it issues reports to insiders, an organization need not satisfy externally imposed standards or adhere to specific accounting principles. The number, frequency, and content of reports can be determined at the discretion of management.

This text deals primarily with financial accounting. Management accounting is left to other texts and courses. The boundaries between the two are not, however, nearly as distinct as may be implied by the organization of the typical accounting curriculum. It is important for a manager to be as comfortable with financial accounting as with management accounting, since most transactions have both managerial and financial accounting ramifications. For example, the decision to sell a division of a company is conventionally considered an issue of management accounting. How to report the event in the financial statements—an important factor to be considered in making the decision—is a topic of financial accounting.

GENERALLY ACCEPTED ACCOUNTING PRINCIPLES AND GENERAL-PURPOSE FINANCIAL REPORTS

The phrase *generally accepted accounting principles (GAAP)* refers both to accounting practices that are in widespread use because of convention and tradition and to those that are specifically mandated by recognized rule-making authorities.

Generally accepted accounting principles apply to general-purpose external financial reports. *General-purpose external financial reports* are intended primarily for investment decisions, although, of course, they may be appropriate for other kinds of decisions as well. They are designed for external users who lack the authority to prescribe the specific information they need. They are not, therefore, directed to boards of directors, taxing authorities, banks, and regulatory agencies. In contrast to most investors, these groups have the power to stipulate the form and content of the reports they require.

General-purpose financial reports provide information about an enterprise's financial performance *during* a period as well as its financial condition *at the end* of the period. These reports address such specific questions as:

- How much better off is a firm at the end of a period than it was at the start? What were its revenues (inflows of resources) during the period? What were its related expenses (outflows of resources)? What was its income (the difference between the two)?
- What are the firm's economic resources (assets) at the end of the period? What are the claims (liabilities and owners' equities) against those resources by lenders, suppliers, employees, and owners?
- What were the inflows and outflows of cash during the period? (In some respects, cash is accounted for no differently than other resources. Yet because cash is the medium of exchange in our society, it is the focus of considerably greater concern and attention.)

These questions are answered in three primary financial statements and in extensive notes and supplementary schedules to the financial statements. The three primary statements are

1. The *balance sheet,* which indicates, as at a specific date, the entity's financial resources as well as the claims against those resources both by outside parties and by owners

2. The *income statement,* which reports the changes in resources and claims during a specified period

3. The *statement of changes in financial position,* which reports on the receipts and disbursements of cash during a specified period

QUALITATIVE STANDARDS FOR ACCOUNTING

A central theme of this book is that there are few, if any, accounting principles or practices that are inherently correct. Nevertheless, there are several *standards* that accounting information should meet. In practice, the standards are goals toward which accountants strive but can never fully achieve. Often, in fact, realization of one goal can be accomplished only at the expense of the realization of others.

Relevance

Above all, accounting information must be useful. It should have an effect in decision making. Unfortunately, what is relevant for one group of statement users may not be relevant for others. As a consequence, there is no such thing as "all-purpose" financial statements and no accounting principles that are preferable in all circumstances. The "general-purpose" financial statements included in a company's annual report facilitate only a small fraction of the many types of decisions that managers and investors must make.

Suppose, for example, that an equipment manufacturer compensates its sales force through commissions. The sales representatives receive a percentage of the dollar volume of sales that they make. Because the equipment must be custom-made, it is generally not delivered to the customer until six months after it is ordered. Generally accepted accounting principles dictate that, for purposes of public reporting, the firm record a sale in the period in which the equipment is *delivered* to the customer. Until then, the firm cannot know with assurance what the cost of manufacturing the equipment will be and has not yet exerted its primary productive efforts. For purposes of determining the compensation of the sales staff, however, it may make sense to record a sale as soon as a *noncancelable order is placed*. When the order is placed, the sales force has accomplished its mission and merits its reward. It would be perfectly appropriate to apply one principle of sales recognition in reports to shareholders and the general public and another in the statements from which sales commissions will be computed.

Reliability

Accounting information should be reliable. It should faithfully describe what it purports to describe. It should be *objective;* it should be *verifiable.* Qualified individuals, each working independently, should be able to examine the same data and derive similar measures or reach similar conclusions. Information contained in financial reports should not depend on the subjective judgments of the parties that prepare it.

Herein lies a conflict. Information that is most reliable may not be relevant to many decisions, and that which is most relevant may not be reliable. A few questions will illustrate the conflict.

1. Should a corporation report its land at *historical cost* or at *fair market value?* The most objective amount would be historical cost—that which the company paid for the land. This amount is readily verifiable. But of what relevance is it? The company may have bought the land decades ago, and the historical cost provides no indication of what it can be sold for today. Yet any amount other than historical cost (e.g., present market value) would necessarily involve estimates or appraisals and hence be less objective. *Conventional accounting reports are based on historical costs.* Increases in market values are not, as a rule, recognized. Some accountants maintain, however, that assets should be carried at the amounts for which they could be bought or currently sold. Their position will be evaluated in later chapters.

2. Should a firm's statement of annual income reflect as earned revenue the potential selling price of goods that the company has produced but not yet sold? Or, alternatively, should the firm defer recognition of the revenue until it has actually sold the items, or even until it has actually collected the full selling price in cash? Revenue results from the entire process of production and sale, and since the firm is *usually* able to sell what it produces, financial statements in which income has been reported as soon as goods have been produced would be most relevant for most decisions. But the statements would be considerably less objective than those in which revenue recognition is delayed until the goods have been formally sold—and hence a firm sales price has been established—or until cash has actually been collected and the full amount to be received is known with certainty.

3. Should a company's income statement include as current pension expenses only amounts actually paid to retired workers or amounts that will eventually have to be paid to present employees as well? A company provides its employees with retirement benefits. The liability for the pensions is incurred during the productive years of the employees. The actual cash payment, however, does not have to be made until an employee retires, and the actual amount to be paid may depend on the number of years the employee survives after retirement. This amount cannot be determined with certainty until after the employee dies. Should the company report an estimate of the pension expense as the employee "earns" the right to the pension (the most relevant time), or should it wait until it actually disburses the cash (when the expense can be objectively determined—the most reliable time)?

Many accounting issues are attributable to the conflict between the objectives of relevance and reliability. Accountants are continually faced with situations in which they must trade the realization of one goal for that of the other.

Financial Reports Are Not Precise

Reliability does not imply precision. Even if all amounts are shown to the nearest dollar (most major corporations now report in thousands or even millions of dollars), financial statements can never be precise. Financial statements are necessarily based on estimates.

For example, generally accepted accounting principles require that the cost of a capital asset be charged to expense over its useful life. Assume a company purchases a car for $30,000. The car has an expected useful life of five years. The firm would charge an average of $6,000 to expense during each of the five years the car is used. Is it possible, however, to predict with precision how long an asset will last? Were the car estimated to last only four years, then the annual expense would be $7,500 per year ($30,000 divided by four years). This amount is 25 percent greater than the $6,000 derived from the estimate of five years—hardly a trivial difference!

Financial Reports Are Not Certain

Just as financial information cannot be precise, neither can it be certain. Financial reports imply predictions. Whatever other unique characteristics accountants have, they are not clairvoyant.

Financial statements must incorporate forecasts because the resources of a firm have value only insofar as they will provide benefits in the future. Equipment is an asset only because it will be used in productive activities of the future. Accounts receivable are of value to the firm only if they will eventually be collected and transformed into cash. In assigning a value to equipment, the firm and its accountants must forecast its useful life. In measuring accounts receivable, they must predict the likelihood of collection. Since these forecasts can never be completely certain, neither can the financial statements based on them.

Neutrality

General-purpose financial reports should be neutral. They should report economic activity as objectively as possible without influencing decisions or behaviour in a particular direction.

Accounting information cannot, of course, fail to influence human behaviour. Indeed, its very purpose is to affect financial decisions. The key is that it should not intentionally influence behaviour *in a particular direction*.

Assume, for example, that proposed accounting rules pertaining to insurance companies would reduce the value of reported assets and owners' equity. As a consequence, some insurance companies might no longer be able to satisfy minimum statutory capital requirements and, counter to national economic interests, would be forced to cease operations. The standard of neutrality would dictate that rule-making authorities should not reject the proposals merely because they would be harmful to either the insurance companies or to the national economy.

General-purpose accounting reports are comparable to automobile speedometers. They should reflect phenomena, either economic or physical, as faithfully as possible. It makes little sense to try to reduce highway speeds by intentionally miscalibrating speedometers. Drivers would eventually see through the ruse and adjust their actual speed accordingly. Correspondingly, it is equally foolhardy to attempt to control economic behaviour by "miscalibrating" financial statements—the gauges of business activity.

Comparability

Financial statements should facilitate two types of comparisons: (1) comparisons among firms and (2) comparisons within a single firm over two or more periods of time. Comparability is generally enhanced when similar organizations base their financial reports on the same accounting principles and each adheres to consistent accounting policies over time.

Accounting reports of different organizations are not now as comparable as many financial specialists believe is desirable. The reasons are twofold. First, the accounting rule-making authorities allow individual companies a relatively free hand in selecting among alternative accounting practices. Second, the task of prescribing uniform accounting principles for the myriad transactions in which firms engage is enormously complex, time-consuming, and expensive. Accounting procedures that are appropriate for one transaction may be inappropriate for a transaction that is only slightly different.

In the last decade, the rule-making authorities have substantially increased the number of accounting standards and disclosure requirements. One consequence of this has been a dramatic increase in the amount of society's resources directed to auditing and financial reporting.

ACCOUNTING PRINCIPLES AS FLEXIBLE RULES

Unlike principles of mathematics or physics, accounting "principles" are not basic truths or laws. They are rules and standards selected by rule-making authorities from among many possible rules and standards, some of which are equally defensible.

The example that follows is intended to demonstrate that there are numerous ways of describing economic events and of measuring economic values. The example contains technical terms that will be defined in subsequent chapters. For now, however, even a layperson will have sufficient understanding to appreciate its main points.

Example

Canadian Oils Ltd. purchases sunflower seed oil from a processor and resells it to its customers. The company was established on January 1, 1996. On that date the firm's owners contributed $18 million in cash, receiving in exchange 1,000 shares of common stock (certificates which indicate ownership). The following transactions and events took place during its first year of operations:

1. *Acquisition of long-lived assets.* The company acquired storage tanks, delivery trucks, and other equipment for $10 million (paid in cash). Management estimates that the useful lives of this equipment will be 10 years.

2. *Acquisition of goods intended for resale.* The company purchased oil at two different prices during the year:

36 million litres @ $.59/L	$21,240,000
4 million litres @ $.69/L	2,760,000
40 million litres	$24,000,000

The *weighted average* price of the 40 million litres purchased was 60 cents per litre (total cost of $24 million divided by 40 million litres).

3. *Sales (i.e., deliveries) to customers*

36 million litres @ an average price of $.70/L	$25,200,000

4. *Cash collections from customers.* The company collected $20.8 million as follows:

On the $25.2 million of goods sold	$20,000,000
Customer deposits on oil to be shipped the following year (see item 5)	800,000
Total cash collections	$20,800,000

Since the company made sales of $25.2 million but collected only $20 million, at year end it had $5.2 million in accounts receivable (amounts owed by customers).

5. *Additional orders from customers*

| 1 million litres @ $.80/L | $800,000 |

These orders were placed prior to year end and were accompanied by full payment.

6. *Operating costs for the year.* These costs included labour, selling and administrative costs, and advertising and amounted to $2 million. They were paid in cash.

7. *Year-end inventory.* Since the company purchased 40 million litres of oil and sold only 36 million, it had 4 million litres on hand at year end.

8. *Other information*
   a. Near the end of the year, the sunflower seed oil producers announced a price increase from 69 cents to 75 cents per litre. Correspondingly, Canadian Oils raised its selling price from what was then 80 cents to 85 cents per litre.
   b. At year end the replacement cost (new) of the tanks, trucks, and equipment had increased to $12 million.
   c. The company signed an employment contract with a top-notch sales executive. The new executive will considerably strengthen the firm's management team.

At year end the firm is required to prepare the three primary financial statements: an income statement, a balance sheet, and a statement of changes in financial position. The statements should answer the three basic questions: How much better off is the firm at the end of the year than at the beginning? What are the firm's year-end resources and what are the claims against these resources? What were the inflows and outflows of cash?

Statement of Changes in Financial Position
The last question can be answered most easily and most objectively. The cash flows can be determined by summarizing the firm's chequebook or similar record of cash receipts and disbursements. Exhibit 1-1 presents the cash flows in a standard format.

Income Statement and Balance Sheet
The first two questions are more difficult. One possible set of answers is represented by the income statement and the balance sheet shown in Exhibits 1-2 and 1-3, respectively. The income statement reports on performance during

EXHIBIT 1-1
Statement of Changes in Financial Position

Canadian Oils Ltd.
Statement of Changes in Financial Position
Year Ended December 31, 1996
(all amounts in millions)

Operating Activities

Collections from customers for goods delivered	$ 20.0
Collections from customers for goods ordered	.8
Payments to suppliers for oil	(24.0)
Other operating costs	(2.0)
Cash provided by (used in) operations	$ (5.2)

Investing Activities

Purchases of tanks, trucks, and equipment	(10.0)

Financing Activities

Proceeds from issuance of stock	18.0
Increase in cash	$ 2.8

the year, and the balance sheet on year-end financial position. The statements in Exhibits 1-2 and 1-3 have been prepared in accordance with "generally accepted accounting principles." The following questions, however, suggest that other sets of answers, leading to dramatically different reported results, would be equally defensible:

1. *Which events should give rise to revenue? Revenue* is the inflow or other enhancement of assets from producing and delivering goods and rendering services. In calculating income, the primary measure of periodic performance, should "sales revenue" be recorded when the firm

   a. receives a customer order?
   b. delivers the goods to the customer?
   c. collects the cash from the sale?

   Moreover, should the firm recognize revenue as the result of

   a. increases in the replacement cost of the goods on hand at year end?

EXHIBIT 1-2
Income Statement

Canadian Oils Ltd.
Income Statement
Year Ended December 31, 1996
(all amounts in millions)

Sales revenue		$25.2
Less: Expenses		
Cost of goods sold	$21.6	
Amortization expense	1.0	
Other operating expenses	2.0	24.6
Net income		$ 0.6

EXHIBIT 1-3
Balance Sheet

Canadian Oils Ltd.
Balance Sheet
As at December 31, 1996
(all amounts in millions)

Assets		
Cash		$ 2.8
Accounts receivable		5.2
Inventory		2.4
Tanks, trucks, and equipment	$10.0	
Less: accumulated amortization	1.0	9.0
Total assets		$19.4
Liabilities and owners' equity		
Customer deposits (oil to be delivered to customers)		0.8
Common stock (owners' initial contribution)		18.0
Retained earnings (income for year)		0.6
Total liabilities and owners' equity		$19.4

b. anticipated changes in the selling price of goods on hand?

c. improvements in the firm's executive team?

Undeniably, each of these events had a material impact on the firm's fiscal well-being. However, per today's accepted accounting principles, revenue would ordinarily be recognized only upon the *delivery* of goods to a customer. It would *not* be recognized as a consequence of customer orders (even if accompanied by cash), increases in replacement costs of goods on hand, anticipated changes in selling prices, or improvements in management. The reasons for these practices will be made clear throughout this text, as will the resultant limitations they impose on financial reports.

Under conventional accounting, therefore, the sales revenue to be reported on the income statement would be $25.2 million, the selling price of the oil delivered. The difference of $5.2 million between the sales revenue of $25.2 million and the $20 million of cash actually collected would be recognized on the balance sheet as an asset: "Accounts receivable, $5.2 million."

2. *Which costs should be matched to revenues?* The company sold (delivered) 36 million litres of oil. As will be explained later in the text, to determine income the expenses incurred in earning revenues must be deducted from the revenues. The most significant expense in this example is the cost of the oil sold.

During the year the company acquired 40 million litres of oil. Of this, 36 million was acquired at 59 cents per litre and 4 million at 69 cents per litre. Which oil should be assumed to be sold first? That purchased first or that purchased last?

If we assume that the oil purchased first was sold first, then the cost of the goods sold would be $21,240,000:

| 36 million litres @ $.59/L | $21,240,000 |

If, by contrast, we assume that the oil purchased last was sold first, then the cost of the goods sold would be $21,640,000:

4 million litres @ $.69/L	$ 2,760,000
+ 32 million litres @ $.59/L	18,880,000
Total	$21,640,000

Alternatively, if we assume that the oil was mixed together, the cost assigned to the goods sold would be the *weighted average* of the two purchases. As indicated, the *weighted average* purchase price was 60 cents per litre. Hence the cost of 36 million litres would be $21,600,000:

| 36 million litres @ $.60/L | $21,600,000 |

Conventional practice would permit a firm to make any of these three assumptions as to flow of costs regardless of which oil was actually sold first. The income statement in Exhibit 1-2 reports cost of goods sold on the assumption that all oil sold was at the weighted average cost of 60 cents per litre.

3. *How should the cost of long-lived assets be allocated to the periods which they will benefit?* The firm acquired $10 million in tanks, trucks, and equipment. These assets have an estimated useful life of 10 years. Because they will benefit 10 years, accepted accounting principles require that their costs be spread over their estimated useful lives. In that way they will be matched to *all* the revenues that they help to generate, not only to those of the year of acquisition. The process of allocating an asset's cost over its useful life is known as *amortization*.

Must equal amounts ($1 million) be charged as amortization expense each year or may the amounts vary? Although it is convenient to charge equal amounts each year, it is unlikely that the productivity of the assets will be the same. As the assets get older, for example, they will require greater maintenance and there will be more "down time" for repairs.

The income statement in Exhibit 1-2 reports amortization expense on a *straight-line* basis (i.e., it spreads the cost evenly among the 10 periods). Conventional practice, however, also permits the cost allocation to be made in any pattern that is systematic and rational. Under one pattern that is particularly popular, the amortization charge in the first year would be $2 million rather than $1 million (a difference of 100 percent!). This seemingly minor change would transform the net income from a profit of .6 million to a loss of .4 million. It must be noted that all amortization patterns eventually charge the same amount (i.e., $10 million) to expense. It is only the timing of the charge to expense that is an issue, not the amount to be charged in total.

4. *What values should be assigned to assets?* Should assets be reported at the amount the firm paid for them (i.e., at their historical cost) or at their value in the marketplace (e.g., the amount that would have to be paid to replace them)?

As indicated in the discussion under question 1, today's accounting principles do not generally permit increases in the market prices of a firm's assets to be recognized in the financial statements. Thus the 4 million litres of oil that remain on hand at year end will be reported on the balance sheet at the average cost paid, 60 cents per litre, rather than at the year-end replacement value of 75 cents per litre. Were market values to be incorporated into the accounts, the inventory would be stated at $3 million rather than $2.4 million. Correspondingly, both revenues and income would be $.6 million greater.

Similarly, were market values taken into account, the tanks, trucks, and equipment would be reported at the replacement value of $12 million rather than at the acquisition cost of $10 million. This increase, like that in the value of the oil, would also be reflected in the computation of income, the measure of the change in resources that takes place during the period.

Some choices among alternative accounting principles have been made by the rule-making authorities of the profession and imposed upon all firms within their jurisdiction. Others are left up to individual firms. There are a multitude of possible combinations of principles, each producing a unique set of financial reports. Although this text highlights the principles that are generally accepted today, it also presents alternatives. A continuing message is that no single set of statements can capture the full range of economic events affecting a firm. Therefore the manager or investor must be willing to seek out supplementary data from other sources and to recast the statements to properly serve his or her own unique information requirements.

ECONOMIC CONSEQUENCES OF ACCOUNTING ALTERNATIVES

An Economic Event as Distinguished from the Description of That Event

As with any occurrence, the event itself must be distinguished from the description of it. The way in which a transaction is described will affect the *appearance* of an entity's fiscal performance or status but have no direct effect on its actual well-being. Yet because substantive economic decisions will be based on the description, the indirect economic consequences may be profound.

In the preceding example, the choices among the various ways of determining income would have no direct impact on the inherent financial worth of the enterprise or its first-year performance. The firm's year-end inventory has increased in market value regardless of whether or not the change is incorporated into reported income. Similarly, the firm is better off for having received customer orders even if it doesn't recognize them as revenues. Obviously the firm will *appear* to be better off if it recognizes the increases in market value or takes account of the goods ordered. But the accounting description, by itself, will not affect the firm's financial condition.

Suppose, however, the company faces any one of the following circumstances. Here the indirect ramifications of accounting choices would be formidable.

- Federal and provincial income taxes are based on reported income.
- The firm is subject to financial restrictions imposed by a lender. The lender specifies that the borrower must maintain certain financial relationships (e.g., a stipulated ratio of liabilities to assets).
- The company ties the salary and bonuses of executives to reported income.
- The company's prices are established by a government regulatory authority. The authority sets prices so as to allow the firm a fair rate of return (i.e., income as a percentage of assets).
- The company and its labour union agree to submit a wage dispute to a mediator for resolution. The labour union asserts that the company can afford wage increases; the company contends that it cannot. The mediator will rely on the financial statements to determine which side is correct.

Under these circumstances, accounting choices will affect not only what is reported on the financial statements but substantive economic determinations as well. Indeed, the perception of financial condition will govern the reality.

As pointed out previously, neutrality is a widely accepted standard of general-purpose financial reporting. But changes in accounting principles will rarely, if ever, be "neutral" in their economic impact. Almost always, they will affect the distribution of resources in our society and thereby enrich some parties at the expense of others.

Accounting Principles and Advocacy Proceedings

Neutrality is a standard that applies to general-purpose reports, not necessarily to special-purpose reports. Therefore accountants, along with managers, lawyers, and other parties involved in advocacy proceedings, should be alert to opportunities to use accounting principles to their advantage. Whenever financial determinations are tied to accounting numbers, negotiators should do their best to assure that the underlying accounting principles produce the results that are the most favourable to their side. Accounting principles should be assessed and negotiated as carefully as any other contract terms. At the very least, negotiators should never yield control over accounting principles to the opposition.

Accounting Principles and the Stock Market

An overriding question faced by accounting standard setters is whether it really matters to investors if they prescribe one accounting principle rather than another. Since investors wish to maximize their return on capital, the amount they will be willing to pay for a firm's common stock (which represents an ownership interest) depends on their expectations as to the firm's future performance. The greater the anticipated returns, the greater the amount investors will be willing to pay. Correspondingly, the brighter the future of the firm, the greater the ease with which it can attract investment capital.

As stated before, reported earnings of the past are widely accepted as a primary predictor of earnings of the future. Different accounting principles, however, result in different determinations of earnings. And, one might hypothesize that the market price of the stock of a firm that *reports* higher earnings as a consequence of adopting more liberal accounting principles will be relatively higher than those of more conservative counterparts. If the hypothesis is correct, then the capital markets can be "fooled" by accounting information, and a measure of inefficiency is thereby introduced into the market system.

There is a substantial body of literature to suggest, however, that the capital markets are not so fooled—that, in fact, investors are aware of differences in earnings as a result of differences in accounting principles and adjust accordingly. Assume, for example, that the common stock of firms in a specific industry were being traded, on average, at a price that was equal to 10 times annual earnings. If a company reported earnings of $5 per share, its common stock could be expected to sell for $50 per share. If it reported earnings of $4 per share, it could be expected to sell for $40 per share. But suppose that a company reported earnings of $5 per share because, relative to other firms in the industry, it adhered to more liberal accounting principles. Otherwise, it would have reported earnings of only $4 per share. Would its stock still be traded at $50 per share? Accounting researchers have conducted numerous statistical studies in which stock prices have been related to reported earnings. The evidence is persuasive that, in general, the market takes into account differences in accounting principles. Thus it is likely that the common stock would be traded at only $40 per share.

The market-oriented accounting studies suggest that the accounting profession need not be as concerned about mandating specific practices as was once generally believed. Regardless of the accounting alternatives that firms select, investors usually (the studies have shown apparent exceptions) make the adjustments necessary to make the earnings of one company comparable with those of others. Obviously, however, investors can make the necessary adjustments only if they have the requisite information—the details of the underlying transactions—to do so. If, therefore, the studies imply that the accounting profession need not be especially concerned about specifying particular accounting practices, they also make clear that it should be very concerned with assuring that corporations disclose enough about their operations and financial position to enable investors to evaluate the results of transactions as they see fit.

The studies do *not* provide evidence that *individual* investors properly interpret financial statements. They deal exclusively with *investors as a group*. Moreover, they in no way imply that determinations other than investment decisions based on reported earnings will be unaffected by choices among accounting principles.

THE RULE-MAKING AUTHORITIES

The Accounting Standards Board

Who are the rule-making authorities responsible for selecting the accounting standards that form the basis of generally accepted accounting principles? In

Canada, the reponsibility for the development and continued evolution of generally accepted accounting principles (GAAP) has been largely assumed by the *Canadian Institute of Chartered Accountants (CICA)*. The CICA, through its Accounting Standards Board, is responsible for setting accounting standards. These standards are published as recommendations in the *CICA Handbook*. Although these recommendations are issued by a self-regulated body (the CICA), they have regulatory authority since the Canada Business Corporations Act and provincial securities commissions have designated the recommendations of the *CICA Handbook* as GAAP in Canada.

The *Accounting Standards Board (ASB)* consists of 13 volunteer voting members representing users, preparers, and auditors of financial information in the various regions of the country. Eight members are appointed by the CICA, along with one member invited from each of the The Society of Management Accountants of Canada, The Certified General Accountants' Association of Canada, The Financial Executives Institute Canada, The Canadian Academic Accounting Association, and The Canadian Council of Financial Analysts. When a new standard, or a change to an existing one, is contemplated, the ASB researches the issue thoroughly and issues its preliminary recommendations in the form of an exposure draft. The exposure draft is made available to all interested users for their comments. Based upon this feedback, the exposure draft is revised, if necessary, and then issued in final form as new or modified recommendations in the *CICA Handbook*.

The U.S. Financial Accounting Standards Board

Because of the close economic links between Canada and the United States, it is also important to have a general understanding of the accounting standard-setting process in the United States. As mentioned earlier, GAAP refers both to accounting practices that are accepted because of convention and to the specific rules mandated. There are many situations in Canada in which the ASB has not made specific recommendations. Often, preparers of financial statements in Canada will look to the accounting standards of another country (particularly the United States) to see if the situation has been addressed there. This referral to other countries' standards is an important source of Canadian GAAP.

The process of setting accounting standards in the United States is similar to that described above for Canada. The Financial Accounting Standards Board (FASB) is the designated standard-setting organization in the private sector. It derives its authority from the Securities and Exchange Commission (SEC) and the American Institute of Certified Public Accountants (AICPA). Unlike the Canadian ASB, the seven members of the FASB are full-time, paid employees. The members are drawn from industry, the accounting profession, academia, and government. They are appointed by an independent board of trustees, the members of which are nominated by six sponsoring organizations that have a direct interest in financial reporting. In Canada, the government has relied exclusively on the self-regulating CICA to be the sole rule-making authority in the setting of accounting standards. In the United

States, however, the government has not relied to the same extent on the self-regulated accounting profession. The SEC has statutory authority, under the Securities and Exchange Act of 1934 and the Public Utility Holding Company Act of 1935, to control practices of financial reporting. Throughout its history, the SEC has generally relied upon the private sector (i.e., the FASB and its predecessors) to carry out the function of standard setting. At times, however, the SEC has exercised its statutory authority and taken an activist role in issuing accounting standards.

The International Accounting Standards Committee

With the increasing globalization of business, there is a significant number of multinational corporations with operations in many parts of the world. In order to raise capital to finance their operations, many of these multinationals list their shares on different stock exchanges around the world. As a result, the multinationals may be required to prepare financial statements for reporting to one stock exchange using different accounting standards from those they used in preparing statements for another stock exchange in a different country. In order to improve the consistency of financial reporting by multinational corporations, the International Accounting Standards Committee (IASC) was formed with members from most of the leading accounting organizations around the world. The objective of the IASC is to develop a set of international accounting standards for multinational firms that would be acceptable around the world. So far, they have succeeded in developing a number of standards. However, most countries still insist that corporations reporting in their jurisdictions use their accounting standards. Many countries, including Canada, attempt to ensure that their national accounting standards are harmonized with international accounting standards, where appropriate.

The Conceptual Framework

In an effort to reduce controversy over each new or revised standard, the accounting profession has embarked on a long-range project to develop a "conceptual framework" of financial reporting. The profession believes that widespread agreement on the objectives of financial reporting, the bases of accounting measurement, the definitions of the key elements of financial statements, and similar issues that underlie virtually all accounting questions will facilitate the resolution of specific problems. In Canada, the concepts underlying the development and use of accounting standards in general-purpose financial statements are summarized in *Section 1000* of the *CICA Handbook*, "Financial Statement Concepts." In the United States, the FASB has issued six *Statements of Concepts*. Among their titles are "Objectives of Financial Reporting by Business Enterprises," "Qualitative Characteristics of Accounting Information," "Elements of Financial Statements of Business Organizations," and "Recognition and Measurement in Financial Statements of Business Enterprises."

Political Influence and the Rule-Making Authorities

Because accounting principles have economic consequences, firms expend considerable resources trying to persuade the rule-making authorities to take positions that will serve their interests. As a result, standard setting is not carried out through detached theorizing alone. It is very much a political process, of which lobbying is an integral part. Much of this lobbying occurs during the exposure draft stage of standard setting.

Most commonly, firms oppose changes in accounting standards that will postpone recognition of income, reduce the reported value of assets, increase the reported value of liabilities, and accentuate year-to-year fluctuations of income. They fear that such changes will decrease a firm's attractiveness to investors and creditors or make it more difficult to meet financial requirements imposed by lenders or regulatory authorities. For example, Canadian and U.S. firms with extensive foreign operations lobbied, eventually successfully, against proposed Canadian and U.S. standards that would require earlier and more frequent recognition of gains or losses on changes in the values of foreign currencies. In the United States, small oil companies objected to a proposed standard that mandated that drilling costs, previously recognizable over a number of years, be shown as an expense as they were incurred (although large oil companies that already used that method favoured the new standard).

But concern with accounting standards is not confined only to the firms to which they apply directly. Agencies of the U.S. government, for example, once fought proposals to reduce the reported value of banks and savings and loan associations. They presented evidence that the new rules would decrease the net worth of many financial institutions below the minimum required by regulatory authorities. They feared that forced liquidations of the institutions (or mergers with more financially sound entities) would further disrupt an already ailing industry and a depressed economy.

The rule-making authorities give considerable weight to the views of their constituents. Nevertheless, they have not been sympathetic to appeals that a proposed standard be rejected or modified because of a potentially adverse impact on a particular industry. Instead, they have attempted to establish principles that most faithfully reflect the relevant economic events, regardless of repercussions. They see the mission of accounting as unbiased reporting and recognize that once the profession waivers from this responsibility, even in the interest of a worthy cause, it will lose its credibility.

THE ACCOUNTING PROFESSION: A BRIEF BACKGROUND

Accountants serve in private industry, government, and nonprofit organizations. The title *accountant* is used to designate persons who provide a wide range of different services—from clerks who perform routine clerical functions to high-level executives who make major financial decisions. The cornerstone of the accounting profession, however, is the public accountant. *Public accountants* are those who make their services available to the public at large rather than to a single employer.

In Canada there are three national accounting organizations: The Canadian Institute of Chartered Accountants, The Society of Management Accountants of Canada, and The Certified General Accountants' Association of Canada. Members of the respective organizations who have satisfied various provincial education and experience requirements, and have successfully completed national examinations, are recognized as chartered accountants (CAs), certified management accountants(CMAs), and certified general accountants(CGAs), respectively. Most public accounting in Canada is performed by CAs, although CGAs are involved in public accounting as well. CMAs are principally engaged in private, or internal, accounting.

Modern accounting can trace its roots at least as far back as 1494, when an Italian monk named Luca Pacioli described a "double-entry" accounting procedure that forms the basis for accounting practice today. But public accounting as a profession is relatively new. The development of the profession was spurred primarily by new forms of economic activity associated with the Industrial Revolution. Many of the significant developments in the early stages of the profession's growth took place in Great Britain. By the latter half of the eighteenth century, small associations of professional accountants began to develop. In the early part of the twentieth century, the momentum for growth and innovation shifted to North America. Since 1900 the number of public accountants in Canada has grown exponentially.

In the eyes of the general public, public accountants are most commonly associated with income taxes. In truth, public accountants perform three primary functions: audits, management advisory services, and tax services. It is the audit function that is unique to, and most characteristic of, the public accounting profession.

Auditing and Financial Reporting

The purpose of the audit function is to enhance the credibility of financial reports. Report users want assurance that statements "present fairly" the results of the economic activities that they purport to describe.

Regulatory agencies such as the Ontario Securities Commission and the Toronto Stock Exchange require that publicly held corporations under their jurisdiction have an *independent* party—a public accountant—*attest to,* or vouch for, the fairness of the financial statements the companies issue to their shareholders. Similarly, banks, insurance companies, and other investors and lenders of funds also demand that financial statements on which they intend to rely be audited, or attested to, by public accountants.

Although the public accounting firm is *not* assigned the responsibility of preparing external financial reports—*corporate management* is so charged—its influence over them is paramount. In Canada, many corporations include a management report in their annual report to shareholders to clarify that it is management's responsibility to prepare the external financial reports. The public accounting firm does not verify each of the transactions underlying the financial statements. In a large corporation the number of transactions in a year would make that an impossible task. Instead, the public accounting firm reviews the accounting systems used to accumulate and summarize the underlying data, tests a substantial number of transactions (especially those involving large dollar amounts), and, most important, makes certain that the financial statements have been prepared in conformity with generally accepted accounting principles. The end product of the independent public accountant's examination is the *auditor's report,* an opinion on the financial statements. A typical report is shown in Exhibit 1-4. If auditors are unable to obtain sufficient evidential matter on which to base an opinion, a denial of opinion is required. If they take exception to the information as presented, they are required to either qualify their opinion or express an "adverse" opinion (e.g., "In our opinion these consolidated financial statements do *not* present fairly the financial position ...").

EXHIBIT 1-4
Report of KPMG Peat Marwick Thorne, Independent Auditors

To the Shareholders of TransCanada Pipelines Limited

We have audited the consolidated statements of financial position of TransCanada Pipelines Limited as at December 31, 1993 and December 31, 1992 and the consolidated statements of income, contributed surplus and retained earnings and changes in financial position for each of the years in the three-year period ended December 31, 1993. These financial statements are the responsibility of the Company's management. Our responsibility is to express an opinion on these financial statements based on our audits.

We conducted our audits in accordance with generally accepted auditing standards. Those standards require that we plan and perform an audit to obtain reasonable assurance whether the financial statements are free of material misstatement. An audit includes examining, on a test basis, evidence supporting the amounts and

disclosures in the financial statements. An audit also includes assessing the accounting principles used and significant estimates made by management, as well as evaluating the overall financial statement presentation.

In our opinion, these consolidated financial statements present fairly, in all material respects, the financial position of the Company as at December 31, 1993 and December 31, 1992 and the results of its operations and the changes in its financial position for each of the years in the three-year period ended December 31, 1993 in accordance with Canadian generally accepted accounting principles.

KPMG Peat Marwick Thorne
Chartered Accountants

Calgary, Canada
January 20, 1994

Public accounting firms in Canada range in size from those with a single practitioner to those with nearly a thousand partners and thousands of professional staff. The largest have annual revenues of nearly half a billion dollars. Canada's largest public accounting firms are shown in Exhibit 1-5. The largest public accounting firms in Canada are affiliated with international accounting firms that have operations around the world. Because of their size and the international scope of their operations, the six largest international public accounting firms have had a predominant impact on the practice of accounting and the establishment of accounting principles throughout the world. They are commonly designated the Big Six.

As professionals, public accountants are expected to adhere to the standards of their profession. The various provincial institutes of public accountants in Canada have adopted codes of ethics to help assure that their members conduct themselves in a manner that is acceptable to their clients, their colleagues, and the public at large. In addition, the Canadian Institute of

EXHIBIT 1-5
Canada's Largest Public Accounting Firms

Canada's Largest Public Accounting Firms (Based on 1993 Revenue) (all amounts in millions)	
1. KPMG Peat Marwick Thorne	$475
2. Deloitte & Touche	$409
3. Ernst & Young	$381
4. Coopers & Lybrand	$267
5. Price Waterhouse	$240
6. Doane Raymond	$202
7. Arthur Andersen & Co.	$193
8. BDO Dunwoody Ward Malette	$186
9. Richter, Usher & Vineberg	$ 45
10. Collins Barrow	$ 29

Source: "The Financial Post 500 (1994)," The Financial Post Company, 1994.

Chartered Accountants has issued standards of auditing. *Standards of auditing* deal with the manner in which public accountants carry out independent examinations of financial statements. They differ from standards of accounting, which pertain to the preparation of the statements themselves.

Management Advisory Services

Most public accountants serve as financial advisers to their clients. Large public accounting firms have separate management consulting divisions that provide a wide range of services to both industry and government. Although most consulting engagements are directly related to the accounting and reporting systems of their clients (a large number, for example, involve installation of computerized management information systems), some are in such diverse fields as marketing, pensions, insurance, and production management. Smaller public accounting firms often provide day-to-day business advice to their clients; some establish the accounting systems used by their clients and maintain a close watch over them to make certain that they are operating as planned.

In recent years the consulting activities of many firms, especially the larger ones, have come under fire for being incompatible with the primary function of public accountants, that of attesting to financial reports. Critics assert that public accountants who provide consulting services cannot be sufficiently independent of their clients to provide unbiased audit services. They question, for example, whether a public accounting firm that has advised a client on means of increasing income, and has seen such advice followed unsuccessfully, could be sufficiently objective in auditing the financial reports that reflect the results of its own poor advice. Public accountants respond that they have developed professional guidelines that minimize the possibility of bias and that the benefits of consulting services to their clients—and hence to society—far outweigh the risk of diminished independence.

Tax Services

For most large Canadian corporations the effective income tax rate, taking into account federal income taxes as well as provincial taxes, is typically close to 50 percent of income. For their foreign operations it may be considerably higher. It is critical therefore that managers assess the tax implications of proposed transactions *before* they enter into them, while they still have an opportunity to minimize the tax burden.

Accountants provide tax services both as members of internal tax staffs and as outside advisers. They do, of course, prepare tax returns for their companies or their clients, but their more important function is counselling managers or individuals of the likely tax consequences *in advance* of a business undertaking.

Accountants in Industry

Accountants who are employed by business enterprises commonly serve in a staff capacity. They provide advice and service to virtually all units of the organization. The industrial accountants of today are likely to be responsible for maintaining financial records. In all probability, however, they will do much more. They will be key members of the management team, counselling on a wide range of corporate activities. The chief accountant of a company is often known as the *controller*. The following list is suggestive of the functions that are carried out by a controller's department:

- Long-range and strategic financial planning
- Data processing and information processing
- Tax planning and administration
- Budgeting
- Reporting to shareholders and government departments
- Evaluating financial performance

The distinction between a *controller* and a *treasurer* varies from firm to firm, but in general the treasurer is concerned with relations between the company and its shareholders, bankers, and other creditors as well as with the administration of the firm's investments and insurance policies.

Many accountants in industry serve as *internal auditors*. Corporate internal audit departments have traditionally been responsible for verifying the accuracy and reliability of internal accounting reports and records. Today, they still perform that function. Their role has expanded, however, to include reviews of the efficiency and effectiveness of all corporate operating and management systems. In more progressive firms internal auditors function as a team of internal management consultants.

Accountants in Nonprofit Organizations

Government and other nonprofit organizations are unconcerned with the computation of net income; they are interested in public service, not profit. Yet financial budgets, accounting controls, and quantitative measures of performance are as necessary in nonprofit as in profit-making organizations.

Unfortunately, many nonprofit organizations have been slow in realizing the importance of adequate accounting systems and reports. Today, however, they are attempting to make rapid reforms in the area of financial management, and as a result job opportunities in such organizations are abundant.

Nonprofit accounting is an especially challenging field. Administrators of nonprofit organizations require the same types of information as their counterparts in private industry to carry out effectively the functions of management. On a day-to-day basis, problems of planning, controlling, and evaluating performance in nonprofit organizations are remarkably similar to those in industry. Managing a government-owned electric utility is not very different from managing a comparable private utility. Controlling clerical costs in the tax-collection division of a municipality has much in common with controlling clerical costs in the billings office of a large insurance company.

The Public Sector Accounting and Auditing Committee (PSAAC) of the CICA is in charge of establishing accounting, reporting, and auditing standards for the federal, provincial, territorial, and local governments. The PSAAC is the sister organization of the ASB and has comparable authority. The ASB is responsible for setting standards for nonprofit organizations that are not part of a government unit.

Litigation against Accountants

Public accountants are continually the target of lawsuits charging them with negligence in carrying out their audits. Both statutory law and case precedent make it clear that accountants are expected to adhere to the standards of their profession. Should they deviate from these standards, and thereby fail to detect or report material errors in their clients' financial statements, they may be liable for the resultant losses suffered by statement users.

It has become increasingly common for both shareholders and creditors who have incurred losses as a consequence of a corporate collapse to look to the failed firm's auditors for recompense. In part, this is because public accounting firms have "deep pockets." They are insured for losses and, in contrast to the failed company itself, can serve as a source of indemnification.

Public accountants, it must be emphasized, are accountable only for *audit* failures, not *business* failures. An *audit failure* occurs when the auditor issues an inappropriate report on a client's financial statements. A *business failure,* by contrast, occurs when a firm is unable to meet its financial obligations. Auditors do not guarantee the fiscal health or even the survivability of their clients. They assure only that a firm's financial statements can be relied upon.

As painful as the proliferation of litigation has been to the accounting profession, it has provided the impetus for a quantum leap in the quality of audits. As a result of the judgments against it, the profession has assumed greater responsibility for the content of financial statements and has established standards that are both more specific and more rigorous than those of the past. Although, as might be expected, the audit failures generate the headlines in the financial press, the number of failures in relation to total audits is remarkably small.

To the student considering accounting as a career, the possibility of litigation underscores the trust that society places in the accounting profession and the responsibility assumed by its individual members.

Accounting is obviously a profession concerned primarily with practice, but it has an important research component as well.

Until the early 1970s, accounting researchers focused mainly on developing and prescribing "optimum" accounting principles. Typical of the questions accounting researchers addressed were those set forth in the example earlier in this chapter:

- Should changes in prices be recognized in the accounts? If so, when and how?
- How should the cost of long-lived assets be allocated over their useful lives?
- What assumptions as to flows of costs should be used in calculating both the cost of goods sold and year-end inventory?

In one mode of research, academics attempted to answer these questions by identifying the decisions made by statement users and deducing the information that would be required to facilitate those decisions. In another, researchers sought to develop a "conceptual framework," maintaining that specific accounting issues could be resolved only after general principles were established. Akin to the models used in mathematical disciplines such as geometry, the frameworks of some researchers were built upon definitions, axioms, and postulates. This type of research was helpful in assuring a logical consistency to accounting principles. However, neither the resultant framework nor specific principles could be readily tested empirically for preferability, and, therefore, the research did not yield definitive conclusions.

Starting in the 1970s, accounting research took a number of new directions. Some researchers, abandoning what they considered a futile search for optimum principles, focused instead on observing accounting practices and explaining their consequences. One ongoing line of research relates to the impact on stock prices of alternative accounting principles or of previously undisclosed news and information. Researchers might hypothesize, for example, that the stock market takes into account changes in the current market values of a firm's assets. Using exceedingly sophisticated statistical models, they then try to measure the extent to which current value information explains variations in stock prices that cannot be explained equally well by historical cost data. If the analysis supports the hypothesis, then the researcher has reason to believe that investors find the current value information useful; if the data do not support the hypothesis, then the utility of the current value information is seen as problematic.

In another line of study, researchers might attempt to explain why some firms opt for one accounting method while others opt for an alternative method. For example, researchers might hypothesize that because senior executives control reporting practices, firms in which executive compensation is tied to earnings will select more liberal (earnings-enhancing) accounting principles than those in which it is not.

In a third line of research, researchers might employ the techniques of psychologists to investigate how decisions of individual users are affected by the amount of accounting data presented to them or by the style of presentation.

Although such research has been carried out for a relatively short period of time, the results have already provided considerable insight into why corporations select certain accounting practices over others and the consequences of the choices.

Summary

Accounting plays an essential role in our economy. It facilitates the allocation of resources both within and among organizations. It provides the information necessary to evaluate the performance of entities and the persons who manage them. Although accounting reports on what happened in the past, it is relied upon to make decisions that affect the future.

Accounting conveys information to a variety of users for a variety of purposes. There can be a number of ways in which to describe financial events. The most appropriate way depends on the requirements of the specific parties who will use the information. Above all else, accounting reports must be *relevant*; they must bear upon the decisions at hand. As a consequence, there is no single set of accounting principles that is inherently better than others.

Accounting information should be *reliable*. It should be objective and verifiable. But information that is most relevant for a particular decision may not always be the most reliable. Thus, in selecting among accounting principles, firms and their accountants must balance these two competing standards. Financial reports should also be *neutral*; they should not influence decisions in a particular direction. Moreover, they should be *comparable* with those of other firms and of the same firm in different periods.

A key objective of this chapter has been to emphasize that the study of accounting requires much more than becoming cognizant of generally accepted accounting principles. Generally accepted accounting principles are not universal truths. Many are rules selected by designated authorities from among other possibilities that are equally defensible. They are subject to change. They lead to financial reports that may be most appropriate for some purposes, but certainly not for all. It is essential therefore that persons who use financial reports in their personal or professional lives not only understand the reasons why financial reports are prepared as they are but are aware of their limitations. They must be able to distinguish the economic substance of events from the way in which the events are reported. They must be able to reformulate financial reports so that the reports most effectively serve their own unique information needs.

Questions for Review and Discussion

1. On January 15, the controller (the chief accounting officer) of the Highland Hills Corp. reported to the president that company income for the previous year was $1.5 million. Two months later, after conducting an examination of the company's books and records, Hunter and Co., Chartered Accountants, determined that the company had earned only $900,000. Upon receiving the report of the CAs, the president declared

that she was going to get either a new controller or a new CA firm. "One of the two," she commented, "must be either dishonest or incompetent." Is she right?

2. The financial vice-president of a corporation recently urged that all amounts in the firm's annual report to shareholders be rounded to the nearest thousand dollars. "It is misleading," he said, "to give shareholders a report in which all figures are carried out to the last penny." Explain what the financial vice-president most likely had in mind by his comment.

3. The Mid-Western Broadcasting Co. recently submitted statements of income to shareholders, to Revenue Canada Taxation, and to the Canadian Radio-television and Telecommunications Commission. In no two of the reports was net income the same, even though the period covered by the reports was identical. Release of all three reports was approved by the firm's public accountants. How is it possible for all three reports to be "correct"?

4. In preparing a financial statement to accompany his loan application to the bank, Howard Johnson was uncertain as to whether he should report his home as having a value of $95,000 or $210,000. Johnson purchased his house 10 years ago at a price of $95,000; similar homes in his neighbour-hood have recently been sold for between $190,000 and $230,000. Which amount do you think would be more useful to the bank? Which amount would be the more objective?

5. Accounting statements report on the past. Yet they incorporate predictions of the future. How? Provide examples.

6. General-purpose financial reports should be *neutral*. What is meant by "neutral" as it applies to financial reports? Why is neutrality a characteristic of financial reports that accountants can only strive toward but never fully achieve?

7. Provide two examples of how managers can use financial reports to their advantage in advocacy proceedings.

8. What do recent studies regarding the effect of alternative accounting practices on stock market prices suggest about the ability of investors to distinguish between an economic event and the description of it? What are the implications of these studies for the accounting rule-making authorities?

9. In the early stages of the development of the accounting profession, independent auditors would "certify" to the "accuracy" of a company's financial statements. Today independent auditors express an "opinion" that the company's financial statements "present fairly" the firm's financial position and results of its operations. Why do you suppose public accountants are reluctant to "certify" to the "accuracy" of a company's financial statements?

10. What role does the Accounting Standards Board play in the development of accounting standards? What role does the Ontario Securities Commission play?

11. What three primary services do public accounting firms render to their clients? Why are such services sometimes thought to be in conflict with one another?

12. Wilbur Wood is concerned about his prospects for re-election as mayor of the town of Spring River. Mayor Wood had promised the citizens of Spring River that as long as he was in charge of fiscal affairs, the town would never run a deficit—that is, expenditures would never exceed revenues. Yet in 1996 the town did, in fact, report a deficit of $1,800,000. The deficit was attributable entirely to the fleet of nine buses purchased by the town. The town purchased and paid for the nine buses in November 1996. At the time the town ordered the buses, it had met all requirements for a provincial grant for the full cost of the vehicles, but as the result of a bureaucratic snarl, payment of the grant was delayed until the following year.

The town's accounting system requires that revenues be recognized only upon actual receipt of cash and that expenses be recorded upon cash payment.

a. What deficiencies do you see in Spring River's accounting system? What revisions would you suggest?

b. Suppose alternatively that the town does not receive a provincial grant to pay for the buses. It is the policy of the town to pay cash (not to borrow) for transportation vehicles and equipment. The useful life of the buses is approximately five years. In those years in which new buses must be acquired, reported municipal expenditures are substantially greater than in those in which buses are not acquired. As a consequence, some citizens believe that the operating efficiency of the town is less in the years in which buses are replaced than in others. Do you believe that the town is really less efficient by virtue of its acquisition of new buses? How might the financial reporting practices of the town be changed so as to reduce the confusion on the part of some of its citizens?

13. Critics of traditional financial accounting have asserted that financial reports are biased in that they fail to account for certain "social" benefits and costs incurred. They recommend that corporations prepare and distribute a "socioeconomic operating statement." The statement might take the following form:

Social benefits		
Improvement in the environment	$xxxx	
Employment equity hiring program	xxxx	
Day-care centre	xxxx	
Staff services donated to hospitals	xxxx	$xxxx
Social costs		
Damage to the environment	$xxxx	
Work-related injuries and illness	xxxx	
Failure to install recommended		
safety equipment	xxxx	xxxx
Social surplus (deficit) for		
the year		$xxxx

Comment on the proposed financial report in terms of the dual accounting goals of relevancy and reliability.

1. *Financial statements are based on estimates. The impact of the estimates on reported earnings may be substantial.*

    Western Canada Airlines Co. owns and operates 8 passenger jet planes. Each plane had cost the company $9 million. The company's income statement for 1996 reported the following:

Revenue from passenger fares		$40,000,000
Operating expenses (including salaries, maintenance costs, terminal expenses, etc.)	$22,000,000	
Amortization of planes	6,000,000	28,000,000
Income before taxes		$12,000,000

    Each plane has an estimated useful life of 12 years. The $6 million amortization charge was calculated by dividing the cost of each plane ($9 million) by its useful life (12 years). The result ($750,000) was multiplied by the number of planes owned (8).

    a. Suppose that the estimated useful life of each plane was 8 years rather than 12 years. Determine income before taxes for 1996. By what percent is income less than that just computed?

    b. Suppose that the estimated useful life of each plane was 15 years. Determine income before taxes for 1996. By what percent is income greater than that originally computed?

    c. It is sometimes said that accountants must be concerned that financial statements are precise to the penny. Based on your computations, do you agree?

2. *It is not always obvious when a company is "better off" by virtue of its production and sales efforts.*

    In January, its first month of operations, the Wonder Computer Co. manufactured 200 laptop computers at a cost of $1,400 each. Although it completed all 200 computers by the end of the month, it had not yet sold any of them.

    In February the company produced 400 computers. It sold and delivered to customers both the 200 computers manufactured in January and the 400 manufactured in February. Selling price of the computers was $2,000 each.

    a. Determine income for each of January and February.

    b. Assume instead that on January 2 the company signed a noncancelable contract to sell 600 computers at $2,000 each to a major chain of department stores. The contract called for delivery in February. The company completed but did not deliver 200 of the computers by January 31. It completed the remainder and delivered all 600 by February 28. Determine income for each of the two months.

3. *The most relevant information may not always be the most reliable.*

    The president and sole owner of the Conner Brewery asked his public accountant to audit (i.e., to express her opinion on the fairness of) the financial statements of his company. The audited financial statements had been requested by the bank to facilitate review of the company's application for a loan to finance the installation of a new bottling line.

The controller of the company, who had actually prepared the statements, included among the firm's assets "Land—$3,000,000." According to the controller, the land was reported at a value of $3 million since the company had recently received offers of approximately that amount from several potential buyers.

After reviewing the land account, the public accountant told the president that she could not express the usual "unqualified" opinion on the financial statements as long as land was valued at $3 million. Instead, she would have to express an "adverse" opinion ("the financial statements do *not* present fairly ...") unless the land was valued at $150,000, the amount the company had actually paid for it.

The president was dumbfounded. The land, he told the public accountant, was purchased in 1921 and was located in the downtown section of a major city.

  a. At what amount do you think the land should be recorded? Explain. Which amount is likely to be the more relevant to the banker? Which amount is the more objective?

  b. Which amount should be reported if the statements are to be prepared in accordance with "generally accepted accounting principles"?

4. *Sometimes it is easy to assign specific costs to specific items sold; sometimes it is more difficult. Choice of method used to determine cost affects the determination of reported income.*

  a. The Best Used Car Co. purchased four cars in the month of June and sold three cars. Purchase prices and sale prices are as follows:

	Purchase Price	Sale Price
Car 1	$4,000	$ 6,000
Car 2	6,500	8,500
Car 3	5,000	—
Car 4	9,000	11,500

  b. The Natural Foods Grocery Store purchased 400 kilograms of nutrient grain in the month of June and sold 300 kilograms. The grain is not prepackaged. Instead, as it is purchased, it is added to a single barrel; as it is sold, it is scooped out and given to the customer in a paper bag. During June, 100 kilograms of grain were purchased on each of four separate dates. Purchase prices, in sequence, were $4.00, $4.50, $5.00, and $5.50 per kilogram. All sales were at $7.00 per kilogram.

    Determine the income of the two merchants for the month of June. (Ignore other costs not indicated.)

    Are there other assumptions that you might have made regarding the cost of the goods actually sold? Would income remain the same?

5. *Accounting reports that are suitable for making a long-term investment decision may not be appropriate for deciding whether to discontinue a product line.*

  John Williams sells greeting cards. Operating out of a garage that he rents for $8,000 per year, he purchases greeting cards from a wholesaler and distributes them door to door. In 1995 he sold 1,000 boxes of cards at $10 per box. The cost of the cards from the wholesaler was $4 per box.

In 1996 Williams decided to expand his product line to include candy. In that year he sold 400 boxes of candy for $20 per box. The candy cost him $12 per box. By making efficient use of his garage, he found that he was able to store his inventory of cards in one half of the garage; thus he could use the other half for his candy. His sales of cards neither benefited nor suffered as the result of the new product. Card sales in 1996 were the same as in 1995.

At the conclusion of 1996 Williams had to decide whether to continue selling candy or to return to selling cards only. His friend Fulton, an occasional accountant, prepared the following income statement for 1996 candy sales for him.

Sales of candy (400 boxes @ $20)		$8,000
Less costs		
Cost of candy sold (400 boxes @ $12)	$4,800	
Rent (.50 of $8,000)	4,000	8,800
Net loss on sale of candy		($ 800)

On the basis of the report Williams decided to abandon his line of candy.
a. Do you think he made the correct decision? Explain.
b. Prepare a report comparing the total earnings of Williams in 1996 with those in 1995. How do you reconcile the apparent contradiction between your report and that of Fulton?

6. *Higher reported earnings for a particular year can sometimes be achieved by actions that do not serve the long-run interests of the enterprise.*

Don Watson, president of a construction corporation, was concerned about the poor performance of his company in the first 11 months of the year. If the company continued at its present pace, reported profits for the year would be down substantially from those of the previous year. Thinking of ways to increase reported earnings, the president hit upon what he considered to be an ingenious scheme: Three years earlier the company had purchased a crane at a cost of $400,000. Since the crane was now three years old and had an estimated useful life of 10 years, it was currently reported on the company's books at seven-tenths of $400,000, or $280,000. Prices of cranes had increased substantially in the last three years, and the crane could be sold for $420,000. The president suggested that the company sell the crane for $420,000 and thereby realize a gain on the sale of $140,000 ($420,000 less the book value of $280,000). Of course, the company would have to buy a new crane—and new cranes were currently selling for $520,000—but the cost of the new crane could be spread out over its useful life of 10 years. In future years, the president realized, amortization charges would increase from $40,000 on the old crane ($400,000 divided by 10) to $52,000 on the new ($520,000 divided by 10). In the current year, however, the company would report a gain on sale of $140,000 and thereby increase reported income by that amount.
a. The scheme of the president is, in fact, consistent with generally accepted accounting principles. Do you think, however, that the company would really be $140,000 better off if it sold the old crane and purchased a new one than if it held on to the old one? Comment.

b. Would the scheme of the president be in the best interest of the shareholders "in the long run"?

c. Assume that generally accepted accounting principles require that assets, such as the crane, be reported on corporate books at the price at which they could currently be sold (i.e., $420,000). Would the scheme of the president accomplish its desired results? Why do you suppose generally accepted accounting principles do not permit such assets to be valued at the prices at which they can be sold?

7. *Choices among a few accounting principles may result in a great number of possible reported incomes.*

Custom Exteriors contracts with homeowners to provide a special protective coating for the outside walls of their homes. The company, however, is primarily a sales organization. It subcontracts the actual work to a painting company. Custom Exteriors charges customers $800 per home; it pays the painting company $600 per home. Per the contract, customers do not have to pay for the work until 30 days after the job is completed. Custom Exteriors, however, must pay the painting company part of the contract price at the start of work and part upon completion.

During a recent year Custom Exteriors signed contracts to provide service to 300 homes. Work was completed on 280 homes; collections were made for work done on 240 homes.

During the year Custom Exteriors made cash payments of $173,000 to the painting firm. Of this amount, $168,000 was for homes that were completed and $5,000 was for homes that were still being serviced.

Custom Exteriors is uncertain whether, in calculating income, it should report revenues as earned when it signs a contract, when the work on a house is completed, or when it collects cash from a customer. Similarly it is unsure whether it should report as an expense the total cash payments made to the paint company or only that portion of the payment representing homes completed. If it recognized only that portion representing homes completed, then any payments made on a home before work was completed would be accounted for as a "prepaid expense" (i.e., an asset) rather than an expense.

a. Indicate three possible amounts that the company could report as "revenue from contracts" for the year.

b. Indicate two possible amounts that the company could report as "expenses."

c. Based on your responses to parts (a) and (b), indicate six possible amounts that could be reported as "income" (revenues less expenses).

8. *Unless a contract specifies accounting principles, each side is free to argue for those that best serve its interest.*

Bantham joins with nine others to form a partnership that trades in wheat. The partnership agreement provides that in the event a partner wants to leave the firm, the remaining partners will purchase his or her interest at an amount equal to the partner's original contribution plus any undistributed income.

Each partner contributes $100,000 to the partnership. During its first year of operations, the partnership engages in the following transactions:

January 10: Buys 30,000 bushels of wheat at $4.25 per bushel.
August 11: Buys 70,000 bushels of wheat at $4.00 per bushel.
September 2: Sells 20,000 bushels of wheat at $4.50 per bushel.

On December 31 the price of wheat is $4.80 per bushel. On that date Bantham decides that he wants to leave the partnership. He requests that in accordance with the partnership agreement, the other partners should pay him $100,000 (his original contribution) plus 10 percent of the partnership's income for the year. He and the partners agree that income is revenue less the cost of the 20,000 bushels that were sold. They agree that revenue should be recognized only upon sale of the wheat. They disagree, however, on how the cost of the 20,000 bushels of wheat sold should be determined.

a. Suppose that you represent Bantham in negotiations with the partnership. How much income would you assert that the partnership earned during the year? Explain and justify your response.

b. Suppose instead that you represent the partnership. You wish to minimize the amount that the partnership has to pay Bantham. How much income would you say the partnership has earned? Explain and justify your response.

9. *Disputes over accounting principles can exacerbate domestic quarrels.*

Susan and Jeff agree to a divorce settlement in which the two will split their property equally. It is agreed that Susan will be granted all the assets. She will then make a cash payment to Jeff in the amount of one-half of the value of the total assets.

Susan's accountant has prepared the following financial report of their common assets as at December 31, 1996, the agreed-upon settlement date:

Cash	$240,000
Automobile	36,000
House	210,000
Stocks and bonds	60,000
Total	$546,000

A note to the financial statement indicates that the value of all assets, other than cash, represents the amounts paid to acquire them.

According to real-estate specialists, the house has a market value of $300,000. The "blue book" of used-car prices indicates that the car could be sold (to a dealer) for $22,000; it could be purchased (from a dealer) for $26,000. The stocks and bonds had a market value on December 31, 1996, of $80,000. On that day, however, securities prices were at an unusually high level. On average during 1996 they had a market value of only $66,000. On the day the accountant prepared his report (February 15, 1997), the securities had a market value of $74,000.

a. Suppose that you were the accountant for Jeff. Prepare a statement of assets that would be in Jeff's best interests.

b. What is the amount of the cash payment to which you would assert that Jeff is entitled?

2

The Accounting Equation and the Three Fundamental Financial Statements

In Chapter 1, we introduced the three principal financial statements found in financial reports and examined the framework for financial reporting. In this chapter, we analyze the three financial statements in more detail by relating them to the fundamental accounting equation. Using the fundamental accounting equation as the basis, we learn how to prepare the balance sheet, the income statement, and the statement of changes in financial position.

After studying this chapter, you will be able to

- State and understand the fundamental accounting equation, Assets = Liabilities + Owners' Equity
- Define the terms assets, liabilities, and owners' equity
- Define the terms revenues and expenses
- Understand how revenues and expenses fit into the accounting equation
- Prepare financial statements using only the fundamental accounting equation as the basis
- Understand the difference between the balance sheet and the income statement

THE FUNDAMENTAL ACCOUNTING EQUATION

A firm's *assets (A)* are the resources which it owns or controls. Its *liabilities (L)* are the resources owed to others. Its *owners' equity (OE)* is the residual difference between the two—the interest of the owners in the firm's resources. Thus

$$\text{Assets} - \text{Liabilities} = \text{Owners' equity}$$

or

$$A - L = OE$$

This equation is the fundamental equation of accounting. It lies at the heart of almost everything that is done in the discipline. It is a *tautology,* an expression that is true by definition. What an entity (an individual, business, or government) owns in the way of resources (for example, cash, inventory, plant, or equipment) minus what it owes to others (for example, accounts or notes payable) composes the entity's financial net worth (i.e., the interest of the owners).

In an alternative form, the liabilities are moved to the right-hand side of the equal sign. Thus

$$A = L + OE$$

The fundamental equation now shows the firm's existing resources on the left and tells how these resources have been financed on the right. Assets *(A)* must have been financed either by borrowed capital *(L)* or contributed capital *(OE)*. Liabilities are often termed *creditor equities*. Thus total equities equal the sum of liabilities and owners' equity. In a third alternative form, the equation says simply that *assets* equal *equities*.

THE BALANCE SHEET

In either form, the fundamental equation of accounting yields an expression of an individual's or firm's financial position at a *moment in time*. When the expression is expanded to list specific assets and equities, it is called a *statement of position* or, more commonly, a *balance sheet*. Exhibit 2-1 illustrates a simple balance sheet.

Assets, Liabilities, and Owners' Equity Defined

What gives a resource sufficient value to be accorded accounting recognition? Generally it is that the resource is expected to yield *future economic benefits*. These economic benefits, either directly or indirectly, are *cash flows*. For example, merchandise inventory (in a trading entity) is an economic resource because it is expected to be sold in the future for cash. Raw materials inven-

EXHIBIT 2-1

	The Calgary Company Balance Sheet As at June 30, 1996		
Assets		**Equities**	
Cash	$ 270,000	Liabilities	
Accounts receivable	450,000	Accounts payable	$ 490,000
Merchandise inventory	360,000	Wages payable	25,000
Buildings	1,610,000	Bonds payable	2,045,000
Equipment	650,000	Total liabilities	$2,560,000
Patents and copyrights	800,000	Owners' equity	1,580,000
Total assets	$4,140,000	Total equities	$4,140,000

tory (in a manufacturing concern) is an economic resource because it will be used in the production of goods that will be sold for cash. Plant and equipment have economic value because, like raw materials inventory, they will be used to provide goods or services that will generate cash. Cash itself is a resource because it can be used to purchase inventory, plant and equipment, and other resources that can be expected to generate additional cash. Moreover, cash is the resource of ultimate concern to the owners of a business because it is the medium of exchange in our society.

Assets have been defined in many ways. Consider one particularly rigorous definition:

> ***Resources or rights incontestably controlled by an entity at the accounting date that are expected to yield it future economic benefits***[1]

Similarly, *liabilities* are

> ***Obligations of an entity at the accounting date to make future transfers of assets or services (sometimes uncertain as to timing and amount) to other entities***

Owners' equity, then, is the difference between the two:

> ***The residual interest in the assets of an entity that remains after deducting its liabilities, that is, the interests of the owners in a business enterprise***

Classification of Assets and Liabilities

Assets and liabilities may be categorized by several different characteristics:

- *Liquidity,* which can be current or noncurrent: A *current* asset can be sold or transformed into cash and a *current* liability can be satisfied within one year or within the normal operating cycle of the business. *Noncurrent* assets and liabilities are not so liquid.

[1]David Solomons, "Guidelines for Financial Reporting Standards," a paper prepared for the Research Board of the Institute of Chartered Accountants in England and Wales, 1989.

- *Physical form,* which can be tangible or intangible: A *tangible* asset has physical existence (such as buildings and equipment), whereas an *intangible* asset is characterized by legal rights (such as notes receivable or patents).
- *Valuation,* which can be monetary or nonmonetary: A *monetary* asset or liability has a *fixed* exchange value in terms of cash; examples are accounts receivable or payable. A *nonmonetary* asset or liability has no fixed exchange value, the amount of cash to be received or paid being dependent upon economic conditions; examples are plant and equipment and inventory.

Because *liquidity,* the ability to transform assets into cash, is such an important factor in economic decisions, balance sheets conventionally employ the *current versus noncurrent* classification. Balance sheets do not typically reflect either the monetary/nonmonetary or the tangible/intangible distinctions. The monetary/nonmonetary distinction, however, is essential to an understanding of some key accounting issues (such as how to account for transactions in foreign currencies) to be addressed later in the text. The tangible/intangible distinction is one that is perhaps the easiest to make in that it is based on physical form. Yet it is the least significant in accounting. The principles of accounting for intangible assets are indistinguishable from those for tangible assets.

Current Assets

Current assets include cash and such other assets that will either be transformed into cash or will be sold or consumed within one year or within the *normal operating cycle* of the business if longer than one year. For most businesses the normal operating cycle is one year, but for some (such as those in the tobacco and distilling industries where the products must be aged for a period of several years) it may be longer. *Cash* includes not only currency but bank deposits as well. Disbursements of cash include payments by cheque, bank transfer, and currency.

Marketable securities are shares of stock, bonds, treasury bills, and commercial paper held by the firm as short-term investments. They are ordinarily stated on the balance sheet at original cost. If, however, the market value of the portfolio of securities held is less than original cost, then they are presented at the lower, more conservative value. But increases in value of marketable securities from original cost are not ordinarily recognized. Due to the ease with which marketable securities can be sold and thereby transformed into cash, the market value of the securities must be disclosed in the financial statements, either parenthetically or in supplementary notes.

Accounts receivable are the claims upon customers that can be expected to be collected within the normal operating cycle (those expected to be collected after the normal operating cycle are included among noncurrent assets). Deducted from accounts receivable is an *allowance for doubtful accounts*—an estimate of the amounts owed to the company that will be uncollectable. Thus the accounts receivable reported on the balance sheet is not the total amount owed to the firm but only the portion that the firm estimates is actually collectable.

Inventories include both items available for sale to customers and raw materials, parts, and supplies to be used in production. Inventories are ordinarily reported at the cost incurred to either purchase or produce them. But in the event that the cost of replacing such items has declined, then the inventories may be "written down" to reflect the decline in value. As with marketable securities, increases in value are not ordinarily recognized.

Prepaid expenses are services or rights to services paid for but not yet consumed. As they are consumed they will be "charged off" as actual expenses. A firm might, for example, purchase a one-year insurance policy for $1,200 ($100 per month). At the time of payment it would record the policy as a current asset, "Prepaid insurance—$1,200." Each month it would reduce the asset by one-twelfth of the original amount ($100) and would charge insurance expense with the same amount. Thus, after eight months, the balance in the prepaid insurance account would be only $400 (four months remaining times $100 per month) and there would be $800 charged to insurance expense. Other common prepaid expense items are prepaid interest, prepaid advertising, and prepaid rent. Prepaid expenses are one type of *deferred charge*—outlays made in one period to benefit future periods.

Noncurrent Assets

Noncurrent assets are resources that *cannot* be expected to be sold or consumed within the normal operating cycle of the business. Noncurrent assets are usually considered to be *long-lived*. Capital assets include property, plant, and equipment and intangible properties.

Property, plant, and *equipment* are recorded on the balance sheet at original cost. Deducted from each of the assets, other than land, is *accumulated amortization*—an allowance to reflect the "consumption" of the assets over time by wear and tear as well as by technological obsolescence.

Amortization is the process of allocating (spreading) the cost of a capital asset over its useful life. Amortization on each individual asset or group of similar assets is computed separately, and the total amount accumulated is a function of the original cost, age, and expected useful life of the asset. No amortization is provided for land since it is not consumed over time and seldom declines in utility. However, as more and more land is polluted or otherwise consumed by companies' operations, the non-amortization of land is increasingly being challenged.

Investments and *other assets* include amounts owed to the company by outsiders that are not due for at least one year and amounts that the company has invested in other companies. If, for example, a company owns 30 percent of the voting shares of another company, its interest would ordinarily be included among investments and other assets. An interest in another company, however, may be classified as either "Marketable securities," a current asset, or as "Long-term investments," a noncurrent asset. The decision as to how the investment should be classified depends to a large extent on the *intent* of the investing company's management. If it intends to maintain its interest for a relatively long period of time and views ownership as a long-term investment, then the amounts owned should be classified as a noncurrent asset. If, on the other hand, the company purchases the interest with the intention of selling it as soon as additional cash might be needed (for example, if it purchases a few hundred shares of Bombardier Inc. stock as a temporary investment with no intention of exercising significant influence over the company), then the amount owned should be classified as a current asset.

Deferred charges such as prepaid expenses may also be included among noncurrent assets. If, for example, a company purchased an insurance policy or a licence that had more than a one-year life, then the percentage of original cost representing the unexpired portion of the insurance policy or licence would be included among noncurrent assets.

Some deferred charges represent outlays that will benefit future accounting periods but for which both the number of such periods and the value of the benefits are exceedingly difficult to measure. Consider the costs incurred to organize a corporation: the legal fees required to draw up the documents of incorporation, the costs of printing the shares of stock to be issued, and the fees paid to the province upon filing for a certificate of incorporation. These costs—like those of buildings and equipment—are incurred to benefit the business over a long period of time. Just as income of a single year of operations would be understated if the entire cost of a building were charged as an expense at the time it was purchased, income would also be distorted if the costs of organizing the corporation were charged off in a single year. As a result, organizational costs are frequently reported as assets of the company, and each year a portion of the costs are *amortized* and charged off as an expense.

Deferred charges representing benefits that will accrue to the firm over a long period of time in the future are often a source of confusion. Deferred charges, unlike most other assets, are intangible and frequently have no market value. Amounts spent as organizational costs, for example, cannot readily be transferred to any other business entity; they cannot be sold to outsiders. How, then, can they be considered assets?

The question must be answered in terms of the nature of all assets. Assets can be defined as future services to be received in money or benefits convertible into money. They can readily be viewed as "bundles of services" available for use or sale by a particular entity. The determination of service potential is made with respect to the business entity issuing the financial reports—not with respect to the world at large.

In accordance with currently employed practices of valuation (alternative practices will be discussed in subsequent chapters), assets are measured and recorded at the time they are acquired at the price paid for them. As their service potential declines over time (e.g., as the assets are consumed), the reported value is reduced *proportionately* through the process of amortization. If one-third of the services have been consumed, then the asset is reported at two-thirds its original cost. As long as the asset is not intended for sale to outsiders, market value seldom enters into the determination of the amount at which an asset is reported. Indeed, an automobile owned by a business might be reported at an amount either greater or less than the price at which similar used cars are being traded.

The outlay for organizational costs will benefit many accounting periods. To the extent that it has "future service potential"—the corporation would not exist without it—the outlay can properly be considered an asset. Even though it may have no value to outsiders, it should be reported on the balance sheet at initial cost less that fraction of cost representing services already consumed.

Current Liabilities

Liabilities are also categorized as either current or noncurrent. *Current liabilities* are expected to be satisfied out of current assets within a relatively short period of time, usually one year, or within the *normal operating cycle* of the business if longer than one year. Most common categories of current liabilities are amounts owed to employees for wages and salaries; to suppliers for services, supplies, merchandise inventory, and raw materials purchased (conventionally called trade accounts, or simply *accounts payable*); to the government for taxes (taxes payable); and to banks or other lenders for loans (notes payable) and for interest on the loans (interest payable) that is payable within one year.

Noncurrent Liabilities

Noncurrent liabilities include all other amounts owed, such as long-term notes and bonds. Bonds are similar to long-term notes, but they differ in that the promise to pay is usually included in a more formal legal instrument and in that the term of the loan is often longer. The same bond or note may be classified as both a current and a noncurrent liability. The portion that is due within one year would be considered current; the portion due beyond one year would be noncurrent.

Amounts that a company pays in advance to receive goods or services in the future are considered to be assets of the company. In the same sense, amounts that others pay to the company for goods and services to be provided in the future are considered to be liabilities. Suppose, for example, that an airline sells a ticket for a trip the traveller intends to take a month after purchase. At the time of sale the airline receives an asset (cash or accounts receivable) equal to the price of the ticket. At the time of sale it also incurs an obligation to provide services (i.e., one airline trip) to the customer. To be sure, the obligation is not a liability in the usual sense, in that the airline has no monetary debt outstanding to the customer. But it is an obligation to provide a service. These amounts are reported among the liabilities and may be labelled as appropriate: "Advances from customers," "Revenues received but not yet earned," or, less descriptively but more generally, *unearned revenue*. They are classified as *current* if the obligation is likely to be satisfied within one year; otherwise they are classified as *noncurrent*.

"Nonassets and Nonliabilities"

Not all amounts that a firm will have to pay to others if it continues in business are recorded as liabilities, nor are all amounts that it can expect to receive recorded as assets. If a firm signs a three-year contract with a new president, for example, and promises to pay him or her $300,000 per year, the firm may be legally liable for the full $900,000 as long as the new president is willing to provide the required services. The firm would not, however, record the full amount as a liability. Only as the president "earns" the salary—that is, performs his or her side of the bargain—would the firm record as a liability amounts earned but not paid. Similarly accounted for would be a transaction in which a firm borrows $1,000 from a bank at a 12 percent rate of interest and gives the bank a one-year note payable. At the end of the one-year period, the firm will owe the bank $1,120—the principal of $1,000 plus interest of $120. At the time the note is signed, however, the only liability that would be recorded is the $1,000 actually borrowed. Each month, as the company has use of the borrowed funds, an additional $10 interest for one month will be recorded as a liability. The bank, for its part, would record as an asset a note receivable for $1,000. It, too, would recognize an asset, "interest receivable," only as it earns the interest revenue with the passage of time.

In general, assets and liabilities arising out of *executory contracts* (those contingent upon the mutual performance of the two sides to the contract) are recorded only to the extent that one of the parties has fulfilled its contractual obligations. The reason for such limited accounting recognition of assets and liabilities will become considerably clearer as the relationship between balance sheet and income statement accounts is discussed more fully in subsequent chapters.

Owners' Equity

In the corporate form of organization, owners' equity is called shareholders' equity, reflecting the fact that the corporation's owners are shareholders. The shareholders' equity section of the corporate balance sheet is typically divided into two main parts. The first indicates the *capital contributed by shareholders*— either at the time the corporation was formed or when additional shares of stock were issued in the course of the corporation's existence. Corporations may issue several different types of stock.

Common stock generally gives its owners the right to vote for members of the corporation's board of directors as well as on numerous other corporate matters and the right to share in corporate profits whenever dividends are declared by the board of directors.

Preferred stock, on the other hand, generally does *not* carry voting rights, but it does ordinarily mean that the owner will receive dividends of at least a minimum amount each year. The dividend rate is fixed at the time the stock is issued. It is important to note that dividends on common and preferred stock need never be paid. They only become a legal liability of the corporation when declared by the board of directors.

Shares of both common and preferred stock are sometimes arbitrarily assigned a *par* or *stated* value (e.g., $100 per share). These values have some legal, but little economic, significance, and shares are often issued for amounts above or below these arbitrarily assigned values. Amounts that the company receives above the par values of the shares are categorized as *premium on capital stock,* or *contributed surplus,* and those below (almost always for preferred stock) as a *discount* on the shares issued. The issuance of shares for less than par value is not allowed in most jurisdictions in Canada. Par value shares are no longer common in Canada, due to changes in the various corporations acts.

The second part of the shareholders' equity section of the corporate balance sheet, *retained earnings,* indicates the accumulated earnings of the business less the cumulative amount of dividends declared since incorporation. Retained earnings will be commented on in greater detail later in this chapter.

If the firm is not a corporation, that is, if it is a *sole proprietorship* (a firm owned by a single individual) or a *partnership* (a firm owned by two or more parties), then the owners' equity section of the balance sheet may take a somewhat different form. Since such enterprises do not issue stock and are not bound by many of the legal restrictions that apply to firms that do, it is generally most useful to readers of the financial reports to indicate the entire equity of each of the owners in a single separate account. The owners' equity section of a company owned by two partners, W. King and F. Prince, might appear as follows:

Partners' capital	
W. King, capital	$ 9,525,347
F. Prince, capital	7,526,322
Total partners' capital	$17,051,669

Recognition of Assets and Liabilities

When does an entity recognize the existence of an asset or a liability? That is, when does it enter (or change) its value on the balance sheet? Almost all accounting issues centre on this key question.

In most circumstances, the value of an asset is based upon an *arm's-length transaction that has taken place in the past*. An "arm's-length" transaction is one with a party that is independent of the reporting entity (e.g., with a party other than an affiliate, owner, or officer of the entity).

Sometimes, however, it is necessary to recognize changes in value resulting from *economic events* in addition to those from transactions to which the reporting entity has been a party. For example, when a firm purchases merchandise inventory, it will record the inventory at the acquisition cost—the amount based upon the arm's-length purchase transaction. Suppose, however, that subsequent to purchase, the market value of the inventory were to decline. The firm would be required to reduce the carrying value of the inventory to the new market value, even if it never acquired additional inventory at the new price. Correspondingly, information that a loan is likely uncollectable would lead the lender to reduce the recorded value of the note receivable even though the lender has engaged in no transactions with the borrower since making the loan.

For the most part, however, accountants have been reluctant to recognize *increases* in values that are not the result of past transactions. For example, whereas the decline in inventory would be recorded, a corresponding increase would not. Due to the potential adverse consequences of overstating assets (or understating liabilities), the accounting profession has traditionally been conservative. It has established more rigorous standards of evidential reliability for asset increases than for decreases. In this respect the accounting professions in Canada and the United States has been more reluctant than many of its overseas counterparts to record increases in values in the absence of arm's-length transactions. For example, British and Australian companies are sometimes permitted to assign values to trademarks, even though the values are attributable to customer loyalty rather than specific purchase transactions. Nevertheless, as shall be pointed out throughout this text, even Canadian standards require asset values to be enhanced in some situations.

The balance sheet is, in essence, an expression of the fundamental accounting equation ($A = L + OE$). It is affected by *all* economic events that are given accounting recognition.

Ever since the early Renaissance, the *double-entry* system has been central to accounting practice and theory. The double-entry system is a manifestation of the accounting equation. Every transaction or event that increases (or decreases) the left side of the accounting equation (assets) must increase (or decrease) the right side of the equation (liabilities and owners' equity) by an identical amount. Thus an increase in assets must be matched by an increase in claims against the assets either by creditors (liabilities L) or by the owners (owners' equity OE). Some transactions or events may affect only one side of the equation. But these involve only an exchange of one asset for another asset or one equity for another equity. Every transaction therefore must be recorded at least twice. A change in one element of the accounting equation must be matched by a change in another. *The equation must be maintained in balance.*

Formation of a Business Entity

Suppose that in March 1996 the Schaefer family establishes the Schaefer Corporation to open and operate a bookstore. The company will commence ongoing operations in April 1996. Adam Schaefer contributes $30,000 cash in exchange for 200 shares of common stock. Bonnie Schaefer contributes land that is worth $50,000 and a building that is worth $100,000 in exchange for 1,000 shares. (These values are indicative of what the new company would have to pay for the land and building in the marketplace.)

The initial contribution of resources must be recorded on the books of the corporation to show both the new assets and the claims against the assets. In this example, the assets are financed entirely by the owners. Hence the transactions result in an increase in assets (cash, building, and land) and in owners' equity (common stock). The common stock is assigned a value of $180,000, which, of course, corresponds to the market value of the contributed assets. The changes on the right side of the equation must equal those on the left. (Change is represented by the Δ.) Thus

Increase

$$
\begin{array}{ccccc}
\text{Land} & & & & \\
\text{+\$50,000} & & & & \\
\uparrow & & & & \\
\text{Building} & & \text{Common stock: Bonnie Schaefer} & & \\
\text{+\$100,000} & & \text{+\$150,000} & & \\
\uparrow & & \uparrow & & \\
\text{Cash} & & \text{Common stock: Adam Schaefer} & & \\
\text{+\$30,000} & & \text{+\$30,000} & & \\
\uparrow & & \uparrow & & \\
\Delta A & = & \Delta L & + & \Delta OE
\end{array}
\qquad (1)
$$

Decrease

In this and subsequent transactions, increases in accounts will be shown above the accounting equation, decreases below. After the formation of the Schaefer Corporation, the following additional transactions occur.

Payment of Utility Deposits

Schaefer Corporation pays $600 in cash to its hydro company as a security deposit. The transaction causes a decrease in cash and an increase in an asset, "utility deposits." The utility deposits are comparable to accounts or notes receivable. Schaefer Corporation is owed the funds (albeit at no specified date) from the hydro company. Thus

Increase

$$
\begin{array}{c}
\text{Utility deposits} \\
\text{+\$600} \\
\uparrow \\
\Delta A \quad = \quad \Delta L \quad + \quad \Delta OE \\
\downarrow \\
\text{Cash} \\
\text{-\$600}
\end{array}
\qquad (2)
$$

Decrease

Prepaid Insurance

Schaefer Corporation purchases a one-year fire insurance policy on its building and equipment, paying $3,600 cash. The policy is to go into effect on April 1, which is when the corporation expects to commence operations. The insurance policy is an asset, comparable to buildings and equipment. The company anticipates receiving economic benefits (insurance coverage) from it over the following 12 months. Thus

Increase

$$
\begin{array}{c}
\text{Prepaid insurance} \\
\text{+\$3,600} \\
\uparrow \\
\Delta A \quad = \quad \Delta L \quad + \quad \Delta OE \\
\downarrow \\
\text{Cash} \\
\text{-\$3,600}
\end{array}
\qquad (3)
$$

Decrease

Purchase of Merchandise Inventory

The company acquires $40,000 of new books as inventory. All acquisitions are "on account" (the company will pay at a later date). The transaction results in an increase in an asset and a corresponding increase in a liability. The inventory is an asset since it will provide a future economic benefit when it is sold. Thus

Increase

$$
\begin{array}{ccccc}
\text{Merchandise} & & \text{Accounts} & & \\
\text{inventory} & & \text{payable} & & \\
+\$40,000 & & +\$40,000 & & \\
\uparrow & & \uparrow & & \\
\Delta A & = & \Delta L & + & \Delta OE \qquad (4)
\end{array}
$$

Decrease

Acquisition of Equipment

The company purchases computer equipment for $28,000, an amount which includes delivery and installation. It pays $4,000 and gives a note payable of $24,000 for the balance. The note is to be repaid in 12 monthly instalments beginning April 30. Interest is to be charged at a rate of 18 percent annually (1.5 percent per month) on the unpaid balance. Thus

Increase

$$
\begin{array}{ccccc}
\text{Equipment} & & \text{Note payable} & & \\
+\$28,000 & & +\$24,000 & & \\
\uparrow & & \uparrow & & \\
\Delta A & = & \Delta L & + & \Delta OE \qquad (5) \\
\downarrow & & & & \\
\text{Cash} & & & & \\
-\$4,000 & & & &
\end{array}
$$

Decrease

The delivery and installation charges are included in the cost of the asset as long as they are necessary to bring the equipment to a serviceable condition.

The note payable is classified as a current liability since it is to be repaid within one year. The interest to be paid, although most definitely an obligation of the company, is not, at this time, given accounting recognition because the company has not yet had the use of the borrowed funds and has not yet benefited from them.

Improvements to Building

The company contracts with a construction company to remodel its building. The agreed-upon price is $20,000. The company pays the contractor $10,500 while the work is in process. When the project is completed, Schaefer Corporation receives the final bill, still unpaid at month's end, of $9,500. Thus

Increase

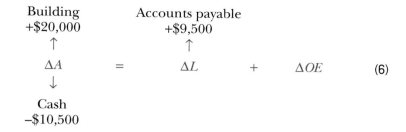

Building
+$20,000
↑
ΔA = ΔL + ΔOE (6)
↓
Cash
−$10,500

Accounts payable
+$9,500
↑

Decrease

The improvements to the building are as much an asset as the building itself, since they have been undertaken to benefit future accounting periods.

Long-Term Borrowing

Recognizing that it will be required to make substantial cash payments once it begins operations, the company borrows $50,000 from the bank and signs a five-year note payable. Interest is to be paid monthly at an annual rate of 12 percent—that is, $6,000 per year, or $500 per month. Interest for the first month will be recorded when paid (as discussed later in this chapter). Thus

Increase

Cash
+$50,000
↑
ΔA = ΔL + ΔOE (7)

Note payable
+$50,000
↑

Decrease

Purchase of Marketable Securities

Rather than deposit in its chequing account the entire $50,000 that it has borrowed from the bank, the company purchases $10,000 in Government of Canada bonds. By doing so, the company is able to earn a higher rate of interest than what it could earn from the bank. Thus

Increase

Marketable securities
+$10,000
↑
ΔA = ΔL + ΔOE (8)
↓
Cash
−$10,000

Decrease

Recognition of Organization Costs

Schaefer Corporation engages a lawyer to file the necessary documents of incorporation and provide legal assistance on a number of matters relating to the establishment of the business. Total costs, which the company pays in cash, are $6,000.

These costs, like the improvements to the building, will benefit the company only when it begins operations (in April). Therefore the costs must be *capitalized*—that is, recorded as an asset. Thus

Increase

$$
\begin{array}{c}
\text{Organization costs} \\
+\$6,000 \\
\uparrow
\end{array}
$$

$$\Delta A \quad = \quad \Delta L \quad + \quad \Delta OE \tag{9}$$

$$
\begin{array}{c}
\downarrow \\
\text{Cash} \\
-\$6,000
\end{array}
$$

Decrease

Organization costs are an *intangible* asset. Unlike most other assets, both tangible and intangible, organization costs cannot be sold or traded; nevertheless, they are an asset because (according to the definition of an asset) they are expected to yield *future economic benefits*.

Preparing a Balance Sheet

To prepare a balance sheet it is necessary only to sum the increases and decreases in each account and to list and classify the accounts and balances. All of the amounts in the balance sheet are the result of one transaction, except for the cash and accounts payable balances. The cash balance of $45,300 results from the following transactions:

Issue of common stock (1)	+ $30,000
Payment of utility deposit (2)	− 600
Payment of insurance premium (3)	− 3,600
Payment for equipment (5)	− 4,000
Payment for building improvements (6)	− 10,500
Cash borrowed from bank (7)	+ 50,000
Payment for marketable securities (8)	− 10,000
Payment for organization costs (9)	− 6,000
	$ 45,300

The $49,500 balance in accounts payable at March 31, 1996, results from the $40,000 payable created on the purchase of merchandise inventory on account plus the $9,500 still unpaid for the building improvements at March 31, 1996.

Exhibit 2-2 presents the Schaefer Corporation balance sheet as at March 31, 1996. (Balance sheets as well as other financial statements are *always* prepared at year end, but they may also be prepared as at any other date.)

EXHIBIT 2-2

The Schaefer Corporation Balance Sheet As at March 31, 1996			
Assets		**Equities**	
Current		Liabilities	
Cash	$ 45,300	Current	
Marketable securities	10,000	Accounts payable	$ 49,500
Merchandise inventory	40,000	Note payable	24,000
Prepaid insurance	3,600	Total, current	$ 73,500
Total, current	$ 98,900		
		Noncurrent	
Noncurrent		Note payable	50,000
Utility deposit	600	Total liabilities	$123,500
Organization costs	6,000	Shareholders' equity	
Land	50,000	Common stock	180,000
Buildings	120,000		
Equipment	28,000		
Total, noncurrent	$204,600		
Total assets	$303,500	Total equities	$303,500

THE INCOME STATEMENT

The accounting equation and the balance sheet indicate net assets (assets less liabilities) and the owners' claims against such net assets at a *point* in time. The income statement, on the other hand, indicates changes in owners' equity (and thus changes in net assets) over a *period* of time resulting from the operations of the business, *excluding* contributions or withdrawals on the part of the owners. The income statement indicates the revenues of the period and the expenses incurred in earning the revenues; an income statement (*not* for the Schaefer Corporation, since so far it has neither earned revenues nor incurred expenses), in condensed form, is shown in Exhibit 2-3.

EXHIBIT 2-3

The Calgary Company Income Statement Year Ended June 30, 1996			
Revenue from sales			$1,220,000
Cost of merchandise sold	$700,000		
Wages and salaries	150,000		
Advertising	30,000		
Rent	40,000	$920,000	
Taxes		120,000	1,040,000
Net income			$ 180,000

Revenues and Expenses

Revenues are the inflows of cash or other assets attributable to the goods or services provided by the enterprise. Most commonly, revenues are derived from the sale of the company's product or service, but they can also be realized (recognized) from interest on loans to outsiders, dividends received on shares of stock of other companies, royalties earned on patents or licences, or rent earned from properties owned.

Expenses are the outflows of cash or other assets attributable to the profit-directed activities of an enterprise. Expenses are a measure of the effort exerted on the part of the enterprise in its attempt to realize revenues. More formally,

> *Revenues are increases in economic resources, either by way of inflows or enhancements of assets or reductions of liabilities, resulting from the ordinary activities of an entity. Revenues of entities normally arise from the sale of goods, the rendering of services or the use by others of the entity resources yielding rent, interest, royalties or dividends.*
>
> *Expenses are decreases in economic resources, either by way of outflows or reductions of assets or incurrences of liabilities, resulting from an entity's ordinary revenue generating or service delivery activities.*[2]

Gains and Losses

Gains and losses are similar, but not identical, to revenues and expenses. *Gains* and *losses* are increases or decreases in net assets resulting from transactions that are not typical of a firm's day-to-day transactions. Suppose, for example, that a retail store sells some office equipment that it had used in its own accounting department. The difference between the selling price and its book value (where book value is defined as the difference between the office equipment account and the accumulated amortization on office equipment account) at time of sale would be recorded as a gain or loss. By contrast, however, if the firm were to sell ordinary merchandise, then the amount for which it was sold would be recorded as revenue; the cost of the goods sold would be reported as an expense.

Gains and losses that are not typical of the entity's normal business activities, are not expected to occur frequently, and do not depend primarily on decisions made by management or owners are classified as *extraordinary items*. Examples are losses from fires, natural disasters, and expropriations of corporate property by governments. To make certain that such extraordinary events do not distort comparisons of performance in past years and predictions of earnings in the future, they are reported separately in the statement of income.

[2] "Financial Statement Concepts," *Sections 1000.37 and .38, CICA Handbook,* 1991.

Stocks versus Flows

Contrast the manner in which the date appears on the income statement with the way it appears on the balance sheet. The income statement of the Calgary Company is *for the year ended* June 30, 1996—it describes what has happened over a one-year period. The balance sheet is *as at* June 30, 1996—it describes the business as at a particular moment in time.

The relationship between the balance sheet and the income statement can be explained by analogy to a household bathtub filled with water. The water in the bathtub is comparable to the owners' equity—or, alternatively, to the firm's net assets (assets less liabilities). In describing the level of water in the tub one could say that at a given moment the tub contains *x* litres of water. Similarly, one could describe a firm as having a particular level of net assets. Indeed, the balance sheet of a firm does exactly that. It indicates, and describes, at a particular point in time, the level of assets, of liabilities, and of the difference between the two—owners' equity.

Suppose, however, that the water is entering the tub through the faucets at the same time it is leaving through the drain. It would still be possible—and indeed necessary if comprehensive information is to be presented—to describe the level of water in the tub. One could say, for example, that at 11:03 P.M. there were 40 litres of water in the tub. But this information would hardly constitute a very complete description of activity in the tub. Also needed would be data as to the rate at which the water level is rising or falling. More complete information might be as follows: Water is entering the tub at the rate of 10 litres per minute; it is leaving at the rate of 8 litres per minute; hence it is rising at the rate of 2 litres per minute.

So also with the firm. Information is required as to the *rate* at which the equity of the owners is increasing or decreasing. The water entering the

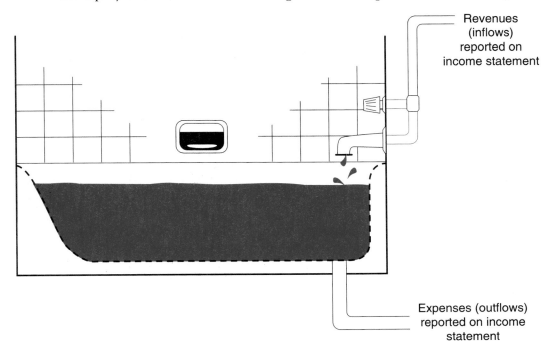

Revenues (inflows) reported on income statement

Expenses (outflows) reported on income statement

tub might be compared to revenues; the water leaving, to expenses; and the difference between the two, to income. Thus it might be said that assets are entering the firm at the *rate* of $10 million per year (i.e., revenues for the year are $10 million), that assets are leaving the firm at the *rate* of $8 million per year (i.e., expenses for the year are $8 million), and that the change in net assets (owners' equity) for the year is $2 million (i.e., income for the year is $2 million).

If the amount of water in the bathtub at 11:03 P.M. is 40 litres and it is increasing at the rate of 2 litres per minute, then the amount at the end of the minute will be 42 litres. The beginning amount plus the net amount added during the period equals the ending amount.

So too with the firm. If the owners' equity at January 1, 1996, is $40 million and income for the year is $2 million, then owners' equity at the end of the year will be $42 million.

The balance sheet indicates the equity that the owners have in the firm at any given *point* in time. Such a point of time is usually the end of a month or the end of a year. The balance sheet also indicates the assets and the liabilities that result in the particular level of owners' equity.

The income statement indicates the *rate* at which the equity of the owners is changing. It reveals the revenues, the expenses, and the resultant income for the period. Assuming that no assets or liabilities entered or left the firm from other sources (i.e., the owners neither contributed nor withdrew assets), then owners' equity at the beginning of the period (per the balance sheet) plus income for the period (per the income statement) must equal owners' equity at the end of the period (per the new balance sheet). In general, the equation is:

$$\begin{array}{l} \text{Owners' equity, beginning of period} \\ +(-)\ \text{Income (or loss) for the period} \\ +(-)\ \text{Additional contributions (or withdrawals)} \\ \qquad\quad \text{of owners during the period} \\ \hline = \text{Owners' equity, end of period} \end{array}$$

The owners' equity of the Calgary Company as at June 30, 1996 (see Exhibit 2-1), was $1,580,000. If, during the following year—that ending June 30, 1997—the company had income of $250,000 and paid dividends of (that is, the owners withdrew) $190,000, then owners' equity as at June 30, 1997, would be $1,640,000:

Owners' equity 30/6/96		Income		Dividends		Owners' equity 30/6/97
$1,580,000	+	$250,000	−	$190,000	=	$1,640,000

Effect of Revenues and Expenses on the Accounting Equation

The key to understanding the relationship between the income statement and the balance sheet is in recognizing that revenues, by definition, are inflows or other enhancements of net assets $(A - L)$. Therefore they *must*, at the same time, be matched by an *increase* in owners' equity (*OE*), since $A - L = OE$. Correspondingly, expenses are outflows or reductions in net assets. They *must* be matched by a *decrease* in owners' equity.

The income statement explains the changes (excluding contributions to, or withdrawals by, the owners) in *retained earnings* that take place in an accounting period. Retained earnings, as indicated in the discussion of owners' equity, is one of the major divisions of owners' equity. It indicates the undistributed earnings of the business accumulated since its inception. The revenues are increases in retained earnings, the expenses decreases.

For example, with the exception of the initial contribution of capital (the issuance of the stock), the transactions in which the Schaefer Corporation engages in March do not affect owners' equity. The company has not yet begun operations. It has not yet earned any revenues or incurred any expenses. All of its costs are intended to benefit future accounting periods, when the company carries out its planned activities. Therefore all of its costs are capitalized (recorded as assets). Indeed, after the firm receives its initial contribution of capital, the "level" of net assets (and therefore owners' equity) remains unchanged during March.

Consider now the transactions in which the Schaefer Company engages in April, after it has begun operations.

Purchase of Additional Merchandise
The company purchases additional merchandise on account for $110,000.

Increase

$$
\begin{array}{ccccc}
\text{Merchandise} & & \text{Accounts} & & \\
\text{inventory} & & \text{payable} & & \\
+\$110,000 & & +\$110,000 & & \\
\uparrow & & \uparrow & & \\
\Delta A & = & \Delta L & + & \Delta OE \qquad (10)
\end{array}
$$

Decrease

Payment of Amount Owed
The company pays the publishers $106,000 of what is owed for the books that it purchased.

Increase

$$
\begin{array}{ccccc}
\Delta A & = & \Delta L & + & \Delta OE \qquad (11) \\
\downarrow & & \downarrow & & \\
\text{Cash} & & \text{Accounts payable} & & \\
-\$106,000 & & -\$106,000 & &
\end{array}
$$

Decrease

These last two transactions are similar to those that took place in March. They result in changes in both assets and liabilities but do not affect net assets $(A - L)$. Therefore they do not affect owners' equity.

Sales Revenue and Cost of Goods Sold

During April the company sells books for $144,000. The books that are sold have cost the company $90,000. The customers pay cash of $32,000 and receive credit for the balance of $112,000.

As a result of these transactions, the net assets of the company increase by $54,000 ($144,000 less $90,000). The firm receives cash and claims to cash of $144,000. It surrenders assets of only $90,000. Because net assets have increased by $54,000, so also must owners' equity (more specifically, retained earnings).

The transaction may be recorded in two steps. The first will recognize the sale and the concurrent receipt of cash and creation of accounts receivable. The second will record the cost of the books sold and the associated reduction in merchandise inventory.

The increase in owners' equity ($144,000) attributable to the sale will be reported in parentheses as "sales revenue." Sales revenue, as will be explained in greater detail in the next chapter, may be interpreted as a subaccount of retained earnings. It provides information on the reason for the change in retained earnings. This information is required for preparation of the income statement—the statement that explains the increase in owners' equity attributable to the operations of the enterprise.

The reduction in owners' equity ($90,000) associated with the reduction in merchandise inventory will be reported in parentheses as "cost of goods sold." Cost of goods sold, like sales revenue and all other revenues and expenses, may also be seen as a subaccount of retained earnings.

To record the sale, we have

Increase

$$
\begin{array}{ccccc}
\text{Cash} \\
+\$32,000 \\
\uparrow \\
& & & \text{Retained earnings} \\
\text{Accounts receivable} & & & \text{(sales revenue)} \\
+\$112,000 & & & +\$144,000 \\
\uparrow & & & \uparrow \\
\Delta A & = & \Delta L & + & \Delta OE \\
\end{array}
\qquad (12)
$$

Decrease

To record the costs related to the sale, we have

Increase

$$
\begin{array}{ccccc}
\Delta A & = & \Delta L & + & \Delta OE \\
\downarrow & & & & \downarrow \\
\text{Merchandise inventory} & & & & \text{Retained earnings} \\
-\$90,000 & & & & \text{(cost of goods sold)} \\
& & & & -\$90,000 \\
\end{array}
\qquad (13)
$$

Decrease

Collection of Accounts Receivable

The Schaefer Corporation collects $68,000 that was owed to it by its customers. As a consequence, it exchanges one asset (accounts receivable) for another (cash). This transaction has no impact on the equity of the owners (OE); the net assets ($A - L$) remained unchanged.

Increase

$$\text{Cash} \atop +\$68,000$$

$$\uparrow$$

$$\Delta A \quad = \quad \Delta L \quad + \quad \Delta OE \qquad (14)$$

$$\downarrow$$

$$\text{Accounts receivable} \atop -\$68,000$$

Decrease

Wages and Salary Expense

During April the firm incurs $34,000 in wages and salary expense. Of this amount, $30,000 is paid in cash. The balance is to be paid in early May.

The April wages and salaries reduce an asset (cash) by $30,000 and increase a liability (wages and salaries payable) by $4,000. Net assets ($A - L$) decrease by $34,000. Therefore owners' equity must also decrease by $34,000. Particularly notable about this transaction is that the wages and salary expense (the reduction in retained earnings) is determined by the wages and salaries *earned* by the employees—not by the amount of cash actually paid.

Increase

$$\text{Wages and salaries} \atop \text{payable} \atop +\$4,000$$

$$\uparrow$$

$$\Delta A \quad = \quad \Delta L \quad + \quad \Delta OE \qquad (15)$$

$$\downarrow \qquad\qquad\qquad\qquad \downarrow$$

Cash   Retained earnings
−$30,000   (wages and salary expense)
−$34,000

Decrease

Insurance Expense

As previously noted, in March the Schaefer Corporation acquired a one-year (12-month) insurance policy at a cost of $3,600. The cost of the policy is recorded as "prepaid insurance," an asset. It is stated at $3,600 on the March 31 balance sheet. During April, one month of the insurance protection expires. Hence the asset, prepaid insurance, must be reduced by one-twelfth

($300) of its initial value. Correspondingly, owners' equity (insurance expense) must be reduced by the same amount.

Increase

$$\Delta A \qquad = \qquad \Delta L \qquad + \qquad \Delta OE \qquad\qquad (16)$$
$$\downarrow \qquad\qquad\qquad\qquad\qquad\qquad\qquad \downarrow$$

Prepaid insurance   Retained earnings
−$300   (insurance expense)
−$300

Decrease

Payment of Interest on Noncurrent Note Payable

The company pays interest of $500 on its noncurrent note payable. The payment reduces cash and has no effect on any other asset or liability. It therefore reduces owners' equity (interest expense).

Increase

$$\Delta A \qquad = \qquad \Delta L \qquad + \qquad \Delta OE \qquad\qquad (17)$$
$$\downarrow \qquad\qquad\qquad\qquad\qquad\qquad\qquad \downarrow$$

Cash   Retained earnings
−$500   (interest expense)
−$500

Decrease

Repayment of Current Note Payable and Payment of Interest

As required by the short-term note payable issued to acquire computer equipment, the company repays $2,000 of the principal (the amount borrowed) and pays $360 in interest. The repayment of the principal reduces both cash and the note payable. It has no impact on either net assets or owners' equity. The payment of the interest, by contrast, reduces cash but does not reduce a corresponding liability. Therefore it reduces owners' equity (interest expense).

Increase

$$\Delta A \qquad = \qquad \Delta L \qquad + \qquad \Delta OE \qquad\qquad (18)$$
$$\downarrow \qquad\qquad\qquad \downarrow \qquad\qquad\qquad \downarrow$$

Cash   Note payable, current   Retained earnings
−$2,360   −$2,000   (interest expense)
−$360

Decrease

Sale of Marketable Securities and Recognition of Interest

The company redeems the $10,000 in marketable Government of Canada bonds that it acquired in March as a temporary investment. It receives $10,100, the additional $100 representing interest for the period.

Interest revenue has the same characteristics as sales revenue. It leads to an increase in net assets and a reciprocal increase in owners' equity (interest revenue).

Increase

$$
\begin{array}{ccccc}
\text{Cash} & & & \text{Retained earnings} & \\
\text{+\$10,100} & & & \text{(interest revenue)} & \\
& & & \text{+\$100} & \\
\uparrow & & & \uparrow & \\
\Delta A & = & \Delta L & + & \Delta OE \quad (19) \\
\downarrow & & & & \\
\text{Marketable securities} & & & & \\
\text{-\$10,000} & & & &
\end{array}
$$

Decrease

Amortization of Building and Equipment

The firm previously acquired and properly recorded a building at a total cost of $120,000 (including remodelling costs) and equipment at a cost of $28,000. The company estimates that the building will have an economic life of 20 years (240 months), after which it will have no value. Similarly it estimates that the equipment will have an economic life of five years (60 months), after which it too will have no value.

In effect, during April the firm "uses up" a portion of both the building and equipment—just as it consumes a share of the 12-month insurance policy. The costs of the building and equipment must therefore be spread over their useful lives. Thus, the stated value of the building and equipment must be reduced by 1/240 and 1/60, respectively. The reduction in the assets ($500 and $467) is offset by an equal reduction in owners' equity (amortization expense).

The process of allocating the cost of an asset to the accounting periods in which it provides its benefits is referred to as *amortization*.

Increase

$$
\begin{array}{ccccc}
\Delta A & = & \Delta L & + & \Delta OE \quad (20) \\
\downarrow & & & & \downarrow \\
\text{Building} & & & & \text{Retained earnings} \\
\text{-\$500} & & & & \text{(amortization expense)} \\
\downarrow & & & & \text{-\$967} \\
\text{Equipment} & & & & \\
\text{-\$467} & & & &
\end{array}
$$

Decrease

There is no need to record amortization on land, since it does not ordinarily become less serviceable with time or use. Land, unlike most other assets, is assumed to have an unlimited useful life.

Amortization of Organizational Costs

The number of years over which organizational costs benefit a corporation is not easily determined. But, like tangible assets, the cost of intangible assets must be allocated, despite the difficulty of making the required estimates.

Schaefer Corporation elects to *amortize* its $6,000 in organizational costs over a period of five years (60 months). Hence amortization expense is $100 per month.

Increase

$$\Delta A \quad = \quad \Delta L \quad + \quad \Delta OE \qquad (21)$$

$$\downarrow \qquad\qquad\qquad\qquad\qquad \downarrow$$

Organization costs   Retained earnings
   −$100   (amortization expense)
                                     −$100

Decrease

APPLYING THE EQUATION: PREPARING THE BALANCE SHEET AND THE INCOME STATEMENT

Preparing the Balance Sheet

Exhibit 2-4 summarizes the changes that take place in each of the Schaefer Corporation balance sheet accounts during April. The beginning balance in an account plus the increases, less the decreases, equals the ending balance.

The revenue and expense accounts are *not* reported on a balance sheet. They have been included in Exhibit 2-4 (which is a worksheet, not a balance sheet) to emphasize that revenues increase retained earnings and expenses decrease retained earnings. (The minus sign to the left of an expense in the exhibit indicates a decrease in retained earnings, not a decrease in the expense.)

A balance sheet as at April 30 can be prepared directly from the column in Exhibit 2-4 marked "Balance, April 30." Exhibit 2-5 presents such a balance sheet.

Preparing an Income Statement

The income statement indicates the changes in owners' equity attributable to the operations of the enterprise. It excludes contributions and withdrawals by the owners.

The income statement may be prepared by summarizing the transactions that affect retained earnings (excluding any dividends). In our illustration, these transactions have been conveniently set forth in Exhibit 2-4. An income statement, such as that presented in Exhibit 2-6, can be prepared by recasting the entries to retained earnings. For most firms, a worksheet of the type in

Exhibit 2-4 would be inadequate to accommodate all of the transactions of an accounting period. A more efficient means of keeping track of transactions is set forth in the following chapter.

EXHIBIT 2-4

The Schaefer Corporation
Changes in Accounts in April 1996

	Balance, March 31	Changes during Month Increases		Decreases		Balance, April 30
Assets						
Cash	$ 45,300	+ $ 32,000	(12)	– $106,000	(11) ⎫	
		+ 68,000	(14)	– 30,000	(15) ⎪	$ 16,540
		+ 10,100	(19)	– 500	(17) ⎬	
				– 2,360	(18) ⎭	
Marketable securities	10,000			– 10,000	(19)	0
Accounts receivable		+ 112,000	(12)	– 68,000	(14)	44,000
Merchandise inventory	40,000	+ 110,000	(10)	– 90,000	(13)	60,000
Prepaid insurance	3,600			– 300	(16)	3,300
Utility deposit	600					600
Organization costs	6,000			– 100	(21)	5,900
Land	50,000					50,000
Buildings	120,000			– 500	(20)	119,500
Equipment	28,000			– 467	(20)	27,533
Total assets	$303,500	$332,100		$308,227		$327,373
Equities						
Wages and salaries payable		+ $ 4,000	(15)			$ 4,000
Accounts payable	$ 49,500	+ 110,000	(10)	– $106,000	(11)	53,500
Note payable (current)	24,000			– 2,000	(18)	22,000
Note payable (noncurrent)	50,000					50,000
Common stock	180,000					180,000
Retained earnings*						
Sales revenue		+ 144,000	(12)			
Interest revenue		+ 100	(19)			
Cost of goods sold				– 90,000	(13) ⎫	
Wages and salary expense				– 34,000	(15) ⎪	
Insurance expense				– 300	(16) ⎬ 17,873	
Interest expense				– 500	(17) ⎪	
				– 360	(18) ⎭	
Amortization expense—buildings and equipment				– 967	(20)	
Amortization expense— organization costs				– 100	(21)	
Total equities	$303,500	$258,100		$234,227		$327,373

*The balance as of March 31 in retained earnings for the Schaefer Corporation is zero; the company has not yet begun operations and therefore does not yet have earnings.

EXHIBIT 2-5

The Schaefer Corporation
Balance Sheet
As at April 30, 1996

Assets			Equities		
Current			**Liabilities**		
Cash	$ 16,540		Current		
Accounts receivable	44,000		Accounts payable	$ 53,500	
Merchandise inventory	60,000		Wages and salaries payable	4,000	
Prepaid insurance	3,300		Note payable	22,000	
Total, current	$123,840		Total, current	$ 79,500	
Noncurrent			**Noncurrent**		
Utility deposit	600		Note payable	50,000	
Organization costs	5,900		Total liabilities	$129,500	
Land	50,000				
Buildings	119,500		**Shareholders' equity**		
Equipment	27,533		Common stock	180,000	
Total, noncurrent	$203,533		Retained earnings	17,873	
Total assets	$327,373		Total shareholders' equity	$197,873	
			Total equities	$327,373	

EXHIBIT 2-6

The Schaefer Corporation
Income Statement
Month Ended April 30, 1996

Revenues		
Sales revenue	$144,000	
Interest revenue	100	
Total revenue	$144,100	
Expenses		
Cost of goods sold	90,000	
Wages and salaries	34,000	
Insurance expense	300	
Interest expense	860	
Amortization of building and equipment	967	
Amortization of organization costs	100	
Total expenses	$126,227	
Net income	$ 17,873	

THE STATEMENT OF CHANGES IN FINANCIAL POSITION

The third primary financial statement is the statement of changes in financial position. The statement of changes in financial position reports on changes in the entity's cash position during a period of time. It tells how a company acquired cash and what it did with it. It accounts for the difference between the cash on hand at the beginning of a period and that on hand at the end.

Cash is an asset that is of special concern in assessing a corporation's fiscal health and performance. It is the objective of a corporation to generate cash. Owners contribute cash to an enterprise with the intention of eventually withdrawing more cash than they put in. Cash is the asset required to meet day-to-day operating costs, to pay interest and dividends, and to satisfy debts. Consequently, a primary objective of financial statements is to enable users to predict the ability of the entity to generate future cash flows.

Distinction between Income and Cash Flow

As is evident from our illustration, the income statement does not provide information on cash flows. As shown in Exhibit 2-6, the Schaefer Company would report income for April of $17,873. However, as shown in the schedule in Exhibit 2-4 the beginning-of-the-month cash balance was $45,300; the ending balance was $16,540. Cash *decreased* by $28,760.

The reasons for the difference between cash flow and income are apparent from an analysis of how different events affected each. Some events that affected owners' equity (and thus income) had no impact on cash. Other events affected cash but had no impact on income. To cite but a few examples:

- *Entry 11.* The company paid suppliers. This transaction reduced cash but did not affect owners' equity. Owners' equity was reduced only when the company sold the goods acquired (entry 13).
- *Entry 12.* The company sold merchandise. The sale increased owners' equity by the full amount of the sale, but cash was increased only as it was collected. In entry 14, the company collected a portion of its receivables from customers, but the increase in cash had no impact on owners' equity.
- *Entry 16.* The company recorded the expiration of a portion of its insurance policy. This decreased owners' equity, but the cash payment for the policy had been recorded the previous month.
- *Entry 20.* The company amortized its building and equipment. The amortization reduced owners' equity but not cash.

It is not uncommon for firms, especially new businesses, to experience severe cash crises, even while reporting substantial earnings. For example, a firm that has developed an innovative product may expand rapidly to meet expected demand. It may face significant cash outflows in acquiring plant, equipment and inventory, in advertising, and in training. It may experience delays in collecting from its customers. Thus, even though its long-term prospects may be bright and even though it may be profitable, it may be unable to meet its current obligations.

Preparing a Statement of Changes in Financial Position

The statement of changes in financial position is conceptually simple. It is a summary of cash receipts and disbursements—all of the transactions that affect the cash account. The transactions are classified into three groups:

1. *Operating activities.* These include the firm's production, selling, and administrative activities.

2. *Investing activities.* These encompass the purchase and sale of property, plant and equipment.

3. *Financing activities.* These incorporate transactions that change the size and composition of the firm's capital structure, both debt and equity (i.e., the issue and redemption of capital stock, bonds payable, or noncurrent notes payable).

The Schaefer Corporation's statement of changes in financial position for April is presented in Exhibit 2-7. As can be seen, the statement encompasses each of the entries to the cash account in the Exhibit 2-4 worksheet.

The statement of changes in financial position will be discussed in detail in Chapter 14.

EXHIBIT 2-7

Schaefer Corporation Statement of Changes in Financial Position Month Ended April 30, 1996	
Operating Activities	
Collections from customers	$ 100,000
Receipt of interest from marketable securities	100
Payments to suppliers	(106,000)
Payment of wages and salaries	(30,000)
Payment of interest	(860)
Cash used for operating activities	$(36,760)
Investing Activities	
Sale of marketable securities	$ 10,000
Financing Activities	
Repayment of loan	$(2,000)
Decrease in cash	$(28,760)

CHANGES IN RETAINED EARNINGS AND OTHER CONTRIBUTED CAPITAL ACCOUNTS

If a firm has engaged in transactions with its owners, then neither the balance sheet nor the income statement may fully explain the changes in owners' equity accounts. Changes in retained earnings are summarized in the *statement of retained earnings.* Changes to contributed capital account balances, the other component of owners' equity, are generally summarized in a note to the financial statements, rather than as a separate financial statement. Both disclosures provide a reconciliation of the beginning and ending balances in the accounts to which they pertain.

Statement of Retained Earnings

The statement of retained earnings (Exhibit 2-8) is the link between the income statement and the balance sheet. The basic accounting equation can be expanded to show the two components of owners' equity:

Owners' equity

$$\text{Assets} - \text{Liabilities} = \overbrace{\text{Capital contributed by owners} + \text{Retained earnings}}$$

EXHIBIT 2-8

Schaefer Corporation
Statement of Retained Earnings
Month Ended April 30, 1996

Balance, April 1, 1996	$ 0
Net income for April 1996	17,873
	17,873
Less: Dividends declared	1,200
Balance, April 30, 1996	$16,673

In practice, the statement of retained earnings may take several forms. It may be included as a separate statement along with the balance sheet, income statement, and statement of changes in financial position. Alternatively, the statement of retained earnings is often presented at the bottom of the income statement to create a single statement of income and retained earnings.

Retained earnings are the sum of the earnings of the accounting periods for which the company has been in existence less the cumulative amounts declared as dividends to shareholders. The retained earnings per the balance sheet at the beginning of the period (which, of course, must be identical to the retained earnings at the end of the previous period), plus the income for that period per the income statement, less any dividends declared during the period, equal the retained earnings at the end of the period:

Retained earnings, balance at beginning of period + Income

      − Dividends declared = Retained earnings, balance at end of period

Retained Earnings Contrasted to Assets

Retained earnings *do not* represent resources of the firm. Retained earnings per se cannot be distributed to shareholders. They cannot be used to purchase goods or services. Only cash or other assets are media of exchange. Retained earnings are nothing more than what remains after liabilities and other owners' equity accounts are subtracted from total assets. Retained earnings may be interpreted as a residual claim against assets—what is left for the owners after all liabilities and claims represented by other owners' equity accounts have been satisfied. However, *there is no specific relationship between particular assets and particular claims*. The existence of retained earnings in no way implies the availability of cash for distributions to shareholders or for other corporate purposes. Moreover, the stated values of assets are not necessarily indicative of the amounts for which the assets could be sold if the business were dissolved. Hence retained earnings are unlikely to show the value of cash or other assets that may remain for shareholders.

Dividends

Dividends are distributions of the assets of the enterprise to its owners. The asset distributed most often is cash, but it could, in fact, be any asset of the firm. As the assets of the firm are reduced upon distribution to the owners, so also are the claims of the owners against such assets.

Suppose that during April, Schaefer Corporation declares dividends of $1 per share. Since there are 1,200 shares of stock outstanding, total dividends are $1,200. The dividends are paid in cash. The effect on the accounting equation is then

Increase

$$\Delta A \qquad = \qquad \Delta L \qquad + \qquad \Delta OE$$
$$\downarrow \qquad\qquad\qquad\qquad\qquad\qquad \downarrow$$

Cash   Retained earnings
−$1,200   (dividends)
                                  −$1,200

Decrease

The statement of retained earnings will appear as presented in Exhibit 2-8.

If the dividend transaction were recorded in April, along with the other transactions of the month, then in the balance sheet presented in Exhibit 2-5 both cash and retained earnings would have been reduced by $1,200.

The amount shown as the ending balance in Exhibit 2-8 would be the balance in retained earnings on the April 30, 1993, balance sheet. The balance sheet presented in Exhibit 2-5 does not incorporate the dividend transaction; hence retained earnings (and, correspondingly, cash) are greater by $1,200, the amount of the dividend.

Changes in Contributed Capital Accounts

The reconciliation of changes in the contributed capital accounts reports changes in a firm's capital structure. The required note disclosure reconciles the beginning and ending balances of the various contributed capital accounts in the owners' equity section of the balance sheet. It indicates the increases or decreases in capital accounts that result when a firm issues or retires common stock or preferred stock. Firms may issue new stock to raise funds to expand the scale of operations, to compensate employees under stock option plans, and to acquire new businesses. They may retire stock to decrease the size of the company, to reduce the number of shareholders (e.g., to eliminate the interest of shareholders who are not members of a controlling group), and to alter their capital structures (e.g., to change proportions of common and preferred stock).

In this chapter we have presented an overview of the three primary financial statements—the *balance sheet* (also called the statement of financial position), the *income statement,* and the *statement of changes in financial position.* We also considered the secondary statement, the *statement of retained earnings,* and the reconciliation in the notes to the financial statements of changes in the contributed capital accounts. The chapter is intended to familiarize you with the purposes of each statement, with its basic format, and with the terminology conventionally employed.

The key to understanding both the balance sheet and the income statement is the accounting equation:

$$\text{Assets} = \text{Liabilities} + \text{Owners' equity}$$

The balance sheet is nothing more than an expression of the accounting equation. It lists the assets, the liabilities, and various classifications of owners' equity as at a particular date. A main theme of this chapter is that *all* accounting transactions have an impact on the accounting equation and thus on the balance sheet.

The income statement reports the changes in the retained earnings component of owners' equity, excluding dividends, during a period of time. It lists the revenues (increases in retained earnings) and the expenses (decreases in retained earnings). The difference between the revenues and expenses is the *income* for the period.

The statement of changes in financial position sets forth the changes in cash during a period. Cash, although accounted for and reported like other assets on the balance sheet, is of particular importance in evaluating the fiscal health of a corporation. It is the medium of exchange in our society. Indeed it is a primary objective of a corporation to generate cash.

The statement of retained earnings accounts for the changes in retained earnings during the accounting period. It reconciles retained earnings at the beginning of the period with those at the end. As reflected in the statement, retained earnings are increased by net income and decreased by dividends.

Changes in a firm's capital structure are disclosed in the notes to the financial statements through the reconciliation of the contributed capital accounts. This reconciliation indicates the increases or decreases in the capital stock accounts when a firm issues or retires its common or preferred stock.

Exercise for Review and Self-Testing

(The solutions to this exercise—and similar exercises in other chapters—will be found following the last problem in the chapter.)

1. A group of entrepreneurs forms a corporation. Together the owners contribute to the enterprise $200,000 cash. To provide evidence of their investment, the corporation issues to them 20,000 shares of no par value common stock.
   a. What are the total assets of the corporation immediately after it has been formed?

b. What are the total equities of the corporation? That is, what are the total claims of the owners against these assets?

2. The corporation borrows $100,000 from a bank.
   a. What are the total assets of the corporation now?
   b. What are the total claims against these assets? Of these total claims (equities), how much are claims of outsiders (liabilities)? How much are the residual claims of the owners?

3. The company acquires an automobile for $20,000 cash.
   a. What are the total assets of the corporation now?
   b. What are the corporation's liabilities now?
   c. What is its owners' equity now?

4. The company acquires 1,000 units of inventory at a cost of $5 per unit. The purchase is made "on account," with the firm promising to pay for the goods within 30 days.
   a. What are the total assets of the corporation now?
   b. What are its liabilities now?
   c. What is its owners' equity now?

5. The firm sells 800 of the units of inventory for $7 per unit. The purchasers pay cash.
   a. What are the total assets of the corporation now?
   b. What are the corporation's liabilities now?
   c. What is its owners' equity now?

6. By how much has the equity of the owners increased since they made their initial contribution of cash? How much "better off" is the corporation (and thus its owners) since the owners made their contribution? What was the "income" of the corporation during the period in which the transactions took place?

Questions for Review and Discussion

1. Explain why the balance sheet of a firm might be dated "*as at* December 31, 1997," but the income statement is dated "*for the year ended* December 31, 1997."

2. What is meant by owners' equity? Why is owners' equity not necessarily indicative of the amount of cash that would be returned to the owners if the assets of a business were to be sold and the creditors paid the amounts owed to them?

3. A bookkeeper recently totalled up the recorded assets of a firm and found that they came to $1,398,576. The total liabilities came to $600,000 and the total owners' equity to $800,000. Are such totals possible in the context of the double-entry bookkeeping process if no error has been made? Suppose instead that assets were equal to liabilities plus owners' equity. Do such totals assure that no accounting errors have been made?

4. Which of the following events will be recognized on the books of United Electric Co.?

a. The firm signs a three-year contract with its union.

b. The firm issues 1,000 additional shares of common stock.

c. An officer of United Electric sells on the open market 3,000 shares of company stock from her personal holdings.

d. The passage of another year has reduced the remaining useful life of plant and equipment.

e. The wholesale price of copper wire has *increased.* United Electric Co. has 100,000 feet of copper wire in inventory.

f. The wholesale price of copper wire has *decreased.* United Electric Co. has 100,000 feet of copper wire in inventory.

5. Included among a firm's noncurrent assets are "unamortized corporate organizational costs, $25,000." What is meant by such an asset? Is it possible to sell such an asset? If not, why is it considered an asset?

6. A firm has recorded among its current liabilities "advances from customers, $3,000." Why is such an amount a liability? What impact did receipt of the $3,000 have on the accounting equation?

7. A company reported substantial earnings for the last several years, yet it is about to file for bankruptcy. How is such a situation possible?

8. A firm recently received a cheque from a customer for $10,000, yet it did not record the receipt as revenue. What are two possible reasons why cash received is not recorded as revenue?

9. A firm recently purchased equipment for $120,000 cash yet did not record an expense. Why not? Will the amount paid ever be reported as an expense? When?

10. What is meant by a *current asset?* How is it possible that shares of the common stock of XYZ Company owned by one company may be recorded as a current asset but those owned by another may be recorded as a noncurrent asset?

11. What is meant by *preferred stock?* What preferences do preferred shareholders have over common shareholders? What rights do common shareholders have that preferred shareholders generally do not have?

12. What are *extraordinary items?* Why are they reported on the income statement separate from ordinary operating revenues and expenses?

13. Is it possible for a firm to have a substantial balance in retained earnings and still be unable to declare a cash dividend? Why?

Problems

1. *Balance sheet accounts indicate the value assigned to resources or obligations as at a particular point in time. Income statement accounts provide information on inflows and outflows of resources during a particular period of time.*

   Some accounts are reported on the balance sheet; others are reported on the income statement. For each of the accounts indicated below, specify whether it would ordinarily be reported on the income statement or on the balance sheet.

a. Sales revenue
b. Accounts receivable
c. Rent expense
d. Prepaid rent
e. Inventories
f. Cost of goods sold
g. Amortization expense
h. Accumulated amortization
i. Interest expense
j. Notes payable
k. Retained earnings
l. Investment in shares of Company X

2. *Account titles generally provide an indication of whether the account represents a "stock" (and is thereby reported on the balance sheet) or a "flow" (and is thereby reported on the income statement). Problem 2 presents information for a sole proprietorship form of organization and Problem 3 is based on the corporate form of organization. The only difference in format between the two is in the owners' equity section of the balance sheet.*

From the following account balances, taken from the books and records of the Julie Company, a sole proprietorship, as at December 31, 1997, prepare an income statement and a balance sheet. Title and date the statements as appropriate, and, insofar as the information permits, separate assets and liabilities into current and noncurrent classifications.

Cash	$18,000
A. Julie, capital	54,600
Sales	75,000
Cost of goods sold	52,000
Prepaid insurance	1,000
Advances from customers	3,000
Patents	8,000
Amortization expense	2,500
Insurance expense	2,000
Interest revenue	500
Prepaid interest	200
Interest payable	600
Accounts receivable	13,000
Inventory	9,000
Rent expense	6,000
Advertising expense	5,000
Notes payable (due in three years)	8,000
Buildings and equipment	26,000
Notes receivable	10,000
Accounts payable	19,000

3. From the following account balances taken from the books and records of Sunburst Trucking Limited as at June 30, 1997, prepare an income statement and a balance sheet. Title and date the statements as appropriate, and, insofar as the information permits, separate assets and liabilities into current and noncurrent classifications.

Common stock	$100,000
Trucking revenue	200,000
Prepaid rent	2,000
Advances from customers	4,000
Organization costs	6,000
Amortization expense—trucks and equipment	15,000
Insurance expense	12,000
Prepaid interest	1,000
Rent expense	24,000
Interest expense	12,000
Accounts receivable	26,000
Advertising expense	6,000
Wages and salaries expense	65,000
Retained earnings	26,000
Wages and salaries payable	3,000
Notes payable (due in five years)	100,000
Trucks and equipment	45,000
Gas and oil expense	35,000
Truck repair expense	14,000
Accounts payable	12,000
Cash	165,000
Amortization expense—organization costs	1,000

4. *All transactions increase or decrease the balances in some combination of asset, liability, and owners' equity accounts.*

For each of the following transactions, indicate whether assets (*A*), liabilities (*L*), or owners' equity (*OE*) would increase (+) or decrease (−). The first transaction is illustrated for you.

a. A corporation issues common stock in exchange for cash. (*A*+; *OE*+)

b. It issues preferred stock in exchange for a building.

c. It purchases inventory, giving the seller a 30-day note payable for the amount of the merchandise.

d. It collects from a customer the amount the customer owed on goods purchased several months earlier.

e. It exchanges shares of preferred stock for shares of common stock.

f. It repays bondholders by issuing to them shares of common stock.

g. It declares and pays a dividend to shareholders, thereby distributing assets of the company (cash) to the owners.

h. It returns to a manufacturer defective merchandise for credit on its account.

i. It receives from a customer defective merchandise and reduces the balance owed by the customer. The merchandise had been sold at a profit. The goods returned have no value.

5. *The accounting equation, whether in its simplest form (A = L + OE), or in an expanded format, must be satisfied for each transaction or economic event.*

For each of the following economic events indicate, in the schedule that follows, the $ impact on the expanded accounting equation. The first transaction is illustrated for you.

The Puzzle Company began operations on January 1, 1997.

a. On January 1, 1997, the company issues, for cash, 100,000 shares of common stock at $5 per share.

b. On January 1, 1997, the company borrows $500,000 from the local branch of the Bank of Montreal.

c. On January 2, 1997, the company buys office equipment for $120,000 cash. This equipment is expected to last for ten years.

d. On January 2, 1997, the company buys office supplies for $12,000 on account.

e. On January 2, 1997, the company hires five employees, at a monthly salary of $3,000 each, to be paid at month-end.

f. On January 31, 1997, the company bills customers $60,000 for services provided in January.

g. On January 31, 1997, the company pays monthly salaries of $15,000.

h. On January 31, 1997, the company recognizes one month of amortization on the office equipment.

i. Other operating expenses of $14,000 are paid on January 31, 1997.

j. On January 31, 1997, the company pays the $12,000 for the office supplies bought on account on January 2, 1997.

	Cash	+	Other Assets	=	Liabilities	+	Common Stock	+	Retained Earnings
a.	+500,000						+500,000		
b.									
c.									
d.									
e.									
f.									
g.									
h.									
i.									
j.									

6. *Assets must equal liabilities plus owners' equity.*

The balances that follow were taken from the balance sheet of a corporation. Arrange a sheet of paper into three columns, each corresponding to a term in the accounting equation:

Assets = Liabilities + Owners' equity

Place each of the balances in the appropriate column. Total each of the columns to make certain that the equation is in balance.

Marketable securities	$ 20,000
Common stock	200,000
Buildings and equipment	300,000
Bonds payable	250,000
Accounts receivable	190,000
Prepaid rent	15,000
Preferred stock	50,000
Inventories	106,000
Taxes payable	25,000
Advances from customers	3,000
Accounts payable	17,000
Interest payable	8,000
Organization costs	12,000
Retained earnings	90,000

7. *Not all financial events give rise to assets or liabilities. Sometimes, assets or liabilities resulting from contractual arrangements are recognized only upon the performance of either of the parties to the contract.*

Indicate the nature (i.e., descriptive account title) of the assets and liabilities (if any) that would receive accounting recognition on the books of the Sussex Company as a result of the following events or transactions:

a. The Sussex Co. employs six men to perform routine maintenance work at a rate of $15 per hour. The men work a total of 200 hours. They have not yet been paid.

b. The Sussex Co. signs a three-year contract with a security company, which will provide guard service for the company at a cost of $3,000 per month.

c. The security company performs one month's services as promised.

d. The Sussex Co. orders machinery and equipment at a cost of $200,000.

e. The machinery and equipment previously ordered are received and installed as agreed upon by the manufacturer.

f. A customer orders 400 units of the company's product at a price of $30 per unit.

g. Sussex Co. ships the merchandise previously ordered.

h. Sussex Co. borrows $400,000 at an interest rate of 12 percent per year. The company gives the bank a four-year note payable.

i. One year elapses, and the Sussex Co. has paid the bank neither principal nor interest on the note payable.

j. The Sussex Co. guarantees to repair any defective products. During the year it sells 10,000 units of product. It estimates from previous experience that 5 percent of such units will be returned for repair work. It estimates also that the cost of such repairs will be $10 per unit.

8. *Retained earnings may be derived from other balance sheet accounts.*

From the following accounts, taken from the books and records of the Finch Company on December 31, 1997, prepare both an income statement and a balance sheet. Derive the amount of retained earnings.

Cash	$18,000
Accounts payable	12,000
Building and equipment	90,000
Cost of goods sold	70,000
Notes payable	5,000
Wages and salaries payable	3,000
Preferred stock	20,000
Common stock	50,000
Marketable securities	18,000
Inventory	22,000
Sales revenue	102,000
Tax expense	4,000
Taxes payable	1,000
Rent expense	12,000
Prepaid rent	1,000
Retained earnings	?

9. *In the absence of additional contributions by owners, owners' equity is increased by earnings and decreased by dividends and losses.*

The Gail Company was organized as a partnership on January 2, 1996. Each of its two owners contributed $200,000 in cash to start the business. After one year of operations the company had on hand the following assets: cash, $250,000; accounts receivable, $30,000; inventory available for sale, $200,000; furniture and fixtures, $250,000.

The company owed suppliers (i.e., accounts payable) $80,000 and had notes payable outstanding to a bank (due in 1998) of $220,000.

a. Prepare a balance sheet as at December 31, 1996.

b. Assuming that the owners neither made additional contributions of capital to the business nor made any withdrawals, compute income for 1996.

c. Assume instead that during the year the owners withdrew $75,000 from the business. Compute income for 1996.

10. *Owners' equity equals assets minus liabilities. Owners' equity is affected by income (or loss), capital contributions, and capital withdrawals (dividends).*

Fill in the missing amounts. Assume that there were no capital contributions by owners during 1997. (*Hint:* First compute owners' equity as at December 31, 1997.)

	(a)	(b)	(c)
Assets, December 31, 1997	$125,000	$50,000	?
Liabilities, December 31, 1997	80,000	10,000	$30,000
Owners' equity, January 1, 1997	20,000	?	90,000
Income, 1997	40,000	8,000	25,000
Dividends declared, 1997	?	4,000	30,000

11. *The balance sheet is closely related to the income statement.*

The balance sheets and income statements of the Ames Corp. for the years ending December 31, 1994, through 1997 are shown in the table following. Also indicated are dividends paid during those years. Some critical figures, however, have been omitted. You are to provide the missing figures. The Ames Corp. began operations on January 1, 1994.

	1997	1996	1995	1994
	Balance Sheet			
Assets				
Cash	$300	$?	$200	$100
Accounts receivable	100	300	100	200
Inventory	100	100	?	350
Building and equipment	400	800	900	600
Liabilities and owners' equity				
Accounts payable	$300	$200	$100	$200
Notes payable	100	300	600	?
Common stock	300	200	200	200
Retained earnings	?	?	400	100
	Income Statement			
Sales	$1,200	$?	$1,000	$?
Cost of goods sold and other operating expenses	?	600	?	500
Net income	300	400	?	?
Dividends paid	$?	$200	$ 150	$ 0

12. *Retained earnings must not be associated with cash or any other specific assets.*

As at December 31, 1996, the balance sheet of the Morgan Motors Co. appeared as follows (in thousands of dollars):

Cash	$ 85,000
Other current assets	75,000
Other assets, including buildings, land, and equipment	670,000
Total assets	$830,000
Liabilities	$220,000
Common stock (10,000,000 issued and outstanding)	10,000
Retained earnings	600,000
Total equities	$830,000

In 1996 the company had net income of $40 million. Since there were 10 million shares of common stock outstanding, earnings per share were $4. In 1996 the company declared no dividends since the directors claimed funds were needed for expansion.

Shortly after the close of the year, the president of the company received a letter from a shareholder protesting the company's refusal to declare a dividend. The letter said in part,

> When I studied accounting, "retained earnings" were called "surplus." No amount of name changing can obscure the fact that the company has $600 million available for distribution to shareholders.

a. How would you respond to the angry shareholder? Does the company have $600 million available for distribution to shareholders?

b. Suppose the company did declare a dividend of $60 per share ($600 million). What effect would such a dividend most likely have on corporate operations?

c. Does the balance sheet provide assurance that the company could, in fact, declare a dividend of $60 per share even if it wanted to? Why?

d. Suppose that instead of earnings of $40 million the company had a loss of $10 million. The company nevertheless declared a dividend of $2.00 per share. A disgruntled shareholder questioned the decision and wrote to the president: "Dividends are supposed to be distributions of earnings. How is it possible to pay a dividend in a year in which there were no earnings?" How would you respond to his question?

13. *The balance sheet is nothing more than a detailed expression of the accounting equation.*

Arrange a sheet of paper into three columns, each corresponding to a term in the accounting equation:

$$\text{Assets} = \text{Liabilities} + \text{Owners' equity}$$

Indicate the impact that each of the following transactions would have on the accounting equation. Suggest titles for the specific accounts that would be affected.

a. Whitman and Farell form a corporation. The corporation issues 1,000 shares of common stock and sells 500 shares to each of the founders for $6 per share.

b. The corporation borrows $20,000 from a bank, giving the bank a one-year note payable.

c. The corporation purchases furniture and fixtures for $5,000. The company pays $1,000 cash and gives a six-month note payable for the balance.

d. The corporation rents a building. It pays, in advance, the first month's rent of $700.

e. The corporation purchases office supplies for $400 cash.

f. The corporation purchases inventory for future sale to customers for $9,600 cash.

Compute the balance in each of the accounts. Summarize the balances in the form of a balance sheet.

14. *Some transactions affect the composition of net assets (assets less liabilities) without affecting the level of net assets. Others increase or decrease the level of net assets—and thereby increase or decrease owners' equity.*

Arrange a sheet of paper into three columns, each corresponding to a term in the accounting equation. Indicate the impact that each of the following transactions would have on the accounting equation. Suggest titles for each of the specific accounts that would be affected.

a. Petrified Products, Inc., purchases furniture and fixtures for $30,000 cash.

b. The company purchases "on account" merchandise inventory for $15,000.

c. The firm, realizing that it has purchased an excessive amount of furniture, sells a portion of it. It sells for $3,000 (cash) furniture that had initially cost $3,000.

d. The firm sells an additional amount of furniture. It sells for $6,000 (cash) furniture that had initially cost $2,000. (Has the "level" of net assets increased as the result of this transaction?)

e. The firm sells for $800 "on account" merchandise inventory that had been purchased for $600.

f. The firm purchases supplies for $300 on account.

g. The firm uses supplies that had originally cost $200.

h. The firm collects $700 of the amount owed to it by customers.

i. The firm pays one month's rent in advance, $500.

j. At the end of one month, the firm wishes to give accounting recognition to the fact that it has occupied the rented premises for the one month paid for in advance.

15. *The beginning balance in an account plus increases and minus decreases in that account during a period equals the ending balance.*

The table following is a condensed balance sheet of the Withington Corporation as at December 31, 1996. On a sheet of paper, copy the account titles and the initial balances. Leave room for seven additional columns of figures. Label six of the columns Transaction 1, 2, 3, and so on, and the seventh column "Balance, 31/1/97."

	Balance 31/12/96	Withington Corporation Transaction						Balance 31/1/97
		1	2	3	4	5	6	
Cash	$ 40,000							
Accounts receivable	25,000							
Inventory	57,000	+8,000						
Prepaid rent	2,000							
Equipment	85,000							
Building	200,000							
	$409,000							
Accounts payable	$ 19,000	+8,000						
Wages payable	4,000							
Notes payable	38,000							
Bonds payable	150,000							
Common stock	45,000							
Retained earnings	153,000							
	$409,000							

The following six transactions take place in January 1997. Indicate the effect that each will have on the balance sheet. Summarize the effects of the six transactions on the December 31, 1996, balance by adding across the rows, and indicate the new balance in the column marked "Balance, 31/1/97."

a. The company purchases inventory on account, $8,000. (Transaction 1 is done for you.)

b. The company purchases equipment for $16,000, giving the seller a two-year note payable.

c. The company pays its employees the $4,000 owed.

d. The company declares and pays a dividend of $20,000.

e. The company reaches an agreement with its bondholders. In exchange for their bonds, they agree to accept shares of common stock that have a market value of $150,000.

f. The company collects $5,000 that was owed by its customers.

16. *Cash and retained earnings are the most significant assets and equities. The statement of changes in financial position accounts for changes in cash; the statement of income accounts for the changes (excluding dividends) in retained earnings.*

The accounting equation can be recast so as to emphasize the changes in cash and retained earnings. For each of the transactions described, indicate how it will affect the accounting equation as presented. The first transaction is done for you as an illustration.

a. The company purchases equipment for $70,000 cash.

b. It borrows $30,000 and issues a 60-day note payable.

c. It purchases inventory for $10,000 and promises to pay for it within 30 days.

d. It purchases inventory for $6,000 cash.

e. It purchases a building for $100,000 cash at the beginning of the year.

f. It records first-year amortization on the building. The building has a 25-year life.

g. It sells for $5,000 goods that had been carried in inventory at $4,000. The customer agrees to pay within 30 days. (Analyze this transaction in two steps: the increase in the asset received and the decrease in the asset surrendered.)

h. It issues preferred stock for $100,000 cash.

i. It pays a utility bill (not previously recorded) of $1,000.

	Cash	+	Other Assets	=	Liabilities	+	Retained Earnings	+	Other Owners' Equities
a.	−70		Equipment +70						
b.									
c.									
d.									
e.									
f.									
g.									
h.									
i.									

17. *Underlying transactions can be reconstructed from a firm's statements of income and changes in financial position. Preparation of a balance sheet helps assure that all transactions have been accounted for.*

Nuth, Inc., began operations on January 1, 1996. Its statement of changes in financial position and statement of income for the first year of operations are presented below.

a. Show the effect on the accounting equation of each receipt and disbursement of cash and each revenue and expense. Indicate the specific assets, liabilities, and owners' equities that would be increased or decreased.

Assume that all of the company's sales to customers were on credit (i.e., resulted in creation of accounts receivable). Assume also that the merchandise inventory, the insurance policy, and the buildings and

Nuth, Inc.
Statement of Changes in Financial Position
Year Ended December 31, 1996

Operating Activities	
Collections from customers	$ 880,000
Payments to suppliers for merchandise inventory purchased	(500,000)
Payment of wages and salaries	(150,000)
Purchase of 2–year insurance policy	(16,000)
Payment of interest	(6,000)
Cash provided by operating activities	$ 208,000
Investing Activities	
Purchase of building and equipment	$ (900,000)
Financing Activities	
Issuance of stock	$ 600,000
Loan from bank	100,000
Cash provided by financing activities	$ 700,000
Increase in cash	$ 8,000

Nuth, Inc.
Income Statement
Year Ended December 31, 1996

Sales revenues	$950,000
Expenses	
Cost of goods sold	420,000
Wages and salaries expense	154,000
Insurance expense	8,000
Interest expense	12,000
Amortization expense	30,000
Total expenses	$624,000
Net income	$326,000

equipment were acquired for cash. By contrast, the wages and salaries and the interest initially resulted in increases in liability accounts (i.e., "wages and salaries payable" and "interest payable"). These obligations were satisfied during the year to the extent indicated on the statement of changes in financial position.

b. Summarize in the form of a balance sheet the increases and decreases to each of the specific asset, liability, and owners' equity accounts. Be sure that the retained earnings account is equal to reported income and that cash is equal to the increase in cash.

18. *Transactions that affect income do not necessarily affect cash; those that affect cash do not necessarily affect income.*

A company engaged in the transactions set forth in the schedule that follows. (All dollar amounts are in thousands.)

	Cash Flow	Retained Earnings
1. The firm purchased merchandise, on account, for $800	$ 0	$ 0
2. It paid its suppliers $680 for the merchandise it purchased.	−680	0
3. The firm made sales of $750, all of which were on account.		
4. The cost of the merchandise sold was $550.		
5. The firm received $600 from customers in payment on their account.		
6. It purchased a three–year insurance policy. Cost of the policy, paid for in cash, was $30.		
7. The firm gave recognition to the expiration of one–third of the insurance policy.		
8. It borrowed $8,000 from a bank.		
9. It paid (in cash) $40 interest on the bank loan.		
10. It purchased equipment for $200 (cash).		
11. It gave recognition to the expiration of one–fifth of the useful life of the equipment.		
12. The firm incurred $380 in wages and salary costs. Of this amount, it paid only $360, with the balance to be paid in the following accounting period.		
Net cash flow	___	___
Net income (impact on retained earnings)	═══	═══

a. Complete the schedule so as to indicate the impact, if any, that each transaction would have upon (1) cash flow and (2) retained earning. The first two transactions are done for you as examples.

b. Compute the firm's income for the period. Compute its net cash flow.

19. *The three primary financial statements can be derived from transactions as they affect the accounting equation.*

A computer service corporation has just completed its first month of operations. The impact on the accounting equation of all the transactions in which the company engaged is summarized in the schedule that follows. From the information in the schedule prepare

a. an income statement

b. a statement of changes in financial position

c. a balance sheet

The schedule does not indicate the specific revenues and expenses that caused the increases and decreases in retained earnings. You should be able to determine them, however, from the asset or liability account with which the change in retained earnings is associated. (All dollar amounts are in thousands.)

Assets	=	Liabilities	+	Owners' Equity
1. Cash, +150				Common stock, +150
2. Customer accounts receivable, +120				Retained earnings, +120
3. Cash, +90				
Customer accounts receivable, –90				
4.		Salaries payable, +40		Retained earnings, –40
5. Cash, –25		Salaries payable, –25		
6. Prepaid rent, +30				
Cash, –30				
7. Prepaid rent, –15				Retained earnings, –15
8. Equipment, +60				
Cash, –60.				
9. Equipment, –1				Retained earnings, –1

20. *Amounts reported on the statement of changes in financial position are also reflected on either or both the balance sheet and the income statement.*

The following statement of changes in financial position is in slightly different form from the one illustrated in the text (Exhibit 2-7). In the statement illustrated there, the specific cash flows associated with income were listed individually. In the statement below, these cash flows are combined into one amount, "net income." Net income is then adjusted for revenues or expenses that did not involve the receipt or disbursement of cash.

For each item on the statement, indicate how it would be reflected on the income statement and the balance sheet. For example, amortization would be reported as an expense on the income statement and would decrease capital assets and retained earnings on the balance sheet.

Statement of Changes in Financial Position Year Ended December 31, 1996 (in millions)		
Operating Activities		
Net income		$ 299
Add: Amortization	$215	
Income taxes charged as an expense but not payable until the future	45	
Excess of sales over collections from customers	(30)	
Other adjustments to income	17	247
Cash provided by operating activities		$ 546
Investing Activities		
Purchase of buildings and equipment		$(869)
Investments in other companies		(105)
Sale of buildings and equipment (at a gain)		12
Sale of investments (at a loss)		11
Cash used in investing activities		$(951)
Financing Activities		
Issuance of stock		$ 50
Loan from bank		782
Repayments of debt		(130)
Payment of dividends		(184)
Cash provided by financing activities		$ 518
Increase in cash		$ 113

21. *The distinction between income and cash flow is critical. The differences can be accounted for by focusing on the changes in the related balance sheet accounts.*

An income statement and comparative balance sheet for the Todd Company are presented below. The following additional information pertains to financial events that took place during 1997. (All dollar amounts are in thousands.)

- The company purchased equipment (for cash) at a cost of $35,000.
- It sold a parcel of land for $10,000 (cash), the same amount that it had paid for the land.
- It borrowed $15,000.
- It paid cash dividends of $12,000.

Todd Company Statement of Income Year Ended December 31, 1997 (in thousands of dollars)		
Sales revenue		$200,000
Expenses		
Cost of goods sold	$100,000	
Wages and salaries	32,000	
Amortization	15,000	
Rent	10,000	
Interest	6,000	163,000
Net Income		$ 37,000

Todd Company Balance Sheet		
As at	December 31, 1997	December 31, 1996
	(in thousands of dollars)	
Assets		
Current assets		
Cash	$ 20,000	$ 30,000
Accounts receivable	70,000	40,000
Inventory	44,000	39,000
Prepaid rent	5,000	5,000
	$139,000	$114,000
Noncurrent assets		
Land	$ 40,000	$ 50,000
Building	150,000	160,000
Equipment	45,000	15,000
	$235,000	$225,000
Total assets	$374,000	$339,000
Liabilities and owners' equity		
Current liabilities		
Accounts payable	$ 68,000	$ 71,000
Wages payable	4,000	5,000
Interest payable	2,000	3,000
	$ 74,000	$ 79,000
Noncurrent liabilities		
Notes payable	$ 75,000	$ 60,000
Owners' equity	225,000	200,000
Total liabilities and owners' equity	$374,000	$339,000

a. Did the sales of the company exceed its cash collections? By how much? (*Hint:* What balance sheet account would increase when customers increase their indebtedness to the company?)

b. Did the firm's purchases of inventory exceed the amount charged as cost of goods sold? By how much? (*Hint:* Which balance sheet account would be affected by purchases and sales of merchandise?)

c. Did the company's payments to suppliers exceed the amount of purchases? By how much? (*Hint:* In which balance sheet account would amounts owed to suppliers be recorded?)

d. Did the company pay more in wages than it recorded as wages and salary expense? By how much?

e. Did it pay more in interest than it recorded as interest expense?

f. The company reported an amortization expense of $15,000. Was this expense associated with a decrease in cash? (*Hint:* Consider the impact of amortization on the components of the accounting equation.)

g. What other transactions increased or decreased cash but had no impact on income?

h. Based on your responses above, complete the following schedule, which explains why the company's cash decreased by $10,000 in the face of $37,000 in reported income.

Net income	$ 37,000
Add: Amortization (an expense not requiring the use of cash)	
Subtract	
Amount by which sales exceeded collections	
Amount by which purchases of inventory exceeded cost of goods sold	
Amount by which payments to suppliers exceeded purchases	
Amount by which wages paid exceeded wage expense	
Amount by which interest paid exceeded interest expense	
Add or subtract transactions that affected cash but had no impact on income	
Net decrease in cash	$(10,000)

22. *Information about income, dividends, and new shares issued can be derived from the shareholders' equity section of the balance sheet.*

The following is taken from the owners' equity section of the balance sheet of a manufacturer of trucks and automobile parts and equipment:

	December 31, 1997	December 31, 1996
Common stock, par value $1.00 share		
Authorized 40,000,000 shares		
Issued 12,839,166 and 12,749,128 shares at		
December 31, 1997, and 1996, respectively	$ 12,839,166	$ 12,749,128
Premium on capital stock	226,807,615	225,144,160
Earnings retained for use in the business	301,611,199	241,679,609
Cost of 630,883 shares of common stock held in		
treasury (deduction)	(15,678,303)	(15,678,303)
Total shareholders' equity	$525,579,677	$463,894,594

The firm's common stock is traded on the Toronto Stock Exchange. The company reported earnings in 1997 of $88,692,900.

a. What was the total amount of dividends that the company declared in 1997?

b. How many additional shares of common stock did the firm issue in 1997?

c. What was the average amount per share for which the additional shares were issued? (*Hint:* Consider changes in *both* the common stock and the premium on capital stock accounts.)

d. How many shares of stock were issued *and* outstanding as at December 31, 1997? (Shares of stock that a company holds in its treasury are not considered to be outstanding.)

e. What was the approximate amount of earnings per share in 1997? Earnings per share is the earnings for the year per each share of common stock outstanding (i.e., earnings divided by number of common shares outstanding). Base the computation on number of shares outstanding on December 31, 1997.

1. a. Assets = $200,000
   b. Equities = $200,000

2. a. Assets = $300,000
   b. Total equities = $300,000; those of owners = $200,000; those of outsiders = $100,000

3. a. Assets = $300,000 (This transaction decreases "cash" and increases "capital assets"—i.e., the automobile.)
   b. Liabilities = $100,000
   c. Owners' equity = $200,000

4. a. Assets = $305,000
   b. Liabilities = $105,000
   c. Owners' equity = $200,000

5. a. Assets = $306,600 ($305,000 per above, plus $5,600 cash received upon sale, minus $4,000 of goods surrendered.)
   b. Liabilities = $105,000
   c. Owners' equity = $201,600 (The "level" of assets increased by $1,600 as a consequence of the sale of 800 units. Liabilities remained unchanged but the equity of the owners must have increased by $1,600.)

6. Owners' equity has increased by $1,600; the company is therefore $1,600 "better off," and income, a measure of how much better off a company is at the end of a period than at the beginning, is also $1,600.

3

The Accounting Cycle

In Chapter 2, we introduced the fundamental accounting equation, Assets = Liabilities + Owners' Equity. In this chapter we expand upon the fundamental equation to develop an accounting system that is efficient to use in practice. This accounting cycle is described to show the recording process from the incurrence of a transaction through to the reporting of the results of the transaction in the financial statements.

After studying this chapter, you will be able to

- Describe ledger accounts and journal entries
- Understand the significance of the equality, Debits = Credits
- Understand the difference between transactions and economic events
- Describe the nine steps of the accounting cycle
- Understand the nature of accrual accounting and the concept of matching

The accounting cycle is described in terms of conventional books and records. In firms in which the accounting system is computerized, the books and records may not take the physical forms suggested by the descriptions in this chapter. Data may be scattered throughout an electronic data bank rather than recorded in neat columns in a journal or ledger. Nevertheless, the underlying principles, the structure of accounts, and the final products (the financial statements) are virtually the same, regardless of whether the system is maintained manually or electronically.

The basic accounting equation—Assets = Liabilities + Owners' Equity—or the slightly expanded equation—Assets = Liabilities + Capital Contributed by Owners + Retained Earnings—serves as the basis for all accounting transactions. In theory, all accounting transactions that affect a business could be recorded in a single ledger (a book of accounts), derived from the basic equation. Changes in assets would be indicated on the left-hand side of the page; changes in liabilities or owners' equity would be indicated on the right.

Example

1. The CDE Company issues capital stock for $25,000 cash. (An asset, *cash*, is increased; owners' equity, *common stock*, is increased.)

2. The company purchases furniture and fixtures for $10,000 on account. (An asset, *furniture and fixtures*, is increased; a liability, *accounts payable*, is increased.)

3. The company purchases merchandise for resale for $7,000 cash. (An asset, *merchandise inventory*, is increased; an asset, *cash*, is decreased.)

4. The company pays $5,000 of the amount it owes on account. (An asset, *cash*, is decreased; a liability, *accounts payable*, is decreased.)

CDE Company General Ledger			
Assets		**Liabilities and Owners' Equity**	
1. Cash (asset +)	+$25,000	**1.** Common stock (owners' equity +)	+$25,000
2. Furniture and fixtures (asset +)	+ 10,000	**2.** Accounts payable (liability +)	+ 10,000
3. Merchandise inventory (asset +)	+ 7,000		
Cash (asset –)	– 7,000		
4. Cash (asset –)	– 5,000	**4.** Accounts payable (liability –)	– 5,000
	$30,000		$30,000

The ledger indicates that, after the fourth transaction, the firm has assets of $30,000 and liabilities and owners' equity of the same amount. The ledger reveals that the accounts are "in balance" (they would have to be unless an error was made), and it indicates the total assets and the total liabilities and owners' equity. But by itself it provides little information that is useful to either managers or owners. Since each side of the ledger page combines changes in more than one account, the balance in any particular account is not readily available. To find the amount of cash on hand, for example, one would have to search the entire page (or entire book if there were numerous transactions) for all entries affecting cash. How much more convenient it would be if a separate page were provided for each account. Thus

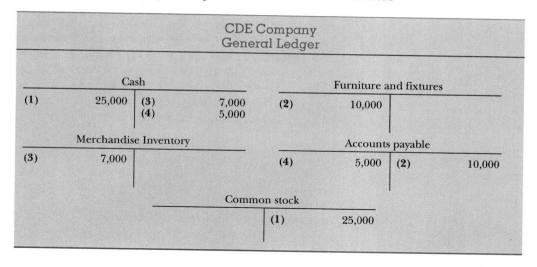

In the illustration each of the "T"s represents a separate page in the general ledger, or book of accounts. There is a separate page or "T account" for cash, furniture and fixtures, accounts payable, etc.

Debits and Credits

You will notice in the CDE Company general ledger above that increases (decreases) to the accounts are not always recorded on the same side of the T account. For example, the $25,000 *increase* in cash from transaction 1 is recorded on the left side of the cash T account. On the other hand, the $10,000 *increase* in accounts payable from transaction 2 is recorded on the right side of the accounts payable T account. It certainly would have been possible to have designated one side of the T account as the increase side and the other side as the decrease side (i.e., increases in any account would have been on the left, for example, and decreases in any account on the right). However, this was not done. Since all transactions must satisfy the accounting equation (Assets = Liabilities + Owners' Equity) it was decided to use this equality to create a secondary equality that would help to ensure accuracy in the recording process. This additional check for accuracy was important in the early days of accounting when the recording process was manual and errors were easy to make. This secondary equality was created by doing the following:

1. Arbitrarily, the left-hand side of the T account was called the *debit* side and the right-hand side of the T account was called the *credit* side.
2. An increase in an asset account would be recorded on the left side of the T account; a decrease in an asset account would be recorded on the right side. Conversely, an increase in a liability or owners' equity account would be recorded on the right side of the T account; a decrease in a liability or owners' equity account would be recorded on the left side.

The effect of this was that debits were forced to equal credits. If they didn't, an error must have been made in the recording process. The accounting equation equality ($A = L + OE$) is now supplemented with another equality, *Debits = Credits*.

Students are often confused by the debit and credit terminology. They understand what accounts are increased or decreased as the result of a transaction or economic event but they are unsure how to record that result in terms of what accounts to debit and credit. This confusion is understandable when one considers that the designation of sides of the account as debit or credit and having different sides be increases or decreases is arbitrary. Because of this arbitrary nature, it is necessary to memorize the rules of debit and credit. Those rules can be summarized as follows:

> *Entries that increase assets are referred to as debits.*
> *Those that decrease assets are known as credits.*
>
> *Entries that increase equities (liabilities and owners' equity) are referred to as credits.*
> *Those that decrease equities are known as debits.*

The following representation of the accounting equation in T account format is a useful device for remembering the relationship between debits and credits and increases and decreases:

Assets			Liabilities			Owners' Equity	
Debit	Credit	=	Debit	Credit	+	Debit	Credit
+	−		−	+		−	+

Use of *debit* to signify an increase in an entity's assets and *credit* to indicate an increase in its liabilities seems odd at first. A *credit* generally means one is *better off*, a *debit* that one is *worse off*. In Italian Renaissance accounting, where the terms originated, however, accounts were kept for those who contributed funds to the enterprise. The terms as they apply to changes in an *entity's equities* are consistent with common parlance when *viewed by the outside holder of the equities*. Thus, when one deposits funds in a bank, one is *credited* with this amount (which is then a liability of the bank). When one withdraws funds, one's account is *debited* (and the bank's liability disappears).

JOURNAL ENTRIES

Each T account represents a separate page in a book of accounts called the *general ledger*. Since transactions affect two or more accounts, each transaction must be recorded on two or more pages. No one page will contain a complete record of the transaction; at best it will indicate only one-half of the transaction. To maintain a comprehensive history of all transactions that affect the various accounts, firms maintain a *journal*—a book that serves as the source of many of the entries to the various accounts. *Journal entries* are ordinarily prepared from source documents, such as *invoices* (bills), *payment vouchers* (internal documents authorizing disbursements), *receiving* or *shipping reports, remittance advices* (documents indicating the receipt of cash), and *credit memoranda* (documents authorizing that a customer be given credit for merchandise damaged or returned or special allowances or discounts to which he or she may be entitled).

The use of journals and journal entries is easily illustrated. For instance, the purchase of merchandise for resale for $7,000 necessitates that a debit entry be made to the merchandise inventory account and a credit entry be made to the cash account. The journal is a convenient place to indicate both accounts affected by the transaction. At the time of purchase, the firm would record the following in the journal:

Debit: Merchandise inventory	$7,000
Credit: Cash	$7,000

The words *debit* and *credit* are conventionally omitted from the entry, and debits are distinguished from credits merely by the placement of the account titles and amounts. The account to be debited is placed along the left-hand margin, and that to be credited is indented slightly to the right. Similarly, the amount to be debited is shown slightly to the left of that to be credited. A brief explanation is often indicated beneath the entry, and the entry is numbered or lettered to facilitate referencing. Thus

(1)

Merchandise inventory $7,000
    Cash $7,000
To record the purchase of merchandise for resale

The amounts indicated in the journal would be posted to or recorded in the appropriate ledger accounts either at the time the transaction is recorded in the journal or, if more convenient, after a number of transactions have been recorded.

Some simple transactions can be used to illustrate the relationship between entries in the journal and those in the various ledger accounts. In this and in several subsequent examples the nature of the account (asset, liability, owners' equity) and whether it has increased (+) or decreased (−) may be indicated in parentheses next to each journal entry. This is done for pedagogical purposes, to emphasize the importance of understanding the effect of the transactions on the accounting equation. In practice, these explanatory notations are omitted.

Example

Brian Heller, an electronics specialist, decides to establish, as a sole proprietorship, a notebook computer repair service. He signs a lease on a store and engages in the following transactions in the month of September, 1996.

1. He takes $50,000 of his personal funds and deposits them in a chequing account in the name of "Heller Computer Service."

2. He purchases tools and test equipment for $25,000. He gives a two-year note payable for the full amount.

3. He purchases parts for $15,000. He pays $10,000 cash and receives 30-days' credit for the balance.

4. He pays rent in advance for the first three months, $1,000 per month.

The *journal entries* that record these transactions include the following:

(1)

| Cash (asset +) .... | $50,000 | |
| Brian Heller, capital (owner's equity +) .... | | $50,000 |

To record the initial contribution of cash

(2)

| Tools and equipment (asset +) .... | $25,000 | |
| Notes payable (liability +)... | | $25,000 |

To record the purchase of tools and equipment

(3)

Parts inventory (asset +)	$15,000	
Cash (asset –)		$10,000
Accounts payable (liability +)..		5,000

To record the purchase of the parts

(Note that a journal entry can consist of more than one debit or credit.) The account "notes payable" is used to record a liability when a written note is given by the borrower. When short-term trade credit is accepted, the liability is recorded as an "account payable."

(4)

| Prepaid rent (asset +) .... | $3,000 | |
| Cash (asset –) .... | | $3,000 |

To record the rent paid in advance

"Prepaid rent" represents the right to use the store for three months. It is a current asset—one that will be "written off," or *amortized,* as it expires over the three-month period.

The journal entries would be *posted* to the various ledger accounts:

Assets		Liabilities and Owner's Equity	
Cash	**Accounts payable**	**Brian Heller, capital**
(1) 50,000 | (3) 10,000	| (3) 5,000	| (1) 50,000
| (4) 3,000		
Tools and equipment	**Notes payable**	
(2) 25,000 |	| (2) 25,000	
Parts inventory		
(3) 15,000 |		
Prepaid rent		
(4) 3,000 |		

If a balance sheet were to be prepared at the end of September after the four transactions had been journalized and posted, then it would be necessary to determine and summarize the balances in each account. The balance in each account can be calculated by subtracting the total credits from the total debits. Thus the balance in the "Cash" account is $50,000 minus the sum of $10,000 and $3,000, or $37,000. Conversely, the balance in each liability or owner's equity account can be calculated by subtracting the total debits from the total credits.

A balance sheet for the business is presented in Exhibit 3-1.

EXHIBIT 3-1

Heller Computer Service
Balance Sheet
As at September 30, 1996

Assets			Liabilities and Owner's Equity		
Current assets			Current liabilities		
Cash in bank	$37,000		Accounts payable	$ 5,000	
Parts inventory	15,000		Noncurrent liabilities		
Prepaid rent	3,000	$55,000	Notes payable	25,000	$30,000
Noncurrent assets			Owner's equity		
Tools and			Brian Heller, capital		50,000
equipment		25,000			
Total assets		$80,000	Total liabilities and owner's equity		$80,000

SPECIAL PROBLEMS OF ACCOUNTING FOR REVENUES AND EXPENSES

Transactions versus Economic Events

Revenues are the inflows of net assets from delivering or producing goods; expenses are the related outflows. Both revenues and expenses can result from economic events *other than* transactions.

A *transaction* is an exchange of one item for another between the accounting entity and another party. Examples of transactions are purchases of inventory and equipment, sales of goods or services, collection of accounts receivable, issuance and repayment of debt. An *economic event* is any occurrence that affects a firm's financial well-being. Economic events include but are not limited to transactions. An earthquake that destroys a company's plant is an economic event but not a transaction. Passage of time is an economic event, not a transaction. Passage of time deteriorates a firm's assets, enables it to earn rent from a tenant, and causes it to owe interest on a loan.

The record-keeping process of accounting entities is quite naturally dominated by transactions. Transactions create financial documents such as cheques and invoices, which trigger entries into journals. Other economic events, by contrast, may not be accompanied by comparable physical or electronic evidence. Often, as with amortization, they are tied to transactions that may have taken place in the distant past (e.g., when an asset was acquired). They will not routinely be signaled by day-to-day business operations. Therefore they must be recognized by special entries, ones that are typically made either periodically (at the end of each month) or whenever financial statements are to be prepared.

The Issue of Recognition

Central to almost all issues of accounting are two intertwined questions:

1. What types of events should cause revenues and expenses to be recognized?

2. When should the revenues and expense be recognized?

As will be illustrated in this and subsequent chapters, the recognition of revenues and expenses is *not* governed primarily by the receipt or disbursement of cash. If it were, income could easily be manipulated. Companies could postpone purchases of inventories and equipment or delay the payment of wages, interest, and rent. Instead, revenues and expenses are recognized when critical events take place. Examples of critical events that typically give rise to revenues and expenses are the *sale* of goods or services (not the collection of cash from customers), the *delivery* of merchandise to customers (not the acquisition of the merchandise or payment for it), the *performance* of services by employees (not the payment of wages), and the *use* of borrowed funds or rented premises (not the payment for them).

The recognition of a revenue or expense (and the related receivable or payable) as a result of an economic event other than a cash transaction involves a difference in *timing* between *revenue earned* and *cash received,* and/or *expense incurred* and *expenditure paid.* There may be an *initial prepayment,* and then a subsequent *expensing* of that prepayment in another period. Or there may be an *initial accrual,* and then the *subsequent payment* in another period of what is owed. The modern accounting system is said, in a general sense, to be on an *accrual* basis, as distinguished from a *cash* basis.

Revenues and expenses are reported on the income statement but are, in essence, subaccounts of retained earnings. The next section will illustrate how common revenues and expenses are recorded. It will also demonstrate how, at the end of an accounting period, the balances in the revenue and expense accounts get transferred to retained earnings.

THE ACCOUNTING CYCLE

There are nine basic steps to the accounting cycle. We shall illustrate these using the Hawthorne Corporation as an example.

The Hawthorne Corporation was organized on June 1, 1996. The financial events described in this example take place during its first month of operation. The usual accounting cycle is one year, at the end of which a firm will prepare a complete set of financial statements. There is no conceptual reason, however, why the accounting cycle cannot be longer or shorter. To simplify our example, it will be assumed that the accounting cycle of the Hawthorne Corporation is one month.

Step 1: Journalizing the Transactions and Other Financial Events

A first set of financial events engaged in by the Hawthorne Corporation is described and journalized in Exhibit 3-2. These transactions are straightforward. Other than transaction 1, which records the issue of common stock, they have no effect on either the level of net assets or on owners' equity. They result in neither inflows nor outflows of net resources to the business and hence in neither revenues nor expenses.

A second set of transactions is more complex and warrants greater discussion, as we see next.

A key part of this first step of the accounting cycle is the analysis of the transaction or economic event to determine the effect (i.e., increase or decrease) on the particular components of the accounting equation (Assets, Liabilities, Owners' equity, Revenues, Expenses). Before the transaction can be recorded in journal entry format, the increase or decrease to the specific accounts must be known. This analysis really is the critical step. If the analysis is wrong, then the remaining steps will all be wrong because those remaining steps are merely mechanical manipulations of data. To emphasize the importance of knowing what accounts increase and decrease, the effect on the accounting equation of each debit and credit is shown in brackets in each journal entry in the Hawthorne Corporation example. This will not be done in practice. It is done here for pedagogical purposes to emphasize the importance of this analysis step.

EXHIBIT 3-2
Hawthorne Corporation, Transactions

The company issues 10,000 shares of common stock to its two cofounders for a price of $50 per share, which is received in cash.

(1)

Cash (asset +).. $500,000
    Common stock (owners' equity +) $500,000
To record the sale of common stock

The company issues $100,000 of long–term bonds, payable on June 1, 2021.

(2)

Cash (asset +).. $100,000
    Bonds payable (liability +) $100,000
To record the issue of long–term bonds

The company purchases a building for $300,000. It gives a down payment of $100,000 and a 10–year note payable for the balance.

(3)

Building (asset +) $300,000
    Cash (asset –).. $100,000
    Notes payable (liability +) $200,000
To record the purchase of the building

The company purchases equipment for $100,000 and incurs installation and transportation costs of $20,000.

(4)

Equipment (asset +)............................... $120,000
    Cash (asset –).. $120,000
To record the purchase of equipment
The installation and transportation costs are assumed to be necessary to bring the equipment to a serviceable condition; hence they are added to the cost of the equipment.

The company rents out a portion of its building. It signs a five–year lease. Rent is to be $1,000 per month, and three months' rent is received in advance. Occupancy is to begin July 1.

(5)

Cash (asset +)... $3,000
    Rent received in advance (liability +) $3,000
To record three months' rent received in advance
The company has received the cash. It is still obligated to provide services to the lessee. "Rent received in advance" can be viewed as "value of rental services yet to be furnished."

EXHIBIT 3-2 (continued)

The company receives an invoice (a bill) from its lawyers—$5,000—for services performed in connection with the filing for the certificate of incorporation and issuing common stock.

(6)

Organization costs (asset +) $5,000
    Accounts payable (liability +) $5,000
To record the costs of organizing the corporation

The organization costs, like the cost of equipment and the building, were incurred in order to benefit future accounting periods. Although they are "intangible"—they cannot be seen or felt—they are nevertheless *assets* of the company. Accounts payable, rather than cash, has been credited because the company has not yet paid the invoice.

The company hires J. Pringle as president. The two parties sign a two–year employment contract requiring the firm to compensate Pringle at a salary of $135,000 per year.

No entry is required.

Although the firm seemingly has incurred a liability of $270,000, the president has not yet performed any services for the company. As indicated previously, accountants generally record liabilities resulting from contracts only to the extent that services have been performed or cash has been paid. Thus, when Pringle has been employed for one month, the company will record a liability of one-twelfth of $135,000—$11,250

The company purchases merchandise for resale for $54,000, on account.

(7)

Merchandise inventory (asset +) $54,000
    Accounts payable (liability +) $54,000
To record the purchase of merchandise

The company purchases for cash 100 shares of BCE stock as a temporary investment. Cost per share is $61.

(8)

Marketable securities (asset +) $6,100
    Cash (asset –) $6,100
To record the purchase of 100 shares of BCE stock

The company pays $5,000 of the amount it owes to its supplier of merchandise inventory.

(9)

Accounts payable (liability –) $5,000
    Cash (asset –) $5,000
To record the payment to the supplier

The company returns defective merchandise to the supplier. The merchandise cost $7,000. The supplier gives the company credit for the merchandise returned.

(10)

Accounts payable (liability –) $7,000
    Merchandise inventory (asset –) $7,000
To record the return of merchandise

The company learns through *The Globe and Mail*'s *Report on Business* that the market price of its BCE stock has increased to $64 per share.

No entry is necessary.

Increases in the market value of assets generally are not recorded—mainly because of accountants' preference toward conservative expressions of value.

The market price of the BCE stock declines to $61 per share. The company sells 50 shares for cash.

(11)

Cash (asset +) $3,050
    Marketable securities (asset –) $3,050
To record the sale of 50 shares of BCE stock

(The stock was sold at original cost; hence there was no gain or loss on the sale.)

Sales Revenue

The Hawthorne Corporation sells merchandise for $83,000 (all sales are "on account"):

(12)

Accounts receivable (asset +) $83,000
    Sales revenue (retained earnings +) $83,000
To record sales for the month

Sales revenue is typically recognized when merchandise is *delivered* to a customer (exceptions will be discussed in later chapters). Recognition of revenue increases net assets and correspondingly increases retained earnings. In this example, "retained earnings" will be parenthetically added to all revenues and expenses so as to emphasize that revenues and expenses are, in essence, increases or decreases in owners' equity.

Collection of Cash from Customers

The company collects $62,000 from its customers:

(13)

Cash (asset +)	$62,000	
Accounts receivable (asset −)		$62,000

To record collection of cash from customers

The collection of cash does *not* create a revenue. The revenue was created when the merchandise was sold. One asset (cash) is exchanged for another (accounts receivable). Net assets, and hence owners' equity, remains unchanged.

Purchase of Merchandise

The company purchases additional merchandise inventory at a cost of $16,000 (on account):

(14)

Merchandise inventory (asset +)	$16,000	
Accounts payable (liability +)		$16,000

To record the purchase of merchandise

Just as the collection of cash does not create a revenue, the acquisition of merchandise does not result in an expense. Instead, the company increases an asset (merchandise inventory) but at the same time increases a liability (accounts payable).

Cost of Goods Sold

The cost of the merchandise sold was $45,000:

(15)

Cost of goods sold (retained earnings −)..	$45,000	
Merchandise inventory (asset −)		$45,000

To record the cost of goods sold as an expense

The cost of merchandise sold is ordinarily recognized as an expense in the same period as the revenue from the sale. Recognition of the expense results in a decrease in net assets and a corresponding decrease in retained earnings.

Many companies do not keep track of the cost of particular items sold. Instead, they take advantage of a basic—and obvious—relationship between account balances and changes during a period:

Beginning balance + Additions − Reductions = Ending balance

As to inventory, the additions are the purchases during the period and the reductions are the goods sold. Thus

Beginning balance + Purchases − Cost of goods sold = Ending balance

And, by rearrangement,

Cost of goods sold = Beginning balance + Purchases − Ending balance

At period end, companies take an *inventory* (physical count) of goods on hand. By referring to invoices or comparable purchase documents, they determine the amount paid for those goods. Inasmuch as they also know the value of the goods on hand at the start of the period (from the financial statements of the previous period) and the amount that was purchased during the period (from purchase records), they can easily compute the cost of the goods that were sold during the period. This is called the *periodic inventory method* of measuring cost of goods sold. Suppose that the Hawthorne Corporation's count of June 30 indicates merchandise inventory of $18,000. Beginning balance on June 1 was $0. Net purchases ($54,000 per entry 7 plus $16,000 per entry 14, less returns of $7,000 per entry 10) are $63,000. Therefore the $45,000 cost of goods sold was derived as follows:

Cost of goods sold = Beginning balance + Purchases − Ending balance

Cost of goods sold = $0 + $63,000 − $18,000

Cost of goods sold = $45,000

Payments to Suppliers

The company pays $38,000 of its amount owing to suppliers:

(16)

Accounts payable (liability −)	$38,000	
Cash (asset −)		$38,000
To record payments to suppliers		

This transaction decreases a liability and a corresponding asset. Of the three events associated with the merchandise (the purchase of the goods, the sale and delivery to the customer, and the payments to the suppliers), only the sale and delivery to customers leads to recognition of an expense. The others result in a reordering of the mix, but no change in the level, of net assets.

Purchase of Advertising Circulars

The company purchases $5,000 of advertising circulars:

(17)

Advertising circulars (asset +)	$5,000	
Cash (asset −)		$5,000
To record the acquisition of advertising circulars		

The advertising circulars are expected to benefit the future. Until consumed, they are an asset.

Advertising Expense

The company distributes $4,000 of the advertising circulars:

(18)

Advertising expense (retained earnings −)	$4,000	
Advertising circulars (asset −)		$4,000
To record consumption of advertising circulars		

The distribution of the circulars prompts the recognition of an expense. This transaction is another example of an expense that is driven by the consumption of, rather than the acquisition of or the payment for, an asset.

Wages and Salaries

The company pays wages and salaries of $13,000. The payment is made on the last day of the month and covers the wages and salaries of the entire period. Therefore the cash paid corresponds to the wage and salary expense.

(19)

Wage and salary expense (retained earnings –)	$13,000	
Cash (asset –)		$13,000
To record wages and salaries		

Had the payment been delayed until the next accounting period, the wage and salary expense would still have been the same. Wage and salary expense is determined by when the employees perform their services, not by when they are paid for them. Were the payment delayed, then the liability "wages and salaries payable," instead of the asset "cash," would have been credited.

Step 2: Updating the Accounts: Recognizing Still Other Economic Events

At month end, the company is to prepare financial statements. Therefore it must bring its accounts up to date by recording the revenues and expenses that are attributable to events other than specific transactions.

Utilities Expense

The company estimates that it consumed $300 in electricity during the month:

(20)

Utilities expense (retained earnings –)	$300	
Accrued utilities payable (liability +)		$300
To record utility costs		

The company must recognize an expense for the electricity used, even if it has not yet received a bill. The term *accrued* is commonly applied to an asset or liability that is not yet contractually receivable or payable, even though the related revenue or expense has been recognized.

Rent Revenue

In early June the company received $3,000 (three months') rent in advance (transaction 5). The amount was recorded as a liability—an obligation to provide services in the future. During the month the company provides one month of service, thereby earning revenue of $1,000:

(21)

Rent received in advance (liability –)	$1,000	
Rent revenue (retained earnings +)		$1,000
To record rent revenue for one month		

Interest Expense

The company must record interest expense, which it calculates to be $3,000, attributable to outstanding bonds and notes payable (entries 2 and 3). It has had the use of the funds, and benefited from them, even if the interest payment is not yet due.

(22)

Interest expense (retained earnings –)	$3,000	
Accrued interest payable (liability +)		$3,000
To record interest expense for one month		

Amortization Expense—Property, Plant, and Equipment

During the month the company purchased a building for $300,000 and equipment for $120,000 (entries 3 and 4). The building has an estimated useful life of 25 years (300 months) and the equipment 5 years (60 months). At the end of June, the company must recognize the consumption of a proportionate share of the assets:

(23)

Amortization expense (retained earnings –) $3,000
      Building (asset –) $1,000
      Equipment (asset –) 2,000
To recognize amortization for one month

Amortization Expense—Organization Costs

Upon its formation, the company paid $5,000 in lawyers' fees (entry 6). The fees were *capitalized* (recorded as an asset) as "organization costs" since, like outlays for buildings and equipment, they were incurred to benefit several accounting periods. They must therefore be amortized over a period of anticipated utility. Due to the difficulties of defining, let alone measuring, the precise benefits provided by organization costs, companies have considerable latitude in determining the amortization period. Current standards allow for any number of years, up to a maximum of 40. The Hawthorne Corporation has elected to amortize the costs over four years (48 months).

(24)

Amortization expense (retained earnings –) $104
      Organization costs (asset –) $104
To recognize amortization for one month

Dividends

The company declared and paid cash dividends of 35 cents per share on its 10,000 shares of common stock outstanding—a total of $3,500. Dividends are distributions of assets to the company's owners. They are not expenses because they are not paid to earn revenue. However, like expenses, they reduce the corporation's net assets and retained earnings.

(25)

Dividends (retained earnings –) $3,500
      Cash (asset –) $3,500
To record the declaration and payment of dividends

Step 3: Posting to Ledger Accounts and Computing Account Balances

The journal entries must be posted (recorded in) the ledger accounts. The ledger accounts as of June 30, in T account form, are presented in Exhibit 3-3. The two sides of all accounts other than revenues and expenses have been totalled and the resultant balances shown beneath the double rules.

EXHIBIT 3-3
Preclosing General Ledger Accounts

| | Assets | | | | Liabilities | | | | Shareholders' Equity (Including Revenues, Expenses, and Dividends) | | |

Assets

Cash

(1)	500,000	(3)	100,000
(2)	100,000	(4)	120,000
(5)	3,000	(8)	6,100
(11)	3,050	(9)	5,000
(13)	62,000	(16)	38,000
		(17)	5,000
		(19)	13,000
		(25)	3,500
	377,450		

Marketable securities

(8)	6,100	(11)	3,050
	3,050		

Accounts receivable

(12)	83,000	(13)	62,000
	21,000		

Advertising circulars

(17)	5,000	(18)	4,000
	1,000		

Merchandise inventory

(7)	54,000	(10)	7,000
(14)	16,000	(15)	45,000
	18,000		

Equipment

(4)	120,000	(23)	2,000
	118,000		

Building

(3)	300,000	(23)	1,000
	299,000		

Organization costs

(6)	5,000	(24)	104
	4,896		

Liabilities

Accounts payable

(9)	5,000	(6)	5,000
(10)	7,000	(7)	54,000
(16)	38,000	(14)	16,000
			25,000

Rent received in advance

(21)	1,000	(5)	3,000
			2,000

Accrued utilities payable

	(20)	300
		300

Accrued interest payable

	(22)	3,000
		3,000

Notes payable

	(3)	200,000
		200,000

Bonds payable

	(2)	100,000
		100,000

Shareholders' Equity (Including Revenues, Expenses, and Dividends)

Common stock

	(1)	500,000
		500,000

Retained earnings

Sales revenue

	(12)	83,000

Rent revenue

	(21)	1,000

Cost of goods sold

(15)	45,000	

Wage and salary expense

(19)	13,000	

Advertising expense

(18)	4,000	

Utilities expense

(20)	300	

EXHIBIT 3-3 (continued)

		Interest expense
(22)	3,000	

		Amortization expense
(23)	3,000	
(24)	104	
	3,104	

		Dividends
(25)	3,500	

Step 4: Taking a Trial Balance

After the journal entries have been posted to the ledger accounts, a trial balance may be taken. A *trial balance* is a complete listing of the balances in each of the ledger accounts. Naturally, the total debit balances must equal the total credit balances. If they do not, then either the accounts or the trial balance is in error.

Unfortunately, the equality of total debits and total credits is a necessary, but not a sufficient, condition for the accounts to be correct. Therefore, even if the debits equal the credits, the records may be in error. The company may have failed to record relevant financial events, recorded them in incorrect amounts, or debited or credited improper accounts.

A trial balance may be taken at any time. A trial balance taken before the end-of-period updating and correcting entries (correcting entries will be discussed in the next chapter) have been made is called an *unadjusted* trial balance. One prepared after the updating and correcting entries have been made is referred to as an *adjusted* trial balance.

A trial balance taken before the closing entries are made is called a *preclosing* trial balance; one taken after is known as a *postclosing* trial balance. Closing entries transfer the balances in revenue, expense, and dividend accounts to retained earnings. Thus a *preclosing* trial balance will include revenue, expense, and dividend accounts. Retained earnings will not yet have been updated to incorporate income and dividends for the period. In the absence of unusual adjustments, the retained earnings in the preclosing trial balance will be those of the *start* of the period, not the end. The *postclosing* trial balance will *not* include revenue, expense, and dividend accounts, since the balances would have been transferred to retained earnings. Correspondingly, the retained earnings in the postclosing trial balance will be those of the end of the period, having been updated to include the balances transferred from the revenue, expense and dividend accounts.

The *preclosing* trial balance of the Hawthorne Corporation is shown in Exhibit 3-4. The dotted line is included for illustration only. The accounts above the line are asset, liability, and owners' equity accounts. Those below are revenues, expenses, and dividends. The accounts above the line will appear unchanged on both the postclosing trial balance and the balance sheet, with the exception that retained earnings will be updated to incorporate the net sum of the accounts below the line.

The accounts below the line, except for dividends, will constitute the income statement. All of these accounts, including dividends, will be closed at period end and the balances transferred to retained earnings.

EXHIBIT 3-4

Hawthorne Corporation
Preclosing Trial Balance
As at June 30, 1996

	Debit Balances	Credit Balances	
Cash	$377,450		
Marketable securities	3,050		
Accounts receivable	21,000		
Advertising circulars	1,000		
Merchandise inventory	18,000		
Equipment	118,000		
Building	299,000		
Organization costs	4,896		Debits > Credits by $12,096
Accounts payable		$ 25,000	
Rent received in advance		2,000	
Accrued utilities payable		300	
Accrued interest payable		3,000	
Notes payable		200,000	
Bonds payable		100,000	
Common stock		500,000	
Retained earnings (beginning)		0	*
Sales revenue		83,000	
Rent revenue		1,000	
Cost of goods sold	45,000		
Wage and salary expense	13,000		
Advertising expense	4,000		Credits > Debits by $12,096
Interest expense	3,000		
Utilities expense	300		
Amortization expense	3,104		
Dividends	3,500		
	$914,300	$914,300	

*This line is included for illustration only. Accounts above the line are assets, liabilities, and shareholders' equities; those below are revenues, expenses, and dividends.

Step 5: Preparing the Income Statement

To prepare an income statement it is necessary only to extract the revenues and expenses from the *preclosing trial balance*. The income statement of the Hawthorne Corporation is presented in Exhibit 3-5.

EXHIBIT 3-5

Hawthorne Corporation Income Statement Month Ended June 30, 1996		
Revenues		
Sales revenue	$83,000	
Rent revenue	1,000	$84,000
Expenses		
Cost of goods sold	45,000	
Wage and salary expense	13,000	
Advertising expense	4,000	
Interest expense	3,000	
Utilities expense	300	
Amortization expense	3,104	68,404
Net income		$15,596

Step 6: Closing Revenues, Expenses, and Dividends

Revenues and expenses have two characteristics that differentiate them from balance sheet accounts. These two features dictate that they be "closed" at the end of an accounting period.

First, revenues and expenses are subaccounts of retained earnings. Revenues are increases in retained earnings; expenses, decreases. In fact, revenues and expenses could be credited or debited directly to retained earnings. Separate accounts are maintained primarily so that the information required for the income statement can easily be extracted and categorized. Once that is done, the balances in the revenue and expense accounts can be transferred to retained earnings.

Second, revenues and expenses measure flows of resources over a period of time. When that period is completed, the accounts must be "reset" to zero so that the measurement process can begin anew in the next period.

Closing entries therefore accomplish two objectives:

1. They transfer the balances in revenue and expense accounts to retained earnings.

2. They "zero out" the accounts so that those accounts are ready to "meter" the resource flows of the next accounting period.

The revenues and expenses may be closed directly to retained earnings. Many firms, however, close them to an intermediary account, "income summary." They then close "income summary" to retained earnings. "Income summary" is a temporary account. Its main purpose is to combine the revenues and expenses so that only a single entry for income need be made to retained earnings. Thus

(Closing entry 1)

Sales revenue	$83,000	
Rent revenue	1,000	
Income summary		$84,000
To close the revenue accounts		

(Closing entry 2)

Income summary	....	$68,404
Cost of goods sold	....	$45,000
Advertising expense	....	4,000
Wage and salary expense	....	13,000
Interest expense	....	3,000
Amortization expense	....	3,104
Utility expense	....	300

To close the expense accounts

EXHIBIT 3-6
Closing Entries

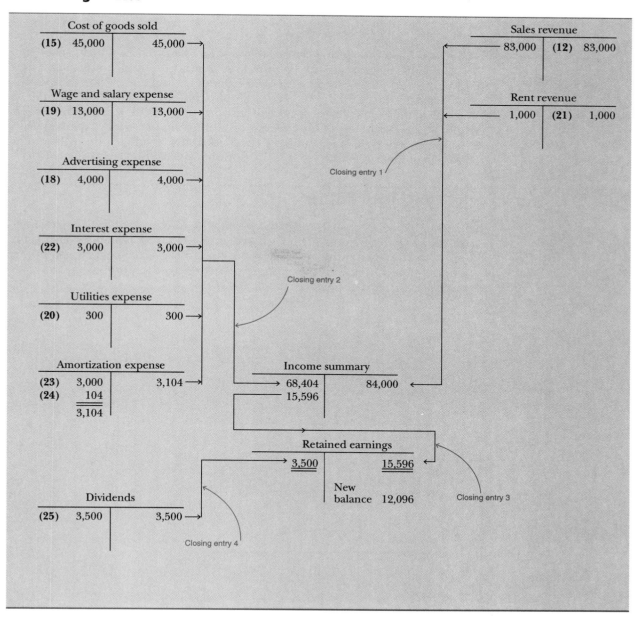

(Closing entry 3)

Income summary $15,596
      Retained earnings $15,596
To close the income summary account and transfer its balance to retained earnings

The dividends account must also be closed. Like revenues and expenses, dividends are a subaccount of retained earnings and measure a flow of resources over a period of time. Dividends do *not* enter in the computation of income. They are a discretionary transfer of resources from the company to its owners. Dividends therefore are closed directly to retained earnings:

(Closing entry 4)

Retained earnings $3,500
      Dividends $3,500
To close the dividends account

Exhibit 3-6 shows the closing entries in diagram form.

The balances in the asset, liability, and common stock accounts need neither be transferred nor zeroed out. The balances at the end of one period will be those at the start of the next. For example, the cash balance of $377,450 at the close of business on June 30 will also be that at the start of July 1. In Exhibit 3-3, to facilitate the summarization of the end-of-period balances, double lines have been drawn beneath the debits and credits. The differences between the sums are shown on the appropriate side of the T accounts.

Step 7: Taking a Postclosing Trial Balance

Exhibit 3-7 presents a *postclosing* trial balance. It includes only balance sheet accounts, since the income statement accounts as well as dividends have been closed to retained earnings. Whereas the preclosing trial balance shows the beginning-of-period retained earnings balance ($0), the postclosing trial balance reports the end-of-period balance ($12,096).

EXHIBIT 3-7

	Hawthorne Corporation Postclosing Trial Balance As at June 30, 1996	
Cash	$377,450	
Marketable securities	3,050	
Accounts receivable	21,000	
Advertising circulars	1,000	
Merchandise inventory	18,000	
Equipment	118,000	
Building	299,000	
Organization costs	4,896	
Accounts payable		$ 25,000
Rent received in advance		2,000
Accrued utilities payable		300
Accrued interest payable		3,000
Notes payable		200,000
Bonds payable		100,000
Common stock		500,000
Retained earnings		12,096
	$842,396	$842,396

Step 8: Preparing a Balance Sheet

The balance sheet (also called a *statement of position*) is, in essence, a postclosing trial balance. The significant difference between the two is in the nature of the balancing. The balance sheet is arranged according to the fundamental accounting equation, Assets = Liabilities + Owners' Equity, while the postclosing trial balance is based on the Debits = Credits equality. As can be seen in Exhibit 3-8, the account balances are the same; they have merely been classified and reordered.

EXHIBIT 3-8

Hawthorne Corporation
Balance Sheet
As at June 30, 1996

Assets

Current assets		
Cash	$377,450	
Marketable securities	3,050	
Accounts receivable	21,000	
Advertising circulars	1,000	
Merchandise inventory	18,000	$420,500
Noncurrent assets		
Equipment	118,000	
Building	299,000	
Organization costs	4,896	421,896
Total assets		$842,396

Liabilities and Shareholders' Equity

Current liabilities		
Accounts payable	$ 25,000	
Rent received in advance	2,000	
Accrued utilities payable	300	
Accrued interest payable	3,000	$ 30,300
Noncurrent liabilities		
Notes payable	200,000	
Bonds payable	100,000	300,000
Total liabilities		330,300
Shareholders' equity		
Common stock, 10,000 shares		
issued and outstanding	500,000	
Retained earnings	12,096	512,096
Total equities		$842,396

Step 9: Preparing a Statement of Changes in Financial Position and a Statement of Retained Earnings

The third primary statement, the statement of changes in financial position, is conceptually straightforward. The statement summarizes and classifies each of the entries to the cash account. If there are a large number of transactions affecting cash, detailed analysis of the cash account can become mechanically complex. Means of simplifying the process will be explained in Chapter 14.

Exhibit 3-9 presents a statement of changes in financial position, in this instance prepared directly from the entries to the cash account.

Exhibit 3-10 presents a statement of retained earnings. The information was derived from the entries to the retained earnings account in Exhibit 3-3.

The accounting cycle is now complete, and a new accounting period can begin.

EXHIBIT 3-9

Hawthorne Corporation
Statement of Changes in Financial Position
Month Ended June 30, 1996

Operating Activities	
Collections from customers	$ 62,000
Payments to suppliers	(43,000)
Payment of wages and salaries	(13,000)
Collection of rent (in advance)	3,000
Purchase of advertising circulars	(5,000)
Cash provided by operating activities	$ 4,000
Investing Activities	
Purchase of building	$ (100,000)
Purchase of equipment	(120,000)
Purchase of marketable securities	(6,100)
Sales of marketable securities	3,050
Cash used for investing activities	$ (223,050)
Financing Activities	
Issue of common stock	$ 500,000
Issue of bonds payable	100,000
Payment of dividends	(3,500)
Cash provided by financing activities	$ 596,500
Increase in cash	$ 377,450

EXHIBIT 3-10

Hawthorne Corporation
Statement of Retained Earnings
Month Ended June 30, 1996

Balance, June 1	$ 0
Net income, month of June	15,596
Dividends declared in June	(3,500)
Balance, June 30	$12,096

CONTRA ACCOUNTS

Contra (meaning against or opposite) *accounts* are offset accounts. They are associated with specific asset or liability accounts, from which their balances are subtracted.

In the Hawthorne illustration, amortization (entry **23**) was recorded with a debit to amortization expense and a credit to building and to equipment.

While the entry is correct, most firms would credit the contra accounts "building—accumulated amortization" and "equipment—accumulated amortization" rather than the asset accounts, "building" and "equipment." Whereas the building and the equipment accounts would have debit balances, the contra accounts would always have credit balances. The asset accounts would indicate the amounts paid for the buildings and equipment, the contra accounts the expired portion of the cost. The differences between the two would reflect the unexpired costs (i.e., the *book values* of the assets). The contra accounts would be reported beneath the related assets:

Equipment	$120,000	
Less: Accumulated amortization	2,000	$118,000
Building	300,000	
Less: Accumulated amortization	1,000	$299,000

The advantage of crediting the contra accounts rather than the asset accounts is that the balance sheet will show the original cost of the assets as well as the portion that has been amortized. This additional information enables statement users to determine the percentage of asset costs that have already been amortized (for example, 2/120, or 1.7 percent, of the equipment).

When an asset is sold or retired, both the accumulated amortization and the asset cost must be removed from the accounts. Suppose, for example, that the equipment is sold for $125,000. The book value at the time of sale is $118,000. Hence there is a gain of $7,000. The following entry would be in order:

Cash	$125,000	
Accumulated amortization	2,000	
Equipment		$120,000
Gain on sale of equipment		7,000
To record the sale of equipment		

BASIC BOOKS OF ACCOUNTS

The basic accounting information-processing system is simple and straightforward. Relatively few books and records need be maintained or prepared—regardless of the size of the business enterprise and regardless of whether the system will be manually or electronically maintained.

If the enterprise maintains a computerized accounting system, the journals or ledgers will not, of course, take the form illustrated here. They would, however, serve the same function and be designed to accommodate the same information.

As we noted earlier in this chapter, the fundamental means of recording economic events and transactions is the *journal entry*. Journal entries are *posted* to the *general ledger*, a book in which all balance sheet and income statement accounts are maintained. General ledger accounts are represented in this text by T accounts. Posting involves nothing more than transcribing the entries from the journals to the appropriate general ledger accounts.

Special Journals

Although conceptually there is need for only a single, or *general,* journal in which to record transactions, in practice, most firms find that record keeping is facilitated by several supplementary, often called *special,* journals. Since a firm may enter into numerous transactions that affect identical accounts, it is relatively easy to combine the transactions into a single journal entry and periodically make but one entry to the accounts affected. Supplementary journals enable the firm to do just that. Most firms, for example, maintain a sales journal to record all sales made on account. The sales journal may be designed as follows:

Date		Purchaser	Invoice #	Amount
Jan.	3	Burnet, Inc.	101	12 580 00
	4	Silver Creek Co.	102	8 000 00
	4	Bertram Manufacturing	103	2 170 00
	5	Leander Processing	104	15 275 00

As each sale is made, the firm enters the date of the sale; the name of the customer to whom the sale was made; the sales invoice number; and the amount of the sale in the "Amount" column. Only one "Amount" column is required in the sales journal since every sale on account requires a debit to Accounts receivable and an equal credit to the Sales account. At the end of each month, the "Amount" column is totalled and then either the following entry is made in the general journal or the amounts are posted directly to the appropriate general ledger accounts:

Accounts receivable	xxxx	
Sales		xxxx

Note that the "Amount" total is interpreted as both a debit to Accounts receivable and as credit to Sales.

Similarly, a firm might maintain a *cash receipts book* and a *cash disbursements book,* both of which are also supplementary journals. One column would indicate the amount of cash received or disbursed; other columns would be reserved for the accounts that are the most frequent corresponding elements of the journal entry. As with the sales journal, the columns are periodically totalled, and either a single summary entry is made in the general journal or the totals are posted directly to the general ledger accounts affected.

Subsidiary Ledgers

A firm almost always finds it necessary to keep records of each customer for whom it holds a receivable, each capital asset owned, and each supplier to whom it is indebted. But it would obviously necessitate a general ledger of massive proportions if separate accounts were maintained for each customer, supplier, or capital asset. Most firms maintain, in the general ledger, *control accounts* that summarize the numerous individual accounts. Control accounts are typically maintained for accounts receivable, accounts payable, and capital assets. The individual accounts are maintained in *subsidiary ledgers*. The subsidiary ledger may be a book or electronic file, one page or record for each subsidiary account. Obviously, the sum of the balances in a *subsidiary ledger* must equal the balance in the general ledger control account for which the subsidiary ledger provides support. Each time an entry is made to the general ledger control account, one or more entries of equal amount must be made to the subsidiary accounts.

Suppose, for example, that in the course of a month a firm makes sales, all on account, to a number of different customers. In the general ledger the firm would debit accounts receivable for the total amount of the sales. In the accounts receivable subsidiary ledger, the firm would debit the individual accounts of the various customers for the amount of each sale. As the customers pay the balances in their accounts, the firm would credit accounts receivable in the general ledger for the total amount collected within a period and credit the individual accounts for the amount of each remittance.

Summary

This chapter has emphasized that revenues and expenses are the inflows and outflows of resources from the production and delivery of goods and services. Recognition of revenues and expenses may be triggered by a specific transaction, such as the sale of goods, as well as by less specific economic events, such as the passage of time. Modern financial accounting is on an *accrual* rather than a cash basis. Therefore the recognition of revenues and expenses may not coincide with the receipt and disbursement of cash.

The chapter also described the fundamental *accounting cycle,* which consists of nine steps:

1. Transactions and other financial events are recorded in journals.

2. At the end of an accounting period, the accounts are updated to recognize other economic events that have not been recorded in the normal course of operations.

3. The journal entries are posted to ledger accounts and the account balances computed.

4. The balances in the accounts are summarized in a *preclosing* trial balance. The sum of the debits must equal the sum of the credits. Otherwise the accounting equation would be out of balance, a condition indicative of an error.

5. On the basis of the balances in the revenue and expense accounts of the preclosing trial balance, an income statement is prepared.

6. The revenue, expense, and dividend accounts are "closed" by transferring the balances to retained earnings.

7. The balances in the remaining accounts are summarized in the form of a *postclosing* trial balance.

8. From the balances in the postclosing trial balance, a balance sheet is prepared.

9. The statements of changes in financial position and retained earnings are prepared.

In addition, the chapter has provided an overview of the books and records maintained by business enterprises. The two basic books of account are the *general journal* and the *general ledger.* Transactions are recorded in the general journal and are then posted to the affected accounts, which are kept in the general ledger. To make it easier to process a multitude of diverse transactions, most firms also maintain specialized journals and ledgers, which support and supplement the general journals and ledgers.

Exercise for Review and Self-Testing

The balance sheet of a company as at August 1 is as follows:

Assets		
Current assets		
Cash	$150,000	
Accounts receivable	100,000	
Inventory	250,000	500,000
Noncurrent assets		
Buildings and equipment	$800,000	
Less: Accumulated amortization	280,000	520,000
		$1,020,000
Equities		
Liabilities		
Accounts payable		$ 220,000
Shareholders' equity		
Contributed capital	$200,000	
Retained earnings	600,000	800,000
		$1,020,000

1. Prepare journal entries to record the following financial events that took place in August:
   a. The company purchased merchandise inventory for $320,000, on account.
   b. It made sales of $290,000, on account.
   c. The merchandise sold had originally cost $230,000.
   d. It collected $310,000 from customers.
   e. It paid suppliers $300,000.
   f. It recognized amortization of $10,000.
   g. Employees earned wages and salaries of $20,000. They were paid only $15,000.

2. Post the entries to T accounts, each of which represents a ledger account. Determine the month-end balance in each account.

3. Prepare a preclosing trial balance.

4. Prepare an income statement for the month of August.

5. Prepare journal entries to close the revenue and expense accounts. Post them to the appropriate T accounts. Indicate postclosing balances in affected accounts.

6. Prepare a postclosing trial balance.

7. Prepare a balance sheet as at August 31.

8. Prepare a statement of changes in financial position for the month of August.

Questions for Review and Discussion

1. "All accounting transactions can be recorded directly to balance sheet accounts. There is no reason to maintain income statement accounts." Do you agree? Explain.

2. What is the purpose of *closing entries*? Why must revenue and expense accounts have a zero balance at the start of each accounting period? Why aren't balance sheet accounts "closed" at the end of each accounting period?

3. If, prior to the end of an accounting period (before closing entries have been made), one were to take a trial balance of all *balance sheet* accounts (assets, liabilities, owners' equity), the debits would probably not equal the credits. Why not?

4. Virtually all transactions in which a firm engages trigger journal entries. But not all journal entries are triggered by specific transactions. Explain and give examples of journal entries that are not triggered by specific transactions.

5. What is meant by an *accrual*?

6. How does the accrual basis of accounting differ from the cash basis?

7. On January 1, a firm purchases a three-year insurance policy for $54,000. It pays in cash. What would be the impact of this transaction on each of the following December 31 financial statements?
   a. income statement
   b. balance sheet
   c. statement of changes in financial position

8. The retained earnings account is generally one of the least active on the balance sheet. What types of transactions or financial events require an entry directly to the retained earnings account?

9. A company purchases merchandise listed in a catalogue at a price of $50,000. It incurs shipping costs of $2,000, taxes and duties of $500, and insurance of $750. At what value should the goods be recorded on the company books? What general rule governs the values at which assets such as merchandise inventory and plant equipment should be initially recorded?

10. Do you agree with either or both of these statements? Explain.

a. If at the end of an accounting period the trial balance is not in balance (the debits do not equal the credits), then an accounting error has been made.

b. If at the end of an accounting period the trial balance is in balance, then an accounting error has not been made.

11. What accounting recognition would be given to each of the following financial events on the books of International Electric Co.?

a. International Electric Co. owns 3,000 shares of Northern Telecom Ltd. common stock. In the course of a year, the market price of the stock increases from $50 per share to $60.

b. International Electric Co. has outstanding 20,000 shares of its own common stock. In the course of a year, the market price of the stock increases from $45 per share to $50 per share.

c. William Barefield, a shareholder, sells 100 shares of International Electric Co. to Jill Abelson for $45 per share.

12. What are *contra accounts?* Why are they used?

13. What is a *sales journal?* Why is it used?

Problems

1. *Financial accounting requires an understanding of only nine basic types of transactions.*

An accounting transaction, when analyzed in terms of the basic accounting equation, can have only nine possible effects, summarized as follows:

(1) Asset + ; asset −

(2) Asset + ; liability +

(3) Asset + ; owners' equity +

(4) Asset − ; liability −

(5) Asset − ; owners' equity −

(6) Liability + ; liability −

(7) Liability − ; owners' equity +

(8) Liability + ; owners' equity −

(9) Owners' equity + ; owners' equity −

Analyze each of the financial events listed below, and indicate which of the nine effects is best described. Make the assumption that each transaction is being entered directly into balance sheet accounts (i.e., the income statement is bypassed), but indicate which of the transactions would, in fact, ordinarily be reported on the income statement.

a. Collection of an account receivable

b. Purchase of merchandise on account

c. Sale of merchandise on account

d. Recognition of the cost of goods that have been sold

e. Declaration (but not payment) of a dividend

f. Payment of a dividend that had been previously declared

g. Recognition of one year's amortization on a company-owned truck

h. Payment of one month's rent on the company's rental premises.

i. Issuance of 1,000 shares of the company's own common stock in exchange for forgiveness of a $100,000 note payable

j. Exchange of 1,000 shares of the company's own common stock for 2,000 shares of its preferred stock

2. *A familiarity with the "mechanics" of accounting facilitates an understanding of its underlying concepts, principles, and issues.*

Complete the following table by specifying whether each of the accounts would ordinarily be increased or decreased by a debit and a credit. The first one is done for you as an example.

	Would a *debit* increase/decrease the account?	Would a *credit* increase/decrease the account?
1. Cash	Increase	Decrease
2. Interest payable		
3. Interest receivable		
4. Interest revenue		
5. Interest expense		
6. Marketable securities		
7. Common stock		
8. Retained earnings		

3. *A preclosing trial balance summarizes the balances in all ledger accounts; only some of the accounts, however, are affected by year-end closing entries.*

Indicated in the table below is the December 31 *preclosing* trial balance of the Montreal Company (in thousands of dollars).

a. Prepare required year-end closing entries. What was the company's income for the year?

b. What will be the balance in retained earnings after closing entries have been made?

	Debits	Credits
Cash	$20,000	
Accounts receivable	12,000	
Inventory	5,000	
Supplies	1,000	
Prepaid rent	800	
Accounts payable		$ 4,000
Accrued interest payable		200
Notes payable		2,000
Common stock		10,000
Retained earnings		23,600
Sales revenue		48,000
Cost of goods sold	35,000	
Supplies expense	4,000	
Rent expense	9,600	
Interest expense	400	
	$87,800	$87,800

4. *The net income or loss for the period may be determined from the information in the preclosing trial balance.*

Following is the December 31, 1996, preclosing trial balance of the Johnson Company.

a. Prepare an income statement, in good format, for the Johnson Company for the year ended December 31, 1996.

---

b. What will be the December 31, 1996, balance in retained earnings after the closing entries have been made?

	Debits	Credits
Cash	$ 60,000	
Marketable securities	15,000	
Accounts receivable	40,000	
Inventory	60,000	
Supplies	2,000	
Prepaid insurance	4,000	
Equipment	80,000	
Notes receivable, due 2001	60,000	
Accounts payable		$ 62,000
Common stock		40,000
Retained earnings		189,000
Sales revenue		240,000
Interest revenue		6,000
Cost of goods sold	120,000	
Salaries expense	46,000	
Amortization expense	20,000	
Rent expense	18,000	
Insurance expense	12,000	
	$537,000	$537,000

5. *Not all of the economic events described in this problem require accounting recognition, but those that do affect only balance sheet accounts.*

Prepare journal entries (as necessary) to reflect the following economic events pertaining to the Edinburg Corporation in the month of June 1997.
a. The company issues $300,000 in long-term bonds payable. The bonds provide for the payment of interest twice each year at an annual rate of 9 percent. The bonds are payable 10 years from date of issue.
b. The company purchases a new typewriter. Suggested retail price of the typewriter is $400, but because the machine is on sale, the company pays only $350, in cash.
c. The company signs a contract with the Watchdog Security Service to receive guard service for the period July 1, 1997 to June 30, 1998. The contract calls for payment of $4,000 per month, payable 15 days after the close of the month in which the service is provided.
d. The firm receives a cheque for $5,000 from one of its customers for payment on merchandise that was delivered in January. The amount owed is included among the company's accounts receivable.
e. The firm purchases 100 shares of Imperial Oil Ltd. common stock for $54 per share as a short-term investment.
f. *The Globe and Mail* reports that the price of Imperial Oil stock has increased to $58 per share.
g. The company purchases manufacturing equipment for $90,000, pays $20,000 in cash and gives a three-year note payable for the balance. In addition, the company incurs costs (paid in cash) of $2,000 to install the equipment.
h. The company issues 10,000 shares of its no par value common stock for $12 per share.

i. The company pays $600 rent on its office space. The rent is applicable to the month of May and had previously been recorded as a liability, "Accrued rent payable."

j. The company returns to the manufacturer raw materials that it deems defective. The company had been billed $900 for the materials and had recorded the amount as a liability.

6. *Revenues and expenses result in an increase or decrease in net assets (assets minus liabilities) as well as in owners' equity.*

If the basic accounting equation is expressed in the form, Assets – Liabilities = Owners' equity, then which of the following transactions increase or decrease the right side (owners' equity) of the equation? Which transactions would represent revenues or expenses as opposed to only changes in asset and liability accounts?

a. A firm purchases fuel oil for cash.

b. It purchases fuel oil on account.

c. It uses the fuel oil previously purchased.

d. It pays for the fuel oil previously purchased on account.

e. It receives and pays the electric bill; no previous accounting recognition has been given to electric costs.

f. It provides services for a customer and bills him.

g. It collects the amount previously billed.

h. It borrows an amount from a bank.

i. It repays the amount borrowed.

j. It gives accounting recognition to interest on the amount borrowed from the bank and makes the interest payment.

7. *Transactions that affect only asset and liability accounts must be distinguished from those that involve revenue and expense accounts.*

Prepare journal entries to reflect the following transactions. Be certain to indicate the nature (i.e., asset, liability, or retained earnings) of each account affected.

a. A company purchases supplies for $1,000 cash.

b. The company uses $700 of the supplies.

c. The company purchases merchandise for $12,000 on account.

d. The company pays $4,000 of the $12,000 owed to suppliers.

e. The company sells for $16,000, on account, merchandise that had initially cost $12,000. (Two entries are required.)

f. The company collects the $16,000 from its customers.

g. It borrows $10,000 at 8 percent annual interest.

h. The company pays one year's interest.

i. The company purchases for cash a machine for $18,000. The machine has an estimated useful life of three years.

j. The company gives accounting recognition to the use of the machine for one year.

8. *An income statement may be prepared by looking at only those transactions and economic events that affect revenue and expense.*

The following transactions, among others, occurred during a company's *first* year of operation:

(a) The company sells for $140,000, on account, merchandise that had cost it $76,000.

(b) Employees were paid $24,000 in wages and salaries. There were no unpaid salaries or wages at year end.

(c) The company rented office space for 12 months at $1,000 per month. Rent payments of $12,000 were made during the year.

(d) Other expenses of $4,000 were paid during the year.

(e) The company gave accounting recognition to the use of its equipment for one year. The equipment was purchased at the beginning of the year at a cost of $120,000 and has an estimated useful life of 8 years.

a. Prepare journal entries to record the above transactions or economic events.

b. Prepare an income statement for the company's first year of operations.

9. *Balance sheet accounts for the end of one year can be derived from data pertaining to the following year.*

The following data pertain to Fowler, Inc. (in millions):

	1997	1996
Assets, December 31	$2,000	$?
Liabilities, December 31	900	?
Common stock, December 31	500	500
Retained earnings, December 31	600	?
Revenues	1,200	1,000
Expenses	800	700
Dividends	200	200

The expenses for 1997 include $300 million that has not yet been paid as of December 31. Other than this amount, there were no changes in liabilities during 1997.

a. Prepare in summary form the entries to close the revenues and expenses accounts of 1997.

b. Determine the missing amounts for 1996.

10. *From the perspective of banks and trust companies, customer deposits are liabilities and mortgage loans are assets.*

The following balance sheet is from the financial statements of Montreal Trustco, Inc. (in thousands):

Consolidated Balance Sheet as at December 31	
Assets	
Cash and short–term securities	$ 1,134,553
Bonds and debentures	771,459
Stocks	666,659
Real estate	55,571
Corporate and commercial loans	2,525,800
Mortgages	6,915,759
Other assets	313,534
Total assets	$12,383,335

Liabilities and shareholders' equity	
Liabilities	
Demand deposits	$ 1,070,886
Investment certificates and borrowings	10,548,460
Other liabilities	115,376
Debentures due 2084	60,000
Subordinated notes	47,014
Total liabilities	11,841,736
Shareholders' equity	
Preferred shares	100,000
Common shares	206,383
Contributed surplus	6,217
Retained earnings	228,999
Total liabilities and shareholders' equity	$12,383,335

Prepare the journal entries that Montreal Trustco would make to record the following transactions:

a. A depositor adds $1,000 to a chequing account.

b. Montreal Trustco makes a mortgage loan of $242,000 on a residential home.

c. A borrower makes a monthly mortgage payment of $1,620, comprising the following:

Interest	$1,450
Repayment of loan balance	170

d. A depositor buys a $1,000,000 10%, 5-year guaranteed investment certificate.

e. Montreal Trustco purchases $150,000 additional stock in The Bank of Nova Scotia.

11. *When a firm returns merchandise, it receives "credit" on its account.*

Prepare journal entries to reflect the following events on the books of both Wholesale, Inc., and Retail, Inc.

a. Wholesale, Inc., sells for $5,000 on account to Retail, Inc., merchandise that cost Wholesale, Inc., $4,000.

b. Upon discovering that some of the merchandise does not meets its specifications, Retail, Inc., returns it to Wholesale, Inc. The returned merchandise had been sold to Retail for $1,000 and had cost Wholesale $800.

c. Retail, Inc., pays the balance due on its account.

12. *The basic relationship, beginning balance + additions − reductions = ending balance, can be used to derive a considerable amount of information.*

The following data were drawn from a company's general ledger balance sheet accounts.

	Beginning Balance	Additions	Reductions	Ending Balance
Accounts receivable	$200	$1,900	$?	$100
Merchandise inventory	80	?	1,100	100
Wages payable	30	800	?	55
Interest payable	12	11	?	13
Rent receivable	24	?	190	26
Accounts payable				
(for purchases of merchandise)	60	?	?	70

By analyzing the data and giving recognition to the financial events that cause an account to increase and decrease, determine
   a. Purchases of merchandise
   b. Cost of goods sold
   c. Sales revenue (All sales were initially "on account.")
   d. Collections from customers
   e. Rent revenue
   f. Collections of rent
   g. Wage expense
   h. Wages paid
   i. Interest expense
   j. Interest paid
   k. Payments to suppliers of merchandise

13. *The cash basis of accounting must be distinguished from the accrual basis.*
   A firm engages in the following summary transactions in its first year of operations:
   a. It purchases furniture and fixtures at a cost of $80,000 (cash). Estimated useful life of the assets is eight years.
   b. It acquires inventory for $300,000. It pays $280,000 and owes the remaining $20,000.
   c. It sells merchandise for $380,000. Cost of the goods sold is $290,000. It collects $330,000 and is owed the remaining $50,000.
   d. It leases its premises at a rate of $3,000 per month. During the year it makes 13 rent payments, including one payment for the first month of the following year.
   Prepare two income statements for the year, one on a cash basis, the other on an accrual basis. Under the cash basis, revenues and expenses should be recognized only as cash is received or disbursed. Under the accrual basis, they should be recognized as significant economic events, including the passage of time, take place.

14. *A balance sheet prepared from a preclosing trial balance will not balance.*
   The preclosing trial balance of Frost, Inc., as at December 31, 1996, is as follows:

	Debits	Credits
Cash	$ 3,000	
Accounts receivable	5,000	
Other assets	12,000	
Accounts payable		$ 5,000
Other liabilities		2,000
Capital contributed by shareholders		4,000
Retained earnings		6,000
Sales revenue		25,000
Cost of goods sold	18,000	
Other expenses	4,000	
	$42,000	$42,000

   a. If, from the trial balance, you were to prepare an income statement and a balance sheet, which accounts would have to be adjusted? Why?
   b. Prepare an income statement.

c. Make the necessary closing entries.

d. Prepare a balance sheet, taking into account the effect of the closing entries.

15. *In the first year of operations, retained earnings at the end of the year will be equal to net income for the first year, assuming no dividends were declared during the first year.*

    The preclosing trial balance of Pinetop Limited at December 31, 1996, the end of its first year of operations, is as follows:

	Debits	Credits
Cash	$ 57,000	
Accounts receivable	60,000	
Prepaid rent	3,000	
Equipment	152,000	
Accounts payable		$ 24,000
Notes payable, due 2001		100,000
Common stock		100,000
Retained earnings		0
Sales revenue		214,000
Salaries expense	90,000	
Rent expense	36,000	
Other expense	24,000	
Interest expense	8,000	
Amortization expense	8,000	
	$438,000	$438,000

a. Prepare an income statement for Pinetop Limited, in good format, for the year ended December 31, 1996.

b. Prepare the required year-end closing entries.

c. What is the balance in Retained earnings at December 31, 1996, after closing entries have been made?

d. Prepare a balance sheet at December 31, 1996, in good format, for Pinetop Limited.

16. *The basic accounting equation can be expanded so as to highlight the relationship among the various balance sheet accounts and revenues, expenses, and dividends.*

    Arrange a piece of paper in columns with the following headings, each of which corresponds to a term in the accounting equation:

    Assets = Liabilities + Contributed capital + Retained earnings, beginning of period + Revenues − Expenses − Dividends

a. Indicate the effect of each of the following events or other items of information on the accounting equation.

   (1) At the beginning of the accounting period a firm reported assets of $400,000, liabilities of $200,000, contributed capital of $10,000, and retained earnings of $190,000.

   (2) The firm purchased merchandise, on account, for $80,000.

   (3) It issued additional common stock for $40,000 cash.

   (4) It borrowed $10,000.

   (5) It made sales of $98,000, all of which were for cash.

   (6) The cost of merchandise sold was $50,000.

   (7) It incurred interest costs, which were paid in cash, of $7,000.

(8) Taxes assessed for the period, payable the following period, were $11,000.

(9) It declared and paid dividends of $4,000.

b. Determine, by summing the columns, the financial position of the firm at the end of the accounting period as well as the revenues, expenses, and dividends of the period.

c. Compute income for the period.

d. Determine the end-of-period balance in retained earnings after the opening balance is adjusted to reflect the revenues, expenses, and dividends of the period.

17. *Owners' equity increases whenever net assets (assets minus liabilities) increase, and decreases whenever net assets decrease.*

Indicate the effect (if any) that each of the several transactions described would have on owners' equity (after closing entries have been made):

a. The firm sold for $100 merchandise that had cost $80.

b. The firm purchased merchandise for $2,000.

c. The firm purchased a truck for $12,000 cash.

d. The firm purchased and used $300 of supplies.

e. The firm paid its advertising agency $600 for ads that had been run (and had been given accounting recognition) the previous month.

f. The firm received $750 in dividends on 1,000 shares of XYZ Co. stock that it owns.

g. The firm paid $45 interest on $1,000 that it had previously borrowed from a local bank.

18. *Because of the logical relationships inherent in an accounting system, lost data can be reconstructed.*

Given the following data about a company over a period of three years, determine the missing amounts.

	1996	1995	1994
Retained earnings, Jan. 1	$?	$6,000	$2,000
Revenues for the year	?	?	8,000
Expenses for the year	8,000	5,000	?
Income for the year	4,000	?	6,000
Dividends declared during the year	3,000	2,000	?
Retained earnings, Dec. 31	?	8,000	6,000

19. *Entries to revenue and expense accounts can be viewed as entries to retained earnings.*

Assume that a company maintains only four accounts: assets, liabilities, contributed capital, and retained earnings. The following transactions occurred during its first month of operations:

(1) The owners of the company contributed a total of $100,000 to establish the business.

(2) The company issued bonds payable for $50,000; that is, it borrowed $50,000.

(3) The company purchased equipment for $60,000, giving the seller a note payable for the full amount.

(4) The company purchased merchandise for cash, $40,000.

(5) The company had sales of $30,000. Cash sales were $25,000, and those on account, $5,000.

(6) The company paid $2,000 rent for the current month.

(7) The company paid one month's interest on the bonds, $250.

(8) The company recognized one month's amortization on the equipment purchased. The estimated useful life of the equipment is 60 months.

(9) The company paid insurance premiums for two months—the current month and the following month—$300 per month.

(10) The company collected $2,000 of the accounts receivable from customers.

(11) The company learned that $500 of the amount owed by customers would not be collectable owing to the bankruptcy of one customer.

(12) The company determined that of the merchandise purchased $22,000 remained on hand, unsold, at the end of the month.

a. Establish T accounts for each of the four accounts. Prepare a journal entry to record each of the transactions, and post the entries to the appropriate T accounts. Compute end-of-month balances in each account.

b. Determine net income for the month.

c. Suppose that the company had paid a dividend of $2,000 to its owners. How would that affect the balance in the retained earnings account? How would it affect income for the month?

20. *Some errors affect only the income statement or the balance sheet; those that affect both are generally more serious.*

A bookkeeper made several errors as described below. For each, indicate whether, for the period in which they were made, they would cause a misstatement on the balance sheet only, on the income statement only, or on both the balance sheet and the income statement.

a. Failed to record a sale of $3,000, on account, to a customer.

b. Failed to record the collection of $200 owed by a customer for a purchase he had made several weeks earlier.

c. Incorrectly recorded the issuance of 1,000 shares of common stock at $2 per share; made the following journal entry:

Cash $2,000
    Marketable securities $2,000

d. Recorded the purchase of a new carburetor for a company-owned vehicle as an addition to capital assets rather than as a repair expense.

e. Recorded funds given to a salesperson to entertain customers as a miscellaneous expense rather than a sales expense.

f. Failed to record the purchase of a new truck.

g. Failed to record amortization on a company-owned car.

h. Incorrectly counted merchandise inventory on hand at year end.

i. Failed to record repayment of the company's loan from a bank.

j. Failed to record payment of interest on the same loan.

21. *At the conclusion of an accounting period, a firm must record economic events that did not automatically trigger journal entries during the period.*

The following events may not always be recognized during the accounting period. Hence they would be recorded at the end of the period.

Prepare the necessary journal entries implied by the facts that follow. The firm's fiscal year ends December 31.

a. On August 1 a company purchased as an investment $1 million in bonds that pay interest on January 31 and July 31. The annual rate of interest is 10 percent (5 percent per semiannual period). The purchase of the bonds was properly recorded, but no interest was recognized during the year.

b. The company owns equipment that has an estimated useful life of five years. The equipment was purchased three years earlier at a cost of $600,000. No amortization has been recognized for the current year.

c. The company paid both its December and January rent of $4,500 per month on December 1. The entire $9,000 payment was added (debited) to rent expense.

d. The company has not yet recorded as an expense the cost of the goods that were sold during the year. At year end, a physical count indicates goods on hand that cost $8 million. Financial statements of the previous year indicated goods on hand at the end of that year of $6.4 million. During the current year the company purchased goods for $25 million. The purchases were added (debited) to inventory. (Thus the December 31 balance in the inventory account was $31.4 million.)

e. The company pays its employees once a month on the fifth day of the month following that in which the wages and salaries were earned. Wages and salaries earned during December totalled $38,000.

f. On January 15 of the new year, the company receives a phone bill of $545 for December service. The company does not close its books until mid-February to avoid having to estimate December charges prior to receipt of phone, utility, and similar bills.

g. During the year the company purchased office supplies for $3,000 cash. The purchase was added (debited) to office supplies inventory (an asset account). At year end a physical count indicated office supplies on hand of $400. No entries were made during the year as office supplies were used up.

22. *A balance sheet may not balance until a certain key account has been updated.*

Arrange a sheet of paper as indicated in the table below. Leave room for additional accounts that might be required. The first column indicates balances as of January 1. All accounts have the "normal" debit or credit balance.

Account	(1) Balance Jan. 1	(2) Transactions in January Dr.	(3) Cr.	(4) Income Statement for January Dr.	(5) Cr.	(6) Balance Sheet, Jan. 31 Dr.	(7) Cr.
Cash	$40,000						
Accounts receivable	50,000						
Merchandise inventory	15,000						
Capital assets	60,000						
Accounts payable	30,000						
Notes payable	25,000						
Common stock	2,000						
Retained earnings	108,000						

a. Record the effect of the transactions described, all of which occurred in the month of January, in columns 2 and 3. Indicate the month-end balances in the accounts in columns 4 through 7 as appropriate. Record the total of each column.

(1) Sales for the month, all on credit, were $70,000.

(2) Collections from customers totalled $80,000.

(3) Purchases of merchandise intended for sale were $45,000. All purchases were "on account."

(4) Goods on hand at the month's end totalled $5,000.

(5) Other operating expenses were $15,000. They were paid in cash.

(6) Amortization expense, in addition to other operating expenses, was based on an estimated useful life of five years (60 months) for all capital assets. (Assume capital assets were all purchased on January 1.)

b. Why doesn't the balance sheet balance after all transactions have been posted?

c. Prepare a journal entry to close accounts as necessary.

23. *Most firms close their books once a year. Financial statements, however, can be prepared at any time and for any time period. The balance sheet and the income statement may be derived from a preclosing rather than a postclosing trial balance. Retained earnings, however, must be adjusted for the income or loss of the period.*

Computer Rental Service, Inc., began operations on January 1, 1996. During its first month of operations, the following events took place:

(1) The company issued 2,000 shares of common stock at $100 per share.

(2) The company rented a store for $2,000 per month. It paid the first month's rent.

(3) The company purchased 20 computers at a price of $5,000 each. The company paid cash of $40,000 and promised to pay the balance within 60 days.

(4) The company purchased, on account, supplies for $5,000.

(5) The company rented out the computers. Total revenues for the month were $12,000. Of this amount $2,000 was collected in cash.

(6) The company paid $1,500 cash to cover other operating expenses.

(7) A count at month end indicated that $2,500 in supplies remained on hand.

(8) At month end the company gave accounting recognition to the amortization of one month on its computers. The useful life of the computers is estimated at 36 months.

a. Prepare journal entries to recognize these transactions.

b. Post the journal entries to T accounts.

c. Prepare a preclosing trial balance.

d. Prepare an income statement and a statement of position (balance sheet).

24. *This example, based on an actual incident, stresses the need to distinguish between sales revenues and cash collections.*

Boscoble Auto Parts began operations in December 1995. According to records maintained by the proprietor, sales for January 1996, the first full month of operation, were $98,000. The company made sales both for cash and credit. At the end of each day, the proprietor recorded the day's "sales" in a book he called the "sales journal." The single figure recorded each day was the sum of the sales for cash, the sales for credit, and the subsequent cash collections on previous sales for credit.

Per supplementary records, which may be assumed to be correct, at the beginning of January the company had accounts receivable from customers of $8,000; at the end of January, accounts receivable had increased to $10,000. During the month, $22,000 had been collected from customers who had made purchases on credit.

On January 31, a count of the parts on hand revealed that the company had an inventory of parts that cost $25,000. A count on January 1 had revealed an inventory of $15,000. During the month, the company had purchased from suppliers parts that cost a total of $65,000. Other cash operating expenses for January were $23,000.

In an effort to assist the proprietor, you have been engaged as a consultant to evaluate the firm's record-keeping system.

a. What is the primary deficiency in the firm's accounting system? How can it be eliminated? What entry in a journal should the proprietor make each time (1) a cash sale is made, (2) a credit sale is made, (3) cash is collected on a previously recorded credit sale?

b. Determine first total cash sales and then total credit sales for January. By how much were January sales overstated? The firm paid sales taxes to the province based on the amount recorded in the sales journal. The sales tax rate was 10 percent. How much of a refund from the province should the proprietor request?

c. What was the cost of goods actually sold in January?

d. What was the correct income (loss) for the month?

25. *This problem reviews the accounting cycle.*

Upon receiving a gift of $8,000, J. Keats decides to enter the copy business. During the first month of operations, the following events take place:

(1) Keats places the entire $8,000 in a bank account in the name of "Fast-Copy Co."

(2) She signs a three-year lease on a store. Rent is to be at the rate of $400 per month. Keats pays four months' rent at the time she signs the lease, $400 for the current month, and $1,200 in advance.

(3) She purchases furniture and fixtures for $1,500, paying $500 at the time of purchase and promising to pay the balance within 60 days.

(4) She signs a rental agreement with a manufacturer of copy equipment. The agreement stipulates that Keats will pay $200 per month plus 2 cents for each copy made.

(5) She places advertisements in the local newspapers. The cost of the ads is $600, paid in cash.

(6) She purchases paper and other supplies for $800 on account.

(7) She makes her first copies for customers. She sells 30,000 copies at 5 cents each. Customers pay cash for all copies.

(8) She takes an end-of-month inventory and finds $200 of supplies on hand.

(9) She withdraws $200 from the business to meet personal expenses.

(10) She pays the amount due the manufacturer of the copy equipment for the first month's operations.

(11) She gives accounting recognition to the use of the furniture and fixtures for one month. The furniture and fixtures have an estimated useful life of five years.

a. Prepare journal entries to record the transactions of the first month of operations.
b. Post the journal entries to T accounts.
c. Prepare an income statement for the month.
d. Prepare any closing entries that would be necessary if the books were to be closed at the end of the month. (Ordinarily books would be closed only at the end of a full accounting period, usually one year.)
e. Prepare a statement of position (a balance sheet).

26. *This problem not only reviews the accounting cycle but also highlights a key deficiency of income as a measure of financial strength.*

The shareholders of Regal Gifts, Inc., were extremely gratified to receive an income statement from management. It revealed that in its first year of operations, the company, which operates a gift shop, had earnings that far exceeded original expectations. Two months after receipt of the income statement, the company was forced to declare bankruptcy. The following information summarizes the major financial events of the company's first year of operations:

(1) The company issued 1,000 shares of common stock at a price of $100 per share.
(2) The company leased a store in a shopping centre. Monthly rent was $1,000. During the year rent payments of $12,000 were made.
(3) The company purchased furniture and fixtures for the store at a cost of $60,000. The company paid cash of $20,000 and gave a one-year note payable for the balance. The estimated useful life of the furniture and fixtures is 10 years.
(4) In the course of the year the company purchased, at a cost of $260,000, merchandise intended for sale. The company paid $210,000 cash for the merchandise; at year end, the balance was owed.
(5) The company had sales of $290,000. Sales were made for both cash and credit. At year end, the company had outstanding receivables from customers of $50,000.
(6) The company paid salaries of $40,000.
(7) The company incurred and paid other operating costs of $15,000.
(8) At year end, the company had $80,000 of merchandise still on hand.

a. Prepare journal entries to reflect the financial events of the company's first year of operations.
b. Prepare an income statement and a balance sheet.
c. Prepare a statement of changes in financial position.
d. Explain why the company may have been forced to declare bankruptcy.

27. *Transactions, in summary form, may be derived from the financial statements.*

Robertson, Inc., was organized on January 1, 1996. After one year of operations, the following balance sheet and income statement were prepared.

Robertson, Inc.
Balance Sheet as at December 31, 1996

Assets		
Current assets		
Cash	$ 199,000	
Accounts receivable (from customers)	150,000	
Inventory	180,000	529,000
Noncurrent assets		
Plant and equipment	$2,000,000	
Less: Accumulated amortization	200,000	1,800,000
Total assets		$2,329,000
Liabilities and shareholders' equity		
Current liabilities		
Rent payable		$ 1,000
Noncurrent liabilities		
Notes payable (to bank)		900,000
Shareholders' equity		
Common stock		1,200,000
Retained earnings		228,000
Total liabilities and shareholders' equity		$2,329,000

Income Statement
Year Ended December 31, 1996

Sales revenue		$1,500,000
Expenses		
Cost of goods sold	$1,000,000	
Amortization expense	200,000	
Interest expense	60,000	
Rent expense	12,000	1,272,000
Net income		$ 228,000

a. Prepare journal entries to reflect the financial transactions and economic events that occurred during the first year of operations. The entries may summarize a series of transactions or events. For example, in a single entry, you may record all sales for the year, including those for which cash has already been received as well as those for which the company still has a receivable.

b. Prepare a statement of changes in financial position.

28. *This problem, based on data from an annual report of Sun Ice Limited, is intended to demonstrate the relationship between the balance sheet and the statement of changes in financial position.*

The following are Sun Ice Limited's balance sheet as at January 31, 1990, and its statement of changes in financial position for the year ended January 31, 1991. The statement of changes in financial position is presented in *indirect form,* which has not yet been discussed. In contrast to the *direct form,* it shows net income as a source of cash from operating activities. Net income is then adjusted to take into account revenues and expenses that were greater or less than the related cash flows. Based on the data in the two statements, prepare a balance sheet of Sun Ice Limited as at January 31, 1991.

Balance Sheet
As at January 31, 1990
(in thousands of dollars)

Assets

Current assets	
Cash and term deposits	$ 1,288
Accounts receivable	8,941
Income taxes refundable	311
Inventory	6,021
Prepaid expenses and deposits	480
Total current assets	$17,041
Fixed assets at cost less accumulated amortization	5,368
Other assets	227
Total assets	$22,636

Liabilities and Shareholders' Equity

Current liabilities	
Accounts payable	$ 1,678
Total current liabilities	$ 1,678
Long-term debt	315
Deferred tax	283
Common stock	11,356
Retained earnings	9,004
Total liabilities and shareholders' equity	$22,636

Statement of Changes in Financial Position
Year Ended January 31, 1991
(in thousands of dollars)

Operating Activities	
Net income (loss)	$(1,795)
Adjustments to net income for revenues and expenses not involving cash	
Amount by which customer collections exceed sales (decrease in accounts receivable)	1,981
Inventory and miscellaneous purchases not yet paid for (increase in accounts payable)	127
Inventory purchased in a prior period charged to cost of goods sold in 1991 (decrease in inventory)	126
Income tax refunds promised but not yet received (increase in income taxes refundable)	(1,186)
Income taxes payable in excess of income tax expense (decrease in deferred income taxes)	(33)
Expiration of prepaid expenses (decrease in prepaid expenses)	235
Amortization of fixed assets (decrease in fixed assets)	506
Amortization of other assets (decrease in other assets)	139
Cash provided by operating activities	$ 100
Investing Activities	
Purchases of fixed assets, net of government grants and investment tax credits	$ (1,891)
Purchases of other assets	(53)
Cash used for investing activities	$ (1,944)

Financing Activities	
Issue of long-term debt	827
Repurchase of shares	(21)
Cash provided by financing activities	$ 806
Decrease in cash	$ (1,038)

1.

(a)

Inventory	$320,000	
Accounts payable		$320,000

To record purchase of merchandise inventory

(b)

Accounts receivable	$290,000	
Sales revenue		$290,000

To record sales

(c)

Cost of goods sold	$230,000	
Inventory		$230,000

To record cost of sales

(d)

Cash	$310,000	
Accounts receivable		$310,000

To record collections

(e)

Accounts payable	$300,000	
Cash		$300,000

To record payments to suppliers

(f)

Amortization expense	$10,000	
Accumulated amortization		$10,000

To recognize amortization for one month

(g)

Wage and salary expense	$20,000	
Wages and salaries payable		$ 5,000
Cash		15,000

To record wages and salaries

2. See Exhibit 3-11.

EXHIBIT 3-11

Cash			
Bal. Aug. 1	150,000	(e)	300,000
(d)	310,000	(g)	15,000
Bal Aug. 31	145,000		

Accounts payable			
(e)	300,000	Bal. Aug. 1	220,000
		(a)	320,000
		Bal. Aug. 31	240,000

Accounts receivable			
Bal. Aug. 1	100,000	(d)	310,000
(b)	290,000		
Bal. Aug. 31	80,000		

Wages and salaries payable			
		(g)	5,000
		Bal. Aug. 31	5,000

Contributed capital			
		Bal. Aug. 1	200,000
		Bal. Aug. 31	200,000

Inventory			
Bal. Aug. 1	250,000	(c)	230,000
(a)	320,000		
Bal. Aug. 31	340,000		

Retained earnings			
		Bal. Aug. 1	600,000

Buildings and equipment			
Bal. Aug. 1	800,000		
Bal. Aug. 31	800,000		

Sales revenue			
		(b)	290,000

Accumulated amortization			
		Bal. Aug. 1	280,000
		(f)	10,000
		Bal. Aug. 31	290,000

Cost of goods sold			
(c)	230,000		

Wages and salary expense			
(g)	20,000		

Amortization expense			
(f)	10,000		

3.

Preclosing Trial Balance		
Cash	$ 145,000	
Accounts receivable	80,000	
Inventory	340,000	
Buildings and equipment	800,000	
Accumulated amortization		$ 290,000
Accounts payable		240,000
Wages and salaries payable		5,000
Contributed capital		200,000
Retained earnings		600,000
Sales revenue		290,000
Cost of goods sold	230,000	
Wage and salary expense	20,000	
Amortization expense	10,000	
	$1,625,000	$1,625,000

4.

Income Statement for August		
Sales revenue		$290,000
Expenses		
Cost of goods sold	$230,000	
Wage and salary expense	20,000	
Amortization expense	10,000	260,000
Net Income		$ 30,000

5.

(cl 1)

Sales revenue	$290,000	
Income summary		$290,000

To close revenue account

(cl 2)

Income summary	$260,000	
Cost of goods sold		$230,000
Wage and salary expense		20,000
Amortization expense		10,000

To close expense accounts

(cl 3)

Income summary	$30,000	
Retained earnings		$30,000

To close income summary account and transfer balance to retained earnings

	Sales revenue					Cost of goods sold		
(cl 1)	290,000	**(b)**	290,000		**(c)**	230,000	**(cl 2)**	230,000

	Wage and salary expense					Amortization expense		
(g)	20,000	**(cl 2)**	20,000		**(f)**	10,000	**(cl 2)**	10,000

	Income summary					Retained earnings		
(cl 2)	260,000	**(cl 1)**	290,000				Bal. Aug. 1	600,000
(cl 3)	30,000						**(cl 3)**	30,000
							Bal. Aug. 31	630,000

6.

Postclosing Trial Balance		
Cash	$ 145,000	
Accounts receivable	80,000	
Inventory	340,000	
Buildings and equipment	800,000	
Accumulated amortization		$ 290,000
Accounts payable		240,000
Wages and salaries payable		5,000
Contributed capital		200,000
Retained earnings		630,000
	$1,365,000	$1,365,000

7.

Balance Sheet as at August 31		
Assets		
Current assets		
Cash	$145,000	
Accounts receivable	80,000	
Inventory	340,000	565,000
Noncurrent assets		
Buildings and equipment	$800,000	
Less: Accumulated amortization	290,000	510,000
		$1,075,000
Liabilities and shareholders' equity		
Current liabilities		
Accounts payable		$240,000
Wages and salaries payable		5,000
		245,000
Shareholders' equity		
Contributed capital		200,000
Retained earnings		630,000
		$1,075,000

8.

Statement of Changes in Financial Position for August	
Cash Flow from Operating Activities	
Collections from customers	$ 310,000
Payments to suppliers	(300,000)
Payments to employees	(15,000)
Decrease in cash	$ 5,000

4

Accruing Revenues and Expenses

In Chapter 3, we introduced the steps of the accounting cycle and went through some of the bookkeeping devices used to capture the results of transactions and economic events and assist in the preparation of financial statements. The primary purpose of this chapter is to examine in detail the accrual method of accounting and its implications for financial reporting.

After studying this chapter, you will be able to

- Explain the difference between the cash basis and the accrual basis of accounting
- Understand the link between the income statement and the balance sheet
- Prepare appropriate period-end adjusting entries
- Understand the nature of the cost of goods sold account
- Distinguish between period costs and product costs
- Calculate and interpret certain measures of an entity's financial performance and health

The *accrual basis* of accounting is the method whereby revenues and expenses are recognized at the time that they have their primary economic impact, *not necessarily when cash is received or disbursed*. Revenues are assigned to the accounting period in which a critical event, such as the rendering of services or the sale of goods, takes place. Costs are charged as expenses in the period in which the organization benefits from them. In commercial organizations, costs are incurred to generate revenues. Thus, to the extent practical, costs are matched to the revenues to which they are related.

The chapter first contrasts the accrual and cash bases of accounting. It then shows how all revenue and expenses are closely tied to assets and liabilities. These relationships between income statement and balance sheet accounts provide firms with considerable flexibility in how and when they record financial events. The chapter illustrates how a firm can employ any of several competing bookkeeping procedures at the date of the transaction as long as it updates and corrects its accounts at year end.

The chapter directs particular attention to cost of goods sold. Cost of goods sold is of special interest because it encompasses several subcategories of costs, all of which must be matched to revenues.

The chapter also introduces the general topic of financial statement analysis. It describes how the accounting structure allows an analyst to derive considerably more information about a company's performance than it may explicitly report. In addition, the chapter highlights several key ratios that are used by financial analysts.

DEFICIENCIES OF THE CASH BASIS

The superiority of the accrual method can be appreciated by comparing it with the cash method. With cash basis accounting, the critical economic event is the collection or disbursement of cash. Revenues attributable to the sale of goods or the provision of services are considered to be *realized* (and given accounting recognition) at the time that cash is collected from customers. Costs are charged as expenses only as actual payment is made for goods or services acquired.

The cash basis of accounting is deficient because it focuses on activities—the receipt or disbursement of cash—that by themselves have relatively little economic significance and that can be easily manipulated by management. When a firm acquires goods or services, the timing of payments is often discretionary. If a firm acquires goods near the end of one period, it can delay recording an expense simply by waiting until the start of the next period to write a cheque. The Province of Ontario, for example, delayed a $584 million pension payment from March 1993 to April 1993 in an attempt to keep the deficit under $10 billion for the fiscal year ending March 31, 1993. By postponing the payment of the $584 million to the next fiscal year, it was trying to give a better picture of its deficit position (i.e., the $584 million was not recorded as an expense until the next fiscal year when it was paid). However, the Auditor General of Ontario recognized that this use of the cash basis of accounting was unacceptable. The government was reprimanded for "the use of permissive accounting rules."[1]

The distorting effects of the cash basis are most pronounced when a cash disbursement is intended to benefit a large number of accounting periods. If a firm were to acquire equipment that was expected to be used for several years, then the entire expenditure would be reported as expense in the year

[1] *The Toronto Sun*, December 8, 1993.

of payment. The revenues generated by the goods produced by the machine would be recognized, however, over the life of the machine.

ADVANTAGES OF THE ACCRUAL BASIS

Under the accrual concept, revenues are *recognized* when there is evidence that the firm is economically better off due to its production and sales activities. The criteria for recognizing revenues will be discussed in the next chapter.

Costs are charged as expenses in the same period as the revenues to which they relate are recognized. If it is impractical to relate specific costs to specific revenues, then the costs are charged as expenses in the period in which the goods are consumed or the services provided. Costs which are intended to provide future benefits are *capitalized*—that is, recorded as assets (bundles of "prepaid" expenses)—until the benefits are actually realized. At the time office supplies are purchased, their cost is stored in an asset account, "supplies inventory." It is recorded as an expense only as the supplies are consumed. The supplies could be consumed either before or after they are actually paid for.

Similarly, the cost of services provided by an office staff is generally recorded as an expense during the period in which the firm benefits from their services even though their paycheques may be drawn in a subsequent (or for that matter a previous) accounting period.

Accrual accounting is as advantageous to managers as it is to investors. Both groups use financial reports to assess organizational performance of the past in order to predict and make plans for the future. Accrual accounting, inasmuch as it reports on inflows and outflows of all types of resources, not exclusively cash, generally provides a superior match of efforts to accomplishments. As noted in Chapter 2, cash flow prediction is also a primary purpose of financial accounting. Prediction of cash flow is necessary since cash is the asset required to pay obligations as they come due. We will see in Chapter 14 that the cash basis statement of changes in financial position can be prepared from the accrual-based accounting records.

THE RECORDING PROCESS IN PERSPECTIVE

In the previous chapter it was pointed out that routine journal entries are triggered by transactions, which often involve receipts and disbursements of cash. But revenues and expenses may be generated by economic events other than transactions. Indeed, accountants must identify the *critical event*—that which is central to the activity involved—in order to determine when to recognize a revenue or expense. For example, cash for rent may be received before, during, or after the period for which it is applicable. Rent revenue, however, must be recognized in the period earned regardless of when the cash is received. Similarly, equipment may be purchased in one period but used over several. The use of the equipment, not the purchase, produces the expense.

Virtually all revenues and expenses are linked to specific assets and liabilities. Whenever a firm receives or dispenses resources but does not recognize a corresponding revenue or expense, it must add to, or subtract from, the related asset or liability.

Asset and liability accounts accommodate *timing* differences between cash flows and recognition of revenues and expenses. Under the cash basis of accounting, there is no need for assets and liabilities other than cash. Revenues coincide with cash receipts, expenses with cash disbursements. Neither resources other than cash nor obligations to provide goods or service are recognized as having value.

Four brief examples will illustrate the relationship, under accrual accounting, between income statement and balance sheet accounts.

Example 1: Resources Are Acquired before They Are Expensed

A company purchases a three-year insurance policy for $9,000, a transaction which, by itself, does not produce an expense. The cost must therefore be "stored" in an *asset account,* "prepaid insurance":

(a)

Prepaid insurance $9,000
    Accounts payable $9,000
To record the purchase of a three-year insurance policy

Over the course of the policy period an expense must be recognized and the prepaid insurance reduced:

(b)

Insurance expense $3,000
    Prepaid insurance $3,000
To record the expiration of one year of the insurance policy

When the policy is paid for (another transaction that does not result in an expense), an asset (cash) and a liability (accounts payable) will be reduced.

Example 2: Resources Are Disbursed after They Are Expensed

A firm maintains a loan balance of $100,000 for a year but pays the required interest of $12,000 in the following year. The use of the funds, not the payment of the interest, generates the interest expense. Therefore an expense of $12,000 must be charged in the current year and a corresponding amount reported in a *liability account,* "accrued interest payable":

(a)

Interest expense $12,000
    Accrued interest payable $12,000
To record the interest expense for one year

When the interest is paid the following year, the liability is eliminated:

(b)

Accrued interest payable $12,000
    Cash $12,000
To record the payment of interest

Example 3: Resources Are Received before Revenue Is Recognized

A firm receives an advance of $25,000 for merchandise that it will sell (deliver) to a customer in a subsequent accounting period.

Revenue from sales is commonly recognized upon delivery of goods to the customer. Since the goods have not yet been delivered to the customer, the cash received must be offset by a *liability,* "advances from customers":

(a)

Cash	$25,000	
Advances from customers		$25,000

To record an advance payment from a customer for merchandise to be delivered in a subsequent period

When the merchandise is delivered, revenue must be recognized and the liability eliminated:

(b)

Advances from customers	$25,000	
Sales revenues		$25,000

To record a sale upon delivery of merchandise to the customer

Example 4: Resources Are Received after Revenue Is Recognized

A consulting firm performs services for which it expects to bill a client $100,000 upon completion of the engagement. The critical economic event, that which generates the revenue, is the performance of the services. The revenue must be offset by an *asset,* "accrued consulting revenues":

(a)

Accrued consulting revenues	$100,000	
Consulting revenues		$100,000

To record revenue from consulting

When the firm bills the client, it will convert the accrued consulting revenues to an account receivable:

(b)

Accounts receivable	$100,000	
Accrued consulting revenues		$100,000

To record the customer billing

When it collects its cash, the firm will eliminate the receivable:

(c)

Cash	$100,000	
Accounts receivable		$100,000

To record collection of cash

To expand upon the relationship between income statement and balance sheet accounts under accrual accounting, we note that when a firm acquires more supplies than it uses, the cost of supplies *used* will be charged as an expense; the cost of the remaining supplies must be added to supplies inventory. Conversely, if the firm uses more supplies than it acquires, the difference will be deducted from supplies inventory. Thus

$$\text{Supplies acquired} = \text{Supplies expense} +(-) \Delta\text{Supplies inventory}$$

In slightly modified form,

$$\begin{aligned}\text{Supplies expense} = &\ \text{Supplies acquired} + \text{Supplies on hand,}\\ &\ \text{beginning of period} - \text{Supplies on hand, end of period}\end{aligned}$$

Assume that a firm begins a period with a supplies inventory of $100. During the year it acquires supplies of $3,000. At end of year it has supplies on hand of $500. Therefore supplies expense (the amount consumed) must be $2,600:

Supplies acquired	$3,000	
+ Supplies on hand, beginning of period	100	$3,100
− Supplies on hand, end of period		500
= Supplies expense		$2,600

This basic relationship is equally applicable to all other accounts. Sales revenue, for example, would be the difference between cash collected from customers and the increase or decrease in accounts receivable or advances from customers:

$$\begin{aligned}\text{Sales revenue} = &\ \text{Cash collections} +(-) \Delta\text{Accounts receivable}\\ &\ (\textit{less} +(-) \Delta\text{Advances from customers})\end{aligned}$$

Suppose, for example, that a firm begins a year with accounts receivable of $3 million. During the year it collects $40 million from customers. At year end it has no outstanding accounts receivable but $6 million in new advances from customers. Sales revenue would therefore be $31 million:

Cash collections	$ 40	
+ Accounts receivable, end of period	0	
− Advances from customer, end of period	(6)	$34
− Accounts receivable, beginning of period		3
= Sales revenue		$31

As will be demonstrated later in the chapter, this association between balance sheet and income statement accounts is especially useful in deriving "missing" information. As long as three of the four elements of the equation are known, the fourth can easily be calculated.

Because each revenue and expense can be linked to an asset and liability, firms have considerable flexibility in maintaining their accounts. First, as illustrated in Chapter 3, firms can postpone recording economic events such as the passage of time until the end of a fiscal period. Then, when financial statements must be prepared, they can bring the accounts up to date with simple end-of-period adjustments.

Second, throughout the year firms can record transactions in ways that may be convenient but are conceptually in error. At year end, they can rectify their "mistakes" with correcting entries that are similar to the updating entries.

This section illustrates three methods of accounting for supplies. Only the first leads to balances in supplies expense and the related supplies inventory that are perpetually current. The other two permit the firm to make fewer journal entries during the year, but they result in accounts that are always out of date and need to be adjusted before financial statements can be prepared.

Suppose that at the beginning of an accounting period a company has on hand $1,000 in supplies. During the accounting period it purchases, for cash, $4,000 of supplies and consumes $2,000. The correct ending balance in the supplies account would be $3,000; supplies expense for the period would be $2,000 (the amount consumed):

Balance, supplies inventory, 1/1	$1,000	
Purchases 1/1–31/12	4,000	$5,000
Supplies used (expense), 1/1–31/12		2,000
Balance, supplies inventory, 31/12		$3,000

Perpetual Method: No Year-End Adjustment Required

The most direct and conceptually correct means of accounting for supplies would be to increase the supplies inventory account each time supplies were purchased and to decrease the account each time supplies were withdrawn and presumably used. Thus

(a) Various Dates

Supplies inventory $4,000
    Cash $4,000
To record the purchase of supplies throughout the year

(If the $4,000 of supplies represents the sum of several purchases, then similar journal entries would be made for each purchase.)

(b) Various Dates

Supplies expense $2,000
    Supplies inventory $2,000
To record the use of $2,000 of supplies

At the end of the year, the accounts would appear as follows:

Supplies inventory				Supplies expense	
Bal. 1/1	1,000	(b) Var. dates	2,000	(b) Var. dates	2,000
(a) Var. dates	4,000				
	3,000				

		Cash		
Bal. 1/1	xxx	(a) Var. dates	4,000	

The accounts correctly reflect the ending inventory of $3,000 and supplies expense of $2,000. No adjusting entries are required at the end of the year. It is necessary only to "close" the supplies expense account. The problem with this method is that if supplies are withdrawn in small amounts at frequent intervals, record keeping in the course of the year becomes burdensome since a separate entry must be made for both each purchase and each withdrawal.

Periodic Method: Asset Account Overstated

As an alternative, a company can avoid making an accounting entry each time supplies are *withdrawn* from the storeroom. Instead of recording both the purchase and the use of supplies, it would record only the purchase. In the course of the year, the supplies inventory account would only be debited— never credited. At the end of the year, however, the firm would take a *physical inventory* (count) to determine the actual amount of supplies on hand. The company would assume that all supplies purchased plus those on hand at the beginning of the year must have been used during the year if they are not physically present at the conclusion of the year. It would adjust the accounts by crediting supplies inventory to reflect the inventory actually on hand and by debiting supplies expense with the same amount—the amount presumably used during the year. Thus

(a) Various Dates

Supplies inventory $4,000
    Cash $4,000
To record the purchase of supplies throughout the year

At the end of the year, prior to the physical inventory count, the accounts would show the following:

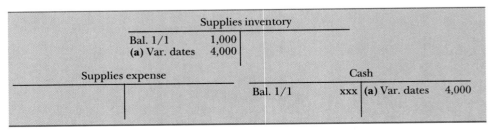

Supplies inventory			
Bal. 1/1	1,000		
(a) Var. dates	4,000		

Supplies expense				Cash		
				Bal. 1/1	xxx	(a) Var. dates 4,000

Assume that a physical count at year end reveals supplies on hand of $3,000. Therefore $2,000 of supplies ($5,000 per the accounts less $3,000 on hand) must have been consumed. The appropriate adjusting journal entry would be

(b) 31/12

Supplies expense	$2,000	
Supplies inventory		$2,000

To adjust the accounts at year end to reflect the physical count of supplies

Supplies inventory				Supplies expense		
Bal. 1/1	1,000	**(b)** 31/12	2,000	**(b)** 31/12	2,000	
(a) Var. dates	4,000					
	3,000					

Once the adjusting entries have been posted, the account balances would be identical to those derived from the procedure illustrated previously.[2] The former approach is often referred to as a *perpetual* method, since the inventory account is always reflective of the actual quantity on hand, and the latter approach as a *periodic* method, since periodic counts are necessary to bring the inventory account up to date.

Periodic Method: Expense Account Overstated

The same results could be obtained by a third procedure, which is also widely used. Instead of charging (debiting) all purchases of supplies to supplies inventory, a company could charge them to *supplies expense.*

At year end, the balance in the supplies inventory account would still equal the beginning balance; no entries to the account would have been made during the year. The firm would then take a year-end count of supplies on hand. To adjust the supplies inventory account to reflect the actual inventory on hand,

[2] Many firms use a modified version of this approach. Instead of initially debiting supplies inventory for purchases, they first debit an account called "purchases." At year end, they close the purchases account to supplies inventory. Then they adjust the new balance in the supplies inventory account to reflect the actual amount of goods on hand. Thus

(a) Various Dates

Purchases	$4,000	
Cash		$4,000

To record the purchase of supplies throughout the year

(b) 31/12

Supplies inventory	$4,000	
Purchases		$4,000

To transfer the balance in the purchases account to supplies inventory

(c) 31/12

Supplies expense	$2,000	
Supplies inventory		$2,000

To adjust the accounts at year end to reflect the physical count of supplies

The advantage of this modification is that it provides, in the purchases account, direct information on total purchases during the year.

it would debit (increase) or credit (decrease) the account to bring it up or down to the quantity indicated by the physical count. It would make the corresponding credit (or debit) to supplies expense. If more supplies were purchased than were actually used, then the firm would have to increase (debit) the supplies inventory account and decrease (credit) the supplies expense account. If more were used than purchased, then it would have to decrease (credit) the supplies inventory account and increase (debit) the supplies expense account.

(a) Various Dates

Supplies expense $4,000
    Cash $4,000
To record the purchase of supplies throughout the year

At the end of the year, before the adjusting entries were made, the accounts would appear as follows:

Supplies inventory		Supplies expense	
Bal. 1/1 1,000		**(a)** Var. dates 4,000	

	Cash	
Bal. 1/1 xxx	**(a)** Var. dates 4,000	

If, as before, the physical count at year end revealed that $3,000 of supplies were on hand, then supplies inventory would be understated by $2,000. Correspondingly, supplies expense would be overstated by that same amount. The required adjusting entry would therefore be

(b) 31/12

Supplies inventory $2,000
    Supplies expense $2,000
To adjust the inventory and expense accounts for the excess of the physical count over the balance in the unadjusted supplies inventory account

Supplies inventory		Supplies expense	
Bal. 1/1 1,000		**(a)** Var. dates 4,000	**(b)** 31/12 2,000
(b) 31/12 2,000		2,000	
3,000			

The adjusted balances would, of course, be in accord with those derived by the other two methods.

The key point about the above supplies inventory/expense example is that the answer is the same in all three cases. The answer is a supplies expense of $2,000 for the year ended December 31 and supplies inventory at the end of the year of $3,000. This answer is related to the economic reality; $2,000 worth of supplies were consumed in the period (an expense) and there is $3,000 worth of supplies left at the end of the period (an asset). The three methods above show that items may be accounted for differently during an accounting period as long as the appropriate adjusting entries are made at the end of the period. In each case, the adjusting entries will be different but the answer will be the same. An efficient way of determining the appropriate adjusting entry required at the end of the accounting period is as follows:

1. Examine the unadjusted trial balance to determine the account balance before adjustments.
2. Determine what the balance in the accounts *should be* at the end of the period (i.e., what should the answer be?).
3. Prepare an adjusting entry to get from the unadjusted balance to the desired balance.

A Reminder

In making either updating or adjusting entries, accounting students are often unsure of the accounts to be adjusted. Although it may be obvious to them that one account must be corrected, they are unsure of the corresponding half of the entry. There is a temptation, in the face of uncertainty, to debit or credit either "Cash" or "Retained earnings." In fact, neither is likely to be affected by periodic adjustments. "Cash" needs to be debited or credited only upon the actual receipt or disbursement of cash. Indeed, unless the student can actually envision a transfer of cash—by cheque, in currency, or by notification of credits or charges by the bank—he or she can be reasonably certain that it is not "Cash" that should be debited or credited. Similarly, retained earnings in the ordinary course of business is affected directly by only two types of events: the declaration of a dividend and the posting of year-end closing entries. Updating or adjusting entries affect either an asset or a liability account and its related expense or revenue account.

YEAR-END ADJUSTMENTS—AN EXAMPLE

Exhibit 4-1 indicates the December 31, 1996, trial balance of the Muskoka Appliance Company, a retail store, before year-end adjustments have been made. The following additional information that requires accounting recognition is available to the accountant in charge of preparing annual financial statements.

EXHIBIT 4-1

Muskoka Appliance Company
Trial Balance
As at December 31, 1996

	Debits	Credits
Cash	$ 105,000	
Accounts receivable	437,500	
Allowance for doubtful accounts		$ 45,000
Merchandise inventory	652,000	
Prepaid insurance	40,000	
Supplies inventory	5,000	
Land	100,000	
Building	450,000	

EXHIBIT 4-1 (continued)

Accumulated amortization, building		110,000
Furniture and fixtures	47,000	
Accumulated amortization, furniture and fixtures		14,100
Notes receivable	20,000	
Accounts payable		182,000
Sales taxes payable		2,000
Advances from customers		5,000
Common stock		250,000
Retained earnings		873,650
Sales revenue		3,302,000
Gain on sale of furniture and fixtures		12,000
Cost of goods sold	2,179,000	
Wages and salaries expense	567,000	
Delivery and shipping charges	33,500	
Amortization expense	12,850	
Property taxes expense	1,800	
Supplies expense	9,400	
Other expenses	35,700	
Income taxes expense	100,000	
	$4,795,750	$4,795,750

Unexpired Insurance

The prepaid insurance ($40,000) indicated on the trial balance represents the unexpired portion of a three-year policy purchased at the beginning of 1995. The required insurance expense of $20,000 has not yet been charged for 1996. The following adjusts the accounts and brings them up to date:

(a)

Insurance expense $20,000
       Prepaid insurance $20,000
To record the expiration of one-third of a three-year insurance policy

Amortization

The company charges amortization semiannually, June 30 and December 31. The building, which originally cost $450,000, is being amortized over a 30-year period; furniture and fixtures, which originally cost $47,000, are being amortized over a 10-year period. Thus amortization charges for a full year are $15,000 and $4,700, respectively—for a half-year, $7,500 and $2,350.[3]

(b)

Amortization expense $9,850
       Accumulated amortization, building $7,500
       Accumulated amortization, furniture and fixtures $2,350
To record amortization expense for one-half year

Interest Earned

The note receivable, $20,000, is a one-year note and was received from a commercial customer on November 1, 1996. The note bears interest at a rate of 12 per-

[3] The amount to be charged for the second half of the year is less than that charged for the first; thus the $12,850 per "amortization expense" on the trial balance. As indicated by the account "gain on sale of furniture and fixtures," some capital assets were sold during the year.

cent per annum. Interest is payable at the expiration of the note. Interest earned in the two months in 1996 during which the company held the note must be recognized. Interest earned would be two-twelfths of 12 percent of $20,000, or $400.

(c)

Accrued interest receivable $400	
Interest revenue	$400
To record the interest earned but not yet collected	

Property Taxes

The company makes property tax payments once a year, on January 31. Total taxes payable on January 31, 1997, will be $22,800. Accounting recognition must be given to the portion—eleven-twelfths of $22,800—applicable to 1996. Additional tax expense for 1996, to be added to the expense of $1,800, which was recorded when the January 31, 1996, tax bill was paid, is therefore $20,900, and total tax expense for the year will be $22,700:

(d)

Property taxes expense $20,900	
Accrued property taxes payable	$20,900
To record the portion of property taxes due in 1997 applicable to 1996	

Supplies

A physical count indicated supplies on hand of $3,000. Supplies purchased during the year were charged entirely to supplies expense. The supplies inventory account must be credited by $2,000 to reflect the difference between the current balance in the account ($5,000 per the trial balance) and actual supplies in stock: Since the supplies inventory has decreased during the year (from $5,000 to $3,000) this means more supplies were consumed during the year than purchased. Since the current amount in supplies expense ($9,400) represents only the amount purchased, the expense must be increased by $2,000 to reflect the drawdown of supplies inventory.

(e)

Supplies expense $2,000	
Supplies inventory	$2,000
To adjust the accounts to reflect the physical count of supplies on hand	

Wages and Salaries

The company pays its employees every two weeks. At year end, employees have worked four days for which they will not be paid until the first payday of the new year. Wages and salaries applicable to the four-day period total $10,900:

(f)

Wages and salaries expense $10,900	
Accrued wages and salaries payable	$10,900
To record wages and salaries earned by employees but not yet paid	

Inventory Shortage

The company maintains its merchandise inventory on a *perpetual* basis. Each time an item is sold, an entry is made in which merchandise inventory is reduced by the cost of the item sold, and cost of goods sold is charged for the same amount. Thus, at year end, the amount recorded in the merchandise inventory account should be in agreement with that actually on hand. However, an actual count of merchandise on hand reveals an unexplained shortage of $6,000. Whether the $6,000 shortage is the result of an accounting error or the result of theft of inventory (which wouldn't have been accounted for!), an expense must be recognized for the additional consumption of inventory:

(g)

Inventory shortage expense	$6,000	
Merchandise inventory		$6,000

To adjust the accounts to reflect the physical count of merchandise on hand

Income Taxes

Based on a preliminary computation, corporate income taxes (both federal and provincial) for the year will total $155,000. To date, the company has made payments of $100,000 based on quarterly estimates of earnings. The company now forecasts that additional payments of $55,000 will be required. Although such payments need not be made until March 31, 1997, they represent an expense of the current year, 1996:

(h)

Income taxes expense	$55,000	
Accrued income taxes payable		$55,000

To record additional income tax expense based on a preliminary computation

Capturing the Adjustments and Preparing the Statements

Exhibit 4-2 illustrates a worksheet that can be used to capture the adjustments and prepare the income statement and the balance sheet. The worksheet is a functional means of summarizing the adjustments and their impact upon the general ledger accounts. It eliminates the inconvenience of taking a new trial balance each time the need for an additional adjustment is uncovered. It does not, however, save the firm from having ultimately to post the adjustments to the actual general ledger accounts.

Note the following features of the worksheet:

- The first two columns (after the account titles) reflect the trial balance amounts (per Exhibit 4-1) prior to the adjustments. The balances are obviously "preclosing" (if they were not, the amounts in the revenue and expense accounts would be zero). Therefore the balance in the retained earnings account does not yet incorporate income for the year.
- The second two columns summarize the year-end adjustments (journal entries **a** through **h**). Accounts that were affected by the adjusting entries, but which previously had zero balances and therefore were not included in the trial balance shown in Exhibit 4-1, are listed beneath the accounts which were included. The sums of the debits and credits in these columns are equal. If they were not, then an error must have been made in either the entries themselves or in posting the entries to the worksheet.

EXHIBIT 4-2

Muskoka Appliance Company
Worksheet
Year Ended December 31, 1996

	Unadjusted Trial Balance Dr. (1)	Cr. (2)	Adjustments Dr. (3)	Cr. (4)	Balance Sheet Dr. (5)	Cr. (6)	Income Statement Dr. (7)	Cr. (8)
Cash	105,000				105,000			
Accounts receivable	437,500				437,500			
Allowance for doubtful accounts		45,000				45,000		
Merchandise inventory	652,000			6,000 (g)	646,000			
Prepaid insurance	40,000			20,000 (a)	20,000			
Supplies inventory	5,000			2,000 (e)	3,000			
Land	100,000				100,000			
Building	450,000				450,000			
Accumulated amortization, building		110,000		7,500 (b)		117,500		
Furniture and fixtures	47,000				47,000			
Accumulated amortization, furniture and fixtures		14,100		2,350 (b)		16,450		
Notes receivable	20,000				20,000			
Accounts payable		182,000				182,000		
Sales tax payable		2,000				2,000		
Advances from customers		5,000				5,000		
Common stock		250,000				250,000		
Retained earnings		873,650				873,650		
Sales revenue		3,302,000						3,302,000
Gain on sale of furniture and fixtures		12,000						12,000
Cost of goods sold	2,179,000						2,179,000	
Wages and salaries expense	567,000		10,900 (f)				577,900	
Delivery and shipping charges	33,500						33,500	
Amortization expense	12,850		9,850 (b)				22,700	
Property taxes expense	1,800		20,900 (d)				22,700	
Supplies expense	9,400		2,000 (e)				11,400	
Other expenses	35,700						35,700	
Income taxes expense	100,000		55,000 (h)				155,000	
Unadjusted totals	4,795,750	4,795,750						
Insurance expense			20,000 (a)				20,000	
Accrued interest receivable			400 (c)		400			
Interest revenue				400 (c)				400
Accrued property taxes payable				20,900 (d)		20,900		
Inventory shortage expense			6,000 (g)				6,000	
Accrued wages and salaries payable				10,900 (f)		10,900		
Accrued income taxes payable				55,000 (h)		55,000		
Totals			125,050	125,050	1,828,900	1,578,400	3,063,900	3,314,400
Net income						250,500	250,500	
Adjusted totals					1,828,900	1,828,900	3,314,400	3,314,400

EXHIBIT 4-3

General Ledger Accounts (Only Those Affected by Adjusting Entries)

Accrued interest receivable

(c) 400	
400	

Prepaid insurance

Bal. 40,000	**(a)** 20,000
20,000	

Supplies inventory

Bal. 5,000	**(e)** 2,000
3,000	

Merchandise inventory

Bal. 652,000	**(g)** 6,000
646,000	

Accumulated amortization, building

	Bal. 110,000
	(b) 7,500
	117,500

Accumulated amortization, furniture and fixtures

	Bal. 14,100
	(b) 2,350
	16,450

Accrued wages and salaries payable

	(f) 10,900
	10,900

Accrued income taxes payable

	(h) 55,000
	55,000

Accrued property taxes payable

	(d) 20,900
	20,900

Interest revenue

	(c) 400
	400

Inventory shortage expense

(g) 6,000	
6,000	

Income taxes expense

Bal. 100,000	
(h) 55,000	
155,000	

Insurance expense

(a) 20,000	
20,000	

Amortization expense

Bal. 12,850	
(b) 9,850	
22,700	

Property taxes expense

Bal. 1,800	
(d) 20,900	
22,700	

Supplies expense

Bal. 9,400	
(e) 2,000	
11,400	

Wages and salaries expense

Bal. 567,000	
(f) 10,900	
577,900	

EXHIBIT 4-4

Muskoka Appliance Company
Worksheet—Closing Entries
Year Ended December 31, 1996

	Adjusted Trial Balance		Closing Entries		Postclosing Trial Balance	
	Dr.	Cr.	Dr.	Cr.	Dr.	Cr.
Cash	105,000				105,000	
Accounts receivable	437,500				437,500	
Allowance for doubtful accounts		45,000				45,000
Accrued interest receivable	400				400	
Merchandise inventory	646,000				646,000	
Supplies inventory	3,000				3,000	
Prepaid insurance	20,000				20,000	
Land	100,000				100,000	
Building	450,000				450,000	
Accumulated amortization, building		117,500				117,500
Furniture and fixtures	47,000				47,000	
Accumulated amortization, furniture and fixtures		16,450				16,450
Notes receivable	20,000				20,000	
Accounts payable		182,000				182,000
Sales taxes payable		2,000				2,000
Advances from customers		5,000				5,000
Accrued property taxes payable		20,900				20,900
Accrued wages and salaries payable		10,900				10,900
Accrued income taxes payable		55,000				55,000
Common stock		250,000				250,000
Retained earnings		873,650		250,500 (c3)		1,124,150
Sales revenue		3,302,000	3,302,000 (c1)			0
Gain on sale of furniture and fixtures		12,000	12,000 (c1)			0
Interest revenue		400	400 (c1)			0
Cost of goods sold	2,179,000			2,179,000 (c2)	0	
Wages and salaries expense	577,900			577,900 (c2)	0	
Delivery and shipping charges	33,500			33,500 (c2)	0	
Amortization expense	22,700			22,700 (c2)	0	
Property taxes expense	22,700			22,700 (c2)	0	
Supplies expense	11,400			11,400 (c2)	0	
Other expenses	35,700			35,700 (c2)	0	
Income taxes expense	155,000			155,000 (c2)	0	
Insurance expense	20,000			20,000 (c2)	0	
Inventory shortage expense	6,000			6,000 (c2)	0	
Income summary	0		3,063,900 (c2) 250,500 (c3)	3,314,400 (c1)		0
Totals	4,892,800	4,892,800	6,628,800	6,628,800	1,828,900	1,828,900

EXHIBIT 4-5

Closing Entries		
(c1)		
Sales revenue	$3,302,000	
Gain on sale of furniture and fixtures	12,000	
Interest revenue	400	
Income summary		$3,314,400
To close the revenue accounts		
(c2)		
Income summary	$3,063,900	
Cost of goods sold		$2,179,000
Wages and salaries expense		577,900
Delivery and shipping charges		33,500
Amortization expense		22,700
Property taxes expense		22,700
Supplies expense		11,400
Other expenses		35,700
Income taxes expense		155,000
Inventory shortage expense		6,000
Insurance expense		20,000
To close the expense accounts		
(c3)		
Income summary	$250,500	
Retained earnings		$250,500
To transfer income to retained earnings		

- Columns 5 and 6 indicate the adjusted balance sheet accounts and columns 7 and 8 indicate the adjusted income statement accounts. The debit and credit columns of both the income statement and the balance sheet are "out of balance." The credit column of the income statement exceeds the debit column by the income for the year ($250,500). Correspondingly, the debit column of the balance sheet exceeds the credit column by the same amount. As pointed out in the illustration of the accounting cycle in the previous chapter, this imbalance exists because the retained earnings account has not yet been updated. When the revenue and expense accounts for the year are "closed" to retained earnings, the inequality will be eliminated.

Exhibit 4-3 depicts the affected accounts of the company after the foregoing transactions have been posted. Exhibit 4-4 illustrates another worksheet. In this worksheet, the first two columns are a preclosing trial balance after the adjustments have been posted. These amounts are identical to those in the income statement and balance sheet accounts in the right-hand columns of Exhibit 4-2. Therefore the worksheets of Exhibits 4-2 and 4-4 could easily have been combined.

The next two columns of Exhibit 4-4 include the closing entries (which are shown in Exhibit 4-5). The last two columns report the postclosing balances. The postclosing balances include only balance sheet accounts. The income statement balances have all been "zeroed out." Exhibit 4-6 presents the income statement and balance sheet, which incorporate the year-end adjustments.

EXHIBIT 4-6

Muskoka Appliance Company
Income Statement
Year Ended December 31, 1996

Revenues		
Sales	$3,302,000	
Interest	400	
Gain on sale of furniture and fixtures	12,000	
Total revenue		$3,314,400
Expenses		
Cost of goods sold	2,179,000	
Wages and salaries expense	577,900	
Delivery and shipping charges	33,500	
Amortization expense	22,700	
Property taxes expense	22,700	
Supplies expense	11,400	
Insurance expense	20,000	
Inventory shortage expense	6,000	
Other expenses	35,700	
Total expenses		2,908,900
Income before taxes		$ 405,500
Income taxes		155,000
Net income		$ 250,500

Muskoka Appliance Company
Balance Sheet
As at December 31, 1996

Assets

Current assets		
Cash		$ 105,000
Accounts receivable	$437,500	
Less: Allowance for doubtful accounts	45,000	392,500
Accrued interest receivable		400
Merchandise inventory		646,000
Supplies inventory		3,000
Prepaid insurance		20,000
Total current assets		$1,166,900
Noncurrent assets		
Land		$ 100,000
Building	$450,000	
Less: Accumulated amortization	117,500	332,500
Furniture and fixtures	47,000	
Less: Accumulated amortization	16,450	30,550
Notes receivable		20,000
Total noncurrent assets		$ 483,050
Total assets		$1,649,950

Liabilities and Shareholders' Equity

Current liabilities		
Accounts payable		$ 182,000
Sales tax payable		2,000
Advances from customer		5,000
Accrued property taxes payable		20,900
Accrued wages and salaries payable		10,900
Accrued income taxes payable		55,000
Total current liabilities		$ 275,800
Shareholders' equity		
Common stock		$ 250,000
Retained earnings		1,124,150
Total shareholders' equity		$1,374,150
Total liabilities and shareholders' equity		$1,649,950

Organizations do, unfortunately, sometimes make errors. An examination of some common types of errors and their impact on financial reports provides additional insight into the accounting process.

Some errors are easily detectable. An entry to a journal may be made in which the debits do not equal the credits. Incorrect amounts may be posted to the ledger accounts. Then, when a trial balance is taken, the sum of the general ledger debits will not equal the sum of the credits.

Other errors, most particularly those related to updating or adjusting entries, are less easily detectable and are likely to affect both balance sheet and income statement accounts. Many such errors are, however, *self-correcting* over time. They will automatically be eliminated either upon the liquidation of the offending asset or liability or when other routine adjustments to the accounts are made. The errors may nonetheless be serious because the intervening financial statements will have been incorrect.

Consider a firm that maintains its inventory records on a periodic basis. The firm physically counts merchandise on hand at the end of each fiscal year. During the year it maintains accurate records of all purchases. In determining the cost of goods sold for the year, it computes goods available for sale (beginning inventory plus purchases during the year) and subtracts goods that remain unsold at the end of the year (ending inventory). If beginning inventory was $3 million, purchases were $30 million, and ending inventory was $6 million, then cost of goods sold during the year would be $27 million:

Beginning inventory	$ 3
Purchases	30
Cost of goods available for sale	33
Less: Ending inventory	6
Cost of goods sold	$27

If, in the following year, purchases were $35 million and ending inventory was $2 million, then the cost of goods sold would be $39 million.

Beginning inventory (same as ending inventory of previous year)	$ 6
Purchases	35
Cost of goods available for sale	$41
Less: Ending inventory	2
Cost of goods sold	$39

Suppose, however, that at the end of the first year the firm miscounted its inventory. Instead of $6 million, the firm counted goods on hand of $5 million. As a result of the miscount, cost of goods sold during the first year would have been reported as $28 million—*overstated* by $1 million. In the second year, the *beginning inventory* would have been understated by $1 million. Cost of goods sold for the second year (assuming a correct count at the end of the second year) would have been reported at $38 million—*understated* by $1 million (I = incorrect; C = correct):

	Year 1		Year 2	
Beginning inventory	$ 3	(C)	$ 5	(I)
Purchases	30	(C)	$35	(C)
Cost of goods available for sale	33	(C)	$40	(I)
Less: Ending inventory	5	(I)	2	(C)
Cost of goods sold	$28	(I)	$38	(I)

Cost of goods sold—and thus income—would be correctly stated for the two-year period combined but incorrectly stated for each of the two individual periods. Both current assets (inventory) and retained earnings would be in error after the first year, but correct after the second.

Consider also a firm that received a two-year, $1,000 note receivable in June 1996. The note carried an interest rate of 14 percent. Interest was receivable annually each June; the principal, in its entirety, was due from the borrower at the expiration of the note in June 1998. The firm has a December 31 fiscal year end.

If the firm made proper adjusting entries, then revenue from the note would be $70 in 1996 (six months' interest), $140 in 1997 (one year's interest), and $70 in 1998 (six months' interest)—regardless of when the annual cash interest payments were received. Suppose, however, that the firm neglected to "accrue" interest at the end of 1996 and instead recognized revenue only upon the receipt of the cash interest payments. For the year ended 1996, revenues, current assets (accrued interest receivable), and retained earnings each would be understated by $70. For the year ended 1997, revenues would be correctly stated, as the firm would have recorded $140 interest revenue upon the receipt of the cash interest payment in June 1997. However, since the cash payment represented interest for the period June 1996 to June 1997, current assets, and thus retained earnings, at December 31, 1997, would still be understated by $70—the interest for the period June 1997 to December 1997. For the year ended 1998, however, revenues would be *overstated* by $70, as the entire June 1998 cash interest payment of $140 would be recorded as revenue. Current assets (accrued interest receivable would be zero), however, would now be correctly stated; so, too, would retained earnings. The differences are summarized in Exhibit 4-7.

Although in the *long run* many errors may be self-correcting, a primary purpose of accounting is to report changes in the welfare of an enterprise in the course of specific, relatively short, periods of time. Firms are not permitted the luxury of allowing the passage of the years to compensate for their errors and omissions.

DERIVING MISSING INFORMATION

A complete set of financial statements, prepared in accordance with generally accepted accounting principles, contains an abundance of information as to a firm's operations and financial position. Sometimes, however, the data

EXHIBIT 4-7
Impact of Failure to Accrue Interest Revenue

On June 30, 1996, a company receives a two-year note receivable for $1,000 at 14 percent interest. Interest payments of $140 are due on June 30, 1997, and June 30, 1998.

	Company Correctly Accrues Interest at Year End	Company Recognizes Interest Revenue Only as Cash Is Received	Difference
Accrued interest receivable, 1/1/96	$ 0	$ 0	$ 0
Interest revenue, 1996	70	0	70
Interest (cash) received, 1996	(0)	(0)	(0)
Accrued interest receivable, 31/12/96	70	0	70
Interest revenue, 1997	140	140	0
Interest (cash) received, 1997	(140)	(140)	(0)
Accrued interest receivable, 31/12/97	70	0	70
Interest revenue, 1998	70	140	(70)
Interest (cash) received, 1998	(140)	(140)	(0)
Accrued interest receivable, 31/12/98	$ 0	$ 0	$ 0
Total interest (cash) received	$280	$280	$ 0
Total interest revenue recognized	$280	$280	$ 0

sought by an analyst are not available, perhaps because they are of a type not incorporated into one of the primary financial statements or perhaps because they got subsumed in the summary and aggregation of individual accounts. Moreover, managers and investors must sometimes make do, especially in the case of companies not publicly traded, with financial reports that are missing one of the primary statements or contain other material omissions. The following two examples illustrate how the fundamental relationships between income statement and balance sheet accounts enable an analyst to derive missing data.

Example 1: Purchases of Inventory

An analyst needs to determine the amount of inventory *purchased* by a firm. The firm's comparative balance sheets report beginning-of-year and end-of-year inventory on hand of $5 million and $10 million, respectively. Its income statement discloses cost of goods sold of $50 million. Its statement of changes in financial position indicates payments to suppliers, but none of the three primary statements reveals purchases.

Using the relationship between inventory and cost of goods sold, the analyst can easily derive purchases. If

Beginning inventory + Purchases − Cost of goods sold = Ending inventory

then purchases equal cost of goods sold plus the increase in inventory:

Purchases = Cost of goods sold + Ending inventory − Beginning inventory
= $50 + $10 − $5
= $55

Thus, in summary:

Beginning inventory	$ 5
+ Purchases	55
= Goods available for sale	60
− Cost of goods sold	(50)
= Ending inventory	$10

Example 2: Sale of Equipment

As to equipment sold, an analyst needs to determine its initial cost, its accumulated amortization, and the gain or loss on sale. This information may help the analyst confirm a suspicion that the firm is disposing of relatively new equipment which has decreased in value, perhaps because it is prematurely obsolete. The firm's financial statements reveal the following (in thousands):

	Balance Sheets		Income Statement	Statement of Changes in Financial Position
	Beginning	Ending		
Equipment	$500	$720		
Less: Accumulated amortization	(300)	(530)		
Net book value	$200	$190		
Acquisitions				$(480)
Cash received upon sale of equipment				125
Amortization expense			$250	

A useful means of deriving missing data is to reconstruct the journal entry to record the relevant transaction. If all elements of the entry but one are known, the missing amount can easily be determined. In this case, the entry to record the sale of equipment, including the amount known from the information in the financial statements, would be

Cash	$125
Loss on sale of equipment	?
Accumulated amortization	?
Equipment	$?
To record sale of equipment	

In this situation, three of the four elements of the entry are unknown. The analyst must therefore pursue additional sources of information.

Accumulated amortization is increased only by annual amortization charges. It is decreased only by the sale or retirement of assets, when the accumulated amortization applicable to the disposed-of asset is removed from the account (as in the entry just presented). Therefore, as to accumulated amortization,

Beginning balance + Amortization expense − Accumulated amortization on assets retired during the year = Ending balance

By rearrangement,

Accumulated amortization on assets retired during the year

> = Beginning balance + Amortization expense − Ending balance

Based on the data in the financial statements,

> Accumulated amortization on assets retired during the year
> = $300 + $250 − $530
>
> = $20

Using similar logic, the analyst can deduce from the equipment account the initial cost of the equipment sold:

> Beginning balance + Acquisitions − Retirements = Ending balance

By rearrangement,

> Retirements = Beginning balance + Acquisitions − Ending balance

Based on data in the financial statements, the analyst can find

> Retirements = $500 + $480 − $720
>
> = $260

With information on three of the four components of the journal entry to record the sale of the equipment, the fourth, the loss on sale, can easily be calculated:

Cash		$125
Loss on sale of equipment		?
Accumulated amortization	20	
Equipment		$260
To record sale of equipment		

If the entry is to balance, the loss must have been $115: $260 − ($125 + $20).

Thus the analyst finds that during the year the company sold for $125 equipment that had cost $260. Since book value of the equipment (initial cost less amortization) is $240, the sale has resulted in a loss of $115. The equipment was relatively new in that only $20 (7 percent of initial cost of $260) had been amortized.

COST OF GOODS SOLD

It has been previously pointed out that, in accordance with the accrual concept, costs are *capitalized* as assets until the intended benefits are actually realized. In a business enterprise costs are incurred to generate revenues. Hence costs should be recognized as expenses at the same time that the benefits that they produce are recognized as revenues. In other words, costs should be *matched* with revenues.

In a retail sales operation the major cost incurred in the generation of revenue is that of the goods to be sold. As the goods to be sold are received, their cost is *stored* in an asset account, "Merchandise inventory." Only when they are actually sold, and when sales revenue is recognized, is the cost of the goods sold charged as an expense. In the period of sale, the following entry is made:

Cost of goods sold (expense +) xxxx
    Merchandise inventory (asset –) xxxx

It follows that in a manufacturing operation all costs of producing the goods intended for sale should also be stored as assets until the goods are actually sold. This means that not only should costs of raw materials be capitalized as assets, but so too should costs of labour, maintenance, machines used (i.e., amortization), and all other costs that can be identified with the production process.

When raw materials are purchased, their cost is charged initially to an asset account, "raw materials." As they are placed in production, their cost is transferred to "work in process," another asset account, and when the goods are completed their cost is transferred to "finished goods," also an asset account.

This is also true of labour costs. Although labour, unlike raw materials, cannot be physically stored, the *cost* of labour, like the cost of raw materials, *can* be stored in an asset account. Labour costs are conventionally recorded initially in an asset account, "labour," and then transferred immediately (since labour cannot be physically stored) to "work in process." The labour account, although perhaps unnecessary since the costs are transferred immediately to work in process, is ordinarily maintained because it facilitates cost control by providing management with a record of labour costs incurred.

So also with other manufacturing costs. Even that portion of manufacturing equipment considered to be consumed in the accounting period must be capitalized as part of the cost of the goods produced. The equipment benefits the periods in which the goods that it has been used to produce are actually sold. Costs of using up the equipment (i.e., amortization) must be added to work in process (an asset account) and thereby included in the cost of the finished goods. They will be charged as an expense (as part of cost of goods sold) when the finished goods are actually sold.

The published financial statements of many major corporations do not include as expenses either amortization or wages and salaries. These costs are, of course, reflected in the income statement. However, along with other manufacturing costs they are initially incorporated into inventory and eventually reported as part of cost of goods sold.

The manufacturing cycle is depicted graphically in Exhibit 4-8. The key point that the exhibit illustrates is that cost of goods sold represents a conglomerate of several different types of costs. All such costs, even those of services that contribute to the value of the product but cannot be physically stored (labour and utility costs, for example), are accumulated and retained in asset accounts (such as factory labour, work in process, and finished goods) until the time of sale. Upon sale, when the goods are transferred to a customer, an asset account (finished goods) is reduced (credited) by the cost to manufacture the goods sold and an expense (cost of goods sold) is increased (debited).

The principles and issues relating to manufacturing costs are typically dealt with in courses in "management" and "cost" accounting.

Principle of Matching

Central to modern accounting is the *principle of matching*. Insofar as it is practical, all costs should be associated with particular revenues. They should be recorded as expenses in the same periods in which the related revenues are recognized. Costs that are associated with revenues to be recognized in the future are to be maintained in asset accounts until such time as recognition is accorded the revenues and the costs can properly be charged as expenses.

Expenses can be defined as the goods or services consumed in the creation of revenues. Indeed, *all* costs are incurred in the hope of generating revenues. If the objective of determining periodic income is to be best served, then all costs incurred by the firm should be capitalized as assets (i.e., charged initially to "work in process" or otherwise added to the cost of goods held in inventory) and recorded as expenses only as the goods are actually sold. Costs of borrowing necessary funds (interest), administering corporate headquarters,

EXHIBIT 4-8
Manufacturing Cycle

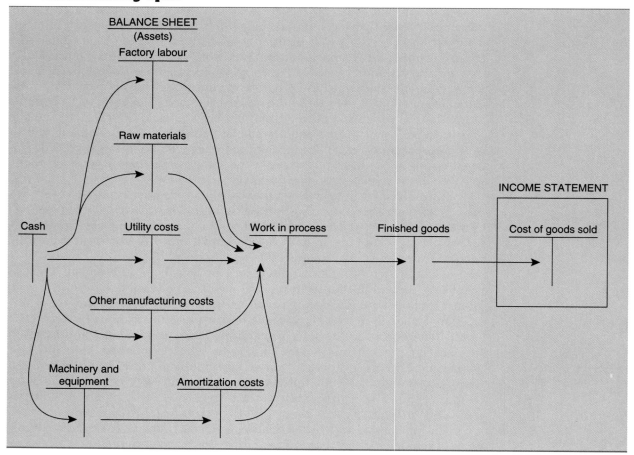

and advertising the products contribute as much to the generation of revenue as those of manufacturing products. Logically, such costs should also be added to the cost of goods to be sold.

In practice, however, many types of costs are not capitalized as assets. Instead they are charged as expenses in the period in which they are incurred, regardless of when the related products are sold. The inconsistency of capitalizing some costs but not others has by no means been lost upon accountants. They have yielded to practical exigencies, however. It is simply too difficult to associate meaningfully—to match—certain costs with specific revenues.

Consider, for example, costs of administration—the salaries of officers, secretaries, computer operators, and accountants; the fees paid to outside lawyers and auditors; the costs of renting office space and equipment. If a firm manufactured numerous types of products, it would be difficult, to say the least, to allocate such costs to specific products. Or consider sales costs. A salesperson might make numerous calls on customers before he or she receives an order. Is it possible, in any meaningful way, to associate costs of the unsuccessful calls with specific revenues to be generated in the future? Or consider interest costs. Funds borrowed benefit the entire company. Can the costs of borrowing be reasonably identified with sales of specific products?

Conventions

To reduce the need to make these troublesome allocations, while still achieving reasonable matching, accountants have adopted certain conventions as to which types of costs should be added to the cost of the product and which should be charged off as expenses in the period in which they are incurred. These conventions apply only to reports intended for external parties. They need not be applied to internal financial reports. Although there is no universal agreement on the conventions, as a general rule, *direct* manufacturing costs, such as factory labour and raw materials, are always charged to the product (i.e., included in "work in process"). So are several types of *indirect* manufacturing costs such as amortization on manufacturing equipment, factory utility costs, rent on the factory building, and salaries of employees who are directly concerned with manufacturing operations. These are called *product* costs. On the other hand, costs of selling, advertising and promotion, interest, employee health and recreational facilities, most taxes, and most other administrative costs are ordinarily considered to be *period* costs, which are charged as expenses as incurred.

The widely followed conventions do not, by any means, eliminate the need to allocate all common costs to specific products. *Factory overhead* costs (those which cannot readily be identified with specific products), such as supervision, utilities, maintenance, and rent, must still be allocated. And, as a consequence of the conventions, seemingly similar types of costs are sometimes accounted for differently. Amortization on tables and chairs in a factory is considered to be a product cost; that on table and chairs in the corporate headquarters is considered to be a period cost; salaries of accountants who deal with factory costs are included among product costs; those of accountants who work with other types of costs are included as period costs.

Impact on Financial Statements

When a firm considers whether to include a specific cost as a product or a period cost, one relevant question must always be raised: What would be the impact of alternative classifications on both the income statement and the balance sheet?

If, within an accounting period, the enterprise sells the *same* number of goods that it produces (assuming no change in per unit costs from one period to the next), then it makes no difference whether a cost is classified as a product or a period cost. Suppose, for example, the salary of an accountant is $48,000 per year. During the year the firm produces and sells 48,000 units. If the salary is considered a period cost, then $48,000 will be reported as an expense among "administrative" expenses; if it is considered a product cost, then $48,000 will first be capitalized as "work in process," then transferred to "finished goods inventory," and finally reported in the same period as an expense, "cost of goods sold."

If the enterprise sells *fewer* goods than it produces, then reported expenses will be *greater* if the costs are categorized as period costs than if they are treated as product costs. Assume that the same firm produces 48,000 units but sells only 40,000 units. If the $48,000 salary of the accountant is classified as a period cost, then the full $48,000 will be charged off as an expense. If, however, it is classified as a product cost, then $1 ($48,000 divided by the number of units produced) will be added to the cost of each unit produced. Since 40,000 units are sold, only $40,000 will be included among cost of goods sold. The remaining $8,000 will be *stored* on the balance sheet, included in "Finished goods inventory." Hence current assets, specifically inventory, will be $8,000 greater than if the salary were accounted for as a period cost.

EXHIBIT 4-9

Product versus Period Costs	Year 1 Production = Sales	Year 2 Production > Sales	Year 3 Production < Sales
Number of units produced	48,000	48,000	48,000
Number of units sold	48,000	40,000	56,000
Manufacturing costs other than salary of accountant ($10 per unit)	$480,000	$480,000	$480,000
Salary of accountant	48,000	48,000	48,000
I. Salary of accountant charged as a product cost			
Cost of goods manufactured	$528,000	$528,000	$528,000
Cost per unit of goods manufactured	11	11	11
Cost of goods sold	528,000	440,000	616,000
Ending inventory	0	88,000	0
Period costs (salary of accountant)	0	0	0
II. Salary of accountant charged as a period cost			
Cost of goods manufactured	$480,000	$480,000	$480,000
Cost per unit of goods manufactured	10	10	10
Cost of goods sold	480,000	400,000	560,000
Ending inventory	0	80,000	0
Period costs (salary of accountant)	48,000	48,000	48,000
Differences (I – II)			
Cost of goods sold	$ 48,000	$ 40,000	$ 56,000
Period costs (salary of accountant)	(48,000)	(48,000)	(48,000)
Net difference in costs	$ 0	($ 8,000)	$ 8,000

If the enterprise sells more goods than it produces, then the reverse will be true. Reported expenses will be less if certain costs are treated as period rather than as product costs. Assume that in the following year the firm produces 48,000 units but sells 56,000 units, taking the additional 8,000 units from inventory. If the accountant's salary is treated as a period cost, then, as previously, the $48,000 will be reported as an expense. But if it is treated as a product cost, $56,000 of salary costs will be charged off as expense—$1 per unit produced and sold in the current period (48,000 units) plus $1 per unit of the goods sold in the current period but produced in the previous period (8,000 units).

Exhibit 4-9 illustrates the example in more detail.

MEASURES OF FINANCIAL PERFORMANCE AND HEALTH

The performance of a business over a *period* of time as well as its well-being at a *particular* time can never be evaluated by examining any single dollar amount that is reported in the firm's financial statements. Net income by itself, for example, tells nothing about how well a company has employed the resources within its command. A large company may have several times the earnings of a smaller company, yet relative to size, the performance of the smaller firm may be better.

Financial performance and fiscal health can best be described by ratios that relate one aspect of a firm's performance or status to another. Some of these ratios are, either by convention or requirement, reported in the body of the financial statements or in the accompanying supplementary data. Others must be calculated by the party engaged in the evaluation.

It is important that investors, creditors, managers, and accountants be familiar with the most widely used of the financial ratios. The ratios can be the basis for evaluating not only a business as a whole, but also its component units and the activities in which it engages. They can warn of fiscal stress. They can point to companies or components of companies to which (or away from which) resources should be directed. Moreover, it is essential that managers be aware of the criteria that outsiders will employ in evaluating their company in order that they can consider the impact on those criteria of any actions that they take. It is equally crucial that independent auditors be knowledgeable of the ratios because they may indicate fiscal stress and areas of high risk.

Ratios themselves, however, must never be evaluated in a vacuum. What are important are trends over time and comparisons with firms in the same or related industries. Should a key ratio or series of ratios increase or decrease from one year to the next, it may be a sign of either financial deterioration or improvement.

There are no fixed minimum or maximum values below which a ratio should not fall or above which it should not rise. But whenever the ratio of a particular firm is substantially out of line with those common in the industry, the analyst should be alert to either potential financial difficulty or unusual financial strength. Normal ranges for most ratios and percentages vary considerably from industry to industry. Some industries, electric utilities for example, require large amounts of invested capital to support their operations. Other industries, supermarkets for instance, require relatively small amounts of permanent capital. As a consequence, supermarkets can be expected to have a much higher ratio of sales to total capital assets than would electric utilities.

Supermarkets, on the other hand, tend to earn a relatively small profit on each dollar of sales since the *markup* on grocery products is relatively small. By contrast, once the physical facilities have been acquired, the cost of generating electricity is relatively low. Thus electric utilities would generally have a much higher ratio of net income to sales revenue (return on sales) than would supermarkets. Industry norms for a number of key indicators can be obtained from publications of industry trade associations or of financial service bureaus such as Dun & Bradstreet Canada Limited.

The ratios that are to be described in this chapter are among the most fundamental of performance indicators. Other ratios will be discussed throughout the text in the sections pertaining to the accounts or activities on which the ratios focus.

The ratios are based on three primary groups of measures:

1. *Profitability and activity measures.* These indicate how well a firm is employing its assets. These measures may relate to specific assets, such as accounts receivable or inventory, or to all the resources within the firm's command.

2. *Liquidity ratios.* These indicate the ability of a firm to meet its obligations as they come due. They relate a firm's *liquid assets* (cash and assets that are most easily converted to cash) to its liabilities.

3. *Financing ratios.* These reveal the proportion of assets financed by creditors as opposed to owners and indicate the ability of the firm to meet its fixed finance charges such as interest.

Profitability and Activity Measures

Earnings per Share

Earnings per share (EPS) is reported in the financial statements of public companies directly beneath net income. It is computed by dividing net income by the weighted average number of common shares outstanding during the period.[4] Earnings per share figures allow individual shareholders to determine their interests in total corporate earnings by multiplying EPS by the number of shares they own. It facilitates comparisons of performance among years in which a greater or lesser number of shares may be outstanding.

To determine earnings per share, we look to an earlier example: Per its income statement (Exhibit 4-6), Muskoka Appliance Company had net income of $250,500 for the year ended December 31, 1996. Assume that there were 10,000 shares of stock outstanding. Earnings per share were therefore $25.05:

$$\text{Earnings per share} = \frac{\text{Net income}}{\text{Shares of common stock outstanding}}$$

$$= \frac{\$250,500}{10,000} = \$25.05$$

---

[4] The computation of earnings per share can be quite complex. The computation of EPS will be expanded upon and discussed in greater detail in Chapter 12.

Return on Investment

The measure of corporate performance that is generally considered most relevant to both managers and investors is *return on investment*. Return on investment relates the earnings of the enterprise to the resources provided by its owners. The resources provided by the owners are measured by their equity—which, of course, is equivalent to net assets (i.e., assets less liabilities). Thus

$$\text{Return on investment (ROI)} = \frac{\text{Net income}}{\text{Owners' equity}^5}$$

The balance sheet of Muskoka Appliance Company, Exhibit 4-6, indicates that the total investment of shareholders at the end of 1996 was $1,374,150. This amount includes the direct contributions of shareholders plus the resources that have been earned over the years and retained in the business (retained earnings). Net income was $250,500. Hence return on investment is 18.2 percent:

$$\text{Return on investment} = \frac{\$250,500}{\$1,374,150} = 18.2\%$$

Other means of computing return on investment, specifically tailored to managers or selected classes of shareholders, will be presented in Chapter 16.

Profit Margins

Profit margins relate income to sales. *Gross profit* is defined as sales minus cost of goods sold. The *gross profit margin* is gross profit divided by sales. Returning to our earlier example, we see that Muskoka's gross profit is

Sales	$3,302,000
Less: Cost of goods sold	2,179,000
Gross profit	$1,123,000

Its gross profit *margin* is 34 percent:

$$\text{Gross profit margin} = \frac{\$1,123,000}{\$3,302,000} = .34$$

The *net profit margin* relates net income to sales:

$$\text{Net profit margin} = \frac{\text{Net income}}{\text{Sales}}$$

Muskoka's net profit margin is 7.6 percent:

$$\text{Net profit margin} = \frac{\$250,500}{\$3,302,000} = .076$$

[5] Preferably, owners' equity should be computed by calculating the average owners' equity during the year. This refinement is ignored for the sake of simplicity in this section of the text.

Other performance and activity ratios compare individual revenues and expense with the assets or liabilities to which they relate (e.g., sales to accounts receivable, cost of goods sold to inventory, and interest to debt). These will be discussed in subsequent chapters.

Still other ratios are tied to stock market measures. The price/earnings (P/E) ratio, for example, compares earnings per share with the stock market price per share. The importance of the P/E ratio is indicated by its being incorporated in the daily stock market tables of *The Globe and Mail's Report on Business* as well as many other financial periodicals.

Suppose that on December 31, 1996, the market price per share of Muskoka was $320. Earnings per share, as just calculated, was $25.05. The price/earnings ratio would be approximately 12.8 to 1:

$$\text{Price/earnings ratio} = \frac{\text{Market price per share of common stock}}{\text{Earnings per share}}$$

$$= \frac{\$320.00}{\$25.05} = 12.8 \text{ to } 1$$

Liquidity Ratios

The most widely used measure of liquidity is the *current ratio*, which provides an insight into the ability of the enterprise to meet its short-term debts. As such it is especially meaningful to parties considering whether to extend credit to the firm. The current ratio compares current assets to current liabilities; that is, it relates cash and the assets that are most likely to be transformed into cash within a single business cycle to the debts that will fall due within that period:

$$\text{Current ratio} = \frac{\text{Current assets}}{\text{Current liabilities}}$$

The current ratio of Muskoka is 4.2 to 1:

$$\text{Current ratio} = \frac{\$1,166,900}{\$275,800} = 4.2 : 1$$

Other, more stringent, tests of liquidity include in current assets only cash and assets that are more easily transformed into cash. The numerator of the *quick ratio*, for example, comprises only cash, marketable securities, and accounts receivable.

Financing Ratios

Financing ratios assess the extent to which a firm is "leveraged"—that is, the extent to which it has financed its assets with debt rather than with the contributed or earned (reinvested) capital of owners. The debt-to-equity ratio, for example, compares total debt to total contributed capital:

$$\text{Debt-to-equity ratio} = \frac{\text{Total debt}}{\text{Total owners' equity}}$$

Muskoka's debt-to-equity ratio is 0.2 to 1:

$$\text{Debt-to-equity ratio} = \frac{\$275,800}{\$1,374,150} = 0.2 \text{ to } 1$$

Importance of Comparisons

Financial statements provide an insight into a company's past operating performance and future earnings potential that is perhaps unmatched by any that can be obtained from other sources. But the picture presented has meaning only when viewed from the proper perspective. Managers, investors, and other users of the statements must be able to examine the financial data with reference to financial position and results of operations of both previous years and of other companies in the same or related industries. No set of dollar amounts, ratios, or other indicators of financial health have meaning in and of themselves. They are of significance only when compared with similar indicators of the same company in other years and of other companies in the same or related industries. Toward this end, corporate annual reports include complete financial statements for the year immediately prior to that being reported upon as well as summary information for a period of 5 to 10 years.

Financial statements are often "rounded" to the nearest thousand or even million dollars, depending on the size of the actual balances. The practice of rounding highlights the imprecision of financial statements; they are necessarily based on a number of estimates and judgmental determinations. Although such estimates and judgmental determinations unquestionably permit a degree of subjectivity to enter into the financial statements, and perhaps make them less comparable with those of other firms, they serve at the same time to make them more relevant for most decisions that they will be used to facilitate.

Summary

The primary purpose of this chapter has been to elaborate upon the accrual concept and to demonstrate some of its many ramifications for accounting practice. The *accrual concept* requires that transactions and other financial events be recognized at the time they have their primary economic impact, not necessarily when cash is received or disbursed. Revenues are assigned to the periods in which they are earned. Costs are matched to the revenues that they generate and are charged as expenses in the periods in which the related revenues are recognized.

The economic benefits attributable to a cost may be both acquired and paid for in periods other than those in which the revenues to which they must be matched are recognized. The benefits attributable to supplies, for example, may be acquired (purchased) in one period, consumed in a second, and paid for in a third. The double-entry accounting system allows for costs that will benefit future periods to be *stored* in asset accounts and charged as expenses only as the revenues with which they are associated are recognized. Similarly, the obligation for the payment may be maintained in a liability account until such time as the required cash disbursement is actually made.

To reduce bookkeeping costs, accounting records are not always kept up to date. For instance, it is more convenient to record the use of supplies periodically rather than each time supplies are consumed. So too in the case of rent and interest revenue, where the benefits accrue over time; it would be impractical to update the books on an around-the-clock basis. As a consequence, firms must periodically bring the records to a current status by means of updating and adjusting entries.

The manner in which costs are accounted for in a manufacturing operation is another manifestation of the accrual concept and the related principle of matching. All manufacturing costs are maintained in asset accounts (e.g., raw materials, labour, work in process, finished goods) until the period in which they can properly be matched to revenues from the sale of the product and charged as expenses (cost of goods sold).

Not all costs are matched directly with specific revenues. The relationships between some costs and revenues are sufficiently indirect that accountants have surrendered to practical exigencies and make no attempt to match certain costs with particular revenues. These costs, often referred to as *period* costs, are charged as expenses in the periods in which they are incurred, regardless of the amount of revenues recognized in that particular period.

A secondary objective of this chapter has been to introduce the general area of financial analysis. Financial statements typically reveal considerably more information about a firm's fiscal wherewithal than is readily apparent. Skilled financial analysts are able to take advantage of the relationships among income statement and balance sheet accounts to derive data that companies have not disclosed. They are also able to use financial ratios to compare the health and performance of a single company over several years and of two or more companies in the same year.

In the following chapter we shall expand still further upon the accrual concept by considering the specific criteria for recognition of revenue.

Exercise for Review and Self-Testing

Global Real Estate leases an office building to a corporate tenant for $200,000 per month. As of January 1, 1997, the tenant had paid two months' rent in advance and Global included among its liabilities "Unearned rent, $400,000."

1. Assuming that the tenant occupied the apartment for 12 months in 1997, how much rent revenue should Global recognize during the year? Does it matter how much cash the firm collected from the tenant?

2. Prepare a journal entry that Global should make at the end of January, 1997, in order for it to be able to prepare financial statements for the month ended January 31, 1997, assuming that it received from the tenant no cash during the month.

3. Suppose instead that during 1997 Global Real Estate received a total of $1,600,000 cash from its tenant. Each time cash was collected, Global made an entry in the following form:

Cash.. xxx
      Rent revenue xxx

It made no other entries with respect to rent during the year.
   a. How much rent revenue should properly have been recognized during the year? By how much is rent revenue understated?
   b. At year end, what should be the balance in "Unearned rent"?
   c. What should be the balance in "Rent receivable"?
   d. Prepare a journal entry to adjust and update the accounts.

4. Global contracted with a maintenance company to perform cleaning services at an annual cost of $120,000. At year end, what amounts should Global report in its income statement account, "Cleaning expense," and its related balance sheet account, either "Cleaning costs payable" or "Prepaid cleaning costs," if it actually made cash payments of
   a. $130,000?
   b. $90,000?
   The maintenance company performed its services throughout the entire year.

5. What determines the amount reported as a revenue or expense for services received or provided? What determines the amount that is added to or subtracted from the related asset or liability account?

Questions for Review and Discussion

1. What is meant by the *accrual method* of accounting? How does it differ from the cash method?

2. Why does the accrual method provide greater insight into organizational performance than does the cash method?

3. What are *adjusting entries?* Why are they necessary?

4. What is a *periodic* method of inventory? How does it differ from a perpetual method?

5. A company charges all purchases of merchandise intended for sale to "Cost of goods sold." Is such practice acceptable? What year-end adjusting entry would be necessary to "correct" the accounts?

6. A bookkeeper incorrectly charges a prepayment of January 1997 rent made on December 28, 1996, to "Rent expense." What would be the impact of this error on the financial statements of the year ended December 1996 and that ended December 1997?

7. A manager of a manufacturing company noticed that the account "Labour cost" was included in the general ledger among the asset accounts. Since she was unable to visually inspect labour costs, she wondered how they could possibly be considered to be an asset. How would you answer her?

8. What is meant by the *matching principle?* If a company were to recognize revenue upon the collection of cash from the customer rather than upon the delivery of goods, when would you recommend that the cost of the goods sold be charged as an expense?

9. Distinguish between product costs and period costs. How would you defend the position of accountants who claim that amortization should sometimes be accounted for as a product cost and sometimes as a period cost?

10. Suppose that in a particular accounting period a company sells the same number of goods that it produces. Would it make any difference insofar as net income is concerned if amortization on office equipment used in the factory were considered a product or a period cost? What if the company sells only a portion of the goods that it produces in a particular accounting period?

11. What are the three primary groups of financial measures and ratios? Give examples of each.

12. An accountant attempted to prepare both an income statement and a balance sheet from an adjusted trial balance. Closing entries had not yet been made. He was unable, however, to get his balance sheet to balance. Assets exceeded liabilities plus owners' equity by an amount exactly equal to income for the year. Which account was most likely in error? Why?

Problems

1. *Expenses must be recognized even if invoices have not yet been received.*

As you are getting ready to prepare year-end financial statements, you learn that your company has not yet received invoices (bills) for services it received in December. The company estimates that in January it will receive invoices as follows:

From the telephone company	$ 700
From the hydro company	3,640
From the outside maintenance service	2,000

a. Prepare any journal entries that you would consider necessary.
b. Suppose that you failed to make such journal entries. What effect would that have on income of the year, income of the following year, and current liabilities?

2. *All costs must be divided between the income statement and the balance sheet.*

A firm made the following payments during its first year of operation:

For rent	$10,000
For interest	8,000
For advertising	3,000
For manufacturing products	96,000

The firm's accountant has determined that the following amounts should properly be reported as expenses:

Rent expense	$12,000
Interest expense	7,000
Advertising expense	6,000
Cost of goods sold	80,000

Determine the amounts that should be reported in balance sheet accounts that correspond to each of the reported expenses.

3. *Costs may be accounted for in three ways.*

The December 31 balance sheet of a company reported accrued interest payable of $3,000 in connection with bonds outstanding of $100,000. Interest, at a rate of 12 percent per year, is payable semiannually on April 1 and October 1.

Prepare all required journal entries for the next year, including year-end adjusting entries, assuming that cash payments are made when due if, alternatively,

a. The company makes appropriate *accrual* entries every three months.
b. The company debits "interest expense" with the full amount of each cash payment.
c. The company debits "accrued interest payable" with the full amount of each cash payment.

4. *The accounting for the purchase and sale of merchandise inventory may be done differently during the accounting period. The required year-end adjustments will be different depending on how the accounting was done during the period.*

At the beginning of 1996 Windswept Company had $65,000 of merchandise inventory on hand. During the year it purchased additional merchandise inventory at a cost of $460,000. A physical count at December 31, 1996, revealed $85,000 of merchandise inventory on hand.

Prepare the required December 31, 1996, adjusting journal entries (if any) that would be required in each of the following independent cases:

a. Windswept recorded purchases of merchandise inventory as increases (debits) to the merchandise inventory (asset) account. No accounting recognition for the consumption of inventory was made at the time of the sale of the inventory to Windswept customers.
b. Windswept recorded purchases of merchandise inventory as increases (debits) to the cost of goods sold (expense) account. No accounting recognition for the consumption of inventory was made at the time of the sale of the inventory to Windswept customers.
c. Windswept recorded purchases of merchandise inventory as increases (debits) to the merchandise inventory (asset) account. At the time of sale of the inventory, Windswept decreased (credited) the merchandise inventory account and increased (debited) the cost of goods sold account for the cost of the merchandise sold. At December 31, there was a debit balance of $82,000 in the merchandise inventory account.

5. *Alternative accounting practices can lead to the same results as long as proper end-of-year adjustments are made.*

Three companies each account for insurance costs differently. Each began the year with a balance of $200 in prepaid insurance costs, which represented one month of insurance remaining on a one-year policy. Upon the expiration of the policy, each renewed for another year, paying $3,600 in cash. The general ledgers of the three companies reported the following balances at year end, prior to adjustment:

	Company A	Company B	Company C
Prepaid insurance	$ 200	$3,800	$ 300
Insurance expense	3,600	0	3,500

a. Explain how each of the companies accounts for insurance costs.
b. Determine the "correct" amounts that should be reported as "Prepaid insurance" and "insurance expense."
c. Prepare the adjusting entries, if any, that should be made by each of the firms.

6. *Consider the relationship, if any, between revenue earned and cash collected.*

A company holds a note receivable of $100,000 from a customer. Interest is payable each month at a rate of 12 percent per year ($1,000 per month). For each of the following independent situations indicate the amounts that the company should report on its December 31, 1996, financial statements for interest revenue, interest receivable, and unearned interest.

a. The balance in interest receivable as at January 1, 1996, was $2,000. The company collects $12,000 in interest payments.
b. The balance in interest receivable as at January 1, 1996, was $2,000. The company collects $14,000 in interest payments.
c. The balance in interest receivable as at January 1, 1996, was $2,000. The company collects $15,000 in interest payments.
d. The balance in unearned interest (interest paid by the borrower in advance) as at January 1, 1996, was $3,000. The company collects $9,000 in interest payments.
e. The balance in unearned interest as at January 1, 1996, was $3,000. The company collects $8,000 in interest payments.

7. *Costs must be matched with revenues.*

During the first three years of its existence, Bravo Company's manufacturing costs, end-of-year inventories, and sales were as follows:

Year	Manufacturing Costs	End-of-Year Inventories	Sales
1	$80,000	$ 80,000	None
2	90,000	130,000	$ 70,000
3	30,000	None	260,000

Ignoring all other costs and revenues, determine the income of Bravo Company for each of the three years.

8. *The significant economic (and therefore accounting) event is the declaration of a dividend, not the payment. Which event will reduce retained earnings?*

On December 12, 1996, the board of directors of a company declares a dividend of $0.75 per share of common stock. The dividend will be payable on January 18, 1997, to the "shareholders of record" (i.e., to those who owned the stock on a particular date) of January 10, 1997. The company has 100,000 shares of common stock outstanding.

a. Prepare an appropriate journal entry to record the declaration of the dividend on December 13, 1996.

b. Prepare an appropriate closing entry as of December 31, 1996.

c. Prepare an appropriate journal entry to record payment of the dividend on January 18, 1997.

9. *This exercise reviews the basic entries required to account for long-lived assets.*

Prepare journal entries to record the following events:

a. A company purchases two trucks, each for $30,000 cash. The estimated useful life of the trucks is five years, after which they have negligible scrap or resale value.

b. The company records first-year amortization on the trucks.

c. At the beginning of the second year, the company sells one of the trucks for $27,000 cash.

d. The company records second-year amortization on the remaining truck.

e. At the beginning of the third year, the company sells the second truck for $16,000 cash.

10. *Should a dance studio recognize revenue when it signs a contract and collects cash or when it provides its services? Which is the more significant economic event?*

Foxtrot Dance Studio offers customers a "One-Year Learn-to-Dance Special." Customers pay $1,200 at the time they sign a contract and are entitled to four lessons per month for one year.

In November, 10 customers sign contracts and pay "tuition" for the series of lessons. In December, each of the customers takes four lessons.

a. Prepare a journal entry to record the sales of the contracts and the collection of the cash. Assume that revenue is to be recognized only as customers actually take their lessons.

b. Prepare any entries that will be appropriate when the customers take their first four lessons in December. (Ignore expenses incurred in connection with the lessons.)

c. Prepare any *closing* entries that might be necessary on December 31.

d. Suppose that the sales representatives of the firm are entitled to sales commissions based on the dollar amount of contracts signed. From the perspective of a sales manager, which is the more significant economic event—the signing of a contract, the collection of cash, or the providing of lessons? Comment on why different means of recognizing revenues or expenses are appropriate for financial statements that will be used for different purposes (e.g., evaluating the performance of salespeople as opposed to evaluating the performance of the organization as a whole).

11. *Firms do not have to give instantaneous accounting recognition to all economic events (including the passage of time), but prior to preparing financial statements they must bring the books up to date.*

In each of the following independent situations, prepare any necessary journal entries that would be required either to adjust a company's books or to bring them up to date in order to prepare year-end (December 31) financial statements. Assume that closing entries have not yet been made.

a. At the beginning of the year, supplies on hand amounted to $1,000. During the year the company purchased supplies at a cost of $4,200. All purchases of supplies were recorded as increases (debits) to the supplies expense account. A year-end physical count indicated supplies on hand of $800.

b. Employees are paid each Monday for wages earned during the previous week. December 31 falls on a Wednesday. Weekly payroll (for a five-day workweek) is $6,000.

c. As heating oil was purchased it was debited to "fuel expense." At the end of the year, heating oil that had cost $400 was still on hand.

d. On April 1, the company purchased a one-year fire insurance policy at a cost of $3,600 paid in cash. The entire cost of the policy was charged to "insurance expense."

e. The company is on a periodic inventory basis. After taking year-end inventory and making appropriate adjustments to its accounts, it discovered that $400 of inventory was incorrectly omitted from the count.

f. The company is on a periodic inventory basis. After taking year-end inventory and making appropriate adjustments to its accounts, it discovered that goods that had cost $2,000 had just recently been purchased. No accounting recognition, however, had been given to either the purchase or the corresponding liability for payment. (Note that since the adjustment to the accounts resulting from the physical inventory count had already been made, the inventory account is *properly* stated.)

g. The company ran an advertisement in the December 30 edition of the local newspaper. The company has not yet received a bill for the advertisement or given it any other accounting recognition. The cost of the advertisement was $250.

h. The company is on a periodic inventory basis. After taking year-end inventory and making appropriate adjustments to its accounts, it discovered that a purchase of equipment was incorrectly debited to "inventory" rather than to "equipment." The cost of the equipment was $4,200. (The *physical* count was correctly taken; hence the inventory account is correctly stated.)

i. On May 1 the company borrowed $10,000 from a bank. It paid the entire interest for one year ($1,200) in advance at the time it signed the note. The advance payment of interest was properly recorded, but no entries pertaining to the interest have been made since the date of payment.

j. On November 1 customers placed orders for merchandise with a selling price of $19,500. The customers paid in advance, and their payment was properly recorded. The goods were delivered on December

29, but no accounting recognition has been given to the delivery. The company uses a periodic inventory method, and the goods were not included in the December 31 inventory count. (Hence both inventory and cost of goods sold are correctly stated.)

12. *It is important to distinguish between the recording of the financial transaction itself and any adjusting entry that may be required at the end of the accounting period to bring the accounts up-to-date.*

   For each of the following independent situations, prepare *both* the journal entry that would have been recorded at the time of the original transaction and any adjusting entry that may be required to bring the company's books up-to-date at December 31. Be sure to include journal entry explanations with your answer. The first one is done for you.

   a. On January 1 the company purchased a new delivery truck for $48,000 cash. Amortization of capital assets is recorded annually on December 31. The truck has an estimated useful life of six years with no expected salvage value.

   January 1

   Trucks $48,000
       Cash $48,000
   To record purchase of truck

   December 31

   Amortization expense $8,000
       Accumulated amortization—truck $8,000
   To record one year of amortization of the delivery truck

   b. There was $45,000 of merchandise inventory on hand at January 1. During the year the company purchased, for cash, merchandise inventory for $475,000. All purchases of merchandise inventory were added (debited) to the merchandise inventory account. The company uses the periodic inventory method. During the year the company sold, on account, merchandise for $800,000. A physical count at year end revealed merchandise inventory on hand of $90,000.

   c. On January 1, the company purchased a one-year fire insurance policy for $3,600 cash. The purchase price was added (debited) to insurance expense.

   d. During the year the company rented office space at a cost of $3,000 per month. It paid the rent, in cash, for the months of January to November, inclusive. It has not yet given accounting recognition to the unpaid rent at December 31.

   e. On July 1, the company issued $2,000,000 of ten-year 12% bonds payable. Interest is payable annually on June 30.

   f. On December 15, the company received a payment of $6,000 from a customer for services to be rendered in the future. The company added (credited) the receipt to service revenue. At December 31, the company still had not provided the service.

13. *Does choice of accounting method affect total reported earnings over the life of an enterprise?*

   Suppose that a company was organized on January 1, 1996. In each of the next 10 years it had sales of $100,000; the costs of the goods sold were $80,000 per year. In each year, the company collected in cash 75 percent of the sales of that year plus 25 percent of the sales of the previous year. Similarly, in each year the company paid in cash 75 percent of the costs incurred in that year plus 25 percent of the costs incurred in the previous year. The company ceased operations at the end of year 10. It remained in business in year 11 only to collect outstanding receivables and to liquidate remaining debts.

a. Assuming that the company maintained its accounts on an *accrual* basis, compute total income for the 11-year period. Determine income for each of the 11 individual years.

b. Assume instead that the company maintained its accounts on a cash basis (i.e., recognized revenues and expenses as cash was received or disbursed). Determine total income for the 11-year period as well as income for each of the 11 individual years.

14. *The impact of a change from cash to accrual accounting may affect earnings and financial ratios in a manner that is not obvious.*

In the years prior to 1996, Western Insurance Co. accounted for the commissions of its sales staff on a pay-as-you-go basis. Amounts paid to the sales staff as commissions were recorded as expenses in the period in which the cash disbursements were made.

In 1996, however, the company engaged a new firm of auditors. The new firm advised Western Insurance that to comply with generally accepted accounting principles, the company would have to report commissions as expenses in the year in which the salespersons had earned them. At the end of each year, the firm would have to show as a liability the amount of commissions earned in that year but not yet paid. The liability would ordinarily be liquidated in the following year when the commissions were actually paid.

As at both December 31, 1995, and December 31, 1996, the sales staff had earned $10 million in commissions that had not yet been paid. During both 1995 and 1996, the company *paid* salespersons a total of $80 million in commissions.

Western Insurance Co. has loans outstanding from banks and other lending institutions. Included in the debt agreements are two covenants relating to the firm's financial position and activities:

- The company shall not in any year pay dividends in an amount greater than reported earnings for the year.
- The company shall maintain a ratio of total debts to total owners' equity no greater than 1 to 1.

The firm calculated its earnings of 1996—*without* accruing the commissions as required by the new firm of auditors—to be $180 million. It paid dividends of $175 million.

As at December 31, 1996, the total liabilities of the company were $300 million; total shareholders' equity was $318 million. These amounts, like earnings, were computed without taking into account the accruals demanded by the new auditors.

The president of the firm has asked your opinion as to whether the accounting change (to be made retroactive to January 1, 1995) would place the firm in violation of either or both of the debt covenants.

a. What would be the effect of the change on each of the covenants? Explain and show computations.
b. Would the change have any effect on the economic well-being of the firm? Comment.

15. *This problem provides insight into how, in practice, accruals may be reported.*

Footnote 7 of the 1996 annual report of a textbook publisher reads as follows (all amounts in thousands):

Other Accrued Expenses	1996	1995
Payroll, commissions, etc.	$11,960	$11,092
Profit sharing	8,084	7,760
Future service costs on rental contracts receivable	8,001	7,865
Book manufacturing costs	6,237	4,488
Other taxes	2,098	2,222
Miscellaneous	2,795	3,385
Total	$39,175	$36,812

a. In which section of the balance sheet (assets, liabilities, owners' equity) should the accrued expenses be shown?
b. The firm's income statement contains only four lines relating to expenses: cost of goods sold; selling, general, and administrative expenses; interest; and income taxes. How are the accrued expenses most likely reflected in income?
c. There is no explanation in the annual report of the accrual, "Future service costs on rental contracts receivable." Indicate, in very general terms, the nature of this item. Show the entry, without using specific numbers, that the company must have made to record this accrual.

16. *An actual annual report highlights the relationships between accrued liabilities and both dividends and expenses.*

Note 11 of the 1990 financial statements of Potash Corporation of Saskatchewan Inc. is as follows (all dollar amounts are in thousands):

Accounts Payable and Accrued Liabilities

	December 31	
	1990	1989
Trade accounts	$29,133	$28,914
Dividends payable	6,980	6,300
Accrued interest	2,050	2,959
Accrued payroll	4,215	4,486
	$42,378	$42,659

a. The statement of consolidated retained earnings reports that the company *declared* dividends of $26,520 in the year ended December 31, 1990. How much did it actually pay in dividends in the year ended December 31, 1990?

b. Information derived from the income statement and another note reveals that interest expense for the year ended December 31, 1990 was $21,875. How much interest did the firm *pay* in the year ended December 31, 1990?

17. *Many companies charge (debit) an account called "Purchases" for all acquisitions of merchandise inventory (instead of debiting "Merchandise Inventory"). This practice is acceptable but requires that an adjusting entry be made at year end to eliminate the balance in the purchases account.*

Examination of a company's general ledger as at the end of the year reveals the following account balances (both debit balances) pertaining to merchandise inventory:

| Inventory | $120,000 |
| Purchases | 720,000 |

Upon inquiry, you learn that the balance in inventory represents that at the *beginning* of the year. No entries were made to that account during the year. All purchases during the year were debited to "Purchases." You also learn that a physical count at the end of the year revealed goods on hand of $80,000.

What adjusting entry would you propose, assuming that you want to eliminate the balance in the purchases account, to have the inventory account reflect the correct balance of goods on hand at year end, and to have a cost of goods sold account reveal the cost of merchandise sold during the year?

18. *A company can report a profit yet still experience a reduction in cash.*

Comparative balance sheets for House of Clothes, a chain of sportswear shops, for the years 1996 and 1997 are presented in the accompanying table. Also presented is an income statement for 1997. All sales were recorded initially as charge sales. All purchases of merchandise were made "on account."

a. Compute the amount of cash collections made in 1997 as a result of either current (1997) year or prior (1996) year sales. Be sure to relate sales to accounts receivable (that is, accounts receivable, 31/12/96 + 1997 sales – 1997 cash collections = accounts receivable, 31/12/97).

b. Compute the amount of cash disbursed in connection with each of the expenses. Be especially careful in computing cash expended, if any, in connection with purchases of inventory and with amortization. (*Hint:* Compute first the amount of goods actually purchased.) Be sure to relate each expense to a corresponding asset or liability account (e.g., rent expense to prepaid rent; cost of goods sold to inventory.)

c. Does the difference between cash received and cash disbursed equal the difference between cash on hand at the beginning of 1997 and cash on hand at the end? (If not, review your computations.)

d. Comment on why net income cannot be used as a measure of cash received or disbursed.

House of Clothes
Balance Sheet
(in thousands)

		As at		
		31/12/97		31/12/96
Cash		$ 3,800		$ 4,000
Accounts receivable		44,000		28,000
Prepaid rent		—		1,000
Inventory		14,000		17,000
Furniture and fixtures	$20,000		$20,000	
Less: Accumulated amortization	8,000	12,000	4,000	16,000
Total assets		$73,800		$66,000
Accounts payable		$ 4,000		$ 2,000
Accrued salaries payable		1,000		3,500
Accrued interest payable		100		200
Accrued rent payable		2,000		—
Notes payable		4,800		4,800
Common stock		10,000		10,000
Retained earnings		51,900		45,500
Total liabilities and owners' equity		$73,800		$66,000

Income Statement
Year Ended 31/12/97
(in thousands)

Sales		$220,000
Cost of goods sold		130,000
Gross margin		$ 90,000
Other expenses:		
Salaries	$67,000	
Interest	600	
Rent	12,000	
Amortization	4,000	83,600
Net income		$ 6,400

19. *Incorrect journal entries can subsequently be corrected without having to first reverse the original entry.*

As management was about to prepare year-end (December 31) financial statements, the journal entries indicated below, which were made by an inexperienced bookkeeper, came to its attention. You are to make the journal entries that would be required to correct the errors (*Hint:* First determine the entry that should have been made; then determine the most efficient means of eliminating the incorrect, and adding the correct, amounts.)

a. A customer made a payment to reduce the balance in his account.

Cash $5,700	
Sales revenue $5,700	

b. The company sold for $3,000 a machine that had originally cost $6,000 when purchased three years earlier. Accumulated amortization on the asset at the time of sale amounted to $2,000.

Cash $3,000
    Sales revenue $3,000

c. In January the company paid rent for the previous December. Before preparing the year-end financial statements as at the previous December 31, the company had correctly accrued rent for December of that year.

Rent expense $5,000
    Cash $5,000

d. The company charged amortization of one year on equipment that had cost $6,000 and had a useful life of three years with no salvage value.

Accumulated amortization $2,000
    Amortization expense $2,000

e. The company paid a bill received from its advertising agency for an ad that it had run the previous year. The company had properly accounted for the ad at the time it was run.

Advertising expense $6,750
    Cash $6,750

f. The company paid $13,000 to Cooks Flight Service for repairs to its corporate jet. It had given no previous accounting recognition to the repair costs.

Capital assets, airplane $13,000
    Accounts receivable $13,000

20. *The ability to evaluate the effect of errors on the income statement and the balance sheet is persuasive evidence of an understanding of the double-entry bookkeeping system.*

On December 31, at the end of the 1996 annual accounting period, a firm made the errors listed below.

Under the assumption that none of the errors was explicitly discovered and corrected in 1997 but that some of the errors would automatically be corrected if normal accounting procedures were followed, indicate the effect of each error on the financial statements listed in the table below. In each case, indicate the amount of the overstatement or understatement the error would cause in the assets, liabilities, owners' equity, revenues, expenses, and net income. If the error would have no effect on an item, then so state. [The first error (part a) is posted for you as an example in the table below.]

	1996 Income Statement			December 31, 1996 Balance Sheet			1997 Income Statement			December 31, 1997 Balance Sheet		
Error	Revenues	Expense	Net income	Assets	Liabilities	Owners' equity	Revenues	Expense	Net income	Assets	Liabilities	Owners' equity
a.	None	Under $9,000	Over $9,000	None	Under $9,000	Over $9,000	None	Over $9,000	Under $9,000	None	None	None

a. It failed to record $9,000 of accrued salaries. The salaries were paid in 1997.

b. A portion of the company's warehouse was rented on December 1, 1996, at $15,000 per month to a tenant who paid the December and January rents in advance. The firm did not make an adjustment for the unearned rent on December 31, which had been credited on receipt to the "rent revenue" account.

c. Through an oversight, the firm failed to record $214,500 of amortization expense on store equipment. The equipment had a useful life of an additional five years. Amortization expense was properly recorded in 1997 and no equipment was sold in 1997.

d. The firm failed to accrue one-half year's interest on a note receivable. The $1,000 note was received on July 1, 1995, and was due on June 30, 1997. Interest was at the rate of 8 percent per year, payable each year on June 30.

e. The firm made an error in adding the amounts on the year-end inventory sheets, which caused a $8,500 understatement in the merchandise inventory. (Inventory on December 31, 1997 was properly stated.)

f. On January 2, 1996, the company purchased a two-year fire insurance policy for $8,000. It charged the entire amount to "insurance expense." No adjustment was made at December 31.

g. On December 31, 1996, the company declared a dividend of $600,000 payable on January 15, 1997. The bookkeeper failed to record the declaration.

h. The company owned 2,000 shares of Bank of Montreal common stock. On December 20, the company received notification from Nesbitt Burns Inc., the firm's stockbroker, that the Bank of Montreal had declared and paid a dividend of $0.60 per share. Since Nesbitt Burns holds in its own name the shares owned by the company, it credited the company's account for $1,200. The bookkeeper first recorded the dividend in January 1997 when the cash was forwarded to the company.

21. *This problem provides a review of the accounting cycle from unadjusted trial balance to financial statements.*

The following table gives the unadjusted trial balance of the Coronet Company as at December 31, 1997. Other pertinent information is listed below the table.

The Coronet Company Unadjusted Trial Balance As at 31/12/97		
Cash	$ 3,000	
Accounts receivable	5,000	
Merchandise inventory	155,000	
Prepaid rent	1,500	
Furniture and fixtures	15,000	
Accumulated amortization		$ 6,000
Accounts payable		9,000
Notes payable		6,000
Sales revenue		220,000

Selling expenses	55,000	
General expenses	18,200	
Interest expense	600	
Income tax expense	3,500	
Common stock		6,000
Retained earnings		9,800
	$256,800	$256,800

(1) Interest on the note payable, at a rate of 12 percent per annum, is due semiannually, April 30 and October 31.

(2) Estimated useful life of the furniture and fixtures is five years with no salvage value. Amortization for the year has not yet been recorded.

(3) The company employs a periodic inventory system. A physical count at year end indicates merchandise on hand of $42,000.

(4) The company last paid its rent on December 1. Such payment was intended to cover the month of December. (Rent expense is included among "general expenses." The payment was properly recorded.)

(5) On December 31, the board of directors declared a cash dividend, payable January 12, of $4,000.

(6) Advertising costs of $700 were incorrectly charged to "general expenses" rather than "selling expenses."

(7) Estimated income taxes for the year are $8,500. Of these only $3,500 have been paid.

a. Prepare all necessary updating and adjusting entries.

b. Post the entries to T accounts.

c. Prepare a year-end income statement, balance sheet, and statement of retained earnings.

22. *This problem reviews the basic steps in the preparation of a worksheet.*

The end-of-year *unadjusted* trial balance of the Columbia Flying Service is presented on the following page. The accompanying additional information has come to your attention:

(1) Instructor salaries for the last week of December, 1996, have not yet been recorded. They will be payable the first week of the new year. Salaries for the one week are $15,500.

(2) In the course of the last two weeks of December, 1996, lessons were given that had been paid for in advance. The amount charged for the lessons was $16,500. No accounting recognition has yet been given for the service provided.

(3) No amortization has been recorded in 1996. The useful life of the planes is estimated at 10 years (no salvage value) and that of the equipment at 7 years (also no salvage value).

(4) Rent for December, $1,000, has not yet been paid.

(5) The company purchases a one-year insurance policy each year which takes effect on July 1. The entire cost of the current year's policy has been charged to "Insurance expense." The December 31, 1996, balance in "Prepaid insurance" was the same as that on January 1, 1996. No entries to the account have been made during the year.

(6) Interest on the $60,000 note payable outstanding is payable twice each year, April 1 and October 1. The annual rate of interest is 8

```
                    Columbia Flying Service
                    Unadjusted Trial Balance
                    As at December 31, 1996

Cash                                          $    37,500
Accounts receivable                                45,000
Supplies inventory                                  2,000
Parts inventory                                    24,000
Equipment                                          42,000
Equipment, accumulated amortization                            $     6,000
Planes                                            216,000
Planes, accumulated amortization                                    71,000
Prepaid insurance                                  15,000
Accounts payable                                                     8,000
Lessons paid for by customers but not yet given                     28,000
Notes payable                                                       60,000
Common stock                                                        10,000
Retained earnings                                                   78,100
Revenues from lessons                                              895,000
Revenues from charters                                            156,000
Salaries                                          623,000
Fuel expense                                      189,000
Maintenance expense                                51,000
Supplies expense                                    6,000
Insurance expense                                  34,000
Advertising expense                                13,000
Rent expense                                       11,000
Interest expense                                    2,400
Licences and fees                                   1,200
                                              $1,312,100         $1,312,100
```

percent. The note was issued on April 1, 1996; the amount of interest expense represents the first interest payment, which was made on October 1.

(7) A physical count of parts on hand indicated an unexplained shortage of parts that had cost $2,000. An adjustment to parts inventory has not yet been made.

(8) All purchases of supplies are charged (debited) to "Supplies expense." The balance in "Supplies inventory" represents supplies on hand at the beginning of the year. A physical count on December 31, 1996, indicated supplies currently on hand of $4,000.

(9) On December 30, the company flew a charter for which it has not yet billed the customer and which it has not yet recorded in the accounts. The customer will be charged $6,800.

(10) Based on preliminary computations, the firm estimates that income tax expense for the year will be $22,000.

a. Prepare all journal entries that would be necessary to adjust and bring the accounts up to date. (Add any additional account titles that you believe to be necessary.)

b. On a 10-column sheet of accounting paper (or on an electronic spreadsheet), copy the unadjusted trial balance given here. Leave an additional six or seven rows between the last account balance and the totals to accommodate accounts to be added by the adjusting entries. Use two columns for the account titles and two for the unadjusted account balances. Label the next two columns "Adjustments" (debits and credits), the next two "Income statement" (debits and credits), and the last two "Balance sheet" (debits and credits).

c. Instead of posting the journal entries to T accounts, post them to the appropriate accounts in the column "Adjustments." When you have finished posting the entries, sum the two columns and make certain that the totals of debits and credits are equal.

d. Add (or subtract, as required) across the columns, and indicate the total of each account in the appropriate column under the income statement or balance sheet. Take care. Remember that credits have to be subtracted from debits. Make certain that amounts are transferred to the proper column; it is easy to make an error.

e. Add each of the four income statement and balance sheet columns. The difference between the debit and credit columns of the income statement should be the net income for the year. The difference between the debit and credit columns of the balance sheet should also be the income for the year. If the two differences are not equal, then an error has been made. Why shouldn't the balance sheet balance? That is, why shouldn't the debits of the balance sheet equal the credits? Look carefully at the balance indicated for retained earnings. Is the balance the before or after "closing balance"? Does it include income of the current year?

f. From the worksheet, prepare in good form both an income statement and a balance sheet. Remember that retained earnings have to be adjusted to take into account income for the current year.

23. *An electronic spreadsheet helps to make clear the impact of adjusting entries on the income statement, the balance sheet, and key ratios.*

The trial balance of the Silver Creek Sales Company as at December 31, 1996, is presented on the next page. (All dollar amounts are in thousands.) The trial balance was made before the company took into account the following information, which will require the firm to make adjusting entries:

(1) The company miscounted ending inventory. The correct ending inventory was $759 rather than $958.

(2) A review of insurance policies indicated that prepaid insurance should have been $22, not $15. (Insurance expense, like other expenses for which there is no specific account, is included in "other expenses.")

(3) The firm neglected to charge amortization of $12 on certain items of furniture and fixtures.

(4) The firm failed to record $16 of sales. The sales had been made "on account."

(5) The firm pays December salaries of several employees in the first week in January and makes appropriate year-end accrual entries. It incorrectly omitted the wages of one employee, $2, from its accrual entry.

(6) Several customers gave deposits totalling $14 on merchandise which was not in stock. It is the policy of the company to debit cash, and credit advances from customers, upon receiving customer deposits. The company inadvertently credited sales for the deposits.

Silver Creek Sales Company
Trial Balance
As at December 31, 1996
(in thousands)

	Dr.	Cr.
Cash	$ 230	
Accounts receivable	550	
Allowance for doubtful accounts		$ 129
Accrued interest receivable	4	
Merchandise inventory	958	
Prepaid insurance	15	
Furniture and fixtures	368	
Accumulated amortization, furniture and fixtures		90
Note receivable	236	
Accounts payable		190
Sales taxes payable		23
Advances from customers		12
Accrued wages and salaries payable		8
Common stock		500
Retained earnings		1,097
Sales revenue		3,500
Cost of goods sold	2,500	
Wages and salaries	288	
Other expenses	400	
Totals	$5,549	$5,549

a. Using an electronic spreadsheet such as Lotus 1-2-3, set up a worksheet comparable to that illustrated in Exhibit 4-2.
   - Make certain that the amounts in the last four columns (for the income statement and the balance sheet) will be calculated automatically as the amounts per the trial balance, plus or minus the amounts in the appropriate adjustment columns.
   - Include a row to indicate the sums of each of the columns.
   - Do not include a row for "net income." Instead, add a cell beneath the total of the expense column to indicate "income." This cell should be specified as the difference between the sum of the revenues and the sum of the expenses.
   - Specify "retained earnings" in the adjusted balance sheet as the initial balance, plus or minus the adjustments, *plus* the income (per the income cell). In that way, retained earnings will automatically include income for the year and the balance sheet should always be "in balance."

b. Prepare adjusting entries to reflect the information presented above. Post the entries, one at a time, to the adjustment columns of the worksheet. After you post each of the entries, compute and/or note the following:
   - Income
   - Retained earnings
   - The current ratio [Consider as current all assets and liabilities except for furniture and fixtures (net of amortization) and notes receivable.]

- Return on investment (income as a percentage of the sum of common stock and end-of-year retained earnings)

Be sure to use the capabilities of the spreadsheet to compute automatically the current ratio and the return on investment.

24. *The following two problems highlight the relationships among the three basic statements. They demonstrate that, given two of the three statements, the third can be derived.*

Shown are the statements of income and changes in financial position of United General Corp. for 1996. Shown also is the firm's balance sheet as at December 31, 1995.

United General Corp.
Statement of Income for 1996
(in thousands)

Sales	$1,234
Other revenues (from royalties)	40
Total revenues	1,274
Expenses	
Cost of goods sold	757
Selling and administrative expenses	166
Amortization expense	70
Interest expense	13
Income tax expense	126
Total expenses	1,132
Net income	$ 142

Statement of Changes in Financial Position
Year Ended December 31, 1996
(in thousands)

Operating Activities	
Collections from customers	$ 1,507
Collection of royalties	35
Payment of interest	(10)
Payment of selling and administrative costs	(150)
Payment of income taxes	(120)
Payments on account (liquidation of accounts payable)	(810)
Cash provided by operating activities	$ 452
Investing Activities	
Purchase of equipment	(100)
Sale of land (at no gain or loss)	80
Cash used for investing activities	(20)
Financing Activities	
Issuance of bonds	200
Payment of dividends	(50)
Cash provided by financing activities	150
Increase in cash	$ 582

Balance Sheet
As at December 31, 1995
(in thousands)

Assets		
Cash		$ 310
Accounts receivable		481
Merchandise inventory		227
Royalties receivable		3
Prepaid selling and administrative expense		46
Equipment	$450	
Less: Accumulated amortization	130	320
Land		200
Total assets		$1,587
Equities		
Accounts payable (for merchandise inventory only)		$ 80
Interest payable		5
Income taxes payable		9
Common stock		400
Retained earnings		1,093
Total equities		$1,587

Based on the statements provided, prepare the firm's balance sheet as at December 31, 1996. Although there are many approaches that you might take to prepare the balance sheet, one that is recommended is to prepare journal entries that relate each of the elements of the statement of income to one on the statement of changes in financial position. The offsetting debit or credit is likely to represent an addition to or subtraction from a balance sheet account (for example, debit cash, $1,507; credit sales revenue, $1,234; credit accounts receivable, $273).

Take note of the following additional item of information: During 1996 the firm *purchased* merchandise inventory at a cost of $800,000.

25. The following are a firm's statement of changes in financial position for a year and balance sheets for the beginning and end of that year. During the year, the firm purchased merchandise inventory at a cost of $2,400,000.

Statement of Changes in Financial Position
Year Ended December 31, 1996
(in thousands)

Operating Activities	
Collections from customers	$ 4,521
Collection of royalties	105
Payment of interest	(30)
Payment of selling and administrative costs	(450)
Payment of income taxes	(360)
Payments on account (liquidation of accounts payable)	(2,430)
Cash provided by operating activities	$ 1,356
Investing Activities	
Purchase of equipment	(300)
Sale of land (at no gain or loss)	240
Cash used for investing activities	$ (60)

Financing Activities		
Issuance of bonds		600
Payment of dividends		(150)
Cash provided by financing activities		$ 450
Increase in cash		$ 1,746

Balance Sheet
As at December 31
(in thousands)

	1996		1995	
Assets				
Cash		$2,676		$ 930
Accounts receivable		624		1,443
Merchandise inventory		810		681
Royalties receivable		24		9
Prepaid selling and administrative				
expenses		90		138
Equipment	$1,750		$1,450	
Less: Accumulated amortization	600	1,150	390	1,060
Land		260		500
Total assets		$5,634		$4,761
Equities				
Accounts payable (for merchandise				
inventory only)		$ 210		$ 240
Interest payable		24		15
Income taxes payable		45		27
Bonds payable		600		0
Common stock		1,200		1,200
Retained earnings		3,555		3,279
Total equities		$5,634		$4,761

a. Reconstruct, in summary form, the transactions that took place during the year and record them as journal entries. From the information provided in the statements and in the preceding paragraph pertaining to purchases, derive the revenues and expenses for the year. For example, if you know the net change during the year in accounts receivable and the reductions in the account during the year (the collections from customers), it is possible to determine the additions (the sales). Be sure that your entries, taken together, reflect the net change in cash.

b. Prepare an income statement for the year ended December 31, 1996.

26. *The accounting cycle in manufacturing firms is no different from that in other types of enterprises, but it is especially important that period costs be distinguished from product costs.*

The Highbridge Products Co. began operations on January 1, 1996. The following events took place in January:

(1) On January 2 the owners of the company contributed $250,000 in cash to start the business.

(2) The company borrowed $200,000 from the Bank of Montreal. It agreed to make annual interest payments at an annual rate of 12 percent and to repay the loan in its entirety at the end of three years.

(3) The company rented manufacturing and office space. It paid three months' rent in advance. Rent is $4,000 per month.

(4) The company purchased manufacturing equipment at a cost of $35,000 and office furniture and equipment at a cost of $4,800. Both purchases were made on account.

(5) The firm purchased raw materials at a cost of $14,000 cash. Of these, raw materials that cost $12,000 were placed in production (added to "work in process").

(6) The firm hired and paid in cash factory workers, $6,000, and office workers, $1,500. The costs of the factory wages were added to "work in process"; the costs of the office workers were considered to be period costs and thereby charged directly to an expense account.

(7) Factory maintenance costs incurred during the month were $450; factory utility costs were $600. Neither costs have yet been paid. Both were added to work in process.

(8) The company recorded amortization for the month: manufacturing equipment, $1,000; office equipment and furniture, $100. The amortization costs on the manufacturing equipment were added to "work in process"; those on the office equipment and furniture were considered to be period costs and charged directly to an expense account.

(9) The company gave recognition to interest and rent costs for the month (see events 2 and 3 and determine the appropriate charge for one month). Seventy-five percent of the rent costs were allocated to the factory and added to "work in process." The remaining portion of the rent costs, as well as the entire amount of the interest costs, were considered period costs.

(10) The company completed, and transferred from "work in process" to "finished goods inventory," goods that had cost $19,000 to manufacture.

(11) The company sold for $30,000 (on account) goods that had cost $18,000 to manufacture.

(12) Selling and other administrative costs paid in cash were $1,000.

a. Prepare journal entries to reflect the events that took place in January.

b. Post the journal entries to T accounts.

c. Prepare a month-end income statement and balance sheet.

27. *Cost of goods sold combines all costs associated with the manufacture of a product. Convention often determines whether a particular type of cost is associated with the manufacture of a product or with the other activities engaged in by a firm.*

During March a company incurred the following costs, all of which were related directly to the manufacture of its product:

Raw materials	$100,000
Factory labour	200,000
Utility costs for factory	4,000
Amortization on factory equipment	10,000
Rent on factory building	50,000

The company started and completed 10,000 units of product. There was no opening inventory.

a. How much cost should have been added during the month to "work in process"?

b. How much cost should have been transferred to "finished goods"?

c. Assume that the company sold 8,000 units. What amount should it report as "cost of goods sold"? What amount as "finished goods inventory"?

d. Assume that at the end of the month the company discovered that it had failed to record the wages of two secretaries. One was employed in the office of the factory, the other in the office of the marketing department. Each was paid $1,500. Comment on how the omission would affect cost of goods sold and finished goods inventory, assuming 8,000 units were sold in the month.

28. *The effects of classifying a cost as a product rather than a period cost will depend upon the relationship between number of units produced and number of units sold.*

Management of a corporation is uncertain as to whether certain administrative, transportation, and amortization costs should be classified as *product* or *period* costs. Such costs average approximately $120,000 per year. It asks your advice as to the significance over the next two years of its decision. Labour and material costs are estimated at $6 per unit. Selling price of the product is $10 per unit.

a. Suppose that in both year 1 and year 2 the company expects to produce and sell 40,000 units per year. What would be the resultant differences in income, ending inventory, and retained earnings for (or after) each of the two years if the company classified the costs as period rather than product costs?

b. Suppose instead that the company expected in year 1 to produce 40,000 units but sell only 30,000 units and in year 2 to produce 30,000 units and sell 40,000 units. What would be the resultant differences in income, ending inventory, and retained earnings for (or after) each of the two years if the company classified the costs as period rather than product costs?

29. *Under conventional accounting practices, the greater the number of units produced, the less the cost per unit—and the less the reported cost of goods sold.*

The Prettyman Doll Co. requires $2 of raw materials and $4 of factory labour to produce each doll. In addition, the company estimates that amortization costs on the factory building and equipment as well as other *fixed* factory costs total $40,000 per year. ("Fixed" factory costs, although considered product costs, do not vary with number of units produced. They would be the same regardless of whether the company produced 10,000 or 50,000 dolls per year.) Sales price per doll is $10.

a. In both 1996 and 1997 the company produced 20,000 dolls and sold 20,000 dolls. Compute the manufacturing cost per doll. Determine also gross margin (sales less cost of goods sold) for each of the two periods.

b. Assume instead that in 1996 the company produced 30,000 dolls but sold 20,000 dolls; in 1997 the company produced 10,000 dolls and sold 20,000 dolls. Determine the manufacturing cost per doll in each of the two years. Compute the amount that should be reported as "Finished goods inventory" at the end of 1996. Determine also the gross margin for each of the two years.

c. Suppose that the company planned to issue additional capital stock in January 1997. The company controller thought it important that the firm impress potential purchasers with a significant growth in earnings. On the basis of this analysis, what steps might company management have taken in 1996 to give the appearance of improved performance?

30. *This is a challenging exercise that requires an understanding of the flow of costs in a manufacturing operation.*

 The following table gives information taken from the ledger accounts of the Wright Manufacturing Co. The figures reported are the total amounts debited or credited to the various accounts during a year. The figures do *not* represent ending balances and do *not* include beginning balances. Some amounts have been omitted. On the basis of your knowledge of the accounting flows in a manufacturing operation, you are to fill in the missing amounts. That is, you are to determine which accounts are normally associated with debits or credits to other accounts. (For example, by knowing the amount *credited* to accounts payable, you can determine the amount *debited* to raw materials inventory.) No closing entries have yet been made.

	Debits	Credits
Accumulated amortization (factory)	$ 0	$ 17,000
Amortization cost (factory)	?	?
Raw materials inventory	?	95,000
Factory labour cost	107,000	107,000
Work in process	?	?
Finished goods	212,000	?
Cost of goods sold	197,000	0
Factory wages payable	105,000	?
Accounts payable*	85,000	110,000

*Includes only amounts owed in connection with purchases of raw materials.

31. *Corporate performance may be evaluated by relating income to the investment of the owners, which may be expressed in terms of "book" or "market" values.*

 Mr. Sweep Company, a manufacturer of vacuum cleaners, had, as of December 31, $491,091,068 in assets and $263,376,708 in liabilities. Net income for the year was $39,263,333. The common stock of the company, which is traded "over the counter," closed on December 31 at 12¾ . There were 12,114,995 shares of common stock outstanding.
 a. Compute the return on the shareholders' equity (ROI).
 b. Compute the price/earnings ratio. Compute also the reciprocal of the price/earnings ratio (i.e., earnings/price) and express it as a percentage.

32. *Alternative borrowing arrangements have different effects upon the current ratio.*

 The balance sheet of the First Corporation as at December 31, 1996, follows.
 a. Compute the current ratio as at December 31, 1996.
 b. Suppose that the company were to borrow an additional $100,000 and give the bank a six-month note payable. How would that affect the current ratio?
 c. Suppose instead that the company were to borrow $100,000 and give a note payable in full at the end of two years. How would that affect the current ratio?

d. Suppose instead that the company were to issue bonds for $400,000 and use the proceeds to purchase a new plant. How would that affect the current ratio?

First Corporation Balance Sheet
As at December 31, 1996

Assets		Liabilities and Shareholders' Equity	
Current assets		Current liabilities	
Cash	$ 10,000	Accounts payable	$ 30,000
Accounts receivable	20,000	Notes payable	20,000
Note receivable	50,000		
Marketable securities	15,000		$ 50,000
Inventories	5,000		
		Noncurrent liabilities	
	$100,000	Bonds payable	$100,000
Noncurrent assets		Shareholders' equity	
Plant and equipment	$120,000	Common stock	$200,000
Land	70,000	Retained earnings	20,000
Investment in			
subsidiaries	80,000		220,000
	$270,000		
		Total liabilities and	
Total assets	$370,000	shareholders' equity	$370,000

33. *Alternative financing arrangements may have substantially different effects on the accounting equation as well as on earnings per share.*

The following information relates to the Emerson Corp.

Total assets, 31/12/96	$20,000,000
Total liabilities, 31/12/96	4,000,000
Total owners' equity, 31/12/96	16,000,000
Net income 1996	2,000,000
Number of shares of common	
stock outstanding	200,000

a. Determine earnings per share for 1996.
b. The Emerson Corp. is currently negotiating to purchase a new manufacturing facility. The present owners of the plant are asking $4,000,000 for the facility. Emerson Corp. estimates that the increased capacity of the new plant would add $600,000 annually to its income (prior to deducting financing costs). To purchase the plant, it would have to borrow the $4,000,000. It estimates that it could issue long-term bonds at an annual interest rate of 11 percent (i.e., $440,000 per year).
   (1) If the company were to purchase the plant and borrow the necessary funds, what effect would the purchase (excluding effects on earnings) have on "the accounting equation"?
   (2) What effect would it have on earnings per share (assuming that income would otherwise have been the same as in 1996)? Ignore income tax considerations.
c. Assume instead that Emerson is considering an alternative means of purchasing the new plant. Instead of offering the present owners of

the plant $4,000,000 in cash, it would offer them common stock of the Emerson Corp. that has a present market value of $4,000,000. The common stock of the Emerson Corp. is currently being traded on a major stock exchange at $200 per share. The Emerson Corp. would issue 20,000 new shares of common stock. Obviously, the company would no longer have to issue the bonds.

    (1) What effect would the alternative purchase plan have on the accounting equation?

    (2) If you were a present shareholder of Emerson Corp. concerned primarily with earnings per share, would you prefer the original purchase plan or the alternative proposal? Why?

34. *The following three problems require a careful look at a set of financial statements.*

    Summit Industries, Inc., is a diversified international manufacturer and marketer of major home appliances and industrial equipment and machinery. The income statement and balance sheet shown below and on page 188 appeared in the company's 1993 annual report.

  a. Explain, as best you can from the information provided, the reason for the improvement in earnings in 1993 over 1992.

  b. Did each major group of expenses increase in proportion to the increase in sales revenue?

  c. How do you account for the increase in income before extraordinary item by a greater percentage than net income *per common share* before extraordinary item?

  d. What percentage of income (before extraordinary item) was income tax expense in 1993?

Summit Industries, Inc. Statement of Income		
	Year Ended December 31	
	1993	1992
Net sales	$2,010,114,000	$1,655,979,000
Other income, net	9,588,000	9,309,000
	$2,019,702,000	$1,665,288,000
Expenses		
Cost of products sold	1,657,748,000	1,363,339,000
Selling, general and administrative expenses	214,318,000	170,564,000
Interest	31,064,000	30,216,000
	$1,903,130,000	$1,564,119,000
Income before income taxes and extraordinary item	116,572,000	101,169,000
Income taxes	53,650,000	46,651,000
Income before extraordinary item	62,922,000	54,518,000
Extraordinary item	12,783,000	—
Net income	$ 75,705,000	$ 54,518,000
Net income per common share		
Based on average shares outstanding:		
Before extraordinary item	$ 4.87	$ 4.33
Extraordinary item	1.08	—
Net income	$ 5.95	$ 4.33

Summit Industries, Inc.,
Balance Sheets

Assets

	As at December 31	
	1993	1992
Assets		
Current assets		
Cash	$ 18,242,000	$ 20,116,000
Income tax claim receivable	16,061,000	—
Trade receivables (less allowances of $7,615,000 in 1993 and $6,458,000 in 1992)	275,300,000	250,419,000
Inventories	484,386,000	395,149,000
Prepaid expenses and other current assets	3,551,000	3,935,000
Total current assets	$ 797,540,000	$669,619,000
Investments and other assets		
Investments in foreign companies and other assets	9,634,000	8,314,000
Goodwill	17,087,000	17,087,000
	$ 26,721,000	$ 25,401,000
Property, plant and equipment		
Land	11,147,000	11,294,000
Buildings	172,279,000	157,130,000
Machinery and equipment	361,918,000	328,614,000
	$ 545,344,000	$497,038,000
Less: Allowances for amortization	208,500,000	196,918,000
	$ 336,844,000	$300,120,000
Total assets	$1,161,105,000	$995,140,000

Liabilities and equity

	As at December 31	
	1993	1992
Liabilities and equity		
Current liabilities		
Trade accounts payable	$ 143,603,000	$ 92,922,000
Accrued payroll and payroll taxes	38,438,000	31,009,000
Other payables and accruals	137,562,000	111,349,000
Accrued and deferred income taxes	3,941,000	1,555,000
Current maturities of long-term debt and redeemable preferred stock	14,339,000	11,131,000
Total current liabilities	$ 337,883,000	$247,966,000
Long-term debt	272,505,000	252,496,000
Convertible subordinated debentures	5,196,000	47,279,000
Deferred income taxes	20,673,000	18,650,000
Long-term warranties, pensions, and other liabilities	52,736,000	48,961,000
Shareholders' equity:		
Redeemable preferred stock	67,059,000	72,168,000
Common stock, no-par value, 50,000,000 shares authorized Issued 13,696,091 shares at December 31, 1993 and 11,850,660 shares at December 31, 1992	13,696,000	11,850,000
Contributed surplus	139,994,000	99,379,000
Retained earnings	257,492,000	202,520,000
	$ 478,241,000	$385,917,000
Less: Cost of 436,500 shares of common stock in treasury	6,129,000	6,129,000
	$ 472,112,000	$379,788,000
Total liabilities and equity	$1,161,105,000	$995,140,000

e. The extraordinary item represents a gain on disposal of company land that was expropriated by a municipal government. What justification can there be for treating the gain as an "extraordinary item" as opposed to including it in "other income, net"?

35. Refer to the financial statements of Summit Industries, Inc., as presented on pages 187 and 188.
    a. Compare the ability of the company to meet its current obligations as they come due in 1993 with its ability in 1992. Why might the current ratio have declined between December 31, 1993, and 1992, even though reported income was substantially greater in 1993 than in 1992?
    b. Compare the return on the investment of shareholders in 1993 with that in 1992.
    c. Did the firm issue additional shares of common stock in 1993? How can you tell?
    d. Did the firm declare dividends in 1993? What was the probable amount? How can you tell?
    e. Suppose that the price at which the common stock of the firm was traded was $24 on December 31, 1993, and $17 on December 31, 1992. What were the price/earnings ratios (excluding the "extraordinary item") as at those dates? How would the increase in the market price of the shares be reflected in the financial reports of the firm?
    f. Based on number of shares of common stock outstanding and the market price per share ($24) on December 31, 1993, what was the total value of the shares outstanding? What was the total value of the equity of the common shareholders per the firm's balance sheet? Why are the two amounts not the same?
    g. Was the firm more highly "leveraged" in 1993 than in 1992?

36. *The financial statements reveal more data than are reported.*
    Review the financial statements of Summit Industries, Inc. Determine the following for 1993:
    a. Purchases of inventories.
    b. Collections from customers. Assume all sales were on account. Ignore the allowances pertaining to trade receivables.
    c. Gain or loss on sale of equipment. The statement of changes in financial position for the year ended December 31, 1993 indicates the following:

Amortization expense	$27,131,000
Proceeds from sale of property, plant, and equipment	6,746,000
Additions to property, plant, and equipment	67,101,000

    d. Income taxes paid. The obligation for income taxes is reported as both a current and a noncurrent liability.

1. $2,400,000 (12 months × $200,000 per month), regardless of how much cash was actually collected.

2. Unearned rent $200,000
       Rent revenue $200,000
   To recognize rent revenue in January

3. a. $2,400,000 (12 months × $200,000 per month) should have been recognized in rent revenue. Rent revenue is understated by $800,000 ($2,400,000 minus the $1,600,000 of revenue actually recognized).
   b. The balance in "Unearned rent" should be zero: The tenant is no longer "ahead" in rent payments.
   c. The balance in "Rent receivable" should be $400,000. The firm began the year "owing" the tenant $400,000 in services; it earned $2,400,000 and was entitled to $2,000,000 from the tenant. It collected, however, only $1,600,000; it is owed the remaining $400,000.
   d. Unearned rent $400,000
       Rent receivable 400,000
           Rent revenue $800,000
   To adjust the year-end rent accounts

4. $120,000 should be reported as "Cleaning expense" regardless of the amount of cash paid.
   a. $10,000 should be reported as an asset, "Prepaid cleaning costs."
   b. $30,000 should be reported as a liability, "Cleaning costs payable."

5. The reported revenue or expense depends upon the value of the services provided or received, regardless of the amount of cash received or paid. The difference between the value of the services provided or received and the amount of cash received or paid would be added to or subtracted from a related asset or liability account.

5

Measuring and Reporting Revenues

In the previous chapter, we were introduced to the nature of accrual accounting. In this chapter, we focus on the key component of accrual accounting: the issue of revenue recognition. In particular, we will examine the criteria for determining when revenue should be considered to be earned.

After studying this chapter, you will be able to

- Understand the need for periodic financial reporting
- Explain the concept of matching
- Identify the criteria for revenue recognition
- List four points where revenue might be considered to be realized
- Explain the concept of conservatism
- Understand the effect on income of recognizing revenue at various points
- Describe different revenue recognition criteria for specific industries

THE ISSUE IN PERSPECTIVE

The Earnings Process

In the previous chapters it was emphasized that revenues should be *recognized* (given accounting recognition and considered to result in an increase in net assets) when *earned*, not necessarily when the related cash is received. Omitted, however, was a discussion of *when* revenues should be considered to be "earned."

Recall the essence of the definition of revenues:

The inflow of assets into the firm as a result of production or delivery of goods or the rendering of services

In the illustrations up to this point, revenues have been recognized either with the *passage of time* (when earned as rent or interest) or when goods or services have been *delivered*.

Recognition based on passage of time or delivery is appropriate for most, but by no means all, types of revenues. The two sets of circumstances that follow illustrate the issue:

> Company A produces ships under contract to the Department of National Defence. On January 2, 1996, the company signed a contract to produce one vessel at a sales price of $800 million. During 1996 and 1997 the company constructed the ship. In 1998 it delivered the vessel to the government. Cost of production was $600 million.

If the company were to report revenue at the time of sale (when the ship was delivered to the government), then it would report zero revenue in both 1996 and 1997, the years of construction prior to delivery. In 1998, when the ship was delivered, it would report $800 million in revenue. Costs of production would be *capitalized* and remain in asset accounts until charged as an expense in the period in which the revenue was recognized. Hence, ignoring certain *period* costs, the company would report expenses of zero in 1996 and 1997 and of $600 million in 1998. Income would be zero in 1996 and 1997 and $200 million in 1998:

	1996	1997	1998
Construction revenue	$0	$0	$800 million
Cost of ship construction (expense)	0	0	600 million
Income	$0	$0	$200 million

There is nothing to suggest that the performance of the company was, in fact, $200 million better in 1998 than it was in either 1996 or 1997. The company probably exerted its main productive effort evenly through the three-year period. Were revenue to be recognized only at the time of sale, income in the first two years would be understated, while that in the third year would be overstated. The financial statements of neither the first two years nor the third year would serve adequately as a basis for predicting future annual cash flows, one of the principal uses of financial statements. They would, therefore, be of diminished utility to investors and other groups of statement users.

> Company B sells parcels of land in an undeveloped area. Sales representatives use high-pressure sales tactics to get customers to buy. A customer is permitted to make a small down payment (10 percent of the purchase price) and pay the balance over 10 years. The company transfers title to the land to the customer only upon collection of the full sales price. Many customers have second thoughts about the wisdom of their acquisitions and fail to pay the balances on their obligations. When a customer defaults, the company retains title to the land as well as the amounts already paid. But it makes no effort to force further payment. The company has

not been in existence sufficiently long to be able to make reliable estimates of the percentage of sales that will eventually be collected. In 1996 the company made "sales" of $50 million; on these sales, it collected only $12 million in cash. Cost of the land sold was $4 million. Other operating costs were $10 million.

If this company were to report revenues at the time of sale, then on the sales of 1996, it would report revenues of $50 million, cost of land sold (an expense) of $4 million, and other operating expenses of $10. Reported income would be $36 million:

		1996
Sales revenue		$50 million
Expenses		
Cost of land sold	$ 4 million	
Other operating expenses	10 million	14 million
Income		$36 million

As indicated, however, collection of the $38 million balance on the sales ($50 million – $12 million) is problematic. Hence the net worth of the company is most definitely not $36 million greater at the end of the period than at the beginning.

Conservatism dictates that this company delay recognition of revenue until it actually has cash in hand. Recognition of the full amount of a sale at the time a contract is signed would clearly overstate the value of the assets to be received from the transaction. At the same time, there could be little justification for delaying recognition of revenue until the title to the land is delivered to the customer. Once the company has received cash, then it is unquestionably better off. It has no further fiscal obligation to the customer.

On the other hand, many companies make sales on account and have enough experience to estimate what percent of the sale's proceeds will never be collected. As long as allowance is made for the uncollectable portion of the receivable, there is no justification for not recognizing revenue at the time of the sale.

Need for Periodic Reports

The problem of determining when and how much revenue has been earned exists only because managers, investors, and other users of financial information insist on receiving *periodic* reports of income to assist them with their decision making. If they were content to receive a single report of profit or loss *after* the enterprise had completed its operations and was ready to return to shareholders their original investment plus any accumulated earnings, then determination of income would be simple: Subtract from the total amount either available or already distributed to shareholders the amount of their total contributions to the firm. The difference would be income over the life of the enterprise. Indeed, in the sixteenth and seventeenth centuries, companies were frequently formed with an expected useful life of only a few years—perhaps to carry out a specific mission, such as the charter of a ship for a single voyage.

Investors in these companies were satisfied to wait until the companies were liquidated to get reports of their earnings.

Most companies today have indeterminate lives, and both owners and managers demand periodic reports of economic progress. Since many transactions are not completed in the same accounting period in which they are started, accountants are forced to make determinations of when and how much revenue should be assigned to specific periods. The shorter the time period (i.e., one month versus one year), the more important is the question of revenue recognition.

IMPACT UPON RELATED ACCOUNTS

Expenses

The issue of revenue realization does not, of course, have an impact solely upon revenue accounts. Directly affected also are expense accounts and, equally significantly, balance sheet accounts. As pointed out previously, the question of when to recognize *expenses* is inherently tied to that of when *revenues* are recognized.

Costs that *cannot* be associated directly with specific revenues are considered *period* costs. They are charged as expenses in the periods in which they are incurred. For example, it is generally not possible to determine what specific sales resulted directly from a specific advertising campaign. Therefore advertising costs are expensed when incurred.

Costs that *can* be associated directly with specific revenues are *matched* to those revenues and are charged as expenses as the related revenues are recognized. Most commonly, these types of costs are incurred prior to the point at which the revenues are recognized. In a previous chapter, for example, it was indicated that the costs of production in a manufacturing concern are typically incurred before the point of sale. At the point of sale, revenues are recognized and the portion of the costs related to those sales can properly be charged as expenses. Until they are charged as expenses, the costs are stored in asset accounts, such as "raw materials," "work in process," or "finished goods inventory." It should be becoming evident that many expenses are the result of the using up, or consumption, of assets. For example, cost of goods sold is the expense that is recognized when finished goods inventory is used up (i.e., when it is sold).

Many situations also occur, however, in which costs should properly be reported as expenses in a period earlier than that in which they are incurred. Suppose that a company sells and delivers manufacturing equipment. The company guarantees to provide maintenance service on the machines for one year after sale. The cost of providing the maintenance service can be directly associated with the revenue generated by the sale of the equipment. It follows, therefore, that it should be *matched* with the sales revenue and charged as an expense (even if an estimate of the actual cost has to be made) in the same accounting period as that in which the related revenue is recognized. The journal entries required to implement this matching approach will be illustrated later in this chapter.

Discussion of the issues pertaining to expense recognition will be deferred to subsequent chapters when they are addressed in conjunction with the assets to which they relate.

Balance Sheet Accounts

The valuation of assets, liabilities, and owners' equity is also related to the recognition of revenue. Revenue has been defined as an inflow of cash or other assets attributable to the production or delivery of goods or services. When revenues are recognized, so also must the resultant increase in assets or decrease in liabilities. Indeed, recognition of revenues is equivalent to the recognition of an increase of owners' equity (i.e., in retained earnings). An increase of owners' equity must be accompanied by an increase in assets or a decrease in liabilities. Remember the accounting equation, $A = L + OE$.

Exhibit 5-1 illustrates the operating cycle of a typical manufacturing business. The enterprise starts with an asset, generally cash, and continuously transforms it into other assets—first to materials, equipment, and labour and then to work in process, finished goods, accounts receivable, and eventually back to cash. If the company earns a profit, then ending cash is greater than beginning cash (i.e., assets have increased). The critical questions facing the firm are at which point (or points) in the production cycle should the increase in the "size" of the asset package be recognized; at which point is the enterprise "better off" than it was before; which are the *critical events* that trigger recognition of revenues?

EXHIBIT 5-1

Operating Cycle of a Manufacturing Business

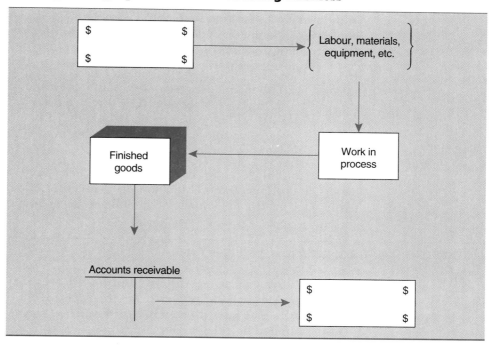

Most commonly, especially in a manufacturing or retail operation, the firm recognizes the increase in the value of the assets at time of sale—when goods or services are delivered to customers. By selecting that point as the critical event, however, it is implicitly ignoring the value of the entire production cycle up to that point. It is asserting that all previous transactions involved nothing more than exchanges of assets and liabilities of equal magnitude—that the level of net assets remained unchanged. It is also implying that all subsequent transactions (e.g., collection of cash, fulfilment of warranty obligations) will also involve nothing more than exchanges of assets and liabilities of equal magnitude and that such exchanges will have no effect on the new level of net assets.

Time of sale is a *convenient* point to recognize revenues for *most* business-es; it is clearly not suitable for some businesses. It is inappropriate in situations in which delivery of goods provides little assurance that the amount owed by the customer will be collectable. It may be equally inappropriate where the enterprise has completed a significant portion of its economic activity and eventual collection of cash from a known customer is certain but the goods have not yet been delivered.

CRITERIA FOR REVENUE RECOGNITION

There are two widely accepted criteria as to when revenues should be recognized. Consistent with these guidelines, the FASB in the United States has issued guidelines as to when revenues should be recognized in numerous specific situations. But they have addressed only a small fraction of all possible transactions. In Canada, the CICA has not addressed the issue of revenue recognition in specific industries to the same extent. Rather, consistent with the standard-setting process in Canada, it has provided the general criteria of revenue recognition and left the specific application to the professional judgment of the accountants. Hence, individual companies and their accountants still must assume responsibility for interpreting and applying the general criteria.

Revenues should be recognized as soon as

1. The firm has exerted a substantial portion of its production and/or sales effort as measured by the proportion of costs already incurred to those expected to be incurred. To be able to do this, the firm must be able to estimate the remaining costs with reasonable reliability and precision.

2. The revenues can be objectively measured, and eventual collection of a substantial portion of cash can reasonably be assured. An estimate can be made of amounts that will be uncollectable.

Rationale for the Criteria

The criteria reflect both the definition of "revenue" and the standards of reporting set forth in Chapter 1. Revenues, by definition, stem from the entire production and sales process in which a firm engages. Ideally, therefore, revenues should be recognized continuously throughout the production and sales process. This would provide the most relevant information. Each step in the production and sales process leaves the firm better off—closer to the ultimate realization of cash. Per the standards, however, accounting information must also be reliable. Except in unusual situations, the benefit to the firm and its owners from the activities in which it engages cannot be determined with reliability until there has been an exchange transaction with outsiders. By virtue of an exchange with outsiders, the value of the consideration to be received by the firm is established. Without an exchange transaction, there can be no assurance that goods intended for sale will actually be sold—and if they can be sold, no assurance of the sales price. Because of their concern for reliability, accountants are exceedingly reluctant to acknowledge increments in asset value without the validation of a transaction with an independent party. Only in unusual circumstances are firms permitted to recognize changes in the values of assets until those assets have been sold. Thus, the issue of revenue recognition is intertwined with the relevance/reliability issue discussed in Chapter 1.

To be sure, an exchange transaction in no way guarantees the eventual realization of anticipated cash. There are any number of reasons why customers will not pay the agreed-upon price for the goods or services purchased. And, at the same time, there are some situations (to be illustrated shortly) in which the consideration to be received can be reliably determined even in the absence of an exchange transaction. Hence the criteria are flexible. They provide that revenues can be recognized as soon as they can be measured objectively. Such time may be either prior or subsequent to the exchange transaction.

Correspondingly, the determination of income requires that costs be matched to revenues. If reported income is to be reliable, then estimates of costs must also be reliable. By requiring that a substantial portion of the costs be incurred before revenue is recognized at any point prior to the completion of a transaction, the guidelines enhance the probability that the amount of revenue recognized will, in fact, ultimately be earned.

Ultimate reliability in the calculation of earnings cannot, of course, be obtained until *all* cash inflows and outflows associated with a transaction have occurred. That point may not be reached, however, until long after the main elements of the transaction have been completed. Were the financial statements not to recognize earnings until then, their relevance—their utility—to most groups of users would be severely diminished. Thus the criteria do not require certainty with respect to costs and revenues. Revenues can be recognized as soon as reliable *estimates* of costs and cash receipts can be made.

SELECTED POINTS OF REVENUE RECOGNITION

The two criteria for revenue recognition may be first satisfied when production begins, when all phases of the transaction are completed, or at any point in between. Four common points (or periods) of revenue recognition are

1. During production

2. At the completion of production

3. At the time of sale

4. At some point after sale and/or delivery of goods, such as upon collection of cash

These four revenue recognition points can be easily seen in the time line in Exhibit 5-2.

EXHIBIT 5-2
Selected Revenue Recognition Points

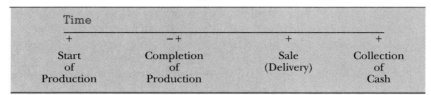

In the first part of this section, we shall provide an overview of these four points. In the second, we shall illustrate the impact on income of using the different revenue recognition points.

Recognition during Production

For some firms, especially those that provide goods or services under long-term contracts, the two criteria of revenue recognition are satisfied as production occurs—prior to point of sale. Recognition of revenue during the entire production process enables firms to avoid the erratic—and often misleading—pattern of income that may result from point of delivery revenue recognition (as was illustrated earlier in the shipbuilding example).

Percentage of Completion Method

A widely used means of recognizing revenue throughout the entire production process is known as the *percentage of completion method*. On any given contract, the proportion of total contract price to be recognized as revenue in each accounting period is the percentage of the total project completed during that period. Percentage completed is usually determined by dividing costs incurred to date by total anticipated costs. If 20 percent of the project is completed in a particular year, then 20 percent of the expected total revenues from the project would be recognized in that year.

The percentage of completion or any other production-oriented means of revenue recognition is appropriate only when total costs of completing the project can be estimated with reasonable reliability and precision, the contract price is fixed and certain to be collected (as is often the case when the contract is with a government department or major corporation), and there can be no question about the ability of the firm to complete the project and to have it accepted by the customer.

Another example of a situation in which revenues could be recognized in the course of production would be that in which a public accounting firm undertakes a large audit engagement. Assuming that the public accounting firm bills its clients on the basis of number of hours of service rendered, then the revenue recognition criteria would be reasonably satisfied as the audit engagement progresses.

Recognition at Completion of Production

When a company is certain as to the price and quantity of its sales, it may recognize revenue at the completion of production.

Suppose, for example, that an electronics supplier contracted with a manufacturer to furnish a specified quantity of custom-designed components at an agreed-upon price. The manufacturer, however, maintains a "just-in-time" manufacturing system. Instead of maintaining a costly inventory of raw materials, it requires its suppliers to deliver their components just in time to be used in the assembly process.

Upon completion of production, the supplier has satisfied the criteria for revenue recognition. It has exerted virtually all of its production and sales efforts; its revenues can be objectively measured and as long as the number of components returned is low and the customer is creditworthy, the eventual collection of cash is reasonably assured.

Recognition at Time of Sale

For most manufacturing and retail concerns, the two criteria of revenue recognition are first satisfied at the point of sale, when the goods are *delivered* to the customer. At that time the firm has exerted a major portion of its economic activity, including its sales efforts. Most of the costs have been incurred, even though there might be additional costs, such as those pertaining to product warranties, guaranteed maintenance, and collection of receivables, that might be incurred in the future. A firm price has been established. Collection of cash can usually be reasonably assured, although the firm may have to estimate and make allowances for merchandise that will be returned and customers who will default on their accounts.

Recognition Subsequent to Sale

A number of circumstances may require that recognition of revenue be delayed until a time subsequent to sale. In some industries firms allow customers unlimited rights of return so that a sale is not final until long after merchandise has been delivered. A book publisher, for example, might permit a retailer to return all unsold copies of a particular title. In other situations, firms may have extensive warranty or other postsale obligations. A computer company, for example, may provide employee training and system-implementation assistance. In these situations, the criteria for revenue recognition may not be satisfied until cash has been collected and/or the postsale obligations fulfilled.

Instalment Basis

In the illustration on page 192, Company B sold parcels of land to customers who frequently elected not to fulfil their payment obligations. Hence the collection of cash could not be reasonably assured, and the revenue from sales could not be objectively measured until cash was actually in hand. Revenues could properly be recognized only as cash was collected—that is, using the instalment basis of accounting.

The cash collection or *instalment* basis of revenue recognition is *not* widely used today to account for routine merchandise sales—not even those in which the customer pays "on time" or on the "instalment plan—since it is generally possible to make reasonable estimates of credit losses. It is, however, used for real estate or other property transactions in which the collectability of the receivable held by the seller is questionable. A builder, for example, might sell a recently constructed shopping centre. The builder accepts from the purchaser a note receivable for a portion of the selling price with the understanding that the purchaser will be able to make the required payments only if the stores in the shopping centre are successfully leased. If there is uncertainty as to whether sufficient space in the shopping centre can be rented to enable the purchaser to make payments on their note, the builder would delay recognition of the sales revenue until cash is actually in hand.

CONSERVATISM

The widely accepted practices of revenue and expense recognition, as well as the corresponding means of asset and liability valuation, are reflective of the accountant's bias toward *conservatism*. Because the concept of conservatism has such a wide-ranging effect on financial reporting, it is important that managers and investors be aware of how it should—and should not—be applied.

Conservatism is widely regarded as one of the pervasive attitudes which underlie financial reports. *Conservatism,* as it relates to accounting, means that it is generally preferable that any possible errors in measurement be in the direction of understatement rather than overstatement of net income and net assets. In matters of doubt, the recognition of favourable events should be delayed and that of unfavourable occurrences should be hastened.

Conservatism has its roots in the uncertainty that pervades all accrual accounting measurements. It has been widely held that the interests of investors and creditors would be more adversely affected by overstatements of assets and profits than by understatements. More harm would accrue to them from an unforeseen or unreported loss than from an unanticipated gain. Moreover, it has sometimes been asserted that corporate managers are inherently optimistic. It is the role of the accountant to contain their optimism and to make certain that it does not spill over onto the company's financial statements.

The convention of conservatism must be applied judiciously. Insofar as accounting measurements are taken from a perspective of pessimism, they may easily be distorted. And to the extent that similar transactions (those which happen to result in gains rather than losses) are accounted for differently, the resultant financial statements may be internally inconsistent.

Moreover, understatement of earnings in one period may lead to overstatement in a subsequent period. It is not uncommon for newly appointed management teams to intentionally delay recognition of revenues to future periods and to charge costs of the future as current expenses. This practice, of course, reduces earnings in the year that the new management group takes over—a poor showing that can be blamed on the previous managers. But it also increases earnings of the future by adding revenues that should properly have been recognized in the past and eliminating expenses that should not have been previously charged. This type of manipulation—including early write-off of a substantial amount of costs previously treated as assets, sometimes referred to as "taking a big bath"—does as much to destroy the credibility of corporations and their accountants as the use of excessively liberal accounting methods.

ANALYSIS OF TRANSACTIONS

The impact of the alternative bases of revenue recognition on revenues and expenses as well as on assets and liabilities can readily be seen when transactions are analyzed, either in journal entry format, or through analysis of the impact on the accounting equation.

The journal entry is an expression of the principles previously set forth. The journal entry process may sometimes appear a bit tricky, but it can be simplified if a few guidelines are kept in mind:

1. In those periods in which revenues are recognized (and *only* in those periods), a revenue account must be credited. Since recognition of revenue implies an enhancement of net assets, a corresponding debit must be made to an asset or liability account.

2. In the periods in which revenues are recognized (and *only* in such periods), an expense account must be debited to give recognition to the related costs. The proportion of total expected costs that is charged as an expense in any particular period would be equal to the proportion of total anticipated revenues that is recognized in that period. Since recognition of expenses implies a reduction in net assets, a corresponding credit must be made to either an asset or a liability account. (This guideline gives effect to the *matching principle,* which holds that expenses must be matched with the revenues with which they can be associated.)

3. In all periods in which revenues are *not* recognized, transactions involve *only* exchanges of assets and liabilities; hence only asset and liability accounts should be debited or credited.

Example 1 below illustrates the journal entry analysis.

Example 1: Recognition of Revenues at Time of Sale—Warranty Obligation Outstanding

In 1996 the Orange Equipment Co. purchases equipment (intended for resale) for $100,000 cash. In 1997 it sells the equipment for $160,000 on account, giving the buyer a one-year warranty against defects. Orange Equipment Co. estimates that its total cost of making repairs under the warranty will be $10,000. In 1998 the company collects the full sales price from the purchaser and incurs $10,000 in repair costs prior to the expiration of the warranty.

1996
(a)

Merchandise inventory (asset +)	$100,000	
Cash (asset −)		$100,000

To record the purchase of the equipment

One asset has been exchanged for another.

1997
(b)

Accounts receivable (asset +)	$160,000	
Sales revenue (revenue +)		$160,000

To record the sale of the equipment

Revenue is recognized at time of sale.

(c)

Cost of goods sold (expense +)	$100,000	
Warranty expense (expense +)	10,000	
Merchandise inventory (asset −)		$100,000
Estimated warranty costs (liability +)		10,000

To record the expenses associated with the revenue recognized

Every expense associated with the revenue must be recognized. The warranty expense charged and the estimated warranty costs credited represent an *estimate* of costs to be incurred in the future. Since these costs can be directly related to the sales revenue, they must be recorded in the same accounting period in which that revenue is recorded. The estimated warranty costs are reported as a liability. They are an obligation to provide future services.

1998
(d)

Cash (asset +)	$160,000	
Accounts receivable (asset −)		$160,000

To record customer payment

One asset has been exchanged for another.

(e)

Estimated warranty costs (liability −)	$10,000	
Cash (asset −)		$10,000

To record costs incurred to fulfil the warranty obligations

The costs incurred to make repairs required under the warranty are *charged* (debited) against the liability that was established at the time the costs were charged as expenses. No additional revenues or expenses are recognized when repairs are actually made. The level of net assets remains the same. If the original estimate of warranty costs proves to be incorrect, then an adjustment can be made as soon as the error becomes known. Thus, if costs were greater than $10,000, the additional amount would be charged as an expense when incurred. If less, then at the expiration of the warranty, the estimated warranty costs account would be debited (decreased) and the warranty expense account credited (decreased) for the difference. The credit to the warranty expense account will have the effect of reducing warranty expenses in a year subsequent to that in which the initial sale was made. No retroactive adjustment is made since, at the time the warranty expense account was debited, it was the best estimate of warranty expense related to sales of that year.

Analysis of the transactions in terms of the accounting equation allows us to determine the effect on revenues, expenses, and net assets of alternative revenue recognition policies, without getting bogged down in the journal entry detail. The journal entries are not difficult, but many new accounts need to be introduced to describe the impact of using the alternative revenue recognition points. To perform the analysis in terms of impact on the accounting equation, the following guidelines need to be observed:

1. In those periods in which revenues are recognized, net assets must increase. The recognition of revenue means that *OE* (Owners' Equity) has increased. Therefore, $A - L$ (net assets) must also increase.

2. In the periods in which revenues are recognized, expenses must be recognized to give recognition to the related costs. The recognition of expenses must be accompanied by a reduction in net assets. This is because the recognition of expenses means that *OE* has decreased. Therefore, $A - L$ (net assets) must also decrease.

3. In all periods in which revenues are not recognized, transactions involve only exchanges of assets and liabilities; hence there is no change in the level of net assets.

Examples 2 and 3 below illustrate the accounting equation analysis of alternative revenue recognition points.

Example 2: Recognition of Revenues at Completion of Production

In 1996 Toronto Instruments Co. receives an order from an electronics manufacturer to provide 10,000 units of a part. The purchaser agrees to pay $10 a unit, but under the terms of the contract Toronto Instruments is to store and retain title to the goods until they are needed by the purchaser. Payment is to be made upon delivery of the goods. Cost of producing the part is $6 per unit. Toronto Instruments elects to recognize revenues upon completion of production.

Toronto Instruments begins production of the parts in 1996 and completes and delivers them in 1997. The following is a summary of the effect on revenues, expenses, and net assets when revenue is recognized at completion of production.

During Production—1996, 1997

As the $60,000 is spent to produce the part, one asset (cash) is being exchanged for another (inventory). No revenue will be recognized and the level of net assets will not change.

Therefore,

Revenue from production	$0
Expenses related to production	0
Income	$0

At Completion of Production—1997

When production is completed, the revenue is recognized. The revenue of $100,000 can only be recognized if there is a corresponding increase in the level of net assets. Therefore, the inventory is increased to its sales price of $100,000 (from the cost of $60,000). As soon as revenue is recognized, the expense must be recognized to give recognition to the related costs. Thus, the $60,000 cost of the inventory is transferred to cost of goods sold. Therefore,

Revenue from production	$100,000
Cost of goods sold (an expense)	60,000
Income	$ 40,000

At Time of Delivery—1997

When the parts are delivered, the asset inventory is converted to another asset, accounts receivable. There is no increase in the level of net assets and therefore, no additional revenue or expense recognized.

At Time of Payment—1997

When payment of $100,000 is received, it is just an exchange of assets. The $100,000 accounts receivable is exchanged for $100,000 cash. Since there is no change in the level of net assets, there is no additional revenue or expense recognized.

Example 3: Recognition of Revenues during Production

The construction of the naval vessel described on page 192 can be used to illustrate the approach to recognizing revenues in which the amount of revenues recognized in any given period depends on the percentage of the entire project completed in that period. A company contracts to build a ship at a price of $800 million. It estimates that total construction costs will be $600 million. In 1996 it begins construction and incurs $120 million in costs; in 1997 it incurs $300 million, and in 1998 it incurs $180 million and completes the project. In 1998, the company collects the full contract price from the government.[1]

---

[1] The example is simplified for purposes of illustration. In practice, the goverment would make periodic cash payments to the contractor during construction of the vessel. The timing of the cash collections, however, would have no impact upon the timing of the revenue recognition.

1996

The company has completed 20 percent of the project (percentage of completion assumed to be equal to the percentage of estimated total costs that have already been incurred). It is therefore appropriate to recognize 20 percent of *both* total revenues and total estimated expenses. Therefore,

Revenues from construction	$160 million	(20% of $800 million)
Expenses related to construction	120 million	
Income	$ 40 million	

Since $40 million of income has been recognized, the level of net assets has to be increased by $40 million. Therefore, the vessel under construction must be carried on the books at a value of $160 million (asset value).

1997

In 1997 an additional 50 percent of construction is completed; hence it is necessary to recognize 50 percent of *both* total revenues and total estimated expenses. Therefore,

Revenues from construction	$400 million	(50% of $800 million)
Expenses related to construction	300 million	
Income	$100 million	

Since $100 million of income has been recognized, the level of net assets has to be increased by $100 million. Therefore, the vessel under construction must be carried on the books at a value of $560 million ($160 million at end of 1996 + $300 million spent in 1997 + $100 million of income recognized in 1997).

1998

In 1998 the remaining 30 percent of construction is completed; hence it is necessary to recognize 30 percent of total revenues and the remainder of the construction expenses. Therefore,

Revenues from construction	$240 million	(30% of $800 million)
Expenses related to construction	180 million	
Income	$ 60 million	

Since $60 million of income has been recognized, the level of net assets has to be increased by $60 million. Therefore, on completion the vessel must be carried on the books at $800 million ($560 million at beginning of year + $180 million spent in 1998 + $60 million of income recognized in 1998).

When the ship is delivered to the government, the $800 million asset (completed vessel) is exchanged for an asset of the same value (accounts receivable). There is no increase in the level of net assets and, hence, no additional revenue or expense is recognized.

When payment is received for the vessel, the $800 million asset (accounts receivable) is exchanged for another asset of the same value, cash. Since there is no increase in the value of net assets, there is no additional revenue or expense recognized.

In summary, over the three years the company has earned income of $200 million and its level of net assets has increased by $200 million (i.e., it spent $600 million to build the vessel and got $800 million in exchange).

Example 4: Recognition of Revenues upon Collection of Cash (the Instalment Basis)

In 1996 a real estate company sells a parcel of land to a developer for $2 million. The original cost of the land to the real estate company was $1.5 million. Under the terms of the sales contract, the seller is to receive 5 percent of the selling price at the time of closing and transfer of title, 60 percent at the end of 1997, and the remaining 35 percent at the end of 1998. Because the ultimate collectability of cash is highly uncertain, the company must recognize revenues only upon actual receipt of cash.[2]

At Time of Sale and Collection of First Payment—1996

Since 5 percent of the sales proceeds have been received in cash, 5 percent of the total revenue should be recognized. Also, for matching purposes, 5 percent of the cost of the land must be recognized as an expense in the same period. Therefore,

Revenue from land sale	$100,000	(5% of $2 million)
Cost of land sold (expense)	75,000	(5% of $1.5 million)
Income	$ 25,000	

There is also a corresponding increase in net assets of $25,000. The $25,000 increase is equal to the $100,000 of cash received less the $75,000 of land assumed to be used up (i.e., sold).

At Time of Collection of Second Payment—1997

Since 60 percent of the sales proceeds have been received in this period, 60 percent of the total revenue should be recognized. Also, for matching purposes, 60 percent of the cost of the land must be recognized as an expense in the same period. Therefore,

Revenue from land sale	$1,200,000	(60% of $2 million)
Cost of land sold (expense)	900,000	(60% of $1.5 million)
Income	$ 300,000	

There is also a corresponding increase in net assets of $300,000. The $300,000 increase is equal to the $1,200,000 of cash received less the $900,000 of land assumed to be used up (i.e., sold).

---

[2] This practice is consistent with Section 402.11.3 of *Recommended Accounting Practices for Real Estate Investment and Development Companies* published by the Canadian Institute of Public Real Estate Companies (CIPREC). CIPREC publishes these recommendations to assist the Canadian real estate investment and development companies in interpreting the generally accepted accounting principles in the *CICA Handbook*.

Since the remaining 35 percent of the sales proceeds have been received in this period, 35 percent of the total revenue should be recognized. Also, for matching purposes, 35 percent of the cost of the land should be recognized as an expense in the same period. Therefore,

Revenue from land sale	$700,000	(35% of $2 million)
Cost of land sold (expense)	525,000	(35% of $1.5 million)
Income	$175,000	

There is also a corresponding increase in net assets of $175,000. The $175,000 increase is equal to the $700,000 of cash received less the $525,000 of land assumed to be used up (i.e., sold).

By the time the final payment has been made, the company will have recorded revenues of $2 million, expenses of $1.5 million, and income of $500,000. It will report on the balance sheet an overall increase in cash of $2,000,000 and a decrease in land of $1.5 million.

REVENUE RECOGNITION—SELECTED INDUSTRY PROBLEMS

The criteria for revenue recognition cannot always be easily applied. The illustrations that follow are designed to demonstrate the difficulties of implementation. To a large extent, decisions as to the timing of revenue recognition are left to the good judgment of corporate managers and their accountants. As a consequence, companies in similar industries or even in the same industry have frequently drawn different conclusions as to the most appropriate basis of revenue recognition.

The rule-making bodies of the accounting profession in the United States—the Financial Accounting Standards Board and the American Institute of Certified Public Accountants—have issued a number of pronouncements and industry audit guides that have done much to narrow the alternatives available to companies in some industries. Nonetheless, differences in practice in other industries are still widespread and are likely to remain so in the foreseeable future. As noted earlier, the CICA in Canada promulgates only the general criteria of revenue recognition and does not attempt to recommend any industry specific standards. The CICA has, however, issued *Accounting Guidelines* from time to time. These guidelines are intended to be interpretations of existing *CICA Handbook* recommendations or opinions on topical areas not currently covered by the recommendations. Two of the current guidelines deal with revenue recognition: franchise fee revenue, which will be covered in Chapter 7, and lending fees, which will be discussed below. It is useful to look at some of the U.S. pronouncements and the lending fees accounting guideline as examples of how the general criteria are applied in practice.

Motion Picture Industry: Program Material for Television

When a motion picture studio produces feature films or other types of programs for television, it does not sell them outright. Instead, it licenses to the broadcasting companies the rights to exhibit the materials over a specified time period.

Over the years, motion picture studios have had diverse practices of revenue recognition on licences of program materials. At least four points or periods of revenue recognition have been used and justified:

1. *Upon signing a licence agreement with a broadcaster.* At that time, an exchange transaction has taken place, and the amount of revenue to be earned is generally known. If the program material has already been produced, the costs are also known; if not, they can generally be estimated.

2. *Upon completion of the program material* (assuming that a licence agreement has already been signed). By now the revenues and costs are known and all significant production efforts have been exerted.

3. *At the start of the licensing period.* The material is transferred to the broadcaster and made available for its use. This point is comparable to the time when merchandise is delivered to the customer in the usual sales transaction.

4. *Over the period in which the licensee has the right to show the material.* The material is produced in order to be shown over a period of time. Recognizing revenues over the licensing period is comparable to recognizing rent over the rental period.

The Financial Accounting Standards Board has ruled in favour of option 3. Revenues should be recognized *at the start of the licence period,* provided, however, that all the following conditions are met:

1. The licence fee for each film is known.

2. The cost of each film is known or can be reasonably determined.

3. Collectability of the full licence fee is reasonably assured.

4. The film has been accepted by the licensee in accordance with conditions of the licence agreement.

5. The film is available for its first showing.[3]

The board took a somewhat different position with respect to motion pictures that are to be shown in theatres rather than on television. The board stipulated that revenue from films shown in theatres should be recognized on the dates of exhibition rather than at the start of the licence period. This applies to licences in which the required payment is a percentage of box office receipts as well as a flat fee. The contractual arrangements between a motion picture producer and both broadcasters and theatre owners obviously have much in common. But the board most likely considered the licence fees to be generated by exhibitions in theatres rather than on television to be more difficult to estimate and less certain of ultimate collection.

Insurance Industry

A property insurance company typically insures property owners against losses from fire, theft, accident, and similar types of casualties. The policies that it

---

[3] "Financial Reporting by Producers and Distributors of Motion Picture Films," Financial Accounting Standards Board *Statement of Financial Accounting Standards No. 53,* 1981.

writes are for a specified duration, often one to three years. Because the period of coverage is fixed, the company knows in advance how much revenue it will earn on each policy. It cannot, of course, determine the costs associated with a policy until the expiration of the policy and upon settlement of all claims. But based on its own experience, or that of other firms in the industry, it can usually make reliable estimates of the total losses that it will be required to cover.

A life insurance company, by contrast, may provide coverage for an indeterminate period (i.e., the life of the policyholder). It typically engages in a broader range of functions than the property company. Sales activities tend to be relatively more important, and many types of life insurance policies require the company to provide savings and investment services in addition to insurance coverage. The period over which the policyholder pays premiums may not be known with certainty when the policy is written since it may be for her or his entire life or such an extended period that there is considerable risk that the insured will either not survive for the full payment period or cancel the policy prior to dying. Moreover, the company may be obligated to provide both insurance coverage and related services for many years beyond the period during which the policyholder is liable for premiums. Nevertheless, both revenues and claims can be estimated on the basis of actuarial experience.

There are several bases for revenue recognition that can be justified and have, in fact, been used within the industry. Revenue may be recognized

1. Evenly throughout the known or estimated period of coverage. This basis is rooted in the assumption that the primary activity of the company is insurance coverage. The company provides the coverage uniformly over the life of a policy and therefore should recognize revenues over its life.

2. In part when the policy is written, in part evenly over the life of the policy. This basis gives recognition both to the service provided in the insurance coverage itself and to the substantial efforts incurred by a company in selling and writing a policy. These efforts may include sales and advertising, investigations, medical examinations, and initial clerical costs.

3. As premiums are due from policyholders. This basis takes into account the uncertainties involved in determining total revenues to be generated. For policies on which the premiums are paid throughout the policy period, the basis provides a reasonable match of revenues recognized and services provided.

In 1982, to reduce diversity of practice, the FASB ruled that revenue on *short-duration* policies, such as those for property coverage, should be recognized *evenly over the period for which the insurance protection is provided*. For *long-duration* policies, such as those for life insurance, revenue should be recognized *as the premiums are due from policyholders*. For both types of policies, estimates of costs, including anticipated claims, must be made and charged as expense in proportion to the revenues recognized.[4]

---

[4] "Accounting and Reporting by Insurance Enterprises," Financial Accounting Standards Board *Statement of Financial Accounting Standards No. 60*, 1982.

The different approaches taken by the FASB toward the two types of motion picture licences and toward insurance coverage illustrate the difficulties of establishing specific rules of revenue recognition for firms in the same industry, let alone for all firms. Seemingly subtle differences in the types of products sold or services provided may justify significant differences in the basis of revenue recognition.

Lending Fees

When a financial institution makes a loan, it often charges an *origination fee*. This fee is typically expressed in *points*. Each "point" is equal to 1 percent of the amount of the loan. For example, a fee of three points on a loan of $1 million would be 3 percent of $1 million, or $30,000. The fee is generally paid by the borrower at the time the loan is made and is in addition to the usual interest that will be charged over the term of the loan.

To most lenders and borrowers the fee is a form of additional interest. It compensates the lender both for using its funds and for making and administering the loan. Financial institutions charge points, rather than incorporate all compensation into the interest rate, for a number of reasons. One is that many borrowers like to be charged the *prime lending rate*—that charged to the most creditworthy customers—even though they may not qualify for it. By charging points, the financial institution can quote the prime rate but receive total compensation that reflects the borrower's actual credit status. Another is that the fee actually raises the real interest rate because the amount loaned is not the face amount of the loan but the face amount *less* the amount of the origination fee. The actual interest earned by the lender is the difference between the amount actually placed at the disposal of the borrower at the beginning of the period and the amount that the borrower must repay at the end of the period.

The issue of revenue recognition that is controversial is whether points should be recorded as revenue when they are received or over the term of the loan. Prior to the applicable CICA Accounting Guideline, many financial institutions recognized the revenue when the points were paid—that is, "up front." The CICA, however, is of the opinion that, in economic substance, loan origination fees are just another form of interest and should therefore be recognized as revenue over the term of the loan.[5]

Summary

Revenues should be realized when earned; costs should be charged as expenses at the time the revenues to which they are related are realized. This chapter has addressed the question of *when* revenues should be considered to be earned. We have not attempted to provide answers; indeed, there are no definitive answers. Instead, we have explored the nature of the problems and set forth general guidelines for their resolution.

[5] "Fees and Costs Associated with Lending Activities," *CICA Handbook*, Accounting Guideline, 1987.

Revenues are commonly *recognized* (considered to result in an increase in net assets) at time of sale. They may also be recognized, however, during the process of production, at the completion of the process, or upon events subsequent to the sale. As a rule, revenues should be recognized as soon as

1. The firm has exerted a substantial portion of its production and/or sales effort as measured by the proportion of costs already incurred to those expected to be incurred. To do this, the firm must be able to estimate the remaining costs with reasonable reliability and precision.

2. The revenues can be objectively measured and eventual collection of a substantial portion of cash can reasonably be assured. An estimate can be made of amounts that will be uncollectable.

We have tried to show some of the difficulties of applying these two criteria of revenue recognition by describing issues that have arisen in three specific industries. The issues are not of the type that can be resolved by methods that would be appropriate in the sciences. At best, a "resolution"—such as an edict by a rule-making authority—can represent a compromise among competing accounting standards and objectives or an arbitrary choice made in the interests of comparability among firms.

Specific issues of asset and liability valuation (and, necessarily, expense recognition) will be addressed in Chapters 6 through 10.

Exercise for Review and Self-Testing

Surfside Construction Co. contracts with the city of Vancouver to construct five municipal swimming pools. Contract price is $1 million ($200,000 per pool); estimated total cost of construction is $800,000 ($160,000 per pool). The contract requires that the pools be turned over to the city when all five have been completed and that payment be made at that time.

Surfside elects to recognize revenues on the basis of number of units completed.

1. In 1996 Surfside incurs $500,000 in construction costs and completes two pools. The cost of each of the completed pools was as estimated, $160,000.
   a. Prepare an income statement for 1996 that reflects the recognition of revenue on the basis of the number of units completed.
   b. At what value will Surfside Construction Co. carry its inventory of swimming pools at December 31, 1996?

2. In 1997 Surfside incurs the $300,000 in estimated additional costs and completes the remaining three pools.
   a. Prepare an income statement for 1997 that reflects the recognition of revenue on the basis of the number of units completed.
   b. Would the receipt of periodic progress payments from the City of Vancouver have any impact on the revenue recognition pattern?

1. Over the life of an enterprise, it matters little on what bases revenues and expenses are recognized; it is only because investors and others demand periodic reports of performance that problems of revenue and expense recognition arise. Do you agree? Explain.

2. "If financial statements are to be objective, then it is inappropriate to recognize revenues on a transaction until the seller has cash in hand; recognition of revenues at any point prior to collection of cash necessarily involves estimates of the amount of cash that will actually be collected." Do you agree? Explain.

3. What are the two criteria as to when revenues should be recognized? What is the rationale behind each of them?

4. The question of revenue and expense recognition is inherently intertwined with that of asset and liability valuation. Explain.

5. Accounting statements are said to be "conservative." What is meant by conservatism as the concept is applied to financial reports? How does the accountant justify being conservative? What problems might such conservatism create?

6. The FASB has ruled that premiums from insurance policies of short duration, such as those on property, should be accounted for differently from premiums for policies of long-term duration, such as those on lives. What is the position of the FASB as to revenues from insurance premiums, and why should length of policy be a characteristic that justifies different bases of revenue recognition?

7. The Evergreen Forest Co. raises trees intended for sale as Christmas trees. Trees are sold approximately five years after they have been planted. What special problems of income determination does the company face if it is to prepare annual financial statements?

8. A greeting card company produces cards for the various holidays and commemorative occasions throughout the year. The cards are perishable; if they are not sold by the day for which they are intended, it is not feasible to save them until the next year. For cards to be sold to consumers, they must be displayed at retail outlets. Due to the risk that they will not be sold, merchants are understandably reluctant to carry a large inventory of cards. To reduce merchants' risk, the greeting card company has agreed to repurchase all cards that remain unsold by the occasion for which they are intended at the full price paid by the merchant. The company estimates that 20 percent of all cards shipped to merchants will eventually be returned. On what basis do you think the company should recognize revenues? Would your response be different if 50 percent were to be returned?

9. A consumer finance company makes instalment loans of small amounts (up to $10,000) to individuals. The loans are for periods up to 36 months. The company faces intense competition from other firms in the industry

and directs considerable resources to advertising and other sales efforts. When a customer applies for a loan, the company incurs substantial costs in conducting credit investigations and in completing the necessary clerical work to initiate the loan. Customers are charged interest on the outstanding balances of their loans. Although the rate of default on loans is low, many customers do not pay their instalments on time. Collection costs are high. The company presently recognizes as revenue 20 percent of the expected total interest from a loan at the time it makes the loan. Thereafter it recognizes interest revenue on a cash collection basis. A portion of each payment made by the customer is considered to be for interest. Conventionally, interest revenue (or, correspondingly, interest expense) is recognized uniformly over the period of a loan in proportion to the loan balance outstanding. How can this company justify recognizing as revenue 20 percent of estimated total interest at the time it first makes a loan and the balance only as cash is collected?

10. The following statement of accounting policy was included in an annual report of Santa Fe Industries:

> Revenues from rail operations are recognized in income upon completion of service. Expenses relating to shipments for which service has not been completed are charged to income and not deferred.

Why might such policy be considered objectionable? What "principle" does it violate? How do you suspect the controller of Santa Fe Industries would defend the policy?

Problems

1. *This problem compares the effects of alternative bases of revenue recognition on earnings of a particular period as well as on earnings over the life of a project.*

   The Anderson Construction Company agreed to construct six playgrounds for the city of Waterloo. Total contract price was $2.0 million. Total estimated costs were $1,600,000.

   The following schedule indicates for the three-year period during which construction took place the number of units completed, the actual costs incurred, and the amounts of cash received from the City of Waterloo.

	Year		
	1	2	3
Units completed	1	2	3
Costs incurred	$800,000	$480,000	$ 320,000
Cash collected	400,000	600,000	1,000,000

a. Determine revenues, expenses, and income for each of the three years under each of the following alternatives:

   (1) Revenues recognized on the basis of the percentage of the project completed (Percentage of costs incurred indicates degree of completion.)

(2) Revenues recognized as soon as each playground is completed

(3) Revenues recognized upon the collection of cash

b. Are total earnings the same over the life of the project? Why?

2. *When should the liability and expense associated with interest and loan origination fees be charged?*

On December 31, 1997, a bank loans a customer $100,000. The term of the loan is two years and it cannot be prepaid. Interest, at a simple rate of 10 percent per annum, is payable in full at the time the loan matures. Thus, at the end of two years, the customer will be required to pay $100,000 (the amount borrowed) plus $20,000 interest—a total of $120,000. The customer is a sound credit risk. There is little question about its ability to make the required payments.

a. At what amount should the receivable be recorded on a balance sheet of the bank as at December 31, 1997? Justify your response in light of the bank's legally enforceable claim against the customer for $120,000.

b. Suppose that the bank charges the company a loan origination fee of two points (2 percent of the amount loaned). The fee of $2,000 is paid by the customer on December 31, 1997. What is the amount of revenue on the origination fee that the bank should recognize in 1997? Justify your response, indicating specifically any assumptions that you might make as to the economic substance of the fee.

3. *Under the percentage of completion method, the percentage of total estimated costs recognized as expenses in each year must equal the percentage of total contract value recognized as revenues.*

On January 3, 1997, Eastern Electric Co. contracted with United Power Company to produce generating equipment. Estimated cost of the equipment was $4.8 million; contract price was $5.6 million. Eastern Electric recognizes revenues on such contracts on a percentage of completion basis.

In 1997 Eastern Electric incurred $3.6 million in costs on the project; in 1998 it incurred the remaining $1,200,000. In 1997 it received from United Power $1,600,000 in cash (which may be accounted for as an advance payment), and in 1998 it received the remaining $4 million.

a. Prepare a journal entry to recognize the costs incurred (added to work in process) in 1997. Assume that they were paid in cash.

b. Determine the percentage of revenues and expenses that should be recognized in 1997.

c. How much income will be recognized in 1997?

d. Prepare a journal entry to recognize the cash collected in 1997.

e. How much income will be recognized in 1998?

4. *The journal entries associated with the percentage of completion method highlight the relationships among revenue recognition, expense recognition, and asset valuation.*

The Moshulu Construction Co. contracts with the Pelham Corporation to construct an office building. The contract price is $50 million. The Moshulu Co. estimates that the building will cost $40 million and will take three years to complete. The contract calls for the Pelham Corporation to make cash advances of $10 million during each of the first two years of construction and to make a final payment of $30 million upon completion of the building; these cash advances are to be accounted for on the books of Moshulu Co. as a liability until the project is completed.

The company elects to recognize revenues on the percentage of completion basis. At the end of 1996 and 1997, the company still estimates total construction costs at $40 million. Actual expenditures over the three-year period are as follows:

1996	$10,000,000
1997	25,000,000
1998	7,000,000

Prepare an income statement and a balance sheet for each of the three years. Assume that at the start of the project the only asset of the company is cash of $20 million.

5. *It is sometimes necessary to recognize costs as expenses before they have actually been incurred.*

On December 31, 1996, the Valentine Roofing Co. reported among its liabilities the following balance:

Estimated costs to fulfil roof guarantees $40,000

During 1997 Valentine constructed roofs for which it billed customers $3 million. It estimates that, on average, it incurs repair costs, under its two-year guarantee, of 2 percent of the initial contract price of its roofs. In 1997 the company actually incurred repair costs of $65,000, which were applicable to roofs constructed both in 1997 and in prior years.

a. Analyze both the liability and expense accounts pertaining to roof repairs in journal entry and T account format for the year 1997.

b. How can a company justify charging repair expenses before the costs are actually incurred, based only on an estimate of what actual costs will be?

6. *Costs of fulfilling warranty obligations must be matched to the revenues with which they are associated.*

In 1996 the Gerard Company sold for cash 20 printing presses at a price of $200,000 each. The presses cost $160,000 to manufacture. The company guaranteed each press for a period of two years starting from the date of sale. The company estimated that the costs of making repairs as required by the guarantee would be approximately 2 percent of sales.

Actual expenditures for repairs of presses sold in 1996 were as follows: 1996, $28,000; 1997, $38,000; 1998, $24,000.

Prepare journal entries to record the sale of the presses and the subsequent repair costs.

7. *The differences between a warranty and a service contract may not be great, yet they may be sufficient to justify different bases of revenue and expense recognition.*

  a. Copco manufactures and sells office equipment. Its copy machine sells for $18,000. The selling price includes a three-year warranty. The company estimates that, on average, it will have to make one service call per month over the warranty period. A service call costs the company $50. The cost to manufacture the machine is $12,000.

  On June 30, the company sells one machine (for cash). On July 15 it makes its first service call on that machine. The cost of the call is paid in cash. During August Copco does not make a service call.

  Prepare the required journal entries for June, July, and August.

  b. Copco sells its mail machine for $18,000. The selling price also includes a three-year service contract. However, the company estimates that it will have to make *four* service calls per month at a cost of $50 each. The mail machine costs only $7,200 to manufacture. The company also sells both the mail machine and the service contract separate from each other. However, the price of the two together is slightly less than each independently.

  On June 30 Copco sells one machine for cash. During July the company makes four service calls on that machine. During August it is not required to make any service calls.

  Prepare the required journal entries for June, July, and August. State any assumptions that you might make. (Use your best judgment; several possible sets of entries would be equally defensible.)

  c. Justify your bases of revenue recognition and, if appropriate, explain any difference in the ways you accounted for the two Copco machines. Also explain how and why you allocated expenses as you did.

8. *Under the completion of production method, as with other methods, expenses are matched with revenues.*

  Lawncare, Inc., sells to Jaymart Stores lawn mowers that are specially manufactured for sale under a Jaymart brand name. A recent contract requires Lawncare to produce and deliver to Jaymart 1,000 mowers at a price of $300 per unit. Lawncare estimates that its manufacturing costs will be $200 per unit.

  a. Lawncare recognizes revenues and expenses on a completion of production basis inasmuch as sale and collection are assured when production is completed. Compute income for the month in which the following occur.

    (1) In a particular month Lawncare incurs $180,000 in production costs, all of which are added to work in process. All costs are paid in cash.

    (2) It completes 400 units and transfers them to finished goods inventory. The costs of the finished mowers were as estimated, $200 each. Lawncare gives accounting recognition to the associated revenues, expenses, and increase in the carrying value of the inventory.

    (3) It delivers to Jaymart 300 mowers and bills Jaymart for the items delivered.

  b. Lawncare also manufacturers lawn mowers under its own brand name for sale to department stores and lawn specialty shops. Sales to these stores are not made under any special contractual arrangements. Goods are shipped as ordered. Do you think that Lawncare should use the completion of production method to recognize revenues on these sales? Would the firm be consistent if it used another method?

9. *On what basis should a manufacturer of custom products recognize revenues?*

The Harrison Co. manufactures video display monitors for sale to Save-More Discount Stores. Save-More sell the units under its own brand name. In 1996 Harrison Co. signed a contract to deliver Save-More 40,000 units at a price of $120 per unit over the next three years. By the end of 1996 Harrison had not yet delivered any units to Save-More but had 20,000 units 80 percent complete. In 1997 Harrison completed and delivered to Save-More 33,000 units—the 20,000 units started in the previous year plus 13,000 units started in 1997. In 1998 Harrison completed and delivered the remaining 7,000 units.

Each unit cost Harrison $80 to manufacture. As agreed upon in the contract, Save-More made cash payments of $1.6 million to Harrison in each of the three years.

a. Determine revenues, expenses, and income for each of the three years if revenue were to be recognized (1) in the course of production, (2) at time of delivery, (3) at time of cash collection. Are total revenues, expenses, and income (for all three years combined) the same under each of the three methods?

b. Which basis of revenue recognition do you think results in the most reliable and relevant determination of corporate performance?

10. *The impact of alternative accounting practices on income as well as retained earnings (and thus on assets and liabilities) must be evaluated.*

Kitchener Construction Co. begins operations in 1996. The company constructs bridges. Each bridge takes three years to complete, and construction is spread evenly over the three-year period. The contract price of each bridge is $3 million. In the period between 1996 and 2000 the firm begins construction of one bridge at the start of each year. Each bridge is started on January 1 and is completed after three years; for example, the bridge started on January 1, 1996, is completed on December 31, 1998.

a. Assume that the firm recognizes revenues only upon the completion of a bridge. Determine annual revenues for the period 1998 to 2000.

b. Assume that the firm recognizes revenue on a percentage of completion basis (one-third of the revenue on each bridge is recognized each year). Determine annual revenues for the period 1998 to 2000.

c. Is there a difference in reported revenues?

d. Determine the balance in retained earnings that the firm would report at the end of 2000 under each of the two methods. Be sure to take into account any revenues that would have been recognized in 1996 and 1997. Assume that no dividends have been declared; ignore expenses related to the revenues.

e. Suppose that starting in 2001 the firm begins construction on two bridges each year. Determine annual revenues for the years 2001 to 2003 under each of the two methods of revenue recognition.

f. Under what circumstances does choice of accounting method have an impact upon reported revenues?

11. *The effect on income of using a convenient, but theoretically unacceptable, method of accounting may be immaterial; the effect on assets and retained earnings may be substantially greater.*

Midwest Energy Company does not recognize revenues at the time it delivers electricity to customers. Instead, it recognizes revenues as it bills its customers for the electricity used. The company ordinarily bills customers on the fifteenth of each month for electricity that they used in the previous month.

As of December 31, 1996, the company had delivered electricity for which it would bill customers on January 15, 1997, for $86 million. As of December 31, 1997, the company had delivered electricity for which it would bill customers, on January 15, 1998, for $90 million.

In response to a suggestion by its auditors that the company adjust its books at the end of each year to take into account the unbilled revenues, the company controller argued that the adjustments would have but an "immaterial" impact on the financial statements. In 1997 the company had revenues of $1.1 billion and income before taxes of $140 million. The company reported current assets of $170 million and retained earnings of $830 million at December 31, 1997.

Suppose that the company consistently followed the practice of recognizing revenues in the year in which electricity was delivered rather than that in which it was billed.

a. Compute the impact of the alternative procedure, in both absolute and percentage amounts, on revenues and profits of 1997 (ignore income taxes).

b. Compute the impact on current assets and retained earnings at the end of 1997.

c. Prepare any journal entries necessary to adjust the accounts on December 31, 1997, so that revenues are recognized at the time electricity is delivered rather than when it is billed.

12. *If revenues from the sale of an asset are to be associated with the collection of cash, so too must the cost of the asset sold.*

Land Developers, Inc., sells a parcel of land for $250,000. Terms of the contract require that the buyer make a down payment of $50,000 at the time the agreement is signed and pay the remaining balance in two instalments at the end of each of the next two years. In addition, the contract requires the buyer to pay interest at a rate of 10 percent on the balance outstanding at the time of each of the two instalment payments.

Land Developers, Inc., had purchased the land for $150,000.

Determine the revenues and expenses that the company should report upon each of the cash collections, assuming that it elects to recognize revenues on an instalment (cash collection) basis.

13. *On what basis should revenues from membership fees be recognized?*

The Beautiful Person Health Club charges members an annual $240 membership fee. The fee, which is payable in advance, entitles the member to visit the club as many times as he or she wishes.

Selected membership data for the three-month period January to March 1997 are indicated in the table following:

	Jan.	Feb.	March
Number of new memberships sold	200	300	100
Number of renewals	500	200	100
Number of expirations (including members who renewed)	500	400	100
Total number of active members at end of month	6,000	6,100	6,200

Members who renew their contracts must also pay the $240 annual fee in advance of their membership year.

Monthly costs of operating the health facilities are approximately as follows:

Rent	$ 10,000
Salaries	50,000
Advertising and promotion	30,000
Depreciation and other operating costs	15,000
	$105,000

The company controller and its external auditor disagree over the basis on which revenues should be recognized. The auditor argues that since members can use the facilities over a 12-month period, revenues from each member should be spread over a 12-month period (i.e., $20 per month per member). The controller, on the other hand, asserts that the entire membership fee should be recognized in the month the member either joins or renews. A major portion of the corporate effort, he argues, is exerted *before* and *at* the time a new member actually joins the club. He points out that the company spends over $30,000 per month in direct advertising and promotion costs, and, in addition, a significant portion of the time of several club employees (whose salaries are included in the $50,000 of salary costs) is directed to promoting new memberships and processing both new applications and renewals.

a. Determine, for the three-month period for which data are provided, the monthly income that would result from adopting each of the two positions.
b. Which position do you favour for external financial reporting purposes?
c. Is a compromise between the two positions possible? Would such a compromise be consistent with what you believe to be sound principles of financial reporting?
d. Suppose that you were the president of the Club. Why might you prefer to receive internal reports that reflect as revenue the full amount of a membership fee in the month that the member either joins or renews?

14. *Changing conditions require changes in accounting practices.*

The following statement appeared in the footnotes to the financial statements of Macmillan Publishing Company, Inc.

> During the year, the Company changed its definition of the unit of sale for the domestic home-study business from the entire contract amount to each individual cash payment, which is generally made when the lesson is delivered.

Changing industry regulations affecting refund and cancellation policies and changing patterns of payment were proving to have such unpredictable effects on ultimate contract collectability that the continued use of prior historical patterns to establish allowances for cancellations and doubtful accounts could have caused serious distortions in the matching of revenues and expenses.

a. Which of the two definitions of unit of sale would result in the more "conservative" practice of revenue recognition?

b. Assume that in a particular month a customer contracts to take a home-study course consisting of 30 lessons. Total contract price for the entire course is $900. The customer remits $30 for the first lesson.

(1) If the unit of sale is considered to be the entire contract and the entire amount of revenue is to be recognized at time of sale, prepare one entry to recognize the signing of the contract and another to recognize the delivery of the first lesson and the collection of cash. Ignore the costs applicable to the revenues.

(2) If the unit of sale is considered to be each individual cash payment, prepare an entry to recognize the delivery of the first lesson and the collection of cash. Is it necessary to record the signing of the contract?

15. *On what basis should revenue from the sale of home-study courses be recognized?*

Computer Learning, Inc., develops and sells home-study courses on the use of Worksheet I, a sophisticated spreadsheet program. Each course consists of 10 lessons on computer disks with an accompanying manual. The manual and one disk are mailed to a student upon registration for the course. Thereafter one lesson is shipped to a student every two weeks over a period of approximately five months. After completing the program, the student takes an examination and, if successful, is awarded a certificate.

In 1996 the company developed the course at a cost of $120,000. The development costs were charged to expense accounts as incurred.

The cost of duplicating the manual is $10 per unit. That of copying a disk is $3 per unit ($30 for the set of 10). These costs are incurred as the materials are needed. The cost of administering the exam is $20 per course. Hence the cost per course, excluding development costs, is $60. (Shipping costs are immaterial.)

The price of the course is $400, payable as follows:

$120 when the student registers for the course and receives the manual and first disk
$180 ($20 every two weeks) as the student receives the remaining nine lessons
$100 when the student takes the examination

The company estimated that it would sell 500 courses and that all 500 students would complete the course.

In 1997 the company sold 100 courses. It shipped 100 manuals and lesson 1 disks and a total of 400 additional disks. It collected the entire amount due on the materials shipped (a total of $20,000).

The company is undecided as to a proper basis of revenue recognition.

a. Suppose the company recognized all revenue from the course when a student registered for the course.

(1) How much revenue should it recognize in 1997? Justify this basis of revenue recognition.

(2) How much in expenses should it charge in 1997? Justify your response.

b. Suppose, alternatively, the company recognized 10 percent of total anticipated revenue each time it shipped a lesson.

    (1) How much revenue should it recognize in 1997? Justify this basis of revenue recognition.

    (2) How much in expenses should it charge in 1997? Justify your response.

c. Is there some other basis on which you would recommend that revenue be recognized? Explain.

16. *Financial statements can be cast and recast—from a limited amount of information.*

A management consulting firm contracts with clients to undertake specific projects. It recognizes revenues on a *percentage of completion basis.* Clients are required to pay for an engagement at the time it is completed. The company bills clients at an amount equal to 133 ⅓ percent of costs.

As at January 1, 1996, a summarized version of the firm's balance sheet reflected the following (in millions):

Cash	$ 10.0
Work in progress, contract value	5.0
Total assets	$15.0
Common stock	$10.0
Retained earnings	5.0
Total equities	$15.0

In the year ended December 31, 1996, the firm collected $10 million in cash from customers. It expended $6 million in cash on work related to customer projects.

a. Prepare an income statement for the year ended 1996 and a balance sheet as at December 31, 1996.

b. Another firm in the industry recognizes revenues only upon completion of a project. Convert the two statements required in part (a) to a completed project basis (which for this company is the same as a cash basis). Be sure to take into account adjustments required in the balance sheet of January 1, 1996.

17. *It is often possible to convert statements from one basis to another with little more information than is included in the basic financial statements. This problem may provide a rigorous test of your understanding of the relationships among the accounts reported in the financial statements.*

Mogul Studios, Inc., produces films for television. The company signs a contract with a network prior to beginning production of a film. The contract gives the network the right to broadcast the film over a specified period of time for a flat fee. The licence period begins as soon as the film is completed and usually extends for three to five years. The network is required to pay its fee over the period in which it is entitled to broadcast the film.

The company recognizes revenues from the production and licensing of films on a percentage of completion basis. The schedules that follow are summarized versions of the firm's balance sheets for 1996 and 1997 and its income statement and statement of cash receipts and disbursements for 1997.

The firm matches all costs associated with the production of films to licence revenues. The ratio of costs to revenues has remained constant for several years.

When the firm completes a film, it relieves its inventory of the film (stated at the amount for which it will be licensed) and recognizes a receivable in the same amount.

For simplicity, it may be assumed that all production costs are paid in cash as incurred. Income taxes may be ignored.

Recognition of revenues on a percentage of completion basis is not in accord with a FASB pronouncement which indicates that revenues should be recognized no earlier than the beginning of the licence period.

a. Convert the firm's income statement and balance sheet for 1997 to a basis by which revenues are recognized at the start of licence periods (when production is completed).

b. Convert the same two statements to a cash collection basis of revenue recognition.

Balance Sheets as at December 31
(in millions)

	1997	1996
Cash	$ 22	$ 18
Films in process, contract value	36	54
Licence fees receivable	54	30
Total assets	$112	$102
Common stock	$ 20	$ 20
Retained earnings	92	82
Total equities	$112	$102

Income Statement for Year Ended December 31, 1997
(in millions)

Revenues	$30
Costs applicable to revenues	20
Income	$10

Statement of Cash Receipts and Disbursements for Year Ended December 31, 1997
(in millions)

Collections from broadcasters	$24
Less: Costs incurred in production of films	20
Net increase in cash	$ 4

18. *Licensing practices in the record and music industry present special problems of revenue and expense recognition. This problem enables you to compare your solutions with those of the FASB.*[6]

River City Discs created a star. In 1996 the small P.E.I. recording studio produced a CD featuring Dianne Murray, a local talent. Much to its surprise, the CD went to the top of the charts.

Because River City Discs did not have the distribution channels necessary for the CD to realize its worldwide sales potential, it licensed the production and distribution rights to Northumberland Sounds, a prominent label in country and western music.

a. What would be River City Discs' 1996 revenues from its new hit, assuming each of the three different sets of circumstances presented below. Briefly justify the amount of revenue that you think should be recognized.

(1) The licence agreement provides that River City Discs is to receive $2 for each CD sold by Northumberland Sounds. In 1996 Northumberland Sounds sold 1.5 million CDs.

(2) In 1996, per the licence agreement, Northumberland Sounds made a one-time payment to River City Discs of $10 million. This payment entitles Northumberland Sounds to unlimited production and distribution rights. Northumberland Sounds has no additional obligation to River City Discs.

(3) In 1996, as required by the licence agreement, Northumberland Sounds paid River City Discs a minimum guarantee of $6 million. The contract stipulates that River City Discs is to receive $2 for each CD sold. Hence the $6 million covers the first 3 million in sales. In 1996 Northumberland Sounds sold 2.0 million CDs. River City Discs is reasonably certain that sales in future years will exceed 1.0 million.

b. River City Discs spent $200,000 to produce the "record master" (including outlays for equipment, vocal background, technicians, and supplies) which it provided to Northumberland Sounds.

(1) When, in your opinion, should the costs be charged as expenses? Consider each of the three sets of circumstances.

(2) Would your response differ if, when the initial recording was made, the artist was a proven talent and there was a basis for estimating the cost that would be recovered from future sales?

19. *How should revenues and expenses in the shipping industry be recognized?*

The Cromwell Co. was organized on June 1 for the specific purpose of chartering a ship to undertake a three-month, 10,000 kilometre voyage. On June 1 the founders of the company contributed $600,000 to the company in exchange for common stock. On the same day, the company paid the entire $600,000 to the owners of a ship for the right to use it for a period of three months.

---

[6] In 1981, the FASB issued a pronouncement, "Financial Reporting in the Record and Music Industry," Statement No. 50, which established revenue recognition guidelines. You need not refer to this statement. Instead, use your best judgment as to the most appropriate basis for determining revenue in this problem.

During the three-month period, the chartered ship made several stops.

Indicated in the table following are the number of kilometres travelled and the amount of cargo, in terms of dollar billings to customers, that the firm loaded and unloaded. (For example, in June the company loaded cargo for which it billed customers $500,000. During that same month it unloaded cargo for which it had previously billed customers $300,000.)

	Loaded	Unloaded	Number of Kilometres Travelled
June	$ 500,000	$ 300,000	4,000
July	300,000	100,000	2,500
August	200,000	600,000	3,500
	$1,000,000	$1,000,000	10,000

Operating and administrative expenses, in addition to the charter fee, were $100,000 per month (to be accounted for as a period cost).

The Cromwell Co. was liquidated on August 31. At that time all expenses had been paid and all bills collected.

a. Determine the income of the company over its three-month life.

b. Determine the income of the company during *each* of the three months. Make alternative decisions as to the methods used to recognize revenues and charge expenses.

   (1) Revenue is recognized when cargo is loaded; charter costs ($600,000) are amortized evenly ($200,000 per month) over the three-month period.

   (2) Revenue is recognized when cargo is unloaded; charter costs are amortized evenly over the three-month period.

   (3) Revenue is recognized when cargo is loaded; charter costs are amortized in proportion to number of kilometres travelled.

   (4) Revenue is recognized when cargo is unloaded; charter costs are amortized in proportion to number of kilometres travelled.

c. Which methods are preferable? Why?

d. The Cromwell Co. was unable to estimate, *in advance*, the total *revenues* to be earned during the voyage. If it could, is there another basis, preferable to the other two, by which the $600,000 in charter costs might be allocated?

20. *In the shipping industry revenue may be recognized at the start, during, or at the completion of a voyage.*

   The notes that follow are adopted from annual reports of three shipping companies. Each describes a different basis of revenue recognition.[7]

   Revenues from vessel operations are recognized upon unloading inbound cargoes—that is, on a terminated voyage basis.

   Revenue . . . is recorded on a pro rata basis over a specified period of time.

   Transportation revenues and related voyage expenses are generally recognized at the commencement of a voyage.

[7] The companies are the Lykes Corporation, the Trans Union Corporation, and R. J. Reynolds Industries, Inc., respectively.

Consider the following three sets of circumstances under which a shipping company may operate. Which basis of revenue recognition would you recommend for each of the circumstances? Justify your response.

a. The company time-charters its vessels for a specified number of months.

b. It operates "tramp steamers," which pick up cargo wherever it is found and discharge it wherever required.

c. It operates a cargo shuttle service between two ports.

21. *The trading stamp industry poses particularly interesting questions of revenue recognition.*

In the trading stamp industry, a company such as Sperry and Hutchinson (S&H Green Stamps), sells stamps to retailers. It bills the retailers for the stamps upon delivery. The retailers give the stamps to their customers according to the amount of their purchases. The customers redeem the stamps for merchandise at outlets operated by the trading stamp company.

Assume that a trading stamp company sells $500 million in stamps to retailers. It estimates that 80 percent of the stamps will actually be redeemed for merchandise. The cost of the merchandise is 75 percent of the stamp redemption value. All other operating expenses are $120 million per year. These costs are accounted for as period costs.

A key question facing the trading stamp industry is whether revenue (and related expenses) should be recognized upon sale of stamps to the retailer or upon redemption of the stamps for merchandise by the customer.

a. Present arguments in favour of each of the two points of revenue recognition; indicate the circumstances or assumptions under which each would be appropriate.

b. Prepare two sets of journal entries to record the sale of stamps, the acquisition of merchandise inventory, and the redemption of the stamps. Also give recognition to the operating costs. First recognize revenues and related expenses when the stamps are sold and then when the stamps are redeemed. Assume that the sales of stamps are for cash, that inventory is purchased for cash, and that the other operating costs are paid in cash. Assume also that the stamp redemption rate is as estimated.

22. *Income as determined for one purpose may not be appropriate for another.*

Tom Ogden celebrated Christmas by purchasing a new car. In his first year as sales manager of the newly formed industrial equipment division of the Shakespeare Manufacturing Co., Ogden and his sales force had generated $7.5 million in noncancelable orders for equipment.

Ogden's employment contract provided that he receive an annual bonus equal to 3 percent of his division's profits. He was aware that costs of manufacturing the equipment were approximately 60 percent of sales prices and that the company had budgeted $2.0 million for administrative and all other operating costs. He could afford to splurge on a new car since, according to his rough calculations, his bonus would total at least $30,000.

In mid-January, Ogden received a bonus cheque for $12,000. Stunned, but confident that a clerical error had been made, he placed an urgent call to the company controller. The controller informed him that no error had been made. Although costs were in line with those budgeted, reported sales were only $6 million.

The equipment produced by Shakespeare is special-purpose polishing equipment. Since it must be custom-made, customers must normally wait for delivery at least two months from date of order.

a. Demonstrate how the amount of the bonus was calculated by *both* Ogden and the company controller. What is the most likely explanation of the difference in their sales figures?

b. The company president has asked for your recommendations with respect to the bonus plan. Assuming that the objective of the company is to give reasonably prompt recognition to the accomplishments of its sales manager, on what basis do you think revenue should be recognized for the purpose of computing the sales manager's bonus? Do you think the company should use the same basis for reporting to shareholders? Explain.

23. *Unusual risks assumed by a construction company may justify conservative accounting principles—for some, though not necessarily all, purposes.*

In 1996 a real estate company established a subsidiary, Devco, Inc., to develop and construct shopping centres. Upon forming the new subsidiary, the parent company contributed $25 million in equity capital.

To attract a few key executives, Devco, Inc., offered them employment contracts stipulating that a portion of their compensation would be based on subsidiary earnings. The contracts did not, however, specify the principles by which earnings would be computed.

In 1996 Devco, Inc., contracted with a group of investors to construct two shopping centres, one in Mississauga and the other in Brampton. The contract price of each was to be $20 million. Payment for each was to be according to the following schedule (in millions):

When shopping centre is completed and turned over to purchaser	$ 2.0
Over the following six years ($3.0 million per year, plus interest on outstanding balance)	18.0
Total	$20.0

From the time a shopping centre was delivered to its purchaser until the balance of the purchase price was paid, Devco, Inc., would have a security interest in the property. If the purchaser defaulted on its obligation, the company would repossess its centre. Ultimately, however, the financial wherewithal of the purchaser to meet its obligation would depend on its ability to generate rental revenues by leasing the stores in the centre to creditworthy tenants. Until the shopping centre became well established, there was considerable risk of the purchasers having to default on the required payments.

In 1997 Devco, Inc., began construction on the two shopping centres. By year end, it had completed work on the Mississauga centre, turned it over to the purchaser, and collected the contractually required payment. It had also completed 60 percent of the work on the Brampton centre.

The company estimated (correctly, it turned out) that construction costs would be $15 million per shopping centre.

At the close of 1997 Devco, Inc., and its vice-president of construction disagreed as to the amount of earnings on which her compensation would be based. The company planned to base her compensation on the amount of earnings to be reported in its general-purpose financial statements. Revenues were to be recognized only when their realization would be assured with a high degree of certainty. The vice-president of construction argued that such earnings were an inappropriate basis on which to base her compensation.

a. On what basis do you think the company planned to recognize revenues for purposes of general reporting? In a few sentences, defend this basis. Prepare an appropriate income statement and balance sheet (prior to taking into account the amount to be paid to the vice-president). Assume that all construction costs were paid in cash as incurred.

b. Suppose that you were called upon to represent the vice-president for construction. On what basis might you assert that revenues should be recognized? Indicate why you believe that such a basis is more appropriate for the specific decision at hand. Prepare an income statement and balance sheet that you would present to the company.

24. *How should a computer software company, in the face of uncertainty as to whether its productive efforts will provide returns, recognize revenues and expenses?*

The University Systems Co. developed a series of computer programs designed to simplify the "back office" operations of stock brokerage firms. All costs of developing the programs have been charged to expense accounts as incurred. Although the programs can readily be applied to the operations of all firms in the industry, certain features of the programs must be custom-designed to meet the specific requirements of each customer. It is generally possible to estimate with reasonable reliability the costs of developing the custom features.

In January, analysts of University Systems made a preliminary study of the "back office" operations of Conrad, Roy, Atwood, Smith, and Harris (CRASH), a leading brokerage firm. University Systems hoped that as a result of the study it could demonstrate the savings in costs and increases in efficiency that its programs could bring about and that it could thereby sell its programs to CRASH. It was agreed that the entire costs of the preliminary study would be borne by University Systems; CRASH was under no obligation to either purchase the programs or pay for the preliminary study. Cost of the preliminary study was $100,000.

The preliminary study was successful; on February 2, CRASH placed an order with University Systems for its series of programs; the contract price was $1.5 million.

During February and March, University Systems developed the custom features of the program for CRASH. Costs incurred in February were $80,000 and in March, $120,000. These costs were equal to amounts previously estimated.

On March 15 University Systems delivered the completed series of programs to CRASH, and they were reviewed and accepted by CRASH management.

On April 4, University Systems received a cheque for $500,000 plus a two-year, 8 percent note receivable for the balance.

a. Prepare comparative income statements for the months ending January 31, February 28, March 31, and April 30.

b. In a short paragraph, justify your choice of basis of revenue and expense recognition. Indicate any assumptions that you may have made.

25. *Unconditional guarantees create special problems of revenue recognition.*

Western Art, Inc., produces and sells bronze sculptures of cowboys and other characters associated with western Canada. The company contracts with a well-known artist to sculpt an original work of art; from the original, the company produces a mould from which castings are taken.

The company produces a casting only upon receipt of an order from a customer accompanied by full payment. It offers a buyer an unconditional guarantee of satisfaction for a period of four months from date of sale. During the four months, the customer is entitled to a full refund, no questions asked.

In 1996 the company commissioned artist Frank Winslow to sculpt "Cowboy and His Horse." The contract with the artist stated that his compensation was to be "40 percent of the income (before commissions and taxes) attributable directly to the production and sale of the sculpture during 1996 and 30 percent thereafter." The contract did not specify principles of revenue and expense recognition.

In 1996 the company incurred costs of $60,000 to produce a mould from which to cast "Cowboy and His Horse." Because the company forecast that sales of the sculpture would take place evenly over a period of three years, it decided that the cost of the mould would be depreciated over three years.

The company determined that the cost of producing each casting (not including any share of the cost of the mould) would be $700.

Sales price for each casting was set at $2,000.

In 1996 the company produced and shipped 70 castings. By year end, the four-month guarantee period had expired on 50 of the castings.

Shortly after the close of the year the company prepared and sent to Frank Winslow the following income statement and balance sheet pertaining to "Cowboy and His Horse":

Income Statement for the Year Ended December 31, 1996

Revenues		$100,000
Less: Cost of castings	$35,000	
Amortization of mould	20,000	55,000
Income before commissions		$ 45,000
Commissions @ 40%		18,000
Income		$ 27,000

Balance Sheet as at December 31, 1996

Cash		$31,000
Company interest in castings shipped on which revenues have not been recognized		14,000
Mould	$60,000	
Less: Accumulated amortization	20,000	40,000
Total assets		$85,000
Commissions payable		$18,000
Unearned revenue on castings shipped		40,000
Accumulated earnings to date		27,000
Total liabilities and equities		$85,000

a. On what basis has the company recognized revenues? Can this basis be justified? Comment.

b. In the following year, 1997, the company shipped 50 units. The guarantee period expired on 40 of them. It paid the 1996 commissions due the artist, but not the 1997 commissions. Assuming that the company adhered to the same accounting principles in 1997 as in 1996, prepare an income statement and balance sheet for 1997. (Remember that commissions in 1997 are only 30 percent of income.)

c. Frank Winslow was surprised at the amount of his commissions in 1996. He thought they would be much greater. He asserted that when he produced other sculptures for similar firms, virtually none were ever returned. Prepare an income statement and a balance sheet for 1996 using a basis of revenue recognition that would better serve the interests of Frank Winslow. Justify the basis selected.

Solutions to Exercise for Review and Self-Testing

1. a.

1996 Swimming pool revenue	$400,000	(40% of $1 million since 2 of 5 pools completed)
1996 Swimming pool expenses	320,000	(actual costs incurred to complete 2 pools)
1996 Income	$ 80,000	

b. The swimming pools will be carried at $580,000 at December 31, 1996 ($500,000 of construction costs plus the $80,000 of income recognized). Alternatively, the $580,000 is the sale price of the two completed pools of $400,000 (2 × $200,000) plus the $180,000 spent on unfinished pools ($500,000 − 2 × $160,000).

2. a.

1997 Swimming pool revenue	$600,000	(60% of $1 million since 3 of 5 pools completed)
1997 Swimming pool expenses	480,000	(actual costs to complete 3 pools)
1997 Income	$120,000	

b. The receipt of cash would have no effect on the revenue recognition patterns, as long as revenue is being recognized on the basis of the number of units completed.

6

Valuation of Assets; Cash and Marketable Securities

In previous chapters we introduced the accounting cycle and the nature of accrual accounting. The next series of chapters examines specific balance sheet accounts, focusing on the valuation of the asset or liability and the effect on the related revenue or expense account. In this chapter, we introduce the concept of valuation based on the present value of future cash flows. Also, this chapter introduces the accounting procedures for the most liquid categories of current assets, cash and marketable securities.

After studying this chapter, you will be able to

- Understand the difference between market value and historical cost
- Explain the three alternative concepts of market value: current cost, net realizable value, and net present value
- Calculate the present and future value of cash flows
- List the components of cash and describe the accounting for cash
- Define marketable securities
- Understand the valuation of, and accounting for, marketable securities

PART I. Valuation of Assets

Although accountants have been unable to derive a definition of an asset upon which there has been complete agreement, almost all proposed definitions stress the notion that assets represent rights to future services or economic benefits. The question facing the accountant is what value—what quantitative measure—should be assigned to the potential services or benefits. (This question is, of course, directly related to that discussed in the previous chapter: When should increases or decreases in the value of net assets—those associated with revenues and expenses—be recognized?)

The leading objective of this chapter is to provide insight into the nature of value. *Value,* as it is used in accounting, can have at least three distinctive meanings:

1. An *assigned* or calculated *numerical quantity;* as in mathematics, the quantity or amount for which a symbol stands

2. The *worth* of something sold or exchanged; the worth of a thing in money or goods at a certain time; its fair market price

3. Worth in *usefulness* or *importance* to its possessor; its utility or merit

The accounting profession has not yet reached consensus on criteria of valuation. In fact, in accordance with generally accepted accounting principles, assets may be stated at amounts reflective of any one of the above three definitions of value.

From the perspective of managers and investors, the distinctions among the three concepts of value are crucial. The "value" assigned to an asset on a financial statement may not—indeed is *unlikely* to—be indicative of the amount for which the asset could be sold or of its ultimate worth to the party owning or using it. As a consequence, decisions that will maximize the *reported* value of assets may not always maximize their true economic worth and may be counter to the financial well-being of a firm and its investors.

HISTORICAL COST

The first definition, that value is nothing more than an assigned or calculated numerical quantity, implies that value need have nothing to do with inherent worth; it is simply a numerical quantity assigned on a basis that is, presumably, logical and orderly. It is, in fact, this first meaning that is most consistent with current accounting practice.

Financial statements are *cost-based.* Most assets are initially recorded at the amounts paid for them. Subsequent to date of purchase, assets are, in general (some exceptions will be pointed out later in this chapter), reported at either initial cost or amortized cost. Amortized cost is initial cost less the portion of initial cost (often indicated in a contra account) representing the services of the asset already utilized. Land is an example of an asset that is reported at initial cost; plant and equipment are examples of assets that are reported at amortized cost.

Except at the date assets are purchased, the cost-based amounts reported on a firm's balance sheet do not represent (unless by coincidence) the prices at which they can currently be either purchased or sold. The reported amounts cannot be viewed as approximations of either the fair market value or the worth of the services that the assets will provide. They designate nothing more than initial cost less the portion of initial cost already absorbed as an expense.

The Going-Concern Concept

Once assets have been initially recorded, they are thereafter valued on the assumption that the firm is a *going concern*—one that will continue in operation indefinitely. Assets are measured with respect to the particular firm reporting them—not with respect to the general marketplace. Thus certain assets, "organizational costs," for example, can be expected to benefit the firm on whose books they are recorded, even though they are not readily marketable. The going-concern concept implies that the firm will survive at least long enough to realize the benefits of its recorded assets.

The corollary to the going-concern concept is that when there is evidence that a firm will be unable to survive, its assets should be reported at their *liquidation* values—the amounts that could be realized if the firm were to be dissolved and its assets put up for sale. Thus, if a firm is expected to be dissolved, perhaps as the result of bankruptcy proceedings, the conventional balance sheet would be inappropriate; instead, a balance sheet that indicates net realizable values should be prepared. This is because the firm will not survive long enough to realize the benefits of its recorded assets.

The Principle of Matching

Why do accountants "value" assets at amounts that have nothing to do with either market value or inherent worth? Historical cost valuations are consistent with the concepts of income determination discussed in the previous chapters. The cost of a long-lived asset is charged as an expense as the asset is consumed. The cost is thereby *matched* to the benefits (revenues) that it produces. The portion of cost that has not yet been charged to expense is reported on the balance sheet, awaiting transfer to the income statement in a future accounting period. In this sense, the balance sheet is a statement of *residuals*—costs that have not yet been charged as expenses. In fact, until recently the primary focus of financial reporting was upon *earnings* rather than assets and liabilities. The *statement of income*, not the balance sheet, was the foremost financial statement. Today, however, the rule-making authorities are showing increased concern with the balance sheet, gradually trying to assure that it is a useful statement in its own right rather than merely an adjunct to the income statement.

Concerns over Objectivity

It is often asserted that historical cost valuations are *objective*. This is true but only to a limited extent. The purchase price of a long-lived asset or initial amount of an account receivable can be determined with reliability. But the other factors which determine the values assigned to such assets cannot. Useful life, salvage value, and estimates of uncollectable accounts are subject to managerial judgment. Hence the objectivity of historical cost-based statements may be more illusory than real—arbitrary rules being substituted for judgments required.

Usefulness for Investors and Managers

To managers as well as investors, who are called upon to make decisions that will affect the future, not the past, historical costs are of little significance. There are virtually no decisions for which historical costs are necessary or even useful.[1] Assets, by definition, provide benefits that will be realized in the future. The historical cost of an asset offers no insight into the resources that could be derived by either retaining or selling the asset. It furnishes no basis on which to assess cash flows that the asset will generate in the future or to evaluate the efficiency of management in using the asset. Therefore, it is necessary to at least look at alternatives to historical cost financial statements.

Three Alternatives to Historical Cost

Three of the most frequently proposed alternatives to historical cost are (1) current cost, (2) net realizable value, and (3) net present value. The first two are market-based. They are consistent with the second definition of value—the worth of a thing in money or goods at a certain time, its fair market price. The third alternative expresses value as the cash to be generated by an asset and is thereby consistent with the third definition of value—its worth in usefulness to the asset's particular owner.

MARKET VALUES

Current Cost

Current cost is an asset's replacement cost—the amount that would have to be paid to obtain the same asset or its equivalent. It is an *input* cost. For inventory it would be the cost either to manufacture or to purchase the goods from a supplier. For capital assets it would be the outlays to construct or to purchase the equivalent asset. Current cost indicates the amount that a firm could save by owning an asset rather than having to acquire it, the cost that it would have to incur if it were deprived of the asset. Underlying current costs is the presumption of a going concern, a firm that will continue to use the asset or will otherwise replace it with a similar asset.

---

[1] Historical costs are, of course, necessary to make decisions that must, by statute or policy, be based on them. The tax laws, for example, require that the gain on sale of an asset be calculated as the difference between selling price and historical cost. Banks sometimes insist (unwisely in the view of many accountants and lending specialists) that in order to be eligible for a loan, a borrower must maintain a specified ratio of assets (stated at historical cost) to liabilities.

Net Realizable Value

Net realizable value is the amount for which an asset could be sold less any costs that must be incurred to bring it to a saleable condition. It is an *output* price. For inventory it would be the expected selling price less any costs to complete and sell the product. The difference between an item's current cost and its net realizable value would ordinarily be the seller's margin of profit. For capital assets, net realizable value would be the price for which it could be sold or salvaged less any disposal costs.

Net realizable value is essential in determining whether a firm should continue to retain an asset. It indicates the sacrifice the firm incurs by holding rather than selling an asset. Such sacrifice is referred to as an *opportunity cost*—the cost of using an asset in its "next-best" alternative.

Market Values in Practice

Revenue Recognition prior to Sale

Even though conventional accounting is primarily cost-based, in selected situations firms do report assets at market values. In general, whenever revenue is recognized prior to the point of sale, the related asset is reported at the amount that is expected to be realized on sale, a market value. For example, when revenue is recognized upon completion of production (e.g., upon the removal of a precious mineral from the ground), the completed products are valued at their anticipated selling price. To avoid the distortions in income that would result from delaying recognition of revenue until point of sale, firms estimate the amount of revenue that they will realize. The best projection of this is the current output price as indicated by either a sales contract or trades in the marketplace.

The CICA has experimented with market value alternatives to historical cost. Under Section 4510 of the *CICA Handbook,* large public companies were encouraged to disclose supplementary information about the effects of changing prices, including the current cost of inventory and capital assets. In addition, those companies were encouraged to disclose income calculated on a current cost basis.[2] However, Section 4510 was withdrawn from the *Handbook* in 1992.

Lower of Cost or Market Rule

The concern of accountants with conservatism also leads them to report market values whenever the prevailing price of an asset intended for sale falls below its acquisition cost. Following the rule of *lower of cost or market*, the accountant compares the historical cost of an asset—that which the company paid either to purchase or produce it—with what it would cost to *replace* it (a current *input* cost). If the market—the replacement—price is less than the historical cost, then the asset is *written down* to the market price and the corresponding loss recognized on the income statement. The lower of cost or market rule is applied only to assets, primarily inventories and marketable securities, that the firm actually expects to sell in the normal course

---

[2] "Reporting the Effects of Changing Prices," Section 4510, *CICA Handbook,* 1982.

---

of business. It is grounded on the assumption that financial statements would be misleading if assets were reported at prices higher than those for which the company expects to sell them. The rule is not ordinarily applied to assets, such as plant and equipment, that are not intended for resale. The lower of cost or market rule will be examined in greater detail in the second part of this chapter when we deal with marketable securities and again in Chapter 8 in connection with a discussion of inventories.

NET PRESENT VALUE, OR VALUE TO USER

The third definition of value relates value to worth in terms of usefulness or importance to the individual possessor. It suggests that the value of an asset be determined with respect to the particular party that owns it.

This third concept of value is of utmost concern to managers and investors as it underlies virtually all decision models pertaining to assets. Moreover, it is of interest to all persons involved with business and economics because the factors that contribute to the worth of an asset to a particular individual or firm provide insight into the nature of both assets and market prices.

Value to individual owners has not, in the past, been the common basis for stating assets in general-purpose financial reports. This is mainly because of the difficulty of assessing the future benefits that assets will provide. However, accountants are increasingly taking into account the worth of the services to be rendered by the asset in determining how it should be reported. This is particularly true when neither an exchange transaction nor a market price is available to indicate value.

The economic benefits of an asset ordinarily are cash receipts. An individual invests in the common stock of a corporation in anticipation of cash receipts greater than the cash disbursement required by the initial purchase. The cash receipts will be from periodic cash dividends paid by the company, from the proceeds resulting from the sale of the stock, or from both. Similarly, a manufacturer purchases a machine with the expectation that it will contribute to the production of goods which will be sold for cash. The value of an asset to its owner is, therefore, the value of the net cash receipts that the asset is expected to generate. The challenge to the accountant or manager is, first, to identify and measure the cash receipts. This may be difficult considering that most assets generate cash only when used in conjunction with other assets and that, in a world of uncertainty, future sales and costs cannot easily be estimated. And, second, the challenge is to determine the present value of those cash receipts.

Although it might appear as if the value of expected cash receipts is simply the sum of all anticipated receipts, an analysis of some fundamental concepts of compound interest will demonstrate that this is not so. Since cash may be placed in interest-bearing bank accounts or used to acquire securities that will provide a periodic return, it has a value in time. Funds to be received in distant years are of less value than those to be received at present. An economically rational person would prefer to receive $1 today rather in one year, since the $1 received today can be invested so as to increase to some greater amount one year from today.

Future Value of a Single Sum

Suppose that an individual deposited $1 in a bank savings account. The bank pays interest at the rate of 6 percent per year. Interest is *compounded* (computed) annually at the end of each year. To how much would the deposit have grown at the end of one year?

The accumulated value of the deposit at the end of one year would be $1 × 1.06 = $1.06.

In more general terms,

$$a = (1 + i)^n$$

where a represents the final accumulation of the initial investment of $1 after
n interest periods
i indicates the rate of interest

As indicated in Exhibit 6-1, after two years the initial deposit would have accumulated to $1.12—the $1.06 on deposit at the beginning of the second year times 1.06. After three years it would have accumulated to $1.19—the $1.12 on deposit at the beginning of the third year again times 1.06.

EXHIBIT 6-1

Future Value of $1 Invested Today, 6% Return (rounded to nearest cent) Year						
0	1	2	3	4	5	6
$1.00→	$1.06→	$1.12→	$1.19→	$1.26→	$1.34→	$1.42

Employing the general formula (and rounding to the nearest cent), we find:
At the end of two years,

$$a = (1 + i)^n$$
$$= (1 + .06)^2 = \$1.12$$

At the end of three years,

$$a = (1 + i)^n$$
$$= (1 + .06)^3 = \$1.19$$

At the end of six years,

$$a = (1 + i)^n$$
$$= (1 + .06)^6 = \$1.42$$

If an amount other than $1 was deposited, the accumulated amount could be computed simply by multiplying the future value of $1 by that amount. Thus $200 deposited in a bank paying interest at a rate of 6 percent per year, compounded annually, would grow to $200 times $(1.06)^6$, or $283.70, at the end of six years. Common notation for compound interest is

$$a_{\overline{n}|i} = (1 + i)^n$$

To facilitate computations of compound interest, tables have been developed and are available in almost all accounting textbooks as well as numerous books of financial tables. Moreover, many business calculators and computer software packages are programmed with time value of money routines. Table 1 in the Appendix of this textbook indicates the amounts to which $1 will accumulate at various interest rates and at the end of different numbers of periods. The number at the intersection of the 6 percent column and the 6 periods row indicates that $1 would accumulate to $1.4185 if invested at 6 percent annual interest for 6 years. Two hundred dollars would accumulate to $200 times that amount, or $200 × 1.4185 = $283.70.

The following examples illustrate the concept of future value.

Example 1

A company sells a parcel of land for $50,000. The purchaser asks to be allowed to delay all payments for a period of three years. The company agrees to accept a note receivable from the purchaser for $50,000 plus interest compounded at an annual rate of 8 percent. What amount would the purchaser be required to pay at the end of three years?

As indicated in Table 1 in the Appendix (8 percent column, 3 periods row), $1 will accumulate to $1.2597. Hence $50,000 will grow to $50,000 times 1.2597, or $62,985. The purchaser would be required to pay $62,985:

$$50,000a_{\overline{3}|.08} = \$50,000(1 + .08)^3$$
$$= \$62,985$$

Example 2

An individual deposits $30,000 in a bank certificate of deposit. The bank pays interest at an annual rate of 12 percent *compounded semiannually*. To what amount will the deposit accumulate at the end of 10 years?

If interest is compounded semiannually and the *annual* rate of interest is 12 percent, then interest is computed *twice* each year at 6 percent—*one-half* the annual rate. (Interest is almost always stated at an *annual* rate even when compounded semiannually or quarterly.) Each interest period would be six months, rather than a year, so that over a 10-year span there would be 20 interest periods. Table 1 in the Appendix indicates that at an interest rate of 6 percent, $1 will accumulate to $3.2071 after 20 periods. Hence $30,000 will grow to $30,000 times 3.2071, or $96,213. As a general rule, whenever interest is compounded semiannually, the interest rate must be halved and the number of years doubled to get the appropriate number of interest periods:

$$30,000a_{\overline{20}|.06} = \$30,000(1 + .06)^{20}$$
$$= \$96,213$$

Example 3

A corporation invests $10,000 and expects to earn a return of 8 percent compounded annually for the next 60 years. To how much will the $10,000 accumulate over the 60-year period?

Table 1 in the Appendix does not indicate accumulations over 60 periods. However, the table does indicate that $1 invested at 8 percent for 50 periods would accumulate to $46.9016. Over 50 periods $10,000 would accumulate to $469,016. The table also indicates that $1 invested at 8 percent for 10 periods would accumulate to $2.1589. If at the end of 50 periods $469,016 were invested for an additional 10 periods, it would increase in value to 2.1589 times $469,016, or $1,012,558:

$$\$10,000 a_{\overline{50}|.08} = \$10,000(1 + .08)^{50}$$

$$= \$469,016$$

$$\$469,016 a_{\overline{10}|.08} = \$469,016(1 + .08)^{10}$$

$$= \$1,012,558$$

Example 4

A corporation reached an agreement to sell a warehouse. The purchaser agreed to pay $800,000 for the warehouse but only if payment could be delayed for four years. The corporation, however, was in immediate need of cash and agreed to accept a lesser amount if payment was made at time of sale. The corporation estimated that it would otherwise have to borrow the needed funds at an annual interest rate of 15 percent. What amount should the corporation be willing to accept if cash payment was made at the time of sale rather than delayed for four years?

The question can be stated in an alternative form. What amount if invested today at an annual interest rate of 15 percent would accumulate to $800,000 in four years? From Table 1 in the Appendix it may be seen that $1 invested today would increase to $1.7490. Hence some amount (x) times 1.7490 would increase to $800,000:

$$1.7490x = \$800,000$$

Solving for x (i.e., dividing $800,000 by 1.7490) indicates that amount to be $457,404. Thus the company would be equally well off if it accepted payment of $457,404 today as it would be if it waited four years to receive the full $800,000. In other words, $457,404 deposited in a bank today at a 15 percent annual interest rate would increase in value to $800,000 after four years:

$$xa_{\overline{4}|.15} = \$800,000$$

$$a_{\overline{4}|.15} = (1 + .15)^4$$

$$= 1.7490$$

$$1.7490x = \$800,000$$

$$x = \$457,404$$

Present Value

As implied in Example 4, it is frequently necessary to compute the *present value* of a sum of money to be received in the future. That is, one may want to know the amount which if invested today at a certain rate of return would be the equivalent of a fixed amount to be received in a specific number of years hence.

In simple terms, an example can be formulated as follows. If a bank pays interest at the rate of 6 percent annually, how much cash would an individual have to deposit today in order to have that amount accumulate to $1 one year from now? Example 4 illustrated one means of computation. In more general terms, the present value of a future sum can be calculated by taking the reciprocal of the basic formula for future value: $a_{\overline{n}|i} = (1 + i)^n$. Thus, for $1,

$$p_{\overline{n}|i} = \frac{1}{(1 + i)^n}$$

where n indicates the number of periods
i indicates the rate of interest (which when used in connection with present value computations is often referred to as a *discount* rate, since a future payment will be *discounted* to a present value)
p indicates the required initial deposit or investment

Therefore, the present value of $1 to be received one year in the future at a discount rate of 6 percent would be

$$p_{\overline{1}|.06} = \frac{1}{(1 + .06)^1} = \$.94$$

The present value of $1 to be received two years in the future at a discount rate of 6 percent would be

$$p_{\overline{2}|.06} = \frac{1}{(1 + .06)^2} = \$.89$$

The present value of $1 to be received six years in the future at a discount rate of 6 percent would be

$$p_{\overline{3}|.06} = \frac{1}{(1 + .06)^6} = \$.71$$

In other words, as illustrated in Exhibit 6-2, 71 cents invested today at 6 percent interest compounded annually would increase to $1 at the end of six years.

EXHIBIT 6-2

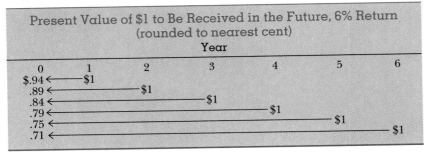

Present Value of $1 to Be Received in the Future, 6% Return (rounded to nearest cent)

Chapter 6   Valuation of Assets; Cash and Marketable Securities

As with future value, if an amount other than $1 were to be received, then its present value could be determined by multiplying the present value of $1 by that amount. Thus, if an individual wanted to receive $200 six years from the present, then the amount he or she would have to invest today at 6 percent interest would be

$$\$200p_{\overline{6}|.06} = \$200 \; \frac{1}{(1.06)^6} = \$141$$

Table 2 in the Appendix indicates the present value of $1 for various discount rates and time periods. The present value of $1 to be received six years from today discounted at the rate of 6 percent would be $.7050. The present value of $200 would be $200 times .7050, or $141.

Concepts of present value are demonstrated in the examples that follow.

Example 1

Assume the same facts as in Example 4 of the previous section. A corporation agreed to sell a warehouse. The purchaser was willing to pay $800,000 four years hence or some lesser amount at time of sale. Assuming that the corporation would have to borrow the needed funds at an annual rate of 15 percent, what equivalent amount should it be willing to accept if payment were made at time of sale?

Per Table 2, the present value of $1 to be received in four years, at an annual interest rate of 15 percent, is $.5718. The present value of $800,000 is $800,000 × .5718, or $457,440. Except for a $36 rounding difference, the result is identical to that computed in the earlier illustration:

$$\$800,000p_{\overline{4}|.15} = \$800,000 \left[\frac{1}{(1 + .15)^4} \right]$$

$$= \$457,440$$

Example 2

A man wishes to give his nephew a gift of the cost of a university education. The nephew will enter university in six years. It is estimated that when he enters university, tuition and other charges will be approximately $80,000 for a degree program. The gift will be placed in a certificate of deposit, which pays interest at an annual rate of 12 percent, compounded *quarterly*. What size gift is required if the full $80,000 is to be available to the nephew at the start of his university career?

Since interest is compounded quarterly, the question to be answered is as follows: What is the present value of $80,000 to be received 24 (4 times six years) periods away if discounted at a rate of 3 percent per period? Per Table 2, the present value of $1 to be received 24 periods in the future, discounted at a rate of 3 percent, is $.4919. The present value of $80,000 is, therefore, $80,000 times .4919, or $39,352. That is,

$$\$80,000p_{\overline{24}|.03} = \$39,352$$

(*Check:* Per Table 1, the future value of $1 to be received in 24 periods if invested at a rate of 3 percent is $2.0328. We find that $39,352 times 2.0328 is, with allowance for rounding, $80,000.)

Future Value of an Annuity

Commercial transactions frequently involve not just a single deposit or future payment but a series of equal payments spaced evenly apart. For example, a company interested in accumulating a specified amount of cash would be concerned with the deposit that it would be required to make during each of a certain number of years to attain its goal. A series of *equal* payments at fixed intervals is known as an *annuity*. An annuity in which the payments are made or received at the *end* of each period is known as an *ordinary annuity* or an *annuity in arrears*. One in which the payments are made or received at the *beginning* of each period is known as an *annuity due* or an *annuity in advance*. Unless otherwise indicated, the examples in this chapter will be based on the assumption that payments are made or received at the *end* of each period. (Annuity tables in the Appendix contain interest factors for ordinary annuities.)

Suppose that at the *end* of each of four years a person deposits $1 in a savings account. The account pays interest at the rate of 6 percent per year, compounded annually. How much will be available for withdrawal at the end of the fourth year?

As shown in Exhibit 6-3, the $1 deposited at the end of the first period will accumulate interest for a total of three years. As indicated in Table 1, it will increase in value to $1.19. The deposit at the end of the second year will grow to $1.12, and that at the end of the third year will grow to $1.06. The payment made at the end of the fourth year will not have earned any interest by the end of the fourth year. As revealed in the diagram, the series of four $1 payments will be worth $4.37 at the end of the fourth year.

EXHIBIT 6-3

Future Value of $1 Invested at the End of Each of Four Periods, 6% Return (rounded to nearest cent)				
			Year	
	1	2	3	4
	$1.00 →	$1.06 →	$1.12 →	$1.19
		$1.00 →	1.06 →	1.12
			1.00 →	1.06
				1.00
Amount available for withdrawal	$1.00	$2.06	$3.18	$4.37

The mathematical expression for the future value (A) of a series of payments of $1 compounded at an interest rate (i) over a given number of periods (n) is

$$A_{\overline{n}|i} = \frac{(1+i)^n - 1}{i}$$

(Note that the uppercase A signifies an annuity, while the lowercase a denotes a single sum.) The value at the end of four years of $1 deposited at the end of each of four years compounded at an annual rate of 6 percent is

$$A_{\overline{4}|.06} = \frac{(1 + .06)^4 - 1}{.06} = \$4.37$$

Table 3 in the Appendix indicates the future values of annuities of $1 for various rates of return. The number at the intersection of the 6 percent column and the 4 periods row indicates that an annuity of $1 would accumulate to $4.3746 in four years. The next three examples illustrate the concept of the future value of an annuity.

Example 1

A corporation has agreed to deposit 10 percent of an employee's salary into a retirement fund. The fund will be invested in a portfolio of stocks and bonds that is expected to provide a return of 8 percent compounded annually. How much will be available to the employee upon retirement in 20 years, assuming that the employee earns $30,000 per year?

The future value of an annuity of $1 per year compounded annually at a rate of 8 percent per year for 20 years is $45.7620. Hence the future value of an annuity of $3,000 (10 percent of $30,000) is $3,000 times 45.7620, or $137,286. That is,

$$\$3,000A_{\overline{20}|.08} = \$137,286$$

Example 2

An individual invests $1,000 every three months in securities that yield 20 percent per year compounded quarterly. To how much will these investments accumulate at the end of 15 years (60 quarters)?

Table 3 in the Appendix does not specifically indicate values for 60 periods. However, per Table 3, $1,000 deposited at the end of each of 50 periods at a rate of 5 percent will accumulate to $1,000 times 209.3480, or $209,348. At the end of 50 quarters, therefore, the individual will have $209,348 invested in securities. Per Table 1, that sum will increase to $209,348 times 1.6289, or $341,007, by the end of the 10 additional quarters. The $1,000 deposited at the end of quarters 51 through 60—an ordinary annuity for 10 periods—will accumulate, per Table 3, to $1,000 times 12.5779, or $12,578. The total amount that will have accumulated over the 15-year (60-quarter) period is the sum of the two amounts, $341,007 and $12,578, or $353,585. In notation,

$$\$1000A_{\overline{50}|.05} = \$209,348 \text{ and } \$209,348a_{\overline{10}|.05} = \$341,007$$
$$\$1,000A_{\overline{10}|.05} = \underline{12,578}$$
$$\text{Total} = \underline{\underline{\$353,585}}$$

Example 3

A municipality has an obligation to repay $200,000 in bonds upon their maturity in 20 years. The municipality wishes to make annual cash payments to a fund to assure that when the bonds are due it will have the necessary cash on hand. The municipality intends to invest the fund in securities that will yield a return of 8 percent, compounded annually.

The required payment of $200,000 can be interpreted as the future value of an annuity. That is, some amount (x) deposited annually to return 8 percent must accumulate at the end of 20 years to $200,000. From Table 3, it can be seen that $1 invested annually at 8 percent would accumulate in 20 years to $45.7620. Therefore some amount (x) times 45.7620 would accumulate to $200,000:

$$45.7620x = \$200,000$$
$$x = \frac{\$200,000}{45.7620}$$
$$= \$4,370$$

If deposited annually into a fund that earns a return of 8 percent, compounded annually, $4,370 would accumulate to $200,000 in 20 years.

Present Value of an Annuity

Just as it is sometimes necessary to know the present value of a single payment to be received sometime in the future, so also there is sometimes interest in the present value of a stream of payments. An investor or creditor may wish to know the amount to be received today that would be the equivalent of a stream of payments to be received in the future.

The present value, discounted at 6 percent, of $1 to be received at the end of each of the future four periods is depicted diagrammatically in Exhibit 6-4. The present value of the stream of receipts, $3.46, is the sum of the present values of the individual receipts. The present values of the individual receipts, which are indicated in the left-hand column, could be taken directly from Table 2.

EXHIBIT 6-4

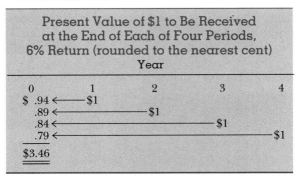

The mathematical formula for the present value P of an annuity of $1 per period compounded at a rate of i for n periods is

$$P_{\overline{n}|i} = \frac{1 - (1 + i)^{-n}}{i}$$

The present value of an annuity of $1 per period for four periods compounded at a rate of 6 percent is

$$P_{\overline{4}|.06} = \frac{1 - (1 + .06)^{-4}}{.06} = \$3.46$$

Consistent with the notation for future values, the uppercase P signifies an annuity, the lowercase p a single amount.

Table 4 in the Appendix indicates the present values of annuities in arrears (i.e., payments received at the *end* of each period) at various rates of return. Each amount in Table 4 is simply the sum, up to that period, of the amounts in Table 2. The number at the intersection of the 6 percent column and the 4 periods row indicates that the present value of an annuity of $1 for 4 years is $3.4651.

The application of the concept of the present value of an annuity is demonstrated in the examples that follow.

Example 1

A mother wishes to give her daughter a gift of a sum of money, so that if the daughter deposits the sum in a bank, she would be able to withdraw $8,000 at the end of each of four years to meet her university expenses. The bank pays interest at the rate of 5 percent per year compounded annually. What is the single amount that the mother should give her daughter that would be the equivalent of four annual payments of $8,000 each?

The present value of an annuity of $1 per year for four years compounded at a rate of 5 percent is, per Table 4, $3.5460. The present value of an annuity of $8,000 is $8,000 times 3.5460, or $28,368. That is,

$$\$8,000P_{\overline{4}|.05} = \$28,368$$

The result can be verified as follows:

Initial deposit	$28,368
First-year earnings (5%)	1,418
Balance at end of first year before withdrawal	$29,786
First-year withdrawal	(8,000)
Balance at end of first year	$21,786
Second-year earnings (5%)	1,089
Balance at end of second year before withdrawal	$22,875
Second-year withdrawal	(8,000)
Balance at end of second year	$14,875
Third-year earnings (5%)	744
Balance at end of third year before withdrawal	$15,619
Third-year withdrawal	(8,000)
Balance at end of third year	$ 7,619
Fourth-year earnings (5%)	381
Balance at end of fourth year before withdrawal	$ 8,000
Fourth-year withdrawal	(8,000)
Balance at end of fourth year	$ 0

Example 2

A corporation has a choice: It can either lease its new plant at an annual rental fee of $30,000 for 20 years or it can purchase it. Assuming that the company estimates that it could earn 14 percent annually on any funds not invested in the plant, what would be the equivalent cost of purchasing the plant? Assume also that the plant would have no value at the end of 20 years.

The present value of a stream of payments of $1 per year, compounded at a rate of 14 percent, for 20 years, is, per Table 4, $6.6231. The present value of a twenty-year stream of payments of $30,000 is $30,000 times 6.6231, or $198,693. The company would be as well off renting the plant for $30,000 per year as it would be purchasing it for $198,693 (ignoring, of course, both tax and risk factors).

Example 3

A corporation issues a security (e.g., a bond) that contains the following provision: The corporation agrees to pay the purchaser $20,000 every six months for 20 years and make an additional single lump-sum payment of $500,000 at the end of the 20-year period. How much would an investor be willing to pay for such a security, assuming that if he did not purchase the security he could, alternatively, invest the funds in other securities which would provide an annual return of 10 percent compounded semiannually?

The company promises to pay an annuity of $20,000 per period for 40 six-month periods. The present value of such an annuity when discounted at a rate of 5 percent (the *semiannual* alternative rate of return) is, with reference to Table 4,

$$\$20,000 \times 17.1591 = \$343,182$$

The present value of a single payment of $500,000, 40 periods hence, discounted at a semiannual rate of 5 percent is, with reference to Table 2,

$$\$500,000 \times .1420 = \$71,000$$

The present value of the stream of payments *and* the single lump-sum payment is therefore $343,182 plus $71,000, or $414,182. This is the amount the investor would be willing to pay:

$$\$20,000 P_{\overline{40}|.05} = \$343,182$$
$$\$500,000 p_{\overline{40}|.05} = \underline{71,000}$$
$$\text{Total} = \underline{\underline{\$414,182}}$$

Similar examples will be presented in Chapter 10; they help to explain why a bond with a certain face value (e.g., $500,000) might sell in the open market at a greater or lesser amount (e.g., $414,182).

Example 4

A company wishes to contribute an amount to a pension fund so that each employee will have an annual income of $24,000 upon retirement. The firm's consulting actuary estimates that an average employee will survive 15 years after his or her retirement and will be employed 20 years prior to retirement. The company anticipates that it will be able to obtain a return of 12 percent per year on contributions to the fund. How much should the company contribute each year, per employee, to the pension fund?

Upon the retirement of an employee, the company must have in its pension fund an amount equivalent to a stream of payments of $24,000 for 15 years. Per Table 4, the present value of a stream of payments of $1 per year, for 15 years, discounted at a rate of 12 percent is $6.8109. The present value of the stream of $24,000 payments is $24,000 times 6.8109, or $163,461:

$$\$24,000 P_{\overline{15}|.12} = \$163,461$$

The company must therefore make equal annual payments so that the accumulated value of the payments after 20 years (the expected number of years an employee will work prior to retirement) will be $163,461. According to Table 3, a stream of payments of $1, invested to yield a return of 12 percent, will accumulate to $72.0524 after 20 years. That is,

$$A_{\overline{20}|.12} = \$72.0524$$

Hence, some amount (x) times 72.0524 will accumulate to $163,461:

$$72.0524x = \$163,461$$
$$x = \$2,269$$

The firm would have to make 20 annual payments of $2,269 to be able to subsequently withdraw $24,000 per year for 15 years.

Discounted Cash Flow as a Means of Determining the Value of Assets

The procedures described in the preceding section in which a stream of future cash flows is *discounted* back to the present can be employed to determine the value to a particular firm of either individual assets or groups of assets.

Example 1

A firm is contemplating the purchase of new equipment. The company has determined that a new machine will enable it to reduce out-of-pocket production costs, after taxes, by $8,000 per year. If the machine will have a useful life of five years and the firm requires a return of at least 10 percent per year on all invested funds, what is the maximum amount it should be willing to pay for the machine?

The present value of the stream of equal cash savings is (per Table 4) 3.7908 times $8,000, or $30,326. The company should be willing to pay no more than that for the new machine.

Example 2

A company is evaluating the feasibility of acquiring another firm. Management estimates that the firm to be acquired will provide after-tax cash receipts to the purchasing company of $11 million per year for the first four years after it is acquired. Thereafter, however, it will lose certain competitive advantages, and the cash that it will be able to generate will be reduced to $7 million per year. It may be assumed that the $7 million annual cash flow will be permanent. What is the most that the company should be willing to pay for the new business, assuming that the company requires a return of 14 percent (compounded annually) on invested capital?

The stream of cash receipts can be evaluated in two parts: a permanent (infinite) flow of $7 million and a temporary "bonus" flow of $4 million for each of the first four years. The amount that the company would pay for the infinite flow can be calculated simply by dividing the annual flow by the appropriate discount rate.[3] Thus

$$\frac{\$7,000,000}{.14} = \$50,000,000$$

Were the company to pay $50 million, $7 million would provide a return of exactly 14 percent.

The amount that the company would pay for the temporary flow of $4 million for four years would be the present value of the anticipated cash receipts, that is, the present value of an annuity of $4 million for four years discounted at a rate of 14 percent. Per Table 4, the present value of an annuity of $1 for four years discounted at a rate of 14 percent is $2.9137. Hence the present value of an annuity of $4 million is $4 million times 2.9137, or $11,654,800.

For the business as a whole, the firm should be willing to pay the sum of what it would pay for the permanent and the "bonus" cash receipts:

$$\$50,000,000 + \$11,654,800 = \$61,654,800$$

Example 3

Although the market prices of common stocks, especially those that are traded on national exchanges, may appear to fluctuate irrationally, changes in market prices can be explained (though by no means predicted) by the present values of expected cash flows. In theory, the maximum amount that an investor will pay for a share of stock is that which will allow for an *acceptable return*. An acceptable return is one for which the present value of the expect-

---

[3] The formula for the present value of an annuity is $P_{\overline{n}|i} = [1 - (1 + i)^{-n}]/i$. As n approaches infinity, $(1 + i)^{-n}$ approaches 0. Thus, if $(1 + i)^{-n} = 0$, $P_{\infty|i} = (1 - 0)/i = 1/i$.

ed cash inflows is no less than the security's purchase price. The expected cash flows would typically come from two sources: periodic dividends and single-sum proceeds upon sale or redemption.

Suppose, for example, an institutional investor is considering the purchase of a security that yields dividends of $6 per year. The investor expects to hold the security for five years and anticipates that sales proceeds will be $140. What is the maximum that the investor will be willing to pay for the security, assuming the investor requires a return on investment of 12 percent per year?

The present value of the dividends, an annuity of $6P_{\overline{5}|12}$, is, per Table 4,

$$\$6 \times 3.6048 = \$21.63$$

The present value of the cash from sale, a single sum, $140p_{\overline{5}|12}$, is, per Table 2,

$$\$140 \times .5674 = \$79.44$$

The present value of both estimated sources of cash, and therefore the maximum amount that the investor should be willing to pay, is $101.07.

Similar analyses on the part of other investors would establish the amounts that they would bid for the security and, through the interaction of supply and demand, would determine actual market price. Investors would, of course, incorporate into their analyses their own unique parameters for dividends, selling price, length of time until sale, and discount rate. These parameters would be continually reassessed to take into account the latest economic and corporate developments, such as actual or forecast changes in prevailing interest rates, market trends, and corporate earnings.

SUMMARY OF PART I

In accordance with conventional financial reporting, the value assigned to an asset is ordinarily based on its *historical cost*—the amount paid to acquire it less that portion of initial cost representing the services of the asset already consumed (i.e., allowance for amortization).

Values based on historical costs are consistent with the *matching* concept, by which costs are matched with the revenues that they generate. The portion of asset cost that has not yet been charged as an expense (i.e., matched with revenues) is carried forward on the balance sheet to be expensed in future accounting periods. Thus the historical cost balance sheet is not a statement of current values; it is, instead, a statement of *residuals*—actual costs that have not yet been charged as expenses.

Historical cost values are frequently said to be *objective*. This characterization is correct only as it applies to the initial value assigned to an asset. Thereafter the reported amount of an asset may be affected by managerial judgments. For example, the reported value of plant and equipment depends upon management's estimate of the assets' useful lives and salvage values; the reported value of accounts receivable is influenced by management's estimate of doubtful accounts.

The *market value* of an asset has the advantage over its historical cost value of being more relevant for most managerial and investor decisions, because it is indicative of either the enterprise's economic sacrifice in holding and using the asset or the cost the company would have to incur to replace it. Market value can take one of two forms: current cost or net realizable value. *Current purchase cost* is an *input entry value,* the amount that the firm would have to pay to replace the asset. *Net realizable value* is an *output exit value,* the amount that the firm would receive if it sold the asset, less any costs of disposal.

Market value, however, fails to take into account the utility of an asset to its particular user. An asset may be worth more to a company than either its selling price or replacement cost. A slightly used vehicle, for example, may be almost as valuable to a company as a new one, although its market value will almost certainly be considerably less.

Moreover, the general use of market values (particularly output values) may be inconsistent with the concept that costs should be charged as expenses in the periods associated with the benefits that they provide. Start-up or organizational costs, for example, may not be considered to be assets at all, since they cannot readily be sold in the open market. Under a market-value system, the entire amounts of such costs would be charged as expenses in the periods in which they were incurred.

The value of an asset could also be stated in terms of its *utility* to a specific user. The worth of an asset to a particular user may be defined as the present value of the anticipated cash receipts with which it is associated. The present value of the cash receipts must take into account the "time value of money"—the fact that a dollar received today is worth considerably more than one to be received in the distant future. Determination of the present value of cash flows requires an understanding of the fundamental concepts of compound interest—hence the extended discussion of that topic in this chapter. It is often impractical, however, to determine the present value of a particular asset, since individual assets are not generally associated with specific cash receipts. Thus conventional financial statements seldom express asset values in terms of worth to the individual possessor. Nevertheless, an understanding of the concepts of present values of cash flows provides an appreciation of the underlying forces that determine the worth of assets and is the key to making rational decisions as to whether to purchase or sell assets.

In Part II of this chapter, as well as in the next several chapters, we deal with problems of valuing specific assets, such as cash, marketable securities, accounts receivable, inventories, and plant and equipment.

PART II. Cash and Marketable Securities

CASH

Cash is ordinarily reported at its face value. *Cash* includes currency on hand and funds on deposit in banks that are subject to immediate and unconditional withdrawal (i.e., amounts in chequing accounts). It does not in a strict sense include amounts that may be subject to withdrawal restrictions, such as funds in the form of savings accounts, which may technically require advance notification for withdrawal, or certificates of deposit. Most companies maintain several general ledger accounts for cash. In statements made available to the public, however, most cash and "near-cash" balances are summarized into a single figure.

There are several characteristics of cash that make it of distinctive interest to a manager or investor. It is the ultimate asset of concern to investors as it is the medium of exchange in our society. The business cycle begins and ends with cash. Owners and creditors contribute cash to a firm. The firm, in turn, uses the cash to acquire other assets. It expects that by providing goods and services, it will eventually be able to reconvert these other assets into more cash than was contributed. It then distributes this greater amount of cash to the owners and creditors.

Cash is the most liquid of assets. Indeed, liquidity is a measure of how easily an asset can be converted into cash. Because of its liquid nature, cash must be the subject of especially tight safeguards and controls. As a general rule, for example, the number of persons handling currency should be kept to a minimum, all currency should be deposited in a bank as soon as feasible, and accounting recognition should be given immediately to all cash receipts via a cash register tape or a manual listing. The responsibility for particular cash functions should be assigned to particular individuals, and whenever possible, to assure better that the payments are made to the parties for whom they are intended, disbursements should be made by cheque rather than with currency.

Cash is the accepted medium of paying bills and satisfying obligations. It is essential that a firm have an adequate amount of cash available to meet its debts as they come due and to make the day-to-day payments required of any operating enterprise. Management, as well as financial analysts and creditors, must, therefore, be continually alert to whether the firm's available cash—or assets that can readily be turned into cash—is sufficient to meet foreseeable needs.

Unproductive Asset

Cash, however, is an *unproductive asset*. Cash on hand or on deposit in a chequing account earns little or no interest. If there is inflation in the economy, cash loses its purchasing power. Unlike many other assets, it produces no services and provides no return to its owner. As a consequence, it is to the advantage of a firm to keep as little cash as possible either on hand or in chequing accounts. Cash that is needed for a *safety reserve* or is being held for future purchase of other assets, distribution to shareholders, or payment of outstanding obligations should be invested temporarily in common stocks, short-term government treasury bills, certificates of deposit, or other dividend or interest-bearing securities.

Cash on Hand; Imprest Basis

Cash on hand includes customer receipts that have not yet been deposited, currency necessary to conduct routine business, and petty cash. *Petty cash* represents small amounts of cash maintained to meet disbursements of insufficient size to justify the time and inconvenience of writing a cheque. Petty cash funds are frequently accounted for on an *imprest* basis. That is, the general ledger balance of petty cash will always reflect a fixed amount, $100, for example. At all times the fund itself should contain either cash or payment receipts for that amount. Periodically the fund is restored to its original cash amount by a transfer from general cash, and at that time accounting recognition is given to the particular expenses that have been incurred. The following journal entry might be made to restore $70 to the petty cash fund:

Postage expense	$30	
Entertainment expense	40	
Cash in bank		$70
To replenish petty cash fund		

Cash in Bank

The balance of cash reported in a firm's general ledger is unlikely to be that actually available for withdrawal at a particular time. Conventional practice dictates that a firm reduce the general ledger cash balance when it writes a cheque. However, a period of several days or even weeks may elapse before a cheque reaches and clears the firm's bank. During that period, the balance per the records of the bank will be greater than the balance in the books of the firm by the amount of the cheque. Similarly, a firm may record deposits at the time it mails or delivers them to its bank. The bank will credit the firm's account only when it actually receives the deposit or, if the receipt is after hours, on the next business day. As a consequence, the amount of cash that a firm reports may be either greater or less than that actually available for withdrawal per the records of the bank. Periodically, upon receiving a statement of its account from the bank, the firm must *reconcile* its balance with that of the bank; that is, it must account for any differences between the balance as indicated by its own records and that of the bank. At the same time, it must update its own books to give recognition to any transactions about which it learns from the bank statement. An example and explanation of a bank reconciliation (in one of many possible forms) are provided in Exhibit 6-5.

Classification of Cash

Cash is ordinarily classified as a current asset. In fact, cash is the fundamental current asset in that current assets are defined as those that will be converted into cash within the operating cycle of a business. Nevertheless, there are exceptions. Cash should be considered a current asset only when there are no restrictions—either those imposed by contract or by management intent—upon its use as a medium of exchange within a single operating cycle. Suppose, for example, that a company is required by terms of a bond agreement to maintain a *sinking fund* for the retirement of debt that will mature in 10 years. A sinking fund consists of cash or other assets segregated in the accounts to repay an outstanding debt when it comes due. All such assets, although normally considered current, when set aside in a sinking fund should be classified on the balance sheet as *noncurrent* assets since management has earmarked them for a specific, noncurrent, purpose. The intent of management should be the key criterion for classification.

EXHIBIT 6-5

Bank Reconciliation
December 31

	Per Firm's Own Books	Per Bank Statement
Cash Balance, December 31 (Note 1)	$20,020.53	$16,160.30
Items that explain differences between firm's and bank's balance		
Add: Deposit in transit (Note 2)		12,176.25
Subtract: Outstanding cheques (Note 3)		(6,562.19)
Subtract: Bank service charge (Note 4)	(10.00)	
Subtract: N.S.F. cheque (Note 5)	(236.17)	
Add: Note collected by bank (Note 6)	2,000.00	
Adjusted cash balance, December 31 (Note 7)	$21,774.36	$21,774.36

Note 1. The firm's records indicate a cash balance of $20,020.53; the bank's records indicate a balance of $16,160.30. Assuming that neither is in error, the difference can be explained by transactions about which one party or the other has no knowledge.

Note 2. The firm made a deposit to the bank on December 31, the date of the bank statement. The company recorded the deposit, but the bank has not, most likely because it was received after the close of business on December 31.

Note 3. The company has written cheques on its account that have not yet "cleared" the bank. The bank is unaware of them since these cheques have not yet been presented for payment. When the company wrote the cheques, it credited (reduced) its recorded cash balance. The bank will reduce the balance in the firm's bank account when it makes the required disbursements on behalf of the firm.

Note 4. The bank reduced the firm's balance in the amount of a service charge. The company, perhaps because it only learns of such charge by way of the monthly bank statement, has not yet recorded it.

Note 5. The bank also reduced the firm's balance to reflect an N.S.F. (not sufficient funds) cheque. An N.S.F. cheque is one returned by the bank to the depositor because it has been dishonoured by the bank on which it was drawn. When the firm initially deposited the cheque, the bank, assuming that the cheque would be collectable, credited (increased) the firm's account. Upon learning that the party that wrote the cheque had insufficient funds in its account to cover the payment, the bank returned the dishonoured cheque to the firm and reduced the balance in the firm's account. The firm, when it first deposited the cheque, had also recorded an increase in its cash balance. Unlike the bank, however, it has not yet recorded the return of the dishonoured cheque by reducing the balance in its cash account.

Note 6. The bank collected the proceeds of a customer note for the company and has given the company credit for it. As with the N.S.F. cheque, it did not yet notify the company (or if it did, the company has not yet recorded it by increasing its cash balance).

Note 7. The cash available to the firm is $21,774.36. The company must now record the bank service charge, the N.S.F. cheque and the collection of the note. In the normal course of events, the bank will routinely record the deposit in transit and the outstanding cheques. Then (disregarding all subsequent transactions), the records of both the firm and the bank would agree; they would show a balance of $21,774.36.

The reconciliation points to the need for the firm to update its records to take account of the information provided by the bank statement. The following entry would give effect to that information:

Cash	$1,753.83	
Bank service charge (expense)	10.00	
Accounts receivable	236.17	
Notes receivable		$2,000

To update the cash account for information indicated by the bank reconciliation
(Accounts receivable has been debited by the amount of the N.S.F. cheque because the party which wrote the cheque is again indebted to the company for the amount of the cheque.)

In an effort to obtain a return on what would otherwise be temporarily idle cash, many corporations use such cash to purchase stocks, bonds, or commercial paper (short-term certificates of debt). Temporary investments are ordinarily grouped together in the current asset section of the balance sheet under the heading "marketable securities." If the investment is in shares of voting stock, the balance sheet classification of the investment depends on management's intention. If the firm ordinarily expects to hold the securities for a relatively short period of time, until a need for cash arises, and does not anticipate exercising any significant degree of influence over the company whose shares it may own, the investment would be classified as marketable securities. If the company has other intentions with respect to the securities (i.e., to hold for an indefinite period and/or to exercise significant influence), they should ordinarily be classified as "long-term investments," a noncurrent asset (to be discussed in Chapter 13).

As with most other assets, marketable securities are reported on the balance sheet at their original cost. However, because the company is likely to sell them in the near future, the current market value is disclosed parenthetically on the face of the statement. Thus

Cash	$ 80,000
Marketable securities (current market value, $350,000)	335,000

Gains and losses on the sale of individual securities are ordinarily recognized at the time of sale. No recognition is given to fluctuations in market value. Assume, for example, that a company had purchased 1,000 shares of Seagram Company Ltd. common stock at $50 per share. The stock would be reported on the balance sheet at $50,000. Should the company sell the stock for $65 per share, it would record the sale as follows:

Cash	$65,000	
Marketable securities		$50,000
Gain on sale of marketable securities		15,000
To record the sale of marketable securities		

Revenues from dividends or interest on marketable securities are ordinarily recognized upon receipt. Thus, had Seagram declared and paid a quarterly dividend of $0.25 per share before the company had sold the shares, the following entry would have been appropriate:

Cash	$250	
Dividend revenue		$250
To record receipt of dividend		

Lower of Cost or Market Rule

The one critical exception to the general rule that marketable securities be reported at historical cost is that, where the market value of equity securities (i.e., stocks) is less than cost, the carrying value of the securities should be reduced to the market value, and a corresponding loss should be recognized. The comparison between cost and market value may be applied on either an individual security basis or on a total portfolio basis. This exception to reporting at historical cost represents an application of the guidelines of conservatism. Unfavourable events should be recognized at the earliest possible time.

This "lower of cost or market" rule is stated in the *CICA Handbook*:

> **When the market value of temporary investments has declined below the carrying value, they should be carried at market value.**[4]

Assume, for example, that during 1996 a firm acquired a portfolio of three stocks. As shown, by year end, two of the stocks had declined in value and one had increased:

	Original Cost	Market Value 31/12/96	Lower of Cost or Market
Stock A	$10,000	$12,000	$10,000
Stock B	12,000	8,000	8,000
Stock C	15,000	9,000	9,000
Total	$37,000	$29,000	$27,000

On a portfolio basis, the portfolio would be written down to the market value of the three securities combined, $29,000. Were the lower of cost or market rule to be applied on the basis of individual securities, the portfolio would be written down to $27,000. The portfolio method is less conservative than the individual security method in that gains in some securities are permitted to offset losses in others.

The decline in market value will be recognized in the statement of income as a loss. Although reported like other losses or expenses, the loss would be unrealized—"unrealized" because it has not been confirmed by an actual sale. Correspondingly, the difference between the cost and the market value of the portfolio would be reported in a "valuation allowance." The valuation allowance would be a contra account to marketable securities. The original cost of the securities would be retained in the marketable securities account. The marketable securities account, less the amount in the valuation allowance, would indicate the market value (if lower than cost) of the portfolio.

The following journal entry would record the decline in the value of the portfolio:

Loss on valuation of marketable securities (expense) $8,000
    Allowance for excess of cost of marketable securities
      over market value (contra asset account) $8,000
To recognize a loss equal to the excess of cost ($37,000) over market value ($29,000) of marketable securities

If, in subsequent years, the value of the portfolio increased, then the balance in the allowance account would be reduced. Correspondingly, a gain on recovery would be reported in the income statement. However, a gain on recovery would be recognized only to the extent that unrealized losses were

---

[4] "Temporary Investments," Section 3010.06, *CICA Handbook*, 1978.

previously recognized. The carrying value of the portfolio must never exceed original cost.

Suppose, for example, that during 1997 the market prices of the securities changed to:

	Original Cost	Market Value 31/12/97
Stock A	$10,000	$11,000
Stock B	12,000	10,000
Stock C	15,000	13,000
Total	$37,000	$34,000

The market value of the portfolio increased since year-end 1996 by $5,000 from $29,000 to $34,000. Hence the valuation allowance must be reduced by $5,000 and a recovery gain in that amount recognized as revenue:

Allowance for excess of cost of marketable
   securities over market value (contra asset account) $5,000
     Recovery of previously recognized losses on
       valuation of marketable securities (revenue) $5,000
To recognize increase in market value of security portfolio (i.e., recovery of previously recognized losses)

The balance in the valuation allowance would now be $3,000—the difference between the original cost of $37,000 and market value of $34,000.

Should the company sell a security, it would record a gain or loss on the individual security, just as illustrated previously. Suppose, for example, that in 1998 the firm sells stock C for $14,000. The original cost of stock C was $15,000; hence it would recognize a loss (now a "realized loss") of $1,000:

Cash $14,000
Loss on sale of marketable securities 1,000
   Marketable securities $15,000
To record the sale of marketable securities at a loss

At the conclusion of 1998, the firm would compare the cost and market values of the securities that remain in its portfolio. It would adjust the allowance account to reflect the difference between the two and record a corresponding valuation loss or recovery gain for the amount that must be added to, or subtracted from, the allowance account. If, for example, the combined market value of stocks A and B increased to $25,000, an amount in excess of original cost of $22,000, then the balance in the valuation allowance should be zero. Since the balance at the end of 1997 was $3,000, the following entry would be in order:

Allowance for excess of cost of marketable securities
   over market value (contra asset account) $3,000
     Recovery of previously recognized losses on
       valuation of marketable securities (revenue) $3,000
To recognize increase in market value of security portfolio (i.e., recovery of previously recognized losses)

VALUATION OF MARKETABLE SECURITIES— A PROPOSED ALTERNATIVE

The current practice of generally reporting marketable securities at original cost is consistent with that for other assets. Two characteristics of marketable securities may justify an alternative approach. First, the current market value of marketable securities (at any particular time) can ordinarily be objectively determined. This is especially true of securities that are widely traded, since current prices are available daily in either newspapers or through electronic services. Second, there is always a market in which to sell the securities. Unlike capital assets or inventories, marketable securities can be disposed of at the market price by a single telephone call to a stockbroker. As a consequence of these two characteristics, critics of current practice assert that the dual accounting goals of providing information that is both relevant and objective can best be achieved by valuing securities on the balance sheet at market values rather than historical costs.

Historical costs detract from the utility of both the balance sheet and the income statement. The stated value of the marketable securities may bear no relationship to their current selling prices. In fact, shares in the same company—which could be converted to the same amount of cash—may be valued at different amounts if not acquired at the same time.

Gains or losses from holding an individual security are recorded only when the security is actually sold. In an accounting sense, at least, management is neither credited nor discredited for holding a security as it increases or decreases in market value until the period of sale. The period of sale may be one subsequent to that in which the increase or decrease in value actually took place.

If a firm has in its portfolio one or more securities that have increased in value since they were purchased, management can easily manipulate reported earnings. If management wishes to improve earnings for the current period, it simply sells those securities that have appreciated in value. If, on the other hand, it wishes to give the earnings of the following year a boost, it delays the sale until then. It is questionable, given the ease by which it can be done, that the sale of a security is of greater economic significance than the changes in its market value while it is being held.

The problem of reporting marketable securities is of special concern to industries, such as mutual funds and insurance, in which all or a sizable portion of assets consists of marketable securities. In those industries it is vital that an investor be concerned with unrealized gains or losses. As a consequence, firms in such industries either already give effect to unrealized gains or losses on both the balance sheet and the income statement or otherwise make prominent disclosure in footnotes.

Although the issue of cost versus market value can conveniently be highlighted in a discussion of marketable securities, it is one that bears upon all assets and liabilities. It will be alluded to again in several subsequent chapters.

SUMMARY OF PART II

In Part II of this chapter we have dealt with problems of accounting for and reporting cash and marketable securities, both of which are ordinarily classified as current assets. Cash includes currency on hand as well as demand deposits in banks.

Cash is the asset of greatest interest to managers and investors as it is the means by which goods and services are acquired. Indeed, the paramount objective of most investors is to maximize cash returns. Cash is also the most liquid of assets. As such it must be the subject of especially tight safeguards and controls.

Cash, although generally classified as a current asset, should be grouped with the noncurrent assets in those situations in which it is subject to restrictions upon its withdrawal, regardless of whether the restrictions are imposed by contract or by management itself.

Marketable securities include those securities which a firm holds as temporary investments. The key issue with respect to marketable securities pertains to the value at which they should be reported on the balance sheet and the point at which increases or decreases in value should be recognized on the income statement. Marketable securities are conventionally reported at cost. Increases or decreases in market value are recognized only upon the sale of a security. An exception is made, however, when the market value is less than cost. In accordance with the "lower of cost or market" rule, the marketable securities are written down to market value, on either a portfolio or individual security basis. Alternatively, however, many accountants argue that all changes in the market values of securities should be given accounting recognition and all gains or losses, both *realized* and *unrealized*, should be reflected immediately in enterprise earnings.

Exercise for Review and Self-Testing

Try to complete this exercise without using the future and present value tables in the Appendix.

Assume that today is January 1, 1997. Further assume that the prevailing rate of interest paid by banks on deposits is 7 percent, compounded annually.

1. *Future value of a single amount.* A corporation deposits $50,000 in a bank today.
   a. How much will it have in its account on December 31, 1997?
   b. How much will it have in its account on December 31, 1998?
   c. How much will it have in its account on December 31, 1999?

2. *Future value of an annuity.* A corporation deposits $50,000 in a bank on December 31, 1997.
   a. How much will it have in its account on December 31, 1997, immediately after making the deposit?
   b. It makes another deposit of $50,000 on December 31, 1998. How much will it have in its account after making the deposit?
   c. It makes yet another deposit of $50,000 on December 31, 1999. How much will it have in its account after making the third deposit?

3. *Present value of a single amount.* A corporation wants to be able to withdraw from its account $50,000 on December 31, 1997.
   a. How much should it deposit today?
   b. Assume instead that it wants to be able to withdraw $50,000 on December 31, 1998. How much should it deposit today?

c. Assume alternatively that it wants to be able to withdraw $50,000 on December 31, 1999. How much should it deposit today?

4. *Present value of an annuity.* A corporation wants to be able to withdraw from its account $50,000 on December 31, 1997, $50,000 on December 31, 1998, and $50,000 on December 31, 1999. How much should it deposit today?

Questions for Review and Discussion

1. What is meant by *value* as the term is used in connection with assets reported on the conventional balance sheet?

2. The balance sheet, it is often asserted, provides little indication of a company's inherent worth. Instead, it is nothing more than a compilation of *residuals.* Do you agree?

3. Historical cost values of assets are of little relevance to most decisions faced by management, creditors, or investors. Why, then, do accountants resist efforts to convert to a market-value-oriented balance sheet?

4. Market values can be interpreted as either *input* or *output* prices. What is the distinction between the two? Give an example of each.

5. What are the economic benefits associated with an asset? How can they be quantified?

6. Current assets are defined as those which are reasonably expected to be *realized in cash,* sold, or consumed during the normal operating cycle of the business. Yet cash itself is not always classified as a current asset. Why might this be so?

7. The owner of a small corporation was recently advised by her CA that she "has too much cash in her chequing account." The company has a chequing account balance of $100,000, and the CA told the owner that the account was costing the company "about $10,000 per year." The owner of the corporation insisted that this could not be so; the money was deposited in a "no-charge" chequing account. What do you think the CA had in mind when she made her comment?

8. The general managers of two identical companies each reported operating earnings in 1996 of $100 million, excluding income from the sale of marketable securities. The manager of company A also indicated that on January 5, 1996, his company purchased but had not yet sold 1 million shares of United Mining Co. common stock at $15 per share. On December 31, 1996, United Mining was trading at $45 per share. By contrast, the manager of company B revealed that his company had purchased 1 million shares of United Mining Co. common stock on April 18, 1996 at $35 per share and had sold them on November 25 at $38 per share. If conventional accounting principles are adhered to, which company would report the higher income? Excluding all factors other than those discussed, which company do you think had the superior performance in 1996?

1. *Problems 1–8 are intended to facilitate understanding of the four basic concepts of compound interest.*

    Assuming an interest rate of 8 percent compounded annually, $400,000 is
    a. The present value of what amount to be received in five years?
    b. The value in five years of what amount deposited in a bank today?
    c. The present value of an annuity of what amount to be received over the next five years?
    d. The value in five years of an annuity of what amount deposited in a bank at the end of each of the next five years?

2. The board of directors of a printing company decided that the company should take advantage of an unusually successful year to place in a reserve fund an amount of cash sufficient to enable it to purchase a new printing press in six years. The company determines that the new press would then cost $300,000 and that funds could be invested in securities that would provide a return of 8 percent, compounded annually.
    a. How much should the company place in the fund?
    b. Suppose that the return would be compounded quarterly. How much should the company place in the fund?

3. In anticipation of the need to purchase new equipment, a corporation decided to set aside $60,000 each year in a special fund.
    a. If the amount in the fund could be invested in securities that provide an after-tax return of 5 percent per year, how much would the company have available in eight years?
    b. Assume instead that the company knew that it would require $600,000 to replace the equipment at the end of eight years. How much should it contribute to the fund each year, assuming an annual return of 5 percent?

4. A corporation wishes to provide a research grant to a university so that the university can withdraw $20,000 at the end of each of the next three years. The university will deposit the amount received in an account that earns interest at the rate of 5 percent per year. How much should the corporation give the university? Prepare a schedule in which you indicate the balance in the account at the end of each of the three years after the annual interest income and the $20,000 withdrawal have been accounted for.

5. On the day of a child's birth, the parents deposit $2,000 in a bank savings account. The account pays interest at the rate of 8 percent each year, compounded annually.
    a. How much will be on deposit by the time the child enters university on her eighteenth birthday?
    b. Assume instead that the interest at an annual rate of 8 percent is compounded semiannually. To how much will the original deposit increase in 18 years?

6. A corporation borrows $5,000 from a bank. Principal and interest are payable at the end of five years.

a. What will be the amount of the corporation's payment, assuming that the bank charges interest at a rate of 10 percent and compounds the interest annually?

b. What will be the amount of the corporation's payment if interest at an annual rate of 10 percent is compounded semiannually?

7. You deposit a fixed amount in a bank. How long will it take for your funds to double if the bank pays interest at a rate of
   a. 4 percent compounded annually?
   b. 8 percent compounded annually?
   c. 8 percent compounded semiannually?
   d. 8 percent compounded quarterly?

8. A company wishes to establish a pension plan for its president. The company wants to assure the president or his survivors an income of $50,000 per year for 20 years after his retirement. The president has 15 years to work before he retires. If the company can earn 8 percent per year on the pension fund, how much should it contribute during each remaining working year of the president?

9. *Effective interest rates can be adjusted in a number of different ways.*

   Canadian government treasury bills differ from conventional government or corporate *coupon* bonds in that they do not have attached to them coupons that can periodically be redeemed for interest payments. Instead, they carry a face value of a fixed amount, for example, $100,000. The purchaser buys the bonds at a discount. For example, he or she might pay $75,000 for a $100,000 treasury bill that will mature in 10 years. The difference between what is paid for the treasury bill and its face value represents the interest for the entire period during which the treasury bill is outstanding. Upon maturity the purchaser will present the treasury bill to the government and receive its full face value. The government can adjust the effective interest rate that it pays by varying either the initial selling price of the treasury bill or the number of years the purchaser must hold the treasury bill before he or she can redeem it.

   a. Suppose that the government sells a $100,000 face value treasury bill for $75,000 and establishes a holding period of 10 years. What is the approximate effective rate of interest (assume that interest is compounded annually)?

   b. Suppose instead that the government wishes to establish an effective rate of 8 percent and a holding period of 10 years. At what price should it sell the treasury bill?

   c. If the government wishes to establish an effective rate of 8 percent and a price of $75,000 how long a holding period should it require?

10. *Truth-in-lending laws are designed to eliminate the type of deception suggested by this problem.*

    The Helping Hand Loan Co. placed an advertisement in a local newspaper that read in part, "Borrow up to $10,000 for 5 years at our low, low rate of interest of 6 percent per year." When a customer went to the loan company to borrow the $10,000, he was told that total interest on the five-year loan would be $3,000. That is, $600 per year (6 percent of

$10,000) for five years. Company practice, he was told, requires that the interest be paid in full at the time a loan is made and be deducted from the amount given to the customer. Thus the customer was given only $7,000. The loan was to be repaid in five annual instalments of $2,000.

Do you think that the ad was misleading? What was the actual amount loaned to the customer? Determine what you consider to be the "true" rate of interest.

11. *Rates of discount determine firms' preferences for alternative financing arrangements.*

Company A is presently negotiating with company B to purchase a parcel of land. Three alternative sets of terms are under consideration:

a. Company A will pay $400,000 at time of sale.

b. Company A will pay $50,000 at time of sale and give company B a note payable for $500,000 that matures in five years.

c. Company A will make five annual payments of $100,000 each commencing one year from the date of sale.

Company A can obtain an after-tax return of 7 percent per year on any funds that it has available for investment; company B can obtain a return of 9 percent. Both firms use discount rates to evaluate potential investments that are equal to the rates of return that they can obtain.

Rank the three sets of terms as you would expect them to be preferred by each of the two companies.

12. *Present value techniques can be used to develop a mortgage schedule.* (This problem is intended for solution using an electronic spreadsheet.)

On December 31, 1996, a bank lends a corporate customer $600,000 to acquire a building. The loan is for a period of 10 years and bears interest at the rate of 12 percent. As is typical of mortgage loans, the borrower will be required to repay the loan in equal instalments. In this case, the borrower will make 10 annual payments, the first on December 31, 1997. Each payment will comprise two elements: interest at the rate of 12 percent on the outstanding balance and a reduction of the principal (the loan balance) that is equal to the total payment less the amount applied to interest.

a. Determine the amount of each required payment (i.e., the amount of a 10-year annuity with a present value of $600,000).

b. Prepare a schedule in which you show in appropriate columns:

(1) The balance of the loan at the end of each of the ten years

(2) The annual payment as computed in part (a)

(3) The portion of each payment that is applied to interest (This amount will decrease each year as the principal balance of the loan is reduced.)

(4) The portion of each payment that is applied to the principal and thereby reduces the outstanding balance (This amount will increase each year as the amount applied to interest decreases.)

13. *Present value analysis can be used to determine the worth of an investment in the shares of a nonpublic company.* (This problem is intended for solution using an electronic spreadsheet.)

Under GAAP, a company is required to write down its long-term investments from cost to market value when there is evidence that its market value has been permanently impaired. In 1991 Wertimer Co. acquired Gambs Ltd. for $200 million and until December 31, 1996, reported its investment in Gambs at cost. In consultation with its independent auditor, Wertimer is assessing its investment in Gambs at December 31, 1996, to determine whether a write down to market is required.

Gambs Ltd. has sustained substantial operating losses since being acquired. An independent consultant has determined that for Gambs Ltd. to be profitable it would have to upgrade its facilities substantially. The required funds would have to be provided by Wertimer, Inc. The consultant estimates that if Wertimer, Inc., elects to modernize the facilities, then (under the most optimistic scenario) it can expect cash flows from Gambs (taking into account the modernization costs) to be as follows for the next 20 years (in millions):

1997	($15)
1998	(10)
1999	(3)
2000	2
2001	5
2002–2006	8 per year
2007–2016	12 per year

Suppose that you are asked to assist Wertimer in calculating the market value of Gambs. Wertimer has not received any offers to purchase Gambs; hence there are no offers on which to base an estimate of market value. However, the auditor is willing to accept alternative evidence of market value.

a. Based on the present value of cash flows for the period 1997–2016, what is the maximum value that you would place on Gambs Ltd.? Apply a discount rate of 15 percent.

b. Suppose the auditor claims that the estimates of cash flows for the years 2007 to 2016 are unrealistically low. Recalculate the present value, assuming that the cash flows for that period would be increased by 100 percent from $12 to $24 million per year.

c. Suppose instead that the auditor challenged the cash flows for the years 2002 to 2006 and said that they should be increased by 100 percent, from $8 million to $16 million per year. Recalculate the present value. Comment on the relative significance of an $8 million increase per year in the years 2002 to 2006 as compared with an increase of $12 million per year in the years 2007 to 2016.

14. *The impact of alternative tax proposals can be assessed by discounting resultant cash savings.*

The Department of Finance is considering three alternative tax incentives to encourage investment in certain types of plant and equipment. Your company is planning to acquire a plant, which would be eligible for the benefits. The plant would cost $100 million and is expected to provide a cash return, before taxes, of $25 million per year for 10 years. The proposed tax incentives, and their impact on the investment, would be as follows:

(1) Provide an investment tax credit of 10 percent of the cost of eligible plant. This would save the company $10 million at the time of acquisition.

(2) Reduce the tax on income from the plant from 40 to 30 percent. This would save the firm $2.5 million per year over the 10-year life of the plant.

(3) Reduce the tax on gains from the sale of the plant. This would save the company $10 million when it disposed of the plant at the end of year 10.

The company applies a discount rate of 12 percent to all investment proposals.

a. Calculate the present value of the savings that would result from each of the three proposals.

b. Suppose that the Department of Finance rejected option 1. What would be the amount of annual savings (for option 2) or savings upon sale (for option 3) that would be necessary to provide the equivalent benefits of option 1?

15. *The market value of a firm's common stock is likely to be affected by changes in anticipated cash flows.*

The common stock of the North Sea Oil Company is presently trading at $50 per share. There are 10 million shares outstanding.

The company will soon announce a major new oil find. The new discovery is expected to have the following impact on the firm's cash flows (in millions, per year):

Years 1 and 2 (as the fields are developed)	($10)
Years 3 through 10	18
Years 11 through 20	12

Historically the firm's dividend policy has been directly associated with net cash receipts. Annual dividend payout has been approximately 50 percent of net cash receipts. In valuing the common stock of North Sea, investors as a group have discounted anticipated cash dividends at a rate of 8 percent. Focusing strictly on the limited amount of information provided in the problem, what would you anticipate to be market price of North Sea common stock immediately following the announcement of the new find?

16. *Alternative bases of asset valuation affect both earnings and assets.*

In 1996 the Bloor Street Diamond Mart acquired a gem for resale. The cost of the jewel to the firm was $2 million. By the end of 1996, the firm would have had to pay $2.4 million to acquire a stone of comparable size and quality, and it could have sold the stone to a retail customer for $3.0 million. However, it was certain that if it would wait an additional year to sell the jewel, it could do so for $3.6 million.

a. Indicate the amount at which the firm should report the gem on its balance sheet of December 31, 1996, if it elects to wait one year to sell it, assuming each of the following bases of valuation:

(1) Historical cost

(2) Current cost (an input price)

(3) Net realizable value (an output price)

(4) Value to user (the firm determines the present value of expected cash receipts using a discount rate of 7 percent)

b. Indicate the amount of any gain associated with the stone that the firm would report in 1996, assuming each of the bases indicated.

17. *The basis of asset valuation determines the basis for revenue recognition.*

During 1996, in its first year of operations, the Mann Company purchased, for $60 per unit, 1,000 units of a product. Of these, it sold 800 units at a price of $100 per unit. On December 31, 1996, the company was notified by its supplier that in the following year the wholesale cost per unit would be increased to $70 per unit. As a consequence of the increase, Mann Company determined that the retail price would increase to $120 per unit.

Ignoring other revenues and expenses, determine the ending inventory balance and compute income, assuming that ending inventories are to be valued at

a. Historical cost (generally accepted basis)

b. Current cost (an *input* price)

c. Net realizable value (an *output* price)

In computing income, distinguish between revenue from the actual sale of product and yet to be realized gains from *holding* the product in inventory. Remember that any recorded increases in the value of the inventory must also be reflected in the determination of income (and, more specifically, of revenues).

18. *Present value techniques can be used to determine the value of a business.*

The general ledger of the Odessa Company reflected, in summary form, the following balances (there were no material liabilities):

Current assets (accounts receivable, inventory, etc.)	$ 40,000
Equipment	80,000
Building	120,000
Land	60,000

The Geneva Company purchased the assets of Odessa for a total of $400,000 (cash). Immediately after purchase an independent appraiser estimated the value of the individual assets of Odessa as follows:

Current assets	$ 40,000
Equipment	100,000
Building	160,000
Land	100,000

a. Prepare a journal entry to record the acquisition on the books of the Geneva Company.

b. Assume instead that the Geneva Company is willing to pay for the assets of the Odessa Company an amount such that its return on investment will be 10 percent per year. Geneva estimates that the earnings (net cash inflow) of the Odessa assets will be $50,000 for the first five years following the acquisition and $40,000 for an indefinite period thereafter.

    (1) How much would the Geneva Company be willing to invest to receive a net cash inflow of $40,000 per year for an infinite number of years?

    (2) How much would it be willing to invest in order to receive a net cash inflow of $10,000 (the "bonus" earnings) for a period of five years?

    (3) How much would it be willing to pay for the assets of the Odessa Company?

19. *Rental charges can be established so that lease arrangements are, in economic substance, equivalent to sales.*

    At the request of several of its customers, a heavy equipment manufacturer has decided to give them the option of leasing or buying its products. The company expects a rate of return of 12 percent on all investments. The useful life of its equipment is eight years. Each lessee (that is, customer) will pay all operating costs including taxes, insurance, and maintenance.

    a. The company establishes an annual rental charge of $12,000. What would be the sale price that would leave the company equally well off as if it had leased the equipment for the entire useful life of the equipment?

    b. The company establishes a price for the equipment of $75,000. What annual rental charge would leave the company as well off as if it had sold the equipment?

20. *Businesses, as well as individuals, should at least once a month compare the cash balance per their bank statement with that per their own records, account for all differences, and adjust their books as required. The next two problems are exercises in preparing bank reconciliations.*

    On December 31, 1996, the general ledger of the MacDonald Company indicated that the cash balance in the firm's chequing account at the Bank of Montreal was $108,763. A statement received from the bank, however, indicated that the balance in the account was $147,974. Investigation revealed the following:

    (1) The company had drawn cheques totalling $55,186 that had not been paid by the bank.

    (2) The company made a deposit on the evening of December 31 of $26,102. This deposit was included by the bank in its business of January 2, 1997.

    (3) On December 10, the company had deposited a cheque given to it by a customer for $103. On December 31, the bank returned the cheque to the company marked "N.S.F." (not sufficient funds in customer's account). The company had given no accounting recognition to the return of the cheque.

    (4) The bank debited the account of the company for a monthly service charge of $20. The company had not yet recorded the charge.

    (5) On December 31, the bank collected a customer note of $10,250 for the company. The company did not receive notification of the collection until January 4, 1997.

a. Prepare a schedule that reconciles the balance per the general ledger with that per the bank statement and indicates the balance that should be shown in the general ledger.

b. Prepare a journal entry to bring the general ledger up to date.

21. The general ledger of the McGuire Corp. indicated cash in bank of $3,822.81 as at December 31. A statement from the bank, as at the same date, indicated cash in bank of $5,477.

As at December 31, the company has outstanding cheques of $1,800.00. On December 29, it mailed a deposit of $465.81 to the bank. As at year end, it had not yet been received by the bank. On December 31, the bank collected for the company a note from a customer. As at year end, the bank had not yet notified the company. The amount of the note was $500.

On December 18, the company made a deposit in the amount of $423.50. The bank incorrectly recorded it as $243.50.

a. Prepare a schedule in which you account for the difference between the balance per the company books and that per the bank statement and determine the amount of cash in bank that should be reported in the firm's end-of-year financial statements.

b. Prepare a journal entry to adjust the present balance.

22. *This problem describes a common banking arrangement, whereby a borrower is required to maintain a compensating balance with a lending institution. It suggests an accounting issue associated with the arrangement.*

Indicated as follows are year-end balances from selected general ledger accounts of the Laurier Co.:

Cash, Bank of Nova Scotia	$ 50,000
Note payable, Bank of Nova Scotia	500,000
Interest expense	70,000

The interest expense represents borrowing charges for one year on the note payable to the Bank of Nova Scotia. Per terms of the loan agreement, Laurier will maintain in a special interest-free account an amount equal to 10 percent of any loans outstanding to the Bank of Nova Scotia.

The controller of Laurier Co. has proposed to include the following comment among the footnotes to its published financial statements: "As at December 31, 1996, the company was indebted to the Bank of Nova Scotia for $500,000. The note to the bank matures in 2001. The company pays interest at the rate of 12 percent per year."

The controller indicated that she intends to classify the cash in the special interest-free account with the Bank of Nova Scotia as a current asset.

a. Inasmuch as the note payable with which the special interest-free account is associated will be classified as a noncurrent liability, do you think that the compensating cash balance should be classified as a current asset?

b. How much money did the company really borrow from the bank; how much did it have available for use?

c. How much interest did it pay in 1996? What was the effective interest rate paid?

23. *The lower of cost or market rule can be applied on two different bases, each having a different effect on both assets and earnings.*

The following table indicates the marketable securities (all common stocks) owned by the Alberta Co. on December 31, 1997. All securities were purchased within the previous 12 months. Also shown are the original purchase prices and the current market prices.

Securities	Number of Shares	Purchase Price	Current Market Price
Laidlaw	100	$ 25	$ 30
Telus	200	14	10
CAE	100	7	12
Nova	50	15	10
IBM	20	110	130

a. Prepare a schedule indicating the lower of cost or market value of each security.
b. Prepare a journal entry to apply the lower of cost or market rule.
   (1) Assume that the rule is to be applied on an individual security basis.
   (2) Assume that the rule is to be applied on a portfolio basis .
c. Which basis is likely to be more conservative in that it results in lower asset values? Which minimizes the inconsistency of recognizing decreases in market values but not increases?

24. *Do earnings as computed in accord with established conventions always provide the best measure of economic performance?*

At the start of 1996, a corporation had in its portfolio of marketable securities 100 shares of each of stocks A, B, and C. Acquisition cost per share and unit market prices as at the end of 1996 and 1997 were as follows:

	Acquisition Cost	Market Price	
		31/12/97	31/12/96
Security A	$100	$80	$150
Security B	50	70	80
Security C	60	63	90

During 1996 the company engaged in no securities transactions. During 1997 it sold 100 shares of security C for $65 per share.

a. Determine reported earnings related to securities for 1996 and 1997. Assume the lower of cost or market rule is applied on a portfolio basis.
b. Do you think that reported earnings is an appropriate measure of economic performance? Why?

25. *The lower of cost or market rule affects both the income statement and the balance sheet.*
   a. Prepare a schedule in which you show, as at December 31, 1996 and 1997, the cost, market value, and lower of cost or market value of each security on hand.

b. Prepare journal entries to reflect all events and transactions that would have affected the securities portfolio during 1996 and 1997. Value securities at the lower of cost or market using the portfolio basis. For convenience, combine all 1996 purchases into a single entry.

c. Show how information pertaining to marketable securities would be presented on the balance sheets and income statements for both 1996 and 1997.

d. Repeat part (c), assuming instead that the lower of cost or market rule was to be applied on the basis of individual securities rather than the entire portfolio.

e. Which basis, the portfolio or individual securities, is the more conservative? What results in greater income from the time the first security is purchased to that when the last security is sold?

Security	Date Acquired	Cost	Market Value 31/12/97	Market Value 31/12/96	Sales Date	Sales Amount
A	23/1/96	$140,000	$120,000	$130,000		
B	11/3/96	50,000	40,000	55,000		
C	16/9/96	40,000	—	—	5/11/96	$30,000
D	25/9/96	80,000	60,000	70,000		
E	5/1/97	110,000	170,000	—		

26. *Measures of performance based on amounts reported in the income statement may be misleading.*

On January 1, the Grey Corporation acquired 100 shares of common stock of company A and 100 shares of company B. Price per share of both securities was $200.

During the year companies A and B declared dividends of $16 and $12 per share, respectively. As at December 31, the market price of the stock of company A was $210 per share; that of company B was $230 per share.

a. Determine return on investment of each security based on the dollar amounts that would be reported on the firm's balance sheet and income statement.

b. Determine return on investment taking into account any "unrealized" gains or losses. Use *average* market value as the denominator.

c. Which security do you think was the better investment? Which basis for calculating return on investment do you think provides the better measure of economic performance? Why do you suppose that the market values of marketable securities must be disclosed in financial reports?

27. *Reported earnings may be a poor reflection of "economic" earnings.*

A company has divided its portfolio of marketable securities into two sections. In one, the market value exceeds the cost; in the other, the cost exceeds the market value. Data pertaining to the two sections for a period of three years are presented in the following schedule:

	December 31		
	1998	1997	1996
Market exceeds cost			
Cost	$ 8,000	$ 8,000	$10,000
Market	8,000	17,000	12,000
Cost exceeds market			
Cost	$10,000	$10,000	$10,000
Market	9,000	8,000	6,000

The securities that were eliminated from the portfolio during 1997 were sold for $1,000, an amount equal to their market value as at year end 1996.

a. Prepare all journal entries relating to marketable securities for 1997 and 1998 that would be required under generally accepted accounting principles.

b. Prepare comparative income statements for 1997 and 1998 and comparative balance sheets (assets only) for 1996, 1997, and 1998. Assume that the firm had no assets other than the marketable securities and the cash received upon the sale of the securities in 1997. Assume also that the firm received no dividends from the securities.

c. Repeat part (b), assuming that all securities were to be stated at market value and that all changes in market values were to be incorporated into income.

d. Compare the statements and comment upon the differences.

28. *Underlying transactions in marketable securities may be deduced from balance sheet and supplementary information.*

The balance sheet of the Clark Corporation indicated the following (in thousands):

	December 31	
	1997	1996
Marketable securities at cost	$280	$300
Less: Allowance for excess of		
cost over market value	10	60
Marketable securities, net	$270	$240

During 1997 the company sold for $70,000 marketable securities that had a market value at December 31, 1996, of $60,000. The company reported a realized loss of $30,000 on the transaction.

a. Reconstruct all entries relating to marketable securities that the company would have made during 1997.

b. Compute the amount of unrealized gain or loss during 1997 on the securities that were not sold during the year.

1. a. $50,000 × 1.07 = $53,500
   b. $53,500 × 1.07 = $57,245
   c. $57,245 × 1.07 = $61,252

   Verify your answers by referring to Table 1 in the Appendix, "Future Value of $1."

2. a. $50,000
   b. $50,000 + ($ 50,000 × 1.07) = $103,500
   c. $50,000 + ($103,500 × 1.07) = $160,745

   Verify your answers by referring to Table 3 in the Appendix, "Future Value of an Annuity of $1 in Arrears."

3. a. $50,000 ÷ 1.07 = $46,729
   b. $46,729 ÷ 1.07 = $43,672
   c. $43,672 ÷ 1.07 = $40,815

   Verify your answers by referring to Table 2 in the Appendix, "Present Value of $1."

4. It should deposit the sum of the amounts determined in Exercise 3:

$$\$46,729 + \$43,672 + \$40,815 = \$131,216$$

Verify your answer by referring to Table 4 in the Appendix, "Present Value of an Annuity of $1 in Arrears."

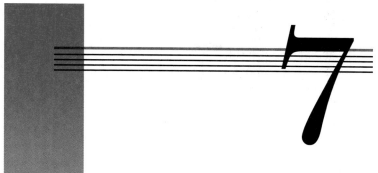

Receivables
and Payables

In the previous chapter, we introduced the concept of asset and liability valuation in general, and looked at cash and marketable securities as specific examples. This chapter is directed toward the measurement of receivables and payables. The primary focus is on the valuation of accounts receivable and the effect of uncollectable accounts on both the balance sheet and income statement. The accounting for payroll is also introduced.

After studying this chapter, you will be able to

- Define receivables and payables
- Understand the two methods of calculating the allowance for doubtful accounts
- Describe the accounting for sales returns
- Account for promissory notes
- Understand the accounting for promissory notes when interest is included in the face value of the note
- Recognize the substance of promissory notes that are noninterest-bearing
- Understand the accounting for payroll
- Calculate and understand the significance of the accounts receivable turnover, the current ratio, and the quick ratio

Definitions

Receivables

Receivables represent claims arising from the sale of goods, performance of services, lending of funds, or some other type of transaction which establishes a relationship whereby one party is indebted to another. Claims resulting from the sale of goods or services and not supported by a written note are categorized as *accounts receivable*. They are distinguished from amounts backed by written notes (which may or may not arise out of a sales transaction) called *notes receivable* and those arising out of myriad other day-to-day business activities, such as *deposits receivable* (e.g., amounts to be received upon return of containers), *amounts due from officers* (perhaps as a consequence of loans), *dividends receivable, rent receivable,* and *interest receivable.* Accounts receivable often do not require payment of interest; notes receivable almost always do.

Payables

Payables represent the corresponding obligations on the part of the recipient of the goods or services. Many of the issues pertaining to the valuation of payables are mirror images of those relating to receivables. The discussion in this chapter will centre largely around receivables, with the expectation that, as appropriate, the reader can generalize to payables.

Current and Noncurrent Receivables and Payables

Receivables and payables that mature within one year (or sometimes one operating cycle of the business if it is greater than one year) are classified as *current* assets or liabilities. Those that mature in a longer period are classified as *noncurrent.*

Significance

Receivables are important to managers and investors for a number of reasons. First, receivables are assets, and financial reports must reflect their value. Second, issues relating to receivables are fundamental to those of income determination and thus performance measurement. Receivables, particularly accounts receivable, often arise out of sales or other revenue-generating transactions. Some may have to be written off as "bad debts." The question of when to recognize increases or decreases in receivables may be viewed alternatively as when to recognize revenues or expenses.

Third, accounts receivable may be unproductive or underproductive assets. They may provide either no return or a return less than could be earned on other types of assets. It is generally to the advantage of a firm to collect its non- or low-interest-bearing accounts as soon as possible and to minimize the resources "tied up" in such accounts.

Correspondingly, the concern of investors and managers with *payables* is that the obligations are fairly presented, that the expenses with which they are associated are recorded in the appropriate accounting period, that payment is made when the liability is due, and that the firm avails itself of all discounts available for prompt payment.

Receivables, like other assets, are reported on the balance sheet in accordance with generally accepted accounting conventions. The resultant values may not necessarily be the same as their face values, their "economic" values, or their market values.

Face versus Economic Values

The *face,* or *stated, value* of a receivable is that which is indicated in the underlying promissory note, sales agreement, or comparable document. The *economic value* (value to user) is the *present value* of the cash that it will provide. It is the cash that the company will receive, discounted to take into account the time value of money. The *market value,* by contrast, is the amount for which the receivable can be sold. Many types of receivables are negotiable; they may be sold or transferred. Companies that prefer not to wait until their receivables mature can sell them for cash to banks or similar financial institutions.

In general, accepted accounting principles require receivables to be recorded initially at amounts that reflect their economic values. Both the economic values of receivables and the amounts at which they are first recorded may differ from their face values for two reasons. First, not all receivables will be collectable. The face values of receivables must therefore be reduced by an estimate of the amounts that will be uncollectable. One of the major causes of corporate bankruptcy is the failure to transform outstanding receivables into cash. Not surprisingly, a considerable number of legal actions against public accounting firms have resulted from alleged overstatements of receivables.

Second, the face value of a receivable may include an element of interest. Face value may indicate the actual amount of cash to be received rather than the present value of such cash. For example, a promise of $100 plus 10 percent interest in one year may sometimes be reflected in a note with a face value of $110. The present value would be the cash to be received less the interest, in this case only the $100. The amount of the interest may be set forth explicitly in the document supporting the receivable, or it may have to be imputed from the circumstances surrounding the transaction from which the receivable arose. As was indicated in previous chapters, interest receivable is not given accounting recognition until it is actually earned. Hence, to arrive at the amount at which a receivable should be recorded initially, the face value must be discounted to eliminate unearned interest. The means by which face values can be reduced to allow for both bad debts and unearned interest are described in sections of this chapter that follow.

Financial accounting is based on historical costs. Therefore, once receivables have been recorded, their values are adjusted only to take into account payments on outstanding balances, interest earned, and (if required) changes in the estimate of the portion that will be uncollectable. They are not adjusted to reflect changes in prevailing rates of interest. Increases in prevailing rates above those incorporated into particular receivables will reduce both the economic value and the market value of those receivables. They will be less desirable both to the firm itself and to other parties to whom they could be sold because they will be providing a return to their holder less than what could be obtained from alternative investments.

Basic Journal Entries

The basic journal entries to establish and to relieve a receivable account are straightforward. Upon the sale of goods and services for $500 on credit, for example, the appropriate journal entry would be

Accounts receivable $500
    Sales revenue $500
To record the sale of goods and services on credit

And upon subsequent receipt of customer payment,

Cash $500
    Accounts receivable $500
To record the collection of accounts receivable

Variations in the terms of sales and the nature of the transactions resulting in the creation of the receivable necessitate considerable modification in the basic entries to accommodate specific circumstances.

UNCOLLECTABLE ACCOUNTS RECEIVABLE

There are two ways of accounting for uncollectable accounts receivable. The first, and generally *unacceptable,* is the *direct write-off* method. It is described here mainly as a basis for comparison with the second, the *allowance* method.

Deficiencies of the Direct Write-Off Method

Under the direct write-off method, when it becomes obvious that an account receivable is uncollectable, it is *written off,* and a *bad-debt expense* is charged. For example, upon learning that a customer from whom it held a receivable of $100 is likely to default on its obligation, a company might give accounting recognition to its loss with the following journal entry:

Bad-debt expense $100
    Accounts receivable $100
To write off an uncollectable account receivable

Concurrently, the firm would also credit the account of the individual customer in the accounts receivable subsidiary ledger. The accounts receivable subsidiary ledger is nothing more than a book or file of the amount owed by each customer. Each element of the file is maintained as a "mini" general ledger account for a specific customer, with debits indicating additional debts incurred by the customer and credits signifying payments made by the customer. The sum of the subsidiary ledger balances due from all customers should, at all times, be equal to the balance in the accounts receivable ledger account (often called the accounts receivable control account). If it is not, an error has been made. In other words, the accounts receivable subsidiary ledger provides the support—or the detail—for the general ledger account.

The direct write-off method, however, is inconsistent with the matching concepts discussed in Chapter 5. For the reasons suggested below, it may lead to misstatements of *both* income and accounts receivable in the period of sale as well as in subsequent periods.

Rationale for the Allowance Method

The *allowance* method of accounting for uncollectable accounts receivable overcomes these deficiencies.

Consider, for example, a company in the retail furniture industry. To attract business, the company grants credit to relatively poor credit risks. The policy results in extensive losses on uncollectable accounts, but the increase in sales which it generates more than offsets the losses. Based on several years' experience, management estimates that for every dollar of credit sales 10 cents will be uncollectable. The company vigorously pursues its delinquent debtors and writes off accounts only after it has made every reasonable attempt at recovery. Few accounts are written off before at least a year has elapsed since a customer has made a payment.

Under the circumstances, it would be inappropriate for the company to include among its assets the entire balance of accounts receivable. After all, only a portion of the balance is likely to be collectable. Similarly, and equally significantly, if in 1996 the company had $5 million in credit sales, it would not be justified in reporting revenues of $5 million when only $4.5 million (90 percent of $5 million) would, in all probability, be fully realized. The individual accounts related to the sales in 1996 would not be written off for at least one or two years subsequent to 1996. But these losses would be the result of decisions—the decisions to sell to customers who prove to be unworthy of credit—made in 1996. The losses would relate directly to sales made in 1996; they should be matched therefore with revenues of 1996.

There are, however, two obstacles to assigning credit losses to the year in which the sales takes place. First, the amount of the loss cannot be known with certainty until several years subsequent to the sales. Normally, however, it can be estimated with reasonable accuracy. Based on the past collection experience of the company—or on that of other firms in similar industries—it is possible to predict the approximate amount of receivables that will be uncollectable. The inability to make precise estimates of the anticipated losses can hardly be a justification for making no estimate at all. For even the roughest of estimates is likely to be more accurate than no estimate—the equivalent of a prediction of zero credit losses.

Second, even though a firm may be able to predict with reasonable precision the overall percentage of bad debts, it certainly is unable to forecast the *specific* accounts that will be uncollectable. After all, if it knew in advance that a particular customer would be unable to pay his or her debts, it would never have made the sale in the first place. If a company were to recognize bad debts as expenses in the same period as the related sales and correspondingly reduce its accounts receivable balance, then which subsidiary ledger accounts would it credit? Since the sum of the balances of the subsidiary ledger accounts must equal the balance in the accounts receivable control account (i.e., the general ledger balance), the firm cannot reduce the balance in the control account without, at the same time, reducing the balances in the accounts of specific customers.

A firm can circumvent this second obstacle by establishing a *contra account,* "allowance for doubtful accounts." This contra asset account will normally have a credit balance (the opposite of the accounts receivable balance) and will always be associated with, and reported directly beneath, its *parent* account, accounts or notes receivable. Instead of reducing or crediting accounts receivable directly, the firm will credit "allowance for doubtful accounts."

Example

To illustrate the procedure, continue the assumption that a firm in 1996 made $5 million in credit sales. At year end the firm estimates that 10 percent ($500,000) of the credit sales will be uncollectable. The following adjusting entry would give accounting recognition to its estimate:

(a)

Bad-debt expense $500,000
    Allowance for doubtful accounts $500,000
To establish an allowance for doubtful accounts

The relevant T accounts would appear as follows:

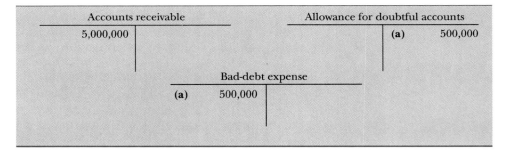

On the balance sheet, accounts receivable (assuming none of the $5 million has yet been collected) and its related contra account would be reported as

Accounts receivable $5,000,000
    Less: Allowance for doubtful accounts 500,000 4,500,000

As soon as the company is aware that a specific account cannot be collected, it is then able to credit the accounts receivable control account as well as the specific accounts receivable subsidiary ledger account. Since the allowance for doubtful accounts was established to accommodate future bad debts, it would now be debited.

Assume that in 1997 specific accounts totalling $70,000 are determined to be uncollectable. The appropriate entry would be

(b)

Allowance for doubtful accounts $70,000
    Accounts receivable $70,000
To write off specific accounts receivable

At the same time, the specific accounts to be written off would be credited in the accounts receivable subsidiary ledger. It is noteworthy that at the time specific accounts are written off no entry is made to *"bad-debt expense." The effect of the uncollectable accounts on income would already have been recognized in the year the sales were made.* Moreover, the entry to write off the specific accounts has no effect on current assets or working capital. The *net* accounts receivable (accounts receivable less allowance for doubtful accounts) remains unchanged by the entry because both the parent account and the related contra account have been reduced by identical amounts. Thus

	Before Write-Off	After Write-Off
Accounts receivable	$5,000,000	$4,930,000
Less: Allowance for doubtful accounts	500,000	430,000
Net receivables	$4,500,000	$4,500,000

If the company wishes to restore a receivable after it has been written off, only the receivable account and the allowance account need be adjusted. The company can simply reverse the entry that was made to write off the account. Suppose that a customer whose receivable of $10,000 had been written off signifies a willingness and ability to make good on his account. The following entry would be in order:

Accounts receivable $10,000
    Allowance for doubtful accounts $10,000
To restore an account previously written off

The customer's account in the subsidiary ledger would, of course, also be restored.

VERIFYING THE ADEQUACY OF THE ALLOWANCE FOR DOUBTFUL ACCOUNTS

The virtue of calculating the annual addition to the allowance account as a percentage of revenues is that the corresponding charge to earnings is a direct function of, and match to, revenues. If, however, the net receivables reported on the balance sheet are to be indicative of actual amounts to be collected, then the allowance must be periodically assessed. If anticipated uncollectable accounts will be greater than the allowance, then the allowance must be increased. If they are anticipated to be less, then it can be reduced.

One means of testing the adequacy of the allowance is by use of an *aging schedule,* which indicates what its name implies—the "age" of each account receivable. That is, it reveals the status of the various accounts—are they current, up to 30 days past due, up to 60 days past due? An aging schedule is illustrated in Exhibit 7-1.

EXHIBIT 7-1

Aging Schedule as at 31/12/96

| Customer Name | Total Balance | Current | No. of Days Past Due | | | |
			1–30	31–60	61–90	Over 90
J. Tremblay	$ 634,780	$ 634,780				
F. Fitzgerald	602,500	261,390	$ 290,000	$ 51,110		
K. Leung	82,220					$ 82,220
G. Brown	116,500				$116,500	
C. Ryder	928,110	292,060	339,300	260,000	36,750	
D. Singh	372,200		372,200			
G. Hawkins	1,101,000	1,101,000				
F. Cohen	1,162,690					1,162,690
	$5,000,000	$2,289,230	$1,001,500	$311,110	$153,250	$1,244,910

Based on the aging schedule, the firm estimates the dollar amount of accounts that will be uncollectable. This amount is indicative of the *total* balance required in the allowance for doubtful accounts account.

As a rule, the longer an account is outstanding—the longer a debtor goes without paying—the less likely it is that the account will be collectable. Thus a considerably greater proportion of accounts that are 90 days past due than those that are current will in all probability be uncollectable. A larger percentage of the balance of accounts 90 days past due must be added to the allowance for doubtful accounts than for accounts that are current. The following summary based on the aging schedule in Exhibit 7-1 reveals the total balance required in the allowance for doubtful accounts:

| Summary of Accounts Receivable as at 31/12/96 | | | |
Number of Days Past Due	Amount	Percent Likely to Be Uncollectable	Required Provision
0 (current)	$2,289,230	2	$ 45,785
1–30	1,001,500	8	80,120
31–60	311,110	12	37,333
61–90	153,250	20	30,650
Over 90	1,244,910	50	622,455
	$5,000,000		$816,343

The total required provision less the balance that is currently in the account is the amount that must be added to the account. Suppose, for example, that the balance in the allowance for doubtful accounts as at December 31 is $500,000. The amount that must be added is $316,343 ($816,343 less $500,000).

The key distinction between the percentage of sales and the aging schedule methods is that under the percentage of sales method the annual addition is determined by multiplying credit sales by a pre-established percentage. The amount of the addition is thereby computed independently of the existing balance in the allowance for doubtful accounts account. Under the aging schedule method, the annual addition is determined by first estimating the *required* balance in the allowance for doubtful accounts account (as revealed by the aging schedule) and then subtracting from the required balance the current balance in the account.

CORRECTING INCORRECT ESTIMATES

If the aging schedule indicates that the balance in the allowance for doubtful accounts account is becoming too high or low, then income of the past also has been misstated; the charges to "bad-debt expense" have been too high or too low. The only conceptually pure way to correct the errors is to restate the financial statements of the years in which the charges were made. The accounting profession, however, frowns upon prior-period adjustments, except in a very limited number of circumstances. It fears that continual revisions of previously reported amounts would undermine user confidence in financial statements. Moreover, it believes that the impact of a correction would be diminished if made only to the statements of previous periods, those to which investors pay little attention compared with current-period reports. The CICA requires that adjustments to the allowance account be made only in a current period, not retroactively.[1] To get the allowance account back in line, a greater or smaller amount than would otherwise be dictated by the current sales volume should be added to the account in the year the out-of-line condition becomes known. Correspondingly, a greater or smaller charge should be made to "bad-debt expense."

If, as in the illustration in the previous section, the aging schedule indicated that the allowance was $316,343 too low, the following entry should be made:

Bad-debt expense $316,343
    Allowance for doubtful accounts $316,343
To correct underestimates of bad debts

This practice has the undesirable effect of correcting prior-period errors by distorting earnings of the year of change. But it serves the positive cause of providing an up-to-date balance sheet without the confusion and complexity that would result from frequent changes in previously issued statements.

Industry Example: Western Canada Bank Failures

The collapse of the Canadian Commercial Bank (CCB) and the Northland Bank in March and September of 1985, respectively, illustrates the need for a healthy scepticism toward allowances for uncollectable accounts. Obviously, receivables are more significant for lending institutions than for other industries because receivables constitute their primary asset. But the caveats are no less applicable to all firms.

In the late 1970s and early 1980s the CCB and Northland Bank lent heavily to the cyclical real estate and energy resource sectors of the economy, primarily in Western Canada. Most of these loans had been given to mid-market commercial borrowers, which provided a higher rate of return than general

[1] "Accounting Changes," Section 1506.25, *CICA Handbook,* 1991.

banking operations but held a higher associated risk. In the initial years, the real-estate and oil industries were in a boom period, which resulted in low default rates and thus correspondingly low allowances for uncollectable accounts. Moreover, the banks were confident that their loans were adequately secured, since the properties and assets pledged as collateral were appraised at values that met or exceeded loan balances.

In the early 1980s, however, the economy moved quickly into recession, hitting the West particularly hard because of falling oil prices, which, in turn, propelled the fall of real-estate values. The default experiences of the past were rendered irrelevant by the new economic realities. As oil and real-estate values plummeted, the incidence of borrower defaults increased to such a point that the number of nonperforming loans within their loan portfolios resulted in a liquidity crisis for the banks. To make things worse, the values of the assets pledged as security against these loans were now far less than the loan balances in the depressed market. In both cases it was the uncollectability of the loans in their portfolios that caused the banks to fail.[2]

Why hadn't the banks adequately reserved against the loan losses even as they became foreseeable? One explanation is that federal regulations mandated that the banks maintain minimum asset-to-capital ratios. Were the institutions to slip below those minimums, regulators would have been forced to shut them down. In an attempt to gain time to strengthen their loan portfolios and wait for the recession to end, bank management, with the awareness of the Office of the Inspector General of Banks, initiated certain "survival tactics," which had the effect of understating their losses and overstating their assets and income. These "survival tactics" were nothing more than accounting manipulation to make uncollectable loans appear collectable. Their policies did nothing, of course, to enhance the collectability of the loans. They did, however, enable the banks to unobtrusively circumvent the government guidelines. The Western bank failures teach accountants and financial analysts at least two important lessons. First, in evaluating the adequacy of an allowance for doubtful accounts, it is risky to rely solely on historical rates of default; the allowance must be sufficient to cover losses of the future, not the past.

Second, the inherent worth of receivables may differ from the balance in either the receivables account or the related allowance for doubtful accounts account. Bookkeeping adjustments do nothing to affect the collectability of the loans. Nevertheless, the *reported* balances of receivables (or any other account, for that matter) can have substantive economic consequences. In the case of the banks, the excessive values attached to the net receivables permitted the banks to meet the regulatory guidelines and thereby remain legally, if not financially, solvent.

SALES RETURNS

Sales returns are accounted for in much the same way as bad debts. If goods that have been sold are expected to be returned in a subsequent

---

[2] "Report of the Inquiry into the Collapse of the CCB and Northland Bank," Canadian Government Publishing Centre, 1986, pages 1–21.

accounting period, the anticipated returns and allowances must be recognized in the same period as the sales. Financial statements that fail to take into account goods to be subsequently returned and refunds to be given to customers would clearly overstate revenues and hence earnings. But as with allowances for doubtful accounts, the necessary accounting entries must reflect the uncertainty that exists until the returns are actually made, of both the amount of the returns and the specific customers who will make them. Thus, as with bad debts, firms must establish an allowance for returns based on an estimate.

Example

Assume that at year end a firm estimates that merchandise that was sold for $1 million will be returned in the following year. An appropriate journal entry would be

(a)

Sales returns	$1,000,000	
Allowance for sales returns		$1,000,000
To record the estimate of sales returns		

Both of the accounts are *contra accounts.* "Sales returns" would be reported on the income statement as a reduction of sales. "Allowance for sales returns" would be reported on the balance sheet as an additional reduction of accounts receivable along with the allowance for doubtful accounts.

If the merchandise to be returned can be resold, then it is necessary to recognize that cost of goods sold, in addition to sales revenue, has been overstated in the year of sale. Assume that the merchandise to be returned had an original cost of $800,000. The required entry to recognize the overstatement of the cost of goods sold related to the anticipated returns would be

(b)

Merchandise to be returned (asset)	$800,000	
Cost of goods sold (expense)		$800,000
To record the cost of goods to be returned		

When the merchandise is actually returned, only balance sheet accounts need to be adjusted; the impact on revenues and expenses would have been accounted for in the year of sale:

(c)

Allowance for sales returns (contra asset)	$1,000,000	
Accounts receivable (asset)		$1,000,000
To give the customer credit for merchandise returned		

(d)

Merchandise inventory (asset)	$800,000	
Merchandise to be returned (asset)		$800,000
To record the receipt of returned merchandise		

If the merchandise returned cannot be resold and has no value, then entries **(b)** and **(d)** need not be made.

The entries as illustrated in the example above are appropriate when a firm expects that returns will be relatively small in relation to sales and it is able to estimate the volume of returns. As indicated in Chapter 5 in the section pertaining to the instalment basis of accounting, when a company grants uncommonly liberal rights of return and cannot make reasonable estimates of the amount of returns, then it should delay recognition of revenue until the rights of return expire. In such a situation, there would be no need to record estimates of returns; the sales themselves would not be recognized until it was certain that there would be no significant further returns.

Industry Example: Sales with Rights of Return

Policies on sales returns form a continuum. At one end are those in which the seller grants no right of return; the sale is final, the merchandise is sold "as is," and the seller provides no warranties as to its condition. At the other end are those in which unlimited rights of return are permitted. Under a *consignment* arrangement, for example, the buyer accepts merchandise which it intends to resell. The buyers are obligated to pay for the goods only if they are able to resell them. Until resale, title remains with the seller, who bears virtually all risks of ownership (e.g., theft, damage, and loss of market value), and the buyer has an unconditional right of return.

When a seller grants no right of return, it is clear that revenue can be recognized upon sale (assuming, of course, that the other criteria of revenue recognition are met). When a seller "sells" on consignment, it is equally obvious that recognition of revenue must be delayed until the buyer has resold the merchandise and no longer has an unrestricted right of return. As with many accounting controversies, it is the "in-between" transactions that challenge the profession's standard setters.

A simple example can be used to illustrate the issue. Clones, Inc., a manufacturer of personal computers, sells its machines to independent computer retailers. The retailers are required to pay for the merchandise within 30 days of receipt. To encourage retailers to stock and display its products, Clones, Inc., grants a one-year unconditional right of return on unsold (and undamaged) goods. Company experience indicates that approximately 10 percent of goods shipped are returned.

Should the company recognize revenue from sales when it ships its computers to the retailers or should it delay recognition until rights of return have expired?

On the one hand, the main criteria for revenue recognition (substantial portions of production and sales effort have been exerted, revenues can be objectively measured, and collection of cash is reasonably assured) appear to be met when the company ships the goods to the retailers. That would suggest recording the sale at the time the goods are shipped.

On the other hand, a critical event in the earnings process is the sale by the retailer to the ultimate consumer. Until that sale is made (or the one-year return period expires), the company is obligated to accept for refund all unsold goods. The company, not the retailer, bears the risks of the marketplace. That would suggest that revenue recognition be delayed until the goods have been resold or the return period has expired.

According to the *CICA Handbook,* it is recommended that the effect of the uncertainty created by returns be treated in the following way:

Revenue would not be recognized when an enterprise is subject to significant and unpredictable amounts of goods being returned, for example, when the market for a returnable good is untested. If an enterprise is exposed to significant and predictable amounts of goods being returned, it may be sufficient to provide therefor.[3]

This suggests that revenue be recognized at the time of shipment of the computers since the amount of returns can be predicted.

In the United States, prior to 1981, there were no specific accounting guidelines as to when, in such circumstances, revenue should be recognized. Some firms took advantage of this gap in standards to artificially inflate reported earnings. They would ship merchandise at the end of one year, fully expecting that it would be returned early in the next. They recorded the shipments as sales of the first year and failed to establish an adequate allowance for returns.

Now, per a 1981 FASB pronouncement, when rights of return exist, revenue can be recognized only when the return privilege has expired *or* all of the following conditions are met:

1. The sales price has been fixed.
2. The buyer has paid the seller, or its obligation to pay the seller is not contingent upon resale of the product.
3. The buyer would have to pay for the goods even if they are stolen or damaged.
4. The amount of future returns can be reasonably estimated.[4]

Applied to the facts as presented, the U.S. guidelines indicate that revenue should be recognized at time of shipment and need not be delayed. To be sure, the conditions for revenue recognition are not as rigorous as some accountants would prefer. Nevertheless, the guidelines have made reporting more uniform and eliminated the more abusive practices of premature revenue recognition. As noted previously, the U.S. standards tend to be more detailed and specific than the comparable Canadian standards.

CASH DISCOUNTS

It is common business practice for companies to offer discounts for prompt payment. For example, a firm may sell under terms such as "2/10, n/30." That is, the total amount is due within 30 days; however, if the customer pays within 10 days, it receives a discount of 2 percent. In economic substance it is difficult to interpret the discount as a true price reduction. A more acceptable explanation is that the customer is penalized for not paying on time.

---

[3] "Revenue," Section 3400.18, *CICA Handbook,* 1986.
[4] "Revenue Recognition When Right of Return Exists," Financial Accounting Board *Statement of Financial Accounting Standards No. 48,* 1981.

Suppose that a customer buys merchandise with a *stated* price of $100 on terms 2/10, n/30. A customer who pays on the thirtieth day following purchase rather than on the tenth day will retain cash for an additional 20 days. Losing the 2 percent discount, the customer pays $100 instead of $98, thereby incurring a cost of $2 to use $98 for 20 days—an effective annual interest rate of 37 percent (365 days/20 days × $2/$98 = .37) Only a company with a severely impaired credit rating would be willing to pay such an extraordinarily high rate. An unbiased observer might suspect therefore that the merchandise had a fair market value not of the stated sales price of $100 but rather of $98, the stated sales price less the discount of $2.

The proper accounting for cash discounts is *not* one of the critical issues facing the accounting profession. It is of interest primarily because it is another example of the importance of distinguishing substance over form.

Net Method and Gross Method

Both purchasers and sellers account for cash discounts in either of two basic ways: the net method or the gross method. The *net* method is theoretically preferable. It requires that both purchases and sales be recorded at the fair market value of the goods traded—that is, sales price *less* the discount—and that payments in excess of the discounted price be recorded separately as a penalty for late payment or as a financing cost.

The *gross* method, by contrast, permits purchases and sales to be recorded at the stated price rather than the fair market value. It thereby inflates both purchases and sales. Purchase discounts taken are credited to an account "purchase discounts." Sales discounts given are debited to an account "sales discounts."

Example

A company purchases merchandise that has a sale price of $100,000 on terms 2/10, n/30:

Net Method		Gross Method	
Inventory	$98,000	Inventory	$100,000
Accounts payable	$98,000	Accounts payable	$100,000
To record the purchase of merchandise			

It pays within the discount period:

Net Method		Gross Method	
Accounts payable	$98,000	Accounts payable	$100,000
Cash	$98,000	Cash	$98,000
		Purchase discounts	2,000
To record payment within the discount period			

Or, alternatively, it fails to pay within the discount period:

Net Method	Gross Method
Accounts payable................$98,000	Accounts payable.......$100,000
Purchase discounts	Cash...............................$100,000
lost (expense)...........................2,000	
Cash..$100,000	
To record payment after the discount period	

The gross method overstates inventory because goods acquired are recorded at gross purchase price, which exceeds the fair market value by the amount of the discount. As a consequence, upon sale of the goods, cost of goods sold is also overstated. The gross method can be justified as a bookkeeping convenience, but only if at year end the overstatements in inventory and cost of goods sold are eliminated. The required entries would have the effect of converting the gross method to the net method.[5]

Additional Advantage of the Net Method

The net method, but not the gross method, contributes to management control. The net method results in a charge to the expense account, "purchase discounts lost," whenever the firm fails to avail itself of the discounts. Management is thereby explicitly made aware of the cost of its negligence in, or policy of, not paying on time. The gross method, by contrast, "buries" the penalty charge in inventory, and it is eventually reflected in cost of goods sold.

The entries recording the sales and subsequent collection from the standpoint of the seller would correspond to those of the purchaser. The gross method would result in the overstatement of both sales and accounts receivable.

PROMISSORY NOTES

When a firm extends credit beyond a short period (two or three months) or makes a loan, it usually requests formal written documentation of the borrower's obligation to make timely payment. The legal instrument that provides such documentation is known as a *promissory note*. A typical promissory note is illustrated in Exhibit 7-2.

A promissory note, unlike an account receivable, generally requires that the maker (the borrower) agree to pay a fee, known as *interest,* for the right to use the funds provided. The promissory note is a legally binding contract. It would specify the following:

- The parties involved in the contract—the payor, who is the person or organization that agrees to make the payment, and the payee, who is

[5] The adjustment would be a credit in the amount of the discount to "merchandise inventory" (or "cost of goods sold" to the extent that the merchandise has been resold) and a debit either to "purchase discounts" (if the discount were taken) or to "purchase discounts lost" (if the discount were lost).

EXHIBIT 7-2
Typical Promissory Note

Bank of Montreal

Variable Rate Personal Loan Plan
Promissory Note

Branch Domicile Stamp

PLEASE PRINT

Full Name of Borrower(s)

PLP Account No. | Date

19 ____

In this promissory note the words "I" and "me" mean the borrower, or if more than one, all borrowers jointly and severally.

On demand I promise to pay to the order of Bank of Montreal at the Branch named above the principal sum of $ _____ . I promise to pay interest on that sum at the rate of _____ % per year above the Bank of Montreal's prime interest rate per year in effect from to time calculated on the dates set out below. At the date of this note such prime interest rate per year is _____ per cent.

Until demand is made I will pay the principal sum and interest by paying $ _____ on _____ , 19 _____ and then by paying $ _____ every _____ starting on _____ , 19 _____ through
(specify frequency)
and including _____ , 19 _____ when I will pay any balance owing.

The Bank's acceptance of any of the payments mentioned above is given solely to acknowledge the borrower's right to make certain payments, but the Bank nevertheless reserves the right to demand the payment of the loan at any time.

I agree that on the yearly anniversary dates of this promissory note the payment amount may be suitably amended at the Bank's discretion to ensure that the principal sum will be paid in full by the date for final payment at the interest rate in effect at the time of amendment.

If I fail to pay any amount when it is due in accordance with the above schedule of payments, I will pay interest at the rate shown above on the amount until such amount is all paid. This interest will be calculated and payable on the dates payments are due until the date for final payment and _____ after that date.
(specify payment frequency)

Signature of Borrower | Signature of Borrower

Optional Insurance

Principal Borrower _____ | Co-Borrower _____
(print name) | (print name)

Life Insurance under Policy 51007-G, Part A, issued by Sun Life Assurance Co. of Canada

Eligibility For Insurance

Insurance is available to individuals under age 70 at the date of application who become indebted to the Creditor under a Personal Loan Plan loan. Insurance is not available to Borrowers who apply for insurance more than 31 days following application for a Personal Loan Plan loan. No more than two Borrowers are eligible for insurance regarding any one Personal Loan Plan loan.

☐ I wish to apply for the Life Insurance Plan offered in connection with the above referenced personal loan. I have read the eligibility criteria above and the description of the insurance coverage described in the Certificate of Creditor Life Insurance Protection on the reverse side, and certify that I meet the eligibility requirements.

Type of insurance coverage (check one)
☐ Joint   ☐ Principal Borrower only   ☐ Co-Borrower only

Net amount of Loan (excluding all insurance premiums)

$ _____ × Premium Factor _____ = $ _____
Total Premium.*
* For Quebec residents premium is subject to Provincial Sales Tax.

☐ I do **not** wish to apply for any insurance.
☐ I, the Principal Borrower am not eligible for insurance coverage.
☐ I, the Co-Borrower am not eligible for insurance coverage.

Date _____ | Signature of Principal Borrower _____

Signature of Co-Borrower _____

Disability Insurance under Policy 21559, issued by Mutual Life of Canada

NOTE : Available to the Principal Borrower Only.
Eligibility For Insurance

Insurance is available to the Principal Borrower if on the date of application for enrolment you are : 1. under age 65; 2. regularly working at least 20 hours each week; 3. capable of performing all the regular duties of the occupation at which you regularly work at least 20 hours each week; 4. your loan has an amortization period of not more than 300 months, and; 5. the date you sign the application for enrolment is not more than 7 days after the new loan was advanced.

☐ I wish to apply for the Disability Insurance Plan offered in connection with the above referenced personal loan. I have read the eligibility criteria above and the description of the insurance coverage described in the Certificate of Disability Insurance on the reverse side, and certify that I meet the eligibility requirements.

Net amount of Loan (excluding all insurance premiums)

$ _____ × Premium Factor _____ = $ _____
Total Premium.*
* For Quebec residents premium is subject to Provincial Sales Tax.

☐ I do **not** wish to apply for any insurance.
☐ I, the Principal Borrower am not eligible for insurance coverage.

Date _____ | Signature of Principal Borrower _____

Prod. 2247808 – Form LF 341 (11/89) Litho. CANADA – 299675

the person or organization to whom the money is owed. (Sometimes a note may be drawn to bearer—that is, payment is made to whomever presents the note to the payor.)
- The date the note was issued and the date payment is due. (Some notes state that payment is due in a specific number of days from the date it was issued.)
- The principal of the note (the amount of credit being extended), often referred to as the face value of the note.
- The rate of interest.
- Any collateral or property that the borrower either pledges or surrenders as security for the note.

Interest on a note is expressed as an annual percentage rate. The formula for translating the percentage rate into the actual dollar amount is[6]

$$\text{Interest} = \text{Principal} \times \text{Rate} \times \frac{\text{Days of loan}}{\text{Total days in one year}}$$

If, for example, a company issues a note for $100,000 that bears interest at an annual interest rate of 8 percent and is payable in 90 days, the actual interest that it will be required to pay can be computed as

$$\$100{,}000 \times .08 \times \frac{90}{360} = \$2{,}000$$

Promissory notes are reported on the balance sheet at their principal, or face, amount. This convention confuses many students since the total obligation of the maker is not only the principal but the interest as well. In the foregoing illustration, for example, the total amount to be paid after 90 days is $100,000 plus $2,000 interest. Yet the note would be recorded on the balance sheet at only $100,000. The logic beyond the convention becomes apparent, however, when the impact of notes and interest on the balance sheet is viewed in conjunction with that on the income statement. Interest is a charge imposed on a borrower for the use of funds over a period of time. From the standpoint of the borrower, therefore, the interest cannot be considered an expense—and hence not a liability—until the borrower has actually had the use of the funds over time. With the passage of time, the borrower will recognize the expense associated with the use of funds—interest expense—and correspondingly the liability—accrued interest payable. Similarly, the lender will periodically recognize the earnings attributable to the funds that it has provided the debtor and concurrently acknowledge the enhancement of an asset, interest receivable.

A brief example may clarify the relationship between income and balance sheet accounts.

Example

On June 1, Echo Co. informs Foxtrot Corp. that it will be unable to make payment on its regular trade account, which on that date has a balance of

---

[6] To facilitate computation, it is common in practice to use 360 days as "total days in one year." We will observe that practice in the examples that follow.

$20,000. Echo requests that Foxtrot accept instead a 60-day note that will bear interest at the rate of 6 percent per annum. Foxtrot agrees.

Upon accepting the note on June 1, Foxtrot Corp. would make the following entry to record the exchange of an account receivable for an interest-bearing note receivable:

```
Notes receivable ............................................................................. $20,000
     Accounts receivable ................................................................ $20,000
     To record acceptance of the note in place of the accounts receivable
```

Thereafter, over time Foxtrot Corp. must account for the revenue that it is earning on its note. Most companies, considering the clerical costs of making frequent journal entries, update their accounts quarterly or at best monthly. Assuming that Foxtrot Corp. updates its accounts monthly, the following entry would be appropriate on June 30:

```
Accrued interest receivable ................................................... $100
     Interest revenue ...................................................................... $100
     To record monthly interest revenue from the note
```

The $100 represents interest for a period for 30 days computed as

$$\$20,000 \times .06 \times \frac{30}{360} = \$100$$

On July 30, the note would fall due. Assuming that both the note and the interest are paid in full, two entries are required to record collection. The first is identical to that made on June 30; it recognizes the interest earned during the one-month period since interest revenue was previously recorded:

```
Accrued interest receivable ................................................... $100
     Interest revenue ...................................................................... $100
     To record monthly interest revenue from the note
```

The balance in the accrued interest receivable account now stands at $200 and that in the notes receivable account at the original $20,000. Upon collection of both interest and principal, the appropriate entry would be

```
Cash ..................................................................................................... $20,200
     Accrued interest receivable ................................................. $200
     Notes receivable ......................................................................... 20,000
     To record the collection of the note and interest (Note that this entry has no effect
     on revenues or expenses.)
```

From the position of the payor—the maker of the note—the journal entries would be a mirror image of those of the payee.

NOTES WITH INTEREST INCLUDED IN THE FACE VALUE

A note may not specifically indicate a rate of interest. Instead, the face value of the note may include not only the amount originally borrowed but also the applicable interest charges as well. A borrower, for example, may give to a bank or other creditor a note for $1,000 in exchange for a 90-day loan. The bank, however, would not give the borrower the full $1,000. Instead, if the agreed-upon interest rate was 12 percent, it would give the borrower only $970.87. If the annual rate of interest was 12 percent, then the interest on a loan of $970.87 for 90 days would be

$$\$970.87 \times .12 \times \frac{90}{360} = \$29.13$$

The interest of $29.13, plus the principal of $970.87, exactly equals the face value of the note, $1,000.

Regardless of how the terms of the loan are stated, the difference between the amount actually received by the borrower and the amount that must eventually be repaid at the maturity of the note represents the cost of borrowing (i.e., interest). In the present example, the actual amount of the loan as well as the interest could have been calculated as follows:

Let x = the actual amount of the loan

If interest is to be at an annual rate of 12 percent, then interest for the 90-day period, approximately one-fourth of a year, would be a total of 3 percent of the actual amount of the loan. The total amount to be repaid is the actual amount of the loan, x, plus the interest, $.03x$. The total amount to be repaid has been established (the face amount of the note) at $1,000. Hence

$$\$1,000 = x + .03x$$

$$\$1,000 = 1.03x$$

$$x = \frac{\$1,000}{1.03} = \$970.87$$

The interest must be the difference between the face amount of the note and the amount actually borrowed: $1,000 minus $970.87, or $29.13.

When the amount actually loaned is less than the face amount of the note—that is, when the face amount includes both principal and interest—the note is known as a *discount note* and the interest rate as a *discount rate*. The journal entries required to record discount notes and the associated interest charges are similar to those for conventional interest-earning instruments.

Assume, for example, that on July 1 a lending institution accepted a three-month discount note of $1,000 in exchange for an actual cash loan of $970.87. The entry for the lending institution to record the loan would be

Notes receivable $1,000.00		
Cash	$970.87	
Discount on notes receivable (contra asset account)	29.13	
To record acceptance of the discount note		

The overall effect of the entry is to record the asset, notes receivable, at the amount actually loaned. "Discount on notes receivable" is a contra account associated with the account, "notes receivable." If a balance sheet were to be drawn up immediately after the loan was made, the relevant accounts would be reported on the balance sheet (among current assets) as

Notes receivable	$1,000.00	
Less: Discount on notes receivable	29.13	$970.87

As with conventional interest-bearing notes, interest must periodically be taken into account. On July 31, the appropriate entry would be (making the simplifying assumptions that one-third of the overall interest charges will be recorded during each of the three months regardless of the actual number of days in the month)

Discount on notes receivable $9.71
    Interest revenue $9.71
To record interest on the note for one month

The effect of this entry is to recognize the interest revenue and also to increase the value of the note (by decreasing the value of the contra account) by the amount of revenue recognized. The entry is similar to that which would have been made had the note had a stated interest rate. The main difference is that with the discount note the recognition of the interest results in the net increase of an asset, notes receivable, whereas with the interest-bearing note it results in the increase of a different asset, interest receivable.

An entry identical to that of July 31 would also be made on August 31 and September 30 to record the interest revenue earned during August and September.

On September 30, the balance in the "discount on notes receivable" account would be reduced to zero.

Discount on notes receivable			
July 31	9.71	29.13	July 1
August 31	9.71		
Sept. 30	9.71		
	29.13		
	0		

Collection of the note would be recorded as follows:

Cash $1,000.00
    Notes receivable $1,000.00
To record collection of the note

If the period of the loan were greater than one year, the present value formulas described in Chapter 6 would have to be used to determine the amount to be advanced to the borrower.

Example

A finance company makes a loan to a customer on a discount basis. The company accepts from the customer a two-year note for $5,000. The actual cash advanced is based on a 12 percent annual rate of interest.

Per Table 2 in the Appendix, the present value of $5,000 discounted at a rate of 12 percent for two years is

$$\$5,000 \times .7972 = \$3,986$$

The finance company would advance the customer $3,986 and record the loan as follows:

Notes receivable	$5,000	
Discount on notes receivable		$1,014
Cash		3,986

To record the loan to the customer

Interest revenue for the first year would be 12 percent of the net balance of the outstanding customer obligation, that is, 12 percent of $3,986, or $478. An appropriate journal entry after the note has been outstanding for one year would be

| Discount on notes receivable | $478 | |
| Interest revenue | | $478 |

To record interest for the first year

Since the customer did not actually remit an interest payment, the effective balance of its obligation would increase after the first year by $478. The increase in the effective balance is accounted for by a decrease of $478 in the discount from $1,014 to $536. After the first year, the note would be reported as follows:

Notes receivable	$5,000	
Less: Discount on notes receivable	536	$4,464

Interest for the second year would be based on the effective customer obligation at the end of the first year. Thus it would be 12 percent of $4,464, or $536. The entry at the end of the second year to record both interest revenue and collection of the full $5,000 would be

Cash	$5,000	
Discount on notes receivable	536	
Notes receivable		$5,000
Interest revenue		536

To record second-year interest and collection of the note

The interest revenue on a discount note would increase from year to year, corresponding to an increase in the effective obligation of the customer. Interest must be paid not only on the original amount borrowed but on any unsatisfied obligations for interest as well. (If the loan is for a relatively short period of time—less than one year—the "interest on the interest" is often ignored because it would be immaterial.)

"NONINTEREST-BEARING NOTES"

Firms sometimes appear to sell on especially generous terms of credit—so generous, in fact, as to defy credibility.

Assume, for example, that a company sells for $100,000 equipment that it no longer needs. The company accepts from the purchaser a five-year "interest-free" note for the full sales price. As emphasized in Chapter 6, $100,000 to be received in five years is worth considerably less than the same amount to be received today. Indeed, per Table 2 in the Appendix, the present value of a single payment of $100,000 five years hence, discounted at a rate of 8 percent, is

$$\$100,000 \times .6806 = \$68,060$$

Recognizing Substance over Form: Impact on Timing and Classification of Revenues and Expenses

It is hardly reasonable to expect a company to provide an interest-free loan to a customer for five years. A more believable interpretation of the transaction is that interest charges are included in the $100,000 selling price. If the prevailing rate for similar types of loans is 8 percent, the "true" selling price of the equipment would be only $68,060. The difference ($31,940) between this amount and the stated selling price of $100,000 represents interest on a five-year loan of $68,060.

If firms are to be concerned with the substance rather than merely the form of transactions, they must divide the $100,000 into its components. They must account separately for the sales price and the interest. They must *impute* interest of $31,940. If the equipment had been recorded on the books of the seller at $50,000, then the following entry would be appropriate:

Notes receivable	$100,000	
Equipment		$50,000
Discount on notes receivable		31,940
Gain on sale of equipment		18,060
To record the sale of the equipment		

During each year that the note was outstanding, the company would accrue interest on the effective balance of the "loan"—the note receivable less the unamortized portion of the discount. Thus, to record interest after one year,

Discount on notes receivable	$5,445	
Interest revenue		$5,445
To record interest for one year on a note of $68,060 at a rate of 8 percent.		

And after the second year,

Discount on notes receivable	$5,880	
Interest revenue		$5,880
To record interest for one year on a note of $73,505 at a rate of 8 percent ($73,505 represents the face value of the note less unamortized discount of $26,495—original discount of $31,940 less first-year amortization of $5,445.)		

Over the life of the note, the firm will recognize earnings on the transaction of $50,000—$100,000 received in cash less the recorded value of the equipment of $50,000—regardless of how the $100,000 is divided between "true" sales price and interest. If the transaction were accounted for in accordance with its form (selling price of $100,000), then a gain of $50,000 would be realized at time of sale. If accounted for in accordance with substance (selling price of $68,060), then a gain of only $18,060 would be recognized in the year of sale. The remaining $31,940 would be recognized as interest and taken into income over the five-year period of the note.

On the books of the purchaser of the equipment, if the entire $100,000 is assigned to the cost of the equipment, then that amount would be subject to amortization and recognized as an expense over the remaining useful life of the equipment—perhaps 10 years. If, however, the interest of $31,940 was taken into account, then only $68,060 would be assigned to the cost of the equipment and expensed as amortization over its useful life. The interest, $31,940, would be charged as an expense over the five-year period of the note. The manner in which the transaction is accounted for has no effect on *total* earnings of either the purchaser or the seller; it does, however, have a significant impact on the timing and classification of such earnings. Exhibit 7-3 indicates the differences in revenues and expenses from the perspective of both buyer and seller.

EXHIBIT 7-3

Impact on Income: Interest Imputed versus Interest Not Computed

Assumptions:
Stated selling price of equipment: $100,000
Total imputed interest (8% per year): $31,940
Selling price if interest is imputed: $68,060 ($100,000 less $31,940)
Estimated useful life of equipment: 10 years
Seller's book value of equipment at time of sale: $50,000

Perspective of Seller

Period	Interest Imputed	Interest not Imputed	Difference
0 (time of sale) Gain on sale	$18,060	$50,000	($31,940)
1 Interest revenue	$ 5,445	0	$ 5,445
2 Interest revenue	5,880	0	5,880
3 Interest revenue	6,350	0	6,350
4 Interest revenue	6,858	0	6,858
5 Interest revenue	7,407	0	7,407
Total interest revenue	$31,940	$ 0	$31,940
Total revenue	$50,000	$50,000	$ 0

Perspective of Buyer

Period	Interest Imputed	Interest not Imputed	Difference
0–10 Annual amortization	$ 6,806	$ 10,000	
Years of useful life	× 10	× 10	
Total amortization	$ 68,060	$100,000	($31,940)
1 Interest expense	5,445	0	5,445
2 Interest expense	5,880	0	5,880
3 Interest expense	6,350	0	6,350
4 Interest expense	6,858	0	6,858
5 Interest expense	7,407	0	7,407
Total interest expense	$ 31,940	$ 0	$31,940
Total expenses	$100,000	$100,000	$ 0

Industry Example: Retail Land Sales Companies

The issue of imputed interest is especially important as it applies to retail land sales companies. Retail land sales companies purchase large tracts of land and subdivide them into small parcels for sale to consumers. They plan communities; install streets, sewers, and utilities; and sometimes construct amenities such as golf courses, clubhouses, motels, and restaurants. Often they engage in extensive promotional efforts (e.g., free dinners or trips to the site), and frequently they direct their sales efforts at those who are interested in either retirement or vacation homes. Retail land sales companies seldom accept interest-free notes. Sometimes, however, they charge relatively low rates of interest. For example, they might charge a purchaser 8 percent interest annually at a time when the *prime rate* (that charged by banks to their most select customers) is 10 percent and the firms' own cost of borrowing is 12 percent.

At one time, it was standard procedure in the industry to record sales at the face value of the note received. This practice, however, overstated sales revenue and understated interest revenue. Since sales revenue is recognized at the time a sales contract is signed and interest revenue is recognized over the term of the note, the effect was to speed up recognition of revenue and to overstate earnings in the year of the sale. Considering that the notes were often for 10 years and that the difference between the rate actually charged and that normally charged for "loans" of similar types may have been as much as 10 percent, the difference in first-year revenues on sales of $1 million could be almost $350,000. This issue is not addressed directly under Canadian GAAP. However, the Canadian Institute of Public Real Estate Companies recommends, where property is *acquired* at a rate of interest different from the prevailing rate of interest for similar types of loans, that the cost of the property be adjusted to reflect the prevailing rate of interest. The difference between the face value of the loan and the amount assigned to the property is considered an adjustment to the interest expense.[7] It would be reasonable to assume that the transaction would be accounted for similarly by the seller and that a portion of the stated sales price of the land be accounted for as interest revenue rather than sales revenue.

Example

Vancouver Island Land Co. sells parcels of land for $50,000. Purchasers must pay $5,000 down and can give a 10-year note, which bears interest at a rate of 4 percent for the $45,000 balance. The note must be paid in 10 annual instalments of $5,550, the annual payment required to repay a loan of $45,000 in equal instalments if interest is charged at a rate of 4 percent per year.

If the company's customers had attempted to borrow the funds from a traditional lending institution, they would have had to pay the prevailing interest rate of 12 percent.

The present value of the consideration—that is, the "true" selling price of the land—can be determined by discounting *all* required payments (both principal and interest) by the *effective* rate of interest, in this example 12 percent:

Present value of $5,000 down payment	$ 5,000
Present value of 10 annual payments of $5,550 discounted at a rate of 12 percent: Per Table 4, $5,550 × 5.6502	31,359
Present value of all payments	$36,359

As a consequence, the firm would recognize sales revenue of only $36,359, which represents the worth at time of sale of all the payments to be received by the company. The difference between that amount and $50,000 represents interest revenue and must be reported as such over the 10-year period that the note is outstanding.

[7] "Non-Market Rate Debt," Section 203.3.1, *Recommended Accounting Practices for Real Estate Investment and Development Companies,* Canadian Institute of Public Real Estate Companies, 1990.

Industry Example: Franchise Companies

The financial arrangements in the franchise industry highlight some of the key issues pertaining to valuation of receivables as well as recognition of revenue.

Franchisors sell to franchisees the right to operate a specific kind of business, to use the name of the franchisor, and to provide goods or services associated with the franchisor. Companies such as McDonald's and Burger King may be among the best-known franchisors, but thousands of establishments throughout the world bear franchised names. Franchisees may be individual businesspersons or may themselves be large corporations.

The revenue of a franchisor ordinarily comes from several sources. First, the franchisor sells franchises to the parties who will operate them. The franchisor receives a small down payment and accepts from the franchisee long-term notes. Second, it receives royalties based on the sales volume of the franchisee. Third, it sells to the franchisee all or a portion of the business's product (e.g., the seasonings for the fried chicken). In return for the payments from the franchisees, the franchisor provides advertising and promotional support, training and business counselling, assistance in site selection, and financial support.

The issues of valuation of receivables and recognition of revenue are especially vexing because the financial well-being of the franchisor and the franchisees is so tightly intertwined. The franchisor can be profitable only if the individual franchisees are successful. The franchisees, however, are dependent upon the goodwill generated, and support provided, by the franchisor. In particular, the franchisor can expect payment on its notes and receivables from franchisees (often a substantial portion of its assets) only as long as it has the financial capacity to promote its name and nurture the franchisees.

The source of revenue that presents the most difficult accounting problems is that from the sale of the franchise. A franchisee may purchase a franchise many months before it is ready to begin operations. During the intervening period and sometimes for years afterward, the franchisor may be obligated to provide services (advertising and management training, for example) to the franchisee. The question arises as to the point at which the revenue from the sale should be recognized and the related receivable should be recorded as an asset. Consistent with the principle that revenue should be related to productive effort, it could be recognized at the time the contract is signed, when the outlet first commences operations, or in the one or more periods in which various services are performed.

Because eventual collection of cash cannot always be reasonably assured, it has sometimes been suggested that revenue be recognized only as the notes are actually collected, that is, on the cash collection or instalment basis. This approach would eliminate the possibility that the assets of the franchisor are overstated by the amounts that will prove uncollectable; it would make certain that revenues are not prematurely realized. But it would also be inconsistent with the general accounting practice of recognizing revenue when a transaction is substantially completed (and, as necessary, making appropriate provisions for uncollectable accounts). The instalment method of accounting is ordinarily reserved for exceptional cases in which there is no reasonable basis for estimating the degree of collectability of outstanding receivables. This approach has been rejected in favour of one permitting recognition prior to collection of cash but not as early as when the contract is signed.

There is a CICA Accounting Guideline for franchise fee revenue that suggests the recognition of revenues from the sale of a franchise be delayed until all material conditions relating to the sale have been substantially performed by the franchisor.[8] Because of the variety of contractual arrangements, there can be no one specific condition or event that is the sole criterion for revenue recognition. The test of substantial performance may be met at a number of different times. Nevertheless, the guideline stipulates that substantial performance "will not normally be met *before the franchisee commences operations,*" which would, therefore be the earliest point for revenue recognition.

PAYROLL TRANSACTIONS

Although payroll transactions present few conceptual considerations that have not already been dealt with, they are worthy of discussion because they are engaged in by almost all profit and non-profit organizations and are of major magnitude.

Characteristic of payroll transactions is that the wage or salary expense pertaining to an individual employee may be considerably *greater* than the amount indicated by her or his wage or salary rate but that the amount actually paid to the employee may be considerably *less*. The business firm must pay payroll taxes that are specifically levied on the employer and, commonly, must provide for *fringe benefits* in addition to regular wage and salary payments. Moreover, the employer must withhold from each employee's wages and salary the employee's share of payroll taxes as well as amounts for other designated purposes. Amounts withheld from the employee ordinarily represent a liability of the employer; they must be remitted either to the government or to a specific fund.

Example

An employee is paid at the rate of $4,000 per month. From her salary must be withheld (either by law or by employee election) the following: income taxes (according to a schedule published annually by Revenue Canada Taxation)—$1080; Canada Pension Plan (CPP) contributions—2.3 percent of gross salary, or $92; Unemployment Insurance (UI) premiums—3 percent of gross salary, or $120; company pension plan at 6 percent of gross salary, or $240; Canada Savings Bond plan—$180. As a consequence of the deductions, monthly *take-home* pay of the employee is $2,288.

In addition, the employer incurs the following voluntary or statutory charges: employer share of CPP contributions—2.3 percent of gross salary, or $92; employer share of UI premiums—4.2 percent of gross salary, or $168; contribution to company pension fund—6 percent of gross salary, or $240.

The following entry would be appropriate on the monthly payroll dates for a group of 1,000 employees, making the simplifying assumption that the payroll deductions for each employee are the same:

[8] "Franchise Fee Revenue," Accounting Guidelines, *CICA Handbook*, 1984.

Salaries expense	$4,000,000	
CPP expense, employer's share	92,000	
UI expense, employer's share	168,000	
Pension expense, employer's share	240,000	
Salaries payable		$2,288,000
Liability for income taxes withheld		1,080,000
Liability for CPP (both employees' and employer's share)		184,000
Liability for Canada Savings Bonds		180,000
Liability for pensions (both employees' and employer's share)		480,000
Liability for UI (both employees' and employer's share)		288,000

To record payroll

When cash payments are made to the employee or to the appropriate funds or government departments, the various liability accounts would be debited; cash would be credited.

When employees take their vacations, the expense of their salaries during the vacations should be allocated to those accounting periods in which they are actually performing services. If, in the example, the employee takes a one-month annual vacation, then the $4,000 that she would be paid while on vacation should be charged as an expense during the 11 months in which she worked. The monthly expense would be $363.63 ($4,000 divided by 11 months). The accrual of vacation pay could be recorded by the following additional entry each month for the group of 1,000 employees:

| Vacation pay (expense) | $363,636 | |
| Provision for vacation pay (liability) | | $363,636 |

To accrue vacation pay—one-eleventh of monthly salaries

When an individual employee takes a vacation, the appropriate entry (which, for simplicity, omits consideration of payroll withholdings and other deductions) would be:

| Provision for vacation pay | $4,000 | |
| Salaries payable | | $4,000 |

To record the amount due an employee for vacation pay

It is particularly important for organizations to spread the costs of vacation pay over the production periods of their employees if they prepare quarterly or semiannual financial reports in addition to annual reports. If they neglect to *accrue* vacation pay, then the cost of operations in the summer months may appear to be considerably higher than in other months. The increase in cost is attributable to the large number of employees who take their vacations in the summer. When they do so, substitute workers must be hired if production levels are to be maintained.

The more interesting and controversial issues pertaining to employee compensation relate to retirement benefits such as pensions, and to bonuses in common stock and other securities. Consideration of these will be delayed until later in the text.

RATIOS

This section is directed to two ratios that are useful in the control and evaluation of accounts receivable.

Accounts Receivable Turnover

Accounts receivable turnover is an activity ratio. *Activity ratios* measure the effectiveness of management in utilizing specific resources under its command. Activity ratios are often referred to as *turnover ratios*. They relate specific asset accounts to sales or to some other revenue or expense accounts with which they are logically associated.

Accounts receivable turnover is the ratio that measures the number of times that receivables are generated and collected during a period. It is computed by dividing sales by average accounts receivable:

$$\text{Accounts receivable turnover} = \frac{\text{Sales}}{\text{Average accounts receivable}}$$

The greater the number of times that accounts receivable turn over, the smaller the amount of funds that the company has "tied up" in accounts receivable and the greater the amount of funds that it can invest in other assets.

The balance sheet and income statement of Sun Ice Limited, a diversified North American active-wear firm based in Canada, are shown in Exhibit 7-4. The company's statement of changes in financial position is presented in Exhibit 14-1 in the chapter directed to statements of changes in financial position. In fiscal 1994 (note that Sun Ice's year end is January 31), Sun Ice had net sales (in thousands) of $15,130. As at January 31, 1994, it held accounts receivable of $5,132 (in thousands); as at January 31, 1993, $4,569 (in thousands). Average accounts receivable were thus $4,850.5—($5,132 + $4,569)/2.[9]

EXHIBIT 7-4

	Consolidated Balance Sheets Sun Ice Limited	
	1994	1993
As at January 31	(Dollar amounts in thousands)	
Assets		
Current Assets		
Cash and term deposits	$ 6,139	$ 6,766
Accounts receivable	5,132	4,569
Income taxes refundable	185	432
Inventory	3,278	1,405
Prepaid expenses and deposits	273	77
Total current assets	15,007	13,249
Capital assets, net of accumulated amortization	4,111	4,842
Other	500	79
Total assets	$19,618	$18,170

[9] Refinements in the calculation of ratios, such as questions of whether instalment contracts receivable should be included among receivables or whether the allowance for doubtful accounts should be deducted, are beyond the scope of this text. Suffice it to say that the specific way a ratio is computed must depend on the analytical function that it will serve. What is most important is that the analyst strive for consistency among firms and over time. This objective is not always possible to achieve because firms are not uniform in their practices of data aggregation and classification.

EXHIBIT 7-4 (continued)

Liabilities and Shareholders' Equity
    Current Liabilities
        Accounts payable
        Current portion of long-term debt

Accounts payable	$ 1,815	$ 1,096
Current portion of long-term debt	50	13
Total current liabilities	1,865	1,109
Long-term debt	200	523
Total liabilities	2,065	1,632
Deferred income taxes	118	204
	2,183	1,836
Share capital	12,122	11,331
Contributed surplus	4	4
Retained earnings	5,309	4,999
Total shareholders' equity	17,435	16,334
Total liabilities and shareholders' equity	$19,618	$18,170

Consolidated Statements of Income and Retained Earnings
Sun Ice Limited

Years Ended January 31	1994	1993
	(in thousands)	
Sales	$15,130	$14,929
Costs of sales	10,011	11,590
Gross profit	5,119	3,339
Expenses		
Selling, general and administrative	4,442	4,055
Interest on long-term debt	25	70
Amortization	705	630
Total expenses	5,172	4,755
Loss from operations	(53)	(1,416)
Interest and other income	100	124
Foreign exchange gain	277	145
Gain on disposal of capital assets	1	243
	378	512
Income (loss) before taxes	325	(904)
Income taxes (recovery)		
Current	243	(295)
Deferred	(85)	(20)
Utilization of loss carryforwards	(143)	(285)
	15	(600)
Net income (loss) for the year	310	(304)
Retained earnings, beginning of the year	4,999	5,303
Retained earnings, end of year	$ 5,309	$ 4,999

$$\text{Accounts receivable turnover} = \frac{\$15,130}{\$4,850.5} = 3.1 \text{ times}$$

Ideally, average receivables should be based on 12 individual months rather than beginning- and end-of-year values. Otherwise, the average may be distorted by seasonal fluctuations. Indeed, many companies intentionally choose to end their fiscal years when business activities are at their slowest.

The same relationship can be expressed in an alternative form, *number of days' sales in accounts receivable* (sometimes called the *average collection period*). Assuming that all sales were made on account, then, on average, Sun Ice Limited made $41.5 thousand in sales per day during 1994.

$$\text{Average sales per day} = \frac{\text{Total sales}}{365}$$

$$= \frac{\$15,130}{365}$$

$$= \$41.5$$

The number of days' sales in accounts receivable may be determined by dividing accounts receivable as of *any particular day* by average sales per day:

$$\frac{\text{Number of days' sales in accounts receivable}}{\text{(Average collection period)}} = \frac{\text{Accounts receivable}}{\text{Average sales per day}}$$

Number of days' sales in accounts receivable as of January 31, 1994

$$= \frac{\$5,132}{\$41.5} = 123.7 \text{ days}$$

Expressed in another way, based on average sales it takes 123.7 days for the company to collect its accounts receivable. Should the collection period increase from one year to the next, or should it be greater than the number of days in the payment period specified in the company's terms of sales, then there would be reason to investigate whether the firm is experiencing difficulty in collecting from its customers.

Current and Quick Ratios

Liquidity ratios measure the ability of a firm to meet its obligations as they mature. As indicated in Chapter 4, the primary measure of liquidity is the *current ratio*. The current ratio compares current assets with current liabilities. The higher the ratio of current assets to current liabilities, the less likely the company will be to default on its obligations. Current assets, however, commonly provide either no direct return to the company or a return smaller than could be obtained if funds were invested and producing assets. If the current ratio is high, therefore, the company may be incurring an *opportunity cost*—it could be losing revenue by tying up funds in current assets rather than by taking advantage of other financial opportunities.

A test of liquidity more severe than the current ratio is the *quick ratio.* The quick ratio compares cash and cash equivalents (such as marketable securities) and accounts receivable to current liabilities. It provides an indication of the ability of the company to satisfy its obligations without taking into account both inventories, which are less readily transformed into cash than other current assets, and prepaid expenses, which save the company from having to disburse cash in the future but which are not themselves transformed into cash. The quick ratio of Sun Ice Limited as at January 31, 1994 is 6.14 to 1:

$$\text{Quick ratio} = \frac{\text{Cash and cash equivalents} + \text{Current receivables}}{\text{Current liabilities}}$$

$$= \frac{\$6,139 + \$5,132 + \$185}{\$1,865}$$

$$= 6.14 : 1$$

Caveats

Both the current and quick ratios are of special interest to short-term creditors, those who are concerned about the firm's ability to meet its obligations within a period of one year. Both ratios, however, should be viewed with considerable care. They are ratios that can readily be manipulated by management. For example, by paying off short-term loans just prior to year end (and subsequently reborrowing at the start of the next year), management may be able to increase its year-end current and quick ratios. It is important to bear in mind that an identical change in both current assets and current liabilities will, in fact, alter the two ratios. If, for example, a firm had current assets of $400,000 and current liabilities of $200,000 and subsequently repaid an outstanding current obligation of $100,000, its current ratio would increase from 2 : 1 prior to repayment to 3 : 1 after payment. The practice of taking deliberate steps to inflate the current and quick ratios is known as *window dressing.*

At the same time, an increase in the current and quick ratios may be symptomatic of financial deterioration rather than improvement. The numerator of the quick ratio includes accounts receivable; that of the current ratio includes accounts receivable as well as inventories. Suppose that a firm's inventory balance is increasing because of an inability to sell its products and its accounts receivable balance is increasing because of a failure to collect outstanding debts. Both the current and quick ratios would also increase, even though the financial condition of the firm is weakening. This increase points to the danger of focusing on individual rather than groups of relationships. If, for example, ratios of sales to inventory and sales to accounts receivable were computed, then the unhealthy buildup of receivables and inventory would become apparent. It would be clear that both balances were increasing at the same time that sales were decreasing.

Three main ideas pervaded the discussion of receivables and payables:

1. Questions of the amounts at which receivables and payables should be stated are directly related to those of when revenues and expenses should be recognized.

   If an enterprise grants credit to customers, it is doubtful that all of its receivables will be transformed into cash. "Losses" on bad debts are a cost of generating revenue. They should be charged as as an expense in the same accounting period in which the related sales are made. Correspondingly, accounts receivable should be reduced by the amount likely to be uncollectable.

   Both sales and receivables should be reduced also by the amount of expected returns, allowances, and discounts of which customers may avail themselves, and interest included in the face value of the receivable but not yet earned. Notes receivable, for example, often include in the stated value an element of interest to be earned during the period over which the notes will be held.

2. The substance of a transaction must take precedence over its form. Accountants and managers must look to the economic rather than the stated values of goods or services exchanged. It is not unusual, for example, for firms to allow customers to delay payments for months or even years and make no explicit charges for interest. Money, however, has a time value, and the right to use funds for an extended period of time is not granted casually. Whenever the sales price of an item is *inflated* by unspecified interest charges, the firm must impute a fair rate of interest and account for the revenue from the sale of the item apart from the revenue from the interest.

3. Proper accounting for receivables and payables requires the good judgment of both managers and accountants. The "correct" value of receivables can never be known with certainty. It is dependent on the amounts that customers will fail to pay, the amount of goods returned, and the amount of cash discounts taken. Reported receivables and revenues are, at best, only estimates.

Exercise for Review and Self-Testing

The LJG Company sells equipment to a customer for $2,000. The customer is permitted to defer payment for one year but is to be charged interest at a rate of 6 percent. The company accepts a note from the customer with a face value of $2,120. This amount represents principal of $2,000 and interest of $120.

   The prevailing rate of interest—the rate normally charged similar customers in similar circumstances—is 12 percent, and the company often sells its equipment for less than $2,000.

1. Determine the fair market value of the equipment, taking into account the prevailing rate of interest. What is the present value of the note (both principal and interest) to the company?

2. Prepare a journal entry to record the sale of the equipment. Be sure that the amount of revenue recognized reflects the value of the consideration received. Any difference between the face amount of the note and the amount of revenue recognized should be classified as "discount on notes receivable."

3. After one year the company collects the entire $2,120 from the customer. Prepare a journal entry to record the collection of the note and to recognize interest revenue for the year. Be sure that the amount of interest revenue recognized reflects the "true" (prevailing) rate of interest.

4. The firm estimates that of the total sales for the year for which notes were accepted, $10,000 will be uncollectable. Prepare a journal entry to add that amount to "allowance for doubtful notes receivable."

5. A review of notes on hand indicates that $1,500 is presently uncollectable. Prepare a journal entry to write off the notes against the allowance provided.

Questions for Review and Discussion

1. Why is it preferable for a firm to maintain an allowance for doubtful accounts rather than simply to write off bad accounts as soon as it is known which specific accounts will be uncollectable?

2. On December 29 a company purchases for $100,000 merchandise intended for resale. The company is granted a 5 percent discount for paying cash within 10 days of purchase. The company records the purchase using the gross method. As at year end, the company has not yet paid for the goods purchased but has resold half of them. The company intends to pay within the specified discount period. Assuming that no adjustment to the accounts has been made, in what way is it likely that the financial statements as at year end are misstated?

3. A company borrows $1,000 for one year at the prevailing interest rate of 6 percent. The note issued to the lender promises payment of $1,000 plus interest of $60 after one year. Upon borrowing the funds, the company records a liability for $1,060. Do you approve of this accounting practice? Explain.

4. A finance company loaned an individual $1,000 on a discount basis. The actual cash given to the borrower was only $920; interest was taken out in advance. At the time of the loan, the finance company recorded its receivable at $1,000, reduced its cash by $920, and recognized revenue of $80. Do you approve of this practice? How would you record the loan? Explain.

5. A retail store places the following ad in a newspaper: "Complete Room of Furniture; $2,000; no money down; take up to 2 years to pay; no interest or finance charges." During a particular month the firm sells 5 sets of the advertised furniture. The company records sales of $10,000. If you were the firm's independent auditor what reservations would you have about the reported sales?

6. A firm acquires a building at a cost of $300,000 and gives the seller a five-year interest-free note for the entire amount. Assuming that the firm would otherwise have had to borrow the funds at a rate of interest of 10 percent compounded annually, at what amount should the building be recorded? What would be the impact of failing to take into account *imputed* interest on reported earnings of the years during which the note is outstanding as well as over the total years of the useful life of the building?

7. After operating successfully in a single city, the owners of Big Top Ice Cream Parlors decide to sell franchises to individual businesspeople in other cities. Within one year the firm signs contracts and receives down payments for 20 franchises. The total sales price of each franchise is $50,000. The required down payment is a small fraction of total sales price. During the first year only five outlets are actually opened. The company reports revenues from sale of franchises of $1 million. What warnings would you give an investor with respect to first-year earnings of the franchisor?

8. The supervisor of a large clerical department in a government agency finds that efficiency in his department always seems to drop during the summer months. He determines efficiency by dividing total payroll costs by the number of documents processed. Total payroll costs include amounts paid to employees on vacation. The department charges all salaries—both those of workers actually on the job and those on vacation—as an expense in the month paid. Why do you suspect efficiency appears to be low during the summer months? What improvements to the accounting system might you recommend?

9. A finance company charges customers 12 percent interest on all balances outstanding. The company continues to accrue interest revenue on outstanding loans (that is, it debits interest receivable and credits interest revenue) even though loan payments might be past due. Only when it writes off a loan does it cease to accrue interest. What dangers are suggested by such practice?

10. The *quick ratio* of a firm has increased substantially from one year to the next. The treasurer of the firm cites the increase as evidence of improved financial health. Why can an increase in the quick ratio be as much of a sign of financial deterioration as of improved financial health? What other ratio or relationship would you look to for insight as to the significance of the increase.

Problems

1. *This is a simple problem in accounting for uncollectable accounts.* The trial balance of the Elton Co. indicates the following:

Sales	$486,000
Accounts receivable	63,000
Allowance for doubtful accounts	11,000

In the current year, bad-debt expense has not yet been recorded.

The firm estimates that approximately 6 percent of sales will be uncollectable. A review of accounts receivable reveals that $21,500 of accounts presently on the books are unlikely to be collected and should therefore be written off.

Prepare any entries that you believe are necessary in light of the facts as presented.

2. *This problem reviews the basic journal entries involved when goods are sold on account, and the accounting for any uncollectable amounts.*

Prepare journal entries to record the following transactions and economic events.

a. During its first year of operations, the Cloud Company made sales of $4,000,000, $3,000,000 of which were on account and the remainder for cash.

b. During the year, $2,400,000 cash from credit sales was collected.

c. Based on industry experience, Cloud expects that 4 percent of credit sales will eventually become uncollectable.

d. During its second year of operations, Cloud identifies customers that will not pay the balances owing to Cloud. These customers' balances total $24,000.

3. *The balance in the allowance for doubtful accounts account must be taken into consideration when the bad-debt expense is determined using the accounts receivable aging schedule.*

During 1997 Stream Incorporated made credit sales of $2,500,000. The accounts receivable balance at December 31, 1997, was $740,000. Based on the aging schedule, the required allowance for uncollectable accounts at December 31, 1997 is $44,400.

The balance in its allowance for doubtful accounts account at December 31, 1997, before the 1997 bad-debt expense provision, was $12,100.

Prepare the journal entry to record bad-debt expense for 1997.

4. *Neither the entries to write off accounts receivable nor those to restore accounts that were previously written off have a direct impact upon earnings.*

Transactions involving accounts receivable and related accounts of Warner's Department Store for 1996 and 1997 can be summarized as follows (in millions):

	1997	1996
Credit sales	$32.00	$41.00
Cash collections on accounts receivable	31.00	28.00
Accounts deemed uncollectable and written off	.65	.30

The firm estimates that 2 percent of annual credit sales will be uncollectable.

Included in the $31 million of cash collections in 1997 is $30,000 from customers whose accounts were written off in 1996. The balances in the accounts when they were written off totalled $80,000. It is the policy of the company to restore in their entirety accounts previously written off upon collection of a partial payment from a customer, since a partial payment is often an indication that payment of the remaining balance will be forthcoming.

a. Prepare summary journal entries to record the activity reported.

b. Compare the impact of credit losses on reported earnings of 1997 with that of 1996.

c. Comment briefly on how your answer to part (b) would differ if the amount to be added to the allowance for doubtful accounts were based on an aging schedule instead of a flat percentage of credit sales.

5. *In the long run, though not in any particular year, charges for bad debts based on an aging schedule should be equal to those based on dollar volume of credit sales.*

The Melrose Co. began operations in January 1993. The following schedule indicates credit sales and end-of-year balances in accounts receivable for 1993 through 1996. The end-of-year balances are broken down by the "age" of the receivables.

				No. of Days Past Due		
Year	Credit Sales	Total	Current	1–30	31–60	Over 60
1993	$12,000	$1,080	$ 800	$100	$150	$ 30
1994	14,000	1,500	1,100	300	50	50
1995	16,000	1,600	900	400	200	100
1996	18,000	1,820	1,280	220	200	120

End-of-Year Balance in Accounts Receivable (in thousands)

The company estimates that approximately 5 percent of all credit sales will be uncollectable. It has also determined that of its accounts receivable balance at any date the following percentages will likely be uncollectable:

Current	15%
1–30 days past due	40
31–60 days past due	50
Over 60 days past due	60

The balance in the "allowance for doubtful accounts" account was zero prior to the adjustment at the end of 1993. Actual write-offs of accounts receivable were as follows (in thousands):

1993	$260
1994	580
1995	815
1996	893

a. Determine bad-debt expense for each of the four years, assuming first that the company bases its addition to the allowance for doubtful accounts on credit sales and alternatively on a schedule of *aged* accounts receivables. Bear in mind that when the sales method is used, the bad-debt expense is determined directly. When the aged accounts receivable method is used, it is necessary to first determine the required balance in the allowance for doubtful accounts account.

b. Compare total bad-debt expense over the combined four-year period under each of the two methods. (They should be the same in this example.) Which method results in the more erratic pattern of bad-debt expense? Why?

6. *Journal entries can be prepared once the missing data are derived.*

The financial records of a firm reveal the following (in thousands):

	1997	1996
Accounts receivable	$ 4,520	$ 3,980
Allowance for doubtful accounts	226	201
Sales (all on account)	54,200	47,500
Restoration of accounts previously written off	27	18

It is the practice of the company to charge "bad-debt expense" with an amount equal to 4 percent of credit sales. Prepare journal entries to summarize all activity in accounts receivable and the related allowance for doubtful accounts in 1997.

7. *Interest on troublesome loans should not be accrued.*

The following comment was included in the notes to the financial statements of the Equitable Life Mortgage and Realty Investors:

> **Nonaccrual of Interest.** When it is not reasonable to expect that interest income will be received, its recognition is discontinued. At that point, interest accrued but not received is reversed, and no further interest is accrued until it is evident that principal and interest will be collected.

a. Why should the company "reverse" interest accrued but not yet received?

b. What is the most likely journal entry made to effect the reversal?

8. *This problem provides an illustration of a firm whose allowance for doubtful loans was inadequate to cover loan losses.*

The annual report of First Winnipeg Corporation contained the following comment and table regarding its provision for loan losses:

> One of the most significant factors adversely affecting 1997 results was the $126.5 million bad-loan expense, up from $118.5 million in 1996. Net loan write-offs were $145.8 million, exceeding the bad-loan expense by $19.3 million.

The allowance for doubtful loans account is summarized below (in thousands).

	1997	1996
Balance, beginning of period	$ 121,352	$ 95,766
Additions (deductions)		
Loans written off	(153,688)	(95,583)
Recoveries	7,874	2,669
Net write–offs	$ (145,814)	$ (92,914)
Bad–loan expense	126,500	118,500
Balance, end of period	$ 102,038	$121,352

a. Prepare journal entries to reflect the activity in the account, "allowance for doubtful loans," in 1997.

b. Based only on the limited information provided, do you think that the balance in the account at the end of 1997 will be adequate to cover losses on loans to be incurred in the future? Explain.

9. *Bad-debt problems can easily be masked by rapid increases in sales.* (Solution of this problem would be facilitated by use of an electronic spreadsheet.)

Throughout the 1980s sales of Northern Co. were level at $100 million per year. Bad debts were approximately 5 percent of annual sales, and the firm maintained an allowance for doubtful accounts equal to one year's bad debts ($5 million). The company made extensive efforts to collect on all receivables, and accounts were typically not written off until three years after the year of sale. Thus receivables from sales of 1987 would not be written off until 1990.

Starting in 1990, the company changed its previously conservative merchandising policies, and sales improved dramatically. From 1990 through 1994 they increased at a compound rate of 20 percent per year ($120 million in 1990, $144 million in 1991, etc.). As a consequence of more liberal credit policies, bad debts increased from 5 percent of sales to 7 percent. Nevertheless, the company continued to add to its allowance for doubtful accounts at the rate of only 5 percent of sales. As in the previous decade, accounts were not actually written off until three years after the year of sale. Thus, beginning in 1993, the company was forced to write off 7 percent of the previous years' sales, but had provided an allowance for doubtful accounts of only 5 percent.

In 1995 sales levelled off and from 1995 to 2001 remained constant at $248.83 million per year.

a. Determine the balances in the allowance for doubtful accounts at year end 1987 through 2001. Calculate the balance as a percentage of sales for the year.

b. Comment on the pattern of changes in the balances and on its significance for financial analysts concerned with the adequacy of the allowance.

10. *In some industries it is especially critical that allowances be made for anticipated returns of merchandise sold.*

Division Products had gross sales in 1996 (its first year of operations) of $8 million and in 1994 of $12 million. At December 31, 1996, the company had accounts receivable of $4 million and as at December 31, 1997, $6 million. The business of the company is highly seasonal; most of its sales are made in the last three months of the year.

The company follows standard practice in its industry. It permits the retailers with whom it deals to return for full credit any merchandise that they are unable to sell within a reasonable period of time. In January 1997, the company accepted for return merchandise that it had sold in 1996 for $800,000. None of the merchandise had yet been paid for by the retailers. A return rate of 10 percent of sales is typical for the industry.

The firm's cost of goods sold is approximately 60 percent of sales. In financial statements prepared for internal use only (and not in accord with generally accepted accounting principles of reporting to the general public), the firm gives accounting recognition to merchandise returned only when it is actually received; it establishes no year-end allowances.

a. Determine for both 1996 and 1997 the difference in income and assets that would result if the company were to establish an allowance for returned merchandise. Assume that all goods returned would be resold at standard prices.

b. Suppose that the company was in a business, such as toys, in which it is extremely difficult to predict the rate of return from pre-Christmas sales. Do you think the company should recognize revenue at time of sale? What alternative point of revenue recognition might be preferable?

c. How else can companies in highly seasonal industries, such as toys, eliminate the danger of misestimating returns in their annual financial reports? Why do you suppose that many department stores report on the basis of a fiscal year ending July 31 rather than on a calendar year?

11. *In mail-order companies, the financial impact of returns may be significant.*

The financial statements of New Process Company (an actual company), which sells clothing by direct mail, contained the following footnote:

> **Returns:** A provision for anticipated returns is recorded monthly as a percentage of gross sales; the percentage is based upon historical experience. Actual returns are charged against the allowance for returns, which is netted against accounts receivable in the balance sheet. The provision for returns charged against income in 1987 and 1986 amounts to $69,470,047 and $68,759,379, respectively.

The financial statements also revealed the following:

	1987	1986
Sales	$362,576,000	$359,609,000
Accounts receivable	71,069,000	66,291,000
Allowances for doubtful accounts and returns	19,776,737	21,785,543

a. Based on the information provided, prepare the journal entries made by the company in 1987 to provide for anticipated returns and to account for actual returns. Assume that, of the allowances for doubtful accounts and returns, 20 percent is for returns and 80 percent for doubtful accounts.

b. Based on the information provided (there is no other with respect to returns included in the financial statements), do you think that the merchandise returned has significant value? Explain.

c. How many days' sales are in accounts receivable as of year end 1987?

12. *Minor differences in return policies may necessitate major differences in accounting practices.*

a. University Textbooks, Inc., sells textbooks to university bookstores. Based on information provided by course instructors, the bookstores order only as many copies as they estimate will be sold. Occasionally, however, they overorder and, as an accommodation, University Textbooks allows them to return unsold books as long as it will be able to resell them. The company estimates that returns are approximately 3 percent of sales.

(1) In December 1996, University Textbooks sold, on account, $10 million in textbooks. Cost of books sold was $6 million. Prepare the appropriate entries.

(2) In January and February 1997, University Textbooks accepted for return books that it had sold in December 1996 for $400,000. Prepare the appropriate entries.

b. Universal Paperbacks sells paperbacks to supermarkets, newsstands, and airport bookstands. To get maximum exposure for its books, the company allows the retailers to return any books that remain unsold 60 days after they have been received and placed on display racks. The company estimates that returns *on average* are 40 percent of sales. However, the range of returns, by title, varies considerably. If a book catches on, there will be few, if any, returns. If it doesn't, almost all copies will be returned.

    (1) In December 1996, Universal Paperbacks shipped $10 million in books. Cost of books sold was $6 million. Prepare the appropriate entries.

    (2) In January and February 1997, Universal Paperbacks accepted for return books that it had sold in December 1993 for $1,200,000. Prepare the appropriate entries.

  c. Justify your entries and comment on any similarities and differences between parts (a) and (b).

13. *The means of accounting for cash discounts may not be the critical issue of our time, but it points up the importance of recognizing the substance of a transaction rather than the form.*

    Manitoba Industrial Supplies reported accounts receivable of $2 million as at December 31, 1996. Of that amount, $1,600,000 represents sales of the final 20 days of the year. The company allows its customers to take a cash discount of 4 percent of sales price on all merchandise paid for within 20 days.

    The company has consistently accounted for cash discounts by the *gross* method. Annual sales and year-end balances in accounts receivable have remained generally constant over the last several years. Approximately 90 percent of the customers take advantage of the cash discount. Comment on whether the firm's sales and accounts receivable are likely to be fairly presented at year end. Indicate the amount of any possible over- or understatement.

14. *The gross method of accounting for cash discounts may not reflect the fair market value of goods traded.*

    The Grimm Co. purchases all of its merchandise from the Anderson Co. Terms of sale are 1/15, n/30. In the month of December the following transactions took place:

Dec. 1	Grimm purchased $160,000 of merchandise on account.
Dec. 10	Grimm remitted payment for the goods purchased Dec. 1.
Dec. 12	Grimm purchased $100,000 of merchandise on account.
Dec. 31	Grimm remitted payment for the goods purchased Dec. 12.

  a. Record the transactions on the books of the Grimm Co. using first the net method and then the gross method.

  b. Record the transactions on the books of the Anderson Co. using first the net method and then the gross method. The entries from the standpoint of the seller were not illustrated in the text. They correspond closely to those of the purchaser, however.

  c. Assuming that no additional adjustments were made to the accounts and that none of the merchandise acquired by Grimm has yet been sold, comment on any distortions of the accounts that might result from use of the gross method.

    Suppose that Grimm had sold all or part of the merchandise that it had acquired. What accounts might be misstated? What information, useful for management control, is highlighted by the net method but obscured by the gross method?

15. *Compute simple and compound interest.*

In each of the following situations, determine the interest revenue that a firm should recognize.

a. It holds for 180 days a $3,000 note that earns interest at an annual rate of 9 percent.

b. It holds for 30 days a $10,000 note that earns interest at an annual rate of 8 percent.

c. It holds for 400 days a $1,000 note that earns interest at an annual rate of 12 percent (interest is not to be charged on interest accrued at the end of the first year).

d. It holds for five years a $5,000 note that earns interest at a rate of 8 percent compounded annually.

16. *The stated price of merchandise is not always the "true" price.*

A firm sells merchandise for a supposed price of $1,000 but sometimes grants unusually generous terms of credit. Prevailing rates of interest are 10 percent. Determine the amount most indicative of "true" selling price of the merchandise if the buyer

a. Pays $1,000 cash today.

b. Pays $1,000 cash one year from today.

c. Pays $1,000 cash plus interest at 4 percent (that is, $1,040) one year from today.

d. Pays $500 six months from today and $500 one year from today.

17. *Compute the amount of discount notes.*

A bank makes a loan to a customer on a discount basis. Determine the amount that should be advanced to the customer in each of the following situations, assuming that the face amount of the note is $10,000 and the rate of discount is 10 percent per year.

a. The period of the loan is 1 year.

b. The period of the loan is 60 days.

c. The period of the loan is 4 years.

18. *The effective rate of interest on discount loans may be substantially higher than the stated rate.*

The Confidential Loan Co. placed an advertisement in a local newspaper. It read, in part, "Borrow up to $24,000. Take up to 3 Years to Repay. Low, Low, 6% Interest Rate."

Upon visiting the loan company you learn that on a three-year, 6 percent loan of $24,000, interest of $4,320 ($1,440 per year) is taken out in advance; you would receive only $19,680 cash. You would be required to repay the loan in three annual instalments of $8,000.

Indicate the main points that you might make in a letter to the Misleading Advertising branch of Consumer and Corporate Affairs Canada. Be sure to specify the approximate effective annual rate of interest charged by the company.

19. *This problem illustrates a borrowing arrangement that, although not specifically discussed in the text, represents an application of the principles which were described.*

Sometimes a firm will "discount" with a bank an interest-bearing note that it has received from a customer. The bank will advance the firm the amount to be received from the customer, less interest charges for the number of days until the note matures. When the note matures, the customer will make payment to the firm and the firm will transfer the amount received to the bank.

Suppose that a firm receives a one-year note from a customer in the amount of $1,000. The note bears interest at the rate of 8 percent. Immediately upon receipt of the note, the firm discounts it with a bank. The bank, however, accepts notes only at a discount rate of 10 percent.

a. Upon the maturity of the note, how much will the customer be required to remit to the firm?

b. What is the amount that the bank will be willing to advance to the firm based on its discount rate of 10 percent?

20. *Even banks and finance companies face difficult questions of revenue recognition.*

Sunrise Finance Co. loaned a customer $20,000 for two years on a discount basis. The customer was to repay $10,000 at the end of each year. The rate of discount (the effective rate of interest) was 10 percent.

a. How much cash would the company actually advance the customer? Prepare a journal entry to record the loan and the receipt by the company of a note for $20,000.

b. How much revenue should the company recognize during the first year of the loan? Prepare a journal entry to record receipt of the first payment of $10,000. At what value will the note be reported (net of discount) after the first year? How much revenue should the company recognize during the second year?

c. Many bankers and managers of finance companies assert that a portion—perhaps 15 percent—of the total revenue to be earned over the two-year period should be recognized at the time the loan is made, without waiting for interest to accrue with the passage of time. In light of the costs of obtaining customers (advertising) and processing loan applications, why do you suspect they feel as they do?

21. *In the real estate industry, it is not uncommon for the selling price of property to include an element of interest.*

The Pearson Co. purchased a building from the Polk Co. The stated selling price of the building was $20 million. Polk Co. agreed to accept from the Pearson Co. an *interest-free* note, which was payable in full five years from the date the transaction was closed.

The building has an estimated useful life of 20 years and zero salvage value after that period. At the time of sale, it had been recorded on the books of the Polk Co. at $8 million. Had Pearson Co. been required to pay cash for the building, it would have had to borrow the funds from a bank at an annual rate of interest of 10 percent.

a. Prepare a journal entry to record the purchase of the building on the books of the Pearson Co. Be certain that the entry recognizes substance over form.

b. Prepare any journal entries that Pearson would be required to make after the first year of ownership to recognize both interest expense and amortization expense.

c. Determine the difference in Pearson Co. earnings of the first year that would result from taking into account, as opposed to ignoring, the *imputed* interest.

d. Determine the difference in Polk Co. earnings of both the first year and second year that would result from taking into account the *imputed* interest. What would be the total difference in earnings in years 1 through 5? (You should not have to compute earnings in each of the five years to answer the question.)

22. *The apparent value of a hotel may be greater than its real value.*

Resorts, Inc., recently acquired the Flamingo Palace, a luxury hotel, at a stated price of $100 million. Two days after the transaction was completed, the hotel was destroyed by fire. Resorts, Inc., has submitted a claim to its casualty insurance company for $100 million.

Assume that you are a claims agent of the insurance company. By examining the purchase contract, you learn that Resorts, Inc., had made a down payment of only $20 million and had given a 4 percent mortgage note for the remaining balance of $80 million. The mortgage note required that the loan be repaid in five annual instalments. As with a conventional household mortgage, the instalments were to be of equal amounts, each representing the repayment of principal plus interest at the rate of 4 percent per annum on the remaining principal balance. With each subsequent payment, the principal balance would decrease. Correspondingly, the proportion of each payment representing principal rather than interest would increase.

You also learn that the prevailing interest rate on comparable types of mortgages is 10 percent.

a. Determine the dollar amount of each required mortgage instalment.
b. What is the maximum amount that you would recommend that the insurance company offer in settlement of the claim? Explain and show all computations.
c. Assume instead that the hotel was not destroyed by fire. The estimated life of the hotel is 20 years (with no residual value). What would be the difference in earnings between what Resorts, Inc., would report if it imputed interest and if it did not (1) in year 1, (2) in year 20, and (3) over the life of the hotel.

23. *Determination of the real value of a business acquired by another may be complex.*

The following note appeared in the 1973 financial report of United Brands Company:

> On December 31, 1973, the Company sold its 83% interest in Baskin-Robbins Ice Cream Company to J. Lyons & Company Limited, a British food company, for a total of $37,600,000 including $30,300,000 in notes. The notes bear interest at 4% per annum and mature in 3 equal annual instalments of $10,100,000 commencing on December 31, 1974. The notes have been recorded in the financial statements at an imputed interest rate of 12%.

a. Determine the present value, discounted at 12 percent, of *all* payments (both principal and interest) that United Brands will receive over the three-year period. Be sure to determine the interest payments as 4 percent of the outstanding balance of the notes at the time of each payment.
b. Prepare a journal entry to record the sale of the 83 percent interest in Baskin-Robbins. Assume that the 83 percent interest had been valued

on the books of United Brands at $20 million. To simplify the journal entry and subsequent computation of interest, record the present value of the expected principal and interest payments to be received in a single account, "notes receivable."

c. Prepare an entry to record the first receipt of principal and interest. Be sure to base the computation of interest earned on the effective rate of 12 percent and the effective balance in the notes receivable account.

d. How much greater or less would the reported income of United Brands have been in both the year of sale and year of collection of the first principal and interest payment had the company not imputed the additional 8 percent interest?

24. *"Interest-free" loans may mislead customers as well as distort financial statements.*

The Davis Land Development Co. sells real estate on terms of 10 percent down, the balance to be paid in annual instalments over a three-year period. Customers are not specifically charged interest on their outstanding balances.

During 1996 the company sold several lots at a stated price of $80,000 each. The original cost to the company of each of the lots was $4,000. The annual interest rate on similar "loans" would be 10 percent.

a. How much *income* per lot do you think the company should recognize at time of sale (upon collection of the 10 percent down payment) assuming recognition of all sales (but not *interest*) revenue at the time of down payment? Prepare a journal entry to record the transaction.

b. How much income per lot should be recognized at the time of each of the three instalment payments? What would be the balances in notes receivable and the related discount account immediately following each payment?

25. *Information that is essential to an evaluation of a franchise is likely to be omitted from the franchisor's financial statements.*

A headline in the *Wall Street Journal* warned, "Jiffy Lube Raises Some Eyebrows with Loans to Its Franchisees for Their Up-Front Expenses." The accompanying column reported that some savvy investors thought the stock of the company, a franchisor of quick-oil-change auto centres, was overpriced. The main concern of the investors was $49 million of notes receivable from franchisees that the company reported as assets. The company had lent franchisees that amount to assist them in paying start-up costs, such as franchise purchase fees, as well as ongoing royalties to the company.

a. Explain why the analysts might be especially sceptical of large amounts of receivables from franchisees? Why are such receivables especially risky?

b. The article also indicated that documents other than Jiffy Lube's financial statements reveal that the company's largest franchisee, which owns 67 outlets, reported a substantial loss in the year that had just ended. Why is this information critical to an assessment of Jiffy Lube's fiscal capability, even if its receivables include no amounts due from the franchisee?

c. Franchisors are not required to report on the financial health of their franchisees, either individually or collectively. In light of the obvious significance of this information, do you believe that they should be? If so, how should the data be presented? What are the major obstacles that a franchisor would face in satisfying such a requirement?

26. *Should a franchisor always recognize revenue at the time it signs a sales contract or are there circumstances that justify a delay?*

The Peter Pan Cheese Co., after successfully operating a single retail cheese store for several years, decided to expand its operations. It offered to sell Peter Pan franchises in several cities for $100,000 each. For that amount, a franchisee acquired the right to sell under the name "Peter Pan" and to purchase from the franchisor several products bearing the company name.

Upon signing a contract, a franchisee gave the company an interest-bearing note for $100,000. The franchisee was required to pay $25,000 upon the opening of the outlet and could pay the $75,000 balance over a period of three years.

The company estimated that the cost of initial services it would be required to provide the franchisee prior to the opening of an outlet would be $80,000. In accord with the provisions of generally accepted accounting principles, it elected to recognize revenue from the sale of a franchise *at the commencement of an outlet's operations.*

In 1996 the company signed sales contracts with 10 franchisees. It estimated that of the $1 million in notes that it received, 6 percent would be uncollectable.

Of the 10 new franchisees, 6 began operations during the year. From these six the company collected a total of $150,000 in cash on the notes that they had signed.

During the year the company incurred $480,000 in costs in connection with the outlets actually opened and $250,000 in connection with those expected to open in the following year. In addition, the company had cash sales of merchandise to the new outlets of $500,000; the cost of merchandise sold was $400,000. The company also collected interest of $35,000 on the interest-bearing notes.

a. Prepare an income statement for 1996 to reflect the company's franchise operations. Be sure to match expenses with revenues.

b. Prepare a balance sheet as at year end. Assume that the company began the year with $500,000 in cash and contributed capital. All costs were paid in cash.

c. Suppose instead that the franchisees were not required to make any payment on their notes when an outlet was opened. Instead they would have to pay off the note at a rate equal to 10 percent of sales each year until the balance was reduced to zero. Moreover, the company was unable to make a reliable estimate of the amounts that would be uncollectable. Do you think the company should recognize revenue on the sale of franchises at the time an outlet commences operations? On what basis do you think it should recognize revenue? Explain.

27. *Reported wage expense is generally greater than the amounts actually disbursed to employees.*

Wellman Manufacturing Co. has 100 hourly employees, each of whom worked 40 hours in a week and was paid $14.50 per hour.

Total income taxes that the company was required to withhold for the week were $14,500.

The Canada Pension Plan (CPP) rate applicable to both employer and employee was 2.3 percent of gross wages.

The company is required to pay 4.2 percent of gross wages into the Unemployment Insurance fund and the employees contribute at the rate of 3 percent.

The company has a matching pension plan. Employees contribute 5 percent of their wages; the company contributes an equal amount.

The firm is required by union contract to withhold from each employee union dues of $2.50 per week.

Twenty employees have elected to join the Canada Savings Bond program. Each week $18 is withdrawn from the wages of each of these twenty employees and used to purchase a savings bond.

The company contributes to a supplementary health insurance plan for each employee. The cost is $8 per week per employee.

a. Prepare a journal entry to record the weekly payroll.

b. Prepare a journal entry to record disbursement of all required payments to the various government departments, insurance companies, pension funds, etc.

28. *The impact of an accounting change on the balance sheet may be substantially greater than on the income statement. An event may have a significant impact on the interim statements but no effect on the annual statements.*

The Sonora Co. has an annual payroll of approximately $2 million. This amount does not include $120,000 paid to employees on vacation. The company does not accrue vacation pay; it charges it to expense as employees take their vacations. The controller has rejected the suggestions of the company's independent auditor that vacation pay be recognized on a week-by-week basis; she claims that such recognition would have no effect on the financial statements; it would only increase clerical costs.

The payroll of the company has remained constant for a number of years. Employees are entitled to three weeks of vacation each year based on work performed in the previous fiscal year, and the vacations must be taken during July and August. Employees receive their regular wages while on vacation, and all employees must be replaced by temporary employees at the same wage rate. The company's fiscal year ends June 30.

a. Is the controller correct in her assertion that accrual of vacation pay would have no impact on the financial statements? Estimate the impact of a change in policy on both the income statement and the balance sheet.

b. Suppose the firm were to issue *interim* financial statements on December 31 for the six months ending on that date. What would be the impact of accruing vacation pay on the income statement and the balance sheet?

29. *An increase in the current ratio may not necessarily be indicative of an improved financial position.*

The president of a company, in requesting a renewal of an outstanding loan, wrote to an officer of a bank: "In spite of a decline in sales and earnings, we were able to strengthen our working capital position." She went on to cite the increase in the current ratio as evidence of the improvement.

The balance sheet of the company reported the following current assets and liabilities:

	December 31, 1997	December 31, 1996
Cash	$ 60,000	$120,000
Accounts receivable	270,000	190,000
Inventories	420,000	300,000
Total current assets	$750,000	$610,000
Accounts payable	$370,000	$330,000
Notes payable	140,000	140,000
Total current liabilities	$510,000	$470,000

The income statement (in summary form) revealed the following:

	1997	1996
Sales	$1,400,000	$1,560,000
Cost of goods sold	$ 840,000	$ 936,000
Other expenses	240,000	260,000
Total expenses	$1,080,000	1,196,000
Net income	$ 320,000	$ 364,000

a. Determine the current ratio for both years.
b. (1) Determine the quick ratio.
   (2) Calculate number of days' sales in accounts receivable.
c. Provide a possible explanation for the increase in accounts receivable and inventories that would undermine the contention of the president that the firm's working capital position has improved. Has the current position of the company really improved?

30. *The manner in which a ratio is computed depends on the purpose to which it is put; conclusions from ratios must be drawn with care.*

The following data (in millions of dollars) were taken from the financial statements of a manufacturer of vacuum cleaners:

	1997	1996
Sales	$754.3	$691.8
Notes and accounts receivables less allowances for doubtful accounts (in millions) of $2.4 in1997 and $2.0 in 1996	143.6	143.7

a. On the basis of accounts receivable turnover, in which year did the firm employ its receivables more efficiently? (Compute receivables turnover *gross*—that is, without reduction for allowances—and use year-end rather than average receivables.)
b. Suppose that the firm sells on terms 2/10, n/30. What concern would be raised by the calculation of number of days' sales in accounts receivable? Inasmuch, however, as the data combine notes receivable and accounts receivable, why might your concern be unwarranted?

c. A question is often raised as to whether ratios involving accounts receivable, such as the current ratio and the quick ratio, should incorporate accounts receivable gross or net of allowances for doubtful accounts. Why might your response be different if you were providing an answer to a banker who is interested primarily in the ability of the firm to collect on its outstanding receivables and repay its debts than if you were responding to a manager who is concerned with minimizing the amount of funds tied up in "unproductive" assets?

Solutions to Exercise for Review and Self-Testing

1. The fair market value of the equipment may be obtained by calculating the value *today* of the note. Per Table 2 in the Appendix, the present value of $1 to be received in one year, discounted at a rate of 12 percent, is $.8929. The present value of the note therefore is $2,120 × .8929, or $1892.95. The fair market value of the equipment therefore would also be $1892.95.

2. Notes receivable $2,120.00
       Discount on notes receivable .... $ 227.05
       Sales revenue 1,892.95
   To record sale of equipment

3. Cash $2,120.00
     Discount on notes receivable 227.05
       Notes receivable $2,120.00
       Interest revenue 227.05
   To record collection of the note and to recognize interest revenue for one year (Interest of $227.05 is 12% of the initial net balance of the note, $1,892.95.)

4. Bad-debt expense $10,000
       Allowance for doubtful notes receivable $10,000
   To record estimate of bad debts

5. Allowance for doubtful notes receivable $1,500
       Notes receivable $1,500
   To write off specific notes that are uncollectable

8

Inventories and Cost of Goods Sold

This is the third chapter that looks at specific balance sheet accounts, along with the related revenue or expense accounts. In this chapter, we introduce the accounting for inventory. Goods manufactured or purchased for resale are included on the balance sheet as inventory, until sold. Once sold, the cost is transferred from the asset, inventory, to the expense, cost of goods sold. We will look at the costs included in the valuation of inventory and the assumptions of cost flow that are used for inventory valuation. Finally, a brief introduction to the use of current costs, rather than historic costs, is provided.

After studying this chapter, you will be able to

- Define inventory and cost of goods sold and understand the relationship between the two accounts
- Value inventory and calculate cost of goods sold under each of the four assumptions of cost flow: specific identification, FIFO, LIFO, and average cost
- Know when to use the lower of cost and market rule for inventory
- Describe the current cost method of accounting for inventory and cost of goods sold
- Calculate and understand the significance of the inventory turnover ratio

The term *inventory* refers to goods that are awaiting sale or are in the various stages of production. It includes the merchandise of a retail concern as well as the finished goods, the work in process, and the raw materials of a manufacturer. In addition, the term includes goods that will be consumed indirectly as the enterprise manufactures its product or provides its service. Thus stores of stationery, cleaning supplies, and lubricants would also be categorized as inventories. Proper accounting for inventories is critical not only because they often compose a substantial portion of a firm's assets but also because they relate directly to what is frequently the firm's major expense—the cost of goods sold. The beginning inventory balance plus purchases of inventory during the period minus the ending inventory balance equals the cost of goods sold. This chapter is directed to several key accounting issues pertaining to inventory, some of which are currently at the centre of active controversy. Among the questions raised are

- What are the objectives of inventory measurement and valuation?
- What costs should be included in inventory?
- How should inventory quantities be determined?
- What assumptions regarding the flow of costs are most appropriate in particular circumstances?
- When and how should changes in the market prices of inventories be recognized?

The discussion of inventories is in the context of generally accepted accounting principles—how inventories are accounted for in practice. But consideration is also given, in a concluding section, to alternatives that have been proposed but are not presently viewed as acceptable.

The overriding objective of conventional inventory accounting is to match the costs of acquiring or producing goods with the revenues that they generate. The emphasis is decidedly on income determination rather than on balance sheet valuation. It is to assure that the resultant measure of income is useful for evaluating performance of the past and making predictions of the future. An unfortunate consequence is that the amounts reported on the balance sheet are indicative of costs incurred in the past—sometimes, in fact, in the very distant past. They provide information on neither the prices that would have to be paid to replace the goods on hand nor those for which they could be sold.

In a typical operating cycle of a firm, the costs of goods that are either manufactured or purchased are included in inventory and reported as an asset. Even though the goods may have been paid for, their costs are not considered to be expenses. Instead the costs are *stored* on the balance sheet until the goods are sold and the costs can be associated with specific revenues. At the end of a year, a portion of the *goods* remains on hand; the rest have been sold to outsiders. A portion of the costs therefore must be assigned to the goods that remain on hand and the rest to the goods that have been sold. That portion of the costs that is assigned to the goods on hand will continue to be carried on the balance sheet, while that assigned to the goods that have been sold will be charged to an expense account, cost of goods sold, and reported on the income statement. The question facing the firm is: "How much of the total costs should be assigned to the goods on hand and how much to the goods that have been sold?" The issue is depicted in Exhibit 8-1.

Insofar as a greater value is placed on the goods in inventory, a lesser amount will be charged as an expense. Insofar as a greater amount is charged as a current expense, then smaller amounts will remain on the balance sheet to be charged as expenses in future years. In other words, only two things can happen to goods that are acquired or manufactured for resale—they can be sold during the period or not sold.

EXHIBIT 8-1

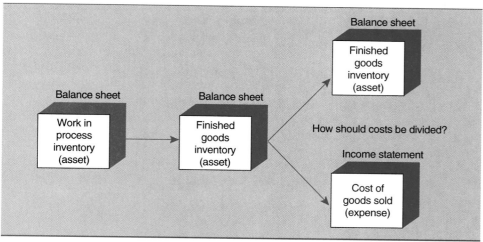

COSTS INCLUDED IN INVENTORY

Inventories are ordinarily stated at historical cost—that of acquisition or production. Cost, as applied to inventories, means the total of the applicable expenditures and charges directly or indirectly incurred to bring an item of inventory to its existing condition and location. If goods are purchased from outsiders, then cost would include not only the invoice price but also costs of packaging and transportation. Trade, cash, or other special discounts or allowances must be deducted from the stated price.

As a rule, all costs that can reasonably be associated with the manufacture or acquisition, with the storage, or with the preparation for sale of goods should be included as part of the cost of such goods. In determining whether a particular item of cost should be added to the reported value of inventory, the impact on both the income statement and the balance sheet should be taken into account. If costs are added to the reported value of goods on hand, they will be charged as expenses (as part of cost of goods sold) in the period in which the merchandise is actually sold. By contrast, if the costs are not assigned to particular items of inventory, they will be charged as expenses in the periods in which they are incurred, regardless of when the merchandise is sold.

Example

A company purchased 100 units of product, for resale, at $20 per unit. It was permitted a trade discount (one granted to all customers in a particular category) of 5 percent but had to pay shipping costs of $300. Cost per unit would be calculated as follows:

Base price (100 units @ $20)	$2,000	
Less trade discount (5%)	100	$1,900
Plus shipping costs		300
Total cost of 100 units		$2,200
Number of units		÷ 100 units
Cost per unit		$ 22

If goods are produced by the company itself, the problem of cost determination is considerably more complex. Cost includes charges for labour and materials that can be directly associated with the product as well as *overhead* such as rent, maintenance, and utilities that may be common to several products produced in the same plant. To determine the cost of a particular product, a company has to allocate these common charges among the various products. In addition, however, the firm has to decide whether certain costs should be considered *product* costs, and thereby added to the carrying value of the goods produced, or *period* costs, and thereby charged off as an expense as incurred. The implications of classifying an outlay as a product rather than a period cost were discussed earlier in Chapter 4 in connection with the discussion of the manufacturing cycle.

ACCOUNTING FOR QUANTITIES ON HAND

Periodic versus Perpetual Bases

In Chapter 4 it was pointed out that inventories may be maintained on a perpetual or a periodic basis. A *perpetual basis* implies that accounting recognition is given to the reduction of inventories each time a sale is made, supplies are consumed, or raw materials are added to production. When goods are removed from inventory upon a sale, for example, the following journal entry would be made:

Cost of goods sold xxxx
　　　Inventory xxxx

The *periodic method,* on the other hand, recognizes the reduction in inventory resulting from the sale or use of goods only periodically, perhaps once a year. The sum of the costs of the beginning inventory and the goods added during the year constitutes a pool of costs that at year end will be divided between the income statement (cost of goods sold) and the balance sheet (inventory).

As goods are added to inventory during the year, the inventory account is debited with their cost.[1] As goods are removed, however, no entry is made to record the reduction in inventory. Throughout the year, therefore, the inventory account misstates the cost of the goods actually on hand. At the end of the period, a physical count of goods on hand is taken. The goods are assigned their acquisition cost, and the inventory account is adjusted to reflect

---

[1] As noted in Chapter 4, many firms, as they acquire inventory, debit an account entitled "purchases" rather than the inventory account itself. At year end, they transfer the balance in the purchases account to the inventory account by debiting "inventory" and crediting "purchases." See page 137 for an example.

the resultant dollar amount. Goods not on hand are assumed to have been sold, and their cost is charged to cost of goods sold.

Assume that a firm begins the year with a balance in inventory of $1 million. During the year it purchases goods of $9 million and debits the purchases to its inventory account. At year end the inventory account would have a balance of $10 million. A physical count, however, reveals only $500,000 of goods on hand. Hence, $9.5 million of the $10 million must be charged to cost of goods sold. The following entry (in millions) would be appropriate:

Cost of goods sold $9.5
    Inventory $9.5
To adjust the year-end inventory account to reflect goods actually on hand

Although this text is not primarily directed toward the record-keeping procedures of enterprises, the two alternative methods of accounting for inventories are explained here because they *may* have an impact on the reported value of inventories at year end. The circumstances in which a difference may occur will be identified in the following discussion of the flows of costs.

FLOWS OF COSTS

The critical issue of inventory accounting, that of flows of costs, arises because the acquisition or production costs of goods do not remain constant. As a consequence, it is sometimes necessary to make assumptions as to which goods have been sold and which remain on hand—those with the higher costs or those with the lower. (Recall the example in the first chapter of the text pertaining to the cost of sunflower oil.) In some situations, identification of specific costs with specific goods presents no problem. The goods have sufficiently different characteristics that they can readily be tagged with specific costs. The costs to retailers of automobiles, appliances, or rare pieces of jewellery, for example, can easily be associated with specific units. Not so, however, with interchangeable goods such as grains or liquids, purchases of which made at different times are mixed together, or with most small items, such as canned goods or items of clothing for which it is inconvenient to account for each unit independently. Moreover, for reasons to be indicated shortly, accountants sometimes find it desirable to make assumptions regarding the flow of *costs* that are in obvious conflict with available information regarding the actual physical flow of the *goods*.

SPECIFIC IDENTIFICATION

The specific identification inventory method requires the enterprise to keep track of the cost of each individual item bought and sold. Ordinarily, a firm would either code the cost directly on the item itself or otherwise tag each item with a control number and maintain a separate record of costs.

EXHIBIT 8-2
Purchases and Sales of a Particular Item

Date	Purchases No. of Units	Purchases Unit Cost	Purchases Total Cost	No. of Units Sold	No. of Units on Hand
Jan. 1 (bal. on hand)	300	$5	$1,500		300
March 2	100	6	600		400
April 20				200	200
May 25	400	8	3,200		600
Sept. 18	200	7	1,400		800
Nov. 8				300	500
Total	1,000		$6,700	500	

Refer, for example, to the data provided in Exhibit 8-2, which indicates quantities of an item purchased and sold on various dates. Also indicated are the opening balance, the prices at which the various acquisitions were made, and the total cost of each acquisition. Assume that of the 200 items that were sold on April 20, 100 units were taken from the lot that was on hand on January 1 and 100 were taken from that purchased on March 2. Of the 300 items sold on November 8, 100 were taken from the lot on hand on January 1 and 200 from that purchased on May 25. The cost of goods sold would be computed as follows:

Sale of April 20		
From lot of Jan. 1	100 @ $5	$ 500
From lot of March 2	100 @ $6	600
	200	$1,100
Sale of Nov. 8		
From lot of Jan. 1	100 @ $5	$ 500
From lot of May 25	200 @ $8	1,600
	300	$2,100
Cost of goods sold	500	$3,200

Total merchandise costs to be accounted for during the year (initial balance plus purchases) are $6,700. If the cost of goods sold is $3,200, then the balance of the total costs must be that of the goods still on hand at year end (i.e., inventory)—$6,700 minus $3,200 = $3,500. This amount can be verified by the following tabulation of ending inventory:

From lot of Jan. 1	100 @ $5	$ 500
From lot of May 25	200 @ $8	1,600
From lot of Sept. 18	200 @ $7	1,400
Ending inventory	500	$3,500

The specific identification method is most appropriate for dealers, such as those of automobiles and appliances, who sell relatively few items of large unit cost. It becomes burdensome to firms that sell large quantities of low-cost

LIFO—The Objections

The effects of LIFO on both the balance sheet and the income statement are, in the view of some managers and accountants, unacceptable. LIFO results in a reported inventory that is continually out of date. If the firm never dips into its base stock (for example, in Exhibit 8-6, the inventory was never reduced below 1,000 units), then the reported inventory would be reflective of prices that existed at the time LIFO was first adopted, decades earlier perhaps. The balance sheet, as continually emphasized in this text, is not purported to be representative of current values. Nevertheless, many accountants feel uncomfortable when values that are preposterously out of date are assigned.

More serious, however, is the impact of LIFO on reported income when the firm is required to dip into its base stock. If the firm is required to sell goods that are valued on the balance sheet at decades-old prices, then the cost of goods sold will be based on the same ancient prices. Refer back to Exhibit 8-6. Suppose that in 1999 the firm was unable to purchase its required 1,000 units. Instead, it sold its goods on hand and thereby reduced its end-of-year inventory to zero. The cost of goods sold would be $100 per unit—the price of the goods on hand when the company first adopted LIFO in 1995—this at a time when the current replacement cost of the goods is $146.41 per unit. If the cost of goods sold is misleadingly low, then reported income would, of course, be correspondingly high. Whatever its advantages when the firm is able to meet current sales out of current purchases, LIFO produces results that are absurd when it becomes necessary to reduce inventory below a level that is historically normal. Many accountants who are opposed to LIFO recognize the need to account for rapid increases in the replacement costs of inventories. They believe, however, that it should be done directly, by adjusting both cost of goods sold and goods on hand to reflect current values. Current cost accounting as it applies to inventories will be discussed later in this chapter.

LIFO—Its Recent Popularity

From the mid-1970s on, several hundred major U.S. firms shifted from either a FIFO or a moving average to a LIFO inventory valuation method. The shifts were motivated almost entirely by the opportunities to reduce the federal income tax burden.

Since 1938, the U.S. Internal Revenue Code has recognized the acceptability of LIFO. In periods of rapid inflation, such as those experienced in many industrial nations in the 1970s and early 1980s, LIFO has been particularly popular in the United States. By basing the cost of goods sold on the most recent purchases, LIFO reduces taxable income. The difference in taxable income between that determined on a FIFO or average cost as opposed to a LIFO basis may not be trivial. Du Pont, for example, estimated that its shift from average cost to LIFO reduced income by over $250 million and reduced its earnings per share by $3.02 (from $11.22 to $8.20). Other major U.S. corporations effected similar reductions in earnings and hence in taxes. Estimates of the overall loss in tax revenues to the U.S. federal government range up to $40 billion per year.

The Income Tax Act in Canada does not allow the use of the LIFO method of inventory valuation for purposes of calculating taxable income. As a result, there has not been as significant a shift to LIFO in Canada as there has been in the United States. However, a few Canadian firms have elected to use the LIFO method of inventory valuation for financial reporting purposes. In particular, Canadian subsidiaries of U.S. companies that use LIFO will likely adopt LIFO for consistency of accounting practices.

As a rule, when there are alternative accounting methods that are generally accepted, businesses are not required to use the same method in reporting to Revenue Canada, Taxation, as they do in reporting to their shareholders. Therefore, Canadian companies may use the LIFO method of inventory valuation for financial reporting to their shareholders, but switch to FIFO for tax reporting purposes. In the United States, however, the U.S. tax code makes an exception with respect to inventory valuation. If a U.S. company adheres to one method of inventory valuation in reporting to the general public, it usually must use the same method in reporting to the U.S. Internal Revenue Service. As a consequence of this ruling, U.S. firms that wish to take advantage of the tax-savings opportunities provided by LIFO are ordinarily required to switch to LIFO for general reporting purposes.

Quite apart from the tax advantages of LIFO available in the United States, some financial analysts consider earnings of LIFO-based companies to be of higher "quality" than those of FIFO or average cost firms. What they mean is that were it not for the "inflated" value of their inventories, the earnings of the non-LIFO firms may have been considerably lower and growth trends somewhat more flat.

LIFO—Can a Firm Afford Not to Adopt It?

Many accountants, in particular accounting researchers, assert that in periods of inflation, the use of any inventory method other than LIFO cannot be justified. LIFO permits, in the United States at least, a company to postpone tax payments and thereby to increase the amount of cash available for other corporate purposes. Failure to switch to LIFO, some say, is the equivalent of making a donation to the taxing authorities. They assert that fears of adverse consequences of the decline in *reported* earnings that results from a switch to LIFO are unwarranted. The benefits of higher reported earnings attributable to non-LIFO methods are at best illusory. There is highly persuasive, if not conclusive, evidence to indicate that investors as a group are not influenced by the higher earnings that would generally be reported by a company using a non-LIFO inventory method. A number of empirical studies have revealed that use of LIFO has no discernible negative impact on the market value of a firm's common stock. Investors are apparently able to "discount" the higher earnings caused solely by choice of inventory method.

It is ironic that non-LIFO methods may enable a firm to report higher earnings and correspondingly greater net worth than LIFO methods. In economic substance, the non-LIFO methods may leave the company worse off. LIFO has no effect on *actual* cost of goods sold (i.e., the cash outlays) or the value (replacement costs or expected selling prices) of the goods on hand. It may, however, enable a company to delay the payment of taxes and thereby to reduce the present value of future tax payments. In economic substance, therefore, the use of LIFO may enhance the net worth of the company in the amount of the present value of the difference in expected tax payments.

Nonetheless, many large U.S. firms, including such large and well-managed companies as IBM and ITT, do not account for the major portion of their inventories on a LIFO basis. Several explanations have been offered by executives of these firms as well as by outside observers:

1. The firms are in industries in which prices are declining. Despite the widespread inflation of recent years, not all goods have increased in price. Prices of electronic equipment, such as computers and calculators, are among the more notable examples of price decreases.

2. Because of special features of the tax laws, firms may not have taxable income even if they have reportable earnings. Thus the firms may not currently be paying taxes and see no need to switch until such time as they are.

3. Firms are fearful of having to sell goods being carried on the books at artificially low values. A "dip into the LIFO base" may be caused by strikes, general economic downturns, or cyclical movements within an industry. This may result in inordinately large increases in taxable income and correspondingly large increases in taxes. The taxes postponed in several previous years may have to be paid in a single year. Although the firms would have benefited over the years from the cash that would otherwise have been paid to the government, their executives believe that the additional problems of cash management (and perhaps costs) are not offset by the present value of the taxes postponed.

4. The reduction in *reported* earnings owing to a shift to LIFO may have adverse *economic consequences* for the firm or its managers. This would be the case when contractual arrangements with lenders or other parties specify that to be eligible for continued funding or other benefits, the firm must maintain its reported earnings or net worth above an established level. Similarly, the shift might reduce the salaries and bonuses of employee groups (including the executives responsible for selecting the inventory method) if compensation is tied to reported earnings. Thus a mere *accounting* change would have genuine *economic* consequences.

LOWER OF COST OR MARKET RULE

Regardless of which of the previously described inventory methods a firm adopts, the application of generally accepted accounting principles requires a departure from cost whenever the utility of the goods on hand has diminished since the date of acquisition. Loss of utility might be the result of physical damage or deterioration, obsolescence, or a general decline in the level of prices. Loss of utility should be given accounting recognition by stating the inventories at *cost* or *market, whichever is lower. Market* should be defined specifically as *replacement cost, net realizable value,* or *net realizable value less normal profit margin.* This lower of cost or market rule is grounded in the convention of *con-*

servatism, which holds that firms should recognize losses as soon as possible but delay recognition of gains.

Example

Suppose that a jewellery retailer purchases a lot of 100 digital watches for $100 each, with the intention of selling them at a price of $125. Prior to sale, however, the wholesale price of the watches drops to $80 and the corresponding retail price to $105. Application of the lower of cost or market rule would require that the stated value of the watches on hand be reduced from original cost of $100 to the current market (replacement) price of $80. The following journal entry would record the decline in price:

Loss on inventory (expense) $2,000
    Inventory (asset) $2,000
To record the loss attributable to the decline in the replacement cost of 100 digital watches from $100 to $80

The lower of cost or market rule may be applied to inventories on an individual (item-by-item) or a group basis. If applied on an individual basis, then the cost of each item in stock is compared with its current replacement cost. If the replacement cost of an item is lower than its original cost, then the item is written down to its replacement cost. If applied on a group basis, then the original cost of the inventory pool (which may be either the entire inventory or a collection of similar items) is compared with its market value, and a reduction in book value is required only if total market value is less than total initial cost. The group basis is likely to result in a considerably higher inventory valuation than the individual basis since it permits the increases in the market prices of some items to offset the decreases in others. The two bases were illustrated in Chapter 6 as part of a discussion regarding the values to be assigned to portfolios of marketable securities.

Some Questions

The lower of cost or market rule has been adopted by the rule-making bodies of the profession, but it has been the subject of widespread attack by accounting theoreticians. Critics assert that the rule sacrifices consistency for conservatism. The rule introduces a measure of inconsistency into financial reports, since it gives prompt recognition to decreases in market values but not to increases. Moreover, they contend that the rule requires that losses be recognized even though not really incurred. In the previous example, the firm purchased watches for $100 and will sell them for $105. Although it will not earn the full $25 profit that was expected, it will nevertheless realize a gain (excluding all other operating costs) of $5 per unit. If the lower of cost or market rule is adhered to, the accounts will reflect a loss of $20 per unit in the period of the write-down and a gain of $25 in the period of sale.[4] Critics contend that, as a consequence,

---

[4] Inventory should not be reduced to a level that will lead to recognition of an unusually high profit in a subsequent period. Thus, if, in the example, the firm estimated that it would be able to sell the watches at retail for $115 rather than $105, it should reduce inventory to no less than $90, which is the *net realizable value less normal profit margin,* as discussed above. If it reduced inventory below $90, its profit in the period of sale would be greater than its "normal" profit of $25 per unit.

earnings of both periods are distorted. In fact, they assert, the company earned a profit of $5 at the time of sale, not a loss of $20 in one period and a gain of $25 in the next.

Application of the lower of cost or market rule would be advantageous for tax purposes. It would enable a taxpayer to report an expense (the loss on inventory) in a period before goods are actually sold and a loss realized. The Income Tax Act in Canada accepts application of the lower of cost or market rule for all accepted methods of inventory valuation. As noted above, the LIFO inventory valuation method is not acceptable for tax purposes in Canada. The U.S. tax code, however, denies the benefits of the lower of cost or market rule to firms that are on a LIFO basis. The conceptual rationale for the lower of cost or market rule is no less sound for the LIFO than for the FIFO or the weighted average flow of cost assumptions. The U.S. taxing authorities do not look to any particular accounting theory for support in denying the benefits of the lower of cost or market rule to LIFO taxpayers. Instead, they contend merely that LIFO itself provides a tax advantage which should not be further enhanced by applications of the lower of cost or market rule. Generally accepted accounting principles, in contrast to the tax requirements, require that the lower of cost or market rule be applied, regardless of inventory method. Thus, in the United States, inventory values may differ between financial statements and tax filings.

PROPOSED ALTERNATIVE: USE OF CURRENT COSTS

Many accountants have proposed that inventories be stated at their current costs. In this way, they suggest, many of the deficiencies of each of the alternative assumptions regarding flow of costs, as well as the inconsistencies of the lower of cost or market rule, can be overcome. Their suggestions are worth attention, not so much because they are likely to be accepted in the foreseeable future—although there is unquestionably a trend in the direction of current value accounting—but rather because they provide an insight into the components of gains or losses attributable to the sale of goods included in inventory.

Assume that on September 1, 1996, a sporting goods outlet purchases 30 cans of tennis balls at $2.00 per can. In the remainder of 1996 it sells 20 cans at $3.00 per can. On December 31, 1996, the wholesale price of tennis balls increases to $2.50 per can. As a consequence, the business raises the retail price to $3.50 per can. In 1997 it sells the 10 cans that remain from 1996. These facts are summarized in Exhibit 8-7. Per conventional practice, the company will record in 1997 a gain of $1.50 for each can (sales price of $3.50 minus cost of $2.00). The $1.50 is composed of two types of gains—a *holding* gain of 50 cents and a *trading* gain of $1.00.

The trading gain arises out of the normal business activities of the firm. It represents a return to the merchant for providing the usual services of a retailer—providing customers with the desired quantity of goods at a convenient time and place. The holding gain, on the other hand, can be attributed to the increase in price between the times the merchant purchased and sold the goods. The magnitude of the holding gain depends on the quantity of goods

EXHIBIT 8-7

Trading Gains versus Holding Gains

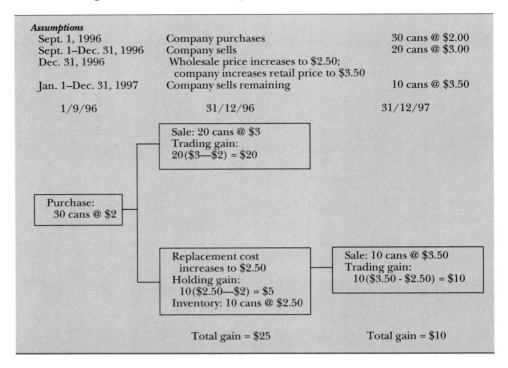

Assumptions

Sept. 1, 1996	Company purchases	30 cans @ $2.00
Sept. 1–Dec. 31, 1996	Company sells	20 cans @ $3.00
Dec. 31, 1996	Wholesale price increases to $2.50; company increases retail price to $3.50	
Jan. 1–Dec. 31, 1997	Company sells remaining	10 cans @ $3.50

1/9/96   31/12/96   31/12/97

Purchase:
30 cans @ $2

Sale: 20 cans @ $3
Trading gain:
20($3—$2) = $20

Replacement cost
increases to $2.50
Holding gain:
10($2.50—$2) = $5
Inventory: 10 cans @ $2.50

Sale: 10 cans @ $3.50
Trading gain:
10($3.50 - $2.50) = $10

Total gain = $25   Total gain = $10

held in inventory and the size of the price increase. Most merchants are required to maintain a stock of goods adequate to service the needs of their customers—that is, to make certain that they have a sufficient number of goods on hand to minimize the risk of outages and to provide customers with an ample choice of styles, sizes, and colours. Some merchants, however, intentionally maintain an inventory greater than necessary to meet their operating needs. Hoping to take advantage of increases in price, they employ inventory as a means of speculation. Speculative holding gains (and of course losses) are especially common in industries that deal in commodities that are subject to frequent and substantial fluctuations in prices—for example, grains and metals.

Were inventories to be stated at their current values, it would be relatively easy to distinguish—and report separately—the holding gains from the trading gains. And more significantly, the holding gains could be identified with the accounting period in which the increase in prices actually took place, rather than delayed until the period of sale. In the example, the holding gain actually occurred in 1996, the year in which the price increase was announced. Management control and evaluation of performance would be facilitated because the elements of profit that are within the control of specific managers could be set forth. Gains or losses arising from changes in prices could be taken into account in appraising the record of management only when they are relevant to its accomplishments.

Exhibit 8-7 depicts the economic substance of the transactions.

The following journal entry would recognize the holding gain of 50 cents per can of tennis balls that took place during 1996.

Inventory $5.00
    Holding gains on inventory (revenue) $5.00
To record the 50 cents holding gain on 10 cans of tennis balls that remained on hand at year end (replacement cost of $2.50 less original cost of $2.00)

When the 10 cans were sold in the following year, the cost of goods sold would be charged, and inventories credited, with their adjusted carrying value of $2.50 per can:

Cost of goods sold $25.00
    Inventory $25.00
To record the cost of goods sold

Comparative income statements which give recognition to the sale in 1996 of 20 cans of tennis balls at $3.00 per can and the sale in 1997 of 10 cans at $3.50 per can would appear as follows:

	1997	1996
Sales	$35.00	$60.00
Cost of goods sold		
10 cans @ $2.50	25.00	—
20 cans @ $2.00	—	40.00
Operating income	$10.00	$20.00
Holding gains on inventory	—	5.00
Comprehensive current income	$10.00	$25.00

Regardless of whether inventory was adjusted to reflect the holding gains or whether conventional procedures were followed, the total income from the sale of the 30 cans of tennis balls would be $35. Conventional income statements, in which the holding gains were not identified, would appear as follows:

	1997	1996
Sales	$35.00	$60.00
Cost of goods sold		
10 cans @ $2	20.00	—
20 cans @ $2	—	40.00
Income	$15.00	$20.00

The effect of increasing the carrying value of the 10 cans in inventory and of concurrently recognizing a holding gain of 50 cents per can would be to shift $5 of income from 1997, the year in which the cans were sold, to 1996, the year in which the price increase took place.

An Advantage of the Current Cost Method

Current cost accounting underscores the limitations of the methods presently used. The example that follows demonstrates how income, computed using either FIFO or LIFO, can be deceiving. It shows how reported income may increase even in the face of both a *decline in sales* and an *increase in costs*. It is designed to warn that increases in income as reported under generally accepted accounting principles may *not* necessarily indicate a true improvement in performance.

The example compares three different inventory procedures—FIFO, LIFO, and current cost. It shows their impact on the earnings of two firms in a single period. The activities of the two firms are the same, with a single exception. Whereas Firm A has sold 100 percent of the merchandise that it purchased, Firm B has sold only 80 percent.

Example

Firm A and Firm B each start the year with 5,000 units of inventory purchased the previous year at $10 per unit. For simplicity, assume they have no other assets. During the year, a period of rising prices, each of the firms acquires inventory as shown in the following schedule:

	Units	Unit Cost	Total
Beginning inventory	5,000	$10.00	$ 50,000
Purchases			
1	10,000	10.50	105,000
2	10,000	11.00	110,000
3	10,000	11.50	115,000
4	10,000	12.00	120,000
5	10,000	12.50	125,000
6	10,000	13.00	130,000
7	10,000	13.50	135,000
Total purchases	70,000		$840,000
Total beginning inventory and purchases	75,000		$890,000

Firm A sells 70,000 units at an *average price* of $12.50. Sales revenue is $875,000. Firm B sells only 56,000 units at the same price. Its revenue is $700,000. The unit cost of inventory at the end of the year is $14.00. Purchases and sales are for cash.

In this example, unlike the sporting goods outlet example, prices increase *during* the year, not just at the end. Under current cost procedures, inventory must be adjusted for each price increase. Cost of goods sold is based on the replacement value of the inventory at time of sale. Operating income is the difference between sales and the *revalued* cost of the goods sold.

Exhibit 8-8 indicates ending inventory, ending net assets, cost of goods sold, and income under each of the three inventory procedures.

The sales of Company A are 25 percent greater than those of Company B. Yet under FIFO, the income of Company A is 15.3 percent *less*—$52,500 versus $62,000. Under LIFO, the income of Company A is 288 percent *greater*—$35,000 versus $9,000. Only under current cost does the percentage difference in operating income (25 percent, or $35,000 versus $28,000) correspond to the percentage difference in sales.

EXHIBIT 8-8

		Company A			Company B	
Beginning Inventory						
(which equals net assets)	5,000 @ $10.00 =	$ 50,000		5,000 @ $10.00 =	$ 50,000	
Purchases (for cash)	70,000		840,000	70,000		840,000
Sales (for cash)	70,000 @ $12.50 =		875,000	56,000 @ $12.50 =	700,000	
Net cash receipts						
(sales less purchases)			$ 35,000			($140,000)
Ending Inventory						
FIFO	5,000 @ $13.50 =	$ 67,500		10,000 @ $13.50	$ 135,000	
				+ 9,000 @ $13.00	117,000	
				19,000	$ 252,000	
LIFO	5,000 @ $10.00 =	$ 50,000		5,000 @ $10.00	$ 50,000	
				+10,000 @ $10.50	105,000	
				+ 4,000 @ $11.00	44,000	
				19,000	$199,000	
Current cost	5,000 @ $14.00 =	$ 70,000		19,000 @ $14.00	$266,000	
Cost of Goods Sold						
FIFO						
Beginning inventory		$ 50,000			$ 50,000	
+ Purchases		840,000			840,000	
− Ending inventory		(67,500)	$822,500		(252,000)	$ 638,000
LIFO						
Beginning inventory		$ 50,000			$ 50,000	
+ Purchases		840,000			840,000	
- Ending inventory		(50,000)	$840,000		(199,000)	$ 691,000
Current cost*						
70,000 units @ $12			$840,000			
56,000 units @ $12						$ 672,000
Operating Income (Sales minus Cost of Goods Sold)						
FIFO			$ 52,500			$ 62,000
LIFO			35,000			9,000
Current cost			35,000			28,000
Ending Net Assets (Ending Inventory plus Net Cash Receipts)						
FIFO			$102,500			$ 112,000
LIFO			85,000			59,000
Current cost			105,000			126,000

*Upon each purchase during the year, the goods in inventory are revalued to reflect the higher cost. Cost of goods sold is based on the most recent acquisition cost. The goods are sold *uniformly throughout the year.* The average acquisition cost—and also therefore the average cost of goods sold—is $12.

The example can be used to note some additional features of current cost accounting. As emphasized in previous chapters of the text, regardless of accounting methods, the income statement must *articulate with* the balance sheet. Income for the period must equal the change in net assets. In this example the change in net assets equals the change in inventory plus the change in cash (the net cash receipts). This relationship holds for FIFO and LIFO but not, apparently, for current cost.

The current cost income statement and balance sheet accounts fully articulate, however, when the *realizable* holding gain is taken into account— that is, when income is specified as *comprehensive current income,* not merely current operating income. Comprehensive current income consists of the current operating income (in essence the *trading gain*) plus the realizable holding gain.

The realizable holding gain is the difference between the outputs into the trading or manufacturing process (the ending inventory and the cost of goods sold) and the inputs (the beginning inventory plus purchases). It is the total holding gain in that it includes the gains on goods sold during the year and goods remaining in year-end inventory.

The realizable holding gain for Company A is $20,000; that for Company B is $48,000:

$$\text{Realizable holding gain} = \text{Outputs} - \text{Inputs}$$

$$\text{Realizable holding gain} = (\text{Ending inventory} + \text{Cost of goods sold})$$
$$- (\text{Beginning inventory} + \text{Purchases})$$

For Company A,

$$\text{Realizable holding gain} = (\$70,000 + \$840,000) - (\$50,000 + \$840,000)$$
$$= \$20,000$$

For Company B,

$$\text{Realizable holding gain} = (\$266,000 + \$672,000) - (\$50,000 + \$840,000)$$
$$= \$48,000$$

The realizable holding gain can also be interpreted as a realizable *cost saving*. It is the amount the firm *saved* by judiciously acquiring the goods in advance of price increases.

Comprehensive current income captures both the trading gain and the holding gain:

$$\text{Comprehensive current income} = \text{Current operating income}$$
$$+ \text{Realizable holding gain}$$

For Company A,

$$\text{Comprehensive current income} = \$35,000 + \$20,000 = \$55,000$$

For Company B,

$$\text{Comprehensive current income} = \$28,000 + \$48,000 = \$76,000$$

For both firms therefore comprehensive income is equal to the change in net assets:

$$\text{Comprehensive current income} = \text{Ending net assets} - \text{Beginning net assets}$$

For Company A,

$$\$55,000 = \$105,000 - \$50,000$$

For Company B,

$$\$76,000 = \$126,000 - \$50,000$$

Under current cost accounting, reported income would mirror economic performance. Holding gains would be captured in the period in which they actually occurred, not when the goods happened to be sold. Cost of goods sold would reflect worth at time of sale.

In the discussion to this point, current cost has been used to mean replacement cost, an *input* value. As indicated in an earlier chapter, however, current cost can be viewed as an *output* value as well as an input value. Thus some theoreticians suggest that inventories be stated at a current *output* value, such as the amount for which they could currently be sold, or at *net realizable* value (the amount for which they are *likely* to be sold in the future, less any costs of bringing the goods to a saleable condition).

Regardless of which particular current value is employed, the suggestion that inventories be valued at some current value should not be viewed as particularly radical. Recall the discussion in Chapter 5 pertaining to recognition of revenue. It was pointed out then that when, in unusual circumstances, revenue is recognized in the course of production (as in long-term construction contracts) or upon completion of production (as in the mining of precious metals), inventory is, in effect, stated at a current value as it also is in "cost or market, whichever is lower." Our example in this section suggests cogent reasons for developing a *generalized framework* for reporting the current values of inventories. At the very least it indicates that changes in current costs are too important for either managers or investors to ignore.

History of the Idea in Practice

In 1982 the CICA issued Section 4510 of the *CICA Handbook,* which required public companies larger than a specified size to disclose the current cost of inventories. The stipulated data on inventories were part of a comprehensive package of information on the effects of changing prices intended to supplement the historical cost statements. The disclosures proved unpopular with the affected companies, who maintained that the cost of the data far exceeded the benefits to statement users. Indeed, several studies indicated that the disclosures were not widely used. In 1991 the CICA withdrew Section 4510 from the *Handbook.*

The elimination of the disclosures should add to, rather than detract from, the importance that analysts place upon understanding and interpreting current value models of accounting. This latest action of the CICA does nothing to eliminate the deficiencies of historical cost accounting, to reduce the differences between historical and current values, or to diminish the utility of current value information. Instead it shifts the burden of compiling the current value data from the preparer—who presumably can do so at least cost and inconvenience—to the user—who must now not only interpret the data but estimate it as well.

INVENTORY TURNOVER

The efficiency with which a firm uses its inventory to support sales can be measured by an activity ratio, *inventory turnover.* Inventory turnover is the number of times the annual cost of goods sold exceeds average inventory. It is computed by dividing cost of goods sold by average inventory:

$$\text{Inventory turnover } = \frac{\text{Cost of goods sold}}{\text{Average inventory}}$$

The greater the number of times per year the inventory *turns over,* the more efficiently the inventory is being used. The smaller the inventory in relation to cost of goods sold, the greater the sales activity that the inventory is able to sustain.

Because inventory is more closely related to cost of goods sold than it is to sales, cost of goods sold rather than sales is the numerator. This is in contrast to the accounts receivable turnover ratio (discussed in Chapter 7) and the capital asset turnover ratio (to be discussed in Chapter 9). As with the accounts receivable turnover ratio, the denominator should ideally be based on a 12-month average (as opposed to a beginning and end-of-year average) to avoid distortions resulting from seasonal fluctuations.

Per its statements included in Chapter 7, Sun Ice Limited reported cost of goods sold in 1994 (in thousands) of $10,011. Average inventory (based on beginning and ending inventory, the only data provided in the annual report) was $2,341 ($\frac{\$3,278 \ + \ \$1,405}{2}$). Inventory turnover was therefore 4.3 times:

$$\text{Inventory turnover } = \frac{\$10,011}{\$2,341} = 4.3 \text{ times}$$

It should be obvious that when a firm uses LIFO to account for its inventory, the usefulness of the inventory turnover ratio as a technique of management control or investment analysis is severely limited. If the inventory is being reported at values representing prices of a distant past, then a comparison of LIFO inventory with cost of goods sold (based on current prices) is of little or no significance. Sun Ice Limited uses FIFO to account for its inventory.

Summary

In this chapter we have dealt primarily with accounting issues pertaining to inventory within the traditional historical cost framework. Because of the overriding importance of inventories to most manufacturing and retail companies, selection of accounting alternatives may have a critical impact on both reported assets and earnings.

The primary objective of conventional accounting is to match the costs of acquiring or producing goods with the revenues that they generate and thereby produce a useful measure of income. To realize this objective, it is necessary to make assumptions as to the flow of costs—whether the cost of goods acquired first, or last, for example, should be associated with the revenues of a particular period. Persuasive arguments can be advanced in favour of or against each of the assumptions, and choice of assumption may have a significant effect on reported cost of goods sold as well as ending inventories.

Regardless of assumption, however, inventories should be restated at the lower of cost or market to reflect declines in their replacement cost. Although some accountants have suggested that accounting recognition be given to increases in market prices as well as to decreases, current practice favours conservatism over consistency, and gains from holding inventories are realized in the accounts only as they are sold.

Exercise for Review and Self-Testing

The inventory records of the Simon Corp. for 1996 indicate the following with respect to a particular item:

Date	Purchases No. of Units	Unit Cost	Total Cost	No. of Units Sold	No. of Units on Hand
Jan. 1*	400	$20	$8,000		400
Feb. 24	200	21	4,200		600
June 16				300	300
Sept. 23	100	22	2,200		400
Nov. 15				300	100
Dec. 28	100	23	2,300		200

* Beginning balance.

1. Determine the total number of units as well as the total costs of inventory to be accounted for during the year.

2. The firm maintains its inventory records on a *periodic* basis. Determine year-end inventory and cost of goods sold, assuming each of the following cost flows:
   a. First in, first out
   b. Weighted average
   c. Last in, first out

3. Suppose that the firm values its inventory on the FIFO basis. On December 31, the price per unit of the item falls to $21 and the anticipated selling price falls by $2. At what amount, in accordance with the lower of cost or market rule, should year-end inventory be stated? What would be the effect of the write-down on earnings of 1996? What would be the effect on earnings of 1997 when the goods are sold?

4. Assume alternatively that the firm were to report inventory at current replacement cost (a practice *not* in accordance with "generally accepted accounting principles") and that the price at year end remained at $23 per unit. At what amount should year-end inventory be stated? How much "holding gain" should be recognized? What would be the effect on cost of goods sold in 1997 of recognizing the holding gain in 1996, assuming that the goods are sold in 1997?

5. Determine inventory turnover for 1996. Assume the firm uses the FIFO inventory method. For convenience, consider average inventory to be one-half the sum of beginning and end-of-year values.

1. "Since it is the objective of asset accounting to assign fair values to goods owned by a firm, LIFO is an inappropriate means of accounting for inventories. LIFO may result in values that are far out of date." Do you agree? Comment.

2. "Firms make assumptions as to the flows of goods only because it is costly and inconvenient to keep records of specific items actually sold. The specific identification method is theoretically superior to any of the other methods and eliminates the possibilities of income manipulation associated with those other methods." Do you agree? Comment.

3. The president of a U.S. firm whose shares are traded on the New York Stock Exchange has asked you for advice on whether the company should shift from FIFO to LIFO. The company is in an industry in which prices have been continually increasing. What is the primary benefit to be gained by a switch to LIFO? Are there any potential costs or risks? How would your answer change if it was a Canadian company?

4. Suppose that the president referred to in Question 3 expresses concern that a switch to LIFO would make it more difficult for her company to raise capital. She points out that LIFO results in lower reported earnings, and she is fearful that the reduction in earnings would have an adverse impact on the market price of her firm's stock price. Are her reservations justified? Comment.

5. It is sometimes asserted that LIFO provides a more meaningful income statement, albeit not necessarily a more meaningful balance sheet. Why does LIFO provide a more meaningful income statement? Does it always? Provide an example of a situation in which it may seriously distort income.

6. What is meant by the term *market* as it is used in the expression *cost or market, whichever is lower*? The lower of cost or market rule is often cited as an example of the possible conflict between conservatism and consistency. Why? Over a period of several years, is the lower of cost or market rule likely to decrease the overall income of a firm? Explain.

7. Suppose that inventories were to be stated on the balance sheet at current replacement cost (which may exceed historical costs). What would be the impact on earnings of the year in which an increase in replacement cost was first recognized? What would be the impact on earnings of the year in which the goods were sold?

8. Conventional accounting requires that inventories be stated at historical cost. How could a financial analyst obtain information on the replacement cost of a firm's inventory?

9. Why does the use of LIFO limit the utility of the inventory turnover ratio?

10. A firm acquires a substantial quantity of inventory on December 31, subsequent to the last sale of the year. The price paid is considerably greater than that of previous purchases. Why might use of the weighted average method, applied on a periodic basis, produce a cost of goods sold that many accountants would claim is overstated?

1. *Frequency of calculations may affect earnings.*

    At the start of a year, a firm had 700 units of product on hand. The stated value was $2,100. During the year the firm had two sales—the first on January 17 of 500 units, and the second on November 11 of 700 units. On March 9 the firm received a shipment of 1,500 units at a cost of $6,000. Assume that the purchases were for cash.

    a. Prepare those journal entries that would affect inventory assuming that the firm uses
       (1) Periodic inventory procedures:
          (a) FIFO
          (b) Weighted average
       (2) Perpetual inventory procedures:
          (a) FIFO
          (b) Weighted average
    b. Compare the total cost of goods sold and the ending inventory under each of the alternatives.

2. *This problem illustrates the three fundamental inventory valuation methods, each applied on both periodic and perpetual bases.*

    During a year the Whitman Co. engaged in the following purchases and sales of an item:

| | Purchases | | Sales |
	No. Units	Cost per Unit	(No. Units)
Jan. 1 (beg. bal.)	500	$5.00	
Feb. 11			150
May 6	200	5.10	
Sept. 8			220
Sept. 30	300	5.20	
Oct. 17			360
Nov. 26	100	5.25	
Dec. 16			50
	1,100		780

    Determine December 31 inventory and cost of goods sold for the year, assuming first that the company maintains inventory on a periodic basis and then on a perpetual basis. Assume also each of the following flows of costs: FIFO, weighted average, LIFO.

    LIFO, applied on a perpetual basis, is not specifically illustrated in the text. The procedures are not difficult, however. Compute the cost of goods sold upon each sale. The goods sold would be assumed to be those that were acquired most recently up to the date of sale. For example, the 220 units sold on September 8 would be considered to be the 200 units acquired on May 6 plus 20 from the balance on hand as of January 1.

3. *The specific identification method, even if clerically feasible, may not be theoretically preferable.*

At December 1, Big Sam Appliance Co. has 300 refrigerators in stock. All are identical; all are priced to sell at $900. Each is tagged with a card indicating in code its cost to Big Sam. Of the 300 refrigerators on hand, 100 were acquired on June 15 at a cost of $800 each, 100 on November 1 at a cost of $650 each, and 100 on December 1 at a cost of $700 per unit. Big Sam estimates that, in the month of December, 200 refrigerators will be sold.

a. Determine cost of goods sold on a FIFO basis, assuming that 200 refrigerators were in fact sold.

b. Suppose that Big Sam uses the specific identification method and wishes to maximize reported earnings for the month. How can it accomplish its objective by judicious selection of the units to be sold?

c. Suppose that Big Sam uses the specific identification method and, to minimize taxes, wishes to minimize reported earnings. How can it accomplish its objective?

4. *The impact of inventory method depends on the direction of price changes.*

Fill in the table that follows with the cost flow assumption—FIFO, LIFO, or average cost—that would produce the results indicated in the rows under the conditions indicated by the columns:

	Inflation	Deflation
Cost of Goods Sold		
Highest		
Lowest		
Ending Inventory		
Highest		
Lowest		
Cash Flow before Taxes		
Highest		
Lowest		

5. *Is the impact of LIFO upon earnings the same in periods of falling prices as in those of rising prices?*

The Simmons Co. began operations on January 1. In its first year the company produced 90,000 units at a cost of $12 per unit and sold 80,000 units. In each of the next three years, it produced 80,000 units and sold 80,000 units. Costs of production were $14, $16, and $18, respectively, in each of the years.

a. Compute both cost of goods sold and year-end inventory for each of the four years, using first FIFO and then LIFO.

b. Do the same as in part (a), assuming this time that production costs were $12, $10, $8, and $6 in each of the four years. (Omit application of the lower of cost or market rule.)

c. What generalizations can be made regarding the impact of LIFO as compared with FIFO on cost of goods sold and inventories in periods of rising prices versus periods of falling prices?

6. *In the long run, choice among accounting principles seldom makes a difference.*

The Westfield Co. existed in business for a period of four years. During that period, purchases and sales were as follows:

Year	Purchases		Sales	
	Units	Unit Cost	Units	Sales Price
1	12,000	$10	8,000	$15
2	14,000	11	15,000	16
3	9,000	12	9,000	17
4	10,000	11	13,000	17

a. Determine income for each of the four years, assuming first that the company uses FIFO and then that it uses LIFO.

b. Determine total income for the four-year period. Over the life of the business, does it matter which method of inventory valuation is used?

7. *Earnings based on LIFO are said to be "higher quality" than those based on FIFO.*

In December 1996, L. Minton established a door-to-door sales company. He invested $12,000 and purchased 2,000 units of inventory at $6 per unit—the minimum number of units required to sustain his business. He made his purchase at a propitious time, for the next day, before he had a chance to make a single sale, the replacement cost per unit of his inventory increased to $7.

During 1997 Minton purchased an additional 10,000 units at $7 per unit and sold 10,000 units at $9 per unit. He withdrew from the business for his personal use *all* cash except that necessary to assure that his inventory was maintained at its minimum level of 2,000 units.

a. Prepare journal entries to reflect the foregoing transactions. First assume that Minton maintained his inventories on a FIFO basis; then assume that he maintained them on a LIFO basis, and indicate any entries that would be different. Prepare income statements and balance sheets comparing results under the two methods.

b. How much cash was Minton able to withdraw during 1997? Compare his cash withdrawals with income as determined by both the FIFO and the LIFO methods. What do you suppose some financial observers mean when they say that in periods of inflation LIFO results in earnings that are of "higher quality"?

8. *An invasion of the LIFO base may seriously distort earnings.*

At January 1, 1996, the Byron Co., a U.S. manufacturer, had 50,000 units of product on hand. Each unit had cost $.80 to produce. During each of the next three years the company produced 100,000 units and sold the same number. In the fourth year, as the result of a strike, the company was able to produce only 60,000 units, though it was able to maintain sales at 100,000. In the fifth year the company, in order to replenish its inventory, produced 140,000 units and again sold 100,000 units. Unit production costs and sales prices are indicated in the accompanying table. The company maintains its inventory on a periodic LIFO basis.

	Units Produced		Units Sold	
	No. Units	Unit Cost	No. Units	Unit Price
1996	100,000	$1.00	100,000	$1.40
1997	100,000	1.20	100,000	1.60
1998	100,000	1.40	100,000	1.80
1999	60,000	1.60	100,000	2.00
2000	140,000	1.80	100,000	2.20

a. Determine the net income *after taxes* for each of the five years. Assume a tax rate of 40 percent of income.

b. Determine the *after-tax cash flow* for each of the five years. That is, determine total cash receipts less total cash disbursements. Assume that all sales were for cash and that all production costs and taxes were paid in cash.

c. In the view of a manager or a financial analyst, of what significance is the net income of the firm for 1999?

d. Compare the total cash flow for 1999 and 2000 with that of the prior two-year period. Why is it lower?

9. *Problems 9 and 10 illustrate the advantages—and disadvantages—of a shift from FIFO to LIFO.*

The annual report of a leading U.S. chemical company contained the following footnote (figures are stated in millions):

> If inventory values were shown at estimated replacement or current cost rather than at LIFO values, inventories would have been $489.9 and $410.6 higher than reported at December 31, 1991, and December 31, 1990, respectively.

a. In periods of rising prices, which valuation method, FIFO or LIFO, results in inventory values which most closely approximate current market prices?

b. Assume that replacement costs are approximately equal to inventory as computed on a FIFO basis. Ignoring the impact of income taxes, how much more, or less, as at December 31, 1990, and 1991, would retained earnings have been had the company remained on FIFO?

c. Considering the effect of the change in valuation method on retained earnings of 1990 and 1991, how much more or less would earnings before taxes have been in 1991 if no change had taken place?

d. Based on your response to part (c) and assuming a tax rate of 40 percent, how much more or less would the tax obligation of the firm have been in 1991?

e. Comment on why, in a period of rising prices, a firm would deliberately select a method of accounting that would adversely affect reported earnings.

10. The same annual report contained the following footnote pertaining to inventories:

> During 1990, inventory quantities were reduced from the abnormally high year-end 1989 level. This reduction resulted in a liquidation of LIFO inventory quantities carried at lower prices prevailing in prior years as compared with 1990 costs, the effect of which increased the 1990 net income by approximately $38.9 million, or $.81 per share.

a. Explain in your own words why a liquidation of inventory increased net income.

b. If the liquidation increased the reported after-tax income by $38.9 million, by how much greater or less was the value of the goods sold based on current (1990) costs than on the historical costs at which they were actually carried on the books? Assume a tax rate of 40 percent.

c. It is clear that in 1990 the use of LIFO seriously distorted the firm's reported income. In fact, management felt compelled to include in its financial statements the previously cited footnote to warn readers of the aberrant earnings. Why did the company not shift to FIFO for 1990 and then shift back to LIFO in subsequent years when earnings would not be distorted by inventory liquidations?

11. *An independent auditor points out that there are no generally accepted standards of "preferability."*

In 1990 (dates changed), the Susquehanna Corporation, a firm whose securities are traded on the American Stock Exchange, changed from the FIFO to the LIFO method of accounting for inventories. The change, according to a footnote to the financial statements, was made "to better match the most recent inventory acquisition costs against current sales, thereby minimizing the effects of inflation on earnings."

In a letter to the firm's board of directors, the company's auditors, Price Waterhouse & Co., wrote the following:

> Note 2 to the consolidated financial statements of The Susquehanna Corporation, included in the Company's Annual Report to its stockholders for the year ended December 31, 1990, and incorporated by reference in the Company's Annual Report on Form 10-K for the year then ended, describes a change from the first-in, first-out method of accounting for inventories to the last-in, first-out method. We concurred with this change in our report dated February 10, 1991, on the consolidated financial statements referred to above. It should be understood that preferability of one acceptable method of inventory accounting over another has not been addressed in any authoritative accounting literature and in arriving at our opinion expressed below, we have relied on management's business planning and judgment. *Based upon our discussions with management and the stated reasons for the change, we believe that such change represents, in your circumstances, adoption of a preferable accounting principle in conformity with Accounting Principles Board Opinion No. 20.*

a. What makes one accounting method preferable to another?
b. If a method of accounting, such as LIFO, is considered preferable to another method, such as FIFO, by both a company and its auditors, how can the use of the alternative method by another company in the same industry, whose financial statements might be examined by the same firm of auditors, be justified?

12. *By shifting to FIFO from LIFO, a company may increase reported earnings but incur a substantial economic cost.*

In November 1970, the president of a "Big Three" U.S. automobile manufacturer became concerned that actual earnings for 1970 would fall short of predicted earnings. In discussions with the corporate controller, he suggested that one way to boost earnings would be to shift from the last-in, first-out method of reporting inventories, which the company was presently using, to the first-in, first-out method.

Upon investigation, the controller found that anticipated inventories at year end would be approximately $100 million if stated on a LIFO basis. If valued on the basis of the cost of the most recent purchases (FIFO), they would be approximately $180 million.

a. What would be the effect on cost of goods sold if inventories for the year 1970 were stated on a FIFO rather than a LIFO basis? Explain.

b. What would be the impact on income tax obligations? Assume a combined federal and state tax rate of 50 percent. (In practice the Internal Revenue Service is likely to allow the company to pay the additional taxes attributable to the shift over a 20-year period.)

c. Comment on any advantages and disadvantages to the company of making the shift.

13. *The LIFO method permits income manipulation.*

At January 1, the Elliot Corp. had 10,000 units of product on hand. Each unit had a carrying value of $20. In November of the same year the president estimated that sales for the year would total 80,000 units. To date, the company had produced 70,000 units, at a cost of $25 per unit. If additional units were to be produced in the remainder of the year, they would cost $26 per unit. The company determines inventory on a periodic LIFO basis.

Determine cost of goods sold for the year if

a. The president ordered that no additional units be produced during the year.

b. The president ordered that 10,000 additional units be produced.

c. The president ordered that 40,000 additional units be produced.

14. *Did General Motors really benefit from LIFO?*

The 1987 financial statements of GM contained the following note:

Inventories are stated generally at cost, which is not in excess of market. The cost of substantially all domestic inventories is determined by the last-in, first-out (LIFO) method. If the first-in, first-out (FIFO) method of inventory valuation had been used for inventories valued at LIFO cost, such inventories would have been $2,359.9 million higher at December 31, 1987, and $2,203.8 million higher at December 31, 1986. As a result of decreases in LIFO U.S. inventories, certain LIFO inventory quantities carried at lower costs prevailing in prior years, as compared with the costs of current purchases, were liquidated in 1986 and 1985. These inventory adjustments favourably affected income before income taxes by approximately $38.2 million in 1986 and $20.9 million in 1985.

Major Classes of Inventories	1987	1986
	(in millions)	
Productive material, work in process, and supplies	$3,876.0	$4,042.5
Finished product, service parts, etc.	4,063.7	3,192.6
Total	$7,939.7	$7,235.1

a. By how much greater or less would pre-tax income have been in 1987 had the company used FIFO rather than LIFO?

b. By how much greater or less would retained earnings have been as at December 31, 1987, had the company used FIFO? Ignore the consequences of income tax benefits.

c. The note indicates that the liquidation of inventories in 1986 and 1985 had a favourable impact on income before taxes. Was the company really better off as a result of the liquidation? What would the adverse consequence have been? What was the main advantage to the company of using LIFO in 1987?

15. *Are differences between "book" and "tax" values a boon or a bane?*

   The 1987 annual report of the Dana Corporation, a U.S. company, reported the following:

   > Inventories are valued at the lower of cost or market. Cost is determined on the last-in, first-out basis for domestic inventories and on the first-in, first-out or average cost basis for international inventories. If all inventories were valued at replacement costs, inventories would be increased by $68,532,000 at December 31, 1987. The valuation of LIFO inventories for financial reporting purposes is $19,166,000 in excess of the valuation for federal income tax purposes.

   Total reported inventories of the company on December 31, 1987, were $726 million.

   Differences between tax and book inventory valuations can result from various technical features of the tax code pertaining to the application of LIFO.

   a. Was the company better or worse off because the book value of its inventory exceeded the tax value? Did the tax regulations which led to the discrepancy work to the benefit or detriment of the company? Explain.

   b. Suppose that in 1988 Dana had been required to substantially reduce its inventory. What would have been the most probable impact, relative to 1987, on

      (1) Cost of goods sold as a percentage of sales? (Would this percentage be useful as a measure of performance?)

      (2) Income tax expense as a percentage of sales?

16. *The advantages of postponing taxes can be expressed in a single dollar amount.*

   Gilling, Inc., a U.S. company, is considering shifting from FIFO to LIFO. The change would be effective January 1, 1996.

   The controller's staff of the company has determined that beginning-of-year inventory on January 1, 1996, will be $100 million, regardless of accounting method.

   Company sales for 1996 were $600 million and cost of goods sold $400 million. The controller's staff forecasts that the number of *units* manufactured and sold will remain constant over the next five years but that manufacturing *costs* and *selling prices* will increase at a compound rate of 10 percent per year.

   The company pays taxes on income at a rate of 40 percent. It uses a discount rate of 7 percent to perform all analyses in which the time value of money must be taken into account.

   Based on the limited information provided (some of which may be extraneous), determine the present value of the tax "savings" that will accrue over the five years beginning January 1, 1996.

17. *An increase in reported earnings may not necessarily be reflected in the market price of a firm's common stock.*

   The president of a publicly held U.S. corporation was considering switching from the FIFO to the LIFO method of accounting for inventory. The shift would enable the firm to reduce its annual income tax payments. The president was reluctant to authorize the shift, however, because it would result in an immediate decline in reported earnings. Such a decline, he thought, might adversely affect the market price of the company's stock and thereby antagonize the shareholders.

At January 1, 1996, the company had 1,000 (000s omitted) units of product on hand. They were carried on the books at $20 per unit, and because the company had recently reduced its inventory to zero, they would be valued at $20 regardless of whether the company remained on FIFO or switched to LIFO.

At January 1, 1996, the president made the following estimate of purchases and sales for the following three years (000s omitted from quantities):

1996	Purchase 1,000 units @ $24; sell 1,000 units @ $32
1997	Purchase 1,000 units @ $26; sell 1,000 units @ $34
1998	Purchase 1,000 units @ $28; sell 1,000 units @ $36

a. Determine annual earnings after taxes for each of the three years, assuming first that the company maintains its inventory on a FIFO basis and second that it shifts to LIFO. The effective rate of taxes is 40 percent. For convenience, disregard all expenses other than cost of goods sold and taxes.
b. Determine the annual cash flows after taxes for each of the three years under both FIFO and LIFO. Compare them with annual earnings. Cash flows should represent sales minus purchases and taxes.
c. Assume that the market price of the firm's stock is based on anticipated corporate cash flows. The total market value of all shares outstanding is equal, at any time, to the present value of expected cash flows for a number of years into the future (in this case assume three years). In calculating the present value of expected cash flows, use a discount rate of 8 percent. Determine the total market value of all shares outstanding, assuming first that the company remains on FIFO and second that it shifts to LIFO. (For convenience assume that all cash flows occur at year end.)
d. Suppose that the company has 100,000 shares of stock outstanding. Determine the expected market price per share under both FIFO and LIFO.
e. If the capital markets are "efficient" (if they recognize or are able to distinguish between economic earnings and reported accounting earnings), are the reservations of the president justified?

18. *A change in inventory method may not have the same impact on flows of cash as on flows of working capital.*

The following table provides selected data from the financial statements of a company that engages in retail sales (all amounts in millions):

	Period		
	1	2	3
Ending inventory	$100	$120	$115
Sales	600	768	732
Cost of goods sold	500	640	610
Accounts receivable	300	340	330

The company maintains its inventory on a FIFO basis. The company pays for all goods in the period following purchase (e.g., goods acquired in period 1 are paid for in period 2). Ignore income taxes.

a. Prepare for period 3 a statement in which you indicate the inflows and outflows of cash attributable to the purchase and sale of merchandise.

b. Prepare for period 3 a statement in which you indicate the inflows and outflows of working capital (current assets less current liabilities).

c. Assume that the company shifts its inventory method from FIFO to LIFO at the start of period 2. Assume also that the quantity of inventory remains constant over the three-year period; the difference from one year to the next in inventory values can be attributed entirely to changes in prices. Convert the inventory and cost of goods sold to a LIFO basis.

d. Repeat parts (a) and (b) based on the values calculated in part (c). Comment on whether cash or working capital is the more objective measure of financial resources.

19. *The difference between reported and replacement values of inventory gives a clue as to accounting method; inventory turnover is altered dramatically when basis of inventory valuation is changed.*

   The financial statements of Deluxe Check Printers, a company whose shares are listed on the New York Stock Exchange, reported the following (dates changed):

	1997	1996
Costs of sales, exclusive of depreciation	$280,894,000	$246,873,000
Inventory (December 31)	14,092,000	13,420,000

   A note to the statements indicated that inventories at December 31, 1997, and 1996, were approximately $8,482,000 and $6,272,000, respectively, less than replacement cost. By contrast, costs of goods sold, based on replacement values, were approximately equal to those reported.

a. Calculate inventory turnover for 1997 based on the average of reported beginning and ending inventories.

b. On which basis, LIFO or FIFO, is it more likely that the company maintained its inventories? Why? There is a substantial difference between inventories as reported and their replacement values. Yet costs of goods sold as reported and those based on replacement values are approximately the same. Can you explain why?

c. Recalculate inventory turnover based on replacement values of inventory. Which calculation do you think would be the more useful for most decisions to be made by investors and managers?

20. *Ratios must be adjusted to take into account inventory basis; often a considerable amount of information pertaining to changes in prices and quantities can be derived from the data in the financial statements.*

   The data that follow were taken from the annual reports of Hasseldine Industries, a U.S. company (all dollar amounts in millions). The company accounts for inventory on the basis of LIFO, which it applies periodically (rather than perpetually). The inventory consists almost entirely of a single product.

Year	Inventory LIFO	Inventory Replacement Value	Cost of Goods Sold	Pretax Income
1	$100	$120	$ 960	$48
2	110	132	1,088	54
3	105	131	1,030	20
4	120	144	1,152	72
5	121	157	1,256	98

a. In which year, if any, did inventory quantities decline? Explain.
b. In which year, if any, did the prices of goods included in inventory decline? Explain.
c. You wish to compare the current ratio of this company in year 5 with that of another firm that reports on a FIFO basis. Hasseldine Industries in year 5 reported current assets of $432 million and current liabilities of $280 million. Based on the information provided, adjust the inventory of Hasseldine so that it would be comparable to that of the other firm. Defend your adjusted inventory as being a reasonable approximation of that which would be reported if the company were on FIFO. Compute the current ratio on both an unadjusted and an adjusted basis.
d. By approximately what percentage did prices increase in year 5? Explain.
e. Suppose that inventory is to be accounted for on the basis of FIFO and that the replacement value of the inventory is approximately equal to its FIFO value. How much greater or less than the reported LIFO amount would cost of goods sold be in year 5? If the tax rate were 40 percent, what would be the impact on after-tax income? Disregarding taxes, what would be the impact on reported retained earnings at the end of year 5? What would be the impact if taxes were taken into account?

21. *The lower of cost or market rule does not reduce the total profits to be realized on the sale of inventories; it only transfers them from one year to the next.*

The Roscoe Corp. started business on January 1, 1996. Its purchases and sales, as well as the replacement cost of goods on hand at year end, for its first three years of operations are

	Purchases Units	Purchases Unit Cost	Sales Units	Sales Unit Price	Unit Replacement Cost at Year End
1996	12,000	$25	10,000	$30	$15
1997	12,000	20	10,000	25	10
1998	6,000	15	10,000	20	5

The company stated its inventory on a FIFO basis and applied the lower of cost or market rule.
a. Determine income for each of the three years.
b. Comment on the effect of the lower of cost or market rule on earnings over an extended period of time.

22. *The lower of cost or market rule provides that declines in the value of inventory be given prompt recognition.*

Indicated in the table following is the December 31 inventory of the Ottawa Company, along with current replacement costs and expected selling prices:

Items	Units	Unit Cost	Replacement Cost	Expected Selling Price
A	6,000	$10	$12	$18
B	4,000	8	6	9
C	12,000	6	4	6
D	2,000	4	2	6

It is the policy of the company to sell at 50 percent above cost, but sometimes market conditions force (or enable) the company to sell at a lower (or higher) price.

Apply the lower of cost or market rule to determine the value at which December 31 inventory should be stated. Apply the rule first on an item-by-item basis and then on a group basis. (In assigning a value to item D, be sure to refer to footnote 4 in this chapter (page 338), which indicates that inventories should never be reduced to a level that will lead to recognition of an unusually high profit in a subsequent period.)

23. *A recent U.S. Supreme Court decision restricted the application of the lower of cost or market rule as it applies to U.S. federal income taxes. Henceforth, a firm will be able to write down its inventory to net realizable value only when it actually intends to make sales at the prices used to determine net realizable value. This ruling may have a significant impact on inventory practices in certain industries. Publishers, for example, may now find it advantageous to sell their books as soon as possible, even if only at greatly reduced prices, rather than to retain them in inventory for sale at later dates at standard prices. There would be no financial incentive for them to carry in stock works of academic and literary merit that are "slow-moving" because of their limited market appeal.*

Art Books, Inc., printed, at a cost of $20 per copy, 20,000 copies of a scholarly art text. In the year of publication, it sold 10,000 copies at a price of $25 per copy. It estimates, however, that sales in the future will be limited to a relatively few collectors and scholars. It predicts that it will be able to sell, at $25 per copy, 1,000 copies per year for 10 years.

The prevailing income tax rate is 40 percent.

a. In your view, is the inventory still worth $20 per copy? What, for example, is the *maximum* amount a buyer would pay for the entire remaining stock of 10,000 books if the decision criterion is the present value of expected cash receipts? Assume a discount rate of 15 percent. In other words, what is the present value of the cash receipts (ignoring taxes) to be received from sales over the period of 10 years?

b. Suppose that Art Books, Inc., has a choice. It could retain the books in inventory and sell them over the period of 10 years. It would be permitted no immediate tax deduction to reflect the loss of the inventory value suggested by your response to part (a). Over the 10-year period, it would, of course, be taxed on profits from the sale of the books (revenue less cost of goods sold) as they are earned. Alternatively, the firm could sell its entire stock of books to a cut-rate bookstore for $10 per copy. The tax loss on the sale (revenue less cost of goods sold) could be used to offset other corporate income. As a consequence, the firm would realize a cash saving equal in amount to 40 percent (the tax rate) of the loss. In an analysis of this course of action, the cash saving could be considered a cash receipt.

(1) What is the present value, after taxes, of the cash to be received from the sale of books at the standard price of $25 over the period of 10 years? Assume a discount rate of 15 percent. The cash receipts for each year are equal to the *revenues* to be received less the taxes to be paid. Cost of goods sold, although an expense, does not require an outlay of cash inasmuch as the books to be sold have already been produced.

(2) What is the present value, after taxes, of the total amount to be received from the immediate sale of the books to the cut-rate bookstore? Because the cash will be received immediately, no discounting is necessary. Be sure to include the tax saving as a cash receipt.

(3) Which course of action is likely to be chosen by management? To simplify the illustration, no mention has been made of the costs of holding the inventory, such as storage and insurance, and of selling and distributing the books. What impact would these costs have on the course of action decided upon? Comment on why the decision of the court would encourage firms to destroy, or sell as salvage, slow-selling works rather than to retain them.

24. *In the precious metals industry, holding gains may dramatically alter operating earnings.*

Engelhard Corporation is a world leader in the development of specialty chemicals and metals. The following data were drawn from its annual report of December 31, 1987:

	1987	1986
	(in thousands)	
Inventories		
Precious metals	$ 104,213	$ 107,021
Nonmetallic minerals and products	57,308	50,640
Other	43,624	30,339
Total inventories	$ 205,145	$ 188,000
Total sales	$2,479,230	$2,289,531
Cost of goods sold	$2,177,317	$2,021,257
Operating earnings		
Specialty chemical business	$ 87,397	$ 76,975
Speciality metals business	22,173	18,644
Other	(4,582)	—
Total operating earnings	$ 104,988	$ 95,619
Total current assets	$ 700,095	$ 603,940
Total current liabilities	$ 297,499	$ 315,976

The financial statements contain the following note:

All precious metals inventories are stated at LIFO cost. The market value of these inventories exceeded the cost by $138.2 million at December 31, 1987, and $118.6 million at December 31, 1986.

a. Determine the approximate value of the precious metals inventory of December 31, 1987, at prices of December 31, 1986. By how much, and by what percent, did the market value of the 1986 inventory increase during 1987?

b. Suppose that the company were to base cost of goods sold on market values of inventories rather than on historical cost. To what extent would cost of goods sold have been different in 1987? Explain. (You need not make specific calculations.) Would your response be the same if the company assumed a FIFO flow of costs?

c. Suppose that the holding gain computed in part (a) were taken into account in determining operating earnings. By how much (in percent) would each of the following have been greater or less?
   (1) Total operating earnings in 1987
   (2) Operating earnings of the specialty metals business in 1987

d. Determine the current ratio as at December 31, 1987, based on historical values. Then recompute, incorporating the current rather than the historical value of the inventories.

e. In your opinion, do the operating earnings and current ratio based on historical costs or on market values provide a more useful measure of corporate performance? Explain.

25. *Identical fiscal performance in different years results in differences in reported income under both LIFO and FIFO. Hence interperiod comparisons are difficult, even within a single firm.*

   The following are selected data as to a firm's sales, purchases, and inventory for a period of four years (number of units and dollar sales are in millions):

	Year 1	Year 2	Year 3	Year 4
Sales				
No. units	24	28	30	24
Sales price	$ 22	$ 21	$ 22.50	$ 22
Dollar sales	$528	$588	$675	$528
Beginning inventory				
No. units	10	6	8	10
Replacement cost	$ 17	$ 16	$ 17.50	$ 17
Purchases				
No. units	20	30	32	20
Unit price	$ 17	$ 16	$ 17.50	$ 17
Ending inventory				
No. units	6	8	10	6
Unit replacement cost	$ 16	$ 17.50	$ 17	$ 16

a. Determine income for each of the four years under both FIFO and LIFO cost-flow assumptions. You need not apply the lower of cost or market rule. Assume that the inventory at the start of year 1 is to be valued at $20 per unit under both FIFO and LIFO.

b. Compare income for years 1 and 4 under each of the assumptions. Note that sales, purchases, and replacement value of beginning and ending inventory were the same in both years. How do you account for differences in reported income in those years under both the FIFO and LIFO cost-flow assumptions?

c. Suppose instead that the firm were to value inventories on the basis of current (i.e., replacement) costs. Would there still be a difference in earnings between years 1 and 4? Explain.

26. *In Great Britain, unlike Canada or the United States, changes in replacement values have been incorporated into the primary financial statements.*

The following data are from the 1987 statement of income of the British Petroleum Company. They are expressed in millions of pounds.

Turnover	£27,578
Replacement cost of sales	(20,758)
Production taxes	(901)
Gross profit	£ 5,919
Distribution and administrative expenses	(3,449)
Exploration expenditures	(469)
	£ 2,001
Other income	784
Replacement cost operating profit	£ 2,785
Stock holding gain	133
Historical cost operating profit	£ 2,918

The following are from a note (amounts also in millions of pounds):

Stocks	1987	1986
Historical cost	£2,716	£2,899
Replacement cost	2,694	3,015

The financial report also contains the following explanation:

Replacement Cost

Replacement cost operating results exclude stock holding gains or losses and reflect the average cost of supplies incurred during the year. Stock holding gains or losses represent the difference between the replacement cost of sales and the historical cost of sales calculated using the first-in, first-out method.

a. What is meant by the terms *turnover* and *stock?*
b. Does "Replacement cost operating profit" include gains or losses from changes in the replacement values of goods held in inventory at year end? Explain.
c. Did replacement values of the firm's products increase or decrease during 1987? Explain.
d. In light of your response to part (c), explain how the company could have a stock holding gain in 1987.

27. *Historical cost accounting may not properly reflect propitious acquisitions of inventory.*

The president of Yarmouth Textiles, Inc., was disappointed to learn from his controller that preliminary data indicated that his firm had suffered a loss of $25,000 in 1997. The president was surprised by the report of the controller since the price of print cloth, the product in which the company trades, had increased substantially during the year.

At January 1, 1997, the company had on hand 400,000 yards of print cloth, for which it had paid 25 cents per yard. The replacement cost of the cloth at that date was 27 cents per yard. At December 31, 1997, the company had in inventory 600,000 yards of cloth for which it had paid 30 cents per yard. If it were to replace the cloth on December 31, 1997 it would have to pay 45 cents per yard.

The president believed that creditors would be misled by financial reports on which inventories were valued, and income determined, strictly on the basis of historical cost. He requested that the controller prepare supplementary reports in which inventories were valued at net realizable value and *holding gains* were specifically recognized in the computation of income.

Determine income for 1997, assuming that inventories were stated at replacement cost in *both* 1996 and 1997.

28. *The conventional income statement can readily be modified to give effect to changes in inventory replacement costs.*

The F. C. Miller Co. trades in scrap metal. The company purchases the scrap from small dealers and sells it in bulk to the major steel manufacturers. As a matter of policy, the company sells the scrap to the manufacturers for $5 per tonne more than the current price it pays the individual dealers. The price of scrap steel is volatile. The following table indicates several price changes that occurred during the year and the transactions engaged in by the F. C. Miller Co. in the periods between the price changes.

Period	Price Paid to Dealers	No. of Tonnes Purchased	Total Cost	No. of Tonnes Sold	Price per Tonne	Total Revenue
1/1	$ 82	5,000 *	$ 410,000			
2/1–11/3	85	16,000	1,360,000	18,000	$ 90	$1,620,000
12/3–4/6	87	25,000	2,175,000	22,000	92	2,024,000
5/6–26/9	93	5,000	465,000	9,000	98	882,000
27/9–30/12	104	17,000	1,768,000	13,000	109	1,417,000
31/12	106	-0-	-0-	-0-		0
		68,000	$6,178,000	62,000		$5,943,000

* Opening inventory.

During the year F. C. Miller incurred operating costs of $325,000.
  a. Prepare a conventional income statement in which gains or losses are recognized only upon actual sales of goods. Use the FIFO method of inventory valuation.
  b. Prepare an income statement in which gains or losses are recognized upon increases in wholesale prices. Cost of goods sold should be based on replacement costs applicable at the time the goods are sold. Be sure to indicate the realizable holding gain (ending inventory plus cost of goods sold less beginning inventory and purchases).

Solutions to Exercise for Review and Self-Testing

1. The total number of units to be accounted for is the sum of beginning balance and the purchases throughout the year—800 units. Similarly, the total cost to be accounted for is $16,700.

2. a. *FIFO*

Ending inventory			
From purchase of Dec. 28	100 @ $23	$2,300	
From purchase of Sept. 23	100 @ 22	2,200	$ 4,500
Cost of goods sold			
From balance of Jan. 1	400 @ $20	$8,000	
From purchase of Feb. 24	200 @ 21	4,200	12,200
Total	800		$16,700

b. *Weighted average:* Average cost = $16,700/800 units = $20.875

Ending inventory	200 @ $20.875	$ 4,175
Cost of goods sold	600 @ $20.875	12,525
Total	800	$16,700

c. *LIFO*

Ending inventory			
From balance of Jan. 1	200 @ $20		$ 4,000
Cost of goods sold			
From purchase of Dec. 28	100 @ $23	$2,300	
From purchase of Sept. 23	100 @ 22	2,200	
From purchase of Feb. 24	200 @ 21	4,200	
From balance of Jan. 1	200 @ 20	4,000	12,700
Total	800		$16,700

3. The 200 units on hand would have to be written down to $21 per unit—$4,200. The write-down from $4,500 would cause earnings of 1996 to decrease by $300. Inasmuch as the carrying value of the inventory would be reduced, cost of goods sold, when the goods are actually sold in 1997, would be reduced by $300 and earnings thereby increased by that amount.

4. The entire inventory must be stated at $23 per unit. The 100 units that would otherwise be reported at $22 per unit would have to be increased in value by $1 per unit—a total of $100. Thus a holding gain of $100 would be recognized. The effect of writing up the inventory by $100 in 1996 would be to increase reported cost of goods sold and reduce reported income in 1997 by the same amount.

5. Beginning inventory is given as $8,000. Ending inventory is calculated in part 2(a) as $4,500. Cost of goods sold is computed in part 2(a) as $12,200:

$$\text{Average inventory} = \frac{\$8,000 + \$4,500}{2} = \$6,250$$

$$\text{Inventory turnover} = \frac{\text{Cost of goods sold}}{\text{Average inventory}}$$

$$= \frac{\$12,200}{\$6,250}$$

$$= 1.95 \text{ times}$$

9

Long-Lived Assets and the Allocation of Their Costs

The previous chapter discussed the last of the significant current asset accounts. This chapter introduces the accounting procedures for the long-lived, or capital, assets. The difference between current and long-lived assets is that the long-lived assets will not be used up or consumed in the next accounting period. The long-lived assets will continue to provide service over a number of accounting periods. The primary issues addressed in this chapter will include what constitutes a capital asset and how to allocate the cost of a capital asset to expense over the period of service (i.e., matching). Examples of common methods of allocating the cost of capital assets to expense will be discussed. The accounting for disposals and trade-ins of capital assets will also be introduced.

After studying this chapter, you will be able to

- Determine which expenditures should be capitalized
- Understand the need to match the cost of the long-lived asset to the revenue generated by the asset
- Describe four types of amortization
- Account for disposals of capital assets
- Account for trade-ins of capital assets
- Calculate and understand the significance of the plant and equipment turnover ratio

Capital assets are long-lived assets that a firm has acquired for use in the business. They are used directly in the production process or to support the administrative function of the business. These assets are expected to be used for a period greater than one year and are not, normally, intended for sale. The capital assets may be tangible—such as property, plant, and equipment—or intangible—such as organization costs and patents.

THE FUNDAMENTAL ISSUES: WHAT IS THE VALUE OF A CAPITAL ASSET? HOW SHOULD ITS COST BE ALLOCATED OVER ITS USEFUL LIFE?

The Economic Value of a Capital Asset to Its Owner

Capital assets may differ considerably in physical form from marketable securities and notes receivable. In economic substance, however, they are quite similar. The value of a note receivable is in the stream of cash flows that it provides. Suppose, for example, a company holds a note that entitles it to annual cash receipts of $100,000 per year for 10 years This amount includes elements of both interest and principal. The value of the note is the present value of an annuity of $100,000 for 10 years. Assuming a discount rate of 10 percent, we find (per Table 4 in the Appendix) that the asset is worth $614,460:

$$\$100,000 \times 6.1446 = \$614,460$$

Suppose instead that the company owns a building that has a remaining useful life of 10 years. The company rents the building to a tenant under a noncancelable 10-year lease. Annual rent is $100,000. The building's economic value to the company is identical to that of the note—the present value of 10 annual cash receipts of $100,000, or $614,460.

Most capital assets cannot be as clearly identified with specific cash flows as can a note receivable or a building on which there is a noncancelable lease for a term exactly equal to remaining useful life. Hence their economic values cannot as easily be determined. This pragmatic obstacle, however, in no way alters the substantive economic characteristics that the capital assets have in common with the other assets.

Generally accepted accounting principles stipulate that capital assets (just like marketable securities, receivables, and inventories) be stated on the balance sheet at amounts based on their *historical* costs rather than their economic values. Of course, other alternatives have been proposed, and they will be addressed later in this chapter.

Allocation of Cost

A long-lived asset, by definition, is purchased in one accounting period but consumed over several. Therefore its cost must be allocated among the periods in which it provides its economic benefits. As the asset is used, a portion of cost must be charged as an expense. The share that has not yet been expensed must be "stored" on the balance sheet.

The cost to be allocated is the original cost of the asset less its *residual* or *salvage* value—the amount estimated to be recoverable when the asset is sold or salvaged. If an asset cost $12,000, but is expected to be sold at the end of its useful life for $2,000, the net amount to be allocated would be $10,000.

The process of allocating the cost of an asset over several accounting periods is referred to as *amortization*. Using the term amortization to define the process of allocating the cost of an asset over several accounting periods is quite recent in Canada. Before a 1990 change in the *CICA Handbook*, separate terms were used for the allocation depending on the type of asset. If the asset was property and equipment, the term was depreciation; if the asset was a natural resource, the term was depletion; and if the asset was an intangible, such as organization costs or a patent, the term was amortization. Under the revised Capital Assets section of the *CICA Handbook*, the word amortization is used for describing the allocation of cost for all types of assets. In this text we will use the word amortization. However, you should be aware that the separate terms of depreciation, depletion, and amortization are still widely used in practice. Certain of the problem material at the end of the chapter will include the separate terms, where they were used in actual annual reports.

Most of this chapter is directed to two related questions: When, and in what amount, should net asset cost be charged as expense? What amount of net cost should remain, and be reported, on the balance sheet?

The basic journal entry to record the acquisition of a long-lived asset such as equipment (assuming the equipment to have cost $12,000) is

Equipment $12,000
    Cash (or notes payable) $12,000
To record the purchase of equipment

The basic entry to record the annual allocation of the cost of the asset over its useful life (assuming a life of 10 years and a residual value of $2,000) is

Amortization expense $1,000
    Accumulated amortization, equipment $1,000
To record annual amortization expense

Capital assets are reported on the balance sheet at original cost less accumulated amortization.

The account for accumulated amortization is a contra asset account and is always reported directly beneath the particular group of assets to which it pertains. Use of the contra account enables the firm to provide information that is more complete than if the balance in the asset account were reduced directly. Thus, after one year, the equipment might be shown on the balance sheet as

Equipment	$12,000	
Less: Accumulated amortization	1,000	$11,000

The standard pattern of accounting for long-lived assets suggests several subsidiary issues which need to be addressed:

1. What should constitute the *acquisition cost* of an asset? What should constitute appropriate adjustments to acquisition cost?
2. How should *useful life* and *residual value* be determined?
3. What basis of *amortization* should be used to allocate the acquisition cost over the asset's useful life?
4. How should the *sale, trade-in,* or *retirement* of an asset be accounted for?

We will discuss these issues as they apply to property, plant, and equipment, but the general concepts apply to all capital assets. Toward the conclusion of the chapter, however, we shall address issues unique to selected other long-lived assets.

ACQUISITION COST OF PROPERTY, PLANT, AND EQUIPMENT

The acquisition cost of property, plant, and equipment is, in general, its stated purchase price. But it is often more, and occasionally less, than that. It includes all costs that are necessary to bring the capital asset to a usable condition. Therefore the cost would include, in addition to actual purchase price, amounts paid for freight, installation, taxes, and title fees. The costs that are included as a part of the capital asset are said to be *capitalized*. They are incurred to benefit several periods, not just one, and should be charged as expenses over the useful life of the asset rather than in the year in which they are incurred.

Interest Excluded

The acquisition cost of an asset generally excludes interest, both implicit and explicit (although some exceptions are noted in a section that follows). Suppose that a firm acquires a capital asset for $1 million but is permitted to delay payment for one year. It is charged interest of $80,000. The asset would be recorded at $1 million; the $80,000 would be reported as interest expense. Suppose, alternatively, that a firm agrees to pay $1 million for a capital asset but is permitted to delay payment for one year with no interest charges. As was pointed out in previous chapters, money has a time value, and businesses cannot be expected to make interest-free loans. Hence the true purchase price can be assumed to be something less than $1 million. If the prevailing rate of interest is 8 percent, then the asset would be recorded at $925,900. That amount is the present value of $1 million discounted for one year at 8 percent. The difference of $74,100 between the stated price of $1 million and the value of the consideration, $925,900, would be accounted for as interest expense.

The catalogue or advertised price of an asset may not always be the relevant purchase price. Often the stated price of an asset is nothing more than the starting point of the bargaining process. Frequently, dealers give trade discounts (not to be confused with trade-in allowances) to customers of a certain category and cash discounts for prompt payment. Such discounts must be deducted from the originally stated price, since the purchase price must be determined on the basis of value actually surrendered by the buyer and received by the seller—that is, the *current cash equivalent*.

Example

Assume that a firm purchases a machine for $10,000 under terms 2/10, n/30 (the company will receive a 2 percent discount if it pays within 10 days, but, in any event, must pay within 30 days). Transportation costs are $300, and the wages of the two workers who install the machine amount to $150. In addition, while the machine is being installed, three employees who work in the vicinity of the new machine are idled for two hours, since power to other machines has to be disconnected. The wages paid to the workers while they are idle are $90. The cost of the new machine would be computed as follows:

Purchase price	$10,000	
Less: 2% discount	200	$ 9,800
Freight		300
Installation costs		150
Payment for idle time		90
		$10,340

It may appear illogical to add the wages of the idle employees to the cost of the machine (and in practice many firms would not bother to do so). But could the machine have been installed without such loss of time? Was the cost necessary to bring the asset to a performing state? If the answer in each case is yes, then such costs have been incurred to benefit future periods, rather than the current period, and should rightfully be capitalized as part of the asset and should be allocated (i.e., amortized) over the useful life of the new machine. If the answer is no, then the wages of the employees should be charged in full as an expense in the period of installation.

Purchases of Land

The same general principle applies to purchases of land. If a company purchases a parcel of land on which it intends to erect a new building, then all costs necessary to make the land ready for its intended use should be capitalized as part of the land. Thus, should a firm purchase land on which stands an old building that must first be torn down before a new building can be constructed, the demolition costs must be added to the purchase price of land; they will benefit future accounting periods.

Example

A company purchases land for $1 million, with the intention of constructing a plant. Before construction can begin, however, an old building on the land must be removed. Demolition costs amount to $100,000, but the firm is able to sell scrap from the old building for $30,000. Title and legal fees incurred in connection with the purchase total $10,000. At what value should the land be recorded?

Purchase price		$1,000,000
Add: Demolition costs	$100,000	
Less: Sale of scrap	30,000	70,000
Title and legal fees		10,000
Net cost of land		$1,080,000

Land is somewhat different from other capital assets in that it does not ordinarily lose either service potential or value with the passage of time. Indeed, most often it *appreciates* in value. Thus the cost of the land should not be amortized or allocated over time as long as there is no evidence of a decline in its service potential or value. If the land does not decline in value and the firm can, at any time, sell the land for the amount that it originally paid, then there is no real cost to the firm and thus no expense need be charged. Land, therefore, is not ordinarily considered an asset subject to amortization.

Construction of Assets

When a firm constructs its own assets, the *theoretical* guidelines to determine cost are quite clear. The firm should include in the cost of the asset all costs necessary to bring it to a serviceable state. Thus the materials used, as well as the wages of all employees who work on the construction project, should be capitalized as part of the asset. It is the *operational* questions that are the most difficult for many firms and their accountants to answer. How should a company account for those costs that are common to a number of activities that are carried out within the firm and cannot be traced directly to the construction of the asset? For example, how should it treat the salary of a general manager who devotes only a portion of his time to supervising the construction project? Or the wages of administrative personnel who maintain records pertaining to both the construction project and other activities of the company? Should these costs be included as part of the asset constructed by the firm or should they be charged to expense as incurred?

The general answer is that the firm should allocate such costs between the capital asset and the other activities. It should make estimates of the proportion of time that the general manager and the administrative personnel performed services relating to the construction project as opposed to the other activities. Only that proportion of overall costs should be added to the cost of the capital asset.

Example

The cost of constructing a minor addition to a plant might be computed (in oversimplified fashion) as follows:

Wages of employees directly associated with construction	$25,000
Materials and supplies used in project	40,000
Salary of plant supervisor (80% of salary for 1 month)	10,000
Wages of administrative personnel (10% of wages for 1 month)	600
	$75,600

Decisions as to what proportions of such *joint* (common) costs should be added to the cost of capital assets are by no means either trivial or academic, especially if the projects involve large dollar amounts. Costs that are included as part of a capital asset will be charged as expenses, through the process of amortization, over the life of the asset. The remaining costs that are allocated to other activities are likely to be charged as expenses in the year in which they are actually incurred. Thus, in this example, if the decision had been made that no portion of the salary of the plant supervisor should be included as part of the asset, then overall company expenses for the year would have been greater, since the entire $10,000 would have been deducted from revenues this year. As it is, only a small portion of the $10,000 (one year's amortization) would be charged against this year's revenues; the remainder would be spread out over the useful life of the asset.

Capitalization of Interest

The question of which costs related to the construction of plant and equipment should be capitalized is reflected in a long-standing dispute among accountants. When a company constructs a major capital asset, such as a new plant, it often has to borrow funds to finance the construction. On the amounts borrowed, it must pay interest. Should the interest be charged as an expense during all the years in which the loan is outstanding, or should the interest, like all other costs of construction, be capitalized as part of the capital asset and charged off, in the form of amortization, over the life of the asset? Some accountants argue that interest costs are no different from labour costs or material costs. They are a necessary cost of construction and should therefore be added to the cost of the asset. Moreover, they assert, the company earns no revenues from the plant while it is under construction; hence the matching principle dictates that it should charge no expenses. The interest costs, they say, will benefit future periods; they should therefore be expensed in future periods.

Other accountants, however, maintain that interest is a special kind of expense. The firm borrows money, they say, for all sorts of purposes. Just as it is impossible to trace capital contributed by shareholders to specific assets, so also is it impossible to trace the proceeds from the issue of bonds or other instruments of debt to particular assets. Thus, they argue, it would be improper to associate the related interest charges to specific construction projects. Interest, they say, should be expensed in the periods during which the loans are outstanding, regardless of the reason for the borrowing.

Opponents of interest capitalization also point out that the practice results in similar assets, both used within the same industry, being recorded at different values because they are financed from different sources. Suppose, for example, that each of two companies constructs identical plants at a cost of $20 million. One finances the new plant by issuing bonds, the other by issuing common stock. The company that issues bonds incurs $2 million in interest costs during the period of construction. The other incurs no interest costs (but, it can be assumed, incurs costs of capital in another form, such as dividends). When the two plants are put into service, the one financed with bonds would be reported at a cost of $22 million, the one financed with common stock at $20 million.

The issue of interest capitalization is of particular importance to public utilities, whose rates are established by regulatory commissions, and to their customers. It is the policy of most regulatory commissions to set user charges at levels that permit the utilities to earn specified rates of return. Rates of return are typically calculated by dividing income by assets.

Public utilities, such as electric, telephone, and gas companies, require large amounts of plant and equipment. The construction of new facilities often takes many years. The firms often incur substantial interest costs while building is in progress.

If a utility were to charge interest as an expense as it is incurred, then expenses during construction periods would be higher than if interest were capitalized. To compensate for the added expenses (and reduced earnings), regulatory commissions would permit the company to increase rates as soon as construction begins. In effect, therefore, the interest costs would be paid by the customers of the utility during the period of construction. If, by contrast, the interest were to be capitalized, then it would be added to the cost of the plant and charged as an expense (amortization) over the life of the plant. The interest charges would not be an allowable expense to be incorporated into the rates charged to customers until the new facilities were on line and the firm began to charge amortization on them. Thus the capitalization of interest would permit the customers to delay having their rates increased to pay the interest costs. Existing consumers usually benefit from capitalization of interest in two ways: first, because the present value of dollars to be paid later is less than that to be paid currently, and second, because the customers of the future may be greater in number than those of the present, thereby enabling the company to spread the costs over a greater number of parties. The latter benefit is particularly important if the new plant is being constructed to extend service into new areas.

The CICA has not made general recommendations with respect to the capitalization of interest. The *Handbook* recommends that interest costs be included in the cost of capital assets acquired or constructed over time, if it is the policy of the company to capitalize interest. Rate-regulated companies, such as those discussed above, are generally required by the regulator (the National Energy Board, for example) to capitalize interest costs incurred to finance construction. For the real-estate sector, CIPREC recommends that interest be capitalized during the development period.[1]

ADDITIONS TO ACQUISITION COST: BETTERMENTS BUT NOT REPAIRS AND MAINTENANCE

Betterments (costs incurred to enhance the service potential of an asset during its useful life) should be accounted for in the same way as initial acquisition costs. They should be added to the original cost of the asset and amortized over the remaining asset life.

Betterments must be distinguished from repairs and maintenance. Betterments extend an asset's useful life, increase its normal rate of output, or lower its operating costs. Maintenance and repairs, by contrast, keep an asset in good operating condition and merely keep up its efficiency. The distinction between the two is not always obvious, but the accounting implications are consequential.

---

[1] "Interest," Section 205.9, *Recommended Accounting Practices for Real Estate Investment and Development Companies,* Canadian Institute of Public Real Estate Companies, 1990.

Maintenance and repair costs are charged off as expenses as they are incurred. Betterment costs are capitalized and charged off as expenses in the periods that they will benefit. The distinction is particularly important from a tax point of view. If the cost is classified as a repair, it will be deductible for tax purposes in the year incurred. If it is classified as a betterment, the cost is capitalized and will only be deductible for tax purposes over the remaining life of the asset.

Example

The Z Company expended $4,500 to recondition the engine of one of its trucks. This reconditioning of the engine will extend the useful life of the truck by three years. At the same time, it spent $400 to paint the truck. The painting of the truck does not extend the useful life of the truck or increase its output. The journal entry to record the repair/betterment combination would be

Trucks (capital asset)	$4,500	
Repairs and maintenance expense	400	
Cash		$4,900
To record repairs and betterments		

The $4,500 spent to recondition the engine will be amortized over three years at $1,500 per year.

The grey area of maintenance involves those costs that routinely recur. Airlines, for example, overhaul engines every several years. Some airlines charge the full cost of an overhaul as an expense in the year in which it is performed, even though the procedure benefits several years. Others capitalize the cost of the overhaul, setting up the repair job as an independent asset. The cost is then amortized over the expected number of years between overhauls; the expense is thereby allocated to the several years benefited by the cost.

USEFUL LIFE AND RESIDUAL VALUE

Useful life is a key determinant of annual amortization charges as well as of the net asset value reported on the balance sheet. In textbook examples, *useful life* is typically stated so cavalierly that a reader can easily be lulled into believing either that its influence upon reported income and assets is insignificant or that it is easy to estimate. Neither is correct.

Annual amortization charges are extremely sensitive to differences in estimates of useful life. Suppose, for example, a firm has $120 million in amortizable equipment. Annual straight-line amortization charges based on a four-year useful life will be $30 million, on a six-year life only $20 million—a difference of 50 percent!

The number of years that a firm will keep an asset depends on more than the ability to maintain it in working order. Physical deterioration is, of course, a relevant consideration, but one of decreasing importance. Of greater significance is technological obsolescence. Improvements in production equipment may permit a company to reduce manufacturing costs. If the company is to remain competitive, it may have no choice but to replace old, but perfectly serviceable, equipment with new. Or advances in the same or related industries may reduce or eliminate the demand for the firm's product—and thereby make many of its production facilities obsolete. The challenges to meaningfully estimating useful life cannot be overstated, but unfortunately neither accountants nor managers are uniquely endowed with powers of prophecy.

The amortization practices of major airlines highlight the subjective nature of estimates of useful life. Whereas Canadian Airlines International Ltd. amortizes substantially all of its flight equipment over a 20-year period, Air Canada does so over periods of 16 to 20 years. The estimates are not necessarily inconsistent. One company may *plan* to use its planes for a shorter time than the other. In fact, estimates are not static and may change with additional information. In 1988, for example, Air Canada increased the estimated service lives of its B-767 aircraft. Airlines, however, are both competitive and capital-intense. Thus the seemingly conflicting policies at the very least raise questions as to the reliability of their estimates and detract from the overall comparability of their financial statements.

In the last decade it has been become common for companies to report write-offs of large amounts of assets. These losses, particularly common during the recession of the early 1990s, often result from closings of entire plants or elimination of product lines. Each write-off is representative of a misestimate of a useful life. If the company had perfect foresight, the plant or equipment would have been amortized down to its residual value by the time it was sold or abandoned, and no write-off would have been necessary.

The problems of estimating *residual value*—the amount to be recovered when an asset is retired—are essentially the same as those of predicting useful life. Residual value is one element of the formula (one exception will be discussed later in this chapter) used to compute amortization. In many industries, the estimates of residual values tend to be only a small percentage of original asset costs. Hence annual amortization charges are not greatly affected by the residual values. In some industries, however, estimates of residual values can be critical. In rental businesses (autos, for example), assets are held for only a short period and sold for a substantial portion of initial purchase price. Residual values are therefore a significant parameter in the amortization calculation.

In most cases, the calculation of periodic amortization expense depends on three factors: acquisition cost, useful life, and residual value. As noted above, useful life and residual value are estimates. Only acquisition cost is known with any degree of certainty. As a result, investors and managers must be cautious when interpreting and comparing amortization expense, essentially an estimate.

AMORTIZATION

Amortization in accordance with generally accepted accounting principles is the process of allocating (in a systematic and rational manner) the cost of a capital asset, less estimated residual value, if any, to expense over the estimated useful life of the asset. Allocation of cost is necessary if costs are to be matched with the revenues that they help to generate.

Amortization is a process of *allocation*, not *valuation*. The original cost of an asset less the accumulated amortization (the amount of amortization taken on an asset up to a given time) is often referred to as the *book value* of an asset.

Accountants do not purport that the book value of an asset represents the value of the asset in the open market. The potential for conflict between the two values can be demonstrated in a simple example involving an automobile.

A company purchases an automobile for $31,000 with the intention of using it for five years. It estimates that the trade-in value of the auto after that time will be $6,000. The amount of amortization expense to be charged each year can be calculated to be $5,000:

$$\frac{\text{Original cost } - \text{ Residual value}}{\text{Useful life}} = \frac{\$31,000 - \$6,000}{5} = \$5,000$$

Exhibit 9-1 shows a comparison of book value to market value at the end of each of the five years of estimated useful life. The market value represents a "typical" pattern of the decline in value of an automobile.

EXHIBIT 9-1

Comparison of Book and Market Values for a Typical Automobile

End of Year	Original Cost	Amortization Taken to Date	Cost Less Accumulated Amortization ("Book" Value)	Estimated Market Value
1	$31,000	$5,000	$26,000	$23,000
2	31,000	10,000	21,000	17,000
3	31,000	15,000	16,000	12,000
4	31,000	20,000	11,000	8,000
5	31,000	25,000	6,000	6,000

Merely because the amounts in the last two columns are not the same, it cannot be said that the decision to amortize the asset at the rate of $5,000 per year was in error. It is *not* the objective of amortization accounting, as it exists under generally accepted accounting principles, to indicate what the asset could be sold for at the end of a year.

It is also not the objective of the amortization process to provide funds with which to replace assets when they must be sold or retired. The absurdity of contending that it is becomes evident by examining the basic journal entry for amortization:

Amortization expense xxxx
    Accumulated amortization xxxx

Cash is neither debited nor credited; it is neither received from outsiders nor moved from one bank account into another. It is not possible for an accountant to assure that a firm will have sufficient cash on hand to purchase a new asset when an old one is retired merely by making an end-of-month or end-of-year adjusting entry.

Only in the most indirect sense can it be said that amortization accounting provides funds for the future replacement of assets. Amortization, like other expenses, is deducted from revenues to calculate annual income. To the extent that it reduces taxable income, it also reduces income taxes. Insofar as it reduces income taxes, it enables the firm to save for asset replacement more cash than it would if it had not recorded amortization. In the same vein, the reduction in income attributable to amortization expense may discourage some firms from declaring cash dividends of the amount they might have if income were greater. In neither case is it the amortization that provides cash. At best, the amortization expense influences decisions that affect cash—cash which may be used to replace assets or for any other corporate purpose.

ACCELERATED AMORTIZATION METHODS

Until this point, the annual amortization charge has been calculated by dividing the total amount to be amortized (cost less residual value, if any, usually called the *amortizable base*) by the number of years that the asset is expected to be in use. The amortization charges are thereby the same during each year of the asset's life. This way of calculating amortization is known as the *straight-line* method. There are, however, other means of allocating the cost of an asset to the various periods during which it will be used that result in unequal annual charges. Two of the most popular are known as the *sum-of-the-years'-digits* method and the *declining balance* method. Both of these result in amortization charges which decline over the life of the asset. That is, amortization expenses are greater in the beginning years of the asset's life than they are at the end. Both are referred to as *accelerated* methods of amortization.

Sum-of-the-Years'-Digits Method

By the *sum-of-the-years'-digits* method, a fraction of the asset's net amortizable cost is charged off each year. The denominator of the fraction remains constant over the life of the asset. It is determined by taking a sum of numbers starting with 1 and continuing to the estimated life of the asset. Thus, if the life of the asset is three years, the denominator will be $1 + 2 + 3 = 6$. If it is five years, it will be $1 + 2 + 3 + 4 + 5 = 15$. A shortcut technique eliminates the need to add the digits. The life of the asset (n) may be multiplied by the life of the asset plus 1 (that is, $n + 1$) and the product divided by 2. For example, the denominator to be used for an asset with five years of useful life would be

$$\frac{n(n + 1)}{2} = \frac{5(6)}{2} = 15$$

The numerator of the fraction would vary over the life of the asset. Each year it would be equal to the number of years remaining in the asset's life. Thus, in the first year of the life of a five-year asset, $\frac{5}{15}$ of the asset's cost (less residual value) would be amortized. In the second year, when the asset has a remaining life of only four years, $\frac{4}{15}$ would be amortized. In subsequent years, $\frac{3}{15}$, $\frac{2}{15}$, and $\frac{1}{15}$, respectively, would be charged to amortization expense.

Example

A firm purchases an auto for $31,000. It estimates that the auto has a useful life of five years, after which it can be sold for $6,000. The net amount to be amortized is $25,000 (original cost less estimated salvage value). Amortization expense using the sum-of-the-years'-digits method would be as follows:

Year	Net Amortizable Amount	Amortization Fraction	Amortization Expense
1	$25,000	$5/15$	$ 8,333
2	25,000	$4/15$	6,667
3	25,000	$3/15$	5,000
4	25,000	$2/15$	3,333
5	25,000	$1/15$	1,667
		$15/15$	$25,000

Declining Balance Method

The *declining balance* method consists of applying to the current book value of the asset (cost less accumulated amortization to date) a percentage rate equal to some proportion of the straight-line amortization rate. If the rate is twice the straight-line rate, it is referred to as the *double declining balance* method.

In the earlier example of straight-line amortization in which the asset had a useful life of five years, one-fifth or 20 percent of the net amortizable cost was charged off each year. Hence the amortization rate could be said to have been 20 percent. The appropriate rate for the double declining balance method would therefore be twice that, or 40 percent. The appropriate rate for 150 percent declining balance amortization would be 1.5 times the straight-line rate, or 30 percent. Unlike the straight-line or sum-of-the-years'-digits methods, the *declining balance procedure requires that the rate be applied initially to the original cost of the asset—not original cost less residual value.*

Example

Again, the asset to be considered cost $31,000 and has a useful life of five years and an estimated residual value of $6,000. Amortization expense using the double declining balance method is based on a rate of 40 percent (twice the straight-line rate of 20 percent). The calculations are shown in Exhibit 9-2.

EXHIBIT 9-2
Double Declining Balance Amortization

Year	Cost Less Accumulated Amortization (Beginning-of-Year Book Value)	Amortization Rate (%)	Amortization Expense	Remaining Book Value End-of-Year
1	$31,000	40	$12,400	$18,600
2	18,600	40	7,440	11,160
3	11,160	40	4,464	6,696
4	6,696	—	696	6,000
5	6,000	—	0	6,000

The declining balance method does not automatically assure that an asset will be amortized exactly down to its estimated residual value at the end of its forecasted useful life. Most frequently, residual value is reached before the end of estimated useful life. When that occurs, an asset should not be amortized below its estimated residual value. In the example, amortization expense in year 4 is limited to $696, rather than $2,678, the full 40 percent of the beginning balance of $6,696. This figure ($696) reduces the remaining book value to the estimated residual value of $6,000. In year 5, no amortization is taken.

For assets for which it is a small percentage of original cost, residual value may not be reached by the end of estimated useful life. In fact, if residual value is zero, then it will never be reached, no matter how long the asset is retained. If a firm holds an asset beyond its originally estimated useful life, then it should continue to amortize the asset until it disposes of the asset or amortizes it to its estimated residual value.

WHICH METHOD IS PREFERABLE?

Official accounting pronouncements permit companies broad discretion in selecting an amortization method. Any method is acceptable as long as it allocates costs in a "systematic and rational manner." The straight-line method is the most widely used for general-purpose financial reporting. The Income Tax Act does not allow the deduction of amortization expense for purposes of calculating taxable income. However, the tax equivalent of amortization, *capital cost allowance,* is used to write off the cost of capital assets for tax purposes. Essentially, capital cost allowance provides that, in the overwhelming majority of instances, the cost of assets be written off on a declining balance basis, with the rate dependent on the category of asset as specified in the Income Tax Act. The system of capital cost allowance (an example of an accelerated method) results in stiff charges to income in the early years of asset life, and therefore, lower taxable income. Hence, in the early years of an asset's life, firms can reap the benefits of accelerated deductions on their tax returns while taking only straight-line deductions on their financial statements.

Accelerated Methods

Many accountants who have given thought to the issue believe that amortization charges should be tied to asset efficiency and productivity. In the periods in which an asset provides the greater output or cost savings, its amortization charges should also be the greater. The efficiency and productivity of most assets decline with age. Vehicles and equipment, for example, are subject to increasing repair costs and "downtime." Residential and commercial buildings are less able to attract premium rents. In the face of declining efficiency and productivity, the accelerated methods provide the closer match between asset benefits and costs. A larger proportion of an asset's cost is expensed in the early years of asset life when the asset output is the greatest.

Straight-Line Method

Even though, as emphasized earlier, the objectives of amortization are more closely tied to the income statement than to the balance sheet, the relationship between amortization and book value cannot be ignored. After all, return on investment, which relates income to net assets (or to shareholders' equity, which is the equivalent of net assets) is one of the most pervasive measures of organizational performance.

When either amortization expense or net income (which is directly affected by amortization expense) is related to the book values of assets, the straight-line method of amortization produces a more stable return on investment than do the accelerated methods. As shown in Exhibit 9-3, if the net revenues (revenues less operating expenses) generated by an asset remain constant, the double declining balance method causes rates of return to increase dramatically over the years of asset life. The increasing return on investment gives the highly misleading impression that the profitability of a firm improves with the age of its assets.[2]

The straight-line method considerably alleviates, but by no means eliminates, the anomaly of rates of return that increase with asset age. As shown in the first part of Exhibit 9-4, when net revenues remain constant, rates of return again rise substantially over the life of the asset. However, in the more realistic case, when net revenues *decline* over asset life (as illustrated in the second part of Exhibit 9-4), the straight-line method yields a constant return on investment.

EXHIBIT 9-3

Example: Rate of Return Based on Double Declining Balance Amortization, Assuming Constant Asset Efficiency and Productivity

Asset cost: $10,000
Useful life: 5 years
Residual value: $0
Amortization rate: 40 percent
Revenues, assumed to be $2,638 per year, represent contributions of asset after deduction of all related expenses other than amortization.

	Period				
	1	2	3	4	5
Revenues	$2,638	$2,638	$2,638	$2,638	$2,638
Amortization expense	4,000	2,400	1,440	864	518
Income	($1,362)	$ 238	$1,198	$1,774	$2,120
Net book value, beginning of period	$10,000	$6,000	$3,600	$2,160	$1,296
Rate of return (income/book value)	(13.6%)	4.0%	33.3%	82.1%	163.6%

[2] The focus herein is on the return of the plant assets alone. The book values of plant assets alone must be distinguished from the book value of the entire firm. If the firm retains, and invests, funds equal to the amortization charges, then both the value of its total assets as well as its income will be greater than what is shown in Exhibit 9-3. The trend of return on investment (total income as a percentage of book value of all assets) will be considerably flatter than what is indicated in the exhibit.

EXHIBIT 9-4

Example: Rate of Return Based on Straight-Line Amortization When Asset Efficiency and Productivity Are Constant and When They Are Decreasing

Asset cost: $10,000
Useful life: 5 years
Residual value: $0
Annual straight-line amortization: $2,000
Revenues represent contributions of asset after deduction of all related expenses other than amortization.

Constant Asset Efficiency and Productivity
(Net Revenues Assumed to Be $2,638 per year)

	Period				
	1	2	3	4	5
Revenues	$2,638	$2,638	$2,638	$2,638	$2,638
Amortization expense	2,000	2,000	2,000	2,000	2,000
Income	$ 638	$ 638	$ 638	$ 638	$ 638
Net book value, beginning of period	$10,000	$8,000	$6,000	$4,000	$2,000
Rate of return (income/book value)	6.4%	8.0%	10.6%	16.0%	31.9%

Decreasing Asset Productivity and Efficiency
(Net Revenues Assumed to Be $3,000 in Year 1 and $200 Less Each Year)

	Period				
	1	2	3	4	5
Revenues	$3,000	$2,800	$2,600	$2,400	$2,200
Amortization expense	2,000	2,000	2,000	2,000	2,000
Income	$1,000	$ 800	$ 600	$ 400	$ 200
Net book value, beginning of period	$10,000	$8,000	$6,000	$4,000	$2,000
Rate of return (income/book value)	10%	10%	10%	10%	10%

The constant rate of return is desirable because it reflects the economic decision made by the firm to acquire the asset. As was illustrated in Chapter 6, the value to the firm of an asset is the present value of its cash inflows (or savings). *Present value* is determined by discounting the cash flows of each year by a constant discount rate. A firm will be willing to acquire an asset as long as the present value of the cash flows, based on that discount rate, is greater than the present value of the cash outflows required to obtain it.

Suppose that, as in the first part of Exhibit 9-4, an asset will provide annual cash returns of $2,638. The discount rate of the firm is 10 percent. Per Table 4 in the Appendix, "Present Value of an Annuity," the value of the asset to the firm is $10,000:

$$\$2,638 \times 3.7908 = \$10,000$$

The $10,000 in this example also happens to be the purchase price. This coincidence is not by chance. In a competitive economy, one might expect the value of an asset to a particular user to approximate its value to the market, at least over the long term.

Compound Interest Amortization

An amortization method known as the *compound interest* method assures that the rate of return on an asset remains constant over its useful life, when the revenues do not decline but rather are constant. It provides for annual amortization charges that *increase* from year to year. It has never been widely accepted in practice because it is counter to both accepted tax methods and the accountant's regard for conservatism. The compound interest method reports as annual amortization expense each year's decline in the present value of expected benefits. When the firm acquires the asset described in the first part of Exhibit 9-4, it expects to receive the equivalent of five cash receipts of $2,638. Based on a discount rate of 10 percent, these are worth $10,000. After one year, the firm anticipates only four receipts of $2,638. These are worth only $8,362:

$$\$2,638 \times 3.1699 = \$8,362$$

Hence the value of the asset to the firm declines by $1,638. This, therefore, is the amount that would be recorded as amortization expense in the first year.

After two years, the firm anticipates three more receipts of $2,638. These are worth $6,560:

$$\$2,638 \times 2.4869 = \$6,560$$

The $1,802 decline in value from $8,362 to $6,560 will be the amortization charge for year 2. The complete amortization schedule is shown in Exhibit 9-5.

EXHIBIT 9-5

Example: Amortization and Rate of Return Based on Compound Interest Amortization, with Annual Decline in Present Value of Anticipated Cash Flows

Asset cost: $10,000
Useful life: 5 years
Residual value: $0
Anticipated annual receipts of $2,638 represent contributions of asset after deduction of all related expenses other than amortization.

Amortization

End of Year	No. of Payments Remaining	Amount of Each Payment	Present Value of Annuity of Remaining Payments (10%)	Present Value of Asset	Decline in Value during Year (Amortization Expense)
0	5	$2,638	3.7908	$10,000	—
1	4	2,638	3.1699	8,362	$ 1,638
2	3	2,638	2.4869	6,560	1,802
3	2	2,638	1.7355	4,578	1,982
4	1	2,638	.9091	2,398	2,180
5	0	—	—	0	2,398
Total amortization expense					$10,000

EXHIBIT 9-5 (continued)

Rate of Return Assuming Constant Asset Efficiency and Productivity					
			Period		
	1	2	3	4	5
Revenues	$ 2,638	$2,638	$2,638	$2,638	$2,638
Amortization expense	1,638	1,802	1,982	2,180	2,398
Income	$ 1,000	$ 836	$ 656	$ 458	$ 240
Net book value, beginning of period	$10,000	$8,362	$6,560	$4,578	$2,398
Rate of return (income/book value)	10%	10%	10%	10%	10%

As can be seen from the second part of the table, return on investment is constant at 10 percent (the discount rate). Were the assumed revenues (which indicate asset productivity) not constant, then a different amortization schedule would have to be developed. In such a schedule, as in the one shown, the amortization charges would be the differences in the present values of the expected cash receipts from one year to the next. Nevertheless, the return on investment would remain constant and be equal to the discount rate used to determine the present values.

ALLOCATION BASED ON HISTORICAL COSTS VERSUS MARKET VALUES

Advantages of Historical Costs

Each of the methods discussed so far is based on historical costs. The amount paid for an asset is allocated to the years it will be in service. As will be discussed (and was indicated in earlier chapters), there are many disadvantages to historical costs. The advantages, however, should be appreciated.

The historical costs to be allocated are objective. In the case of capital assets, they are transaction-based; the amount paid for an asset can be verified by its purchase documents. Total charges to amortization are equal to the net cost (cost less estimated salvage value, if any) of the asset. Resultant financial statements present a historical record based, at least initially, on verifiable arm's-length exchanges.

It is incontrovertible that financial statements based on historical costs do not provide *all* information required for investment or management decisions. It is doubtful, however, whether financial statements prepared on any single basis could do that. The use of historical costs by no means precludes the preparation and release of supplementary statements on other bases.

Limitations of Historical Costs

The limitations of historical costs with regard to capital assets are similar to the limitations of historical costs as applied to inventories, marketable securities, and other assets. But they are especially pronounced when applied to property, plant, and equipment, which have long lives and are slow to turn over. Hence (as with LIFO inventories) the gap between historical and market values is often substantial.

Insofar as the financial reports fail to account for changes in market values, *both* the balance sheet and the income statement may be of limited utility to managers as well as investors. The balance sheet fails to provide information on the total amount of resources available to management for which it should be held accountable. It serves inadequately, therefore, as a basis on which to determine the return generated by the assets. Corporate performance can be meaningfully measured only in current values—not historical values. Current values indicate the alternative uses to which the assets could be put—the amount for which they could be sold and the proceeds invested in other ventures.

"Stealth" Assets

Historical cost accounting permits firms to maintain a reserve of hidden values and profits. If market values exceed book values, then the corporation can capture additional income merely by selling off the understated assets.

Assets that have especially long lives, such as land and buildings, are the most likely to exhibit wide differences between market and book values. One business journal referred to corporate real estate as a "stealth" asset—its value hidden from all but insiders and a few savvy investors.[3] It pointed out that on their books the largest 500 U.S. companies own real estate worth $350 billion, but that is only a fraction of its potential yield. Under pressure to generate short-term gains, many companies sell their properties, fearing that if they do not do so, they will be acquired by corporate raiders who will use the assets as sources of immediate cash. In recent years, the financial press has contained any number of stories of companies that were acquired for their real estate rather than their worth as going concerns. Examples include bus companies, restaurant chains, and department stores whose main business segments were well past their prime, but whose land and buildings were in choice downtown locations.

Distorted Earnings

The historical cost-based income statement provides no information as to the market value of the services consumed as an asset is used. Amortization expense represents the cost of a portion of an asset's service potential. If the annual amortization charge is determined on the basis of outdated historical costs, then in a period in which market values exceed historical costs the charge will understate the market value of the services consumed. A reader of the financial report may be led to infer that the firm is being operated with greater efficiency (less cost) than is in fact the case.

Similarly, a naive manager may improperly conclude that one plant is more cost-effective than another. In fact, its lower costs may be the consequence of lower amortization charges, which are attributable to the use of older and less costly assets. If, however, the current market values of the assets are the same, then the value of resources consumed will also be the same, despite the differences in the accounting numbers assigned to them.

[3] "More Companies Are Living Off the Fat of Their Land," *Business Week*, November 7, 1988, p. 156.

The income statement also fails to provide information on the periodic increases in the value of assets (and thus of corporate net worth) over time. If income is to be a measure of how much "better off" a firm is from one period to the next, then changes in the amount for which assets could be bought or sold may be as important in determining income as actual exchange transactions. Decisions to hold or to sell capital assets may be critical to the long-run welfare of the company. Since historical cost-based income statements omit *holding* gains or losses until the assets are sold or retired, they fail to account for an important dimension of corporate performance.

One of the more telling ironies of the failure to recognize holding gains as they occur is that the reported earnings of airlines actually increase as the result of major air disasters. Airlines, of course, insure their planes for their market values, not their book values. When a plane crashes, the company collects from the insurance company the full market value of the lost plane. It recognizes a gain in the amount of the excess of insurance proceeds over book value. In fact, by virtue of its DC-10 disaster in 1979, American Airlines increased its earnings by $26 million—from $1.25 per share to $2.63 per share.

An Alternative Basis: Current Cost

There are several market-based substitutes for historical costs. One proposed alternative is *current cost.* The current cost of an asset can be one of two values. First, it can be the amount necessary to acquire an asset that is identical to the existing one. The asset would be of the same age and condition and hence have the same *service potential.* This value, called *current reproduction cost,* is easily available for assets (such as motor vehicles and many types of equipment) for which there is an active "used" market. Second, it can be the cost of a similar *new asset.* If this value, called *current replacement cost,* is used, it must be adjusted for any improvements in design and technology that make the new asset more productive than the old. From this cost must be deducted an allowance for amortization to reflect the portion of the existing asset already consumed.

Under a current cost system of asset valuation, income would incorporate not only an expense (amortization) indicative of asset consumption, but also a *holding* gain or loss based on the change in the asset's market value.

Current cost systems have the obvious advantage of reporting on the balance sheet values that are more useful than historical costs for most investment and management decisions. They are likely to be a better measure of an asset's earning potential from either continued use or sale. Current costs do *not* directly indicate the value of an asset to a particular user—that is, the present value of the cash flows that it will generate. The value of an asset to a company that uses it with unusual efficiency might far exceed the price at which it is being traded in current markets. Nevertheless, the price that independent purchasers are willing to pay would, in general, be a reasonable approximation of the present value of the anticipated services. Certainly it is likely to be a more reliable surrogate than historical cost.

Equally important, current cost systems result in an amortization charge that indicates the current value of resources consumed. Historical cost amortization, by contrast, is analogous to historical cost of goods sold, particularly that on a FIFO basis. It values resources expended based on prices that pertained in what might be the distant past.

The following example shows how current costs can be incorporated into the accounts.

Example

A company owns a building that originally cost $1.8 million when purchased 10 years ago. The building has an estimated useful life of 40 years and no salvage value. It is currently reflected on the balance sheet as follows:

Building	$1,800,000
Less: Accumulated amortization (10/40 of $1,800,000)	450,000
	$1,350,000

During each of the 10 years, amortization has been recorded with the conventional journal entry

Amortization expense	$45,000	
Accumulated amortization		$45,000
To record annual amortization expense		

Replacement cost has remained constant for the first 10 years of asset life.

At the end of this tenth year, however, due to increases in construction costs, the replacement cost of the building has increased by $300,000.

The following entry would recognize the increase in replacement cost:

Building	$300,000	
Accumulated amortization		$ 75,000
Realizable holding gain (gain from appreciation)		225,000
To record the increase in replacement cost		

The necessity for crediting accumulated amortization for $75,000 may not be obvious. The useful life of the building has not changed. Thus 25 percent of the building must still be considered as having been amortized, regardless of the value placed on it. The new value of the building is $2.1 million; hence 25 percent (10 years worth—$525,000) of replacement cost must be reported in the accumulated amortization account.

In each of the following 30 years, amortization would be recorded in the standard manner, except that the charge would be $\frac{1}{40}$ of $2.1 million:

Amortization expense	$52,500	
Accumulated amortization		$52,500
To record annual amortization expense		

This example is based on the assumption that there is no market for comparable used buildings. This is the reason for the use of replacement cost rather than reproduction cost. At year end the building will be reported at a net value of $1,575,000 (replacement cost of $2.1 million for a *new* building less accumulated amortization of $525,000). The amount, of course, is only an estimate of what would be required to obtain a comparable 10-year-old facility.

If there is a market for used assets, then the net value assigned to the building would be the market value of a 10-year-old asset. The net charge to income (amortization expense combined with the holding gain or loss) would equal the change in the value during the period.

Objections to Current Cost

A primary objection to the use of current costs is the difficulty of measuring them. Many assets are unique and market prices are not readily available. How, for example, would you determine the current cost of a tract of land? In some cases it may be possible to derive a value based on a recent purchase offer. In others, a reasonable value could be obtained by determining the amount for which similar tracts in the same neighbourhood have recently been sold or by using price indices that reflect a general increase in commercial real estate value. Consider the problem, however, of estimating the value of land on which Stelco Inc.'s Hamilton foundry is located. The tract of land comprises several square miles, and the industrial influence of the plant is felt for many miles around the plant. Whatever value (or lack of it) the surrounding land has is attributable to the steel-making activities of Stelco. It would be impossible to determine the value of the land either by looking at other recent offers (the plant is of such enormous value that it is reasonably certain that there have been few serious offers) or by looking at the sales prices of surrounding land (the Stelco land determines the value of the surrounding land, not the other way around). Current costs may be relevant for many decisions, but they are not often objectively determinable.

The difficulty of establishing current costs for some assets cannot be denied. But the issue that accountants face is whether an approximation, however subjective, of a useful value is to be preferred to an exact measure of a useless one. Current costs, even if arbitrary, convey information that is pertinent to many managerial and investment decisions. Historical values do not.

A second objection is that the firm may have no intention of either selling the assets or replacing them. Moreover, even if it were to dispose of the assets, it might replace them with ones that are more technologically advanced. The significance of information on amounts that are unlikely to be either paid or received is at best problematic.

The response to this objection is that current cost systems do not presuppose that firms intend to sell or replace their assets. Current values express the worth of resources within the command of an entity as measured by criteria of the marketplace, not the individual user. Value to the user, as discussed earlier, requires specification of the cash flows to be generated by the assets, either by sale or by use.

A third objection is that, regardless of theoretical merit, current values have not proved to be of concern to statement users. Perhaps, as implied in this chapter, they *should* use them. But apparently they do not. Thus it is questionable whether the cost of obtaining and gathering the data equals the benefit. This is the objection that was persuasive to the CICA. As discussed in Chapter 8 in relation to inventories, the *Handbook* at one time recommended extensive supplementary current value disclosures. Citing lack of interest, however, the CICA has since removed the recommendations from the *Handbook*.

Upon the retirement of an asset, either by sale or by abandonment, the asset *as well as the related accumulated amortization accounts* must be removed from the books. If the asset is sold for the amount and at the time originally estimated, then the retirement entry is especially simple.

Example

Return once again to the auto that originally cost $31,000 and had an estimated residual value after five years of $6,000. At the end of five years, the asset account would have a debit balance of $31,000 (regardless of the choice of amortization method), and the accumulated amortization account a credit balance of $25,000. If the asset is, in fact, sold for $6,000, then the appropriate journal entry would be

```
Cash ...................................................................................... $ 6,000
Accumulated amortization, automobiles ........................................   25,000
    Automobiles ......................................................................          $31,000
    To record the sale of the automobile
```

If, at any time during its life, the asset is either sold or abandoned for an amount greater or less than its book value, then a gain or loss on retirement would have to be recognized.

Example

The firm had charged amortization on the auto using straightline amortization. At the end of three years, after $15,000 of amortization had been charged, the firm sold the auto for $12,000. The book value of the asset at time of sale would have been $16,000 (i.e., $31,000 less $15,000). Hence the firm has suffered a loss of $4,000:

```
Cash ...................................................................................... $12,000
Accumulated amortization, automobiles ........................................   15,000
Loss on disposal ......................................................................    4,000
    Automobiles ......................................................................          $31,000
    To record the sale of the automobile
```

Bear in mind that if an asset is sold anytime before the close of the year, amortization for the portion of the year that the asset was actually held must first be recorded before any gain or loss on disposal can be computed.

The nature of gains or losses on retirement merits comment. Such gains or losses arise only because a company may not have perfect foresight when it acquires the asset as to the time of retirement and the residual value. If it had such foresight, it would determine its amortization schedule accordingly and hence there would be no gain or loss upon retirement.

In the previous example, the $4,000 loss on retirement indicates that insufficient amortization of $1,333 per year for the three years that the asset was held had been charged. If the firm had known that it would sell the asset (that cost $31,000) for $12,000 after using it for three years, then it would have allocated $19,000 of asset cost ($31,000 cost less $12,000 salvage value) to the three years—instead of the $15,000 actually allocated. Annual amortization expense would thereby have been $6,333 instead of $5,000.

Proper accounting might therefore dictate that, rather than recognize a loss on retirement in the year of sale, the company should correct the earnings of the prior years for the insufficient amortization charges. This type of correction would reduce retained earnings without burdening reported income in the year of retirement. In practice, such an approach is not permitted because it would require an excessive number of prior adjustments and thereby complicate the process of financial reporting. The CICA requires that the effects of changes in any accounting estimates (of which useful life and residual value are two) be accounted for in the year of the change.[4]

TRADE-INS

A special problem is presented when a firm *trades in* an old asset for a new one. For example, a firm surrenders an old car, plus cash, for a newer model. One convenient way of handling a trade-in is to view it as two separate transactions. In the first, the old asset is sold—not for cash but for a *trade-in allowance*. In the second, the new asset is purchased—for cash plus the trade-in allowance. The critical step in implementing such a procedure lies in determining the price for which the old asset was sold. In many instances, the amount that the dealership says it is offering as a trade-in allowance bears no relationship to the actual fair market value of the old asset. In the auto industry, for example, it is common for new car dealers to offer unusually high trade-in allowances on the used vehicles of prospective new car purchasers. If purchasers accept the high trade-in allowance, they may be unable to avail themselves of discounts that are generally granted to purchasers who come without used cars. They may, in effect, have to pay full, or nearly full, *sticker* price for the new car, something they would not ordinarily have to do if they came to the dealer without an old car to trade.

If a meaningful gain or loss on retirement is to be computed, it is essential therefore that the company determine as accurately as possible the actual fair market value of the asset given up. This amount, regardless of representations by the dealer, is the true trade-in allowance. It can usually be derived—or at least estimated—by consulting industry publications, such as the car dealers' "blue book" of used car prices, or by obtaining data on transactions involving similar assets.

Example

The auto which originally cost $31,000 (estimated life of five years, $6,000 salvage value) is traded in for a new car after three years. The dealer grants a trade-in allowance of $18,000, but according to a book of used car prices, the car is worth no more than $13,000. The true trade-in allowance is therefore only $13,000. Correspondingly, the sticker price of the new car is $41,000 but,

[4] "Accounting Changes," Section 1506.25, *CICA Handbook*, 1991.

in fact, an astute buyer would not normally pay more than $36,000. In addition to giving up its old car, the company pays cash of $23,000, thereby surrending cash and a car with a total value of $36,000 ($13,000 + $23,000).

The book value of the old car, assuming straight-line amortization, would, at the time of trade-in, be

Original cost	$31,000
Accumulated amortization (3 years × $5,000)	15,000
Book value	$16,000

Loss on the sale of the old car would therefore be $16,000 less $13,000 (fair market value of the old car), or $3,000.

The "sale" of the old car could be recorded as follows:

(a)

Loss on retirement	$ 3,000	
Accumulated amortization, automobiles (old)	15,000	
Trade-in allowance (a temporary account)	13,000	
Automobiles (old)		$31,000
To record the "sale" of the old automobile		

The entry to record the purchase of the new auto would be

(b)

Automobiles (new)	$36,000	
Cash		$23,000
Trade-in allowance		13,000
To record the purchase of the new automobile		

Clearly, the two entries could be combined (and the trade-in allowance account eliminated).

This method of accounting for trade-ins allows the new asset to be recorded at its fair market value, which is equal to the cash price that an independent buyer would have to pay. At the same time, it permits the gain or loss on retirement of the old asset to be based upon its fair market value. It thereby gives recognition to the economic substance of the transaction, regardless of what amounts the buyer and seller arbitrarily assign to the trade-in allowance and the price of the new asset.

The transaction just illustrated resulted in a reported loss on retirement. If, however, application of the accounting procedure described had resulted in a *gain* rather than a loss, then the new asset would be recorded at an amount equal to the sum of

1. The book value (cost less accumulated amortization) of the old asset
2. Any additional cash paid for the new asset

Suppose, for example, a firm were to exchange the old auto having a book value of $16,000 (cost $31,000, accumulated amortization $15,000) plus cash of $15,500 for a new auto that has a fair market value of $36,000.

These facts imply that the old auto had a market value of $20,500 inasmuch as the dealer was willing to accept it plus $15,500 cash for a new auto worth $36,000. Since the book value of the old auto was only $16,000, the trade-in resulted in an economic gain of $4,500. Nevertheless, the following entry would be in order:

Accumulated amortization, automobiles (old)	$15,000	
Automobiles (new)	31,500	
Automobiles (old)		$31,000
Cash		15,500

To record trade-in of automobile

The entry gives no recognition to either the fair market value of the new asset or the obvious economic difference at the time of the trade between the fair market value and the book value of the old asset. The new balance in the automobile account would be amortized over the useful life of the new auto. The reason for the inconsistent treatment between the gain and loss situation is another example of conservatism.

The different treatment for gains and losses applies only to trades of similar assets—an auto for an auto, for example, but not an auto for a computer. The trading of similar assets suggests that the earnings process has not yet been completed. In the auto example, additional cash is simply being expended to keep an auto (albeit a different one) in service. It is reasonable, therefore, that the new asset be carried at old book value plus any additional cash expended. If the trade is for a dissimilar asset, it is assumed that the earnings process of the old asset is complete and the resultant gain or loss should be recognized. In the past there has been some abuse in the reporting of trades of similar assets. Firms in some industries, such as utilities, were exchanging assets whose market values exceeded their book values. These trades enabled the utilities to report increases in both the book values of their assets and in annual amortization charges. The higher amortization charges (a noncash expense) could then be passed on to customers in the form of increased rates.

The contrast between the two methods is another reminder that many current accounting issues can be attributed to the practice of reporting assets on the basis of historical cost rather than market value. If the reported value of an asset were periodically increased to reflect changes in market conditions, then at the time of retirement or trade there would be little need to recognize a gain or a loss. The reported value of the asset would be nearly identical to the amount for which it could be sold or traded.

PLANT AND EQUIPMENT TURNOVER

The efficiency with which plant and equipment is utilized may be measured by the *plant and equipment turnover ratio,* determined by comparing sales to average book value (cost less accumulated amortization) of plant and equipment:

$$\text{Plant and equipment turnover} = \frac{\text{Sales}}{\text{Average property, plant, and equipment}}$$

For example, Sun Ice Limited in 1994 had average property, plant, and equipment (in thousands) of $4,477 (the average of the beginning balance of $4,842 and the ending balance of $4,111) and sales for the year were $15,130. The balance sheet of Sun Ice Limited presented in Chapter 7 does not give a breakdown of the capital assets number. However, a note to the Sun Ice Limited financial statements indicates that all of the capital assets are property, plant, and equipment and there are no intangible assets. Therefore, the capital assets balance is used for property, plant, and equipment in calculating the plant and equipment turnover ratio.

$$\text{Plant and equipment turnover} = \frac{\$15,130}{\$4,477} = 3.4 \text{ times}$$

The greater the turnover ratio, the more efficiently plant and equipment are being employed. In years when sales are down and physical facilities are not being used to capacity, the ratio will decline. In years when sales are up and the plant is being used to the fullest extent possible, the ratio will increase.

Although plant and equipment are conventionally stated in the ratio at book values, there is no reason why market values could not be used instead. Indeed, if management is concerned with comparing asset utilization among plants of different ages, then market values may provide a more appropriate measure of the resources over which plant executives have stewardship.

NATURAL RESOURCES AND AMORTIZATION

Natural resources, or *wasting assets,* as they are often referred to, are accounted for in a manner similar to property, plant, and equipment. They are recorded initially at acquisition cost, and this value is subsequently reduced as service potential declines.

Units of Output Basis

Like other capital assets, the process of allocating the cost of natural resources over the periods in which they provide benefits is known as *amortization.* The service potential of natural resources can ordinarily be measured more meaningfully in terms of quantity of production (such as tonnes or barrels) than number of years. Hence amortization is generally charged on a units of output basis. As mentioned earlier in the chapter, the old terminology for allocating the cost of natural resources was *depletion.* The word depletion was related to the fact that the natural resource was being used up, or depleted, as it provided its benefit (i.e., the sale of the product). The *units of output* basis may also be used as a method of amortization for property, plant, and equipment where the service potential of the property, plant, and equipment is better estimated in terms of output, rather than time. In fact, it might be argued that the straight-line method of amortization is simply an approximation of the units of output basis where it is assumed that the expected output of the asset will be relatively constant over its expected life. As with other types of long-lived assets, the initial cost of a natural resource may be reported on the balance sheet for as long as it is in service. The accumulated amortization may be indicated in a contra account. In practice, however, a contra account is not always used; often the balance in the natural resource account itself is reduced directly by the amount of the accumulated amortization.

Example

A firm purchases mining properties for $2 million cash. It estimates that the properties will yield 400,000 usable tonnes of ore. During the first year of production, the firm mines 5,000 tonnes.

The following entry would be appropriate to record the purchase of the properties:

```
Mineral deposits ...................................................................... $2,000,000
        Cash ...........................................................................................        $2,000,000
    To record the purchase of the ore deposit
```

Since the deposit will yield an estimated 400,000 tonnes of usable ore, cost assignable to each tonne is

$$\frac{\$2,000,000}{400,000 \text{ tonnes}} = \$5 \text{ per tonne}$$

Amortization cost of the first year is

$$5,000 \text{ (tonnes mined)} \times \$5 \text{ per tonne} = \$25,000$$

The entry to record the amortization would be

```
Amortization cost .......................................................................... $25,000
        Accumulated amortization, mineral deposits .......................................        $25,000
    To record first-year amortization
```

After the first year, the mineral deposits would be reported on the balance sheet as

Mineral deposits	$2,000,000
Less: Accumulated amortization	25,000
	$1,975,000

Amortization of mineral deposits is a cost of production, to be added along with other production costs (labour, amortization of equipment, supplies) to the carrying value of the minerals inventory. It should be charged as an expense (cost of minerals sold) in the accounting period in which the inventory is sold and the revenue from the sale is recognized.

Amortization of Location-Specific Equipment

A mining or drilling company may have to purchase or build equipment or structures that can be used only in connection with the recovery of a specific deposit. If the structures or equipment will be used for as long as the property continues to be exploited (and only so long), then amortization charges should logically be determined using the same units of output basis as used to compute depletion.

Suppose, for example, that mining equipment costs $80,000 and can be used exclusively at a site with estimated ore content of 400,000 tonnes. Amortization would be charged at a rate of 20 cents per tonne mined ($80,000 divided by 400,000 tonnes) regardless of useful life in terms of years.

If in the first year of operation 50,000 tonnes were mined, the amortization charge would be $10,000 (50,000 tonnes @ 20 cents per tonne). Amortization, if based on output, is more likely in such circumstances to assure that the cost of equipment or structures is matched with the revenues realized from the sale of the minerals than if based on useful life in terms of time.

INTANGIBLE ASSETS AND DEFERRED CHARGES

Intangible assets are those assets characterized by the rights, privileges, and benefits of possession rather than by physical existence. Examples of intangible assets are patents, copyrights, trademarks, licences, goodwill, and franchises. Often the service potential of intangible assets is uncertain and exceedingly difficult to measure. As a consequence, intangible assets frequently are the subject of controversy.

Closely related to intangible assets are deferred charges. *Deferred charges* are expenditures not recognized as an expense of the period in which incurred but carried forward as assets to be written off in future periods. Examples of deferred charges that are categorized as long-term assets (because they will be written off over a period greater than one year) are certain product development costs, organization costs, costs of drilling unsuccessful oil wells, and store preopening costs. The distinction between intangible assets and deferred charges is at best vague; in fact, deferred charges can be considered as a type of intangible asset. The basic accounting principles and issues pertaining to them are the same.

In this section we shall deal with only a few selected intangibles and deferred charges. But the principles and issues set forth can be generalized to a wide range of other assets with similar characteristics. (A discussion of goodwill, one of the more controversial intangible assets, will be deferred until the chapter pertaining to ownership interests among corporations, since goodwill conventionally arises only out of the acquisition of one company by another.)

Intangibles are considered to be assets either because they represent rights to future benefits or because the expenditures that were made to acquire or develop them will benefit a number of accounting periods in the future. Hence the costs must be allocated to the periods in which the benefits will be realized.

Intangibles are recorded initially at their acquisition or development costs. The costs are then amortized over (allocated to) the periods in which the benefits will accrue. The general accounting approach to intangibles may be illustrated with respect to copyrights.

Copyrights

A *copyright* is an exclusive right, granted by law, to publish, sell, reproduce, or otherwise control a literary, musical, or artistic work. Canadian copyright law specifies this exclusive right to last for the life of the creator plus 50 years. The cost to secure a copyright from the federal government is minimal; however, the cost to purchase one from its holder on a work that has proved successful— on a best-selling novel or musical recording, for instance—may be substantial.

If a firm were to purchase a copyright, it would record it initially as it would any other asset. Assuming a cost of $20,000, for example, an appropriate journal entry might be

Copyright	$20,000	
Cash		$20,000

To record the purchase of the copyright

If the remaining useful life was 10 years, then the following entry would be appropriate each year to record amortization:

Amortization expense	$2,000	
Accumulated amortization, copyrights		$2,000

To record annual amortization of copyright

Accounting practices as to copyrights focus attention on a question that is raised with many intangibles—that of the number of years over which cost should be amortized. Although the legal life of a copyright may be firmly established, the copyright may be of significant economic value for a considerably shorter period of time. Actual useful life may depend on a multitude of factors such as public taste, critical acclaim, or future success of the author, none of which can readily be assessed. As with other long-lived assets, carrying value of the assets as well as amortization charges (the periodic decline in value) must be based, in large measure, on subjective judgments of corporate management and accountants.

Costs of Drilling Unsuccessful Oil Wells

Accounting practices in the oil and gas industry raise other important issues relating to intangible assets. What is the nature of the costs to be included as part of the asset? How directly must a cost be associated with a future benefit before it should properly be capitalized? How broadly should an asset be defined?

Despite highly sophisticated geological survey techniques, it is usually necessary for oil and gas companies, in their search for new reserves, to drill unsuccessfully in several locations before actually striking oil or gas. Obviously, the cost of drilling the productive wells should be capitalized and amortized over the years during which oil or gas will be withdrawn from the ground. But what about the costs of drilling the dry holes? Should they be written off as incurred, or should they also be capitalized and amortized over the period in which oil is withdrawn from the successful wells? Should they be considered losses (corporate errors in a sense) as opposed to expenditures that are statistically necessary to discover the productive locations? The dry holes may produce no direct benefits to the company, but they are an inevitable cost of finding the productive wells.

If an asset is defined narrowly as a single hole, then there would be little justification for capitalizing the dry hole. It clearly has no future service potential. But if the asset is defined more broadly as an entire oil field, then the dry hole can be interpreted as an element of cost required to bring the field to a serviceable state.

The two methods that have been used to account for the costs associated with unsuccessful prospects (dry holes) are called the *full cost* method and the *successful efforts* method. Full cost accounting includes the costs of the dry holes in the cost of the oil and gas properties. Successful efforts accounting only adds the costs incurred drilling successful wells to the cost of the oil and gas properties; outlays associated with unsuccessful drilling efforts are charged as expenses as soon as it is concluded that the efforts at a particular location are a failure.

Either method of accounting for dry holes is acceptable in Canada, as long as the method selected is applied consistently to all oil and gas properties. In the United States, both methods were used until 1977, when the FASB mandated the use of the successful efforts method. The result of this accounting policy change will be examined in the following section.

Economic Consequences of Accounting Methods in Establishing Drilling Costs

The use of one method rather than the other has no direct economic consequences for a firm. It has no impact on tax liabilities; as with amortization, the allowable tax deductions are independent of the method used for reporting. It has no effect on either the amount of proven reserves or their anticipated selling prices. Reported earnings, of course, would differ, but because the firm is required to disclose the method used, knowledgeable analysts can easily convert earnings to the other basis. One might think therefore that a standard that prescribed one method rather than the other would generate neither controversy nor emotion. In fact, however, it did.

In 1977, the Financial Accounting Standards Board, in *Statement No. 19,* prescribed that all firms must use *only* the *successful efforts* method. The decision of the FASB was a source of consternation to those firms that had been using the full cost method and the federal agencies concerned with administering the antitrust statutes. The full cost method had been used by many small exploration firms. The switch to the successful efforts method resulted, at least in the short run, in reductions in their reported earnings because the costs of unsuccessful wells were written off in the year of failure rather than over a number of succeeding years. The small firms argued that the reduction in reported earnings would make them less attractive to investors and lenders and thereby less able to acquire the capital necessary to compete with the giants of the industry, many of which were already using the successful efforts method. The FASB and its defenders, however, asserted that fears of reduced competition were groundless because the change would affect only *reported* earnings. In terms of economic wealth—the present value of actual oil and gas reserves—the firms would be neither better nor worse off merely because they made use of one accounting method rather than another.

The Securities and Exchange Commission (SEC) failed to support the directive of the FASB that mandated the use of the successful efforts method. It took the position that both the successful efforts and the full cost methods were deficient because they failed to provide adequate information on the economic worth of the oil and gas reserves that had been discovered. The SEC proposed that a third method, *reserve recognition accounting*, be developed. The new method required that proven reserves be reported at the present value of the cash flows that they were likely to generate. It required firms not only to estimate the quantities of oil and gas in their fields, but also to make assumptions as to the prices at which they would be sold and the cost of lifting them from the ground.

Due in large measure to the difficulties of making the necessary estimates, reserve recognition accounting never gained the support of firms in the oil industry, and eventually the SEC abandoned efforts to impose it upon them. In light of the initial opposition to successful efforts accounting on the part of the SEC, the FASB suspended the key provisions of *FAS 19*. Since 1982, firms can use either the full cost or the successful efforts method but must disclose the extent of their reserves.

Accounting researchers have conducted several studies as to whether the small firms were correct in asserting that the lower earnings resulting from the successful efforts method would increase their cost of capital. The results have been mixed, with no clear answer as to whether, in fact, there are indirect economic consequences of choice of accounting method.

Research and Development Costs

Accounting procedures for research and development costs are illustrative of an additional issue common to intangible assets: To what extent must theoretical concepts of intangible assets be tempered by "practical" considerations? Research and development costs are, by nature, incurred to benefit future accounting periods. Expenditures for research and development are made with the expectation that they will lead to new or improved products or processes that will in turn increase revenues or decrease expenses. The matching concept suggests that research and development costs be capitalized as intangible assets and amortized over the periods in which the additional revenues are generated or cost savings effected.

In practice, however, it has proved exceedingly difficult to match specific expenditures for research and development with specific products or processes. Some expenditures are for basic research; they are not intended to produce direct benefits. Others produce no benefits at all or result in benefits which could not have been foreseen at the time they were incurred.

The CICA has chosen to address the problem by separating development costs from research costs, and accounting for each differently. The relevant definitions of the terms are as follows:

> *Research is planned investigation undertaken with the hope of gaining new scientific or technical knowledge and understanding. Such investigation may or may not be directed towards a specific practical aim or application.*

> *Development is the translation of research findings or other knowledge into a plan or design for new or substantially improved materials, devices, products, processes, systems or services prior to the commencement of commercial production or use.*[5]

Research costs are to be charged to expense as incurred whereas development costs, when certain criteria are met, should be deferred and amortized as associated revenues are realized. For development costs to qualify for deferral, the product must be technically feasible, the costs must be identifiable, management must intend to market the product, there must be a clearly defined market for the product, and resources must exist to complete the development. Obviously, these criteria are subject to different interpretations and there will be some lack of uniformity in reporting. However, there is at least some attempt to match costs with

[5] "Research and Development Costs," Section 3450.02, *CICA Handbook*, 1985.

the associated revenues. In the United States, the FASB decided to get uniformity of reporting, at the expense of proper matching, as noted below.

The FASB, in *Statement No. 2* (1974), prescribed that expenditures for most types of research and development costs be charged to expense in the year incurred rather than capitalized as intangible assets. The board was motivated by the great variety of practice among corporations as to the nature of costs that were capitalized and the number of periods over which they were amortized. Given almost unlimited flexibility in accounting for research and development, some firms capitalized costs that were unlikely to provide future benefits; others wrote off large amounts of previously capitalized costs in carefully selected periods so as to avoid burdening other accounting periods with amortization charges.

As a consequence of the board's actions, uniformity of accounting practice among companies has been enhanced. But research and development costs must now be charged as an expense as if they benefit but a single accounting period. And the period in which they are to be charged off—that in which they are incurred—is that which is, in fact, least likely to benefit from the expenditures, since research and development costs are almost always future- rather than present-oriented.

The approach of the board is inconsistent with the concept that costs should be matched to the revenues with which they are associated. It substitutes a precise accounting rule for the professional judgment of managers and accountants. It can hardly be viewed as an ideal solution to the accounting problems related to intangibles. But the board's approach does represent an attempt to ensure greater consistency among firms and to eliminate abusive reporting practices.

Start-Up Costs

A problem common to numerous industries is how to account for start-up costs. *Start-up costs* are outlays incurred prior to the point at which a venture is fully operational.

The issues pertaining to start-up costs are further demonstrative of the practical difficulties of applying the matching concept. The matching concept requires that costs be charged as expenses in the same period as the revenues that they generate are recognized. Start-up costs are incurred before the revenues that they are expected to generate are earned. Therefore they should be recorded as assets and amortized over the periods to be benefited by them. But there is seldom a direct link between the start-up costs and the anticipated revenues. Hence it is almost never obvious what outlays should be capitalized and over how many periods they should be charged as expenses.

The examples that follow show how start-up costs are dealt with in two specific industries.

Retail Industry

Prior to the opening of a new store, retail chains incur costs of site selection, rent, advertising, stocking shelves, and training new employees. Since the store produces no revenues before it opens, the costs will provide benefits only in periods thereafter.

There are no specific authoritative pronouncements as to how preopening costs should be accounted for, and practice in the industry is diverse.

Some chains charge preopening costs to expense in the year incurred. This policy is conservative and convenient (the company avoids having to account for the costs for over more than one period), but it otherwise has little to recommend it. It is contrary to the matching principle, since expenses are charged in periods before revenues are earned. Other chains (e.g., Mark's Work Wearhouse Ltd., the Calgary-based retailer of workwear and casual wear) capitalize the preopening costs and charge them to expense in their entirety in the year in which the store is opened. Still others (e.g., Canadian Tire Corporation, Limited) capitalize the costs and amortize them over an arbitrary period, such as three years.

Cable Television Industry

Cable television firms can expect cash outflows to exceed cash inflows for some time after they initiate service in a new market. They must incur costs not only for the capital equipment required to receive and transmit signals, but also for advertising, promotion, general administration, and programming. Many of their costs are "fixed"; they do not vary significantly, regardless of the number of subscribers.

Some types of start-up costs will be incurred in their entirety before revenue is earned from the first subscriber. But others will continue even after the system goes on line. Most cable companies can expect to incur cash deficits until a target number of subscribers have been signed up and the system is operating at a specific level of capacity.

There is no question that equipment costs should be capitalized in full and amortized over their expected useful lives. But advertising, promotion, general administration, and programming costs, especially those incurred after the system goes on line, are usually considered period costs. They are commonly expensed as incurred. When service is extended to a new area, however, they are clearly intended to benefit the future, not the present. Should they nevertheless be expensed as incurred, or should they be capitalized? And if they are to be capitalized, then how should the start-up costs that will benefit the future be distinguished from the normal operating costs that will benefit only the present? What is an acceptable length for the start-up period? Over how many years should the costs that have been capitalized be amortized?

There are no official pronouncements in this area for Canada. In the United States, however, the Financial Accounting Standards Board responded to diversity of practice within the industry by establishing arbitrary (though seemingly quite reasonable) guidelines.[6] The guidelines require a cable firm to establish a "prematurity" period of not more than two years when it begins service to a new geographic area. During the period, "subscriber-related and general and administrative expenses" must be expensed as incurred. Programming and other system costs (including property taxes and costs of renting equipment) must be allocated between current and future operations. The portion allocated to current operations must be expensed as incurred; the remainder capitalized and amortized over the same period used to amortize the main cable television plant. The allocation must be based on a formula developed by the board that relates current to anticipated number of subscribers.

[6] "Financial Reporting by Cable Television Companies," Financial Accounting Standards Board *Statement of Financial Accounting Standards No. 51,* 1981.

Summary

Long-lived assets are used over a number of accounting periods. They are recorded initially at *acquisition cost,* which is the amount necessary to bring them to a serviceable condition. Interest, whether implicit or explicit, is generally excluded from acquisition cost but may be included in that of certain long-term construction projects. Subsequent to acquisition, costs of *betterments,* but not of repairs and maintenance, must be added to initial cost.

Because long-lived assets provide services over more than one period, their costs must be allocated to all the periods that benefit from them. The process of allocation is referred to as *amortization.* Among the several basic methods of allocation are *straight-line, sum-of-the-years'-digits, declining balance,* and *units of output.* An additional method, *compound interest,* provides insight into the economic benefits of assets. However, unlike the others, it results in increasing charges and for that reason is seldom used in practice.

Long-lived assets are reported at historical cost, less the allowance representing the portion of services consumed. This value has the virtue of being based on actual transactions in which the firm engaged but does not provide information that is useful for investment or management decisions. Market values, by contrast, provide more relevant information but must be based on transactions external to the firm.

When an asset is sold at an amount that differs from its book value, a gain or loss must be recognized. This gain or loss results because the firm did not have perfect foresight and failed to correctly predict useful life or residual value.

Regardless of how a long-lived asset is accounted for—its basis of amortization, the estimates of useful life and salvage value, whether changes in market values are recognized—its impact on reported earnings over its entire useful life will be the same. The total cost—the amount to be charged as an expense—will be the price paid less the amount received when it is sold or retired. "Only" the allocations of costs among periods will differ. It is because financial statements must be prepared periodically—and income for each individual period determined—that long-lived assets are the cause of as many issues and controversies as they are.

Exercise for Review and Self-Testing

Airline Freight acquires a cargo plane. The company pays $4 million cash and gives the seller marketable securities with a fair value of $500,000. The company incurs additional costs of $6,000 to have the plane delivered to its home airport and $94,000 to have it fitted with special equipment. The firm plans to keep the plane for 10 years; it estimates that it will be able to sell the cargo plane at the end of 10 years for $900,000.

1. At what amount should the plane be initially recorded?

2. What is the total dollar amount to be allocated as amortization expense over the period during which the plane will be in service?

3. What should be the charge for amortization for each of the 10 years of useful life if the firm were to use the straight-line method?

---

4. What should be the charge for amortization for each of the first three years of useful life if the firm were to use the double declining balance method?

5. Suppose that the firm used the double declining balance method and that at the end of the seventh year of useful life the book value of the plane was $964,690—that is, amortization of $3,635,310 had been charged to date. How much amortization should the firm charge in the eighth year of service? How much in the ninth? Be sure your answers are consistent with your response to part 2.

6. Suppose that after the third year of using the plane the company elected to trade in the old plane for a new one. The company paid $7 million cash for the new plane and surrendered the old cargo plane. Immediately prior to the trade, the firm had received offers from parties who were willing to buy the plane outright. All were willing to pay approximately $1.5 million cash. At the time of the trade, the old plane had a book value of $2,355,200 (initial cost less accumulated amortization of $2,244,800) based on use of the double declining balance method. How much gain or loss should the firm report on the transaction? At what amount should it record the new plane?

Questions for Review and Discussion

1. "Because capital assets are stated on the *balance sheet* at values that are based on historical costs, the *income statement* is of limited value in evaluating corporate performance." Do you agree? Explain.

2. What is the value of an asset to a particular user? Why is it seldom feasible to measure the value of a capital asset to a particular user?

3. It is generally agreed that market values of capital assets are more relevant than are historical values for decisions that must be made by both investors and managers. Why, then, do accountants persist in reporting historical values?

4. A company recently purchased for $350,000 a parcel of land and a building with the intention of razing the building and using the land as a parking lot for employees. The land had an appraised value of $300,000 and the building, $50,000. The company incurred costs of $10,000 to remove the building. The firm recorded the parking lot on its books at $360,000. Can such value be justified?

5. A company purchased a parcel of land for $100,000, but was permitted by the seller to delay payment for one year with no additional interest charges. The prime lending rate at the time was 12 percent per year. Do you think that the company should record the land at $100,000 or at a greater or lesser amount? Explain.

6. The term *reserve* for amortization is sometimes used instead of *accumulated* amortization. Some managers point out that it is essential that firms, through the process of amortization, make periodic additions to such

reserve to make certain that they have the wherewithal to replace assets when they must be retired. Explain why (or why not) amortization assures that a firm will have sufficient resources to acquire new assets as old ones wear out.

7. "Accelerated methods of amortization are generally preferable to the straight-line method because most assets decline in market value more rapidly in the early years of their useful lives than in later years." Do you agree?

8. A taxi company owns a fleet of several vehicles. The president of the company recently observed that the older cabs seemed to be more efficient than the newer ones. He based his conclusion on "return on investment," per vehicle, which he calculated by dividing net revenues (revenues minus expenses, including amortization) by beginning net book value. The firm uses the straight-line method to compute amortization. What might be an explanation, other than greater efficiency, for the older assets providing the greater return on investment?

9. A company incurred $1 million in advertising costs for radio and television ads broadcast during the year. It elected to *capitalize* such costs as an intangible asset and charge them off as expenses over a five-year period. Such practice is *not* in accord with generally accepted accounting principles. What arguments might the firm make, however, in defence of the practice? Why do you suppose that such practice is not generally accepted?

10. As an executive of a firm with two manufacturing plants, you are required to evaluate the efficiency with which the managers of the plants utilize the resources within their control. One criterion by which you judge is plant and equipment turnover. The two plants are of substantially different ages. In computing turnover, why might you find it advantageous to state property, plant, and equipment at market rather than book values?

Problems

1. *Amortization, regardless of the method used, is a means of allocating the cost of an asset over its productive life.*

   The Valentine Construction Corp. purchased a crane for $180,000. The company planned to keep it for approximately five years, after which time it believed it could sell it for $30,000.
   a. Determine amortization expense under each of the following methods for each of the first four years that the crane is in service:
      (1) Straight-line
      (2) Sum-of-the-years'-digits
      (3) Double declining balance
   b. At the start of the fifth year the company sold the crane for $66,000. Determine the gain on retirement under each of the three amortization methods.
   c. Determine for each of the methods the net impact on earnings (total amortization charges less gain on retirement) of using the crane for the four-year period.

2. *Costs incurred at the end of an asset's useful life may be associated with revenues of previous accounting periods.*

   National Auto Company agrees to participate as a major exhibitor at the North American Trade Fair. The company constructs and furnishes its exhibit hall at a cost of $8 million. The fair will last for three years, after which National Auto will be required to remove its building from the fairgrounds. National estimates that removal costs will be approximately $100,000 but that the building materials and the exhibits can be sold for $300,000.

   a. Record the construction of the exhibit hall on the books of National Auto. Assume all payments are made in cash.

   b. Calculate first-year amortization expense using the straight-line method.

   c. Record the removal of the exhibit hall at the completion of the fair. Assume that removal costs are as estimated.

   d. Suppose instead that removal costs were estimated to be approximately $700,000 and that the building materials and exhibits could be sold for $300,000. Prepare journal entries to record the construction of the exhibit hall, to account for the hall during the three-year period, and to remove it from the books after the three-year period. Over how many periods should the removal costs (net of the amount to be salvaged) be charged as an expense?

3. *The useful life of one asset may depend upon that of another.*

   The James Co. purchases a small plant for $2.5 million. The plant has an estimated useful life of 25 years with no salvage value. Included in the plant is specialized climate-control equipment. At the time of purchase the company is aware that the remaining useful life of the equipment is 15 years. The firm estimates the value of the equipment to be $250,000.

   a. Record the purchase of the plant.

   b. Record amortization on a straight-line basis during the first year.

   c. At the end of 15 years the climate-control equipment requires replacement, and the firm purchases new equipment for $400,000. The estimated useful life of the new equipment is also 15 years.

   (1) Record the replacement of the old equipment with the new.

   (2) Record amortization during the sixteenth year.

   (3) Over how many years did you decide to amortize the new equipment? What assumptions did you make?

4. *Periodic maintenance costs that benefit more than one accounting period may be accounted for in at least two different ways.*

   Treetop Airlines conducts maintenance overhauls on all aircraft engines every three years. The cost of each overhaul is approximately $100,000. The company owns 24 engines. In 1996 the company overhauls 10 engines; in 1997, 8 engines; and in 1998, 6 engines.

   a. How much expense should the company report in 1998 in connection with engine overhauls?

   b. A financial report of one of Canada's major airlines indicates that "expenditures for major flight equipment overhauls are charged to income (as incurred)." Is the policy of this airline consistent with your response in part (a)? If it is, can you think of, and justify, an alternative policy that might be as acceptable or even preferable? If it is not, then defend your response.

c. Suppose instead that it was company practice to overhaul eight engines each year. Would it matter, as far as reported expense is concerned, which accounting procedure the company used?

5. *It is often unclear whether certain types of costs are necessary to bring an asset to a serviceable condition.*

On January 2, National General Corporation purchased for $20,000 an *option* on a tract of land on which it hoped to construct a plant. The option gave the company the right to purchase the land itself within a given time period and for a fixed price—in this case within 10 months and for $2 million. If the company decided to exercise its option, it would pay the seller an additional $2 million and receive title to the land. If it decided not to purchase the land, then it would let the option lapse and would be unable to recover the $20,000. The option arrangement allows the company additional time to decide whether to make the purchase and at the same time compensates the seller for giving the company the exclusive right to purchase the property.

a. On July 2, National General decided to purchase the tract of land for $2 million. Prepare journal entries to record both the purchase of the option and the subsequent purchase of the land. Should the cost of the option be added to the cost of the land?

b. Suppose instead that on January 2, National General purchased three options—each for $20,000—on three tracts of land. The company expected to purchase and build on only one of the three tracts; however, it wanted to locate its new plant by the side of a proposed highway, and the exact route of the highway had not yet been announced. The company purchased the three options in order to assure itself that the plant could be built adjacent to the road, regardless of which of three routes under consideration was selected for the highway. On July 2, the company exercised its option on one of the three tracts and purchased the land for $2 million. It allowed the other two options to lapse. Prepare journal entries to record the purchase of the three options, the purchase of the land, and the expiration of two of the options. Consider carefully whether the cost of all three options should be included as part of the cost of the land. Present arguments both for and against including the expired options as part of the cost of the land.

6. *The impact on earnings of both alternative amortization practices and errors may depend upon a firm's trend of growth.*

Collins Manufacturing Corporation, established in 1990, uses 15 lathes, each of which costs $20,000 and has a useful life of three years (with no residual value). Each year the company retires five machines and replaces them with five others.

a. Compute total amortization charges on the 15 lathes for the three-year period 1996, 1997, and 1998 using
   (1) The straight-line method
   (2) The double declining balance method

b. Suppose the company used an incorrect useful life in calculating amortization charges. Even though it replaced the machines after a three-year period, it charged amortization over a two-year period. It made no adjustments in the accounts for the "error"; it simply charged zero amortization in the machines' third year. Compute amortization using the straight-line method for the same three-year period.

c. In 1999 the company undertook an expansion program. In each of the next three years (1999, 2000, and 2001) the company purchased six machines and retired five. Thus in 1999, 2000, and 2001 the firm had in operation 16, 17, and 18 machines, respectively. Compute amortization charges for the three-year period using
   (1) The straight-line method
   (2) The double declining balance method

d. Assume again that the firm used an incorrect useful life and amortized the machines over a two-year period instead of three. Compute amortization charges for the three-year period using the straight-line method.

e. What conclusions can you draw regarding the impact of choice of amortization method and estimate of useful life on the income of a firm that is expanding its asset base as opposed to one that is maintaining it at a constant level?

7. *Complete journal entries can be reconstructed from limited amounts of data.*

   The following information relating to capital was taken from an annual report of Magna International Inc. (in thousands):

Property, plant, and equipment	
Balance at beginning of period	$ 993,864
Additions and miscellaneous adjustments	250,842
Balance at end of period	1,153,954
Accumulated amortization, Property, plant, and equipment	
Balance at beginning of period	151,909
Amortization expense and miscellaneous adjustments	74,570
Balance at end of period	213,879

a. Based on the data provided, plus any other amounts that it may be necessary to derive from them, prepare a journal entry that summarizes the retirement of equipment during the period. Assume that the equipment was sold for $81,692 thousand.

b. One of the impacts of inflation, over the long run, is that accumulated amortization is often insufficient to replace fully amortized productive capacity.
   (1) Prepare a journal entry that summarizes amortization expense for the period.
   (2) Is it the purpose of amortization accounting to provide for the replacement of equipment? In what way, if any, does the entry you proposed enable the company to accumulate funds for replacement?

8. *Compound interest amortization results in an amortization charge indicative of the decline in the present value of anticipated cash flows.*

   Machine Rentals, Inc., is considering purchasing a new computer that it will be able to rent to a customer for $20,000 per year for five years. The machine has a useful life of five years and no salvage value. The company expects an annual rate of return of 7 percent on all its assets.

a. What is the maximum amount the firm would be willing to pay for the machine? That is, what is the present value, discounted at a rate of 7 percent, of anticipated future cash receipts?
b. What is the present value of anticipated cash receipts at the end of each of the five years?
c. Suppose that the firm was able to purchase the machine for the amount computed in part (a). It elects to charge amortization on the basis of what the machine is worth to the company (the present value of anticipated cash receipts) at the end of a year as compared with what it was worth at the beginning. How much amortization should it charge during each of the five years? Determine total amortization charges for the five-year period.
d. Comment on the trend of charges by this method of amortization as compared with other methods. This method is not widely used in practice, but is regarded with favour by many theoreticians. How can it be justified?

9. *Straight-line amortization provides a level return on investment only when cash flows decline. (This problem is intended for solution using an electronic spreadsheet.)*

   Computer Rentals, Inc., acquires a computer at a cost of $379,080. It immediately leases the computer to a customer for a term of five years. Annual rent is $100,000. The company believes that the machine will have no significant value when the lease expires.
   a. Determine annual return on investment (i.e., income as a percent of the book value, net of accumulated amortization).
      (1) Assume that the company computes amortization on a straight-line basis.
      (2) Assume instead that the company computes amortization using compound interest amortization. Use a discount rate of 10 percent. Amortization each year should represent the difference between present value of the anticipated cash flows at the beginning and end of the year.
      (3) Comment on the trends in return on investment. Would the apparent problem with straight-line amortization be alleviated or exacerbated by an accelerated method?
   b. Suppose instead that the computer is used internally; it is not leased to outsiders. The company estimates that cash savings attributable to the machine will be $120,000 the first year and will decline by $10,000 per year over the remaining four years.
      (1) Compute return on investment, using the straight-line method. Comment on the difference in return on investment when cash flows decline as the asset ages.
      (2) Comment on the trend in return on investment that would result from use of the compound interest method. You should not have to actually carry out the computations.
      (3) Which pattern of cash flows—equal or declining over asset life—do you think is characteristic of most assets? Consider specifically when and why a company would retire an asset.

10. *Financial analysts must be watchful of amortization practices, especially in capital-intensive industries such as steel.*

Prior to 1969 most major U.S. steel firms amortized their assets on an accelerated basis. In that year several companies shifted to the straight-line basis. Some firms, however, currently use a modified version of the straight-line method. The "Summary of Principal Accounting Policies" in a recent annual report of U.S. Steel, for example, brings out the following:

> For the most part, depreciation expense is related to rates of operation, within a limited range.

In other words, the charge for amortization is determined, in part, by the units of output method. The greater the use of the assets, the greater the charge for amortization.

In 1977, Bethlehem Steel closed several of its plants. It wrote off the unamortized value of assets at the facilities, charging earnings for $167 million. In 1979, U.S. Steel did the same, writing off $218.7 million in plant and equipment. Both firms blamed foreign imports and environmental regulations that would have required substantial capital expenditures to clean up what the firms believed to be marginally profitable facilities.

a. Neither the foreign competition nor the environmental regulations sprung up in a single year. In retrospect, what do the write-offs suggest about the amortization practices of the two companies? How might the firms defend their practices?

b. In light of rapid technological developments in the steel industry, what dangers do you see in the policy of basing amortization, even in part, on units of output? Comment specifically on the adequacy of amortization charges in periods of low output.

c. On what basis can a shift from accelerated to straight-line amortization be justified? What do you suspect was the real motive behind the change?

11. *The method of amortization selected should provide the best possible match of costs to revenues.*

The Strip Mining Co. decides to remove coal from a deposit on property it already owns. The company purchases for cash mining equipment at a cost of $850,000 and constructs a building on the site at a cost of $90,000. The equipment has a useful life of 10 years and an estimated salvage value of $50,000 and can readily be removed to other mining locations. The building has a potential useful life of 12 years but will have to be abandoned when the company ceases operations at the site.

The mine contains approximately 1 million tonnes of coal, and the company plans to remove it over a four-year period according to the following schedule:

Year	
1	450,000 tonnes
2	200,000 tonnes
3	200,000 tonnes
4	150,000 tonnes

The property will be abandoned at the end of the fourth year.

a. Record the purchase of the equipment and the construction of the building.

b. Compute amortization charges for the first year on both the building and equipment. Justify in one or two sentences your choice of amortization method(s) and useful lives.

12. *Amortization costs, like those of labour and materials, may be considered production, rather than period, costs if they can be associated directly with the minerals recovered.*

   Wildcat Minerals, Inc., was incorporated in 1997 for the specific purpose of mining a tract of land. The company acquired the tract at a cost of $7.2 million. It estimated that the tract contained 700,000 tonnes of ore and that after the property was completely mined (in approximately four years) it could be sold as farmland for $900,000.

   The company built various buildings and structures at a cost of $1.4 million. Such improvements have a potential life of 15 years but have utility only when used at the specific mining site; they cannot be moved economically to other locations. In addition, the company purchased other equipment at a cost of $400,000. This equipment has a useful life of five years and an estimated salvage value of $50,000.

   In 1997 the company incurred labour and other production costs of $357,700 and selling and administrative costs of $224,000. It paid taxes of $105,000.

   The company mined 100,000 tonnes and sold 80,000 tonnes of ore in 1997. The selling price per tonne was $19.

   The company elected to charge amortization on a units of output basis.
   a. Determine total amortization costs for 1997.
   b. Determine the cost per tonne of ore sold.
   c. Determine net income.
   d. Determine the ending inventory.

13. *The information in annual reports as to fixed assets may enable an analyst to estimate average useful life of assets but is otherwise quite limited.*

   The 1990 financial statements of Jannock Limited contained the following information regarding fixed assets and depreciation:

From a Footnote, "Fixed Assets":

	December 31 (in millions of dollars)	
	1990	1989
Land	$ 59.0	$ 39.7
Buildings	59.0	61.8
Equipment	199.5	191.6
Other	10.1	9.8
Construction in progress	2.9	1.4
	$330.5	$304.3
Less: Accumulated depreciation	145.5	134.5
	$185.0	$169.8

From the "Statement of Changes in Financial Position":

Depreciation	$21.5	$17.2
Additions to fixed assets, net of disposals	26.2	58.0

From a Note on Accounting Policy as to Fixed Assets:

> Fixed assets are carried at cost less accumulated depreciation. Depreciation, which is based on management's estimate of the assets' useful life, is provided on a straight-line basis at annual rates of 2% to 5% for buildings and 5% to 33% for equipment and other fixed assets.

There was no additional information in the financial statements regarding either fixed assets or depreciation.

a. Based on the information provided, estimate the average useful life of buildings, equipment, and "other" assets.

b. Assume that all assets retired or otherwise disposed of had been fully depreciated.

   (1) What was the initial cost of the assets retired in 1990?

   (2) What were the total additions to fixed assets? (Note that the statement of changes in financial position provides data on "additions, net of disposals.")

14. *A footnote provides insight into depreciation and capitalization practices.*

The following notes are from an annual report of Magna International Inc., a leading supplier of components and systems to the automotive industry.

Fixed Assets

> Fixed assets are recorded at historical cost including, where appropriate, interest capitalized on construction in progress and land held for development, less investment tax credits generated.

> Costs incurred in establishing new facilities which require substantial time to reach commercial production capability are capitalized as deferred preproduction costs. Amortization is being provided over terms ranging from two to five years from the date commercial production capability is achieved.

Research and Development Costs

> Research and development expenses are charged against income in the year of expenditure.

Would you characterize the company's policies as to start-up costs as being "liberal" or "conservative"? How do you explain the apparent inconsistency in that interest and start-up costs are capitalized but research and development costs are not?

15. *Tax laws, as they affect amortization, may encourage firms to sell assets long before the expiration of their useful lives.*

Commuter Airlines, Inc., issued common stock for $24 million and used the funds to purchase six small passenger jets at a total cost of $24 million. The firm plans to use the planes for 10 years, after which it believes they can be sold for a total of $8 million.

a. Compute amortization expense for each of the first three years under each of the following methods:

   (1) Straight-line

   (2) Sum-of-the-years'-digits

(3) 150 percent declining balance

b. Assume that income before amortization and taxes during each of the first three years is $6 million. Compute income taxes payable for those years if the tax rate is 40 percent under each of the three methods, assuming they were allowed for tax purposes. As noted in the chapter, amortization is not deductible for tax purposes; only capital cost allowance is. Which method results in the least tax burden in the early years of asset life?

c. Suppose that at the end of the second year the planes are sold for $20 million. The remaining useful life of the assets is eight years. If the new owner charged amortization for tax purposes using the 150 percent declining balance method, what would be the first-year deduction for amortization? Compare such deduction to that which would be permitted Commuter Airlines if it used the 150 percent declining balance method. Why might it be said that the asset is "worth" more to the new owner than to the previous one?

16. *Capital cost allowance methods differ considerably in the economic value of the tax savings that they provide.* (This problem is intended for solution using an electronic spreadsheet.)

Suppose that you are an executive of an equipment manufacturer. The equipment that your firm sells costs approximately $100,000 and has a useful life of 10 years (with no residual value).

Assume further that the current tax laws require purchasers of the equipment to charge capital cost allowance using a declining balance rate of 20 percent. A Department of Finance committee, however, is considering a proposal which would permit firms to use a declining balance rate of 30 percent. You have been asked to provide evidence as to the economic value of the change to your customers. *Economic value* is interpreted as the difference in the present values of the capital cost allowance deductions. The current tax rate is 30 percent.

a. Prepare two schedules, one for the 20 percent rate and one for the 30 percent rate. In each, show annual capital cost allowance deductions that would be permitted the equipment purchaser. Determine the present values of the two series of capital cost allowance deductions and the difference between them. Use a discount rate of 12 percent. Calculate the after-tax value of the difference.

b. In your testimony to the committee you plan to advocate an additional "technical" adjustment to the proposal. Firms would be permitted to switch from the 30 percent declining balance rate to the straight-line method when the deduction under the straight-line method became greater than that under the declining balance method. In shifting to the straight-line method, a taxpayer would be required to amortize the unamortized balance of the asset over the remaining useful life of the asset. Thus, if the shift was made at the *start* of year 5 and the unamortized asset balance was $24,000, then the firm could write off $4,000 over each of the remaining six years of asset life.

Prepare a schedule in which you determine the optimal year in which a taxpayer would shift to the straight-line method and show the additional economic benefit of the switch.

17. *Utility rates are affected by interest capitalization policies.*

The rates that Northern Electric and Gas is permitted to charge customers are fixed by a public utility board. The board has a policy of establishing rates so that the company realizes a pretax return on assets of 12 percent per year. That is, rates are established that permit the company to generate annual revenues of an amount so that revenues less expenses will equal 12 percent of reported assets.

Prior to 1996, the reported value of the company's assets was $80 million. In 1996, it earned revenues of $29.6 million and incurred expenses (excluding taxes) of $20 million. Operating profit was therefore $9.6 million—12 percent of $80 million. The book value of these assets, and the earnings thereon, is expected to remain constant through 1998.

In 1996, to extend its service area, the company began construction of a new plant. The estimated cost of the plant is $50 million. It will be completed by the end of 1997. During construction, the company will pay a total of $6 million in interest costs on funds borrowed to finance the new plant. They will be incurred as follows:

1996	$2 million
1997	$4 million

On average, the company will have $20 million recorded as construction in progress in 1996 and $40 million in 1997. For purposes of determining rates, construction in progress is included in the asset base.

The company estimates that once the new plant goes "on line" in January 1998, annual operating expenses, excluding amortization but including interest, will be $8 million.

Amortization on the new assets will be charged on a straight-line basis. Estimated life of the new plant is expected to be 40 years (with no salvage value).

An important accounting issue is whether interest costs related to the construction of assets should be *capitalized* (added to the cost of the assets constructed). Interest costs that are not capitalized are charged as expenses in the years incurred.

a. Prepare a table, assuming that interest is not capitalized. Show the following for each of the three years, 1996, 1997 (the two years of construction), and 1998 (the first year the plant goes on line).
   (1) The asset base (on existing and new facilities combined)
   (2) The income that the utility board will permit
   (3) The expenses on the existing plant
   (4) The new interest expense
   (5) The new amortization expense
   (6) The new operating expenses
   (7) The total expenses
   (8) The allowable revenues
   In determining asset base, assume that new assets, with a cost equal to the annual charge for amortization, are acquired each year. Thus, for purposes of calculating the asset base, ignore any reduction that would result from amortization.

b. Do the same, assuming that interest is capitalized.

c. Suppose, first, that you represent a consumer group concerned with holding utility rates to a minimum; suppose, next, that you represent Northern Electric and Gas, which is interested in obtaining maximum revenues as soon as possible. What recommendations would you make to the public utility board as to a policy of capitalization of interest? What arguments would you make in support of your position?

18. *Changes in useful life can have a potent impact on amortization charges and earnings per share.*

The 1987 annual report of TWA contained the following note:

> Effective January 1, 1988, the estimated remaining useful service lives of TWA's owned wide-body aircraft fleets will be extended and the estimated residual values will be reduced to recognize that these aircraft are physically capable of being actively flown into the 21st century. The change reflects an approximate increase in average depreciable lives of six years for owned L1011 aircraft, four years for owned B747 aircraft and nine years for owned B767 aircraft. Such change in estimate does not affect the provision for depreciation expense computed for 1987 and prior years.

> Estimated useful service lives in effect for the three years ended December 31, 1987, for purposes of computing the provision for depreciation, of flight equipment (aircraft and engines, including related spares) were sixteen to twenty-three years.

The firm's balance sheet indicates that the book value of flight equipment, before depreciation, was $2.89 billion. Assume that the average useful life of flight equipment, prior to the change, was 20 years. After the change it would be 28 years.

Determine the approximate impact that the change would have on

a. Earnings before taxes

b. Earnings per share before taxes (The company had 30,506,000 shares outstanding.

To put the magnitude of the change in perspective, it should be noted that in 1987 TWA had net income (after taxes) applicable to common shares of $50,400,000 and earnings per share of $1.65.

19. *As illustrated by an actual annual report, companies have broad discretion in accounting for long-lived assets. Taken together, the policies that they adopt can have a formidable impact on reported earnings.*

The following notes were taken from the 1990 annual report of PWA Corporation, the parent company of Canadian Airlines International.

Property and Equipment

> Costs of repairs, renewals, and replacements, including major flight equipment overhauls, are charged to income except for those expenditures which improve or extend the useful life of the asset. Depreciation is provided at straight-line rates to estimated residual values based on the following estimated useful lives: Flight equipment—20 years; Buildings—10–40 years; Ground equipment—5–10 years.

Route Acquisition Costs

Costs related to the acquisition of international flying rights are being amortized on a straight-line basis over forty years.

Capitalization of Interest

Interest on funds used to finance payments made for the acquisition of flight equipment prior to entry into service and on other advance payments for capital acquisitions is capitalized and included in the cost of the related capital items.

Review each of the notes and identify any policies and practices that are within the discretion of the company. Indicate any alternatives which the company might have selected. Comment on whether the policies and practices adopted by the company appear to be "liberal" (i.e., result in earlier recognition of expenses) or "conservative" (i.e., result in later recognition of expenses).

20. *Trade-in transactions must be accounted for in a manner that reflects economic substance rather than form.*

In January 1996 the Jarvis Co. purchased a copy machine for $12,000. The machine had an estimated useful life of eight years and an estimated salvage value of $1,000. The firm used the double declining balance method to record amortization.

In December 1998 the company decided to trade in the machine for a newer model. The new model had a *list* price of $24,000, but it is common in the industry for purchasers to be given a 15 to 20 percent trade discount off of list price. The manufacturer offered the company a trade-in allowance of $8,000 on its old machine. The company accepted the offer since it was considerably above the several offers of approximately $4,000 that the firm had received from other parties interested in purchasing the machine. The company paid $16,000 in addition to giving up the old machine.

Record the trade-in of the old machine and the purchase of the new. Assume that amortization had already been recorded for 1998.

21. *Disasters can result in increased earnings.*

On October 26, 1996, the Great Hotel was destroyed by fire. Best Hotels, Inc., had purchased the hotel exactly three years earlier at a cost of $50 million. The company had been amortizing the hotel by the double declining balance method, based on an estimated life of 25 years.

The hotel was insured for only 80 percent of its market value. At the time of the fire, market value was $62 million.

a. Indicate the impact of the fire on the financial statements of Best Hotels, Inc.

b. Comment on why seemingly unfavourable events result in reported gains. Assume that Best Hotels, Inc., is a publicly held company whose shares are traded on a major stock exchange. What impact do you think the fire would have on the market price of the firm's stock? How can you reconcile the effect on market price with your response to part (a).

22. *Revaluation of assets to reflect changes in market values would affect not only their recorded values but also the allocation of earnings among the years that the assets were in service.*

   The Rhinegold Chemical Co. constructed a new plant at a cost of $20 million. The plant had an estimated useful life of 20 years, with no salvage value. After the plant had been used for four years, its replacement cost had increased to $24 million. The company decided to recognize in its accounts the increase in the fair market value of the asset. (Such practice is not, of course, in accord with currently acceptable accounting principles.)

   a. Prepare the journal entry to record amortization for each of the first four years.
   b. Prepare an entry to record the revaluation of the plant.
   c. Prepare an entry to record amortization in the fifth year, the first year subsequent to the revaluation.
   d. At the *start* of the eighth year the company accepted an offer to sell the plant for $19 million. Prepare an entry to record the sale.
   e. Suppose that the company had not readjusted its accounts after the fourth year to recognize the increase in market value. How much gain on retirement would it have reported upon sale of the plant? Compare total amortization expense and total gains recognized if the company recognized the increase in market value with those that would have resulted if it had adhered to conventional practice and not recognized the increase in market value.

23. *Two principal accounting practices employed in the oil industry may result in substantial differences in reported earnings and assets, but neither reflects "true" economic values.*

   Panhandle, Inc., in 1996 drilled three exploratory oil wells at a cost of $300,000 each. Of the three, only one proved successful. The company estimates that the property on which the successful well is located will provide a cash inflow of $600,000 per year, after taking into account recovery costs, royalties, and other cash outlays for each of the next 10 years, including 1996. The firm uses a discount rate of 10 percent to evaluate investments.

   a. Determine earnings for 1996, assuming that the firm uses
      (1) The full cost method
      (2) The successful efforts method
   b. Assume that the firm uses the successful efforts method. It does not own the property on which it discovered oil; instead it pays a per barrel royalty to the owner of the property.
      (1) At what value should the oil reserves (including the capitalized drilling costs) be reported on the balance sheet as at the end of 1996?
      (2) Do you think that such value fully and fairly reflects the value of the asset? What is your estimate of the "economic value" of the reserves? What supplementary disclosures would you recommend?

24. *This problem deals with title insurance, an issue recently addressed by the FASB, but not discussed in the text.*

   Title insurance guarantees that the rights to property are properly established. A title insurance policy indemnifies the policyholder against losses incurred in the event that the title (ownership right) to the covered property is deemed invalid. Home buyers, for example, almost always insure against defects in the titles on their homes. Should a purchaser have to surrender a home because the seller did not have authority to sell it (perhaps because many years earlier an owner had not made all tax or mortgage payments), the insurance company covers the losses up to the amount specified by the policy.

Title insurance companies must maintain a *title plant,* a historical record of all matters affecting titles to real estate within a particular area. It contains maps, contracts, copies of prior title insurance policies, and numerous other legal documents. To be useful, the title plant must not only cover an extended period of time but it must be continually kept up to date.

United Title Insurance Co. has decided to extend its service area to a new town. It is able to purchase an existing title plant from another company which is abandoning the title business. Purchase price is $5 million.

The purchased title plant, however, contains numerous gaps and is therefore inadequate. To bring it to a usable condition, United incurs $3 million in research-related costs.

To maintain the title plant during its first year of operations, United spends an additional $1 million. These costs are incurred to add documents on sales and transactions that take place during the year.

a. In your judgment (and without reference to the relevant FASB pronouncement), which, if any, of the costs to acquire and develop the title plant should be capitalized (i.e., recorded as a long-lived asset)? Which should be expensed?
   (1) The $5 million to purchase the existing title plant
   (2) The $3 million to bring the plant up to standard
   (3) The $1 million to maintain the plant
b. If you proposed that the some or all of the costs be capitalized, then over how many years do you recommend the costs be amortized?

Justify your responses in the context of the general principles discussed in this chapter.

25. *The practices of one company are illustrative of ambivalence toward start-up costs.*
   The note that follows was included in a recent financial report of Ball Corporation, a manufacturer of glass jars and other packaging materials:

Deferred Preoperating Costs

> Preoperating costs of new manufacturing facilities are charged to income as incurred except for those facilities and major expansions or modifications thereof which are constructed primarily to serve customers under contractual supply arrangements. The costs deferred, which represent principally training and other startup costs, are amortized over the terms of the related supply contracts of generally five to seven years commencing with commercial production.

The same financial report provided the following additional data about deferred preoperating costs (thousands of dollars).

From the balance sheet, noncurrent assets (dates have been changed):

	1996	1995
Deferred preoperating costs	$5,902	$4,118

From the statement of changes in financial position:

	1996	1995
Amortization of deferred preoperating costs	$1,126	$1,158
Use of financial resources for deferred preoperating costs	2,910	2,270

a. Prepare summary entries to record all activity relating to deferred preoperating costs in 1996.

b. What justification is there for deferring preoperating costs of facilities constructed to serve customers under contractual supply contracts but not other preoperating costs?

26. *Accounting for start-up costs varies among, as well as within, industries.*

Indicate how each of the costs described here should be accounted for. Express an opinion as to whether the cost should be recorded as an asset or an expense. If as an asset, explain how it should be amortized. State the period of amortization or tell how it should be determined. For some of the costs, there are no authoritative pronouncements that provide specific guidance as to how they should be handled. Use your own judgment.

a. A chain of discount stores opens an outlet at a new location. Prior to beginning operations, it incurs $800,000 in advertising, promotion, training, and general administration costs.

b. To celebrate the first anniversary of the opening of its store at the new location, the aforementioned discount chain incurs $100,000 in advertising costs to announce a new line of products. Although the advertisements will be run toward the end of 1996, the new products will not be sold until 1997.

c. On February 1, 1996, an established cable television company acquires franchise rights to provide service to a city in central British Columbia. In the two years following the award of the franchise, the company incurs $10 million in programming, rental, and advertising costs in addition to amounts it spends on plant and equipment. Although the company's system goes on line in December 1997, as is expected it does not reach a profitable level of operations until February 1999.

d. In 1997 the same cable television company upgrades the level of its service to the city by adding additional programs to those previously available. It incurs $5 million in programming and advertising costs to improve the system. It estimates that the costs will be recovered through additional revenues within a period of five years.

e. A hotel chain purchases a rundown hotel with the intention of modernizing it by renovating its rooms and adding new restaurants and convention facilities. Although the physical changes are made within three months of acquisition, the company, consistent with its plans, incurs $2 million in net operating losses in its first two years of operations. The losses were anticipated since it takes at least two years for the hotel to build up its clientele. The losses are in addition to outlays for furniture, fixtures, and other changes to the facilities, which of course have been capitalized.

27. *Under generally accepted practices of cost capitalization, comparable assets are not necessarily reported at comparable values.*

In each of the following situations, indicate whether the outlay described gives rise to an asset that would be reported on the balance sheet. If it does, indicate the amount. Provide a brief explanation of your response.

a. A drug firm incurs $2 million in research costs and $4 million in development costs to develop a new cold tablet. The tablet is brought to the market and is a highly successful product.

b. The same firm purchases the patented formula for a new skin cream from an independent research laboratory. Purchase price is $6 million.

c. A publishing company contracts with an unknown author for the rights to publish his first novel. The author is to receive as royalties 15 percent of sales. The book becomes a bestseller, and the company is offered (but has not yet accepted) $5 million for paperback and movie rights.

d. A paperback publisher purchases for $2 million the rights to publish the paperback version of the novel cited in part (c).

e. A computer firm custom-designs and installs a computer system for an airline. As at the end of a year, the computer firm has incurred $2.5 million for labour and materials and an additional $300,000 in interest on funds borrowed to finance the project. The project is not yet complete and has not been turned over to the customer.

f. The same firm manufacturers microcomputers for sale to the general public. As at the end of the year, it has in inventory 1,000 computers awaiting sale. Cost of the inventory is $2.5 million. This amount excludes interest of $300,000 on funds borrowed to finance the manufacture of the computers.

Solutions to Exercise for Review and Self-Testing

1. The amount at which the plane should be recorded must include the fair market value of all consideration (cash and property) paid to bring the asset to a usable condition. In this case, it includes all amounts indicated: $4 million cash payment; $500,000 in marketable securities; $6,000 in delivery charges; $94,000 in furnishing costs—a total of $4.6 million.

2. The total cost of using the plane for 10 years—the amount to be allocated—is the initial amount recorded ($4.6 million) less the anticipated residual value ($900,000)—$3.7 million.

3. If the straight-line method is used, annual amortization charges will be $3.7 million divided by 10, or $370,000 per year.

4. The straight-line rate of amortization is 10 percent; twice that is 20 percent. This rate would be applied each year to the current book value (cost

less accumulated amortization) *without* regard to residual value (except as suggested in part 5 of this exercise). Thus

Year	Book Value, Start of Year	Amortization Rate (%)	Amortization Expense	Book Value, End of Year
1	$4,600,000	20	$920,000	$3,680,000
2	3,680,000	20	736,000	2,944,000
3	2,944,000	20	588,800	2,355,200

5. Amortization must never be charged so as to reduce the remaining book value below expected salvage value—in this case $900,000. In the eighth year of service, therefore, the firm would charge only $64,690 of amortization ($964,690 less $900,000); in the ninth year, zero.

6. In economic substance the firm sold an asset with a book value of $2,355,200 for $1.5 million—the apparent fair market value of the old plane. Hence it should report a loss of $855,200. The new plane should be recorded at an amount representative of the fair market value of the consideration paid—$7 million cash plus $1.5 million, the fair market value of the plane surrendered—a total of $8.5 million.

10

Liabilities and Related Expenses

The previous four chapters have focused on specific categories of assets and their related expenses. This chapter introduces the principal categories of liabilities that a company may incur. Liabilities were defined in the first chapter to be obligations of the entity to make future transfers of assets or services to other entities. These obligations, legal or otherwise, may arise from the issuing of long-term debt (bonds), the entering into of leases, provisions of the Income Tax Act, and the promise to provide pension benefits to employees. As was the case with assets, the principal accounting issues relating to liabilities are those of recognition and measurement.

After studying this chapter, you will be able to

- Record the issue of bonds, the periodic payment of bond interest, and amortization of related discount or premium
- Calculate and understand the significance of the times interest earned ratio
- Distinguish between an operating lease and capital lease
- Prepare appropriate journal entries to account for operating and capital leases
- Explain the relationship between accounting income and taxable income

- Understand the nature of deferred income taxes
- Understand the calculation of the employers' pension expense for a defined benefit pension plan

Within the past several years, issues relating to liabilities have become the centre of accounting concern and controversy. This new focus can be traced to several ongoing financial developments. First, worldwide corporations have gone on a debt binge, financing with borrowed money activities that previously would have been paid for with funds from investors. Second, due to the magnitude of their obligations, the accounting profession has demanded that companies give explicit accounting recognition to liabilities that previously were recorded "off the balance sheet" (i.e., in footnotes, if at all). Prime among this category of debt are pensions and other benefits promised to retired employees. Third, the Income Tax Act has become increasingly complex and has thereby made the calculation of tax liabilities and expenses even more tangled than it had been previously. Fourth, many new types of financing instruments have been developed and widely adopted. Some, in fact, have been designed specifically to circumvent existing measurement and disclosure rules. Each creates its own unique accounting problems.

AN OVERVIEW

In a previous chapter (see page 35), liabilities were defined as

Obligations of an entity at the accounting date to make future transfers of assets or services (sometimes uncertain as to timing and amount) to other entities.

Liabilities obviously encompass amounts that an entity is legally obligated to pay others. But the accounting and legal concepts of a liability are quite different. Liabilities as interpreted by the accountant include *probable* sacrifices of resources stemming from past events or transactions whether or not there is a binding obligation to make payment.

The accounting issues relating to liabilities mirror those associated with assets. Key questions centre upon the circumstances that give rise to liabilities and the values to be assigned to them.

Issues of Recognition

Liabilities usually result from agreements between the parties to business transactions. The transactions may involve loans, purchases of goods, or the provision of services. Liabilities may also be imposed upon a business by statute (e.g., taxes) and by court action or threat of court action (e.g., lawsuits).

As pointed out in an earlier chapter, accountants today do not record as liabilities all expected future sacrifices of resources even if the amount and dates of payment are known with certainty. Obligations arising from contracts in which neither side has yet fulfilled its side of the bargain are generally not recognized as liabilities. A company may sign a five-year employment contract with an executive for $500,000 per year. At the time the contract is signed, the company need not record a liability. Only as the executive provides the expected services and the company receives the expected benefits must the company report a liability and, of course, a related expense.

As a rule, a firm must record a liability as soon as (1) it has received a benefit from an event or transaction and made an obligation to make a future transfer of assets or services, (2) the amount of the required sacrifice of resources is known, and (3) the due date has been established. But it can also do so even if all the criteria have not been satisfied. The tough accounting questions arise when one or more of these criteria have not yet been met.

Lease arrangements under present-day generally accepted accounting principles are illustrative of the difficulties of determining when to recognize that assets and liabilities have actually been created. When a business rents a store on a year-by-year basis, it does not record the rights to the property as an asset. Nor does it record the required rent payments as a liability. It is assumed that the company will receive the benefits and incur the obligations from the transactions over the course of the lease. But when a long-term lease is structured so that the business acquires virtually all rights of ownership—when it has in economic substance purchased the property—it must record the property as an asset when the lease is first signed. So also, therefore, must it record the lease payments as a liability as if it had borrowed the funds to buy the property. The troublesome accounting issue is: When should a lease be considered an ordinary rental arrangement, a contract in which the business obtains the rights to use the property and incurs the obligation to pay for it over the life of the lease? When should it be considered a purchase-borrow transaction, a contract in which the business obtains the rights and incurs the obligations at the inception of the lease?

Repair warranties and income taxes are illustrative of potential obligations that must be recorded as liabilities, even though it is uncertain whether and in what amount a future sacrifice of resources will be required. Generally accepted accounting principles state that when a firm provides repair warranties, the firm should credit a liability account at the time of sale in the amount of the expected cost to fulfil them. Obviously, the firm cannot be sure what the eventual sacrifice will be, but any estimate is likely to be better than none—which would be an implicit estimate of zero. The practice of setting up a liability for warranty costs is consistent with the matching concept. The cost of the repairs should be reported in the same period as the sales revenue with which it is associated.

As will be discussed later in this chapter, the Income Tax Act permits a firm to postpone the payment of taxes on earnings recognized in a particular period. The taxes will have to be paid only if certain conditions are satisfied or events take place. A source of long-standing conflict among accountants is the extent to which payment must be probable before the tax liability should be recognized. Whereas there is widespread agreement that potential warranty costs should be recorded as liabilities, there is considerable controversy over how deferred taxes should be accounted for.

Issues of Measurement

The economic value of a liability is the present value of the cash that will be required to settle it. As with assets, the expected cash flows must be discounted at an appropriate rate. Assuming a discount rate of 10 percent, a liability of $100 to be paid in two years has a value of $82.64 ($100 × .8264, the present value of $1 discounted at 10 percent for two years). This is the amount that the firm could set aside today in an account that earns interest at 10 percent and be able to pay off the loan when due without having to contribute anything additional.

As with assets, the manner in which liabilities are *reported* may not necessarily reflect their economic values. Liabilities, like assets, are reported at historically based amounts. Long-term liabilities are generally stated at the present value of payments to be made in the future. (Current liabilities are usually reported at actual, rather than present, values, only because the difference between the two is immaterial.) The present value at any time a liability is outstanding is determined by discounting required future payments by the historical rate of interest—i.e., the rate that was in effect at the time the liability was initially recorded. Only at the time the liability is first recorded will its reported value necessarily be equal to its economic value. Thereafter, prevailing interest rates will change. The present value of the future payments discounted at the prevailing rate may be greater or less than that discounted at the *historical* rate. The prevailing rate is the relevant rate for determining economic value. If the firm wanted to have the cash available to pay off the claim at any time prior to its due date, it could place in an interest-bearing bank account funds equal to the present value of the future payments of principal and interest. Assuming that the rate of interest paid by the bank was equal to the prevailing rate and was guaranteed from date of deposit to when the liability matures, the firm would have to make no further payment. The principal and interest could be paid from the funds placed in the bank and the interest that was earned on them.

The Issue of Market Value

Liabilities, like assets, have market values. In previous chapters, it was noted that bonds and similar certificates of indebtedness are often held by firms as marketable securities. Accounts receivable may be purchased and sold. Obviously what is a bond or note receivable to one party is a payable to another. The market for receivables can be viewed, with equal logic, as a market for payables.

Under generally accepted accounting principles, the amounts at which liabilities are stated are seldom adjusted to reflect fluctuations in market prices. The market price of a liability has as much significance as that of an asset, and the arguments in favour of reporting liabilities at market values may be as compelling as those for assets. The market price of a liability represents the amount that would be required for a firm to discharge its debt at a particular time. The firm could purchase the debt from its holder at the prevailing market price. For reasons to be explained shortly, such a price may be greater or less than the book value of the debt. By not purchasing the debt in the market, the firm (like the corresponding asset holder) is taking the risk that subsequent price movements will be in its favour.

Corporations, as well as government units and nonprofit organizations, borrow funds to finance *long-term* projects, such as plant and equipment and major public works projects. Conventionally, borrowers provide the lender with bonds or notes as evidence of their obligations to repay the funds and to make periodic interest payments. A bond is a more formal certificate of indebtedness than a note. Bonds are usually evidence of long-term indebtedness (five years or more), while notes may be issued in connection with short- or long-term borrowings.

Corporate bonds are most commonly issued in denominations of $1,000. The *par* or *face* value of a bond indicates the *principal* amount due at the *maturity*, or due date of the bond. Bonds ordinarily carry a stated annual rate of interest, expressed as a percentage of the principal. Most bond *indentures* (agreements that set forth the legal provisions of the bonds) require that interest be paid semiannually. Thus a corporation that has issued $1,000-denomination bonds that specify an annual rate of interest of 12 percent would pay the holder of a single bond $60 every six months.

Corporate bonds may be secured (collateralized) by property, such as an office building or land. Or they may be unsecured, with the lender relying primarily upon the good faith and financial integrity of the borrower for repayment. Secured bonds may be categorized by the type of legal instrument used to provide the lien on the property that is pledged (e.g., mortgage bonds and equipment trust bonds). Unsecured bonds are commonly called *debentures*.

Virtually all corporate bonds specify a maturity date. However, many corporate issues provide for the early retirement of the bond at the option of the *borrower* (the corporation). Such a *call provision* ordinarily requires the company to pay the lender (the bond holder) a *call premium,* an amount in addition to the par value of the bond, as a penalty for depriving the lender of its "right" to interest payments for the original term of the loan.

Bonds are generally freely negotiable—they can be bought and sold in the open market subsequent to original issue. An active market for government and corporate bonds is maintained by the major investment dealers in Canada. A lender who no longer wishes to have its funds tied up in a loan to the issuer of a bond can sell the bond to an investor who is seeking the type of return provided by that type of bond. The price at which the bond is sold would not be that for which the bond was initially issued. Rather, it would be at a price based on interest rates prevailing at the time of sale.

The Nature of Bonds

Bonds generally provide for periodic interest payments of a fixed amount. Ordinarily, the more financially sound the lender, the lower the rate of interest. Interest rates for securities *within* the same category of risk are determined by the forces of supply and demand—the amount of funds being sought by borrowers and the amount being made available by lenders. Rates of interest that prevail throughout the world fluctuate from day to day and even from hour to hour. Although corporations conventionally set the coupon or stated rate of interest—the amount that will be paid to the lender each interest period—and print it in the bond indentures several weeks prior to the date on which they are to be issued, the actual interest rate is determined at time of sale. The actual interest rate is called the *yield rate* or effective yield. It is established not by changing the coupon rate but rather by adjusting the price at which the bond is sold. Suppose, for example, that a $1,000 bond has a coupon rate of 8 percent—that is, the holder of the bond will be entitled to two interest payments of $40 each year. At the time of sale, however, the prevailing interest rate for that type of bond is 8 ¼ percent. Would purchasers be willing to pay $1,000 for such a bond? Obviously not. They could lend their money to another similar company and receive $82.50 per year rather than $80. Therefore the purchaser would be willing to pay something less than $1,000 for the bond. How much less will be considered in the next section. Similarly, if the prevailing interest rate was lower than 8 percent—7 ½ percent, for example—rational buyers would be willing to pay more than $1,000 for the bond. If they were to purchase the bonds of similar companies, the buyers would receive only $75 per year in interest. They would be willing to pay something above $1,000 to receive a return of $80 per year. If purchasers pay less than the face amount for a bond, then the difference between the face amount and what the purchasers actually pay is referred to as a *bond discount*. If the purchasers pay more than the face amount, then the additional payment is referred to as a *premium*.

Rational purchasers would undertake a similar analysis in deciding how much to pay for a bond that had been issued several years earlier. In this case, the purchase would not be from the issuing company directly but rather from the current holder of the bond. If prevailing interest rates are greater than the coupon rate of the bond, the purchasers would be only willing to pay *less* than the face value of the bond, for they could receive the prevailing rate by purchasing a different bond on which the coupon rate is equal to the prevailing rate. If prevailing rates are less than the coupon rate, the purchasers would be willing to pay more, since the semiannual interest payments would be greater than what they could obtain elsewhere.

> *As prevailing rates of interest (yields) increase, the market prices of outstanding bonds with fixed coupon rates of interest decrease.*
>
> *As prevailing rates of interest (yields) decrease, the market prices of bonds with fixed coupon rates of interest increase.*

Determination of Discount or Premium[1]

Determining the amount that a rational purchaser would pay for a bond requires an understanding of the promises inherent in the bond agreement.

Suppose that on a particular day a corporation seeks bids on two bonds. Bond A bears a coupon rate of 12 percent and bond B a coupon rate of 10 percent. Both bonds will mature in two years. Both pay interest semiannually. The prevailing annual rate of interest is 12 percent.

---

[1] The reader is strongly urged to review the material on compound interest and present value contained in Chapter 6.

Both bonds contain a promise to pay the purchaser $1,000 upon maturity after two years—four semiannual periods hence. The present value of a single cash payment four semiannual periods away, given an interest rate of 6 percent per period, is, per Table 2 in the Appendix, $1,000 × .7921, or $792.10. The 6 percent rate is one-half the annual rate of 12 percent; it reflects the semiannual rather than the annual payment of interest. The 12 percent rate is the *prevailing* rate for bonds of that type, not necessarily the coupon rate on either of the two bonds in question. It is the rate that is relevant to prospective purchasers since it is that which they could receive if they were to turn to alternative investments of comparable risk.

Bond A also promises four semiannual payments of $60. The present value of four semiannual payments, discounted at 6 percent per period (one-half the *prevailing* annual rate), is, per Table 4, $60 × 3.4651, or $207.90. The total present value of the two promises—the promise to pay principal of $1,000 plus the promise to make semiannual interest payments—discounted at the prevailing rate of 6 percent per semiannual period—is $1,000 ($792.10 plus $207.90). The rational buyer would be willing to pay $1,000—in this instance, the face value—for the bond.

Bond B, on the other hand, promises four semiannual payments of only $50, since the coupon rate is 10 percent per year. The present value of four semiannual payments of $50, discounted at 6 percent is, again per Table 4, $50 × 3.4651, or $173.25. The rate of 6 percent is one-half the *prevailing* rate of 12 percent. The *prevailing rate is the one that must be used to evaluate an investment opportunity*, since it (rather than the coupon rate) is indicative of the return that the investor can expect to receive. The present value of the two promises combined is therefore $792.10 plus $173.25, or $965.35. A rational purchaser would be willing to pay only $965.35 for the bond with a face value of $1,000 and a coupon rate of 10 percent. The discount of $34.65 would assure him or her a *yield* of 12 percent per year, even though the coupon rate is only 10 percent per year. The analysis can be summarized as follows:

	Bond A (12% coupon, $60 per period)	Bond B (10% coupon, $50 per period)
Present value of $1,000 to be received at the end of 4 periods, discounted at prevailing per period rate of 6% ($1,000 × .7921 per Table 2)	$ 792.10	$792.10
Present value of $60 to be received at the end of each of 4 periods, discounted at prevailing per period rate of 6% ($60 × 3.4651 per Table 4)	207.90	
Present value of $50 to be received at the end of each of 4 periods, discounted at prevailing per period rate of 6% ($50 × 3.4651 per Table 4)		173.25
Present value of bond	$1,000.00	$965.35

Diagramatically, the two bonds can be depicted as in Exhibit 10-1. Both bonds are evaluated at a rate of 6 percent per period—the prevailing yield on comparable securities. It is assumed that the bonds were issued on January 1,

EXHIBIT 10-1

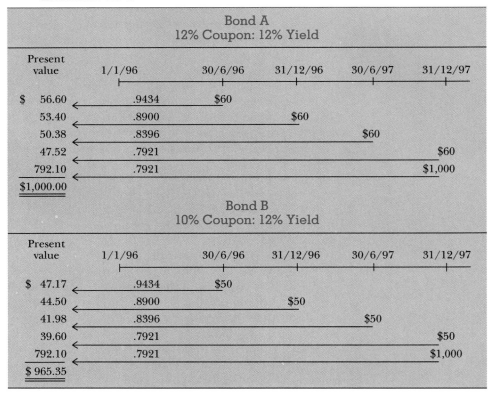

1996. All discount factors are per Table 2. Bond A would sell at face value because its coupon rate is identical to the yield rate. Bond B would sell at a discount because its coupon rate (10 percent) is less than the prevailing rate of interest (12 percent). Any time there is a difference between the coupon and the yield rates, the bonds would be sold at an amount other than face value.

Alternative View

The discount of $34.65 on bond B can be viewed from a slightly different perspective. If a purchaser can obtain a yield of 12 percent per year elsewhere, then from a $1,000 bond he or she expects interest payments of $60 every six months. In fact, bond B will pay only $50 per six months. The purchaser is "losing" $10 per period. The present value of $10 lost for four periods, discounted at a rate of 6 percent per period (one-half the prevailing yield of 12 percent), is, per Table 4, $10 × 3.4651, or $34.65.

Computation of the bond premium or discount can be facilitated by asking four simple questions:

1. How much interest per period (based on the *coupon rate*) is a purchaser of the bond actually going to receive?

2. How much interest (based on the prevailing *yield* of comparable securities) would the purchaser expect to receive?

3. What is the difference between the two amounts?

4. What is the present value, discounted at the prevailing *yield rate,* of such difference?

The present value of the difference between the amounts a purchaser would expect to receive and what he or she will actually receive represents either a premium or a discount:

Interest to be received each period, based on an annual coupon rate of 10%	$50
Less: Interest expected each period, based on an annual yield rate of 12%	60
Interest "lost" each period	$(10)
Present value of an annuity of $1 for 4 periods at a per period yield rate of 6 percent	× 3.4651
Present value of "lost" interest, or bond discount	($34.65)

RECORDING OF BOND ISSUES

The issue of bond B for a price of $965.35 could be recorded by the following journal entry:

Cash (asset) $965.35	
Discount on bonds payable (contra account to bonds payable) 34.65	
Bonds payable (liability) $1,000	
To record issuance of the bond	

If financial statements were prepared immediately after the issuance, the liability would be reported as follows:

Bonds payable	$1,000.00	
Less: Discount	34.65	$965.35

The *net* liability to be reported would be only $965.35, not the $1,000 face value of the bond.

Nature of Premium or Discount

The net liability of the company at the time of issuance of bond B is only $965.35. That is the amount of cash actually received by the issuing company. It may be argued that the company will have to repay $1,000, the face value of the bond, and that that amount therefore is the liability to be reported. The company will, of course, have to pay $1,000 at time of maturity. But if it only borrowed $965.35, then the "extra" $34.65 must represent interest, in addition to the semiannual coupon payments, to be paid to the lender. The additional $34.65 has the effect of increasing the rate of interest paid by the company from 10 percent to 12 percent. Interest is not ordinarily reported as a liability and recorded as an expense until the borrower has had use of the funds. Just as the liability for each of the periodic coupon payments of

$50 will not be recorded until the interest has accrued, neither should the liability for the additional interest of $34.65 to be paid upon maturity of the bond. Instead, it should be added to the liability account over the remaining life of the bond issue—as the firm has use of the funds borrowed.[2] Similarly, if the bonds were sold at a premium, at a price of $1,020, for example, then the amount borrowed by the company is the amount actually received, $1,020. The company will, of course, have to repay only $1,000. The $20 represents a reduction, over the life of the issue, of the firm's borrowing costs and should be accounted for as such.

Recording the Payment of Interest

As a consequence of the price adjustments attributable to the premium or discount at which the bonds were sold, the effective rate of interest to be paid by the company is that established not by the coupon rate but rather by the *yield rate* (the effective rate at time of issue). *The reported interest expense should be based on the yield rate.*

In the previous example, the company borrowed $965.35 at an effective interest rate of 12 percent (6 percent per interest period). Each interest date, however, it must pay the bondholder only $50. On the first interest date, its effective interest expense is 6 percent of $965.35, or $57.92, an amount that is $7.92 greater than the actual payment of $50 to be made to the bondholder. The $7.92 represents the first interest period's share of the $34.65 in additional interest to be paid upon the maturity of the loan. It is therefore the amount of the discount that must be amortized and charged as additional interest expense in the first period. The following journal entry would reflect this interpretation of the bond discount:

Interest expense		$57.92
Cash		$50.00
Discount on bonds payable		7.92

To record payment of interest and amortization of discount

As a result of this entry, the unamortized portion of the bond discount has been reduced from $34.65 to $26.73. The bond would be reported in the liability section of the balance sheet as follows:

Bonds payable	$1,000.00	
Less: Discount	26.73	$973.27

The effective liability of the company has increased from $965.35 to $973.27 because the company now owes not only the original amount borrowed ($965.35) but also a portion of the additional interest which the bondholder has earned during the first period. The additional interest now owed is equal to the effective interest for the period ($57.92) less the amount actually paid ($50.00).

---

[2] It could, of course, be asserted that the company has a legal liability for the full $1,000. Should the company go bankrupt, however, soon after the sale of the bonds, it would be unreasonable for a bankruptcy court to award the full $1,000 to a bondholder who recently had loaned the company only $965.35.

At the end of the second interest period, the interest expense would again be based on the effective interest or yield rate that prevailed at the time the bond was issued. But now the effective liability is not $965.35 as at the end of the first period but rather $973.27, an amount reflective of the amortization of a portion of the original discount. Hence the effective interest expense is 6 percent of $973.27, or $58.40. As in the first period, the actual payment to the bondholder would be only $50.00. The difference between the two represents the portion of additional interest earned by the bondholder but not yet paid to him or her—the amount that must be subtracted from the bond discount and thereby added to the effective liability. The following journal entry would be required on the second interest date:

Interest expense $58.40	
Cash	$50.00
Discount on bonds payable	8.40

To record payment of interest and amortization of discount

As a result of this entry, the unamortized portion of the bond discount has been reduced from $26.73 to $18.33. After the second payment of interest the bond would be reported as follows:

Bonds payable	$1,000.00	
Less: Discount	18.33	$981.67

A history of the bond is summarized in Exhibit 10-2.

The effective liability, as at any date, can be determined by following the same procedures used to calculate the initial issue price of the bond. For example, as at December 31, 1996, there are two interest payments of $50 remaining. The present value of the two payments discounted at the effective interest or yield rate of 6 percent per period is, per Table 4, $50 × 1.8334, or $91.67. The present value of the $1,000 to be received at maturity is, per Table 2, $1,000 × .8900, or $890.00. The present value of the two sets of payments combined is $91.67 plus $890.00, or $981.67.

EXHIBIT 10-2

$1,000 Bond Issued on January 1, 1996; Matures on December 31, 1997; 10% Coupon; Sold to Yield 12% (6% per Semiannual Period)				
Date	Interest Expense (6% of Effective Liability)	Coupon Payment	Discount	Effective Liability
1/1/96	—	—	$34.65	$ 965.35
30/6/96	$57.92	$(50.00)	(7.92)	7.92
31/12/96	58.40	(50.00)	26.73 (8.40)	973.27 8.40
30/6/97	58.90	(50.00)	18.33 (8.90)	981.67 8.90
31/12/97	59.43	(50.00)	9.43 (9.43)	990.57 9.43
			$ 0.00	$1,000.00

The following example deals with a bond to be sold at a premium rather than a discount.

Example

A company wishes to sell 10-year debentures that bear a coupon rate of 10 percent. At the time of sale, bonds of comparable risk are being sold to yield 8 percent.

1. For how much will the company be able to sell each $1,000 bond?

    The present value at the effective *yield* rate of 4 percent per half-year period (8 percent per year) of a single payment of $1,000, 20 periods hence, is, per Table 2, $1,000 × .4564, or $456.40.

    The present value of a stream of 20 payments of $50 each (the required *coupon payment* discounted at the *yield* rate of 4 percent per period) is, per Table 4, $50 × 13.5903, or $679.52. The sum of the two present values is $1,135.92, the amount for which the company will be able to issue the bond:

Present value of $1,000 to be received after 20 periods, discounted at prevailing rate of 4% per period ($1,000 × .4564 per Table 2)	$ 456.40
Present value of $50 to be received at the end of each of 20 periods, discounted at prevailing rate of 4% per period ($50 × 13.5903 per Table 4)	679.52
Present value of bond	$1,135.92

Alternatively, the same result could have been obtained by focusing on the premium. The company is offering the purchaser 20 payments of $50 each. The purchaser, based on the prevailing interest rate of 8 percent, would be willing to accept 20 payments of $40 each. The present value of the series of the $10 "bonuses" is, per Table 4, $10 × 13.5903, or $135.90. The latter figure represents the bond premium; hence the sale price would be the face value of $1,000 plus a premium of $135.90—the same (with allowance for rounding discrepancies) $1,135.92 as computed earlier.

2. Prepare a journal entry to record the sale of one bond.

Cash	$1,135.92	
Bonds payable		$1,000.00
Premium on bonds payable		135.92
To record issuance of the bond		

3. How would the bonds be reported on the balance sheet immediately after sale?

Bonds payable	$1,000.00	
Premium	135.92	$1,135.92

4. Prepare a journal entry to record the first interest payment. The total amount borrowed by the company is $1,135.92. The effective

annual rate of interest, the yield rate, is 8 percent. The effective semi-annual interest would therefore be 4 percent times the outstanding balance of $1,135.92, or $45.43. The amount of interest actually to be paid at the time of the first payment is, based on the coupon rate, $50:

Interest expense	$45.43	
Premium on bonds payable	4.57	
Cash		$50.00

To record payment of interest and amortization of premium

This entry reduces the premium to $131.35.

5. How would the bonds be reported immediately after the first payment of interest?

Bonds payable	$1,000.00	
Premium	131.35	$1,131.35

6. Prepare a journal entry to record the second interest payment. The effective liability just prior to the second payment of interest is $1,131.35. Effective interest expense, based on the yield rate at the time of sale, is $1,131.35 × .04, or $45.25:

Interest expense	$45.25	
Premium on bonds payable	4.75	
Cash		$50.00

To record payment of interest and amortization of premium

The net liability will now be $1,131.35 less that portion ($4.75) of the premium just amortized—$1,126.60.

7. For how much could the bondholder sell the bond immediately after the second payment of interest, assuming that the prevailing interest rate is still 8 percent?

Present value of $1,000, 18 periods away, discounted at 4%, per period (per Table 2), $1,000 × .4936	$ 493.60
Present value of 18 coupon payments of $50 each (per Table 4), $50 × 12.6593	632.97
Price at which the bond could be sold	$1,126.57

This amount is the same amount that would be reported on the books of the issuing company as calculated for part 6 of this example (save for a minor rounding discrepancy). It is the same only because the prevailing interest rate is the same as it was at the time when the bond was first issued—8 percent.

End-of-Year Accruals

If a bond interest payment date does not occur exactly at a company's fiscal year end, it is necessary to accrue interest for the expense incurred from the time of either the issue date or the last payment date to the year end. Suppose, for example, that a 12 percent, 20-year coupon bond was sold on December 1, 1996, for $866.68—a price that would result in a yield of 14 percent. Interest is payable each year on May 31 and November 30. Interest expense for the first full six-month period would be 7 percent of $866.68, or $60.67. That portion of the discount amortized would be the difference between the interest expense of $60.67 and the actual coupon payment of $60.00, or 67 cents. The accrual entry on December 31, 1996, would reflect one-sixth of these amounts:

Interest expense (⅙ of $60.67)	$10.11	
Discount on bonds payable (⅙ of $0.67)		$ 0.11
Accrued interest payable (⅙ of $60.00)		10.00
To record accrual of interest		

The entry on May 31, 1997, when the first payment is made, would be reflective of the remaining five-sixths (note that, consistent with conventional practice, the interest expense on May 31 is *not* based on the effective liability at December 31—after the *partial* amortization of the discount—but rather on the liability as of December 1):

Interest expense (⅚ of $60.67)	$50.56	
Accrued interest payable	10.00	
Discount on bonds payable (⅚ of $0.67)		$ 0.56
Cash		60.00
To record payment of interest and amortization of discount		

The Deficiencies of Straight-Line Amortization

Some firms, instead of determining interest expense and amortization of discount or premium as described in the preceding paragraphs, have in the past amortized the premium or discount on a straight-line basis. Total interest expense for the period is calculated by adding to the cash coupon payment (or subtracting from, in the case of a premium) the portion of the discount (or premium) amortized. The amount of the discount or premium amortized each period is determined simply by dividing the initial discount or premium by the total number of periods for which the bond will be outstanding. As a consequence, effective interest expense remains constant (in dollar amounts) over the life of the issue. In the illustration used earlier, a 10 percent coupon bond was issued at a price of $965.35—a discount of $34.65. Since the bond would be outstanding for four periods, one-fourth of $34.65, or $8.66, would be amortized each period. Total interest expense each period would be $58.66—the portion of the discount amortized plus the $50 coupon payment. The straight-line method is convenient; it eliminates the need to recompute interest each period. But it is deficient in that it results in a constantly changing *rate* of interest when interest expense is compared with effective liability (face value plus or minus discount or premium). Since, in the example, the effective liability would increase by $8.66 each period, the effective interest expense rates over the life of the bond (interest expense ÷ effective liability) would be as follows:

$$\frac{\$58.66}{\$965.35} = 6.08\%; \quad \frac{\$58.66}{\$974.01} = 6.02\%; \quad \frac{\$58.66}{\$982.67} = 5.97\%; \quad \frac{\$58.66}{\$991.33} = 5.92\%$$

In contrast, the effective rate of interest tends to increase over time when a bond is sold at a premium. The CICA is silent on the method of premium or discount amortization. When the difference between the two methods is significant, the effective interest method provides better matching. The straight-line method of amortization, however, is sometimes used in Canada because of its simplicity.

REDEMPTION OF BONDS

When a firm redeems its bonds outstanding upon their maturity, no special accounting problems are presented. Once the interest expense of the final period is recorded, any discount or premium will have been amortized to zero. Thus for a single bond, the following entry would be appropriate:

Bonds payable	$1,000.00	
Cash		$1,000.00
To record redemption of the bond		

If, however, the firm decides to redeem the bonds before they mature, then the accounting questions are more complex.

Assume that 20 years ago a company had issued 30-year, 7 percent coupon bonds at a price of $1,025.50 to yield 6.8 percent. With 10 years remaining until maturity, the firm decides to redeem the bonds since it no longer needs the funds that it borrowed. According to the bond agreement, the company has the right to call the issue any time after 15 years of issuing date at a price of $102. (Bond prices are frequently quoted in terms of $100 even though they are conventionally sold in denominations of $1,000. Thus the company would have to pay $1,020 to redeem a single bond.) The bond was originally issued at a price of $1,025.50; if the company had amortized the premium correctly, the net value of the bond after 20 years (10 years remaining) per the corporate books would be $1,014.34. If the company exercised its option to redeem the bond for $1,020.00, the following entry would be appropriate:

Bonds payable	$1,000.00	
Premium on bonds payable	14.34	
Loss on redemption	5.66	
Cash		$1,020.00
To record redemption of the bond		

The loss on redemption represents a penalty payment that management has elected to make to the bondholders in return for depriving them of the return that their investment in the bonds was providing them.

A corporation may also realize a gain by redeeming its bonds prior to maturity. This is especially true if the company does not officially *call* its outstanding bond issue but instead purchases its bonds in the open market. The company would pay the current bondholders the prevailing price for the security. By purchasing the bonds outstanding, the company would eliminate its liability to outsiders, and it would recognize as a gain the difference between the book value of the bonds and the purchase price.

Fluctuating Nature of Bond Prices

Bond prices, as pointed out earlier, are determined by the relationship between the coupon rate and the prevailing return that an investor is able to obtain elsewhere. It is believed by many that bonds are a relatively riskless investment—that bond prices remain reasonably stable. This is untrue. If, for example, prevailing interest rates increase from 12 percent to 14 percent, then the market price on a bond that bears a coupon rate of 12 percent and has 30 years remaining until maturity could be expected to decline from $100.00 to $85.96—a 14 percent change. If a company had initially issued such a 12 percent coupon bond at a price to yield 12.2 percent, then after 10 years (with 20 years—40 periods—until maturity), the bond would be recorded on its books at a net value of $98.51 (a discount of $1.49 per hundred dollars). The purchase (i.e., the redemption) of a single $1,000 bond at a price of $86.67 (which reflects a market rate of interest of 14 percent) would be recorded as follows:

Bonds payable	$1,000.00	
Cash		$866.70
Discount on bonds payable		14.90
Gain on redemption		118.40
To record redemption of the bond		

Interpreting Gains and Losses on Redemptions

Gains or losses on the redemption of bonds must necessarily be interpreted with care by both managers and independent financial analysts. Such gains or losses are recognized and reported on the income statement in the year in which the redemption takes place. As a result, corporate management can easily time its redemptions so as to provide a source of discretionary income whenever it believes that a boost in reported earnings would be helpful. Assume, for example, that in 1980 a firm issued (at par) $10 million in 5 percent coupon bonds payable in 45 years. In 1995, 15 years later, the prevailing rate of interest for similar securities was 7 percent. A 5 percent bond with 30 years remaining until maturity would be traded in the open market for approximately $75. The company could purchase the entire issue for $7.5 million and thereby realize a $2.5 million gain. If management believes that interest rates will continue to remain substantially above the level of the period in which the bond was issued, it is free to select the year in which it redeems the bonds and thereby reports the gain.

Viewed from another perspective, a gain or loss on redemption of bonds may be seen as being very similar to a gain or loss on the sale of long-term assets. If a company were blessed with perfect foresight and were able to predict exactly when and for how much it will redeem its bonds, it would calculate its periodic charges or credits for the amortization of the bond discount or premium in a manner that would assure that the net book value of the bonds at time of redemption is exactly equal to the redemption price. Thus there would be no gain or loss on redemption. If a company does not have perfect foresight, then, upon redeeming its bonds, it must make adjustment for its failure to amortize correctly the discount or premium in the years that the bond was outstanding. The gain or loss on the retirement of long-lived assets may be interpreted as a correction of amortization expense. Similarly, the gain or loss on redemption of bonds may be considered to be a correction of the amortization of the bond discount or premium and, thus, as an adjustment to the interest expense of previous periods.

The gain on redemption that will be reported on the financial statements does not accrue to the corporation without a price. If the corporation must reborrow the funds used to redeem the outstanding issue, it will have to do so at the prevailing rates of interest—rates that are higher than those that it had been paying in the past. The new rates will, of course, be reflected on income statements of the future as greater interest expense.

Times Interest Earned

Insight into the ability of a company to satisfy its fixed obligations to creditors may be obtained by comparing earnings with interest expense. Although the *times interest earned* ratio may be expressed in a variety of ways, the simplest form indicates the relationship between interest expense and income, *before* deducting both interest expense and income taxes. The objective of the ratio is to indicate the margin of safety afforded bondholders and noteholders. If earnings only barely cover interest expense, then the creditors' promised interest payments are in jeopardy. If, however, earnings are several times greater than interest expense, then, in the absence of a business reversal, their return is reasonably assured.

Since the objective of the ratio is to indicate the earnings available for the payment of interest, it is important that the interest expense itself be added back to net income. Moreover, since interest payments are a deductible expense in the determination of taxable income, income taxes should also be added back. In a sense, the payment of interest takes precedence over the payment of federal and provincial income taxes. Required income tax payments are calculated after deducting payments to creditors. If the firm, after payment of interest, has zero income or a net loss, then the tax liability is zero.

As indicated in the financial statements presented in Chapter 7, Sun Ice Limited had net income (after taxes, in thousands) of $310 in 1994. Income taxes, both federal and provincial, were $15. Interest expense was $25. Times interest earned was

$$\text{Times interest earned} = \frac{\text{Net income} + \text{interest expense} + \text{income taxes}}{\text{Interest expense}}$$

$$= \frac{\$310 + \$25 + \$15}{\$25}$$

$$= \frac{\$350}{\$25} = 14 \text{ times}$$

The company covered its interest expense 14 times. This is a fairly high interest coverage ratio and reflects the fact that Sun Ice has very little long-term debt. Most of Sun Ice Limited's assets have been funded by equity, not debt.

As will be indicated in the next section, many companies are increasing the amount of their debt and correspondingly decreasing the ratio of income to interest expense. It is common to find firms with coverage ratios only slightly better than 1 to 1. Whether these companies will, in fact, be able to meet their interest and debt payments is an open question, and the jury is still out as to whether the fiscal guidelines of the past were unduly conservative and restrictive.

JUNK BONDS AND LBOS

In the mid- and late 1980s, a new wave of corporate acquisitions swept over the Canadian economy as well as the U.S. and several other Western economies. These buyouts differed from traditional takeovers in that they were financed mainly by debt rather than by equity (stock). In a conventional acquisition, the purchasing company exchanges shares of its common stock, often newly issued, for those of the target firm. Alternatively, the purchaser might issue new shares of its own stock in the open market and then use the cash proceeds to buy the stock of the target.

In the new type of transaction, the purchaser puts up little of its own money, perhaps 10 percent or less of the purchase price. The remainder is borrowed.

Transactions that are financed primarily with debt are referred to as *leveraged buyouts (LBOs)*. They can be extremely profitable to the buyers because, as their name implies, they make use of financial leverage. *Leverage* is the use of debt to increase the earnings of the shareholders. The benefits of using debt to finance an acquisition can be explained and illustrated with a simple example.

Suppose Company P has 20 million shares of common stock outstanding and has annual earnings after taxes of $15 million, or 75 cents per share. Company P proposes to acquire Company S at a cost of $400 million. Earnings of Company S have been, and will continue to be, $60 million per year (after taxes).

Company P has two options available to obtain the necessary $400 million for the acquisition of Company S: (1) issue 80 million shares of stock at a price of $5 per share or (2) issue 8 million shares at $5 per share (for $40 million) and borrow the remaining $360 million at an interest rate of 10 percent. Exhibit 10-3 shows the effect of each of the alternatives on the earnings per share of Company P's common stock.

As can be seen, if the company finances the acquisition entirely with additional stock, earnings of Company P remain at 75 cents per share; if it finances the acquisition with 90 percent debt and 10 percent equity, earnings increase to $1.84 per share. The leverage is positive in this example because Company P borrowed $360 at a rate of 10 percent ($36 million before taxes, $23.4 million after taxes) and Company S provided $60 million in earnings. However, leverage is not without risks. The interest is a *fixed* cost; it must be paid regardless of actual earnings. Were earnings of Company S to drop below the required interest payments, then earnings of Company P shareholders would be leveraged downward and the shareholders would be worse off for having financed the acquisition with debt.

As is shown in Exhibit 10-3, the advantages of debt over equity financing are greatly enhanced by provisions of the Income Tax Act which allow interest payments to be tax-deductible. Thus the after-tax cost of interest is significantly less than the before-tax cost. By contrast, payments of dividends (the returns to shareholders) are not tax-deductible. Since many acquiring companies assume formidable amounts of debt, they are able to lighten considerably their tax burdens, often down to zero.

EXHIBIT 10-3

Example of Effective Use of Leverage

P to acquire S for $400 million
Option 1: Issue 80 million shares of stock at $5 per share
Option 2: Issue 8 million shares of stock at $5 per share and borrow $360 at an interest rate of 10 percent

	Earnings per Share of P	
	Option 1 100% Stock	Option 2 10% Stock
	(dollars in millions)	
Projected earnings of P (independent of S)	$15.0	$15.0
Earnings to be contributed by S	60.0	60.0
Total earnings of P before interest	$75.0	$75.0
Interest on debt of $360 (after taxes)*	—	(23.4)
Projected net income	$75.0	$51.6
Number of shares of stock of P currently outstanding (millions)	20	20
Number of additional shares to be issued (millions)	80	8
Projected total shares of P outstanding (millions)	100	28
Projected earnings per share of P (projected net income divided by projected shares outstanding)	$0.75	$1.84

*Assume a corporate tax rate of 35 percent. Total interest is $36.0, but effective interest cost, after taxes, is only $23.4:

Interest cost (10% of $360)	$36.0
Tax deduction @ 35%	12.6
Interest after taxes	$23.4

Because of their risk, the bonds issued in LBOs have been dubbed *junk* bonds. They command high rates of interest and are not considered to be of "investment grade" (i.e., suitable for investors unwilling to take high risks). There have been a few major defaults of junk bonds (i.e., the borrower has been unable to meet its fixed obligations). The most spectacular Canadian example is the Campeau Corporation, which financed its purchases of the U.S. department store chains—Allied Stores Corp. and Federated Department Stores Inc.—largely with junk bonds. Campeau's leveraged buyouts coincided with the recession of the early 1990s, when the depressed earnings of the U.S. department stores became insufficient to cover the interest payments on Campeau's junk bonds. Sharp reductions in corporate earnings during that recession meant that many companies were unable to meet their payments on the junk bonds issued in leveraged buyouts. The jewellers Henry Birks and Sons Ltd. and People's Jewellers Ltd. are two other examples in which junk bond–financed Canadian expansion into the U.S. ran into difficulty when corporate earnings were insufficient to cover interest payments. Leverage is all to the good when corporate earnings are sufficient to cover interest costs; it can spell financial disaster when they are not.

A financial arrangement that is of special concern to managers and accountants is *leasing*. In a strict sense a lease involves the right to use land, buildings, equipment, or other property for a specified period of time in return for rent or other compensation. In practice, however, many lease arrangements are the equivalent of instalment loans or other forms of borrowing.

Acquisition by Purchase

Suppose that a construction company is in need of equipment. The cost of the equipment is $100,000; the estimated useful life is 10 years. Since the company does not have sufficient cash on hand to purchase the equipment, it borrows the full cost. The terms of the loan are that principal and interest will be paid in 10 annual instalments of equal amount. The amount of each payment will be determined on the basis of an annual interest rate of 12 percent. If $100,000 is viewed as the present value of an annuity for 10 periods, discounted at a rate of 12 percent, then the annual payment required to amortize the loan can be determined (per Table 4 of the Appendix) as follows:

$$\$100,000 = 5.6502x$$

$$x = \$17,698$$

Upon purchasing the equipment and borrowing the necessary funds, the company would make the following journal entries:

Cash $100,000
    Note payable $100,000
To record the loan of $100,000

Equipment $100,000
    Cash $100,000
To record the purchase of the equipment

Each year the company would make the required payment on the note and would record amortization on the equipment. The division of the payment between principal and interest would, of course, vary from year to year. As the balance of the loan declines, a smaller portion of the payment would be for interest and a larger portion for reduction of the principal. The interest expense for the first year would be 12 percent of the $100,000 balance of the note, or $12,000. The remainder of the total payment of $17,698 would be a repayment of the principal. The entry for the payment of the first year would be

Interest expense $12,000
Note payable 5,698
    Cash $17,698
To record the first payment of the note

The entry for amortization (assuming the straight-line method is being used) would be

tion costs will total $36 million and that the bridge will be built over a two-year period.

The company estimates that construction and collection of cash will adhere to the following timetable:

	Percent Completed in Year	Percent Cash Collected in Year
1996	20	—
1997	80	25
1998	—	75

The company decides to report earnings from the contract on a percentage of completion basis in its financial statements but elects to report the earnings on an instalment basis (i.e., as cash is collected) on its income tax return.

The tax rate is 40 percent. The required tax payments and income statements are shown in Exhibit 10-5.

In the income statement, the tax expense is based on the reported income before taxes, regardless of the required tax payment. *The tax expense follows the income.*

The following journal entries give effect to the appropriate *allocation* of taxes. It is assumed for convenience that the required tax payment (the current portion of the liability) is made entirely in the year to which it is applicable, although in practice a part of the payment is likely to be delayed until the following year:

Year 1996

Income tax expense $320,000
    Deferred taxes $320,000
To record tax expense (No tax payment need be made in 1993; tax expense represents 40 percent of reported income before taxes of $800,000.)

Year 1997

Income tax expense $1,280,000
    Income taxes payable in current year $400,000
    Deferred taxes 880,000
To record tax expense (Required tax payment is $400,000; tax expense represents 40 percent of reported income before taxes of $3,200,000.)

Income taxes payable in current year $400,000
    Cash $400,000
To record payment of taxes

Year 1998

Deferred taxes.. $1,200,000
    Cash $1,200,000
To record payment of taxes (Required tax payment is $1,200,000; reported income is zero, so no tax expense need be charged.)

EXHIBIT 10-5

Required Tax Payments (Instalment Basis)			
	1996	1997	1998
Revenue	$ 0	$10,000,000 (25%)	$30,000,000 (75%)
Expenses applicable to revenues (36/40 of revenues)	0	9,000,000 (25%)	27,000,000 (75%)
Taxable income	$ 0	$ 1,000,000	$ 3,000,000
Tax rate	40%	40%	40%
Tax	$ 0	$ 400,000	$ 1,200,000

Income Statements for Purposes of Financial Reporting (Percentage of Completion Basis)			
	1996	1997	1998
Revenue	$8,000,000 (20%)	$32,000,000 (80%)	$0
Expenses applicable to revenues (36/40 of revenues)	7,200,000 (20%)	28,800,000 (80%)	$0
Income before taxes	$ 800,000	$ 3,200,000	$0
Tax expense (40%)	320,000	1,280,000	0
Net income	$ 480,000	$ 1,920,000	$0

The liability, "deferred taxes," would be reported on the balance sheet among the current or noncurrent liabilities, depending on when it is likely to be reversed. The balance in the account will increase in those years in which the tax expense exceeds the required tax payments and decrease in those years in which required tax payments exceed the tax expense.

Deferred taxes			
(1998)	1,200,000	(1996)	320,000
		(1997)	880,000

Controversial Nature of Tax Allocation

The issue of tax allocation continues to be controversial and there are many accountants who reject the very concept of tax allocation for some of the reasons outlined below.

Lack of Direct Relationship

Tax allocation is rooted in the matching concept; it assumes that there is a cause-and-effect relationship between income and tax expense. It is intended to prevent companies from reporting a relatively high income in one period only to have to report a correspondingly low income when taxes that have been postponed from the earlier years must be paid. Many accountants maintain, however, that the relationship between required tax payments and

As a general principle, the employer is required to disclose the obligation for pension benefits (the actuarial present value of benefits earned to date) and the market value of the pension fund assets. If the obligation is in excess of the assets, an unfunded liability exists.

The Employer's Pension Expense

An employer's pension expense consists of six components. The first three compose the ongoing pension expense. The remaining three represent the amortization of adjustments to the unfunded obligation for pension benefits.

The Three Components of Ongoing Pension Expense

The three components of ongoing pension expense are service cost, interest cost, and investment income.

1. *Service cost.* Service cost is the actuarial present value of the benefits earned by employees for their service *in the current period.* It is similar to wages and salaries. It differs, however, in two ways. First, it will be paid in the future, when the employees retire. Therefore it must be discounted to its present value. Second, it can only be estimated, since the actual amount to be paid is unknown. The amount to be paid will depend on actuarial factors such as employee turnover and mortality rates.

2. *Interest cost.* Interest cost is the increase in the liability to the employees due to the passage of time. As just indicated, the service cost is the present (discounted) value of the benefits earned. The interest cost represents the annual increase in the present value of the benefits earned *in earlier periods.*

3. *Investment income.* Investment income is the expected return on the fund assets. It includes projections of dividends, interest, and gains in value.

    To avoid abrupt changes in annual pension expense, investment income is based on expected rather than actual earnings. As will be explained in the discussion of the fifth component of the employer's pension expense, experience gains and losses (the difference between actual and expected investment earnings [or losses]) will be charged or credited to income over a number of periods, not just one.

In determining net ongoing pension expense, investment income must be *deducted* from service cost and interest cost. Ongoing pension expense is recorded by a standard payroll-type entry. Suppose, for example, that the ongoing pension expense is $50 million. The following entry would be necessary:

Pension expense $50,000,000
    Accrued pension cost (liability) $50,000,000
To record ongoing pension expense

As the employer *funds* the liability by contributing to the fund, the liability would be reduced. If, for example, the employer contributed $40 million, the entry would be

Thus the remaining liability would express the *unfunded* obligation for pension benefits.

Three Additional Elements of Employer Expense

Each of the three remaining components represents the amortization of a deferred charge or deferred credit. These assets or liabilities are established so that certain economic costs or gains will have an impact on reported pension expense over several periods instead of one. This practice causes income to be smoother than if the costs or gains were fully recognized in a single period.

The pattern of accounting for each of the costs or gains to be deferred is similar. Assume the element is a cost (the accounting for gains is a mirror image). The employer would add the full amount of the cost to its accrued pension liability. It would offset the liability with a deferred charge (asset) of the same amount. For purposes of balance sheet display, the asset and liability would be combined, so initially there would be no net effect on the reported accrued pension liability.[5]

Then, over a predetermined number of years, the deferred charge would be amortized. The amortization would be a component of pension expense. As the offsetting deferred charge is reduced, the net reported pension liability would increase. The reported pension liability itself would be reduced only as it was funded.

4. *Past service costs arising from plan initiation or amendment.* When a company initiates a pension plan or enhances pension benefits, the obligation for pension benefits of the pension fund typically increases immediately. That is because the plan amendments generally apply to all employees presently on the payroll, including those who are near retirement age. The new benefits will be based primarily on these employees' *past service* to the firm.

Section 3460 requires that the employer add to its pension liability the actuarial present value of the new benefits. To avoid a major shock to its earnings, the employer does not, however, have to recognize a corresponding expense immediately. Instead, it would debit a deferred charge, "unamortized past service costs." This asset would be amortized in a rational and systematic way over the expected average remaining service periods of the employees eligible to receive benefits.

Suppose that the employer amended its pension plan. The resultant increase in the actuarial present value of its pension obligation was $5 million. The following entry would be in order:

Unamortized past service costs (deferred charge) $5,000,000
    Accrued pension cost (liability) $5,000,000
To recognize the liability and corresponding deferred charge arising from improvements to pension plan

[5] In practice, much of the accounting for pensions is accomplished by "memo" entries. The only entries that are actually "booked" are those that will affect the net amounts to be reported on the balance sheet or income statement.

For purposes of reporting, the asset and liability would be combined. Therefore the entry would have no impact on the pension liability shown on the balance sheet.

If the unamortized past service costs were to be amortized over 25 years, then each year 1/25th would be reported as an expense:

Pension expense $200,000
    Unamortized past service costs (deferred charge) $200,000
To amortize past service costs

This entry would reduce the deferred charge and thereby increase the net (reported) accrued pension liability.

5. *Experience gains and losses.* Experience gains and losses of a pension plan are of two types: (1) actuarial gains and losses and (2) unexpected returns on plan assets. Like past service costs, they are accorded delayed recognition.

Actuarial gains and losses result from changes in actuarial assumptions. As indicated previously, actuarial assumptions are used to estimate the employer's obligation for pension benefits. Changes in actuarial assumptions increase or decrease this liability. For example, an increase in life expectancy would increase the obligation because the pension benefits would have to be paid for a longer period of time.

Unexpected returns on plan assets result whenever actual earnings are greater or less than the previously projected rate. They could be caused by changes in prevailing interest or dividend rates or by unusual shifts in the values of marketable securities.

Pension plans are accounted for from a long-term perspective. Small changes in actuarial assumptions can have a relatively large impact on the obligation for pension benefits. So too can swings in the stock and bond markets. Section 3460 is grounded on a premise that the year-to-year pension expense should not fluctuate widely in the face of changes in the obligation for pension benefits. The effect of any changes should be spread out over a number of periods.

Experience gains and losses are accounted for similarly to past service costs. Suppose that, because of a broad-based fall in securities prices, the actual return on plan assets was $3 million less than the projected return. The following entry would be in order:

Unamortized experience loss (deferred charge) $3,000,000
    Accrued pension cost (liability) $3,000,000
To record an experience loss in the pension plan

As with the unamortized past service cost, the unamortized experience loss (a deferred charge) would be netted against the accrued pension cost and thereby have no immediate impact on the reported pension liability.

Assuming that the deferred charge was to be amortized over 10 years, the following entry would be appropriate each year:

Pension expense $300,000
    Unamortized experience loss (deferred charge) $300,000
To amortize the experience loss

This entry would increase pension expense and, at the same time, increase the accrued pension cost (the liability) reported on the balance sheet.

6. *Transition gains and losses.* Section 3460 imposed new rules as to how to compute the obligation for pension benefits. Thus a firm might have had to increase or decrease its pension liability in the year it first applied Section 3460. To avoid a sudden jolt to earnings, the CICA prescribed that the change be treated similarly to unamortized past service costs. The employer would offset the change in the liability with a deferred charge or credit, unamortized net transition loss or gain. It would then amortize the deferred charge or credit over the expected average remaining service period of employees covered by the plan.

Suppose that as a consequence of adopting Section 3460, the obligation for pension benefits *decreases* by $4 million. The following entry would be appropriate:

Accrued pension cost (liability) $4,000,000
    Unamortized transition gain (deferred credit) $4,000,000
To record the transition gain

As with the entries to record the past service costs and the experience loss, this entry has no immediate balance sheet effect, since the unamortized transition gain or loss is combined with the accrued pension cost liability.

As the unamortized transition gain is amortized (assume over a period of 10 years), both the annual pension expense and the unamortized transition gain are reduced. So also, therefore, is the net pension liability to be reported on the balance sheet:

Unamortized transition gain (deferred credit) $400,000
    Pension expense $400,000
To amortize the transition gain

Summary of Pension Expense

In summary, the pension expense as defined by Section 3460 captures two categories of costs. The first is the "normal," ongoing costs:

1. Service costs, the benefits earned by the employees during the period

2. Interest cost, the annual increase in the present value of the pension liability

3. Investment income, the *expected* return on pension fund assets

The second is the "unusual" costs:

1. Past service costs, amendments to pension benefits

2. Experience gains and losses, changes in actuarial assumptions, and unexpected returns on pension assets

3. Transition gains and losses, the gains and losses from the initial adoption of Section 3460

The unusual costs are not taken into income all in one year. Instead, they are amortized over time.

Summary of Impact on Reported Pension Liability

The accounting for pensions is driven by the expense, not the liability. The reported liability is an artificial accounting construct. It comprises the *unfunded* obligation for pension benefits plus or minus the three deferred charges or credits. The unfunded obligation for pension benefits is the difference between the obligation for pension benefits and the market value of the fund's investments. The three deferred charges or credits are

1. Unamortized past service costs
2. Unamortized experience gains and losses
3. Unamortized transition gains and losses

Exhibit 10-6 summarizes the impact of this section's illustrative transactions on both the pension expense and the pension liability.

Exhibit 10-7 compares the economic and reporting consequences of selected events and transactions. Note that some have an economic impact on either or both the obligation for pension benefits or the fund assets. Nevertheless, they are given no immediate accounting recognition in that they have no effect on the reported pension expense or liability. They affect the reported pension expense or liability only over time through the process of amortization.

EXHIBIT 10-6

Effect of Journal Entries on Pension Expense and Liability (in millions)

Pension Expense

Net ongoing expense for year (includes service costs, interest cost, and investment income)		$50.0
Add: Amortization of deferred charges and credits		
Past service costs (plan amendments)	$0.2	
Experience loss (less than expected return on plan assets)	0.3	
Transition gain	(0.4)	0.1
Net pension expense		$50.1

Pension Liability

Increase due to ongoing pension expense		$50.0
Add: Increases due to nonroutine events		
Plan amendments	$5.0	
Experience loss	3.0	
Transition gain	(4.0)	4.0
		54.0
Subtract: Increases in offsetting deferred charges and credits, net of amortization		
Past service costs	$4.8	
Experience loss	2.7	
Transition gain	(3.6)	3.9
Increase in pension liability prior to employer contributions		50.1
Employer contribution to plan		(40.0)
Net increase in pension liability		$10.1

EXHIBIT 10-7
Comparison of Economic and Reporting Consequences of Selected Transactions and Events

Transaction or Economic Event	Economic Impact[1]			Impact on Financial Statements of Employer		
	Obligation for Pension Benefits	– Assets of Fund	Unfunded Obligation = for Pension Benefits	Reported Pension Expense	Reported Pension Liability[2]	Net Deferred Charge[3]
Employees earn benefits	I	NE	I	I	I	NE
Interest on pension obligation increases with passage of time	I	NE	I	I	I	NE
Fund investments increased by interest and dividend earnings (at expected rate)	NE	I	D	D	D	NE
Employer makes cash contribution to pension fund	NE	I	D	NE	D	NE
Plan pays benefits to retired employees	D	D	NE	NE	NE	NE
Benefits attributable to past service are enhanced by changes to plan	I	NE	I	NE	NE	I
Past service costs are amortized	NE	NE	NE	I	I	D
Actuary changes assumptions to increase actuarial obligation	I	NE	I	NE	NE	I
Actuarial changes are amortized	NE	NE	NE	I	I	D
Plan investments earn returns greater than expected	NE	I	D	NE	NE	D*
Greater than expected returns are amortized	NE	NE	NE	D	D	I*
Actuary reports adoption of Section 3460 increases acturial obligation	I	NE	I	NE	NE	I
Transition costs are amorized	NE	NE	NE	I	I	D

I = Increase; D = Decrease; NE = No effect.

[1] Calculations of the obligation for pension benefits will be made by the plan's actuary. Information on the market value of the plan's assets will be provided by a trustee who administers the fund. The difference between the obligation for pension benefits and the market value of the assets is the unfunded obligation for pension benefits.

[2] The reported pension liability is the obligation that will be reported on the employer's balance sheet. It represents the unfunded obligation for pension benefits plus or minus the net deferred charge. The deferred items are disclosed in the notes to the financial statements but on the balance sheet they are netted against the unfunded obligation for pension benefits. As a result, transactions and events that increase or decrease both the unfunded obligation for pension benefits and the net deferred charge have no effect on the reported pension liability. The reported pension liability is affected only by events or transactions that affect *either* the unfunded obligation for pension benefits *or* the net deferred charge—but not both.

[3] This column indicates the deferred items. An increase (I) represents either an increase in a deferred cost (charge) or a decrease in a deferred credit. A decrease (D) denotes either a decrease in a deferred charge or an increase in a deferred credit. The items marked by an asterisk (*) would affect deferred credits.

Required Note Disclosures

A typical corporate income statement and balance sheet may reveal nothing of the company's pension fund, since the various pension accounts are aggregated and often combined with nonpension accounts. The information of significance is revealed in the notes to the financial statements. Exhibit 10-8 illustrates the disclosures required by Section 3460.

Part 1 of Exhibit 10-8 disaggregates the pension expense into the three elements of current service cost and the net amortization of the deferred charges and credits.

The second table shows both the *accumulated obligation for pension benefits* and the *obligation for pension benefits*. The *accumulated obligation for pension benefits* (an obligation not previously discussed) is similar to the obligation for pension benefits. It is the actuarial present value of all benefits that have been earned. It differs from the obligation for pension benefits in that the obligation for pension benefits is based on estimated increases in wage and salary levels. Future compensation is relevant to the pension obligation because pension benefits are almost always based on earnings throughout an employee's career. The accumulated obligation for pension benefits, by contrast, incorporates no assumptions as to future rates of compensation. The difference between the two measures, as shown in the second table, is therefore the actuarial value of the benefits attributable to the compensation increases.

EXHIBIT 10-8
Example of Pension Note Disclosures

1. Pension costs of a corporation's domestic operations aggregated $8,819,000 in 1997:

	(in thousands)
Service cost (benefit earned during period)	$12,636
Interest cost	25,454
Actual return on plan assets	(7,799)
Net amortization of transition items and deferrals	(21,472)
Net periodic pension cost	$ 8,819

2. The actuarial present value of obligation for pension benefits and the funded status for the corporation's domestic plans at December 31, 1997, was

	(in thousands)
Obligation for pension benefits:	
Accumulated obligation for pension benefits:	
Vested benefits	$254,200
Nonvested benefits	14,400
	268,600
Projected compensation increases	48,400
Total projected obligation for pension benefits	$317,000
Fair value of plan assets available for benefits, primarily	
Canadian government bonds and equity securities	299,500
Obligation for pension benefits in excess of plan assets	$ 17,500
Unrecognized past service cost (a deferred charge)	(23,300)
Unrecognized net experience gain (a deferred credit)	7,500
Unamortized transition gain (a deferred credit)	5,200
Net pension liability	$ 6,900

3. The actuarial assumptions used in accounting for the corporation's domestic plans at December 31 were as follows:

Weighted average discount rate	8.5%
Rate of increase in compensation	5.5%
Expected long-term rate of return on plan assets	9.0%

Part 2 of Exhibit 10-8 also indicates the investments of the fund, valued at market, that are available for the payment of benefits. Added to, or subtracted from, the investments are the deferred charges and credits. The difference between the obligation for pension benefits and the net assets available for benefits, plus or minus the deferred items, is the *net pension liability*.[6] This is the amount that will be reported as a long-term liability on the balance sheet.

[6] If the net assets available for benefits, plus or minus the deferred items, *exceed* the obligation for pension benefits, then the firm would report a net pension *asset*.

The note also sets forth (see part 3 of Exhibit 10-8) key actuarial assumptions: the rate used to discount the benefits to be paid in the future, the rate of compensation increases used to calculate the obligation for pension benefits, and the expected rate of return on fund investments.

Pension accounting is another example of a problem that has proved exceedingly intractable. The discussion in this text, as was true of that on income taxes, only hints at the complexity of both the issues and the resultant pronouncements.

OTHER POSTEMPLOYMENT BENEFITS

Many progressive companies provide retired employees benefits in addition to pensions. The most common of these are supplemental health care and life insurance. These benefits present accounting challenges that are exceedingly similar to pensions but even less surmountable. Employees earn these benefits, like wages, salaries, and pensions, during their working years. The payment is deferred, however, until they retire. As with pensions, the eventual cost to the employer will depend on actuarial variables such as employee turnover, mortality rates, and investment earnings. Unlike pension benefits, however, the annual amount to be paid on behalf of each employee is beyond the control of the company. The amount that an employee receives each year in pension benefits is a function of salary earned and number of years of service. By contrast, the annual medical insurance premiums paid on behalf of the employee will depend on the cost of medical services at the time. Technological and scientific changes in the field of health care make it beyond the capabilities of employers to predict reliably the form that health care will take in the distant future, let alone its cost.

At present the *CICA Handbook* does not include any recommendations for the accounting for postemployment benefits other than pensions. The Emerging Issues Committee of the CICA considered the issue in 1989 and recommended that disclosure be made of the type of postemployment benefits other than pensions provided by the employer and a description of the method of accounting for such benefits. This issue is less significant in Canada than it is in the United States because of the current system of universal health care provided by the Canadian government. The cost to the corporation of providing supplemental health care is minor compared with the cost of funding all health care, as is the case in the United States.

The FASB has recognized the similarity between health care, life insurance, and pension benefits and has recently released SFAS 106, "Employers' Accounting for Postretirement Benefits Other Than Pensions." SFAS 106 requires that all postemployment benefits be accounted for as they are earned by the employees. They may no longer be accounted for on a pay-as-you-go basis.

The FASB's pronouncement on other postemployment benefits is likely to have a more profound impact on the financial statements of corporations than any other statement that it has issued. Some sources have estimated that the change will add $1 trillion of liability to the balance sheets of U.S. companies. The effect will be so great—greater even than that of the statement on pensions—because most companies have not funded their postemployment benefits as they have been earned by their employees. Thus they will have to "book" the entire obligation when the new rules are adopted and will have no assets set aside to offset the new liability. For example, in the year ended December 31, 1991, International Business Machines Corp. (IBM) took a charge to earnings of $2.3 billion after taxes to account for the future cost of health care benefits for retirees, in conforming to the provisions of SFAS 106.

It is important to note that these huge charges to income did not cause significant declines in the company's share prices when they were announced. This is because the postemployment benefits were not a new liability. Both the companies and their shareholders already knew the cost of the postemployment liabilities; they simply weren't recorded in the financial statements before the implementation of SFAS 106.

Summary

In this chapter we have reviewed the accounting for several types of liabilities—bonds, leases, taxes, pensions, and other postemployment benefits. Each of the liabilities is directly related to an expense—interest expense, income tax expense, and pension and other postemployment expense. The amount at which a liability is stated on the balance sheet is tied to the related expense.

In economic substance, the value of a liability, like that of an asset, is the present value of what will have to be paid. Liabilities, like assets, however, are not necessarily reported on the balance sheet at their economic value. "Deferred taxes," for example, need not be discounted to reflect a present value. Bonds, by contrast, are shown at an amount indicative of their present value (although the present value is based on the discount rate that determined the initial value of the bond, not the discount rate that prevails on the balance sheet date).

Some liabilities, such as for pensions and postemployment health benefits, are subject to especially thorny problems of measurement. The amount to be paid is dependent on a number of actuarial variables, such as employees' turnover and mortality, and on earnings on amounts in the fund established to pay the liabilities.

The guiding principle in accounting for liabilities and their related expenses is that both should be recognized when the obligation is first established and the firm has benefited from the cost. Timing of cash payment should not dictate recognition of either the liability or the expense. Nevertheless, of the liabilities discussed in this chapter, those associated with at least four costs—income taxes, leases, pensions, and postemployment benefits—were not until recently even recorded on the balance sheet. Instead, the costs were accounted for on a pay-as-you-go basis. In large part, the reluctance of the accounting profession to require that they be recorded can be ascribed to the need to estimate their values, since the amount of payment cannot always be known until the distant future. Efforts on the part of the standard-setting authorities to mandate timely recognition of these liabilities and expenses have met with considerable resistance and controversy. Nonetheless, the trend in standard setting is clear. Corporations can no longer keep their obligations off the balance sheet. They must bring them into the light.

On January 1, 1997, a company issued 10 million face value bonds. The bonds had a coupon rate of 8 percent, but they were issued at a price that provided bondholders a return of only 6 percent. The bonds were to mature in 20 years and pay interest semiannually on June 30 and December 31.

1. How much interest will the company be required to pay each six months?

2. How much interest would a bondholder expect to receive semiannually based on the prevailing yields of comparable securities?

3. What is the difference between the two amounts?

4. What is the present value of the difference based on the effective yield rate (compounded semiannually) and the number of periods until maturity?

5. What is the premium or discount at which the bonds will be issued? What is the total issue price?

6. What is the interest, based on the effective yield rate, that the company should record as an expense when, on June 30, 1997, it is required to make the first interest payment?

7. What is the actual required interest payment on June 30, 1997?

8. What is the difference between the interest expense and the required interest payment on June 30, 1997? By how much should the recorded value of the bond premium be reduced?

9. What is the effective liability of the bonds on July 1, 1997?

10. What is the interest expense that the company should record on December 31, 1997, when it is required to make its second payment of interest?

1. A friend recently purchased $10,000 of Canadian Pacific Limited bonds. The company is considered as financially sound as any major Canadian corporation. The bonds are scheduled to mature in 30 years, but your friend intends to sell them within two or three years to provide funds for her child's education. She wants a "safe" investment. She decided not to purchase the common stock of the same company because she viewed it as too risky. Do you think she made a wise decision? Would she have been better off buying Canadian Pacific Limited bonds that matured in only three years? Explain.

2. The account "discount on bonds payable" ordinarily has a debit balance. It has sometimes been argued that bond discount, like most other accounts which have debit balances, should be reported as an asset rather than as *contra* (as an adjustment) to a long-term liability. Considering the nature of bond discounts, do you agree?

3. For many years there has been controversy over the accounting for gains and losses that may arise when a company repurchases or redeems its own

bonds at a price different from the value at which they are recorded on its books. Why have some financial observers charged that major corporations have engaged in repurchases or redemptions to give an artificial boost to earnings? How is this possible?

4. Why are some lease arrangements accounted for as if they were instalment purchases? Why do some accountants believe that almost all long-term noncancelable lease agreements should be *capitalized* (i.e., assets and corresponding liabilities recorded) on the balance sheet? Why might a company believe that it is able to present a more favourable balance sheet by leasing, rather than purchasing, plant or equipment?

5. Why might a company report a tax expense on its income statement that is greater or less than the required tax payment indicated on its income tax return?

6. Why do some financial experts contend that tax allocation results in an overstatement of liabilities, in that amounts that may never have to be paid are included among reported obligations?

7. Distinguish between a defined *contribution* and a defined *benefit* pension plan. Why do defined benefit plans present the more difficult accounting issues?

8. What are the three elements of *ongoing* pension expense? What other elements of cost are incorporated into a firm's total pension expense?

9. As a consequence of a rapid increase in stock prices, the return on investment of a pension fund greatly exceeds expectations. How would the rise in the value of the fund assets affect the pension expense to be reported by the employer in the year of the increase? In subsequent years?

10. Why do postemployment benefits, such as life and health insurance, present virtually the same accounting problems as pension benefits?

11. What is a leveraged buyout? What are "junk bonds"?

Problems

1. *The amount for which a bond is issued, as well as subsequent charges to income, is dependent upon the prevailing yield rate at the time of issue.*

   On January 2, 1997, the Green Company issued 12 percent coupon bonds at a price that provided purchasers a yield of 10 percent. The bonds pay interest on June 30 and December 31 and are scheduled to mature on December 31, 1998.
   a. Record the sale of a single $1,000 bond.
   b. Determine interest expense, per $1,000 bond, for each of the four periods and record the first payment of interest.
   c. Record the redemption on December 31, 1988, per bond (including final interest payment).

2. *The prices at which outstanding bonds can be resold fluctuate with changes in the prevailing rates of interest.*

The Edmonton Co. issued at par (i.e., at a price of $100) $20 million in 6 percent, 20-year coupon bonds. Interest is payable semiannually.

a. At the end of two years, prevailing interest rates had increased to 8 percent. At what price could a bondholder sell a single $1,000 bond in the open market?

b. By the end of the fourth year, prevailing interest rates had increased to 10 percent. At what price could a bondholder now sell a single $1,000 bond?

c. What impact would the increase in prevailing interest rates have upon the reported interest expense of the Edmonton Co.?

d. "In comparison with common stocks, bonds provide a relatively risk-free investment." Do you agree?

3. *Call provisions may establish a ceiling on the prices at which outstanding bonds are traded.*

In 1985 the Universal Drilling Co. issued $4,000,000 of 8 percent, 30-year bonds. The bond indentures provided that the company could redeem the bonds any time after 1995 at a price of $102. Interest is payable semiannually.

In 2000, with 15 years remaining until maturity, the company decided to retire the bonds. Since the prevailing interest rate was 10 percent, the company repurchased the bonds in the open market at the prevailing price.

a. Determine the price that the company would have to pay to redeem the bonds.

b. Assume instead that the prevailing annual interest rate in 2000 was 5 percent. Determine the price that the company would have to pay for the bonds. Be sure to consider the maximum price at which the bonds are likely to trade in light of the call provision.

4. *Years to maturity is a primary influence on bond value—but only up to a point.* (This problem is intended for solution using an electronic spreadsheet.)

As the treasurer of a company, you are estimating the amount of cash your firm will receive from a pending issue of 30-year bonds. The bonds will bear a coupon rate of 9 percent and will pay interest semiannually. The issue price of the bonds will depend on prevailing yields on the date the bonds are actually issued.

a. Prepare a table in which you indicate the issue price of each $1,000 bond, assuming the following yield rates: 8.8 percent; 8.9 percent; 9.0 percent; 9.1 percent; 9.2 percent.

b. Assume instead that the bonds (with the coupon rate of 9 percent) are to be issued to yield 8.8 percent.

   (1) Determine the issue price, assuming the following maturities: 10 years, 20 years, 50 years, 100 years.

   (2) Comment on why years to maturity has a critical impact on issue price (or bond value)—but only up to a point. As the number of years increases, the significance of years to maturity diminishes.

5. *Bonds may also be issued between interest dates, and, although not specifically discussed in the text, the accounting problems associated with such issues are not overly complex.*

The city of Richmond Hill on January 31, 1997, issues $40,000,000 of 8 percent coupon bonds to mature in 20 years. The bonds are sold, at par, to yield 8 percent. The bonds require the payment of interest on June 30 and December 31.

a. What will be the required interest payment on June 30, 1997? (All coupons, including the first, require the payment of the same amount of interest.)

b. Since the bondholders on June 30, 1997, have held the bond for only five months, how much interest would they have earned (i.e., actually "deserve" to receive)?

c. Suppose the bondholders agreed to advance the city the portion of the first interest payment that they did not actually earn. How much would they advance the city?

d. Prepare a journal entry to record the issue of the bonds, assuming that the city received the principal plus the unearned portion of the first interest payment.

e. Prepare a journal entry to record the first interest payment. The interest expense should represent the cost of borrowing funds only for the period during which the city had the use of such funds.

6. *Principles of accounting for financial reporting may not be appropriate for managerial decisions.*

In January 1970, the Bowman Co. issued $100,000 of 6 percent, 30-year coupon bonds. The indentures stipulate that the company has the right to *call* (redeem) the bonds at a price of $103 any time after the bonds have been outstanding for 10 years. Interest is payable semiannually. On January 1, 1995, the bonds were stated on the company's books at a value of $98,300; there was a reported discount of $1,700.

In January 1995, when five years remained until maturity, the company controller debated whether or not the company should refund the entire bond issue—that is, whether it should redeem the bonds and reborrow the entire amount required for the redemption. The controller determined that the company could acquire the entire $103,000 necessary to call the outstanding issue by issuing, at par, bonds that paid interest at an annual rate of 5 percent and mature in five years.

The company uses a discount rate of 8 percent to evaluate all financial opportunities.

a. Prepare a journal entry to record the redemption of the bonds.

b. Because the company would have to report a loss on the redemption of the bonds, the controller decided against redeeming the bonds. Do you agree with the decision? (*Hint:* Identify all cash receipts and disbursements that would result in the next five years—10 semiannual periods—under both of the alternatives. Determine their present value to the company.)

7. *The straight-line method of bond amortization distorts the cost of borrowing.*

In the past, companies wishing to avoid the complexities of the *effective interest* means of accounting for bond premium or discount used the *straight-line* amortization method.

Suppose a company issues 10 percent coupon bonds at a price that will provide a return to the bondholders of 8 percent. The bonds will mature in 20 years. Interest is payable semiannually.

a. Prepare a journal entry to record the issue of a single $1,000 bond.

b. Prepare journal entries to record both the *first* and the *last* payments of interest. Assume first that the company uses the effective interest method and second the straight-line method. Be sure to determine the *effective* liability outstanding at the start of each of the periods.

  c. Determine the effective rate of interest recorded as an expense under each of the two methods for both the first and the last payments. That is, express the recorded interest expense as a percentage of the reported effective liability (bonds payable plus unamortized premium).

8. *By redeeming its debt at a "bargain" price, a firm is able to realize a substantial gain.*

    Suppose the financial statements of a company contained the following note:

> During 1997 [the company] purchased $11.6 million principal amount of its $4\frac{1}{2}$ percent convertible debentures due 2027 at a price of $550 each under a tender offer. The resulting net gain was $2.6 million after related deferred income taxes of $2.4 million.

  a. The firm is financially sound. Why do you suspect that it is able to redeem its outstanding debt at a "bargain" price?

  b. The note makes reference to *deferred* income taxes. What does the use of the term *deferred* suggest about the provisions of the tax laws pertaining to gains on the redemption of bonds?

  c. Suppose that the company is unable to pay off its debt without reducing the scale of its operations. It therefore has to reborrow the amount that it paid to the holders of the $4\frac{1}{2}$ percent debentures. How do you think the rate of interest on the new debt would compare with that on the old (much higher, much lower, etc.)? Will the company really be better off as a consequence of having "refunded" (paid off and reborrowed) its debt? What is the real nature of the gain of $5 million (before taxes)? When did the gain really occur—at the time of refunding or in the several previous accounting periods?

9. *An important issue facing banks and other financial institutions is whether they should give immediate accounting recognition to unfavourable modifications in the terms of debt arrangements.*

    A bank acquired $50 million of the bonds of Gotham City. The bonds paid interest at a rate of 10 percent and were sold to yield 10 percent (that is, they were sold "at par"). The bonds were to mature in five years.

    Shortly after the bank made its investment, Gotham City faced a fiscal crisis. After a series of complex legal manoeuvres, it was able to "restructure" its debt. The city was permitted to extend the maturity of the debt from five years to ten years and to reduce the rate of interest paid from 10 percent to 6 percent. The amount of principal owed (the face value of the bonds) was to remain unchanged.

  a. What is the value to the bank of its Gotham City bonds immediately following the restructuring? That is, what is the present value, discounted at the prevailing yield rate of 10 percent per year (5 percent per period), of the anticipated payment of $50 million in principal and the anticipated 20 semiannual payments of $1,500,000 in interest?

  b. Do you think that the bank should "write down" the carrying value of the bonds from $50 million to the amount determined in part (a) and thereby recognize an immediate loss? If it did, what would be the impact on earnings of the current year and future years as compared with that if it did not? How would total earnings, over the remaining life of the issue, be affected by a decision to recognize an immediate loss? (*Note:* The question of how to account for "restructured debt," although not specifically dealt with in the text, was an important issue in the mid-1970s as a consequence of fiscal crises that faced New York City as well as a large number of firms in the real-estate industry. The FASB, in *Statement No. 15,* ruled that in situations similar to the one described in this problem no write-down would be required. However, in cases where total anticipated receipts of both principal and interest, without regard to their *present* value, are less than the carrying value of the debt, an immediate loss would have to be recognized.)

10. *Bonds can provide substantial returns to their holders—even if they pay zero interest.*

    The *Wall Street Journal* reported that PepsiCo, Inc., planned "to take out a 'loan' on which it won't have to pay any interest for 30 years." According to the *Journal,* the company would issue bonds that would pay no annual interest. Instead the bonds, known as "zero coupon" securities, would be sold at a "deep discount" from face value and would then be redeemed at the full face amount upon maturity. The difference between the two would be the investors' return.

    The *Journal* indicated that PepsiCo would issue $25 million of the new securities. Initially, each bond with a face value of $1,000 would be priced at $270.

    a. Suppose that a 30-year bond was priced to sell for $270. What would be the effective percentage yield (within 1 percent) to the purchaser? (To be able to make use of the tables in the Appendix, assume that interest is compounded annually rather than semiannually).

    b. What would be the primary advantage to the borrower in issuing zero coupon bonds?

    c. Suppose, as in part (a), that a bond was issued for $270. What journal entry would you propose that the firm make to record
       (1) Issuance of the bond?
       (2) First-year interest expense?
       (3) Second-year interest expense?

11. *Principles of liability valuation are essential to assessing the assets of thrifts (savings and loan associations) as well as financial institutions in general.*

    A letter to the *Wall Street Journal* stated,

    > "Threat to Thrifts" [a previous article] skirts the real, present, financial plight of not only thrifts but of banking institutions in general. So-called "net worth" is only an illusion, a distortion of reality resulting from the treatment of 8 percent mortgage loans with 15 years amortization as being worth the principal balance due on them rather than the market value, in today's 15 percent mortgage market, of less than 70 percent of the unpaid balance. (The Penn Central also had an impressive net worth prior to its bankruptcy.)

    The author went on to suggest that a more meaningful measure of the assets (i.e., the mortgage loans outstanding) of a thrift institution would be their current market values.

    Suppose that a thrift institution issued a 30-year mortgage loan of $100,000 at an annual rate of interest of 8 percent. Annual payments on the loan were $8,883. (Although mortgage notes often require monthly payments, assume for convenience in this problem that only one payment per year is required.) Each yearly payment would contain an element of interest (8 percent of the remaining loan balance) and an element of principal.

a. What would be the "book value" (i.e., the remaining principal balance) of the loan after 15 years?

b. What would be the most likely market value of the loan, assuming that prevailing interest rates on mortgage loans had increased to 15 percent?

c. Is the letter writer correct in asserting that market value is likely to be less than 70 percent of the book value (unpaid principal balance)?

12. *The distinction, in economic substance, between an instalment purchase and a financial lease may be trivial.*

The covenants incorporated into the outstanding bonds of the Eastern Machine Co. stipulate the maximum amount of debt that the company can incur. The company wishes to expand its plant and purchase new equipment but has insufficient funds to purchase the equipment outright. Since the company is prohibited by the existing covenants from borrowing the needed funds, its controller has suggested that the firm arrange for the manufacturer of the equipment to sell the equipment to a lending institution. The lending institution would, in turn, lease the equipment to the company. The lending institution would provide no maintenance or related services, and the company would have responsibility for insuring the equipment. Upon the expiration of the lease, the company would have the option of purchasing the equipment at a price of $1. If the company were to acquire the equipment outright, its cost would be $1,500,000. If it were to borrow the funds, it would be required to pay interest at the rate of 9 percent per year. The financial institution has agreed to a noncancelable lease with a term of 12 years, a term corresponding to the useful life of the equipment.

a. If the company decides to lease the equipment, what would be the most probable annual rental payments?

b. How do you suspect the controller intends to account for the acquisition of the equipment? What journal entries do you think she would propose at the time the equipment is acquired? At the time the first payment of rent is made?

c. Do the proposals of the controller in your opinion reflect the substance of the transaction? Are they in accordance with provisions of the CICA? What alternative journal entries would you propose?

13. *Ownership arrangements that are different in form may be similar in economic substance.*

Deception, Inc., currently has a loan outstanding from the Gibraltar Insurance Co. that requires that Deception, Inc., maintain a "debt-to-equity ratio" no greater than 1:1. That is, the balance in all liability accounts can be no greater than that in the share capital and retained earnings accounts. As of December 31, Deception, Inc., had total liabilities of $3 million and total share capital and retained earnings of $3,150,000.

The vice-president of production of Deception, Inc., has proposed that the company purchase new equipment that would cost $303,756. The equipment would have a three-year useful life and no salvage value and during its life would allow for substantial cost savings to the company. Aware that the company is short of cash, the vice-president arranged with the manufacturer of the equipment for the company to give a three-year note for the purchase price. Interest would be at the rate of 9 percent on the unpaid balance. Payments would be made at the end of each of the three years as follows:

Year	Remaining Balance	Payment of Interest at 9%	Payment of Principal	Total Payment
1	$303,756	$27,338	$ 92,662	$120,000
2	211,094	18,998	101,002	120,000
3	110,092	9,908	110,092	120,000
			$303,756	

When the company controller was informed of the proposed purchase, he advised the vice-president that the additional debt would increase the firm's debt-to-equity ratio above the maximum permitted in its loan agreement with Gibraltar Insurance. As an alternative, he recommended an arrangement whereby Deception, Inc., would *lease* the new equipment from the manufacturer. The lease could not be cancelled and would be for a term of three years. Annual rent would be $120,000, but Deception, Inc., would have to pay all maintenance and insurance costs. At the expiration of the lease, Deception, Inc., would have an option to purchase the machine for $1.

a. Prepare all journal entries that would be required on the books of Deception, Inc., if it agreed to *purchase* the machine and issued the note for $303,756. The company records amortization on a straight-line basis.

b. Prepare all journal entries that would be required if the firm agreed to lease the machine and accounted for it as an operating lease.

c. What are the total charges associated with the acquisition of the machine under each of the two alternatives?

d. Comment on the difference, if any, in the *substance* of the two transactions. Viewing the transactions from the point of view of Gibraltar Insurance Co., how would you propose that the firm record the transaction if it decided to *lease* the equipment? What changes would you make to the entries in part (a) above?

14. *Recommendations of the CICA Handbook are intended to prevent firms from avoiding balance sheet disclosure of financial obligations by leasing rather than purchasing long-lived assets.*

The managers of Business Services, Inc., are debating whether to buy or to rent a computer. A computer manufacturer has offered the company the opportunity to lease a machine for $200,000 per year over a period of 6 years. Alternatively, the company would purchase the machine outright and could borrow the purchase price from an insurance company at an annual rate of 8 percent. The note to the insurance company would be repaid in 6 equal annual instalments, each instalment representing both a repayment of principal and a payment of interest on the unpaid balance.

Costs of operating the equipment would be the same under either alternative; the salvage value after 6 years would be negligible.

Currently the company has total assets of $5 million, total liabilities of $2 million, and total owners' equity of $3 million.

a. What is the maximum that the company should be willing to pay to purchase the machine?

b. Suppose that the company paid the maximum amount. Compare total expenses that would be reported during the first year if the company purchased the machine as opposed to leasing it, assuming that it accounts for the transaction as an operating lease (although under current CICA recommendations the lease would satisfy the criteria of a capital lease). The company uses the straight-line method of amortization.

c. Determine the ratio of total debt to total owners' equity under each of the alternatives immediately upon acquisition of the asset (prior to giving effect to first-year expenses).

15. *With the most commonly used methods of amortization, capitalized leases may result in expenses that decline over the life of the lease. (This problem is intended for solution using an electronic spreadsheet.)*

A company leases equipment that has a market value of $900,000. The term of the lease is 10 years, which is also the useful life of the equipment. Annual lease payments are to be based on an implicit interest rate of 10 percent. At the end of the period, the company will have the option to acquire the equipment for a nominal amount.

a. Determine the annual lease payments.

b. Prepare a schedule in which you show
   (1) "Loan" balance at start of year
   (2) Interest expense for year
   (3) Reduction of principal
   (4) Amortization of leasehold (on a straight-line basis)
   (5) Total expense for year

c. Compute total expense for the entire 10-year period. How does it compare with what the total expense would have been had the lease been accounted for as an *operating* lease?

d. Comment on the trend over the 10-year period in annual expenses (interest plus amortization). Is there an amortization method that would result in level annual expenses? Explain.

16. *The perceptive financial analyst would adjust for differences between companies relating to the means of financing and accounting for long-term assets and obligations.*

As a financial analyst, you are reviewing the 1997 annual reports of two discount department store firms. The reports indicate that one of the two companies owns all its stores; the other leases them. A footnote to the financial statements of the firm that leases contains the following information:

> The company operates principally in leased premises. The terms of the leases range from 10 to 20 years. The leases meet the criteria of noncapitalized leases (operating leases) as defined by the *CICA Handbook* and accordingly have not been included among long-term liabilities. Total minimum rental commitments are as follows (in thousands):

1998–2002	$60,000 per year
2003–2012	$50,000 per year
2013–2017	$20,000 per year

An additional note to the financial statements indicates that the company's cost of borrowing is 10 percent.

What adjustments to the assets and liabilities of the firm that leases its stores would make its financial reports comparable to those of the firm that owns the stores?

17. *The leasing note of George Weston Limited highlights the difference between capital and operating leases.*

The following is adapted from the notes to the financial statements of George Weston Limited (1987):

Leases

Minimum lease commitments together with the present value of the obligations under capital leases are

	Minimum Lease Payments (in millions)	
	Capital	Operating
Fiscal year		
1988	$ 17.4	$ 93.7
1989	15.6	86.2
1990	24.4	76.9
1991	13.4	67.4
1992	13.9	57.8
Thereafter to 2054	139.6	277.7
Total minimum lease payments	224.3	659.7
Less: Minimum sublease rental income		(159.9)
Net minimum lease payments	$224.3	$499.8
Less interest at a weighted average rate of 10.4%	(122.9)	
Obligations under capital leases, of which $5.7 million is due within one year	$101.4	

a. How much debt due to capital leases is presently recorded on the balance sheet as lease liabilities? Explain. What is meant by "interest at a weighted average rate of 10.4%" in the schedule of lease commitments?

b. Suppose that the firm were to capitalize all operating leases. How much additional debt would that add to the George Weston Limited balance sheet? Assume a discount rate of 12 percent and that the $277.7 million in payments for "thereafter to 2054" will be spread evenly ($27.8 million per year) over a period of 10 years starting in 1993.

18. *By the time an asset is fully amortized, the balance in the deferred tax account related to that asset should be reduced to zero.*

The Frost Co. purchased equipment in 1996 at a cost of $200,000. The equipment had an estimated useful life of four years with zero salvage value. The company elected to use straight-line amortization for general reporting purposes but decided to take advantage of the maximum capital cost allowance, which is a declining balance rate of 50 percent.

In each of the four years from 1996 through 1999 the company had earnings of $100,000, before both amortization on the equipment and taxes. The tax rate is 40 percent.

a. Determine taxable income and taxes payable for each of the four years. Assume that the asset's undepreciated capital cost goes to zero in the fourth year.

b. Determine reported tax expense and net income for each of the four years, assuming that tax expense is based on reported rather than taxable income.

c. Prepare journal entries to give effect to the allocation of income tax expense for each of the four years. Assume that all taxes are paid in the year in which they are incurred. Determine, and keep track of, the year-end balances in the deferred taxes account.

19. *As long as a company continues to expand, the balance in its deferred tax liability account will continue to increase.*

A company made purchases of capital assets as follows (in millions):

Year	
1	$ 60
2	90
3	120
4	120
5	0
6	0
7	0

The useful lives of all assets are four years. They have no residual value. The income tax rate is 40 percent.

The company uses the straight-line method of amortization for reporting purposes and the maximum capital cost allowance (CCA) deduction, based on a declining balance rate of 50 percent, for tax purposes.

a. Determine, for each of the seven years, total amortization that would be reported on the financial statements and the CCA which would be deductible for tax purposes. Indicate the difference each year.

b. Determine the taxes that would be *saved* (postponed) or would have to be *repaid* during each of the seven years.

c. Determine the amount that would be reported as a deferred tax liability at the end of each year.

d. Suppose that the firm continued to increase its purchases of capital assets after the third year. What would be the effect on the deferred tax liability? Why do you suppose some managers and accountants are opposed to tax allocation?

20. *A liability for taxes that will have to be paid in the future should be established whenever a company is permitted to recognize revenue for financial reporting purposes in one period and for tax purposes in a later period.*

The Central Ontario Land Co. was organized on January 1, 1996. The corporation issued 10,000 shares of common stock for $1 million cash. The company elected to recognize revenue on the instalment basis (i.e., upon collection of cash) for income tax purposes but at time of sale for general accounting and reporting purposes.

In 1996 the company purchased a parcel of land for $1,200,000 cash. In the same year it sold the land for $2 million; the buyer made a down payment of $1,000,000 and paid the balance in 1997.

In 1997 the company purchased another parcel of land for $3.6 million cash and sold it for $4 million. The buyer paid the entire amount in cash at the time of sale.

The effective tax rate is 40 percent. The company pays all taxes in the year to which they are applicable. The company allocates taxes as appropriate.

Prepare a statement of income and a balance sheet for 1996 and 1997.

21. *Information about a corporation's pension costs and obligations is to be found in notes, not the income statement or the balance sheet.*

The following are excerpts from the pension plans note of Placer Dome Inc. for the year ended December 31, 1992. Observe how the company, which has numerous independent plans, has elected to combine them. This form of display, while not typical, is not uncommon. It should be noted that Section 3460 of the CICA Handbook requires disclosure of only the obligation for pension benefits and the value of the pension fund assets. However, many Canadian companies that are listed on one of the U.S. stock exchanges, such as Placer Dome, disclose additional details that would be required under U.S. GAAP.

Placer Dome has both defined benefit and defined contribution pension plans requiring contributions by the Corporation or its subsidiaries. Pension benefits are based, in defined benefit plans, on employees' earnings and years of service. Most of the plans are funded currently based on periodic actuarial estimates and statutory requirements. Pension expense charged against earnings was $8 million in 1992, $7 million in 1991, and $8 million in 1990.

The status of defined benefit plans as at December 31, 1992 is as follows:

	Plans with Assets in Excess of Projected Benefits	Plans with Projected Benefits in Excess of Assets
	(in millions)	
Net assets available for plan benefits, at market values	$86	$ —
Projected benefit obligations, including provision for future pay increases	70	15
Plan assets in excess of (less than) projected benefit obligations	16	(15)
Unamortized January 1, 1986 surplus	(7)	—
Unamortized experience gains	—	2
	$ 9	$ (13)

In determining the present value of accumulated plan benefits and current service pension cost the discount rates and expected rates of return on plan assets used vary from 8.0 percent to 8.5 percent and the salary escalation rates assumed vary from 5.5 percent to 6.0 percent. The rates used reflect management's and actuarial assessments of the economic conditions in each of the countries in which Placer Dome operates. The amortization periods for unrecognized gains, losses, surpluses and deficits associated with pension plans vary from 3 to 25 years and are based on the expected average remaining service life of each employee group.

    a. Would Placer Dome report a net pension asset or liability on its balance sheet? Of what amount?
    b. Has the company's actuarial experience been better or worse than anticipated? Explain.
    c. Did Placer Dome's projected benefit obligation increase or decrease as a result of the company's having adopted Section 3460 in 1986? How can you tell?
    d. By how much does the company expect wages and salaries to increase each year in the future?

22. *Some, but not all, changes in an employer's pension obligation are incorporated into pension expense.*

In reviewing your company's earnings forecast, you became aware of several factors that may influence pension costs. Indicate as best you can from the information provided how each of the following is likely to affect *reported* pension expense. The company maintains a defined benefit plan. It amortizes deferred pension debits and credits over 10 years.

    a. Employees will earn benefits of $20 million attributable to service of the current year. The company plans to contribute $25 million to the pension fund.
    b. The company expects to improve its plan. The change will increase the plan's obligation for pension benefits attributable to prior employee service by $25 million.
    c. The company will earn $2 million on pension investments during the year (as previously projected).
    d. The company will change its actuarial assumptions as to investment earnings and employee turnover. The change will decrease its obligation for pension benefits by $8 million.

23. *This problem tests and reviews the terminology used in a typical pension footnote.*

The information that follows was excerpted from the pension note of Imperial Oil Limited, an oil exploration, refining, and distribution company whose shares are traded on the Toronto Stock Exchange.

Retirement-income benefits are company-paid and cover almost all employees. Benefits are based on years of service and final average earnings. The company's related obligations are met through funded registered retirement plans and through unfunded supplementary benefits that are paid directly to most surviving spouses and certain retirees. The data below include funded benefits provided through the Imperial Oil retirement plans, the Company's share of the Syncrude retirement plan and unfunded benefits.

	Dec. 31, 1993	Dec. 31, 1992
	(in millions)	
Accumulated benefit obligation	$2,118	$2,037
Projected benefit obligation	$2,353	$2,271
Market value of assets	1,979	1,732
Unfunded obligation	$ 374	$ 539

Unfunded obligations/(assets) are amortized over the expected average remaining service of employees, which is currently 14 years (1992—14 years).

The discount rate, long-term return on plan assets, and the rate of pay increase were assumed to be 8.5 percent, 8.5 percent, and 5 percent respectively.

a. Does the information in the note relate to a defined benefit plan or a defined contribution plan? Explain.

b. What is represented by the difference between the accumulated benefit obligation of $2,118 million and the projected benefit obligation of $2,353 million?

c. What is the meaning of the unfunded obligation of $374 million at December 31, 1993?

d. What would be the impact on both the accumulated benefit obligation and the projected benefit obligation of an increase in 1994 in
   (1) The weighted average discount rate?
   (2) The rate of return on the plan's assets?

24. *Why would an individual company, and indeed the country at large, adopt an accounting rule that would severely diminish its net worth?*

On November 21, 1988, the LTV Corporation announced that it would take a special charge of $2.26 billion to reflect estimated costs of health and insurance benefits promised to retirees. The company indicated that it was taking the charge in anticipation of a rule change by the Financial Accounting Standards Board that would require companies to include postemployment obligations on their balance sheets. According to the *New York Times*,[7]

> Instead of forcing companies to recognize all the costs immediately as LTV has done, the standards board will permit companies to average the costs over 15 years. Still, many companies have argued that the rule is too drastic and will bite heavily into the net worth of the nation's industrial base.

a. In the year it recorded the charge for postemployment benefits, LTV was in bankruptcy proceedings and attempting to renegotiate its debt with its creditors. It expected to emerge from the proceedings in reorganized form and to be able to continue operations. Why do you think that LTV voluntarily recorded an obligation when generally accepted accounting principles did not require it to do so?

b. The *New York Times* article implies that the FASB's standard on postemployment benefits may severely reduce the country's industrial net worth. In what way will the country be worse off as a consequence of the new accounting rule?

---

[7] *New York Times*, November 22, 1988, p. 29.

1. 4 percent (½ of 8 percent) of $10 million, or $400,000 payable each six months.

2. 3 percent (½ of 6 percent) of $10 million, or $300,000 interest payment expected each six months.

3. $100,000 difference.

4. The present value of an annuity of $100,000 for 40 semiannual periods at a discount rate of 3 percent is, based on Table 4 in the Appendix,

$$\$100,000 \times 23.1148 = \$2,311,480$$

5. The premium is $2,311,480 and the bonds will be issued for $12,311,480 ($10 million + $2,311,480).

6. 3 percent of $12,311,480, or $369,344.

7. $400,000 (see part 1).

8. $400,000 − $369,344 = $30,656 amortization of bond premium.

9. $12,311,480 − $30,656 = $12,280,824 effective bond liability on July 1, 1997.

10. 3 percent of $12,280,824, or $368,425 interest expense.

11

Transactions between a Firm and Its Owners

The previous five chapters have examined financial reporting issues for significant asset and liability categories of typical entities. The next two chapters focus on the owners' equity accounts in both unincorporated and incorporated entities. In unincorporated entities, there is only one capital account. Incorporated entities generally split the owners' equity into two accounts, contributed capital and retained earnings. This chapter illustrates the basic accounting for unincorporated entities and the accounting by corporations for the issuance of various classes of stock.

After studying this chapter, you will be able to

- Understand the differences between unincorporated and incorporated business enterprises
- Describe the unique features of accounting for partnerships and proprietorships
- Distinguish between common stock and preferred stock
- Record the issuance of common and preferred stock
- Calculate and understand the significance of the debt-to-equity ratio

PROPRIETORSHIPS AND PARTNERSHIPS

There are three major types of business enterprises: the individual proprietorship, the partnership, and the corporation. The *proprietorship* is a business firm owned by a single party. The *partnership* is one owned by two or more parties. The *corporation* is a separate legal entity that operates under articles of incorporation issued by the federal or a provincial government and is owned by one or more shareholders.

The proprietorship is far and away the most common type of business in Canada. However, the corporate entity is the most significant in terms of size. Corporations control the majority of the resources in the economy, the bulk of the business receipts, and the majority of the people employed. In addition, the Canadian economy is dominated by a relatively small number of large public corporations.

No Limits on Size

Corporations are often thought of as large enterprises, proprietorships and partnerships as small. While it is true that most proprietorships and partnerships are small businesses, *most* corporations are also relatively small, often family-owned firms. The corporation is associated with bigness because most large businesses—those that account for the major part of industrial output—are corporations. Nevertheless, many large enterprises are organized as partnerships. Service organizations such as law firms and the large international public accounting firms may be organized as partnerships even though they generate hundreds of millions of dollars in annual revenues.

No Limits on Owner Liability

Proprietorships and partnerships are, in a legal sense, extensions of their owners. One or more parties simply establish a business. They purchase or rent whatever equipment or space is needed, acquire supplies or inventory, and obtain any local operating licences that might be required. No formal charter or federal or provincial certificates are required. If the business is to be operated as a partnership, it is generally wise to have a lawyer draw up a partnership agreement that specifies the rights and obligations of each partner—how profits will be distributed, who will perform what services, how much each partner must contribute initially, what rights of survivorship will accrue to each partner's estate, what limitations there will be upon sale of a partner's interest in the business. But a partnership agreement is for the protection of the individual partners; it is not ordinarily required by law.

A proprietor, as well as each partner of a partnership, is usually personally responsible for all obligations of his or her business. If the enterprise suffers losses, the owners are jointly and severally responsible for all debts incurred. Partners will generally be held liable not only for their own individual shares of the debts but, should their fellow partners be unable to meet their shares of the claims against the business, for the debts of those partners as well. As a consequence, few investors are as willing to purchase an equity interest in a partnership as they might be to purchase one in a corporation. In the event the partnership is liquidated and fellow partners are unable to meet their share of obligations, the personal assets of the investors might be subject to the claims of creditors. Their assets at risk are unlimited, extending beyond their original investment.

There are no limits to the number of parties who might compose a partnership. Because of the extended liability to which each partner is subject, most partnerships are small—two or three members. However, many partnerships are considerably larger. Some international public accounting firms that are organized as partnerships have *thousands* of partners who are located throughout the world.

Tax Liabilities

Neither proprietorships nor partnerships are subject to federal or provincial taxes on income. Instead, the income tax is assessed on the individual owners. If the organization is a partnership, then each partner is taxed on his or her own share of partnership earnings. The rate of tax is determined by the personal tax bracket in which the individual partner falls after taking into account earnings from nonpartnership sources. Each partner is taxed on his or her individual share of the entire earnings of the partnership, not just on withdrawals from the business. Thus, especially if the partnership requires capital for expansion, a partner may be taxed on earnings that are retained in the business and are not available for his or her discretionary use, in addition to funds actually taken from the business.

CORPORATIONS

A Legal "Person"

A corporation, by contrast, is a legal entity separate and distinct from its owners. It is a legal "person" created by the government, either federal or provincial. A corporation is owned by its shareholders, but its shareholders are not compelled to take an active role in its management. In many corporations there is a distinct separation of ownership and operating control, with managers typically holding only a small fraction of total shares outstanding. A corporation has an indefinite life. It continues in existence regardless of the personal fortunes of its owners. Its owners are commonly free to transfer or sell their shares of stock to anyone they wish.

Corporations, unlike proprietorships or partnerships, are creatures of the government. A corporation has the right to own property in its own name, and it can sue or be sued. Upon its formation, it must be chartered by either the federal or a provincial government. Although at one time charters were granted only upon special acts of Parliament or of a legislature, today they are routinely issued upon submission of certificates of incorporation and supplementary application forms, and payment of necessary fees. The certificate of incorporation specifies the name of the proposed corporation, its purposes (most certificates of incorporation are drawn so as to allow the company to engage in an unlimited range of business activities), the number of shares authorized to be issued, and the number of directors.

Once the charter has been issued, the corporation has to adopt formal bylaws, which govern a number of critical areas of operation. The bylaws cover such matters as the issuance and transfer of stock and the conduct of meetings of directors and shareholders.

Limited Liability

The single most significant distinction between corporations and proprietorships or partnerships is that the liability of shareholders of a corporation is limited to the amount of their initial investment in the company, whereas that of the owners of proprietorships or partnerships is unlimited. With few exceptions, the maximum loss that a shareholder can sustain on the purchase of an interest in a corporation is the amount of his or her initial investment. Should the corporation fail, creditors can avail themselves of only the assets of the corporation: they cannot seek redress against the personal assets of the inidividual shareholders. Only in rare circumstances—the involvement of corporate shareholders in fraud, for example—is it possible for creditors or others who may have judgments against the corporation to "pierce the corporate veil" and bring a successful legal action against the individual shareholders. Because it is able to protect investors against unlimited loss, the corporation is a vehicle that is well suited to raising large amounts of capital. Investors may be willing to purchase an ownership interest in a company knowing that they can share in the gains of the company to an unlimited extent but that their losses will be limited by the amount of their direct contributions. They need not be overly concerned with the day-to-day operations of their business, since neither the managers nor their fellow owners can so mismanage the business as to put their personal assets in jeopardy.

Tax Liabilities

Corporations, like other legal persons, are subject to both federal and provincial income taxes. Earnings of a corporation are taxed regardless of whether or not they are distributed to its owners, albeit at rates different from those of individuals. The individual owners of the corporation, unlike those of a partnership, are not taxed on their shares of the earnings that are retained in the corporation; they are, however, taxed on the earnings when corporate assets are distributed to them in the form of dividends. Earnings of a corporation are taxed twice—once when earned by the corporation and again when "earned" as dividends by the shareholders. The effect of this *double taxation* is mitigated somewhat by the dividend tax credit available to individual shareholders of Canadian corporations.

CORPORATIONS VERSUS UNINCORPORATED ENTITIES: DISTINCTIONS IN PERSPECTIVE

It is easy to place too much emphasis on the distinctions between unincorporated entities and corporations. For some businesses, especially smaller enterprises, the differences may be more of form than of substance.

Capital Formation

For a small business the corporate form of organization is unlikely to facilitate acquisition of required capital any more than would the unincorporated form. Most small enterprises have difficulty obtaining equity capital, not so much because potential investors are concerned about subjecting all of their personal assets to possible loss, but rather because they are unwilling to risk any funds on the venture. Small businesses are inherently hazardous, and the corporate form of organization does not by itself enhance prospects for success.

Equally significant, the limited liability feature of the corporate form of organization may actually deter potential suppliers of capital. To a bank or other lending institution, the limitation on owners' liability is an obstacle rather than an inducement to making a loan. The bank, after all, wants assurance that in the event of default it can have access to all the assets of owners, not merely those devoted to the business. As a consequence, many lenders circumvent the limitations on shareholder liability by requiring that the shareholders personally cosign any notes issued by the corporation.

Partners' Liability

The distinction between the corporate and partnership form of organization has been diminished further in recent years by legislation in most provinces that provides for the limitation on the liability of certain partners in selected circumstances. As long as there exists at least one *general* partner whose liability is unlimited, the liability of other partners, particularly those who take no part in the day-to-day management of the enterprise, may be limited.

Stock Transferability

The advantage of a corporation over an unincorporated entity in that shares of ownership are readily transferable may also be more illusory than real. The shares of *public* corporations (i.e., those corporations which have their shares listed on a recognized stock exchange) can be sold without difficulty. The shares of companies that are *closely held* by a small number of shareholders (commonly called private corporations) could probably not be sold any more easily than could a similar interest in a partnership. Indeed, agreements among shareholders of private companies sometimes provide that all sales of shares to outsiders must meet the approval of existing owners.

DISTINCTIVE FEATURES OF PARTNERSHIP ACCOUNTING

There are relatively few differences between accounting for a proprietorship or partnership and a corporation. What differences there are relate primarily to the owners' equity accounts and are more of form than of substance. For accounting purposes the proprietorship may be viewed as a special case of a partnership—a "partnership" with only a single partner.

The owners' equity section of a partnership general ledger usually consists of one capital account for each partner. Each capital account is credited (increased) by the amount of a partner's contributions to the firm and by his or her share of partnership profits. It is debited (decreased) by a partner's withdrawals from the firm and by that individual's share of partnership losses.

Example

Clark and Rae decide to form a partnership. Clark contributes $2 million cash, and Rae contributes a building that has been appraised at $1.5 million but on which there is a mortgage of $500,000. The building had been carried on Rae's personal books at a value of $750,000. The partnership agrees to assume the liability for the mortgage. The following entry would be required to establish the partnership:

(a)

Cash	$2,000,000	
Building	1,500,000	
Mortgage note payable		$ 500,000
Clark, capital		2,000,000
Rae, capital		1,000,000

To record formation of the partnership

Property contributed is recorded at its *fair market value,* regardless of the value at which it might have been carried on the books of the individual partners prior to being assigned to the partnership. In other words, it is recorded at its acquisition cost to the partnership. This fair market value acquisition cost becomes the historic cost to the partnership.

The partners agree to share profits and losses in the same ratio as their initial capital contributions, 2 to 1. During the first year of operations the partnership has revenues of $2.4 million and expenses of $1.8 million—income of $600,000. The following summary *closing entry* would be required, assuming that revenues and expenses were properly recorded throughout the year:

(b)

Revenues (various accounts)	$2,400,000	
Expenses (various accounts)		$1,800,000
Clark, capital		400,000
Rae, capital		200,000

To close the revenue and expense accounts and transfer earnings to the partners' capital accounts

During the year Clark withdraws $280,000 in cash and Rae withdraws $320,000. The appropriate entry would be

(c)

Clark, drawings	$280,000	
Rae, drawings	320,000	
Cash		$600,000

To record partner withdrawals

The year-end entry to close the partners' drawings accounts and transfer the balances to the capital accounts would be

(d)

Clark, capital	$280,000	
Rae, capital	320,000	
Clark, drawings		$280,000
Rae, drawings		320,000
To close the partners' drawings accounts		

Exhibit 11-1 shows in T account form the partners' capital and drawings accounts.

At the conclusion of the year, Clark has a capital balance of $2,120,000 and Rae only $880,000. The capital balances are no longer in the original ratio of 2 to 1 because the drawings were not made in the 2 to 1 ratio.

EXHIBIT 11-1
Partners' Drawings and Capital Accounts

	Clark, capital				Rae, capital		
(d)	280,000	**(a)**	2,000,000	**(d)**	320,000	**(a)**	1,000,000
		(b)	400,000			**(b)**	200,000
			2,120,000				880,000

	Clark, drawings				Rae, drawings		
(c)	280,000	**(d)**	280,000	**(c)**	320,000	**(d)**	320,000

Whether a partner is permitted to draw his or her capital account below a specified level is a question that must be addressed in the partnership agreement. Some partnership agreements provide for the payment of interest *to* any partner who maintains an *excess* capital balance in relation to the other partners or *by* any partner who has a *deficiency*.

It is also essential that a partnership agreement set forth any amounts that the individual partners are to receive in salaries, apart from the percentage of earnings to which they are entitled. Payments of salaries to partners may be accounted for as they would be if they were ordinary expenses. They have no direct impact on the drawings accounts or the individual capital accounts.

Admission of New Partners

The difficult conceptual issues pertaining to partnership accounting relate to the sale of partnership interests and the admission of new partners. The critical question—one to which there is no widespread agreement on an answer—is whether such events demand, or justify, an overall revaluation of partnership assets. Suppose, for example, that at the conclusion of its first year of operations the Clark-Rae partnership decides to admit a third partner, Getty. Getty agrees to pay $2 million for a one-third interest in the partnership. Just prior to his admission, the combined balance in the capital accounts of the original two partners is $3 million ($2,120,000 plus $880,000). Hence reported net assets must also be $3 million. After admission of Getty and acceptance of his contribution of $2 million, net assets of the partnership will be $5 million.

Getty is willing to pay $2 million for a one-third interest in the partnership. In his eyes—and probably those of the marketplace, assuming an arm's-length transaction—the total value of the partnership must be three times $2 million, or $6 million. Yet the reported net assets of the company after his admission will be only $5 million. Should the additional $1 million in value be recognized? If so, how?

Revaluation Approach

There are two probable explanations for the apparent $1 million excess of *market* value over *reported* value. First, the market value of one or more specific assets of the partnership may be worth more than its reported value. For example, plant and equipment recorded at a book value of $2 million may, in fact, have a market value of $3 million. Or, second, the company may possess assets that have not been recognized in the accounting records. More than likely, such assets are intangible—the good name of the firm, special skills of management, an advantageous location or economic environment. Such intangible assets could be grouped together in a broad category called *goodwill.*

The market value of the "new" asset, goodwill, or the increase in the existing assets, plant and equipment, as well as the corresponding increase of the equity of the two original partners, can be recorded with the following journal entry:

Goodwill (or plant and equipment) $1,000,000
    Clark, capital $666,667
    Rae, capital 333,333
To revalue assets on admission of a new partner

The increase in owners' equity is divided among the two partners *in proportion to the agreed-upon* profit/loss sharing ratio, 2 to 1, even though their capital balances are not in such ratio.

The admission of the new partner can now be recorded as follows:

Cash $2,000,000
    Getty, capital $2,000,000
To record admission of a new partner

After his admission, the balance sheet of the partnership would reveal net assets of $6 million and owners' equity as follows:

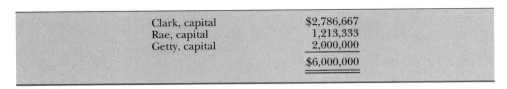

Clark, capital	$2,786,667
Rae, capital	1,213,333
Getty, capital	2,000,000
	$6,000,000

The revaluation approach is based on the assumption that the transfer of the partnership interest in an arm's-length transaction provides an objective means of determining the fair market value of partnership assets. Proponents of the approach assert that the transfer is of sufficient economic significance to justify a restatement of assets. Indeed, they argue, the admission of a new partner is the equivalent of the dissolution of one business entity and the formation of another.

Those who object to the revaluation approach contend that the admission of a new partner may create a new legal entity, but not a new economic one. Hence, they say, the revaluation approach is inconsistent with the historical cost basis of accounting. Assets of an enterprise are generally reported at original cost, less any allowances for amortization. Goodwill developed by the enterprise is never recognized. The balance sheet indicates unexpired costs, not current market values. Moreover, the approach is in violation of accounting principles as applied by corporations. In corporate accounting, neither the sale of existing shares nor the issue of new shares at a price reflective of a market value in excess of book values is considered to be proper occasion for an overall revaluation of corporate assets.

Bonus Approach

As an alternative to recognizing the increase in fair market value, the partnership can account for the additional payment by the new partner as a *bonus* paid to the existing partners. After the admission of the new partner, the net assets of the partnership will be $5 million (the $3 million in assets prior to his admission plus the new partner's contribution of $2 million). For his contribution of $2 million, the new partner will receive a one-third equity in a partnership that has total equity of $5 million. He will be credited, therefore, with a capital interest of one-third of $5 million, or $1,666,667. The difference of $333,333 between his contribution of $2 million and the capital interest with which he will be credited ($1,666,667) may be interpreted as a bonus to be divided among the existing partners *in proportion to their profit/loss sharing ratio* of 2:1. Thus the admission of Getty could be recorded as follows:

Cash $2,000,000		
Getty, capital		$1,666,667
Clark, capital		222,222
Rae, capital		111,111

To record bonus to existing partners on admission of a new partner

After his admission, the balance sheet of the partnership would reveal net assets of $5 million (as compared with $6 million under the *revaluation* approach), and partners' capital accounts would be reported as follows:

Clark, capital	$2,342,222
Rae, capital	991,111
Getty, capital	1,666,667
	$5,000,000

The issue of accounting for the admission of a new partner is not one that is currently under consideration by the rule-making authorities. It is of interest to students of accounting primarily because it is yet another example of the problem that arises when book values are inconsistent with market values.

CORPORATE CAPITAL ACCOUNTS

In contrast to the owners' equity section of a partnership balance sheet, in which the capital balances of the partners are reported, that of a corporation indicates

EXHIBIT 11-2

Bombardier Inc. January 31, 1994 (dollar amounts in millions)	1994	1993
Shareholders' equity		
Series 1 Cumulative Redeemable Preferred Shares, without nominal or par value. The quarterly dividend rate is equal to the greater of (i) 1.875% and (ii) one-quarter of 75% of the average of the prime rates of three designated major Canadian banks for specified three-month periods.		
Authorized, an unlimited number: issued, 1,324,200 shares (1993—1,363,500 shares)	$ 33.1	$34.1
Class A Common Shares (multiple voting), without nominal or par value, ten votes each, convertible at the option of the holder into one Class B Common Subordinate Voting Share.		
Authorized, 224,000,000 shares; issued, 44,736,355 shares (1993—45,207,020 shares)	49.8	50.3
Class B Common Subordinate Voting Shares, without nominal or par value, one vote each with an annual non-cumulative preferential dividend of $0.0125 per share.		
Authorized, 224,000,000 shares; issued, 120,237,996 shares (1993—109,072,645 shares)	648.7	420.5
Total share capital	731.6	504.9
Retained earnings	619.5	484.8
Deferred foreign currency translation adjustments*	32.0	(5.6)
Total shareholders' equity	$1,383.1	$984.1

*To be discussed in Chapter 15.

the different classes of stock authorized, the amount received by the corporation on issue of such shares, and the earnings retained in the business. Exhibit 11-2 illustrates the shareholders' equity section of a typical Canadian corporation. Bombardier Inc., a Canadian company, is a world leader in the manufacture and distribution of transportation equipment including trains, subway cars, airplanes, and personal recreation vehicles.

There are two major categories of capital stock: common stock and preferred stock. *Common stock* is the "usual" type of stock; when only one class of stock is issued, it is almost certain to be common stock. *Preferred stock,* when issued, ordinarily has certain preferences as to dividend payments and rights in liquidation.

The balance sheet disclosure in Exhibit 11-2 includes information on the numbers of shares of each class of stock authorized, issued, and outstanding. More commonly in Canada, this detailed information is found in the notes to the financial statements rather than on the face of the financial statements. The information presented for Bombardier Inc. was, in fact, found in the notes to the financial statements. It is shown on the face of the balance sheet in Exhibit 11-2 for illustration purposes only. The number of shares *authorized* is the maximum number of shares, per its corporate charter, that the company is permitted to issue; the number of shares *issued* is the amount that has actually been put into circulation; the number of shares *outstanding* indicates those currently in circu-

The entry reflects the widely held view among accountants that a company should not include in reported income gains or losses on transactions in its own securities. Such transactions involve nothing more than increases or decreases in the amount of contributed capital. Thus the purchase and sale of treasury stock, like the issue or retirement of other shares, should not result in revenues or expenses to be included in the computation of net income.

If a corporation plans to cancel the reacquired shares immediately, the acquisition is accounted for as a retirement of the stock purchased. First, the common stock account is reduced (debited) by an amount indicative of the percentage of shares being retired. Then retained earnings is reduced (debited) by any amounts in excess of the reduction in the common stock account.

If the price paid to acquire the stock is *less* than the original issue price, then, for each share, common stock would be debited with the original issue price.

Using the data previously presented, for example, we see that the purchase of 1.5 million shares at a price of $22 per share represents the retirement of 10 percent (1.5/15 million) of the outstanding shares. Common stock (no-par value) would be reduced by 10 percent of $180 million—$18 million. Retained earnings would be reduced by the difference between the total amount paid for the shares ($33 million) and the reduction to the common stock account ($18 million) or $15 million. Thus (in thousands),

Common stock $18,000
    Retained earnings 15,000
    Cash $33,000
    To record the purchase of stock for cancellation (1.5 million shares at $22 per share)

Subsequent to the retirement, the capital accounts would appear as follows (again in thousands)

Common stock, no-par value, 13.5 million shares issued and outstanding	$162,000
Retained earnings	45,000
Total shareholders' equity	$207,000

If previously acquired treasury stock was being cancelled, the entry would be the same as above, except the credit of $33 million would be to the previously recorded treasury stock account rather than to cash.

Whether the reacquired shares are initially recorded as treasury stock or immediately as a retirement of the stock purchased is not critical. Both methods result in the same reported assets, liabilities, and total owners' equity. Neither method affects reported revenues or expenses. They vary only in their impact on the components of shareholders' equity.

ISSUANCE OF PREFERRED STOCK

The mechanics of recording the issuance of preferred stock are almost identical with those of recording common stock. However, the amount to be received on issuance of the preferred shares is determined more like the issue price of bonds than with common stock.

The amount that investors will pay for a corporation's common stock is dependent on their expectations of the firm's earnings in the future. Because these investors will share in the *residual* income of the company—that which remains after the claims against earnings of bondholders and preferred shareholders are satisfied—the price that they are willing to pay for a share of common stock will rise and fall with their assessment of the company's earning potential.

Owners of preferred stock, however, are less concerned with anticipated profits of the company. Their dollar share in the income of the company is contractually fixed. They will receive only the dollar amount of the dividend specified on their preferred shares. As long as the company has sufficient earnings to meet its required dividend payments, they will be unaffected by swings in income.

The primary concern of the purchasers of preferred stock is the yield that they will obtain from one company as opposed to another with similar risk characteristics. Suppose, for example, the preferred stock of a company has no-par value and a dividend rate of $6 per year. If similar securities are being sold to yield 7 percent per year, then rational purchasers would be willing to invest in the shares only if they could purchase them at a price to assure a return equivalent to the rate prevailing in the market.

Example

The ABC Co. wishes to issue 1 million shares of no-par value preferred stock, which will pay dividends of $10 each per year. On the day of issue the prevailing yield on similar types of securities is 9 percent. For how much is each share likely to be sold?

Let x = Amount for which each share will be sold

$$.09x = \$10$$

$$x = \frac{\$10}{.09}$$

$$x = \$111.11$$

If the stock that pays dividends of $10 per year is to be sold to yield 9 percent, then it would be sold at $111.11. Since, unlike bonds, there is no maturity date, the return can be assumed to be a *perpetuity* (one for an infinitely long duration); hence there is no need to refer to present value tables to determine the selling price.[1]

CONVERTIBLE SECURITIES

Convertible securities, usually bonds or preferred stock, are hybrids. They have the characteristics of both debt and equity financial instruments. They can be changed, usually at the option of the holder, into the issuer's common stock. The

---

[1] For a different perspective on perpetuities, see footnote 3 in Chapter 6, page 248.

security indentures would specify a *conversion ratio,* which is the number of shares into which the security may be converted. If a $1,000 bond can be tendered for 50 shares of common stock, then the conversion ratio is 50 to 1. The principles and issues pertaining to convertible securities are illustrated here with reference to bonds; the examples and discussions can easily be generalized to preferred stock.

Convertible bonds pay interest, although the rate is generally lower than that on conventional bonds. There are two main features of the conversion right that make it attractive to investors. The first is that it allows the investors to realize the benefits of appreciation in the issuer's common stock. If the value of the common stock into which the bonds can be converted exceeds that of the bonds, then the investors can exchange the bonds for the stock. As a consequence, the market value of the bonds is tied directly to that of the common stock. As the stock appreciates, so also do the bonds. If the stock does not increase in value, then the bondholders need not convert, and they can still be assured of fixed payments of interest and a return of principal.

Consider, for example, the $1,000 bond with the 50-to-1 conversion ratio. If the market price of the stock was to rise to $20, conversion would yield stock with a value of $20 × 50 = $1,000. Any market price for the stock above $20 would yield conversion values exceeding $1,000. Hence it would be in the interest of the bondholders to convert prior to the maturity of the bonds. When the stock price goes above $20, the market value of the bonds can be expected to increase by approximately $50 for every $1 increase in the value of a share of stock over $20.

The second advantage of the conversion right is that it allows the bondholders to share in the rewards of corporate ownership without the corresponding risks. Convertible securities are therefore often used by both new corporations seeking start-up capital and by failing firms attempting to re-establish themselves. Should an issuing company become financially successful, bondholders can exchange their interests as creditors for those of owners. They can thereby share in the subsequent corporate earnings. Should the company fail or become only marginally profitable, the bondholders can continue as creditors. They would be assured payments of interest and principal before any dividends or other distributions of corporate assets were made to shareholders.

The primary benefits of convertible bonds to the issuer are a lower rate of interest and the possible opportunity to avoid repaying the debt by forcing conversion to common stock. The latter can be accomplished by making the bonds *callable.* A call provision included in the bond indenture permits the company to redeem the bonds at a specified price, one that is usually above the face value of the bond. Should the aggregate market value of the stock to be issued on conversion of a bond increase to where it is above the call price of the bond, then the rational investor would have to convert from bonds to stock. Otherwise, the company could redeem the bonds at the call price, leaving the investor worse off than if he or she had taken the stock.

If, for example, in our above illustration, the bond was callable at $1,200, the rational investor would automatically convert if the share price ever went above $24, for $24 × 50 = $1,200, and any share price above $24 would lead to a bond-conversion value exceeding the call value of the bond.

Accounting for the Issuance

When a firm issues convertible bonds, the *generally accepted* entry to record the transaction is identical to that for conventional bonds. Suppose, for example, that a firm issues $100,000 of 8 percent convertible bonds at a premium of $3,000. Each bond has a face value of $1,000 and is convertible into the firm's common stock (no-par value) at a ratio of 50 to 1. Thus the firm has issued 100 bonds that are convertible into a total of 5,000 shares (100 bonds times 50). The market price of the firm's common stock at the time the bonds are issued is $15 per share. The generally accepted entry to record the issuance of the bonds would be

Cash		$103,000
Bonds payable		$100,000
Premium on bonds payable		3,000

To record the issuance of bonds

The theoretical deficiency of this entry is that it assigns the entire amount received to the debt. It is almost certain, however, that the purchasers paid at least a portion of the issue price for the conversion rights—the possibility of sharing in the future earnings of the company and of obtaining other benefits of corporate ownership.

Suppose, for example, that the prevailing yield on bonds that are comparable in all respects to those just described, except that they are not convertible, is slightly *more* than 8 percent. If, like the convertible bonds, their coupon rate was 8 percent, then they would sell at less than the face value of $100,000. Assume that they sold for $98,500, at a *discount* of $1,500. The most plausible explanation as to why the investors were willing to pay the additional $4,500 (the difference between $103,000 and $98,500) for the convertible bonds is that they placed that value upon the conversion rights. Many theoreticians would assert that the $4,500 should be assigned to owners' equity—either contributed surplus or some other appropriately described account. Thus

Cash		$103,000
Discount on bonds payable		
($100,000 − $98,500)	1,500	
Bonds payable		$100,000
Contributed surplus (from issuance of convertible bonds)		4,500

To record the issuance of convertible bonds

This entry is *not*, however, in accordance with generally accepted accounting principles. Although not specifically addressed by the CICA, the Accounting Principles Board in the United States ruled that *no portion* of the proceeds of convertible debt should be accounted for as attributable to the conversion feature. The board pointed to the *practical difficulties* of valuing the conversion rights as well as to the inseparability of the debt and the conversion rights. Neither the debt nor the conversion rights, it argued, can exist independently of one another; the holder cannot sell one right and retain the other.[2]

---

[2] "Convertible Debt and Debt Issued with Stock Purchase Warrants," *Accounting Principles Board Opinion No. 12,* 1966.

Accounting for the Conversion

Assume that the issuance was recorded in accordance with generally accepted accounting principles.

After several years the market price of the firm's common stock increases to $22 per share. By this time, the company has amortized the bond premium down to $2,000; hence the book value of the bonds is $102,000. The market value of the bonds, because of their convertibility feature, could be expected to be $22 × 50 = $1,100 × 100 bonds = $110,000. The investors would exercise their option to convert.

Under generally accepted accounting principles, the conversion may be accounted for on the basis of *either book value or market value.*

Book Value

If the conversion is to be accounted for on the basis of *book* value, then the new common stock to be issued will be recorded at the book value of the bonds that they will replace—in this exchange, $102,000. No gain or loss will be recognized on the trade. Thus

Bonds payable	$100,000	
Premium on bonds payable	2,000	
Common stock		$102,000

To record conversion of bonds (book value method)

The book value method accounts for the conversion as an extension of the previous transaction in which the bonds were first issued. The value assigned to the stock is that of the *bonds* and may bear no relation to the market value of the stock at the time the stock is issued.

Market Value

If the conversion is to be accounted for on the basis of market value, then the new securities will be recorded at their current market prices—in this case $22 per share and a total of $110,000 for the 5,000 shares to be issued. The firm would recognize a loss of $8,000 on the exchange, the difference between the market value of the stock issued and the book value of the bonds retired:

Bonds payable	$100,000	
Premium on bonds payable	2,000	
Loss on conversion of bonds payable	8,000	
Common stock		$110,000

To record conversion of bonds (market value method)

The market value method accounts for the conversion as an independent event, assigning to the new securities a value reflective of what would have been recorded had they been issued for cash at the time of the exchange. The market value method, however, typically requires recognition of a loss. This loss can best be interpreted as an *opportunity cost*. It indicates how much better off the firm would have been had it been able to redeem the bonds at book value and separately issue the common stock at its prevailing market price.

A Comparison

Although the market value method results in what many accountants believe to be a more meaningful presentation of the equity accounts on the balance sheet, the recognition of the loss is understandably objectionable to many firms. After all, it is attributable to *increases* in the market value of the firm's common stock—the higher the market value, the greater the reported loss. Gains in the market value of a firm's common stock are not, of course, otherwise given ongoing accounting recognition. Additional support for the book value method comes from the fact that the cash received on issue of the bonds was for either bonds payable or common shares, depending on whether conversion eventually takes place. In practice, the book value method is used almost exclusively, in large measure, no doubt, because of the necessity of reporting conversion losses under the market value method.

NEW FINANCIAL INSTRUMENTS

One of the significant ongoing challenges to the accounting profession is how to account for and report the new, nonconventional financial instruments. Over the last decade, corporate financing has become exceedingly innovative, with new types of securities being created each year. This trend is almost certain to continue. Many of the new instruments are hybrids. Like convertible securities, they have elements of both debt and equity. Some contain promises that are conditional upon future earnings or appreciation in stock prices.

To cite but one example: Many gold producers have recently arranged gold loans to finance their expansion. Under a typical gold loan, the gold producer borrows gold from a bank or other lender and immediately converts the gold to cash by selling the gold in the market. The loan must be repaid by the borrower in gold, or the eqivalent cash dependent on the gold price at the time of repayment. The interest rate on the gold loan is typically much lower than that on ordinary loans. Some of the questions about the financial reporting for the gold loans are:

1. On the balance sheet, should the loan be classified as debt or as deferred revenue?

2. Should the value of the gold loan be reported at market value (based on the price of gold) in the financial statements?[3]

No general rules can be established as to how a new financial instrument should be accounted for. One key, however, is to determine the economic nature and market value of each of its components. Often that will make clear how the components should be categorized on the balance sheet and what values should be assigned to them. The market-based means of accounting for both the issuance and the conversion of convertible bonds are illustrative of this approach. Although market-based approaches may need to be modified to take into account "practical" realities, they can generally be expected to capture the economic substance of a transaction.

[3] "Gold Loans," EIC-32, CICA, November 20, 1991.

Financing ratios, one of which is the debt-to-equity ratio, compare claims of creditors with the equity of shareholders.

The debt-to-equity ratio relates capital provided by creditors to that supplied by owners. Debt includes all outstanding liabilities, both current and noncurrent. Equity includes balances in all shareholders' equity accounts—common and preferred stock, contributed surplus, and retained earnings.

Example

The total debt of Sun Ice Limited (see its statements in Chapter 7), composed of both the current and the noncurrent liabilities, is (in thousands) $2,183 (including deferred income taxes). Total shareholders' equity is $17,435. The debt-to-equity ratio as of January 31, 1994, therefore, is 0.13 to 1:

$$\text{Debt-to-equity ratio} = \frac{\text{Total debt}}{\text{Shareholders' equity}} = \frac{\$2,183}{\$17,435} = 0.13 : 1$$

The debt-to-equity ratio is of particular concern to creditors. The claims of creditors against the assets of a firm have priority over those of the shareholders. The higher the debt-to-equity ratio, the greater the amount of the *priority* claims against the assets, and in the event the firm is unable to meet all its outstanding obligations, the less likely that any individual claim will be liquidated in full. Moreover, a high debt-to-equity ratio suggests the obligation to make high periodic interest payments. As a consequence, there is an increased risk that corporate earnings will be insufficient to cover all required principal and interest payments.

The debt-to-equity ratio is also of interest to managers and the shareholders they represent. Shareholders can expect no return on their investment, either periodically in the form of dividends or upon liquidation, until all senior claims of creditors have been satisfied. The lower the debt-to-equity ratio, the less the risk of loss assumed by shareholders. But in contrast to the possible preference of shareholders to be assured a return on their investment, there may be a conflicting desire to make use of *leverage*—the ability to take advantage of other people's money to enhance the return on their invested capital. Any earnings on borrowed capital above required interest payments increase the return to shareholders. As discussed in Chapter 10, however, leverage works both ways. Any interest payments in excess of the earnings on the borrowed capital reduce the return to shareholders.

Summary

In this chapter we have focused on the equity accounts of *proprietorships, partnerships,* and *corporations.* Although there are important legal and organizational differences between proprietorships, partnerships, and corporations, the accounting distinctions are relatively minor, affecting primarily the accounts composing the owners' equity section of the balance sheet.

A corporation's transactions involving its own shares are seldom reported on its statement of income. Yet they can have a profound impact on its earnings per share as well as on the value of outstanding shares.

In the 1960s, for example, many companies took advantage of relatively high stock market prices to issue additional shares. Since the prices that the new investors were willing to pay were substantially above the *book* values of the new shares, the added premiums increased the book values of the existing shares. Inasmuch as the cost of the capital acquired was low in relation to the returns that could be generated by the additional capital, sales of the new shares increased overall earnings per share. Numerous firms that were previously privately owned went public to benefit from the ease of obtaining capital through the sale of common stock.

In the late 1980s, when stock market prices were depressed, a number of companies engaged in the reverse process; they reacquired shares that they had issued previously. If the market prices of the shares acquired were less than their intrinsic values, then the proportionate values of the remaining shares increased. Since relatively little capital had to be surrendered to reacquire the shares, the overall earnings capacity of the firms may have declined only slightly. But since earnings now had to be divided among a significantly smaller number of shares, earnings per share may have increased substantially. The desired effect was an increase in the share prices.

The late 1980s was also a period of financial restructuring. There were numerous mergers and acquisitions as well as divisions of firms into smaller, independently owned units. Often the changes were accompanied by new "creative" financial instruments.

Perceptive investors and financial analysts examine carefully the transactions between a company and its owners and the manner in which they are accounted for. This can have a critical effect on a shareholder's interest in past and future corporate earnings. The skilled manager and perceptive investor must be aware of the opportunities and pitfalls inherent in corporate dealings between a company and its owners and must be cognizant of how they are reflected in the financial reports.

Exercise for Review and Self-Testing

Brunswick, Inc., decides to reorganize its corporate structure. To facilitate additional financing, it elects to incorporate one of its divisions. Brunswick will transfer to the new corporation plant and equipment that is presently recorded on its books at a cost of $8.9 million, less accumulated amortization of $4 million, and patents that were developed by the company itself and have not been recognized in the accounts. The fair market value of the plant and equipment is $8.2 million; that of the patents, $2 million.

1. The new company issues 100,000 shares of no-par value common stock. Initially, all the shares will be held by Brunswick, Inc.
   a. What value should the new company assign to the plant and equipment? To the patents?

    b. What value should the new company assign to "common stock"? To "contributed surplus"?

    c. Prepare a journal entry to record the issuance of the common stock.

2. The new company also issues 10,000 shares of preferred stock. The preferred stock is assigned a par value of $100 and pays dividends at a rate of 9 percent per year. At the time the stock is issued, comparable securities are being sold to yield 8.5 percent.

    a. What is the dollar amount per share that the firm will pay in dividends?

    b. How much is an investor likely to pay for a share of stock that pays a dividend of such amount if he or she expects a return of 8.5 percent?

    c. Prepare a journal entry to record the issuance of the preferred stock, assuming that the stock is issued for cash at the price determined in part (b).

3. The company reacquires 20,000 shares of common stock with the intention of retiring them. The company purchases the shares for $160 each. At the time of purchase the company has a balance in its retained earnings account of $2 million.

    a. By what percentage would the number of shares outstanding be reduced?

    b. By what percentage and by what amount should the balance in the account "common stock" be reduced?

    c. By what amount—the difference between total amount paid and the reduction in the "common stock" account—should the balance in "retained earnings" be reduced?

    d. Prepare a journal entry to record the retirement of the shares.

Questions for Review and Discussion

1. The risks of being a *silent partner* (one who takes no active role in management) of a business organized as a partnership are far greater than those of being a silent shareholder of a firm organized as a corporation. Do you agree? Explain.

2. It is often pointed out that the limitations on liability afforded shareholders of a corporation make it easier for a corporation as opposed to a partnership to raise capital. Cite an example of a situation where the limitations of liability may, in fact, make it more difficult for a corporation to acquire needed funds.

3. A corporation, it is said, is a legal "person." Why is a corporation, but not a partnership or a proprietorship, so described?

4. Why is *preferred* stock preferred? What preferences attach to it?

5. A friend wants to purchase "safe" securities for a period of two to three years. He wants assurance that the original amount of his investment will remain intact. Assume that you are satisfied that the company in which he is considering investing is sound—that it is highly unlikely that it will be unable to pay required preferred stock dividends or interest. Would you suggest to him that the preferred stock of the company is necessarily a

safer investment than the common stock? What factors are most likely to influence the market price of the preferred stock, assuming that it is not convertible into common stock?

6. What are the critical accounting problems involved in the formation of a corporation? What warnings would you give to someone who is about to purchase the common stock of a newly organized corporation?

7. Describe the way in which the issuance of convertible bonds is accounted for. Why can it be said that the entry required by GAAP does not allocate the proceeds of the issue in a way that reflects the benefits acquired by the investors?

8. Distinguish between book value and market value methods of accounting for security conversions. What is the rationale for each? What is the weakness of each?

9. What is meant by *leverage?* Which financial ratio provides a measure of leverage? What are the risks of leverage?

Problems

1. *The method of financing used by a "closely held" corporation must take into account the distinctions in the Income Tax Act between dividends and interest.*

   William Elton is the sole shareholder of the Elton Co. Mr. Elton intends to contribute $2 million of his personal funds to the corporation to finance expansion of a plant. He expects that the added capacity of the plant will enable the company to earn $600,000 per year additional income, before federal and provincial income taxes. Mr. Elton has asked your advice as to whether he should have the corporation issue common stock or bonds in return for the $2 million. Mr. Elton intends to withdraw $200,000 of the additional earnings each year, either in the form of interest on bonds or dividends on the common stock. The corporation pays combined federal and provincial income taxes at a rate of 40 percent. Mr. Elton pays income tax personally at a rate of 50 percent. Mr. Elton would be required to pay taxes on all returns from the corporation, regardless of whether in the form of interest or dividends.

   What advice would you give to Mr. Elton?

2. *Accounting principles applicable to partnerships are essentially the same as those applicable to corporations.*

   Simmons and Ross decided to form a partnership to engage in the purchase and sale of real estate. Simmons contributed land that had an appraised value of $400,000; Ross contributed cash of $100,000. The land was subject to a liability of $100,000, which the partnership agreed to assume. The land had been recorded on the personal books of Simmons at a value of $200,000. The partners agreed that profits and losses would be shared in proportion to the initial contributions of the owners. In addition, however, Ross would be paid a management fee of $10,000 per year.

   During its first year of operation, the partnership purchased additional land for $800,000, paying $150,000 cash and giving a note for the balance. It sold for $300,000 land that it had acquired for $200,000. The buyers paid cash of $90,000 and agreed to assume liabilities of $210,000 that the partnership had incurred when it had acquired land.

During the first year the partnership borrowed $80,000 from Simmons. It agreed to pay Simmons interest at the rate of 6 percent per year. As at year end the loan had been outstanding for six months, but the partnership had neither paid nor accrued any interest.

The firm incurred additional interest expenses, paid in cash, of $40,000. At year end, Ross withdrew $30,000 cash from the partnership and, in addition, was paid his management fee; Simmons withdrew nothing. (Assume that all other operating expenses are negligible.)

a. Prepare all necessary journal entries to record the formation of the partnership and to summarize all transactions in which it engaged during its first year of operations. Prepare also any required adjusting and closing entries.

b. Prepare a balance sheet of the partnership as at year end.

3. *Distributions to partners upon liquidation of a partnership must be based upon the balances, after appropriate adjustments, in the partners' capital accounts.*

After 10 years, Freeman Brothers Men's Shop is going out of business. Freeman Brothers is operated as a partnership. Just prior to liquidation, its balance sheet reflected the following:

Cash	$ 200,000
Merchandise inventory	800,000
Total assets	$1,000,000
Current liabilities	$ 50,000
J. Freeman, capital	450,000
L. Freeman, capital	500,000
Total liabilities and owners' equity	$1,000,000

The two Freeman brothers share profits and losses equally.

The firm holds a "going-out-of-business" sale and sells its entire merchandise inventory for $1 million. It pays the creditors and distributes the remaining cash between the two partners.

a. Prepare the required journal entries to record the sale of the merchandise and payment of the liabilities. (Prepare closing entries with respect to revenues and expenses associated with the sale of the merchandise.)

b. Determine the balances in the partners' capital accounts immediately prior to the final distribution of cash between the partners. Explain why, even though the partners share profits and losses equally, their capital balances are not also equal.

c. How much cash should be distributed to each of the partners? Prepare a journal entry to record the final distribution to the partners.

4. *Partners' capital accounts are basically the same as shareholders' equity accounts of corporations.*

The accompanying table is an excerpt from the annual report of Price Waterhouse & Co., one of the major international public accounting firms (dates have been changed).

Worldwide Statement of Changes in Partners' Capital and Undistributed Income, Years Ended June 30, 1993 and 1992 (thousands of dollars)	1993	1992
Partners' capital		
Balance, beginning of year	$ 65,900	$ 53,500
Additional capital provided	10,700	17,900
Repayment of paid-in capital	(3,500)	(5,500)
Balance, end of year	$ 73,100	$ 65,900
Undistributed income		
Balance, beginning of year	$129,200	$119,300
Payments to retired partners	(1,300)	(3,300)
Net income of active partners	186,100	154,800
Distributions to active partners	(164,800)	(141,600)
Balance, end of year	$149,200	$129,200

a. To what corporate account would "partners' capital" be comparable?
b. To what corporate account would "undistributed income" be comparable?
c. What were the net assets of Price Waterhouse as at December 31, 1993?
d. If Price Waterhouse had 1,487 partners worldwide, what would the average earnings per active partner be in 1993? What would the average amount of payments (presumably in cash) be to each of the active partners?

5. *The basic journal entries for the issuance of capital stock by a corporation are illustrated in this problem.*

The Exploration Company Limited was incorporated on January 1, 1996. Its principal business activity is to explore for diamonds in the Northwest Territories. The company obtained a listing on the Toronto Stock Exchange, and to finance its operations it issued, for cash, 3,000,000 no-par value common shares at $8 each. It also issued 1,000,000 shares of $8 preferred stock at $110 cash each.

a. Prepare the journal entries to record the issue of the two classes of capital stock.
b. Prepare a balance sheet of Exploration Company Limited immediately after the issue of the capital stock.
c. Why do you suppose this company raised capital through the issue of capital stock rather than trying to finance its operations with debt (i.e., borrowing money)?

6. *The initial values assigned to the assets of a newly established corporation must be indicative of their fair market values.*

You have recently been offered the chance to purchase 1,000 shares of the common stock of Computer Service Corporation at a price of $15 per share (a price well below book value). The company has just been formed; it has not yet commenced operations. It was organized by three computer systems analysts, who are presently the only shareholders. The company intends to lease office space and computers; it will provide electronic accounting services to small businesses.

A balance sheet provided to you by the company reveals the following:

Cash	$100,000
Inventories and supplies	20,000
Goodwill	300,000
Total assets	$420,000
Common stock, no-par value (20,000 shares authorized, 10,000 shares issued and outstanding)	$420,000
Total equities	$420,000

A footnote to the financial statements indicates that the $300,000 of goodwill represents the accumulated expertise of the founders of the corporation. All three incorporators have had extensive experience with a leading computer manufacturer and have held management positions with other computer service companies. The goodwill was authorized by the firm's board of directors.

a. What reservations might you have about purchasing the stock of the company?

b. Assume instead that you were an independent public accountant called upon to audit the company shortly after its formation. What adjusting journal entry might you propose?

7. *The amounts for which shares of common stock were issued can be derived from information provided upon their retirement.*

The financial report of Sun Ice Limited, contains the following note:

During the year the Company repurchased 12,000 common voting shares at a cost of $20,760 and cancelled them.

From other information in the financial report it can be determined that the share repurchase resulted in a charge of $25,200 to common stock and an increase to contributed surplus of $4,440.

a. How much did the company pay to acquire each share?

b. What was the initial issuance price per share?

c. Prepare a journal entry to record the retirement of the shares.

8. *The price at which preferred stock, like bonds, is issued is reflective of the relationship between prevailing interest yields and the promises inherent in the security.*

The Board of Directors of the Thoreau Electric Co. has voted to issue 200,000 shares of preferred stock that will pay an annual dividend of $6 per share. At the date of issue, similar grades of preferred stock are being sold to provide a return to investors of 5 percent.

a. At what price is the preferred stock of Thoreau likely to be issued?

b. Prepare a journal entry to record the sale of the preferred stock.

c. Prepare an entry to record the payment of the first annual cash dividend.

9. *Preferred stock dividends are usually "cumulative."*

The *Wall Street Journal* reported that Cenco, Inc., which had missed all but one of its preferred dividend payments for five years, now planned to

---

pay the accumulated dividends. According to the *Journal,* "the dividends, totaling about $933,000 at $1.40 a share, will be payable April 27 to stockholders of record February 28." Cenco, the *Journal* indicated, "said the payment is subject to the condition that it won't violate the company's debenture agreements, which call for Cenco to have about $31.4 million in retained earnings before it can pay its preferred dividends." That requirement was the reason that Cenco had been unable to pay its preferred dividends in the past.

Cenco's financial problems were attributable to a $25 million phony profit scheme that involved inflating both inventories and earnings. Several executives had been convicted of conspiracy and fraud.

a. What is meant by the term *accumulated dividends?*
b. How many shares of preferred stock did the company have outstanding?
c. What entries, if any, does the *Wall Street Journal* report suggest that the firm made in those years that it failed to pay its dividends? Explain.

10. *Prices at which securities are issued and acquired can be derived from changes in the balances of owners' equity accounts.*

The shareholders' equity section of the balance sheet of the Intercontinental Corp. reveals the following:

	1997	1996
Common stock, no-par value (120,000 shares in 1997; 100,000 shares in 1996)	$12,700,000	$ 9,900,000
Preferred stock, $100 par value, 8%	500,000	450,000
Contributed surplus		
Preferred stock	8,000	—
Retained earnings	17,970,000	20,090,000
	$31,178,000	$30,440,000

a. How many shares of common stock did the company issue in 1997? What was the issue price per share?
b. How many shares of preferred stock did the company issue in 1997? What was the issue price per share?
c. What would you estimate to be the prevailing yield rate for comparable types of securities at the time the preferred stock was issued? That is, what was the yield rate used to determine the issue price of the preferred stock?

11. *The price at which common stock of a newly formed corporation is issued should reflect the fair market value of the corporate assets.*

Filmore and Francis are partners in a firm that operates a chain of drugstores. They decide to incorporate their business and sell shares in the enterprise to the general public. Filmore has a 60 percent interest in the partnership and Francis a 40 percent interest.

The net assets (assets less liabilities) of the partnership are recorded on the books of the partnership at $8 million. However, after considerable study and consultation with independent appraisers, the partners decide that the fair market value of their business is $14 million. Indeed, just prior to their decision to incorporate they received an offer to sell the firm to an independent party for that amount.

The partners intend to issue 400,000 shares of no-par value common stock. They plan to keep 70 percent of the shares for themselves and sell the rest to the public.

a. At what price should the shares be sold to the public?

b. Prepare any journal entries required to record the formation of the new corporation.

12. *A shift from partnership to corporate status is an event of sufficient economic and legal significance to justify revaluing assets and liabilities.*

Bryan and Moore are partners in a retail stereo business. After several successful years of operation as a partnership, the two decide to incorporate their business as Stereo, Inc. Bryan and Moore share profits and losses in the ratio of 3:1. Prior to the liquidation of the partnership and its subsequent incorporation, the balance sheet of the partnership indicated the following:

Assets		
Cash		$ 120,000
Accounts receivable		260,000
Inventory		830,000
Furniture and fixtures	$ 750,000	
Less: Accumulated amortization	220,000	530,000
Land		180,000
Building	$1,020,000	
Less: Accumulated amortization	600,000	420,000
Total assets		$2,340,000
Liabilities and owners' equity		
Accounts payable		$ 290,000
Notes payable		800,000
Bryan, capital		937,500
Moore, capital		312,500
Total liabilities and owners' equity		$2,340,000

Prior to transferring the assets to the corporation, the partners decide to adjust the books of the partnership to reflect current market values.

The building has a current market value of $850,000; the land, $260,000; and the furniture and fixtures, $300,000.

The firm has not previously provided for uncollectable accounts. However, it is estimated that $40,000 of the accounts are uncollectable. It is also determined that $80,000 of inventory is obsolete. The new corporation is to assume the liabilities of the partnership except as noted below.

The new corporation is authorized to issue 100,000 shares of no-par value common stock. The common stock is to be issued at $100 each, with the number of shares proportionate to the fair market value of one's contribution.

Shares will also be issued to the following parties in addition to the partners:

- To a lawyer for providing services pertaining to the organization of the corporation; the fair market value of the services is $80,000.
- To the party holding the note payable, who has agreed to accept common stock in full payment of his $800,000 note.
- To a venture-capital financial institution, which has agreed to invest $500,000 cash in the new corporation.

a. Prepare journal entries to revalue the partnership, to transfer the assets to the new corporation in exchange for common stock, and to distribute the shares of the common stock to the partners.
b. Prepare journal entries to organize the new corporation.
c. Indicate the number of shares each investor will receive.

13. *Transactions involving a firm's own stock are often based upon the price at which the shares are being traded in the open market.*

The Frost Co. was organized on June 1, 1996. According to the terms of its charter, the firm was authorized to issue capital stock as follows:

Common stock: no-par value, 100,000 shares
Preferred stock: no-par value, $5 dividend, 10,000 shares

During the first year of operation the following transactions that affected capital accounts took place. Prepare journal entries to record the transactions.
a. The corporation issued for cash 70,000 shares of common stock at a price of $25 per share.
b. The corporation issued for cash 10,000 shares of preferred stock at $80 per share.
c. The company purchased a building, giving the seller 10,000 shares of common stock. At the time of the purchase, the common stock of the company was being traded in the open market at $20 per share.
d. The firm's advertising agency agreed to accept 3,000 shares of common stock, rather than cash, in payment for services performed. At the time of payment the market price of the stock was $22 per share.
e. The firm agreed to purchase the stock of a dissident shareholder. The firm purchased 3,000 shares at a price of $30 per share and cancelled it.

14. *United Parcel Service, a U.S. company, explains why it accounts for treasury stock as an asset.*

The balance sheet of United Parcel Service includes the following current asset:

	1987	1986
	(in thousands)	
Treasury stock, at cost	$370,734	$322,153

The company explains this unusual classification in a footnote:

> UPS generally accounts for treasury stock as an asset because it is held for distribution pursuant to awards under the UPS Managers' Incentive Plan and the UPS Incentive Stock Option Plan. The liability for the amount of the annual managers' Incentive award is included in Accrued Wages and Withholdings. Treasury stock in excess of anticipated future requirements, if any, is treated as a reduction of shareowners' equity.

a. Why is the reporting of treasury stock as an asset not allowed under Canadian generally accepted accounting principles?
b. Comment on the company's explanation as to why treasury stock is shown as an asset. Is it reasonable?

15. *Accounting for transactions in a corporation's own shares of common stock is illustrated using information from an actual annual report.*

The December 31, 1987, balance sheet of Canadian Energy Services Ltd. disclosed the following:

Share capital	1987	1986
Authorized capital		
10,000,000 common shares		
without par value		
Issued and fully paid		
2,651,122 common shares	$2,268,002	$2,268,002
Number of shares		
Issued and fully paid	2,651,122	2,651,122
Held by the Company	686,722	646,122
Outstanding	1,964,400	2,005,000

A note reported the following:

> During 1987, the Company purchased 40,600 of its own common shares from the public at a cost of $113,195.

a. Did Canadian Energy cancel the common shares that it repurchased during 1987? How can you tell?

b. What was the purchase price per share?

c. Prepare the entry that the company made in 1987 to record the purchase of the 40,600 shares.

d. What entry would the company make if it subsequently retired the 40,600 shares of reacquired stock?

16. *A corporation can increase the equity of existing (and remaining) shareholders by judiciously issuing and retiring shares of its own common stock.*

In 1996 Mary Bells, Inc., reported earnings of $6 million. Its owners' equity at the end of the year was $30 million. The firm had 1 million shares of common stock issued and outstanding.

At the start of 1997 the company decided to expand its operations. To raise an additional $30 million in capital, it issued additional common stock at a price of $100 per share. The additional capital enabled the firm to increase earnings by $6 million per year after taxes to $12 million.

a. Determine the *book* value per share and earnings per share both before and after the issue of the additional common stock.

b. In 2000 the market price of the firm's common stock fell to $50 per share. The firm decided to reacquire and cancel, at market price, $15 million of common stock. To avoid having to reduce its scale of operations, the firm decided to issue long-term bonds for $15 million. The bonds could be sold at a price such that the effective interest cost to the company, after taxes, would be 5 percent. Determine the book value per share and earnings per share after the reacquisition of the shares and the issue of the bonds. Assume that in the intervening years, including 2000, the firm declared dividends in the amount of earnings and that income in 2000, before taking into account interest on the new bonds, was the same as that in 1997—$12 million.

17. *The value of a business which is about to be acquired by another firm can be established in a number of different ways.*

Alliance Department Stores, Inc., has agreed to purchase McKay Bros. Discount Store. McKay Bros. is operated as a partnership. The owners' equity accounts on the books of the partnership indicate that each of the two partners has a recorded capital balance of $10 million. An independent appraiser has determined that the value of the individual assets of the company (there are no significant liabilities) is $25 million. The partners, however, have had several offers to sell the entire business for $30 million.

Alliance Department Stores, Inc., has offered to purchase the store in exchange for shares of its own common stock. The number of shares to be issued is currently being negotiated between the two parties. Alliance currently has 5 million shares of no-par value common stock outstanding. The company has $40 million in capital stock and $60 million in retained earnings. The current market price for shares of Alliance is $25 per share.

Six possible ways of determining the number of shares to be issued to the McKay Bros. partners are under consideration. The value of a share to be issued by Alliance can be based on either its *book* or its *market* value. The value of the interest to be purchased by Alliance can be based on the book value of McKay Bros.' assets, the appraised value of its assets, or its market value as a going concern.

a. Determine the number of shares to be issued by Alliance under each of the six combinations:

   Value of Alliance shares based on (1) book value or (2) market value* and *Value of McKay Bros. based on (1) book value, (2) appraised value,* or *(3) market value

b. How do you account for the differences between book value, appraised value, and market value?

c. On which basis do you recommend the number of shares should be determined?

18. *Prevailing tax laws are a key factor in a corporation's decision as to whether it should issue bonds or preferred stock.*

A firm wishes to construct a new plant. The estimated cost of the plant is $5 million. The firm is undecided as to whether to raise the required capital by issuing bonds or preferred stock. The current prevailing yield on bonds of similar grade is 8 percent, and that on preferred stock is 10 percent.

What would be the minimum earnings, before taxes, that the firm would have to realize, under both alternatives, if it were to break even on the proposed project? The effective combined federal and provincial income tax rate is 40 percent.

19. *In choosing between alternative instruments of financing, a firm must take into account its expectations as to future earnings.*

A corporation has decided to construct an addition to its plant. The cost of the addition is $5 million; the addition is expected to increase earnings by $900,000 per year before taking into account income taxes.

The firm is considering three means of acquiring the needed $5 million capital:

- The firm can sell bonds; current yield rates are 8 percent per year.
- The firm can issue preferred stock; current yield rates are 12 percent per year.
- The firm can issue common stock; There are currently 600,000 common shares outstanding. The firm estimates that additional shares could be sold at a price of $10 per share. The company has not paid any dividends on common stock in recent years and does not plan to do so in the foreseeable future. The current combined federal and provincial tax rate is 48 percent.

a. Prepare a table that has one column for each of the three options and the following captions for its rows:
   (1) Anticipated additional earnings (before taxes)
   (2) Required interest or dividend payments
   (3) Additional "earnings" less direct cost of capital [(1) − (2)]
   (4) Income taxes
   (5) Net additional earnings [(3) − (4)]
   (6) Shares of common stock outstanding
   (7) Additional earnings per share of common stock [(5) / (6)]

   Which alternative do you think the company ought to select if impact on earnings per share of common stock is to be the most important criterion?
b. Suppose that anticipated earnings from the new addition are $1.5 million per year. Which alternative do you think the firm ought to select? (You need not recompute earnings per share; simply use judgment.)
c. Suppose that estimated additional earnings are $900,000 per year but that the market price of the firm's common stock is $20 per share. Which alternative should now be favoured?

20. *Market-based relationships suggest an alternative means of recording the issuance of convertible bonds.*

Dunedin Corp. issues $1 million of 8 percent coupon bonds at a price of $110 (i.e., $1.1 million). The bonds are convertible, after three years, into the firm's no-par value common stock at a ratio of 40 to 1. The bonds mature in 20 years.

At the time the bonds are issued, the prevailing rate of interest on bonds with the same characteristics, but lacking the conversion feature, is 10 percent.
a. Prepare an entry to record the issuance of the bonds.
b. For what amount would the bonds most probably have been issued if they were not convertible?
c. Why should the purchasers of the bond be willing to pay an amount in addition to that determined in part (b)? Do you think that the extra amount should be classified as "debt"? How else might it be classified?
d. Prepare an alternative entry to record the issuance of the bonds, one that is consistent with your response to part (c). (Note that this entry is not in accord with generally accepted accounting principles.)

21. *Choice of accounting method for convertible bonds affects the classification of owners' equity.*

Rotorua Industries, Inc., issues $1 million of 8 percent convertible bonds at a premium of $200,000. The bonds may be exchanged, any time after four years from the date of issuance, for shares of the firm's no-par value common stock at a ratio of 20 to 1. At the time the bonds are issued, the common stock has a market value of $48 per share.

After four years, the market price of the firm's stock has increased to $60 per share. The bond premium has been amortized down to $180,000. The bondholders elect to convert.

a. Prepare a journal entry to record the issuance of the bonds.

b. Prepare a journal entry to record the conversion using first the book value method and then the market value method.

c. Suppose instead that the market price of the securities at the time of conversion is $63 per share. What is the difference, if any, in each of the entries?

d. What difference in the firm's total owners' equity would result from using the market value rather than the book value method? What difference would result in the distribution among the categories of owners' equity? Explain.

22. *There are a variety of transactions that cause changes to a firm's capital stock accounts.*

The annual report of Laidlaw Inc. a Canadian-based leader in North American waste management and transportation services, contains the following note (modified):

> Material changes in all classes of capital stock since September 1, 1990:
>
> (i) During fiscal 1991, 9,340,248 5% Cumulative Convertible First Preference Shares Series G with a stated value of $137,433,000 were converted to 14,010,366 Class B Non-Voting Common Shares. The proceeds from this conversion were $40,233,000.
>
> (ii) On November 12, 1991, the Company issued 201,857 Class B Non-Voting Common Shares in the amount of $1,768,000 as partial consideration for the acquisition of a business.
>
> (iii) On February 20, 1992, the Company issued 23,650,000 Class B Non-Voting Common Shares for net proceeds of $215,459,000.

Prepare journal entries to record each of these capital stock transactions.

23. *This problem illustrates some special provisions of convertible securities.*

The financial statements of Ivaco Inc., one of North America's largest steel producers, describe its classes of stock, in part, as follows:

> The corporation has authorized an unlimited number of preferred shares issuable in series, second preferred shares issuable in series, subordinated non-voting preferred shares, Class A subordinate voting shares, and Class B voting shares—all without par value.
>
> The $2.72 Series 4 cumulative redeemable exchangeable second preferred shares are exchangeable, at the option of the holder, into one common share of Dofasco Inc. for each Series 4 exchangeable second preferred share. Dividends after April 15, 1990, will be determined by applying to $32.00 a quarterly rate equal to the sum of (i) the cash dividends paid by Dofasco per common share of Dofasco during the three calendar months immediately preceding the dividend payment divided by $32.00 expressed as a percentage, and (ii) 1%. The Company may redeem Series 4 exchangeable second preferred shares after April 14, 1990, at $33.50 per share and after April 14, 1995, at $32.00 per share, provided the market price of Dofasco common shares is greater than $40.00 at that time.

a. Assuming that 3,000,000 exchangeable second preferred $2.72 Series 4 shares were issued for proceeds of $96,000,000, prepare the journal entry to record the issue.

b. If Dofasco paid a common share dividend of $0.16 per share in the first quarter after April 15, 1990, record the payment by Ivaco of the first quarterly dividend on the exchangeable second preferred $2.72 Series 4 shares.

c. From where do you think Ivaco will get the Dofasco shares in order to transfer to those shareholders who elect to convert their exchangeable second preferred $2.72 Series 4 shares?

d. Would Ivaco be able to redeem the exchangeable second preferred $2.72 Series 4 shares when the market value of Dofasco common stock is $16?

e. Prepare the entry that would be made to record the conversion of the entire issue of exchangeable second preferred $2.72 Series 4 shares to the Dofasco common shares. Assume the conversion is to be based on book values.

24. *The journal entry to record the redemption of preferred stock can be reconstructed from the information provided in the notes to the financial statements.*

The 1987 financial statements of Triton Canada Resources Ltd., an oil and gas exploration and development company, included the following note:

Preferred Shares, Series A	Number	Amount
Preferred Shares, Series A Balance, December 31, 1987	771,850	$13,147,000

Preferred Shares, Series A have a stated value of $20.00 per share with cumulative quarterly dividends of $0.4625 per share. They are convertible, at the option of the holder, into 3.0769 Common Shares at any time up to April 14, 1993, or the third business day prior to the date fixed for redemption, whichever is earlier. If the market price of Common Shares is at least 130% of the conversion price, the Preferred Shares, Series A are redeemable by Triton Canada until April 13, 1988, for $21.00 per share plus accrued and unpaid dividends. On or after April 14, 1988, Triton Canada may redeem Preferred Shares, Series A for $20.80 per share which price declines by $0.20 per year to $20.00 and remains constant thereafter. Commencing July 1, 1993, Triton Canada is obligated to purchase for cancellation 1.25% of the Preferred Shares, Series A then outstanding in each quarter for $20.00 per share plus accrued and unpaid dividends.

a. What was the amount per share at which the Preferred Shares, Series A stock was issued? How can you tell?

b. Are the Preferred Shares, Series A likely to be cumulative or non-cumulative? Why?

c. Assuming none of the Preferred Shares, Series A stock had been converted prior to July 1, 1993, give the entry to record the required redemption in the third quarter of 1993.

1. a. The assets should be recorded at their fair market values. Hence plant and equipment, $8.2 million; patents, $2 million.
   b. Common stock: $8.2 million + $2 million = $10.2 million.
      Contributed surplus: $0. Since the common stock is no-par value, all of the stock issue price ($10.2 million) is allocated to the common stock account.
   c. Plant and equipment $8,200,000
      Patents 2,000,000
          Common stock $10,200,000
      To record issuance of common stock

2. a. The firm will pay $9 per share in dividends (9% of $100).
   b. $9 ÷ 0.085 = $105.88, which equals the market value per share of preferred stock.
   c. Cash $1,058,800
          Preferred stock $1,000,000
          Contributed surplus (capital in excess of par value) 58,800
      To record issuance of preferred stock

3. a. 20 percent.
   b. 20 percent; 20% of $10,200,000 = $2,040,000.
   c. 20,000 shares × $160 per share − $2,040,000 = $1,160,000.
   d. Common stock $2,040,000
      Retained earnings 1,160,000
          Cash $3,200,000
      To record retirement of 20,000 shares of common stock

12

Special Problems of Measuring and Reporting Dividends and Earnings

The previous chapter described the accounting for transactions between a corporation and its shareholders where the shareholders were making contributions to the corporation, generally in the form of purchases of stock. This chapter focuses on transactions in the other direction: the transfer of assets from the corporation to the shareholders in the form of dividends. Additional topics include the accounting for stock options, the issue of loss recognition, the calculation of earnings per share, and the accounting for interim periods.

After studying this chapter, you will be able to

- Describe the differences among cash dividends, stock dividends, and stock splits
- Prepare journal entries to record cash and stock dividends
- Understand the criteria for the timing of loss recognition
- Describe the accounting for compensation in the form of stock options
- Understand the criteria for extraordinary item classification
- Calculate basic and fully diluted earnings per share
- Identify the issues pertinent to accounting for interim periods

The issues dealt with are of immediate concern to investors inasmuch as they affect directly both the magnitude and the proportion of their claims to corporate assets. They are of equal importance to managers because managers are the agents (representatives) of investors, and their performance is likely to be evaluated on how competently and equitably they represent their interests. Moreover, the corporations that managers administer may themselves be investors, owning shares in other companies.

CASH DIVIDENDS AND RETAINED EARNINGS

Retained earnings are the total accumulated earnings of a corporation less amounts distributed to shareholders as dividends and any amounts transferred to other capital accounts.

Dividends are distributions of *assets* (or shares of common stock) that reduce retained earnings. They are *declared* by a formal resolution of a firm's board of directors. The announcement of a dividend indicates the *amount per share* to be distributed, the *date of record* (that on which the stock records will be closed and ownership of the outstanding shares determined), and the *date of payment*. A typical announcement reads as follows: "The board of directors of the Bank of Nova Scotia, at its regular meeting of March 27, 1995, declared a quarterly dividend on its common shares of $.31 per share payable on April 26, 1995, to shareholders of record on April 4, 1995."

Basic Entries

The entry to record the declaration of a dividend is straightforward. On the date of declaration, when the legal liability for payment is first established, the entry (in this case to record a dividend of $0.31 per share on 100 million shares outstanding) would be

Common stock dividends $31,000,000
    Dividends payable $31,000,000
To record declaration of the cash dividend on common stock

At year end, "common stock dividends" would be closed to retained earnings. When payment is subsequently made, it would be recorded as follows:

Dividends payable $31,000,000
    Cash $31,000,000
To record payment of the dividend

Dividends and Availability of Cash or Other Assets

Although conventional dividends are *charged* to retained earnings, they are *paid* in cash or other tangible assets. It does not follow that merely because a company has a balance in retained earnings it has the liquid assets to make dividend payments. Retained earnings are a part of shareholders' equity.

Shareholders' equity is the excess of assets over liabilities. It cannot be associated with specific assets to which shareholders have claim.

The nature of retained earnings is a common source of misunderstanding. At one time the term *earned surplus* was used in place of retained earnings. "Surplus" implies something extra—an amount over and above what is needed. Retained earnings rarely, in fact, represent surplus. Rather, a balance in retained earnings is indicative of earnings that have been reinvested in the corporation. By not distributing its earned assets to shareholders, the corporation may have internally financed expansion. The retained earnings, therefore, may not denote the availability of cash or other assets that can readily be distributed to shareholders; instead, the company may have used its available resources to acquire land, buildings, and equipment. The shareholders' equity section of the 1993 Canadian Pacific Limited balance sheet, for example, comprised the following accounts (in millions):

Preference shares	$ 14.9
Ordinary (common) shares	1,247.0
Premium on securities	1,173.9
Other paid-in surplus	154.1
Foreign currency translation adjustments	224.7
Retained earnings	3,216.1
	$6,030.7

Retained earnings, in this case, accounted for 53 percent of owners' equity. It is obvious that distribution of assets represented by the entire $3.2 billion in retained earnings would have forced the company to retrench its operations back to the scale of its early railroad days.

When and how much of a dividend to declare depends on financial requirements and opportunities as well as legal constraints.

The company must first determine whether available and projected cash is sufficient to meet its other operating requirements—the need to meet payrolls, maintain inventories, and replace worn-out equipment. In addition, however, the corporation must consider the interests of shareholders. Insofar as assets are not distributed to shareholders, the shareholders are being forced to increase their investment in the corporation as the corporation generates profit and does not make a return to the shareholders. Whether they wish to increase their investment will depend largely on the return they could obtain from competing investments. If the funds to be retained in the corporation are likely to provide a return greater than shareholders could obtain elsewhere, then shareholders should be willing to permit the company to retain all or a portion of its assets. In fact, many corporations, particularly *growth* companies, omit payment of dividends for years at a time. Shareholders of these companies are willing to forgo immediate cash returns for long-term corporate expansion and enhancement of their investment, through capital appreciation (i.e., an increase in share price).

The payment of dividends is sometimes constrained by statute. The federal and provincial corporation acts generally prohibit firms from paying dividends "out of capital"; they can pay them only "out of earnings." That is, the payment of dividends cannot reduce the shareholders' equity of the company beneath the amount contributed by the shareholders. The motive behind these restrictions is protection of creditors. The laws are designed to make certain that corporations repay their debts to creditors before they distribute assets to shareholders. The shareholders, because of their limited liability, are not individually responsible for the obligations of the corporation.

DIVIDENDS IN KIND

Although dividends are usually paid in cash, it is not uncommon for a company to distribute other types of assets.

A company may own all or a portion of the outstanding stock of a subsidiary. Wishing to divest itself of that firm, it distributes the stock to its own shareholders. The shareholders can then choose to retain their interest in the subsidiary or sell the shares in the open market. Such a transaction is referred to as a *spinoff*. In the 1980s, spinoffs were used extensively by major corporations to rid themselves of unwanted lines of business. Hudson's Bay Co., for example, spun off its real estate arm in 1990 by giving its shareholders a dividend consisting of shares of its real estate subsidiary, Markborough Properties Inc. The 1995 spinoff by Sears Roebuck & Co. of its insurance subsidiary, Allstate Corp., was one of the largest spinoffs in history. At a market value of approximately $29 each, the 360.5 million Allstate shares distributed as a dividend to the shareholders of Sears Roebuck & Co. were worth approximately $10 billion. Shareholders of Sears Roebuck & Co. received approximately 0.93 shares of Allstate Corp. common stock for each share of Sears common stock held.[1] The strategy of the spinoff was to create value for the Sears shareholders and to allow Sears to concentrate on its main business, retailing.

Example

Suppose, for example, the Gamma Co. owns 1 million shares of XYZ Corporation stock. Gamma declares and pays a *dividend in kind* (as such dividends in property are known) of 4 shares of XYZ stock for each of its own 250,000 shares outstanding. If the stock of the XYZ Corporation has been recorded on the books of the Gamma Co. at $5 per share but has a fair market value of $8 per share, then the following two entries would be required:

Investment in XYZ Corporation	$3,000,000	
Gain on investment		$3,000,000
To write up XYZ Corp. stock to reflect market value		

Common stock dividends	$8,000,000	
Investment in XYZ Corporation		$8,000,000
To record declaration and payment of dividend in kind		

As a consequence of the dividend, the corporation will report a holding gain in the amount of the difference between book value and market value of the property distributed.

[1] *Globe and Mail Report on Business,* April 1, 1995.

Many accountants assert, however, that a corporation should *not* be permitted to realize gains or losses as the result of discretionary, non–arm's-length transactions with shareholders. If it were, they contend, it could readily manipulate earnings by distributing to shareholders assets that it could not otherwise sell to outsiders at the value assigned to them. Other accountants point out, however, that "market value" implies an ability to sell the assets to outsiders at the value assigned. Moreover, they observe, a corporation should not have to incur the transaction costs of selling its assets to outsiders to realize a gain. It could as easily transfer them directly to its shareholders, who could sell them for as much cash as they would otherwise receive. There is no Canadian recommendation for this type of transaction, but in the United States the Accounting Principles Board, in *Opinion No. 29*, held that dividends in kind should generally be accounted for at market values and appropriate gains or losses recognized.[2] This would serve to guide practice in Canada.

Distributions of the stock of other companies *(dividends in kind)* should not be confused with *stock dividends*, which will be discussed in a following section.

STOCK SPLITS

Corporations will sometimes *split* their stock; that is, they will issue additional shares for each share outstanding. A firm might, for example, split its stock 3 for 1, meaning that, for each one share presently held, a shareholder will receive an additional two.

Stock splits are ordinarily intended to reduce the market price per share, to obtain a wider distribution of ownership, and to improve the marketability of the outstanding shares. The common stock of a corporation might be trading at $150 per share. The board of directors determines that at such a high price the stock is less attractive to investors than it would be at a lower price. Many investors like to acquire stock in round lots of 100 shares since brokerage commissions are relatively higher when fewer shares are purchased. The board might, therefore, vote a 3-for-1 stock split. Each shareholder will end up with three times as many shares as previously, but the market price per share can be expected to fall to nearly one-third its previous price. Neither the corporation nor the individual shareholder will be intrinsically better or worse off as a result of the split. For example, when the Bank of Montreal split its common stock *two* for *one*, the share price fell from approximately $50 per share to approximately $25 per share. However, there is some empirical evidence that the stock of companies that split their stock provide a higher return to investors than the stock of companies which do not split their stock. In other words, the stock split may be a signal of exceptional performance.

A stock split is the equivalent of an exchange of one $5 bill for five $1 coins. As a consequence, no accounting entries are required to effect the split. A memorandum note will be made to record the fact that the number of shares outstanding has increased. There will be no changes to the shareholders' equity

---

[2] An exception to this general rule is made when a company distributes to its shareholders *all* of the shares of another corporation as part of a reorganization or rescindment of a prior business combination. In this type of transaction, *the distribution of shares should be based on their recorded* value. Hence no gains or losses are recognized.

section of the balance sheet as a result of the stock split, other than a change in the number of shares outstanding. For a company with 1 million shares outstanding, it would report 3 million shares outstanding following a 3-for-1 stock split.

STOCK DIVIDENDS

Motivation

A special form of stock split is known as a *stock dividend*. As with a stock split, a stock dividend results in the issuance of additional shares. Ordinarily the ratio of new shares to outstanding shares is lower for a stock dividend than for a stock split. Seldom does the number of new shares to be issued exceed 20 percent of previously outstanding shares; generally it is less than 5 percent. More significantly, the motivation for a stock dividend is considerably different from that for a stock split. A corporation would not issue a stock dividend to improve the marketability of its shares, but instead to provide its shareholders with tangible evidence of an increase in their ownership interest. A company may view a stock dividend as a substitute for a dividend in cash or other property. Lacking the available cash, it would distribute to each shareholder, on a pro rata basis, additional shares of its own stock. Sometimes, for example, a company that has consistently paid cash dividends may experience a cash shortage. Rather than omit the dividend entirely, the company would distribute additional shares of stock. A stock dividend may also provide a means for a company to *capitalize* a portion of accumulated earnings. The company would transfer a portion of accumulated earnings from the "retained earnings" account (which is sometimes viewed as a temporary capital account) to the "common stock," account (which is considered to be of a more permanent nature). This type of transfer provides formal evidence that resources have been permanently retained in the business and are no longer available for the payment of additional dividends.

In Essence a Stock Split

A stock dividend, like a stock split, has no effect on the intrinsic worth of the corporation. It leaves the shareholders neither better nor worse off than previously. A stock dividend has no effect on corporate assets and liabilities. As a result of the stock dividend, additional shares of common stock are outstanding. But since the net worth of the corporation remains the same, each share of common stock represents a proportionately smaller interest in the corporation.

Suppose, for example, that a corporation, prior to declaration of a stock dividend, had net assets of $100 million and 1 million shares of common stock outstanding. A shareholder who owned 100,000 shares would have held a 10 percent interest in a company with a book value of $100 million. If the corporation declared a 3 percent stock dividend, then that shareholder would receive 3,000 additional shares. She would now own 103,000 shares out of a total of 1,030,000 shares—still a 10 percent interest in a company with a book value of $100 million. Insofar as the market price for the stock is determined rationally, then the market price per share can be expected to be reduced proportionately.

The underlying nature of a stock dividend has been well expressed by the U.S. Supreme Court. In a case in which the court was called upon to rule whether stock dividends constituted income subject to tax under the provisions of the Sixteenth Amendment, Justice Pitney affirmed a judgment in a previous case in which it was held:

> A stock dividend really takes nothing from the property of the corporation, and adds nothing to the interest of the shareholders. Its property is not diminished, and their interests are not increased. . . . The proportional interest of each shareholder remains the same. The only change is in the evidence which represents that interest, the new shares and the original shares together representing the same proportional interest that the original shares represented before the issue of the new ones.[3]

But Accounted for Differently

Although stock dividends are, in essence, a form of stock split, the rule-making authorities of the accounting profession have determined that they should be accounted for differently. Whereas a stock split results only in a change to the number of shares outstanding, a stock dividend is handled as a *reclassification* of the shareholders' equity accounts.

According to generally accepted practice, when a corporation issues less than 20 to 25 percent additional shares as a stock dividend, it should transfer from retained earnings to "permanent" capital an amount equal to the fair value of the shares issued.[4] Assume, as before, a company which previously had 1 million shares of no-par value stock outstanding declared a 3 percent stock dividend. Assume additionally that the market price at the time of the declaration was $150 per share. The fair value of the 30,000 shares to be issued and the accumulated earnings to be capitalized would be 30,000 times $150, or $4.5 million. Because of the relatively small percentage of additional shares to be issued, a company would not consider the distribution to be a stock split and simply adjust the number of shares outstanding. Instead, it would transfer from retained earnings to "common stock," an amount reflective of the fair value of the new shares to be issued—in this example, $4,500,000.

The following entry would give effect to the stock dividend:

Dividends in common stock $4,500,000
    Common stock $4,500,000
To record the issue of a stock dividend

The stock dividends account would then be "closed" to retained earnings:

Retained earnings $4,500,000
    Dividends in common stock $4,500,000
To close stock dividend account

---

[3] Eisner V. Macomber, 252 U.S. 189, 40 S. Ct. 189.
[4] This is an example of a situation in which common practice dictates what generally accepted accounting principles are. There is no recommendation in the *CICA Handbook* to cover the issue, but general practice is to account for stock splits and dividends as noted. This general practice is also consistent with the applicable U.S. pronouncements.

Rationale behind Generally Accepted Practice

The rationale behind the *capitalization* of retained earnings rests largely with the interpretation supposedly placed upon stock dividends by the recipients. A stock dividend does not, in fact, give rise to any change whatsoever in either the corporation's assets or its respective shareholders' proportionate interests. However, according to the professional committee that ruled on the issue in the United States, "it cannot fail to be recognized that, merely as a consequence of the expressed purpose of the transaction and its characterization as a *dividend* in related notices to shareholders and the public at large, many recipients of stock dividends look upon them as distributions of corporate earnings and usually in an amount equivalent to the fair value of the additional shares received."[5]

Moreover, the committee pointed out, in many instances the number of shares issued is sufficiently small in relation to shares previously outstanding so that the market price of the stock does not perceptibly decline. Hence the overall market value of a shareholder's interest may increase by the amount of the market value of the new shares. Because both recipients and the investing public *think* that the dividend shares are of value, the committee said, the corporation should account for them as if they were of value. It should transfer a portion of accumulated earnings from "temporary" to "permanent" capital accounts so as to indicate that such portion of accumulated earnings is no longer available for the payment of dividends. Whatever merit the rationale of the committee might have had when it was first set forth has unquestionably been reduced by the increased sophistication of investors. Today, only the most naive of investors would see the new shares per se as having value—although they do, of course, recognize that the earnings that they represent have enhanced the value of their investment.

WHEN IS A LOSS A LOSS?

Inherent in almost all accounting issues is the question, "When is a company better off than it was previously?" Implicit in this question is its corollary, "When is a company worse off?" Or, to phrase it somewhat differently, "When should a loss be recognized as a loss?"

Suppose, for example, that a Canadian multinational company has been threatened with the expropriation of certain of its foreign manufacturing facilities. Unquestionably, the mere threat of the expropriation leaves the firm worse off than it was previously. No doubt, the market price of the firm's outstanding common stock would fall in reaction to such a threat. But should the mere possibility of expropriation be a cause for the firm to write off its foreign assets and charge income with a "loss from expropriation"?

---

[5] American Institute of Certified Public Accountants, *Accounting Research Bulletin No. 43*, Chapter 7, New York, 1961.

Contingencies

The question of when to recognize *contingencies* (gains and losses that are uncertain as to both occurrence and amount) is particularly troublesome. On the one hand, the convention of conservatism dictates that prompt recognition be given to losses. But, on the other, financial statements must be objective. The probability of many types of losses does not suddenly go from remote to certain. It increases gradually over a period of time. Firms cannot be permitted unlimited discretion in selecting the period in which to recognize losses. If they were, then reported income would be nothing more than an arbitrary determination of corporate management.

The difficulty of establishing guidelines as to when a loss should be recognized arises in large measure because the types of losses that firms incur form a continuum from "likely and estimable" to "unlikely and not estimable." On one end of the continuum are losses such as those arising from warranty obligations and uncollectable accounts receivable. As indicated previously, such losses are conventionally recognized at the time of the related sale of merchandise. They are statistically certain to occur, and the amount of the loss is subject to reasonable estimation, even though the particular account that will have to be written off or the party to whom the warranty service might have to be made is unknown at the time of sale. On the other end of the continuum are losses from fires and natural disasters, which, although sure to occur at some time, are random happenings.

Criteria for Recognizing Loss

The *CICA Handbook*, in Section 3290, "Contingencies," has prescribed that a loss may be charged to income only when

(1) it is likely that a future event will confirm that an asset had been impaired or a liability incurred at the date of the financial statements; and

(2) the amount of loss can be reasonably estimated.

These guidelines are, of course, nonspecific, but the Handbook provides a number of examples as to when various types of losses should be recognized. The Handbook directs that, even if a loss contingency does not satisfy the criteria for formal recording within the accounts, the contingency must nevertheless be *disclosed* in a footnote to the financial statements. The disclosure must indicate the nature of the contingency and give, if possible, an estimate of, or range of, the possible loss.

In keeping with the convention of conservatism, *gain* contingencies are not usually recognized in the accounts until the cash or other resources are actually received. They may, of course, be disclosed in the footnotes of periods prior to those when they are recognized, giving the nature of the contingency and an estimate of the possible gain.

Corporations frequently compensate their employees in shares of stock or in options which permit them to purchase stock on favourable terms. Stock plans take a variety of forms. They have become popular for several reasons. First, they provide employees with tax advantages over straight cash wages in that they permit employees to defer the tax on the compensation. The Income Tax Act provides that the benefit from the stock received is taxable only when the individual sells the shares. Second, by making the employees corporate owners, stock plans can increase loyalty, efficiency, and productivity. Third, they enable the employer to conserve cash by permitting it to substitute stock for cash.

Accounting for Compensation Expense

The *CICA Handbook* makes no recommendations for the accounting for compensation in the form of stock or stock options. Canadian practice, therefore, is influenced by the relevant U.S. pronouncements. The following discussion is based on the U.S. pronouncements. The guiding accounting rule for compensation in stock or stock options is that the total compensation cost is to be measured by the fair market value of the stock or options at the date of the grant. The compensation expense is to be recognized over the period during which the employees perform the related services and thereby earn the stock or option.

Compensation in Stock

The accounting for compensation in stock is relatively straightforward because the value of the stock is known at the time it is earned by the employees.

Example

Assume that in abbreviated form the balance sheet of a corporation is (in millions)

Assets (net of liabilities)	$300
Capital stock (300 million shares)	$200
Retained earnings	100
Total shareholders' equity	$300

The corporation, in addition to paying its employees standard cash wages and salaries, grants them 25 million shares of its own common stock. Market value of the shares (which in this example is the same as book value) is $1 per share.

The corporation would report additional wage and salary expense of $25 million—the market value of 25 million shares at $1 per share and a corresponding increase in capital stock:

```
Wage and salary expense ................................................................................. $25
    Capital stock ..................................................................................................... $25
```
To record employee compensation and the issuance of additional shares of common stock

At year end, wage and salary expense would be closed to retained earnings, thereby reducing retained earnings by $25 million. The accounting for compensation in the form of stock is quite similar to the acccounting for stock dividends discussed previously, the only difference being that the stock dividends go to shareholders and the compensation stock goes to employees (who then, obviously, become shareholders). Both are accounted for as a capitalization of retained earnings.

Note, however, an anomaly. The reported wage expense will be greater than the likely value of the shares to be given the employees. After the new shares have been issued, and wage and salary expense has been closed to retained earnings, the total assets, as well as the total shareholders' equity, will remain at $300 million (capital stock has increased by $25 million and retained earnings has decreased by $25 million). There will now, however, be 325 million shares outstanding. The value per share (both book and market) can be expected to decline to $.9231 per share ($300 million in net assets divided by 325 million shares). Thus from their perspective, the employees receive compensation of only $23.08 million rather than $25 million.

An interesting example of compensation in the form of stock is the case of Ted Newall, the chief executive officer of Nova Corp., an Alberta-based gas transmission and petrochemical company. For the year 1994, Newall decided to risk his annual salary by agreeing to accept shares of Nova's common stock for his 1994 compensation in lieu of cash salary. At the beginning of 1994, when the shares of Nova were trading for approximately $7 per share, his 1994 compensation was set at 68,000 shares of common stock. At a price of $7 per share, this had a value of $476,000, a significant drop from his 1993 cash salary of $609,000. However, during 1994 the share price of Nova common stock rose and, based on the 1994 quarterly closing prices, his compensation was valued at $822,375, *a significant increase* over his 1993 cash salary.[6] The journal entry that Nova Corp. would make to record the issue of the 68,000 shares and the associated salary expense would be:

```
Salary expense ...................................................................................... $822,375
    Common stock ...................................................................................................... $822,375
```
To record chief executive officer compensation and the issuance of 68,000 shares of common stock

Compensation in Stock Options

The issues of accounting for compensation in stock options are considerably more complex than those for the stock itself because of the uncertainty that attaches to the compensation.

---

[6] *Globe and Mail Report on Business,* March 28, 1995.

Stock options take many forms, but typically they permit employees to purchase shares of a company's stock at a fixed price at some date in the future. Although the employees will have to pay for their shares, the price to be paid remains constant regardless of fluctuations in market value. Should the market value of the shares increase above the set price (the *exercise* price), employees could acquire the shares at a considerable savings over what they would otherwise have to pay. Should the market price fall below the exercise price, then they need not exercise their options, but can allow them to lapse.

Measuring Compensation Expense and Determining Share Values

The difficult accounting issues with respect to employee stock options are how to measure the compensation paid and how to value the shares of stock to be issued. If the employees had to exercise the options immediately upon receipt, then the problems of valuation would be reasonably straightforward. The approximate value of each option would be the number of shares that could be purchased times the difference between the current market price of the stock and the exercise price of the option. If, for example, options permitted employees to purchase 100 shares of stock at $40 per share at a time when the stock was being traded at $45 per share, then the employees could "save" $5 per share. The value of each option would be

Current market price	$45	
Less: Exercise price	40	$ 5
Times number of shares that could be purchased		× 100
Value of options		$500

Most stock option plans stipulate that an option can be exercised only after a specified number of years has elapsed and only if the employee has remained with the company during that period. Indeed, one of the primary objectives of stock option plans is to reduce employee turnover. As a result, at the time the option is granted, neither the number of shares to be issued nor the total amount to be received from an employee as payment for the shares is known.

Moreover, once a stock option plan has been adopted, the *exercise price*—the price that the employees will have to pay for their shares—is adjusted only periodically. Because of fluctuations in the market price of the firm's shares, the exercise price may sometimes be *greater* than the market price. For example, the options may allow employees to purchase shares of stock at a price of $40 even though the current market price is only $35. If the value of the options is to be based on the excess of the exercise price over the market price at the time of issue, then it would appear to be negative.

The options, however, clearly have positive value, regardless of the relationship between exercise and market prices. The recipients have the *right* to purchase the shares at $40 per share. If, in the period during which they are eligible to exercise the options, the market price increases to more than $40, they can purchase the shares at a *discount* price. If the price remains below $40 per share, they need not exercise the options; they have lost nothing.

Despite these problems of measurement, the former Accounting Principles Board in the United States has ruled that stock options should be recorded as compensation expense in the periods in which an employee performs the services for which the option is granted. The dictum of the board is intended to ensure that the cost of employee services is matched with the benefits (revenues) that they generate. The value of the option should be determined as of the date that the option is granted.

The board prescribed that the value of each option be measured by the difference between the exercise price and the market price so long as the market price exceeds the exercise price. But, if, as in the situation just described, the exercise price is greater than the market price, then the option and the related compensation expense should be assumed to have a zero value. The board recognized that there is, in fact, value to options that are granted when the exercise price is greater than the market price. However, it considered the practical difficulties of determining such value to be insurmountable.

Example

On December 31, 1996, a firm grants its president the option to purchase 1 million shares of the firm's no-par value common stock at a price of $8 per share. The option is in recognition of service performed during 1996. It can be exercised during the five years beginning January 1, 1997, providing the president is still employed by the firm. The market price of the stock on December 31, 1996, is $10 per share.

The compensation expense and the option would be assigned a value of 1 million times $2 ($10 minus $8), or $2 million, and would be recorded on the date granted as follows:

Executive compensation (expense)	$2,000,000	
Capital received, stock options		$2,000,000

To record the issue of the employee stock options on December 31, 1996

The account "capital received, stock options," would be reported among the other shareholders' equity accounts. It would represent capital contributed by the president in the form of services rather than cash or other property. When the option is actually exercised, the receipt of the $8 million cash from the president and the issue of the 1 million shares would be recorded as follows:

Capital received, stock options	$2,000,000	
Cash	8,000,000	
Common stock		$10,000,000

To record the issue of 1,000,000 shares of common stock

If, alternatively, the president elects not to exercise the option and it lapses, then no entry would be required (although "capital received, stock options," could be reclassified to an account with a title indicative of the lapsed status of the option).

Now suppose that on December 31, 1997, the firm grants the president an identical option. The market price of the stock has now fallen to $7 per share, however. Since the exercise price is greater than the market price, the option, for accounting purposes, is deemed to have a zero value; no journal entry is required to record the grant of the option.

When the option is actually exercised, the issue of the 1 million shares would be recorded with the following entry:

Cash $8,000,000
    Common stock $8,000,000
To record issue of 1,000,000 shares of common stock

Note that the recorded value of the capital received is directly dependent on the market price of the common stock on the *date the options are granted* rather than the date on which the options are exercised and the shares issued. The board's approach to valuing options oversimplifies an intricate economic question. The valuation of options involves more than merely subtracting exercise price from market price. Academic researchers have developed sophisticated mathematical models to determine the value of options. They are widely used by professional option traders. They take into account a number of variables in addition to market price of stock and exercise price of the option. Among them are time to expiration, prevailing rates of interest, and the variability in the market price of the stock. The board, of course, recognizes that the prescribed method is simplistic, but continues to support it because it believes that the benefits of the more elegant methods are outweighed by the implementation costs imposed by their complexity.

EXTRAORDINARY ITEMS

Extraordinary items are those that are *unusual in nature and infrequent in occurrence*. Section 3480 of the *CICA Handbook* directs that extraordinary items be segregated from other revenues and expenses and reported separately on the income statement. It is recommended that they be included as part of the income statement as follows:

Income before extraordinary items	$xxxx
Extraordinary items (less applicable income tax of $ _____) (Explanatory note: _____)	xxxx
Net income	$xxxx

As indicated by the suggested presentation, the income tax associated with the extraordinary items should be presented along with those items. The income tax applicable to the extraordinary items should therefore be excluded from the income tax expense reported in the main body of the income statement.

To help assure uniformity of practice, the CICA has established rigorous criteria as to what constitutes an extraordinary item. To qualify as extraordinary, an item (as set forth in Section 3480) must be *unusual in nature* in that "it does not typify the normal business activities of the entity." It must also be *infrequent in occurrence* in that "it is not expected to occur frequently over several years." In addition, it must not be *at the discretion of management* in that "it does not depend primarily on decisions or determinations by management or owners." This last criterion was added in recently (1989) to remove most of the discretion of management in determining when to classify an item as extraordinary. The discretion previously available had led to difficulties in the comparability of financial statements. As a result of this criterion, very few examples of extraordinary items are now found in the income statements of Canadian corporations.

Examples of events or transactions that would ordinarily be categorized as extraordinary items are losses resulting from major catastrophes such as earthquakes, expropriations of property by foreign governments, or government prohibitions against the sale or use of products which the company had previously manufactured.

Examples of events or transactions that would *not* be categorized as extraordinary items and should thereby be reported along with ordinary expenses are uncollectable accounts receivables, losses on the sale of plant and equipment, and losses from foreign currency revaluations.

EARNINGS PER SHARE

If there is any one single measure of corporate performance that is of primary concern to common shareholders and potential investors, it is unquestionably earnings per share (EPS). In its simplest form, calculation of earnings per share is straightforward:

$$\text{EPS} = \frac{\text{Net income} - \text{Preferred stock dividends}}{\text{Number of shares of common stock outstanding}}$$

Net income should be that after income tax. Preferred stock dividends must be deducted from net income whenever the ratio is being computed for the benefit of common shareholders, since preferred dividends reduce the equity of common shareholders.

Basis: Weighted Average Number of Shares Outstanding

The number of shares outstanding should be based on the *average* number of shares outstanding during the year. The average should be weighted by the number of months the shares may have been outstanding. The *weighted average* number of shares outstanding, rather than simply the number outstanding at year end, must be used in the denominator. That is because the corporation would have had the use of the capital associated with any additional shares issued during the year only for a part of the year. The company's opportunity to generate earnings on the additional capital would have been limited by the number of months it had the use of the capital.

Example

A firm had net income (after taxes) for the year of $800,000. It has a preferred stock dividend requirement of $200,000. It had 200,000 shares of common stock outstanding since January 1. On October 1, it issued an additional 100,000 shares of common stock.

Earnings available to common shareholders would be $600,000 (net income less the preferred dividend requirement).

The weighted average number of shares outstanding would be

200,000 shares × 9 months	1,800,000
300,000 shares × 3 months	900,000
	2,700,000
Divided by 12 months	÷ 12
	225,000 shares

Earnings per share of common stock would be

$$\frac{\$600,000}{225,000 \text{ shares}} = \$2.67$$

Accounting for Potential Dilution

Because of the complex capital structures of many firms, the straightforward computation of earnings per share may be misleading. Although the average number of shares actually outstanding during a year is, by year end, a historical fact, many firms have commitments to issue additional shares in the future. If earnings per share are to have predictive value—if they are to be useful in forecasting future earnings—then the number of shares reasonably expected to be issued in the future must also be taken into account. Otherwise, earnings per share may take a precipitous drop in the period in which the additional shares are issued.

The obligation to issue the additional shares of common stock stems largely from commitments contained in other securities that may be outstanding: stock rights, warrants, and options as well as bonds and preferred stock that might be converted into common stock.

Stock rights, often called *preemptive rights,* represent commitments on the part of a company to issue, at an established price, a specified number of shares of common stock. A company typically grants stock rights to existing shareholders whenever it intends to issue new shares of stock. The rights give the existing shareholders first opportunity to acquire the new shares and thereby to preserve their proportionate interests in the company.

Warrants, like rights, are promises on the part of a company to issue a stated number of shares at a set price. Warrants, however, are usually issued by companies in connection with the sale of bonds to make the bonds more attractive to prospective purchasers.

When a firm has a complex capital structure—one that includes securities that could result in the *dilution* of earnings per share—the calculation of earnings per share becomes both subjective and complicated because the issue of the additional shares will affect not only the number of shares outstanding but overall corporate earnings as well. The CICA, in Section 3500 of the *Handbook*, established specific guidelines for the computation of earnings per share. An overview of these guidelines will indicate some of the difficulties of determining earnings per share when the capital structure is complex.

Must Present Basic and Fully Diluted Earnings per Share

Section 3500 requires that a firm with a complex capital structure present two types of earnings per share data on the face of its income statement. The first would indicate *basic earnings per share* and the second *fully diluted earnings per share*. The calculation of the fully diluted earnings per share figures would take into account the impact of additional shares of common stock that might be issued.

In *basic* earnings per share, the number of shares of common stock outstanding includes all common shares presently outstanding, appropriately weighted if any were issued in the current year.

In *fully diluted* earnings per share, the number of shares of common stock outstanding includes:

1. All common shares presently outstanding, appropriately weighted if issued in the current year

2. Potential common shares to be issued if all convertible securities are converted

3. Potential common shares to be issued from the exercise of rights, warrants, and options and from other contingent issuances

Must Adjust Earnings to Reflect Interest and Preferred Dividends Saved and Income to Be Received from Additional Capital

If, in computing fully diluted earnings per share, it is assumed that certain securities will be converted into common stock and thereby increase the number of common shares outstanding, it is also necessary to consider the impact of the conversion on the *net income* of the company that is available to common shareholders. For example, if outstanding bonds or preferred stock will be converted to common stock, the firm will no longer have to pay interest or dividends on these securities. The amounts saved will increase the earnings in which the common shareholders have an equity interest. In determining the numerator (net income) of the EPS fraction, one must add to the actual net income for the year the interest or dividends on bonds or preferred stock that are assumed to be converted into common stock.

In addition, the imputed earnings, after income taxes, from the cash that would have been received had the shareholders exercised dilutive rights, warrants, and options must be added to the actual net income in calculating fully diluted earnings per share.

Example

A company had outstanding 10 million shares of common stock and 5 million shares of convertible preferred stock. The preferred shares paid annual dividends at the rate of $12 per share and were convertible into common stock at the rate of one share for one share. Net income of the company before payment of preferred dividends was $200 million.

Exhibit 12-1 illustrates the computation of the earnings available to the common shareholders, as well as both the basic and fully diluted earnings per share based on the above information.

Issue: How to Take into Account the Cash to Be Received upon the Exercise of Warrants and Options

Outstanding stock warrants or options permit the holder to *purchase* (for cash) shares of common stock. If, in computing number of shares outstanding, it is assumed that warrants and options will be exercised and additional shares of common stock issued, it is also necessary to take into account the cash that will be received in exchange for the additional shares. Few firms will permit cash to remain idle in a chequing account. Instead, they will invest it in income-producing projects. If the shares to be issued are added to those outstanding, it will also be necessary to add this potential increase in corporate earnings, generated from the additional cash, to actual earnings for the year.

The CICA recognized that the additional income that would be derived from the cash received from the exercise of warrants and options would be a matter of professional judgment. To assure comparability among firms, the CICA required that each firm disclose the rate of return used for imputing additional income along with the dollar amount of the imputed income, after income taxes.

EXHIBIT 12-1
Computation of Earnings (EPS Numerator) and Earnings per Share (Shares and Earnings in Millions)

Basic EPS	
Net income	$ 200
Subtract preferred dividends ($12 on 5 million shares)	(60)
Earnings available to common shareholders	$ 140
Number of common shares	10
EPS (earnings available to common shareholders divided by number of common shares) $= \dfrac{\$140}{10} = \$14.00$	
Fully Diluted EPS	
Earnings after preferred dividends	$ 140
Add back preferred dividends that would not have to be paid if shares were converted	60
Earnings available to common shareholders	$ 200
Number of shares assumed to be outstanding (10 million + 5 million assumed issued on conversion)	15
EPS (earnings available to common shareholders divided by number of common shares) $= \dfrac{\$200}{15} = \$13.33$	

Example

The capital structure of a firm included the following throughout all of 1997.

Common stock: 200,000 shares issued and outstanding.

Preferred stock, Class A: 50,000 shares issued and outstanding. Each share is convertible into one share of common stock. Each share pays a dividend of $2.

Preferred stock, Class B: 100,000 shares issued and outstanding. Each share is convertible into one share of common stock. Each share pays a dividend of $6.

Executive stock options outstanding: Options to purchase 9,000 shares at a price of $40 per share are outstanding.

The rate of return for imputing earnings on the cash received on the exercise of the stock options is assumed to be 10%. The combined income tax rate is assumed to be 40 percent.

The firm had net income of $3 million. Of this amount, $100,000 was paid in dividends to holders of preferred stock, Class A, and $600,000 was paid in dividends to holders of preferred stock, Class B. Earnings available to common shareholders were, therefore, $2.3 million.

The computation of earnings per share, both basic and fully diluted, is shown in Exhibit 12-2.

EXHIBIT 12-2
Computation of Earnings per Share: A Comprehensive Example

Basic Earnings per Share

Number of shares outstanding	
Common stock	200,000 shares
Earnings	
Earnings available to common shareholders (per information provided)	$2,300,000

$$\text{Basic EPS} = \frac{\$2,300,000}{200,000 \text{ shares}} = \$9.20$$

Fully Diluted Earnings per Share

Number of shares outstanding	
Common stock outstanding	200,000 shares
Add: Preferred stock, Class A, convertible into 50,000 shares of common stock	50,000
Preferred stock, Class B, convertible into 100,000 shares of common stock	100,000
Stock options, exercisable into 9,000 shares of common stock	9,000
Shares outstanding for fully diluted EPS calculation	359,000 shares
Earnings	
Earnings available to common shareholders	$2,300,000
Add: Dividends on preferred stock, Class A and B assumed in calculation of number of shares outstanding to be converted into common stock	700,000
Imputed earnings on cash received on assumed exercise of stock options $(9,000 \times \$40 \times 0.1 \times 0.6)$	21,600
Income for fully diluted EPS calculation	$3,021,600

$$\text{Fully diluted EPS} = \frac{\$3,021,600}{359,000 \text{ shares}} = \$8.42$$

Publicly traded corporations are required, and many other firms elect, to issue interim financial reports. *Interim financial reports* are those that cover less than a full year. Commonly they cover a quarter or half-year period. For example, companies listed on the Toronto Stock Exchange are required to report to the Exchange on a quarterly basis. The interim reports of most companies are not nearly as detailed as their annual reports. Generally, an income statement separately disclosing revenue, investment income, amortization, interest expense, income taxes, extraordinary items, net income, and basic and fully diluted earnings per share is required. A statement of changes in financial position is required, but a balance sheet is not.

The accounting principles to be followed in calculating income for a period of a quarter or half year are the same as those followed for a full year. Nevertheless, meaningful determination of income for short periods presents inherent difficulties. In an earlier chapter it was pointed out that over the life of an enterprise determination of income is relatively simple. Most accounting problems arise because of the need for financial information on a periodic basis. Revenues and expenses must be assigned to specific accounting periods long before the full consequences of a transaction are known with certainty. Prepaid and deferred costs must be stored in asset and liability accounts pending allocation to earnings of particular years. To the extent that interim periods are shorter than annual periods, the related problems of income determination and asset valuation are correspondingly greater. It becomes considerably more difficult to associate revenues with productive effort and to match costs with revenues.

Revenues and Expenses May Be Based on Annual Measures

A period of one year will often correspond to a firm's natural business cycle. However, periods shorter than a year may be characterized by seasonal fluctuations in both revenues and expenses, thereby compounding the problems of financial reporting. Indeed, some revenues and expenses are determined on an annual basis; they cannot be calculated accurately for a period less than a year until results for the entire year are known. As a consequence, meaningful interim reports cannot be prepared for any one period without consideration of anticipated financial activities in subsequent periods.

A corporate compensation plan may require a firm to pay year-end bonuses to employees based on annual measures of performance, such as corporate earnings or a salesperson's gross sales. The amount of the bonus cannot be determined, and will not be paid, until the end of the fourth quarter. Yet the bonus unquestionably represents compensation for services rendered throughout the year, not just the final quarter.

Some firms permit customers quantity discounts based on cumulative purchases during the year. The discount may not take effect until the customer has reached a specified level of purchases—a level not likely to be attained until the third or fourth quarter of the year. Prices—and revenues—will appear to be higher in the earlier quarters than the later ones. Unless an adjustment to revenues is made to take into account the discounts to be granted in the future, the interim reports will overstate earnings.

In the same vein, firms may incur certain costs in a particular season. Major repairs, for example, may be undertaken during a firm's "slow" season, but they benefit the entire year. Property taxes may be paid at year end, but they represent an operating cost for the entire year. Unless these expenditures are expensed evenly over the entire year, the interim reports for each individual period may be misleading.

Each Interim Period Should Be Viewed as a Separate Accounting Period

Section 1750 of the *CICA Handbook* deals specifically with interim reports. It emphasizes that each interim period should be viewed as a discrete period. However, it goes on to recommend that appropriate estimates and assumptions should be made to match costs and revenues. This additional recommendation is consistent with the view that the interim period is just a part of the entire year. This lack of consistency means that there is considerable divergence of practice in interim reporting.

Interim reports necessarily are based on an even greater number of subjective assumptions, estimates, and allocations than are annual reports. They provide financial information for a relatively short period of time. Especially if a business is seasonal, they cannot be relied upon as predictors of earnings for the remaining periods of the year. If carefully prepared, they are a useful means of comparing performance in one quarter with that in a corresponding quarter of a prior year, though usually not among quarters of the same year.

Example

The accounting records of a firm indicate (in summary form) the following *first-quarter* data:

Sales		$10,000,000
Cost of goods sold	$6,000,000	
Other expenses	2,500,000	8,500,000
Income before taxes		$ 1,500,000

Several adjustments to the recorded amounts are necessary to match costs and revenues.

1. *Sales Discounts.* The company grants discounts to customers on annual purchases above specified amounts. Customers are allowed a discount of 10 percent on cumulative purchases during the year

of more than $100,000. As at the end of the first quarter, no customer has purchased more than $100,000 of goods. Hence no discounts have been granted. However, the company estimates that on average over the entire year, sales discounts will be 1.5 percent of sales.

Because discounts are as much associated with purchases of the first quarter as of subsequent periods, sales of the first quarter must be adjusted to take into account discounts that will actually be taken in later periods. Sales must be reduced by 1.5 percent, or $150,000.

2. *LIFO Inventory.* The company maintains its inventory on a LIFO basis. In the first quarter of the year, sales exceed production, and the company has to dip into its LIFO base. Hence cost of goods sold includes items acquired at relatively low cost. Of the goods sold, 100,000 units have been carried at $6 per unit. Current replacement cost is $8 per unit. The company is certain that by year end the LIFO base will be restored. Since cost of goods will be determined on a periodic basis at year end, all goods sold will be assumed to have been acquired at current-year prices of $8 per unit.

Cost of goods sold must be increased by $2 for each of the 100,000 units taken out of the LIFO base—thus $200,000.

3. *Expenses That Benefit the Entire Year.* Each year, in the third quarter, the company overhauls certain of its equipment at a cost of $600,000. The overhaul is required because of production carried out throughout the year. Hence 25 percent of the cost, $150,000, must be added to expenses of the first quarter.

4. *Income Taxes.* The company estimates that because it is able to take advantage of various special credits and deductions, its effective tax rate *for the year* will be only 24 percent, a rate considerably below the firm's marginal combined federal and provincial rate of 36 percent. The reported tax expense for the quarter must be based on this effective rate, even though all the conditions for the special tax benefits might not be satisfied until later in the year.

Summary of Adjustments		
Sales ($10,000,000 less 1.5%)		$9,850,000
Cost of goods sold ($6,000,000 plus LIFO adjustment of $200,000)	$6,200,000	
Other expense ($2,500,000 plus share of overhaul, $150,000)	2,650,000	$8,850,000
Income before taxes		$1,000,000
Taxes @ 24%		240,000
Net Income		$ 760,000

Summary

In this chapter we have dealt with distributions of assets, stock options, losses and contingencies, earnings per share, and interim reports. Although we discussed several diverse accounting problems, the general approach to resolving them must, in essence, be the same as the approach to the issues discussed in previous chapters. Accountants must discern the substance, as well as the form, of a transaction; they must measure and assign values to the goods, services, or securities exchanged; and then must make a judgment as to the appropriate accounting period in which to give recognition to the impairment or enhancement of company resources.

Exercise for Review and Self-Testing

A corporation had earnings of $500,000 after taxes and preferred dividends. It had 100,000 shares of no-par value common stock outstanding for the entire year.

The company also had outstanding 10,000 shares of preferred stock. The shares were issued at $100 each and pay a dividend of $4 each. Each share is convertible into one share of common stock.

The firm's capital structure also includes 2,000 convertible bonds, each of which is convertible into 15 shares of common stock—a total of 30,000 shares of common stock. Each bond pays interest at a rate of 8 percent per year. Total annual interest costs are $160,000, but after-tax interest costs are only 60 percent (1 minus an assumed tax rate of 40 percent) of that amount, or $96,000.

1. In determining *basic* earnings per share, how many shares of common stock should be considered outstanding?

2. What would be *basic* earnings per share?

3. How many additional shares of common stock would the company be required to issue if the convertible securities were converted? How many shares of common stock should be considered outstanding in determining *fully diluted* earnings per share?

4. If the bonds were converted into common stock, by how much would interest (after taking into account tax costs) be reduced? If the preferred stock were converted into common stock, by how much would the preferred dividend requirement be reduced? What would now be total earnings available to common shareholders?

5. Based on the calculations in (3) and (4), what would be *fully diluted* earnings per share?

Questions for Review and Discussion

1. The *Wall Street Journal* reported that Gulf & Western Industries, Inc., declared a 100 percent stock dividend, said it intends to raise its quarterly

dividend by the equivalent of 2.5 cents a current share, and predicted record earnings for the coming fiscal year. Explain the significance of each of the three elements of the announcement. Which of the three is of most significance to the economic welfare of the shareholders? Which is of the least?

2. Dividends are sometimes said to be "paid out of retained earnings." Yet for many corporations, especially those that have been in existence for, and have expanded over, a period of several years, the balance in retained earnings is of little consequence in the decision as to the amount of dividends that can be declared. Why?

3. A firm owns 10,000 shares of stock in another corporation. It wishes to distribute the stock to its shareholders as a dividend in kind. The stock was purchased by the company as a temporary investment at a price of $4 per share. It has a present market value of $10 per share. If the company were to distribute the shares to its shareholders, how much gain on the transaction should the company report? Some accountants oppose recognizing gains or losses on distributions to shareholders. Why?

4. The following excerpt of a conversation was overheard in a crowded elevator in a Bay Street office building: "I just heard that Inco Ltd. is going to split its stock 2 for 1. The announcement will be made later this week so you'd better purchase a few hundred shares before everyone else hears about it and the price skyrockets." Assuming that the tip is reliable, is there any reason for the price of Inco to "skyrocket"?

5. Why is it important that accounting recognition be given to executive stock options in the period in which they are first issued? Why would it not be preferable to wait until the period in which the options are exercised—and the company actually receives cash and issues the additional shares—to record the option transaction?

6. In calculating fully diluted earnings per share, why is it necessary to make assumptions as to what a firm will do with any cash received when options are exercised? Why not simply add the potential number of shares to be issued to the number of shares currently outstanding?

7. What is the distinction between basic earnings per share and fully diluted earnings per share?

8. A firm incurred unusual losses on two of its six plants. Each plant had a book value, prior to the loss, of $100 million. One plant was destroyed by flood. Insurance covered only $60 million of the loss. The other plant was sold for $60 million. Should either of the losses be considered *extraordinary*? Explain.

9. Under what circumstances would income taxes for the current year be reported as an extraordinary item? Why?

10. "The deficiencies and limitations of financial statements are magnified many times when they are prepared on a quarterly rather than annual basis." Do you agree? Explain.

1. *Are shareholders really better off if they receive a cash, rather than a stock, dividend?*

    At January 1, 1996, the shareholders' equity section of Arrow Industries contained the following balances:

Common stock, (no-par value, 12,500,000 shares issued and outstanding)	$255,000,000
Retained earnings	300,000,000
	$555,000,000

    In 1996 the company had net income of $40,000,000.

    In 1995 the company had declared cash dividends of $3 per share. In 1996, however, the board of directors wished to use all available cash to expand facilities. It decided instead to issue a stock dividend "equivalent in value" (based on market prices) to the cash dividend.

    The market price for the firm's common stock on December 31, 1996, was $60 per share.

    a. How many additional shares of common stock should the company issue?

    b. Prepare a journal entry to record the distribution of the additional shares.

    c. Comment on whether the shareholders are as well off for having received the stock rather than the cash dividend.

2. *You be the judge: Does a stock dividend represent income to the recipient? Does a cash dividend? Consider the following example from the United States:*

    The case before the court presents the question whether, by virtue of the Sixteenth Amendment, the U.S. Congress has the power to tax, as income of the shareholder, a *stock dividend* made lawfully and in good faith against earnings accumulated by the corporation since March 1, 1913.

    The facts are as follows:

    > On January 1, 1916, the Standard Oil Company of California declared a stock dividend; the company issued additional shares to its shareholders and transferred a portion of its retained earnings to permanent capital (common stock and capital received in excess of par).

    > Plaintiff, a shareholder of Standard Oil Company of California, received her pro rata number of additional shares. She was called on to pay, and did pay under protest, a tax imposed on the shares. The amount of the supposed income was her proportionate share of the retained earnings transferred to the other capital accounts.

    > Plaintiff has brought action against the Collector of taxes to recover the tax. In her complaint she contends that the stock dividend was not income within the meaning of the Sixteenth Amendment.

    a. Put yourself in the position of a judge hearing the case. Outline an opinion in which you decide whether the shareholder can recover the tax paid. The only issue you need to consider is whether a stock dividend constitutes income. Make certain that in your outline you summarize the arguments most likely to be made by *both* plaintiff (shareholder) and defendant (tax collector).

b. Suppose that the court held that a stock dividend does *not* constitute income to the recipient. What arguments could you now make to support a contention that, if a stock dividend does not constitute income, then neither does a cash dividend. Indeed, when is a shareholder "better off" because of the activities of the corporation in which he or she has an interest? (Recall your response to these questions when you study the cost and equity methods of accounting for intercorporate investments in the next chapter. As you will see, the rationale for the equity methods is that a cash dividend does not, in economic substance, enhance the well-being of the recipient when the recipient has substantial influence over the fiscal policies of the company that pays the dividend).

3. *The economic as well as the accounting impacts of three types of dividends of "equal value" may be somewhat different.*

   The balance sheet of Cannon Industries Limited reports the following amounts:

Cash		$ 2,000,000
Marketable securities		4,000,000
Other assets		14,000,000
Total assets		$20,000,000
Liabilities		$ 7,000,000
Common stock (no-par value, 600,000 shares issued and outstanding)	$4,000,000	
Retained earnings	9,000,000	13,000,000
Total liabilities and shareholders' equity		$20,000,000

Marketable securities include 300,000 shares of Consolidated Mines Ltd., which were purchased for $6 per share.

In past years the company has paid annual dividends of $3 per share. This year Cannon Industries is considering two other alternatives to a cash dividend that it hopes will have "equal value" to shareholders:

   (1) A *dividend in kind* of shares of Consolidated Mines Ltd. The market value of the shares is $9 per share. The company would distribute to shareholders one share of Consolidated for each three shares of Cannon held—a total of 200,000 Consolidated shares.

   (2) A *stock dividend.* The market value of Cannon Industries stock is $60 per share. The company would distribute one additional share for each 20 shares held—a total of 30,000 shares.

      a. Prepare journal entries that would be required if the company were to issue (1) the dividend in kind, (2) the stock dividend, (3) the cash dividend of $4 per share.

      b. Comment on any problems the company might face in issuing the cash dividend.

4. *Although a stock dividend is comparable in economic substance to a stock split, it is not accounted for in the same manner.*

   The shareholders' equity section of the Cortland Co. includes the following balances as of June 30:

Common stock (no-par value, 80,000 shares issued and outstanding)	$10,800,000
Retained earnings	30,000,000
	$40,800,000

On June 30 the market price of the firm's stock is $700 per share. On that date the firm issues to its shareholders an additional 20,000 shares.

  a. Record the issuance of the additional shares if the transaction is to be accounted for as (1) a 5-for-4 stock split and (2) a 25% stock dividend.

  b. At what price would you anticipate the common stock would be traded subsequent to the issuance of the new shares?

  c. Comment on how the individual shareholders should account for the additional shares received in their own books and records. How much income should they report for income tax purposes?

5. *The evidence suggests that stocks that split outperform those that do not.*

  A column in *Newsweek* ("The Lure of Stock Splits," October 31, 1983) pointed out that companies, in record numbers, were splitting their stocks—engaging in a "splendid orgy of reproduction." The column raised the question of whether a stock split increases the market value of a company's stock and thereby benefits its shareholders.

  According to the column, "The brokerage community generally insists that you can make money buying into splits." This position seems to run counter to the incontrovertible argument that a stock split, by itself, has no economic significance. It does not change the company's assets, liabilities, or prospects for the future.

  The column cited a 1981 New York Stock Exchange study that asked whether companies that split their stock do better than companies that do not. "The answer was a resounding yes," the column reported. "Between 1963 and 1980, stocks that split rose 2 1/2 times faster in price than nonsplitting stocks." The evidence of the study clearly points to the conclusion that "companies with a history of splits are better buys, on average, than companies that rarely, if ever, split their stocks."

  The column did not, however, recommend that shareholders urge their boards of directors to split their shares. Quite the contrary. It explained why academic experts, while not disputing the evidence or conclusions of the New York Stock Exchange study, have shown that splits per se have little or no impact on the value of a firm's shares.

  a. Which companies—those with the more favourable or less favourable trends in the market values of their shares—would you expect to be more likely to split their shares? Why?

  b. Provide an explanation, consistent with the view that a stock split per se is of no economic significance, as to why stock splits may be *associated with,* although do not necessarily *cause,* strong market performance.

  c. Outline in general terms a study in which you would investigate whether stock splits are, in fact, the prime cause of increases in the market values of companies' shares.

6. *The distinction between a stock split and a stock dividend may be a source of confusion.*

Barron's contained the following two news items in the same article:

McQuay-Perfex, Inc., declared a 50% stock dividend and raised its quarterly cash dividend to 24 cents a share from 20 cents.

Stanley Works directors declared a three-for-two stock split and boosted the cash dividend on presplit shares to 40.5 cents from 36.0 cents.

a. Assume that the shareholders' equity of both firms comprised the following:

Common stock (no-par value, 100,000 shares issued and outstanding)	$1,100,000
Retained earnings	2,000,000
	$3,100,000

Prepare the journal entry, if any, that each of the firms should make to record the stock "dividend" or stock split.

b. Comment on why accountants, businesspeople, and journalists are sometimes accused of using needlessly confusing jargon.

7. *Restrictions on the payment of dividends that are based on balances in retained earnings may be inappropriate for some companies.*

The Mineral Wells Mining Co. has been organized for the sole purpose of extracting ore from a deposit that the company intends to purchase. It is anticipated that after the property is mined, the company will be dissolved.

The company issues 10,000 shares of no-par value common stock at a price of $220 per share. It purchases the properties for $2 million cash.

During its first year of operations the company extracts 25 percent of the available ore. It has sales revenue of $800,000 and operating expenses and income taxes of $200,000, excluding amortization. All revenues are received, and all operating expenses are paid, in cash.

The company estimates that it requires an operating cash balance of $200,000.

a. Prepare an income statement and a balance sheet that would reflect the results of operations for the first year.

b. Based entirely on the cash requirements of the firm, what is the maximum cash dividend it can pay?

c. Prepare a journal entry to record payment of such "dividend." (Debit shareholders' equity accounts directly rather than "dividends.")

d. The various corporations acts generally prohibit companies from paying dividends in amounts greater than the existing balance in retained earnings. The purpose of the restriction is to assure that distributions of corporate assets are not made to shareholders at the expense of creditors. Do you think that such restrictions should apply to companies organized to extract minerals from specific properties? What would be the impact, over time, of such restrictions on the assets of the companies?

8. *The question of how best to report litigation and resultant claims is a troublesome one for accountants.*

Assume the following facts:

In 1993 a major manufacturer of electrical equipment is charged by a group of customers with engaging in pricing practices that are in violation of the federal Competition Act. The alleged illegal activities took place in the years 1990 to 1992. The customers file suit in the Federal Court of Canada; they seek damages totalling $36 million. Lawyers for the defendant confidentially advise their client to be "prepared for a final judgment between $10 million and $20 million."

In 1996, after a lengthy trial, the company is found liable to the plaintiffs for $20 million in damages. The company announces its intention to appeal.

In 1997 the Appeals Division of the Federal Court reverses the decision of the Federal Court and orders a new trial.

In 1998 the company agrees to an out-of-court settlement with the plaintiffs. The firm will pay damages of $6 million.

In 1999 the company pays the agreed-upon amounts to the plaintiffs.

How do you think the company should account for the litigation? Indicate any specific journal entry that the company should make during or at the end of each of the years in question. Consider the possibility of making supplementary disclosures in footnotes to the financial statements. Bear in mind that the financial statements will be public documents, available to the plaintiffs and their lawyers.

9. *When is a gain a gain?*

The following is an excerpt from a financial magazine report:

> Samson International Corp. said net income of 71 cents a share reported for the fiscal fourth quarter included 30 cents a share of what it expects to recover from litigation against two subcontractors. That's about 44% of the earnings.
>
> The company, in its fourth quarter report to shareholders, also disclosed that the Securities and Exchange Commission is investigating the inclusion in earnings of the hoped-for court awards.
>
> As reported earlier this year, Samson is seeking damages exceeding $2,766,000 against Norcomp Systems, Inc., and more than $1,477,000 against Unito, Inc., two subcontractors Samson terminated on a contract in Pueblo, Colo. Samson filed suits against them in federal court in Denver, which are still pending.
>
> Based on the 10.5 million Samson shares outstanding, the expected awards totalled more than $3 million of Samson's earnings of $7.5 million for the fiscal fourth quarter, ending Sept. 30.

a. Based on the limited information provided in the article, what do you think is the basis of the U.S. Securities and Exchange Commission investigation? In what other way might the litigation have been accounted for and reported?

b. How do you think Norcomp Systems, Inc., and Unito, Inc., accounted for and reported the suit?

10. *One firm's loss may not be another's gain.*

The following were taken from the notes to the 1987 financial statements of Pacific Resources Corp.

Note 12. Contingencies

> In February 1988, the U.S. Court of Appeals for the Ninth Circuit reversed in full the antitrust judgment rendered in 1985 against PRI and its subsidiary, GASCO, Inc. In October 1987, the same court had reversed about 75% of

the 1985 judgment. As discussed in Note 4, PRI recorded an extraordinary loss in 1985 to reflect the 1985 judgment and, in 1987, an extraordinary gain to record the partial reversal. The plaintiff is appealing the Ninth Circuit's decision. Special Counsel has advised the Company that it is unlikely that the court will modify its decision or that the U.S. Supreme Court will review this matter if appealed.

Note 4. Extraordinary Item

As a result of the antitrust action discussed in Note 12, the Company recognized an extraordinary loss provision of $3,375,000 in 1985, net of a $3,277,000 deferred income tax benefit. In 1987, as a result of a reversal of part of this antitrust judgment by the U.S. Court of Appeals, the Company reversed $2,086,000 of this extraordinary loss provision, net of $1,614,000 in deferred income taxes. In February 1988, the U.S. Court of Appeals reversed the remainder of the antitrust judgment. The Company will determine the advisability of reversing the remaining provision in 1988.

a. Suppose that you were the independent auditor of the company which was the beneficiary of the antitrust judgment against Pacific Resources Corp. in 1985. Knowing that Pacific Resources would appeal the judgment, would you have recommended that the company recognize the amount of the award as income of that year? Explain. Are your recommendations "symmetrical" to the way in which the litigation was accounted for by Pacific Resources? If not, explain and justify any inconsistencies.

b. Based on the information provided, do you think that Pacific Resources Corp. should record a gain in 1988 to recognize the February 1988 ruling of the U.S. Court of Appeals, or should it defer any further recognition until the appeals process is completed?

11. *Lawsuits that raise "going-concern" questions present special problems of accounting and reporting.*

The 1987 annual financial statements of Union Carbide explain in considerable detail the status of litigation attributable to the tragedy at its Bhopal, India, chemical plant. The disaster left thousands dead, injured, or homeless. What follows is a brief excerpt from the relevant note.

Numerous lawsuits were brought against the Corporation and/or Union Carbide India Limited (UCIL) (50.9% of the stock of which is owned by the Corporation) in Federal and state courts in the United States and in Indian courts alleging, among other things, personal injuries or wrongful death, property damage and economic losses from the emission of gas at UCIL's Bhopal, India, plant in December 1984. Most of the actions in United States courts were filed on behalf of individual plaintiffs and as a purported class action in which plaintiffs claimed to represent large numbers of claimants seeking unspecified compensatory and punitive damages for injuries and deaths, property damage and economic losses from the gas emission.

The Union of India also brought suit against the Corporation in the District Court in Bhopal, India. In that suit, the Union of India seeks punitive damages, damages for injury to the environment, amounts paid for emergency aid provided by the Union of India, economic losses suffered by businesses and individuals, and all personal injury damages recoverable by its citizens. The Corporation is vigorously defending the pending litigation. In its Amended Complaint, the Union of India estimates that the approximate value of the total claims would exceed $3 billion if the suit is tried to judgment.

Given the Corporation's numerous defenses and the evidence that the tragedy was caused by employee sabotage, liability is in dispute.

a. The financial statements of 1987 report that the book value of Union Carbide's assets is $7.9 billion and net worth is $1.25 billion. In light of the magnitude of the potential liability, how would you recommend that the litigation be reflected in the financial statements? Explain. If you believe that additional information is required for you to make a judgment, specify what you would need and how it could be obtained.

b. Suppose that corporate lawyers provided you with the following probability estimates of the eventual amount for which the case will be resolved. They assert that they are unable to be more precise in their estimates.

Probability, %	Amount of Settlement
5	$2 billion or greater
25	$1 billion or greater but less than $2 billion
50	$500 million or greater but less than $1 billion
20	$250 million or greater but less than $500 million

Would the additional information change your response?

12. *Unusual events present unusual problems of accounting and reporting.*

The following four notes were adapted from published financial statements. They differ from the notes as they actually appeared in that the published notes indicated how the issues raised in this problem were resolved.

For each of the notes, discuss the issues of accounting and reporting that the situations present. For example, do you think the companies should recognize a gain or loss in the year of the statements? If you do, should it be ordinary or extraordinary? If you do not, what events must take place before you would recommend that a gain or loss be recognized? If you believe that more information is necessary to resolve an issue, specify what you would need and where you would obtain it.

a. *Itel Corporation:* In July 1987 two former officials of Great Lakes (a wholly owned subsidiary) pleaded guilty to conspiring prior to 1985 to eliminate competition on certain government dredging projects. The company estimates that it will cost $7.3 million to resolve the antitrust charges against Great Lakes.

b. *Georgia Bonded Fibers, Inc.:* In November 1985 a flood damaged the company's domestic manufacturing facility and certain other assets. Substantially all assets and flood-related costs were insured. The company settled its claim with the carrier for an amount that was $354,000 (net of income taxes of $329,000), or 25 cents per share, in excess of the flood-related costs and the net book value of the damaged assets.

c. *Johnson & Johnson:* As a result of criminal tampering with Tylenol Extra-Strength Capsules in February 1986, the company announced the withdrawal of all capsule products made directly available to the consumer. The company also announced that it will no longer manufacture or sell these capsule products and that it has no plans to re-enter this business in the foreseeable future. The costs associated with these decisions are estimated at $140 million ($80 million after income taxes), and include customer returns, inventory handling and disposal costs, and communication expenses to reassure consumers of the safety of noncapsule Tylenol products.

d. *Public Service Company of Colorado:* As of the quarter ended September 30, 1986, the company expected to incur a sizable loss resulting from an anticipated writing down of a substantial portion of the total investment in Fort St. Vrain (a nuclear generating station), recognizing estimated future decommissioning expenses and recognizing estimated unrecoverable operating and capital expenditures. The estimated loss at September 30, 1986, was $93.7 million (net of $89.4 million in related income taxes) and was subsequently increased to $101.4 million (net of $101.5 million in related income taxes) at December 31, 1986. The estimate of amount of the investment in Fort St. Vrain that would have to be written down was based on the assumption that the plant would remain operational until all existing fuel in the reactor and on-site was utilized (approximately three to four years, assuming a continued average annual capacity factor of about 45 percent) and that the reactor would then be decommissioned and the plant converted to a fossil-fuel-burning plant.

Realization of the company's remaining investment in Fort St. Vrain (approximately $70.3 million at December 31, 1987), and the reliability of the estimated future decommissioning expenses and unrecoverable operating and capital expenditures, was dependent on future events, including sustained operations at levels significantly greater than in the past, achieving and maintaining a cost-effective relationship between expenses and revenues from Fort St. Vrain, and satisfactory resolution of various alternatives regarding Fort St. Vrain after the on-site nuclear fuel was utilized.

13. *Employee stock options are a cost of compensating employees. They should be recorded as an expense in the accounting period during which the employees perform the related services.*

The Warwich Co. adopted a stock option plan that entitled selected executives to purchase shares of its common stock for $30 per share, the price at which the stock was being traded in the open market on the date the plan was adopted.

The plan stipulated that the options could be exercised one year after being received, provided the executive was still employed by the company. The options were to lapse, however, 2 1/2 years after they were issued.

Each option entitled the executive to purchase one share of the company's no-par value common stock.

The following transactions or events with respect to the option plan took place over a period of three years:

Dec. 31, 1995: The company issued 1,000 options to its executives. Market price of the stock on that date was $44.

Dec. 31, 1996: The company issued an additional 2,000 options. Market price of the stock was $26.

July 1, 1997: Executives exercised 800 of the options issued in 1995. Market price of the common stock was $33.

March 6, 1998: Executives exercised 1,000 of the options issued in 1996. Market price of the common stock was $39.

June 30, 1998: The remaining 200 of the options issued in 1995 lapsed. Market price of the common stock was $38.

Prepare journal entries, as required, to record these transactions and events.

14. *Due to outstanding stock appreciation rights, an increase in the market price of a firm's shares caused a decrease in reported earnings.*

The *Wall Street Journal* called Texas International, an Oklahoma City–based exploration company, one of the year's "hottest trading stocks." In 1995 (dates changed) and the first quarter of 1996, the price of the stock increased more than fourfold. It traded as high as $46\frac{7}{8}$, which, as the *Wall Street Journal* indicated, was "not bad" for a company that had 1995 earnings of only 76 cents a share.

But the *Journal* pointed to a dark cloud in front of the silver lining. Both the chairman and the president of the company held "stock appreciation rights." These rights entitled the officers to *cash payments* based on the increase in the market value of the company's shares. For each right held, the officers would receive the difference between the per share selling price as of specified dates and a stated exercise price ($4\frac{3}{8}$).

Every fiscal quarter, according to the *Wall Street Journal,* the company must charge to an expense an amount reflective of the stock's rise and the corresponding increase in the firm's obligation to the officers. In the first quarter of 1996, the firm had to charge about $5.2 million to earnings—earnings which, after the charge, were less than $3 million.

a. Distinguish between the stock appreciation rights described in this problem and the employee stock options described in the chapter.

b. Why must Texas International charge an expense each period to reflect the increase in the market price of the shares? Why can't the company record the full amount of compensation expense at the time the rights are granted, as it would if it had granted stock options?

c. Does the charge of $5.2 million against earnings represent a true economic sacrifice? Or could the firm take advantage of the increase in the market price of its shares to acquire, at small cost, the cash to make the required payments to the holders of the rights?

Suppose that first-quarter 1996 earnings, prior to charges relating to stock appreciation rights, were $8.2 million. The firm's obligation to holders of stock appreciation rights increased during the quarter by $5.2 million. The firm had outstanding 9.5 million shares of common stock.

d. The firm decides to acquire the $5.2 million in cash needed to satisfy the rights obligations by issuing new shares of common stock. Assume that the market price per share is $50. How many new shares would the firm have to issue?

e. What would be earnings per share, assuming no charge to earnings for stock appreciation rights, based on 9.5 million shares of common stock outstanding?

f. What would be earnings per share, assuming no charge to earnings for stock appreciation rights, based on the number of shares outstanding after the additional shares had been issued?

15. *An actual firm's footnote pertaining to stock options may be used to demonstrate the journal entries for the granting and exercising of stock options.*

A note to the January 31, 1994, financial statements pertaining to employee stock options of Bombardier Inc. reads as follows:

> Under a share option plan, options are granted to key employees to purchase Class B Subordinate Voting Shares. The exercise price is equal to the average of the closing prices on the stock exchanges during the five trading days preceding the date on which the option was granted. The options are exercisable during a period commencing two years following the date of granting and ending not later than ten years after such date. The right to exercise is acquired gradually over this period.

Issued and outstanding options at year end are is follows:

Granting Period	Exercise Price (dollars)	1994	1993
1987	2.48 to 4.13	1,227,000	1,299,000
1988	4.86 to 6.19	200,000	222,250
1989	4.89 to 5.83	32,000	86,000
1990	6.12 to 7.88	1,397,000	1,420,000
1991	7.08 to 7.66	489,300	600,000
1992	12.45 to 15.25	85,000	90,000
1993	11.17 to 16.50	1,365,000	1,365,000
1994	10.09 to 16.99	765,000	—
		5,560,300	5,082,250

The number of options has varied as follows:

	1994	1993
Balance at beginning of year	5,082,250	4,970,750
Granted	765,000	1,365,000
Exercised	(226,950)	(1,228,500)
Cancelled	(60,000)	(25,000)
Balance at end of year	5,560,300	5,082,250

a. Assuming the 765,000 options granted in 1994 were granted when the share price was $18, prepare the journal entry to record the granting of the options. Assume an average exercise price.

b. Assuming that the 226,950 options exercised in 1994 had an exercise price of $8 and were issued when the share price was $6, prepare the journal entry to record the exercise, assuming the price on the date of exercise was $17.

16. *This problem provides a review of several types of transactions that affect owners' equity.*

At January 1, the shareholders' equity section of the Green Mountain Co. contained the following balances:

Common stock (no-par value, 100,000 shares issued and outstanding)	$1,000,000
Retained earnings	800,000
	$1,800,000

During the year, the following events took place:

a. On January 7, the company issued to executives options to purchase 4,000 shares of common stock at a price of $24 per share. The market price of the common stock on that date was $28 per share.

b. On February 1, the company purchased 4,000 shares of its own stock in the open market at a price of $25 per share and cancelled them.

c. On February 10, the company declared a cash dividend of $1 per share. The dividend was paid on February 23.

d. On March 7, executives exercised options to purchase 4,000 shares. The market price of the common stock on that day was $27 per share.

e. On May 10, in lieu of its usual quarterly cash dividend, the company declared and paid a dividend in kind. The company distributed to shareholders 5,000 shares of Pacific General Co. common stock that had been held as an investment. The prevailing market price for the shares was $12 per share; they had been purchased previously, and recorded on the books of Green Mountain Co., at a price of $2 per share.

f. On August 10, the company declared and paid a stock dividend equal in value (based on the current market price of the shares issued) to the $1 per share of its traditional quarterly dividend. The market price of the shares on that date was $25.

g. On December 17, the company declared a stock split. For each old share owned, shareholders would be given two new shares.

h. On December 28, the company issued to executives options to purchase 8,000 shares at a price of $12 per share. The market price of the common stock on that date was $12 per share.

Prepare journal entries to record these events. (Debit any dividends directly to the shareholders' equity accounts affected rather than to "dividends.")

17. *This problem, based on the statements of a large food company, reviews the impact of key events that affect owners' equity accounts.*

The April 30, 1996, financial statements of Bob Evans Farms, Inc., indicated the following as to shareholders' equity at April 30, 1993 (*dollar* amounts are in thousands):

Common stock	$49,090
Retained earnings	$67,238
Number of shares of common stock outstanding	16,506,378

The financial statements also reported net income and dividends declared per share for each of three years ending April 30:

	Net Income	Dividends per Share (See Note F)
1994	$20,575	$0.18
1995	$21,470	$0.22
1996	$29,329	$0.24

The financial report of April 30, 1996, also contained the following note:

Note F—Shareholders' Equity

> On August 12, 1993, the Board of Directors authorized a 10% stock dividend on all the company's issued common stock as of August 16, 1993. On August 11, 1994, the Board of Directors authorized a 5-for-4 stock split on the company's issued common stock as of September 5, 1994. On August 10, 1995, the Board of Directors authorized a 5-for-4 stock split on the company's issued common stock as of September 11, 1995. *All data as to per share cash dividends have been adjusted for the stock splits.*

For convenience, assume that cash dividends were paid at year end and were based on number of shares outstanding at year end. As a consequence, the dividend per share in the year ending April 30, 1996, was in the amount reported; there is no need to adjust it for the stock split in August 1995. By contrast, the dividends for the years ending April 30, 1994 and 1995, must be restated to their original amounts. (There is no need to adjust dividends per share for the 10 percent stock dividend.)

The reduction in retained earnings attributable to the stock dividend was based on market value per share. The market value on the date of the dividend was $22 per share.

Prepare a schedule which indicates the impact of the information provided on number of shares outstanding and the balances in each of the owners' equity accounts over the three-year period between April 30, 1993, and April 30, 1996.

18. *Beginning and ending balances in shareholders' equity accounts can be reconciled from information on the face of the balance sheet as well as in notes.*

The shareholders' equity section of the Northern Trail Corporation balance sheet reported the following:

	December 31	
	1997	1996
	(thousands of dollars)	
Common stock, no-par value, 450,000,000 shares authorized; issued 195,302,488 shares and 196,575,003 shares, respectively	$ 653,505	$ 651,885
Retained earnings	4,346,542	4,439,473
Total shareholders' equity	$5,000,047	$5,091,358

From other sections of the financial statements you learn:
(1) Net income for 1996 was $518,688,000 and for 1997 was $172,377,000.
(2) In 1996 the company declared dividends for that year of $3.40 per (presplit) share. The average number of shares outstanding was 63,041,000.
(3) In 1996 the company issued 70,000 (presplit) shares of stock for $1,820,000.
(4) The board of directors declared a 3-for-1 stock split effective December 31, 1997.
(5) In 1997, following the split, the company issued 418,000 shares for $7,301,000.
(6) In 1997 the company purchased and retired 1,691,000 shares. The amount paid for these shares was $43,469,000. Assume that this transaction took place at year end. (Due to this assumption, you will be unable to reconcile to the dollar; you will have a "discrepancy" of $23,000.)
(7) In 1997 the company declared dividends of $1.20 per (postsplit) share. The average number of shares outstanding was 189,600,000.

Prepare a schedule in which you reconcile the January 1, 1996, balance in the shareholders' equity accounts with both the December 31, 1996, and December 31, 1997, balances. Use the form that follows. The balances for January 1, 1996 (in thousands) are provided in the schedule.

	Number of Shares	Common Stock	Retained Earnings	Total
Balance, Jan. 1, 1996	65,455	$650,065	$4,135,124	$4,785,189
Balance, Dec. 31, 1996	196,575	$651,885	$4,439,473	$5,091,358
Balance, Dec. 31, 1997	195,302	$653,505	$4,346,542	$5,000,047

19. *End-of-year changes in number of shares outstanding will have but little effect upon earnings per share.*

In November 1997 the controller of a firm estimated that net earnings for the year ending December 31 would be approximately $1,000,000, an amount considerably less than the $1,200,000 for the previous year. Aware that the financial press commonly focuses on earnings per share, the controller devised a scheme to boost EPS. On December 1, the firm would acquire in the open market 20,000 shares of its own common stock. It would immediately retire those shares. The acquisition and retirement would reduce the denominator of the EPS ratio and thereby boost EPS. Throughout 1996 and the first 11 months of 1997, the firm had 100,000 shares of common stock outstanding.
a. Determine EPS for 1996 and 1997, based on 100,000 shares outstanding.
b. Determine EPS for 1997 as the controller apparently expects it will be computed.
c. Will the scheme of the controller be successful? Determine EPS for 1997 in accordance with generally accepted accounting principles.

20. *The procedure for determining earnings per share, although complex, is designed to make certain that potential dilution is taken into account.*

The Sutton Company had net income after taxes and before preferred stock dividends of $500,000. The company has 200,000 shares of common stock outstanding. The corporate income tax rate is 40 percent.

In addition, the company has issued $500,000 of 4% bonds that are convertible into common stock at a rate of 60 shares for each $1,000 bond.

The company also has outstanding 3,000 shares of no-par value convertible preferred stock. Each share of preferred stock may be exchanged for six shares of common stock. The preferred stock carries a dividend rate of $10 per share. The stock was issued at a price of $100 per share.

a. Determine basic earnings per share.
b. Determine fully diluted earnings per share.

21. *In computing earnings per share, a firm must make an assumption as to what it does with cash received when outstanding stock options are exercised.*

Riggs Corporation had net income after taxes of $1,200,000. The company had 300,000 shares of common stock outstanding. The current market price of the common stock was $25 per share.

Years earlier the company had adopted a stock option plan. Outstanding as at the current year end were 5,000 options that would enable the holder to purchase one share each at $20 per share and 10,000 options which could be exercised for one share each at $10 per share. Assume the rate of return to impute earnings on the cash received from the exercise of the options is 10%. The corporate tax rate is 40%.

The company had 10,000 shares of 8 percent convertible preferred stock outstanding. Par value of the stock was $100; each share was convertible into *three* shares of common stock. The year-end market price of the preferred stock was $105.

a. Determine basic earnings per share.
b. Determine fully diluted earnings per share.

22. *Seasonal businesses have special problems of interim reporting.*

Lakeview, Inc., operates a summer resort. The resort is open for guests during the summer months only. All its revenue is earned during the summer months. In the first quarter (January 1 through March 31) of its fiscal year, the company has zero revenues but makes cash disbursements as follows:

Property taxes for the period January 1 to December 31	$ 80,000
Administrative salaries for the first quarter	25,000
Advertising	20,000
Repair and maintenance (annual overhaul of boats and docks)	9,000
Total disbursements	$134,000

a. For each disbursement, consider whether, for purposes of interim reporting, (1) it should be charged as an expense as incurred, (2) it should be allocated evenly to each of the four quarters, or (3) it should be allocated on some other basis. (Use your judgment; the answer cannot be found in the text.)

b. Comment on the special difficulties faced by seasonal businesses in preparing interim reports. (In practice, policies as to the allocation of costs such as those indicated in this problem vary from firm to firm. There are no specific professional guidelines that deal with seasonal industries.)

23. *First-period "interim" earnings must be adjusted to take into account events of subsequent periods.*

For the first three months of the year, the Warwick Company, according to its president, had earnings before taxes of $240,000, determined as follows:

Sales		$520,000
Cost of goods sold	$200,000	
Other expenses	80,000	280,000
Income before taxes		$240,000

The following additional information has come to your attention:

a. The company gives quantity discounts to its customers based on total purchases for the year. No quantity discounts have been allowed to date. The firm estimates that total sales for the year, at *gross* sales prices, will be $2 million. After taking into account quantity discounts, $200,000 of the sales will be at 95 percent of gross sales prices (a discount of $10,000) and $400,000 will be at 90 percent of gross sales prices (a discount of $40,000). Average selling prices for the year are thus somewhat lower than those implied by sales revenue of the first quarter.

b. The company uses the LIFO inventory method and determines year-end inventory and the annual cost of goods sold on the basis of a periodic inventory count, which is taken on December 31 of each year. The cost of goods sold for the quarter ending March 31 was calculated as follows:

Goods on hand, January 1:		
30,000 units @ $5	$150,000	
Production, 1st quarter:		
10,000 units @ $10	100,000	$250,000
Estimated goods on hand,		
March 31: 10,000 units @ $5		50,000
Cost of goods sold, 30,000 units		$200,000

The company estimates that it will complete the year with an inventory of 30,000 units. As a consequence, the ending inventory will be stated at $5 per unit; the firm will not have to "dip into" its LIFO stock. The cost of goods sold for the entire year will be based on current production costs of $10 per unit.

c. The company overhauls its plant once a year in July at a cost of $30,000. The cost of the overhaul has not been taken into account in computing first quarter expenses.

d. Each December the company gives its salaried employees a bonus equal to approximately 10 percent of their annual salaries. First-quarter salaries (included in other expenses), without adjusting for the bonus, amounted to $65,000.

e. Assume that the current combined income tax rate is 22 percent of the first $75,000 of taxable income and 38 percent on all earnings above that amount. The company estimates that taxable income for the entire year will be $120,000. Thus its average effective rate for the year will be different than that based on first-quarter earnings alone.

Determine earnings after taxes for the first quarter of the year as they should be reported to the general public.

Solutions to Exercise for Review and Self-Testing

1. 100,000 shares of common stock, being only those that are currently outstanding.

2. Basic earnings per share = $500,000/100,000 shares = $5.00.

3. 10,000 if the preferred stock was converted + 30,000 if the convertible bonds were converted = 40,000 additional common shares. A total of 140,000 shares of common stock should be considered outstanding in determining fully diluted earnings per share.

4. If the bonds were converted to common stock, the after-tax interest cost would be reduced by $96,000. If the preferred stock was converted to common stock, the preferred dividend requirement would decrease by $40,000 ($4 × 10,000). Total earnings available to common shareholders would be $500,000 + $96,000 + $40,000 = $636,000.

5. Fully diluted earnings per share = $636,000/140,000 shares = $4.54.

13

Intercorporate Investments and Earnings

This chapter examines the reporting requirements for a particular class of asset, the intercorporate investment. An intercorporate investment is any situation in which one business entity has purchased some of the securities of another corporation. If the investment is for only a short period of time, it is classified as a marketable security and accounted for as discussed in Chapter 6. The reporting of long-term intercorporate investments depends on the degree of influence the investor obtains over the investee corporation as a result of the security purchase. Our discussion will focus on the purchase of voting shares as the long-term investment.

After studying this chapter, you will be able to

- Understand the motivation for an investment in the shares of another company
- Identify the situations in which the cost, equity, or consolidation method of reporting is appropriate
- Prepare journal entries to record investments under the cost method and the equity method
- Determine the allocation of the purchase price when a controlling interest is purchased
- Prepare a consolidated balance sheet and income statement using the purchase method
- Recognize when the pooling of interests method of consolidation is appropriate

A corporation may acquire an *equity interest* (ownership of common or preferred stock) in another company for a number of reasons. A company may have cash that is temporarily idle. It may use this cash to purchase a relatively small number of the shares of another company to obtain a short-term return—as an alternative, perhaps, to purchasing short-term government treasury bills or certificates of deposits. Such securities are categorized on the books of the acquiring corporations as "marketable securities." The accounting for current marketable securities was discussed in Chapter 6. On the other hand, a company may purchase the stock of another corporation as a long-term investment.

It may do so for several reasons:

1. *To expand into new markets.* A consumer food products company sees an opportunity to tap the restaurant market. Although it can easily adapt its products for sale to restaurants, it has no direct ties with restaurants. Therefore it acquires an existing company with strong channels of distribution in the restaurant industry.

2. *To develop sources of supply.* An appliance manufacturer purchases electric motors from a number of different suppliers. It believes it could improve the quality and lower the cost of motors if it had greater control over a motor manufacturer. To achieve the greater control, it purchases one of its suppliers.

3. *To secure a return on capital greater than it could obtain through internal expansion.* A cigarette manufacturer recognizes that the long-term profit outlook for its product is bleak. To reduce its dependence on a single product, it invests available funds in firms in other industries. Sometimes it acquires controlling influence in a company; other times it merely holds a minority position. For example, Seagram Co. Ltd.'s 1995 purchase of a controlling interest in entertainment giant MCA Inc. (home of Universal Studios), is an attempt by the liquor company to diversify. The market for liquor products is stagnant while there is perceived to be growth in the entertainment industry.

This chapter pertains to long-term, as opposed to temporary, investments.

A company may acquire the stock of another company by purchasing it for cash or other assets. Or it may exchange shares of its own common stock for those of the company it seeks to acquire. Moreover, a firm may obtain shares of another company simply by organizing such a company and retaining all, or a portion of, the new shares issued.

When a company owns 100 percent of the shares of another firm, it can, if it wishes, dissolve the subsidiary firm and combine its assets with its own. There are several reasons, however, for operating as separate legal entities rather than as a single combined corporation. Among them are

1. *To take advantage of the limitations on corporate liability.* Shareholders of a corporation, be they individuals or other corporations, are generally not liable for losses of the company they own in amounts greater than their original investment. By dividing its operations into several legal entities, a company may be able to protect general corporate assets against liabilities arising from unprofitable operations of a single unit.

2. *To enhance organizational efficiency.* By dividing its operations into separate legal entities, a firm may be able to make the subsidiary units more autonomous than if the company were operated as a single corporation. For example, the individual units might have greater flexibility in obtaining bank loans or in issuing common or preferred shares to outsiders. In many situations, decentralization may contribute to increased performance.

3. *To make it easier to satisfy government regulations.* Federal or provincial regulations can often be more efficiently and effectively met by carrying out certain types of activities in separate corporations. Sometimes a company will find it necessary to maintain separate corporations for activities conducted in each of the provinces in which it does business, as well as in each of the foreign jurisdictions in which it does business. Almost always, separate corporations are established for specialty activities, such as banking and insurance.

LEVEL OF INFLUENCE

The critical determinant of the means by which intercorporate investments are accounted for is the degree of influence that the investor corporation exerts over the acquired company.

If the investor corporation exerts relatively minor influence, the investment, referred to as a *portfolio investment,* would generally be accounted for by the *cost method.*

If it exerts significant influence, the investment would be accounted for by the *equity method.* (Both these methods will be defined and evaluated shortly.)

If the investor company is able to *control* the other company (control ordinarily being defined as ownership of over 50 percent of the voting stock), the investment is commonly reported by means of *consolidated financial statements.* Consolidated financial statements report the financial positions and earnings of two or more corporations as if they were a single entity.

The three methods of accounting for corporate investments—the cost, the equity, and the consolidated statement method—are not, it should be emphasized, categorically consistent. *Since each corporation is a separate legal entity, a separate set of accounting records must, by law, be maintained for it. On the books of the investor corporation, the shares of the other company must be accounted for by either the cost or the equity method. If, however, the investor company has control over another corporation, then, for purposes of reporting, and only for purposes of reporting, the individual financial statements of the two companies can be combined into a single, consolidated set of statements.*

The relationships and distinctions among the methods will be brought out in the next several sections.

Criteria for Presumption of Significant Influence

Where an investor corporation is unable to maintain significant influence over the company in which it owns an interest because of the small proportion of its holdings or for other reasons, then it should account for its investment by the cost method. Evidence of an ability to influence significantly the key financial and operating policies of an investee company can be made manifest by several factors: percentage of shares owned, representation on the corporate board of directors, membership on key policy-making committees, interchange of managerial personnel, material purchases or sales between the two companies, and exchanges of technological information. Even though a company may not own a majority of a corporation's outstanding shares, it can nevertheless exercise a predominant impact on that company's policies. The CICA recognized that degree of influence cannot be objectively measured. To make practice more uniform, however, it prescribed in Section 3050 of the *CICA Handbook* that an investment of less than 20 percent of the shares of the investee should lead to a presumption that the investor does not have the ability to exercise significant influence, unless significant influence can be demonstrated. An ownership of more than 20 percent of the voting shares, on the other hand, does not necessarily mean the investor has significant influence. It is commonly assumed that the 20 percent rule is rigid and that the *cost method* should be used for all investments of less than 20 percent and the *equity method* for all investments greater than 20 percent. However, it is extremely important to realize that the 20% figure is a guideline only. If an investor company can demonstrate that even though it owns 20 percent or more of a firm's stock it has, in fact, little or no influence over the investee's operating and financial policies, then it should use the cost rather than the equity method.

COST METHOD

Under the cost method used for portfolio investments, a company records its investment in the stock of another company at cost—the amount paid to acquire the stock. It recognizes revenue from its investment only to the extent that the investee company actually declares dividends. In the absence of unusual declines in market values, the investment would be maintained on the books of the investor at original cost. The carrying value of the investment would be unaffected by changes either in the market value of shares owned or in the net worth of the company that they represent.

Example

On January 2, 1997, the Adams Company purchases 10,000 of 100,000 (10 percent) shares of the outstanding common stock of the Cain Company. It pays $30 per share. The following entry would be required on the books of the *investor* company, the Adams Company:

(a)

Investment in Cain Company	$300,000	
Cash		$300,000
To record the purchase of 10,000 shares of Cain Company common stock		

On December 31, 1997, the Cain Company announces that earnings for the year were $500,000 ($5 per share of common stock).

No entry is required by the Adams Company to record the announcement of the annual earnings of the Cain Company. The Adams Company recognizes revenue from its portfolio investment only upon the actual declaration of dividends by the company whose shares it owns.

On the same date, December 31, 1997, the Cain Company declares dividends of $3 per share, payable on January 20, 1998. The following entry would be required on the books of the Adams Company:

(b)

Dividends receivable	$30,000	
Dividend revenue from investment in Cain Company		$30,000
To record dividends to be received from the Cain Company		

Loss in Value of an Investment

The *CICA Handbook* Section 3050, "Long-Term Investments" (1991), provides that long-term investments accounted for by the cost or equity method be written down to recognize the loss whenever there is a loss in value that is determined to be other than a temporary decline. Each long-term investment should be accounted for separately, rather than combined in one portfolio as was the case for marketable securities. Since long-term investments are planned to be held for a long period of time, day-to-day fluctuations in market prices are of less significance in valuing long-term than short-term securities (see Chapter 6). Since long-term investments are not expected to be liquidated in the short term, temporary declines in value need not be recognized, since it may be expected that the value will recover in the long term. However, if the decline in value appears to be permanent, a write-down to reflect the loss in value is required. The *Handbook* provides the following examples of conditions that might suggest a decline in value is other than temporary:

    a. a prolonged period during which the quoted market value of the investment is less than its carrying value;
    b. severe losses by the investee in the current year or current and prior years;
    c. continued losses by the investee for a period of years;
    d. suspension of trading in the securities;
    e. liquidity or going concern problems of the investee;
    f. the current fair value of the investment(an appraisal) is less than its carrying value.[1]

In certain cases, such as bankruptcy of the investee, the permanent nature of the decline in value may be more obvious.

When a decline in value is determined to be other than temporary, the write-down in value is a loss to be included in the income statement. The written-down value of the investment becomes the new cost base, and subsequent recoveries in value are not recognized until the investment is sold.

Assume, for example, that on December 31, 2001, following continued losses for three years, the market value of Adams Company's investment in Cain Company is $276,000, which is $24,000 less than cost. It is determined

[1] "Long-term Investments," Section 3050, *CICA Handbook*, 1991.

that the decline in value is other than temporary. The appropriate entry on the books of the Adams Company would be

(c)

Loss in value of investment $24,000
    Investment in Cain Company $24,000
To record permanent loss in value of investment in Cain Company

Suppose that on January 15, 2002, the investment in Cain is sold for $280,000. The appropriate entry on the books of the Adams Company would be

(d)

Cash $280,000
    Gain on sale of long-term investment ($280,000 – $276,000) 4,000
    Investment in Cain Company $276,000
To record sale of shares in Cain Company

The $276,000 that is removed from the Investment in Cain Company account is the amount of the original investment in 1997, $300,000, less the $24,000 write-down made in 2001 to reflect a permanent decline in the value of the investment.

The cost method of maintaining investments in essence consists of the recognition of revenue when investee dividends are declared, the recognition of loss in value for other than temporary declines in value, and the recognition of a gain or loss on disposal of the long-term investment.

EQUITY METHOD

Under the equity method, a company records its investment in the shares of another company at cost (the same as under the cost method). But it periodically adjusts the carrying value of its investment to take into account its share of the investee's earnings and dividends. It recognizes its share of increases or decreases in the book value net worth of the investee as soon as it knows of them.

If net worth increases as a result of investee earnings, then the investor recognizes promptly, on its own books, revenue in the amount of its proportionate share of such earnings; it does not wait until the earnings are distributed in the form of dividends. Since earnings of the investee company benefit the investor, the investor will increase the carrying value of its investment by its share of investor earnings.

If net assets of the investee decrease, then the investor will also recognize a decrease in its investment. Net assets will decrease as a consequence of operating losses. But they will also decrease whenever dividends are declared (a liability for the payment of a dividend is established; retained earnings are decreased). Hence, when the investee declares a dividend, the investor recognizes the dividend receivable and at the same time adjusts downward the carrying value of its investment to reflect the decline in the net assets of the investee. An example will help to clarify the accounting procedures.

those who hold the remaining 20 percent interest in the firm. Consolidated financial statements are prepared from the perspective of the majority shareholders, those of the parent company. From the standpoint of a *majority* shareholder, it would be both confusing and misleading to report on the balance sheet common stock and retained earnings of two companies—those of the parent and those of the subsidiary. Hence the minority interest in each of the shareholders' equity accounts (the amounts that remain after the majority interest has been eliminated) are reclassified into a single account, "minority interest in subsidiary":

Common stock (of subsidiary)	$2,000	
Retained earnings (of subsidiary)	6,000	
Minority interest in subsidiary		$8,000

To reclassify the equity of minority shareholders in the subsidiary

The minority interest in subsidiary account represents the equity of the minority shareholders in the consolidated corporation. It is, in a sense, the minority's portion of the residual interest in the subsidiary. Common practice is to report minority interest in subsidiaries on a single line between long-term liabilities and shareholders' equity. The amounts reported in the shareholders' equity section of the consolidated balance sheet represent only the equity of the parent company shareholders.

Acquisition Price in Excess of Investment Book Value

In the discussion so far, the price paid by the parent to acquire its investment in the subsidiary was exactly equal to its proportionate share of the *book value* (which is equal to the *shareholders' equity*) of the subsidiary. If, as is common, the parent company acquires its interest at an amount greater than the book value of the net assets acquired, then such excess must be transferred to an account indicative of its nature.

Assume now that the parent company pays $45,000 to acquire a 100 percent interest in the subsidiary but that the net assets of the subsidiary, as recorded on its own books, are only $40,000 (see Exhibit 13-3). As in the previous examples, if the financial positions of the two individual companies are to be shown as if a single economic entity, then both the investment of the parent and its corresponding shareholders' equity as recorded on the books of the subsidiary must be eliminated. This time, however, although the investment would be recorded on the books of the parent at $45,000, the corresponding equity would be recorded on the books of the subsidiary at only $40,000.

The portion of the investment ($40,000) that represents value as recorded on the books of the subsidiary can be eliminated against the corresponding shareholders' equity with an entry identical to that made in a previous example. Thus

(a)

Common stock (of subsidiary)	$10,000	
Retained earnings (of subsidiary)	30,000	
Investment in subsidiary (of parent)		$40,000

To eliminate investment in subsidiary and corresponding amounts in subsidiary's shareholders' equity accounts

That leaves $5,000 (the excess of $45,000 paid over the corresponding book value of $40,000) of the investment still to be eliminated.

Specific Tangible or Intangible Assets

This excess of purchase price over book value is often a source of confusion and misunderstanding. There are at least two reasons a firm may pay for an interest in a subsidiary an amount in excess of its corresponding book value. First, the book value of individual assets (and hence the recorded shareholders' equity) is based on historical cost—the amount the subsidiary initially paid to acquire the assets, less amortization. Book value, as frequently emphasized in this text, is not necessarily indicative of market value. Thus the price paid by the parent company to acquire its shares of stock in the subsidiary may be indicative of the market value of the individual assets represented by such shares. If this is the case, then the excess of purchase price over book value should be assigned to the particular assets acquired.

Consistent with the historical cost basis of accounting, assets should be valued at purchase price. The mere fact that the parent company may not have purchased the assets directly, but instead acquired the common stock of the company that has title to the assets, does not change the substance of the transaction. Nor should it change the manner in which the assets are accounted for. Sometimes, in fact, as is the case with intangible assets, the assets acquired may not even be recorded on the books of the subsidiary. In accordance with generally accepted accounting principles, patents, copyrights, and trademarks when developed internally (as opposed to purchased from outsiders) are often not given accounting recognition. When such assets are obtained in connection with the purchase of a subsidiary, they should be reported at their fair market values and an appropriate share of the excess of the purchase price over the book value assigned to them. The following additional adjustment is required if the entire excess of purchase price over book value is to be allocated to specific assets:

(b)

Specific assets (land, buildings, equipment, patents, etc.) $5,000
      Investment in subsidiary $5,000
To allocate the excess of purchase price over book value of investment to specific assets

Subsequent to the acquisition, the consolidated enterprise should report its charges for amortization on the amounts at which the assets are recorded on the consolidated balance sheet. Thus amortization charges may be greater on the consolidated income statement than the sum of the separate amortization charges on the financial statements of the two individual companies. The acquired subsidiary, on its own financial statements, will maintain its assets at historical cost and continue to base amortization on their original values.

Goodwill

A firm may also pay an amount in excess of recorded book value to acquire the shares of another company because the investee company possesses certain intangible assets that cannot be specifically identified. These assets may be favourable customer attitudes toward the company, unusual talents of corporate managers, advantageous business locations, or special monopolistic or political privileges. Or they may exist because the individually identifiable assets when used together are worth considerably more than the sum of the fair market values of the assets employed independently. Whatever their attributes, they enable the firm to earn amounts in excess of "normal" returns. Such assets—that is, the amount of the purchase price in excess of book value that cannot be specifically allocated to other assets—may be classified as *goodwill:*

(b, alternative)

Goodwill $5,000
      Investment in subsidiary $5,000
To allocate the excess of purchase price over book value of investment to goodwill

Goodwill is a residual. It represents that portion of the cost of acquiring a subsidiary that cannot be assigned directly to any specific assets. Goodwill is one asset that arises *only* out of business combinations. Although firms may develop the attributes that compose goodwill over a number of years, they may not, under conventional accounting principles, recognize them. Goodwill may be recorded only when one firm purchases the assets of another, as a going concern, and all of the excess of cost over book value cannot be specifically assigned to other assets.

Because of the very nature of goodwill—it is a residual asset—its useful life is not readily determinable. Nevertheless, the CICA has recommended that firms should make their best efforts to estimate the useful lives of all intangible assets, including goodwill, and that they should be amortized over their useful lives. In no event, however, should the amortization period for goodwill exceed 40 years. Therefore, if a consolidated entity records goodwill, it must each year reduce the balance in the goodwill account (a credit to goodwill) and increase expenses by a like amount (a debit to amortization of goodwill) by no less than one-fortieth of the initial amount recorded. Both the goodwill itself and the charge for amortization would appear only on the consolidated statements, not on those of either the parent or the subsidiary balance sheet. Exhibit 13-3 highlights the required adjustments when the acquisition price exceeds the subsidiary's book value.

EXHIBIT 13-3
Acquisition Price in Excess of Book Value of Investment

	Original Statements		Adjustments		Combined
	Parent	Subsidiary	Debit	Credit	Statements
Investment in subsidiary	$ 45,000			$40,000 **(a)**	
Various assets	105,000	$40,000		5,000 **(b)**	$145,000
Specific tangible or intangible					
assets or goodwill			$ 5,000 **(b)**		5,000
	$150,000	$40,000			$150,000
Common stock	$ 30,000	$10,000	$10,000 **(a)**		$ 30,000
Retained earnings	120,000	30,000	30,000 **(a)**		120,000
	$150,000	$40,000	$45,000	$45,000	$150,000

In essence, the consolidated income statement, like the consolidated balance sheet, presents the sum of the balances in the accounts of the component corporations. However, as with the balance sheet, numerous adjustments and eliminations may be necessary to give effect to transactions among the individual companies.

The consolidated income statement indicates the change in enterprise welfare between two dates subsequent to the acquisition as if the various components of the enterprise were a single economic entity. Principles of revenue and expense recognition must be applied as if the individual companies were, in fact, combined into a single company. Thus revenues and expenses, if they are to be recognized, must be the result only of arm's-length transactions with parties *outside* of the consolidated entity.

Intercompany transactions take many forms; the specific eliminations and adjustments that might be required must be determined in light of their particular nature. The general approach to consolidations may be illustrated with some typical intercompany transactions.

Assume the following statements of income of the parent company and the subsidiary company:

	Parent	Subsidiary
Sales	$400,000	$300,000
Gain on sale (to subsidiary) of capital assets	6,000	
Interest revenue (from subsidiary)	7,000	
Total revenues	$413,000	$300,000
Cost of goods sold	$240,000	$210,000
Interest expense (to parent)		7,000
Other expenses	80,000	53,000
Total expenses	$320,000	$270,000
Net income	$ 93,000	$ 30,000

The parent company owns 80 percent of the subsidiary.

Interest

The individual components of the consolidated entity may enter into arrangements which result in revenues to one and expenses to another but involve no transactions with outsiders. Suppose, for example, that a parent makes a loan to its subsidiary. Interest on the loan would be recognized as a revenue to the parent and as an expense to the subsidiary. From the standpoint of the consolidated entity, the "loan" is nothing more than an intracompany transfer of funds from one "division" to another. Just as any intercompany payable and receivable outstanding at year end would be eliminated from the consolidated balance sheet, so too must the interest revenue and expense be eliminated from the consolidated income statement. If $7,000 of the interest revenue and expense reported on the individual statements were intercompany interest, then the following elimination would be required:

(a)

     Interest revenue (parent) $7,000
          Interest expense (subsidiary) $7,000
     To eliminate intercompany interest

Sales and Cost of Goods Sold

From the standpoint of a consolidated enterprise, a sale of merchandise by one member of a consolidated group to another is not an event worthy of revenue recognition. A sale is recognized only when merchandise is sold to a party outside of the consolidated enterprise. Intercompany sales should, of course, be given accounting recognition on the books of the individual companies; they must, however, be eliminated when reporting on the operations of the companies as a consolidated economic entity.

Assume, for example, that included in the revenues of the parent are $100,000 in sales to the subsidiary. The goods sold to the subsidiary were manufactured by the parent at a cost of $80,000. The subsidiary company in turn sold the goods to outsiders at a price of $120,000. The transactions would be reflected on the books of the two companies as follows:

	Parent (Sales to Subsidiary)	Subsidiary (Sales to Outsiders)
Sales revenue	$100,000	$120,000
Cost of goods sold	80,000	100,000

From the standpoint of the consolidated firm, sales to outsiders were $120,000 and the cost of goods sold only $80,000. It is necessary to eliminate $100,000 in both sales revenue (the sales by the parent to the subsidiary) and cost of goods sold (the cost of the goods sold by the subsidiary to outsiders):

(b)

     Sales revenue (parent) $100,000
          Cost of goods sold (subsidiary) $100,000
     To eliminate intercompany sales

The required adjustments for intercompany sales become considerably more complex when, at year end, one member of the corporate group has not yet sold to outsiders its entire stock of goods purchased from another member. It then becomes necessary to reduce the value of inventory in the amount of any profit recognized on the sale from one company to another. Inventory must be stated at its cost to the consolidated entity, rather than at the intercompany selling price.

Sales of Capital Assets

Capital assets must be reported on the consolidated statements on the basis of their initial cost to the consolidated enterprise. If a capital asset has been sold by one member of the consolidated group to another, then the amount at which the asset is carried on the books of an individual company may be greater or less than that based on original cost.

Assume, for example, that the $6,000 in the account of the parent company, "gain on sale of capital assets," represents in its entirety the gain on the sale of land to the subsidiary. The land was sold to the subsidiary at a price of $45,000; it had originally cost the parent $39,000. After the sale, the land would be recorded on the books of the subsidiary at its purchase price of $45,000—an amount $6,000 greater than that paid for it by the two companies viewed as a single, consolidated entity.

To report the consolidated results of operations and financial positions of the two companies, it is necessary to eliminate the effects of transactions that would be considered nothing more than internal transfers if the two companies were viewed as a single economic entity. Thus

(c)

Gain on sale of capital assets (of parent) $6,000		
Land (of subsidiary) $6,000		
To adjust for gain on intercompany sale of land		

This adjustment, as is the case with many consolidation adjustments, would affect both the income statement and the balance sheet.

The intercompany sale of land will have to be accounted for in the preparation of consolidated statements in years subsequent to that in which the sale took place—in fact, for as long as the asset remains on the books of the subsidiary. The land will continue to be "overvalued" on the books of the subsidiary company by the amount of the gain recognized by the parent. Since, on the books of the parent, the gain will have been *closed* at year end to retained earnings, retained earnings of the parent company also will be permanently overstated.

The adjustments for the sale of capital assets are substantially more complex when the assets transferred are subject to amortization. From the standpoint of the consolidated enterprise, amortization charges must be based on the original cost of the asset to the first member of the consolidated group that acquired it. On the books of the company on which the asset is presently recorded, however, it would be maintained on the basis of the price paid to the seller company, a member of the consolidated entity. If, for example, the capital asset sold was equipment rather than land, then the subsidiary would properly amortize, on its own books, an asset that had cost $45,000. If the useful life was 10 years and salvage value was zero, annual amortization charges would be $4,500. For purposes of consolidated reporting, however, the asset initially cost only $39,000, the original acquisition cost of the parent (seller). Hence annual consolidated amortization charges would be only $3,900. An adjustment on consolidation would be required to reduce annual amortization charges by $600. But, in addition, adjustments would also be required in each year after the first to "correct" for the cumulative effect on "accumulated amortization" of the previous "overstatements" of amortization charges.

Amortization of Goodwill

As was indicated in the discussion relating to the interpretation of the excess of investment cost over book value, *goodwill* is an asset that arises exclusively out of the process of consolidation. Goodwill is recorded only on a consolidated balance sheet, not on the balance sheets of the component companies of a consolidated group. When goodwill is amortized, the amortization expense is reported only on the consolidated income statement, not on the income statements of the individual companies.

EXHIBIT 13-4
Income Statement Adjustments

Parent Company
Consolidated Statement of Income

	Individual Statements		Adjustments That Affect Income Statement		Consolidated Statement of Income
	Parent	Subsidiary	Dr. (Cr.)		Income
Sales	$400,000	$300,000	$100,000	**(b)**	$600,000
Gain on sale of capital assets	6,000		6,000	**(c)***	
Interest revenue	7,000		7,000	**(a)**	
Total revenues	$413,000	$300,000	$113,000		$600,000
Cost of goods sold	$240,000	$210,000	($100,000)	**(b)**	$350,000
Interest expense		7,000	(7,000)	**(a)**	
Other expenses	80,000	53,000			133,000
Amortization of goodwill			500	**(d)** †	500
Total expenses	$320,000	$270,000	($106,500)		$483,500
Total income	$ 93,000	$ 30,000	$ 6,500		$116,500
Less: Minority interest in earnings of subsidiary					6,000
Consolidated income					$110,500

* Corresponding credit would be to land, which would be reported on the consolidated balance sheet.
† Corresponding credit would be to goodwill, which would be reported on the consolidated balance sheet.

Assume that the parent company paid $200,000 for an 80 percent interest in the subsidiary company and that the book value of the subsidiary company was $225,000. The book value of the 80 percent interest is therefore $180,000. The excess of cost over book value—assumed in this case to all represent goodwill—was, at time of acquisition, $20,000.

If the goodwill is to be amortized over 40 years, the maximum amortization period permitted by current professional pronouncements, then the following annual consolidation adjustment would be made:

(d)

Amortization of goodwill (expense)	$500	
Goodwill (asset)		$500
To amortize goodwill		

Minority Interests in Earnings of Subsidiary

Consolidated statements, as already emphasized, are prepared from the perspective of the shareholders of the parent corporation. The parent corporation, however, is entitled to only a portion of the earnings of its subsidiary, based on its ownership interest. The minority shareholders of the subsidiary are entitled to the remaining earnings. Therefore the portion of subsidiary earnings that can be ascribed to the minority shareholders must be deducted from total consolidated income to arrive at net consolidated income.

The earnings of the subsidiary company as indicated in its income statement are $30,000. Since the parent company owns only 80 percent of the outstanding shares of the subsidiary, the minority share of subsidiary earnings would be 20 percent of $30,000, or $6,000.

By summing the amounts reported in the income statements of the individual companies, taking into account the consolidating adjustments, and giving recognition to the minority interest in the earnings of the subsidiary, a consolidated statement of income can be prepared. A worksheet is shown in Exhibit 13-4.

COMPREHENSIVE EXAMPLE

Exhibits 13-5 through 13-8 illustrate in a single example the essentials of preparing both the consolidated income statement and the consolidated balance sheet. Exhibit 13-5 contains the individual financial statements of a parent (Ontario, Inc.) and its subsidiary (Toronto, Inc.) for the year ended December 31, 1997. (All dollar amounts are in millions.) It also provides essential information as to intercompany transactions.

Exhibit 13-6 illustrates a worksheet that can be used to prepare both the consolidated income statement and the consolidated balance sheet. The trial balances in the columns to the left are *preclosing* trial balances. Therefore the balances in retained earnings differ than those shown in the balance sheets. They are less by the amount of earnings of 1997.

Exhibit 13-7 shows the journal entries required to make the consolidating adjustments and eliminations. They have been posted to the worksheet in Exhibit 13-6.

Exhibit 13-8 displays the consolidated balance sheet and income statement of Ontario, Inc., and its subsidiary.

EXHIBIT 13-5

Financial Statements of Individual Companies and Additional Information as to Intercompany Transactions

Balance Sheets
December 31, 1997

	Ontario, Inc.	Toronto, Inc.
Assets		
Cash	$ 10	$ 6
Accounts receivable	80	12
Notes receivable	60	90
Property, plant, and equipment (net of amortization)	400	110
Investment in Toronto, Inc.	152	
Total assets	$702	$218
Liabilities and shareholders' equity		
Accounts and notes payable	$150	$ 58
Common stock	50	85
Retained earnings	502	75
Total liabilities and equities	$702	$218

Statements of Income
Year Ended December 31, 1997

	Ontario, Inc.	Toronto, Inc.
Sales	$700	$ 90
Interest revenue	12	9
Gain on sale of land	28	0
Total revenues	$740	$ 99
Cost of goods sold	600	58
Interest expenses	15	6
Other expenses	48	15
Total expenses	$663	$ 79
Net income	$ 77	$ 20

Other Information

On January 1, 1997, Ontario, Inc., acquired an 80 percent interest in Toronto, Inc., for $152 million. The excess of price paid over book value cannot be assigned to specific assets.

During the year, Ontario, Inc., made sales to its subsidiary of $25 million.

Ontario Inc., made several loans to its subsidiary during the year. At year end the balance in notes receivable from Toronto, Inc., was $10 million. During the year, Ontario, Inc., earned $4 million in interest on notes from its subsidiary.

During the year Toronto, Inc., purchased land from its parent at a price of $15 million. Ontario, Inc., had paid $10 million for the land.

It is the policy of Ontario, Inc., to amortize goodwill over a period of 40 years.

EXHIBIT 13-6
Consolidating Worksheet

	Individual Statements				Adjustments		Consolidated Statements	
	Ontario, Inc.		Toronto, Inc.					
	Dr.	Cr.	Dr.	Cr.	Dr.	Cr.	Dr.	Cr.
Cash	10		6				16	
Accounts receivable	80		12				92	
Notes receivable	60		90			10 (e)	140	
Property, plant, and equipment (net of amortization)	400		110			5 (g)	505	
Investment in Toronto, Inc.	152					40 (a) 112 (b)	0	
Goodwill					40 (a)	1 (h)	39	
Accounts and notes payable		150		58	10 (e)			198
Minority interest in Toronto, Inc.						28 (c)		28
Common stock		50		85	68 (b) 17 (c)			50
Retained earnings, 1/1/97		425		55	44 (b) 11 (c)			425
Sales		700		90	25 (d)			765
Interest revenue		12		9	4 (f)			17
Gain on sale of land		28		0	5 (g)			23
Cost of goods sold	600		58			25 (d)	633	
Interest expense	15		6			4 (f)	17	
Amortization of goodwill					1 (h)		1	
Other expenses	48		15				63	
	1,365	1,365	297	297	225	225	1,506	1,506

EXHIBIT 13-7

Consolidating Journal Entries

(a)

Goodwill $40		
Investment in Toronto, Inc.	$ 40	

To assign excess of purchase price over book value to goodwill

Investment in Toronto, Inc.		$152
Book value of Toronto:		
Common stock	$ 85	
Retained earnings, 1/1/97	55	
Total book value	140	
Percent of ownership	× 80%	
Book value of Ontario's interest		112
Excess of cost over book value		$ 40

(b)

Common stock $68	
Retained earnings 44	
Investment in Toronto, Inc.	$112

To eliminate remaining balance in investment in Toronto, Inc., against corresponding equity in Toronto, Inc.

(c)

Common stock $17	
Retained earnings 11	
Minority interest in Toronto, Inc.	$28

To reclassify minority interest in Toronto, Inc.

(d)

Sales $25	
Cost of goods sold	$25

To eliminate intercompany sales (of Ontario) and corresponding cost of goods sold (of Toronto)

(e)

Accounts and notes payable $10	
Notes receivable	$10

To eliminate intercompany receivable and payable

(f)

Interest revenue $4	
Interest expense	$4

To eliminate intercompany interest revenue and expense

(g)

Gain on sale on land $5	
Property, plant, and equipment...............................	$5

To eliminate gain from intercompany sale on land

(h)

Amortization of goodwill $1	
Goodwill	$1

To amortize goodwill of $40 over 40 years

EXHIBIT 13-8
**Consolidated Financial Statements of
Ontario, Inc., and Subsidiary**

Consolidated Statement of Income
Year Ended December 31, 1997

Sales	$765	
Interest revenue	17	
Gain on sale of land	23	$805
Cost of goods sold	633	
Interest expense	17	
Amortization of goodwill	1	
Other expenses	63	714
Consolidated income		91
Less: Minority interest in earnings of subsidiary (20% of $20,000)		4
Net consolidated income		$ 87

Consolidated Balance Sheet
As at December 31, 1997

Assets	
Cash	$ 16
Accounts receivable	92
Notes receivable	140
Property, plant, and equipment (net of amortization)	505
Goodwill	39
Total assets	$792
Liabilities and shareholders' equity	
Accounts and notes payable	$198
Minority interest in Toronto, Inc. (see note 1)	32
Common stock	50
Retained earnings (see note 2)	512
Total liabilities and equities	$792

Note 1: Minority Interest in Toronto, Inc.

Minority interest in Toronto per worksheet	$ 28
Minority interest in 1997 earnings per statement of income	4
Minority interest in Toronto, Inc.	$ 32

Note 2: Retained Earnings

Retained earnings per worksheet	$425
Net consolidated income	87
Total consolidated retained earnings	$512

INSTANT EARNINGS

A company may, of course, purchase all, or a portion, of the outstanding stock of another corporation for *cash*. But quite often interests in other companies are obtained in exchange for the common stock of the acquiring corporation. If the investment is accounted for as a purchase (an alternative means will be discussed shortly), no special accounting problems are presented. Suppose, for example, Alpha Company acquired all 500,000 shares of Beta Company at a price of $10 per share. In exchange for the shares, Alpha Company issued to Beta Company shareholders 50,000 shares of its own no-par value common stock, each share having a market value of $100. The following journal entry would be required on the books of Alpha Company:

Investment in Beta Co. $5,000,000		
Common stock		$5,000,000
To record purchase of shares of Beta Co. by Alpha Co.		

An acquisition for stock, rather than cash, may have a striking impact on the reported earnings of the parent company. Indeed, acquisitions may result in instant increases in reported profits even in the absence of any substantive improvements in the operations of either the parent or the subsidiary company. Consider the following additional information pertaining to the acquisition of Beta by Alpha:

Selected Financial Data Immediately Prior to Acquisition		
	Alpha	Beta
Number of shares outstanding	100,000 shares	500,000 shares
Net assets	$1,000,000	$5,000,000
Capital stock (no-par value)	$100,000	$500,000
Retained earnings	$900,000	$4,500,000
Book value per share	$10	$10
Latest annual income	$200,000	$500,000
Latest earnings per share	$2	$1
Market price of common stock	$100 per share	$10 per share

Alpha Company is the smaller of the two companies in terms of assets and total earnings. Yet investors obviously consider its prospects for future earnings to be more promising than those of Beta. The price/earnings (P/E) ratio (market price of common stock to earnings per share) of Alpha is 50 to 1 and that of Beta is only 10 to 1. Suppose that the exchange of stock was to be based on the market prices of the shares of the two companies. The 500,000 shares of Beta Company have a total market value of $5 million (500,000 shares at $10 per share). Since each share of Alpha has a market value of $100, the number of shares that Alpha would be required to issue would be $5 million divided by $100, or 50,000.

If Alpha Company was to issue 50,000 additional shares to the owners of Beta Company, then it would have outstanding a total of 150,000 shares. Consolidated earnings in the year subsequent to acquisition, assuming no substantive improvement in the operations of either firm, would be the sum of the earnings of the two individual companies—$700,000 ($200,000 plus $500,000). No amortization of excess of cost over book value is required since the total market price of Beta Company stock is exactly equal to its book value. Earnings per share of Alpha Company, reported on a consolidated basis, would now be $4.66 ($700,000 divided by 150,000 shares)—233 percent of previously reported earnings of $2 per share. Under the purchase method of accounting for a business combination, consolidated income would only include the earnings of the subsidiary from the date of acquisition forward. For example, if P Company purchased 100 percent of the common stock of S Company on December 30, 1996, and accounted for its investment using the purchase method, the consolidated income statement for the year ended December 31, 1996, would include the earnings of S Company from the one day, December 31.

The ramifications of this simplified example are critical to an understanding of the merger movement of the 1960s and 1970s. Many of the acquisitions of that era were for common stock rather than cash, and often, as in the example, a whale of a firm was swallowed up by a minnow. Today, mergers and acquisitions tend to take forms that are both different and more varied than those of the earlier periods. Many acquisitions are for cash, rather than stock; consider, for example, leveraged buyouts. In the case of acquisitions, new and creative financial instruments are issued. In almost all, however, the impact on *reported* income, assets, and liabilities is a prime consideration in premerger analyses.

The acquisition in the example above, as is common in practice, was facilitated by the substantial difference in the price-earnings ratios of the two firms. The P/E ratio of Alpha was considerably higher than that of Beta. Alpha was able to acquire Beta by giving up shares with a market value that exceeded by a considerable amount their book value. Because the number of shares issued was based on market value, not book value, Alpha had to issue only a relatively small number of new shares. It was thereby able to add a relatively large amount of earnings without substantially adding new ownership claims to those earnings.

Stock market prices are likely to be influenced by the trend in earnings over a number of years. The relatively high P/E ratio of Alpha might be explained, at least in part, by a trend of rapidly increasing earnings. The acquisition of Beta would likely help sustain that trend or even accentuate it. The P/E ratio of Alpha may thereby remain high or even increase, thus making it even easier for the firm to acquire additional firms in the future. And future acquisitions may further add to reported earnings per share. To a considerable degree, the merger movement was supported by the circle of acquisition, increase in earnings, increase in market price of stock, additional acquisitions, and so on.

It must be pointed out, however, that the increase in earnings is seldom as dramatic as in the example. If the acquiring corporation pays a price in excess of a firm's book value, then the excess might have to be amortized over a number of years (exceptions will be discussed in the paragraphs that follow), and the charge for amortization would reduce reported consolidated earnings.

POOLING OF INTERESTS

Description and Rationale

In the discussion of business combinations to this point it has been assumed that one company acquires another. The combinations have been accounted for as purchase-type transactions—one company purchases, either for cash or common stock, the outstanding common stock of another. In those instances where a business combination is effected by an exchange of common stock—where one company, be it a new or existing company, acquires substantially all of the voting stock of another in return for its own common stock—the transaction may be accounted for as an alternative type of business combination, a *pooling of interests*. The situations where a business combination in Canada may be accounted for as a pooling of interests are extremely rare, as will be noted later.

A pooling is a union of two companies, with neither acquiring the other. Whereas in a purchase a new basis of accountability is established for the acquired firm, in a pooling both firms carry over the asset and liability values from their own books.

The financial consequences of accounting for a business combination as a pooling of interests rather than a purchase may be profound; reported earnings as well as values assigned to assets may be significantly different.

Underlying the pooling of interests method of accounting for business combinations is the rationale that two firms join together to operate as a single economic enterprise. Neither of the two purchases the other, and the owners of both of the component companies are granted a proportionate interest in the combined enterprise. The combination represents a marriage of equals, or if not exactly of equals, then at least a marriage where one party does not clearly dominate the other.

No Increase in Asset Values

The key feature of the pooling of interests method is that each of the component companies retains its former basis of accounting. That is, the assets and liabilities of neither company are revalued at the time of combination. The recorded assets and liabilities of both companies are carried forward to the consolidated enterprise at their previously recorded amounts. So also are their retained earnings. *No accounting recognition is given to goodwill, nor are other assets written up to their fair market values.* Retention of the former basis of accounting is justified because there has been no sale of the assets of one firm to another; there has merely been a fusion of two companies into one. The pooling of interests method has great appeal to combining firms in that in most circumstances it permits the consolidated enterprise to report higher earnings than if the combination were accounted for as a purchase.

The pooling of interests method may result in higher reported consolidated earnings because it does not require the consolidated enterprise to increase the carrying values of the assets of the acquired firm to reflect an excess of purchase price over book value. No goodwill need be recorded. Therefore the firm does not have to charge amortization on the amounts by which the fair market values of either of the two firms exceed their book values. Even more significant, perhaps, is that consolidated earnings in the year of combination include the subsidiary's earnings for the entire year. The inclusion in earnings is not dependent on when the combination took place since, consistent with the pooling concept, the merging firms are considered to have always been combined. Therefore, in a combination on the last day of the year, accounted for as a pooling of interests, consolidated earnings would include the earnings of the subsidiary for the whole year. This can lead to significant instant earnings. An example can be used to illustrate the pooling of interests approach and to highlight the differences between the pooling of interests and the purchase methods of accounting for business combinations.

Example

Indicated in the following table is selected information about two firms, Delta Corp. and Echo Corp., prior to their merger:

	Balance Sheet	
	Delta Corp.	Echo Corp.
Net assets (assets less liabilities)	$1,000,000	$5,000,000
Common stock, no-par value	400,000	$1,200,000
Retained earnings	600,000	3,800,000
Total shareholders' equity	$1,000,000	$5,000,000
Number of shares outstanding	100,000	500,000
Net income, in year prior to merger	$200,000	$500,000
Earnings per share	$2	$1
Recent market price per share	$100	$20

Delta and Echo agree to combine their operations. Delta Corp. will issue to the current shareholders of Echo Corp. new shares of its own common stock in exchange for their existing shares in Echo Corp. The number of shares to be issued by Delta will be based on the relative market prices of the shares just prior to the negotiations leading to the merger. Since the shares outstanding of Echo Corp. have a current market value of $10 million (500,000 shares at $20 per share), Delta Corp. will have to issue 100,000 shares ($10 million divided by $100, the market price of Delta Corp. stock).

Under the pooling of interests method, the accounting entries are a bit tricky. The consolidated balance sheet, however, would reflect the sum of the assets and liabilities of each of the two companies. The balance in the "retained earnings" account would represent the sum of the previous balances of the two individual companies. The balance in the "common stock" account would, in essence, be a "plug"—whatever amount is required to ensure that assets less liabilities is equal to shareholders' equity. When the common stock is no-par value, as in this case, the consolidated common stock balance is simply the sum of the balances of the two companies.

Delta Corp. and Subsidiary Consolidated Balance Sheet	
Net assets	$6,000,000
Common stock (200,000 shares outstanding)	$1,600,000
Retained earnings	4,400,000
Total shareholders' equity	$6,000,000

The assets and liabilities are stated on the same basis as on the books of the component companies. In contrast to the purchase method, no adjustment has been made to asset values—either by revaluation of specific assets or by the addition of goodwill—to reflect the difference between the market value of the common stock issued by Delta Corp. ($10 million) and the value at which the assets were recorded on the books of the Echo Corp. ($5 million).

If there were no substantive increases in the earnings of the two firms as a consequence of the merger, then annual earnings after the merger would be the sum of the earnings of the two individual firms—$200,000 contributed by Delta, $500,000 contributed by Echo, a total of $700,000. And, as indicated above, even if the merger took place on the last day of the fiscal year, all of the earnings of Echo immediately become part of consolidated earnings.

The earnings per share, based on 200,000 shares of Delta Corp. stock outstanding would be $3.50—an increase of $1.50 per share from the pre-merger EPS. This increase in EPS can be attributed entirely to the *instant earnings* effect described earlier. The shares of Delta were selling at a price/earnings ratio of 50 to 1; those of Echo at only 20 to 1. Delta was thereby able to increase total earnings 3.5 times (from $200,000 to $700,000) by only doubling the number of its outstanding shares (from 100,000 shares to 200,000).

By contrast, if the combination had been accounted for as a purchase, then the combined entity would either have reported goodwill of $5 million or increased the carrying value of specific assets by that amount. If the $5 million in additional assets or in goodwill were amortized over a period of, say 20 years, then earnings would be $250,000 per year lower than under the pooling method. If earnings of the two individual firms after the merger were the same as those prior to the merger, then annual consolidated earnings, if the combination was accounted for as a purchase, would be only $450,000. By contrast, they would be $700,000 if the combination was accounted for as a pooling. Hence earnings per share would be only $450,000 divided by 200,000 shares, or $2.25.

Exhibit 13-9 highlights these differences.

EXHIBIT 13-9

Example of Differences between Pooling and Purchase Accounting

Reported Net Assets		
	Pooling	Purchase
Reported net assets (assets less liabilities) per individual statements		
Book value of Delta	$1,000,000	$ 1,000,000
Book value of Echo	5,000,000	5,000,000
Total book value:	$6,000,000	$ 6,000,000
Excess of purchase price over book value	—	5,000,000*
Consolidated net assets	$6,000,000	$11,000,000

* Market value of stock issued by Echo	
(500,000 shares @ $20)	$10,000,000
Book value of Delta	5,000,000
Excess of purchase price over book value	$ 5,000,000

This amount would be assigned, if possible, to specific assets. If, however, it cannot be associated with specific assets, then it is assigned to goodwill.

EXHIBIT 13-9 **(continued)**

	Reported Earnings	
	Pooling	Purchase
Delta earnings	$200,000	$200,000
Echo earnings	500,000	500,000
Total individual company earnings	$700,000	$700,000
Amortization of goodwill	—	250,000*
Net consolidated earnings	$700,000	$450,000
Number of shares of stock outstanding	200,000	200,000
Earnings per share	$ 3.50	$ 2.25

* Assuming that excess of purchase price over book value is amortized over 20 years.

Note: Companies do not have a choice as to whether to account for a merger or acquisition as a pooling or a purchase. Only in the very rare case where an acquirer cannot be identified would the pooling of interests method of accounting be allowed.

Abuses and Reforms

The term *pooling of interests* was at one time used to describe a type of business combination rather than an accounting method. Two corporations of similar size joined together to carry out their operations. The owners of the two firms obtained, and retained, an interest in the new firm proportionate to their respective contributions, and the new company was managed jointly by the previous managers of the two firms. A pooling of interests was viewed as a merger of two great rivers, as contrasted with a purchase, which was seen as a stream feeding into a river.

In the late 1950s and early 1960s, especially in the United States, the traditional criteria for a pooling of interests began to erode. Business combinations that were not in spirit poolings of interests were accounted for as if they were. First, the relative size test was abandoned. Combinations of giant firms with much smaller firms were treated as poolings of interests. Then the criteria of continuity of ownership and management were disregarded. One of the two firms involved in the combination may have paid sizable amounts of cash, rather than common stock, for a portion of the common stock of the other firm. Thus the owners of one of the firms were, to the extent that they received cash payments, *bought out* by those of the other. Eventually, almost any combination could be accounted for as a pooling. Poolings of interests and purchases came to be recognized as accounting alternatives from which managements could select, rather than as types of business combinations.

Today, as set forth in Section 1580 of the *CICA Handbook,* "Business Combinations," a business combination may be accounted for as a pooling of interests only if *an acquirer cannot be identified.* As long as one of the parties to the business combination can be identified as the acquirer, the combination will be accounted for as a purchase. Whether the combination is effected through the exchange of cash or shares, it is almost always possible to identify one of the parties as the acquirer. Therefore, the use of the pooling of interests method is extremely rare in Canada.

The issue of business combinations remains controversial. The critical issue on which attention is focused relates to the values that should be assigned to the assets of the combining companies—and most particularly those of a company acquired by another. The values assigned to the assets have, of course, a direct bearing on amortization charges and hence on reported earnings. In a pooling, the assets of each company are stated at their previous bases; in a purchase, assets are restated to reflect the consideration paid for them.

SHOULD ALL MAJORITY-OWNED SUBSIDIARIES BE CONSOLIDATED?

A key question that faces the accounting profession is whether a company should consolidate majority-owned subsidiaries that are in unrelated industries.

When companies are in different industries, consolidated statements become less meaningful. This is especially true when one or more of the firms are in specialized industries such as insurance, banking, and real estate, which engage in unique accounting practices. There is a risk that unrelated numbers will be combined into a meaningless hodgepodge. Until recently firms were not required to consolidate heterogeneous subsidiaries. Subsidiaries could be excluded from consolidation when the subsidiaries did not follow generally accepted accounting principles (banks and life insurance companies until recently, for example) or when the consolidated financial statements would not provide the more informative presentation. The presumption was that when the companies had little in common, other than common ownership, separate statements would be more informative.

Manufacturing and merchandising concerns used "nonhomogeneity" as a basis for selectively excluding subsidiaries from their consolidated statements. Often the real motive for not consolidating the subsidiaries was to escape having to report sizable liabilities on the parent's balance sheet. Sometimes, in fact, the subsidiaries were established for the main purpose of providing "off the balance sheet" financing.

In 1991, Section 1590, "Subsidiaries," was added to the *CICA Handbook*. The Section recommends that all subsidiaries be consolidated, except where control is likely to be temporary or where control does not rest with the majority owner.

ECONOMIC CONSEQUENCES OF ACCOUNTING PRACTICES

For the most part, the way a merger or acquisition is accounted for has little impact on corporate cash flows. Hence in economic substance, one accounting method leaves a company no better or worse off than another.[3]

The following discussion of the economic impact of accounting choices is based on a U.S. situation. However, the issue is equally applicable to the Canadian setting. Many investment bankers in the United States are con-

[3] The income tax consequences of mergers and acquisitions are generally independent of the accounting methods used for general reporting. Consolidated tax returns are not allowed in Canada. Each legal entity is required to file its own tax return.

vinced that impact on reported earnings has been the driving force behind many mergers and acquisitions. They contend, in fact, that U.S. accounting standards place domestic companies at a competitive disadvantage relative to firms in other countries. In the United States, mergers have to satisfy rigid criteria before they can be accounted for as poolings of interest. If a merger does not meet the criteria, then it must be reported as a purchase. Under the purchase method, the excess of purchase price over book value must be assigned either to specific assets or to goodwill. If assigned to specific assets, it must be amortized over their useful lives; if to goodwill, it must be amortized over a maximum of 40 years. In Great Britain, goodwill must also be amortized. However, in contrast to U.S. conventions, it need not be expensed. Instead, it can be charged directly to shareholders' equity. Thus no matter how great a premium over book value a company pays for an acquisition, the premium will never affect reported income.

Forbes magazine, in a story entitled "Ill Will,"[4] claimed that the U.S. goodwill amortization rules make acquisitions more attractive for foreign companies than for domestic companies. "By making it tough for U.S. public companies to buy, the rule limits the number of potential bidders when a corporate asset goes on the market. The fewer the bidders, the less the final price."

The contention that the amortization rules have unfavourable economic consequences for U.S. companies is consistent with criticisms that have been cast at other income-reducing provisions: those pertaining to pensions, deferred income taxes, postemployment benefits, and intangible oil drilling costs, to cite but a few. It raises, in yet another context, the issue of whether investors can "see through" variations in *reported* earnings that result solely from differences in accounting practices. As indicated previously, the academic evidence, while by no means either uncontested or conclusive, suggests that investors do take note of the accounting differences. At the very least therefore, the charges that the FASB is undermining the U.S. economy should be met with scepticism. The anecdotal evidence of the investment bankers is still unsubstantiated.

Summary

Intercorporate ownership may take a variety of forms. The objective of accounting is to reveal the economic substance of the relationship between the parties involved.

As a general rule, the manner in which the interest of one company in another is accounted for is determined by the degree of influence that it is able to exercise. If an investor company is unable to exert significant influence over the company whose shares it owns, it would account for its interest in this portfolio investment on the *cost basis*. If it is able to exercise significant influence, it would account for its interest on the *equity basis*.

When a corporation has control over another, then the information needs of the shareholders of the controlling company are usually best served by combining the financial positions and results of operations of the firms into a single set of *consolidated* financial statements.

[4] "Ill Will," *Forbes,* January 23, 1989, p. 41.

EXHIBIT 13-10
Summary of Investor Decisions

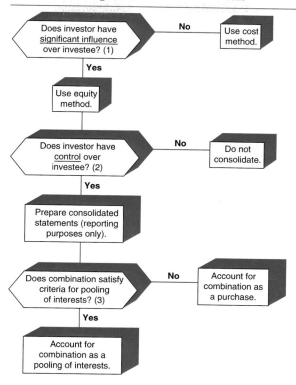

(1) General test is whether investor owns 20% or more of stock of investee.
(2) General test is whether investor owns 50% or more of stock of investee.
(3) Only if an acquirer cannot be identified is it permissible to use the pooling of interests method.

Exhibit 13-10 summarizes in a flowchart the possible intercorporate-ownership relationships and their accounting ramifications for the investor company.

Exercise for Review and Self-Testing

On January 1, 1997, Parent Co. acquired, for cash, 90 percent of the outstanding common stock of Subsidiary Co. Immediately following the acquisition, the balance sheets of the two firms revealed the following:

	Parent Co.	Subsidiary Co.
Investment in Subsidiary Co.	$320,000	—
Other assets	500,000	$300,000
Common stock	200,000	120,000
Retained earnings	620,000	180,000

Subsidiary Co. reported earnings for the year ending December 31, 1997, of $50,000 and declared dividends of $15,000. Parent Co. reported earnings, *excluding* any revenues attributable to Subsidiary Co., of $200,000.

1. Parent Co. maintains its investment in Subsidiary Co. on the equity basis.
   a. What would be the amount that it should report in 1997 as earnings from subsidiary?
   b. At what amount should it value "Investment in Subsidiary Co." on December 31, 1997, after the declaration of the dividend?

2. If the financial statements of Parent Co. and Subsidiary Co. were to be consolidated, what amount should be reported on the balance sheet as excess of purchase price over book value (goodwill) prior to amortizing such excess in 1997? What would be total reported consolidated assets?

3. What would be the amount of Subsidiary Co.'s 1997 earnings that could be ascribed to minority shareholders?

4. If the excess of purchase price over book value were to be amortized over a period of 40 years, by how much would the combined earnings of the two companies be reduced when the income statements of the two firms were consolidated?

5. What would be the consolidated income of the two companies for 1997, assuming that the earnings of the subsidiary company ascribed to minority shareholders were considered as an expense?

6. Suppose alternatively that Parent Co. acquired 100 percent of the stock of Subsidiary Co. in exchange for shares of its own common stock. At time of acquisition, the common stock issued by Parent Co. had a fair market value of $400,000 and the book value of Subsidiary Co. was $300,000. What would now be the consolidated income of the two companies for 1997 assuming that the merger satisfied the conditions of the pooling of interests accounting method? What would be total reported assets?

Questions for Review and Discussion

1. Under what circumstances should a firm account for an investment in another company by the cost method? By the equity method? When should it prepare consolidated financial statements?

2. Why is the cost method considered inappropriate for investments in which the investor can exert significant influence over the operating policies of the investee?

3. Why, under the equity method, does a firm *reduce* its balance in its investment account upon declaration of a dividend by the investee?

4. When, under the equity method, does an investor recognize revenue attributable to the earnings of the company in which it maintains an investment? When under the cost method? When is revenue recognized if consolidated statements are prepared?

5. Why do consolidations relate only to corporate *reports* rather than to the underlying corporate books and records? On which set of books—those of the parent, those of the subsidiary, those of both, or those of neither—are consolidation adjustments made?

6. From the standpoint of which group of shareholders—that of the parent, of the subsidiary, or of both—are consolidated statements prepared?

7. Under what conditions may a company improve its earnings per share simply by acquiring a controlling interest in another company?

8. What is *goodwill*? When is it recorded? From what does it arise? Suppose that a firm acquires an interest in a subsidiary for an amount in excess of the subsidiary's book value. What difference might it make to consolidated net income if the excess was classified as goodwill rather than assigned to specific assets?

9. What is the underlying rationale of a pooling of interests? What critical differences arise in terms of asset valuation and income determination if a combination is accounted for as a pooling rather than as a purchase?

10. What four accounts—two income statement accounts and two balance sheet accounts—appear only on consolidated financial statements, never on those of individual companies?

11. General Cinema Corp. announced that it had purchased 18.9 percent of the outstanding shares of Heublein, Inc. According to the *Wall Street Journal*, "General Cinema's decision to stop buying Heublein stock with a holding of 18.9 percent came as a surprise." Most analysts thought that General Cinema would want a 20 percent holding. What is significant about the 20 percent figure?

Problems

1. *The equity method provides for more timely recognition of subsidiary earnings and losses than does the cost method.*

    On January 2 the Manitoba Co. purchased for $80 per share (cash) 2 million of the 10 million outstanding shares of the Winnipeg Corp.

    On July 5 the Winnipeg Corp. reported earnings of $50 million for the first six months of the year.

    On July 15, the board of directors of the Winnipeg Corp. declared and the company paid, a $2 per share cash dividend.

    On December 31, the Winnipeg Corp. reported a loss of $20 million for the second six months of the year.

    a. Prepare journal entries to account for Manitoba's investment in the Winnipeg Corp. using first the *cost* method and then the *equity* method.

    b. Compare total revenues of the Manitoba Co. attributable to its investment under the two alternative methods. Compare the year-end carrying values of the investment.

2. *Under the cost method of accounting for intercorporate investments, the investment account is not affected by dividends received or the investor's share of the investee's earnings.*

Challenge Inc. purchased 10 percent of the common stock of Meek Limited on March 15, 1996, for $10 million. This 10 percent ownership interest gave Challenge no significant influence over Meek Limited. Beginning in 2000, Meek suffered a number of years of losses. At December 31, 2004, the market value of Challenge's 10 percent interest in Meek has fallen to $5 million and Challenge determines that this loss is not temporary.

a. Prepare the journal entry to record Challenge's loss in the value of its investment in Meek.

b. What is the balance in Challenge's Investment in Meek Ltd. account at December 31, 2004, after the above journal entry?

3. *The earnings of a subsidiary can be derived from information on the carrying value of the investment and dividends declared.*

On January 1, 1994, the Eagleton Co. purchased for $80 million a 40 percent interest (4 million of 10 million shares) in the common stock of Alexander, Inc. The Eagleton Co. uses the equity method to account for its investment in Alexander.

On December 31, 1996, the Eagleton Co. sold 1 million of the shares at a price of $25 per share. It recorded a gain of $2 million on the sale.

On December 31, 1998, the remaining shares were reported on the books of Eagleton at a carrying value of $78 million.

During the five-year period from 1994 through 1998, Alexander, Inc., paid annual dividends of $1.50 per share.

a. Determine the earnings of Alexander, Inc., during the period January 1, 1994, to December 31, 1996.

b. Determine the earnings of Alexander, Inc., during the period January 1, 1997, to December 31, 1998.

4. *The equity method prevents an investor company from regulating its own earnings by manipulating the dividend practices of the investee firm.*

The New Brunswick Co. owned 40 percent (10 million shares) of the voting stock of the Fredericton Corp. and controlled a majority of seats on the latter's board of directors. Toward the end of 1996, the controllers of the two firms estimated that New Brunswick Co. would have earnings for the year of approximately $10 million (exclusive of earnings attributable to Fredericton Corp.) and that Fredericton Corp. would have earnings of approximately $50 million.

The president of New Brunswick Co. was disappointed that his firm would earn only $10 million plus its share of Fredericton Corp. earnings. Prior to 1996, New Brunswick Co. had increased its earnings by 10 percent each year; consistent with that trend, New Brunswick Co. would have to report total earnings in 1996 of $45 million.

a. In accordance with generally accepted accounting principles, New Brunswick Co. accounts for its interest in Fredericton Corp. on the equity basis. If Fredericton Corp. were to declare its usual dividend of $1 per share, what would be the total reported income of New Brunswick Co.?

b. The president of New Brunswick Co. suggested to his controller that Fredericton Corp. be directed to declare a special dividend of $2.50 per share in addition to the regular $1 per share. What impact would the additional dividend have on earnings of New Brunswick Co.?

c. Suppose that New Brunswick Co. accounted for its investment in Fredericton Corp. on the cost basis. What would be the total reported earnings of New Brunswick Co. if the latter declared its regular dividend of $1 per share? What impact would the additional dividend specified in part (b) have on earnings of New Brunswick Co.?

d. Comment on why the equity rather than the cost method is considered appropriate for firms that can exert significant influence over companies in which they have an interest.

5. *A firm is ordered to pay its earnings from a subsidiary to the U.S. Treasury.*

The Federal Trade Commission held that Beatrice Food Co.'s 1978 acquisition of Tropicana Products, Inc., violated federal antitrust laws. The acquisition had been valued at about $490 million.

According to the financial press, an FTC hearing officer ordered Beatrice Foods to divest itself of Tropicana Products, Inc., and "pay its profits to the U.S. Treasury." Although Beatrice did not break out Tropicana's earnings in its financial statements, industry sources estimated that Tropicana contributed about $57 million to Beatrice's income in 1979.

Antitrust specialists speculated that the unusual penalty was imposed in order to discourage other firms from engaging in questionable takeovers. Some companies, they suggested, were willing to make acquisitions that they knew would be challenged by federal authorities because of the profits that could be earned even while a case was in litigation.

a. By which method, cost or equity, is it likely that Beatrice accounted for its interest in Tropicana?

b. Suppose that after being acquired by Beatrice, Tropicana declared dividends of an amount less than annual earnings. Would recorded *earnings* from the subsidiary be a reasonable measure of economic value of the benefits that Beatrice received from Tropicana during the period of ownership? What might be a better measure?

c. Is it really possible for a firm to "pay its *profits* to the U.S. Treasury"? Comment.

6. *Consolidating adjustments may have varying effects on consolidated earnings.*

The consolidated income of a parent company and its subsidiary is the sum of their individual earnings after certain adjustments have been made. For each of the transactions listed, indicate with a brief explanation whether the required adjustments would increase, decrease, or have no effect upon consolidated income as determined simply by summing the earnings of the two individual companies. Assume that Company A owns 100 percent of the outstanding shares of common stock of Company B.

a. Company B acquired $100,000 of bonds issued by Company A. Company A paid Company B interest of $9,000.

b. Company A sold $100,000 of merchandise to Company B. The goods had cost Company A $80,000 to produce. By year end, Company B had resold all of the goods to outsiders.

c. Company A sold $60,000 of merchandise to Company B. The goods had cost Company A $40,000 to produce. At year end, all the goods remained in the inventory of Company B.

d. Company B owned 5,000 shares of the preferred stock of Company A. Company A paid dividends of $3 per share on the preferred stock.

e. Company A sold Company B land for $25,000. The land had cost Company A $40,000.

f. Two years earlier, Company A sold Company B equipment for $20,000. The equipment had cost Company A $12,000. The equipment had an estimated useful life of 10 years and zero salvage value. Company B has been charging amortization based on its cost of $20,000—$2,000 per year.

7. *Consolidated income represents the sum of the earnings of individual firms plus or minus any revenues or expenses that would not have been recognized had the individual firms been divisions of a single entity.*

Vancouver Corp. owns 100 percent of the outstanding stock of the Kitsilano Co. Vancouver Corp. has earnings of $300,000 (exclusive of its share of Kitsilano Co. earnings) and Kitsilano Co. has earnings of $120,000. Given the additional information that follows, determine consolidated earnings:

a. Vancouver Corp. sold merchandise to Kitsilano Co. at a price of $80,000. The cost of the merchandise was $64,000. Kitsilano Co. has not yet resold any of the merchandise.

b. Vancouver made a loan of $100,000 to Kitsilano, which paid interest of $8,000 on the loan.

c. Vancouver Corp. purchased equipment from Kitsilano for $40,000. The equipment has a remaining useful life of 10 years and no anticipated salvage value. The equipment had a net value on the books of Kitsilano of $15,000 (cost of $30,000 less accumulated amortization of $15,000). Kitsilano had been amortizing the equipment over a period of 20 years ($1,500 per year). Vancouver Corp. charged a full year's amortization (based, of course, on its cost).

d. Kitsilano Co. leased office space from Vancouver Corp. and made rent payments of $1,000 per month—a total of $12,000.

e. Vancouver Corp. paid for its investment in Kitsilano an amount that was $80,000 in excess of Kitsilano's book value. The $80,000 was allocated entirely to goodwill and is being amortized over a period of 20 years.

8. *The sale of equipment by one member of a consolidated group of firms to another may result in complex adjustments to a number of accounts for as many years as the equipment is used.*

The Wayside Co. purchased manufacturing equipment from its subsidiary, The Gardner Co. The Wayside Co. paid $80,000. The equipment had been recorded on the books of the Gardner Co. at its cost of $100,000 less accumulated amortization of $50,000. The Gardner Co. had been amortizing the asset over a period of 10 years. The Wayside Co. will amortize the asset over its remaining useful life of five years.

a. At what amount should the Wayside Co. record the asset on its own books? How much amortization should it charge each year?

b. At what amount should Wayside Co. report the asset on its consolidated balance sheet? How much amortization should it report?

c. Suppose that amortization charges on the equipment enter into the computation of cost of goods sold. Explain the nature of any adjustments to cost of goods sold that might have to be made when a consolidated income statement is prepared. Suppose that not all goods manufactured in the course of a year are actually sold. Explain the nature of any adjustments to year-end inventory that might have to be made.

9. *Intercompany sales may require the adjustment of inventory as well as sales and cost of goods sold.*

Retail Co. serves as the marketing division of Manufacturing Co. It purchases all the goods that it sells to outsiders from Manufacturing Co. Manufacturing Co. sells only to Retail Co., at prices that exceed costs by 66 2/3 percent.

The following data were taken from the year-end balances of the two firms:

	Manufacturing Co.	Retail Co.
Sales revenue	$400,000	$432,000
Cost of goods sold	240,000	360,000
Ending inventory	—	40,000

Neither company had inventory on hand at the beginning of the year. The financial statements of the two firms are to be consolidated.
a. What is the total amount that should be reported as sales (i.e., sales to outsiders)?
b. What is the cost to the consolidated entity of the goods sold?
c. What is the amount at which the ending inventory should be reported (i.e., what is its cost to the consolidated entity)?
d. Prepare a journal entry to eliminate intercompany sales and cost of goods sold and to eliminate any "unearned" profit from the ending inventory. Your entry should reduce the combined balances of the two firms to the amounts computed in parts (a), (b), and (c).

10. *By way of intercorporate investments, control over corporate giants can be obtained with small commitments of financial resources.*

Condensed balance sheets of three companies, A, B, and C, are as follows:

	A	B	C
Miscellaneous assets	$490,000	$130,000	$80,000
Investment in B (80 percent)	200,000		
Investment in C (60 percent)		70,000	
Total assets	$690,000	$200,000	$80,000
Common stock	$ 50,000	$ 5,000	$10,000
Retained earnings	640,000	195,000	70,000
Total shareholders' equity	$690,000	$200,000	$80,000

Company A just acquired its interest in Company B; Company B just acquired its interest in Company C.
a. Make any necessary adjustments to eliminate, for purposes of consolidation, the investment of B in C, to recognize goodwill, and to reclassify the interest of the minority shareholders.

b. Make any necessary adjustments to eliminate the investment of A in B, to recognize goodwill, and to reclassify the interest of the minority shareholders.

c. Combine the remaining balances into a consolidated balance sheet.

Suppose that Company A is effectively controlled by a small group of investors. Because the stock of the company is disbursed among many small shareholders, they have been able to establish their control with an ownership interest of only 20 percent of the outstanding shares.

The investors wish to obtain control of Company D. They believe that they could do so by purchasing 10 percent of its outstanding shares. The market value of all outstanding shares of Company D is $8 million. The investors plan to have Company C buy the 10 percent interest for $800,000. The shareholders of Company C will contribute the necessary cash in proportion to their ownership interest. Then, in turn, the shareholders of Companies B and A will make appropriate proportionate contributions to their firms.

d. What will be the required cash contribution by the group of investors to obtain control of Company D?

11. *This problem reviews the various types of adjustments that are generally required to consolidate financial statements.*

Indicated in the table that follows (dollar amounts in thousands) are the preclosing trial balances of X Co. and its subsidiary Y Co. as at December 31, 1997.

	X Co.		Y Co.	
	Dr.	Cr.	Dr.	Cr.
Cash	$ 19,200		$ 3,000	
Accounts and notes receivable	50,000		16,000	
Interest receivable	4,000		3,000	
Inventory	25,000		10,000	
Capital assets	185,000		30,000	
Investment in Y Co.	30,000			
Accounts and notes payable		$ 44,000		$ 17,000
Interest payable		2,000		1,000
Common stock		60,000		30,000
Retained earnings		181,200		15,000
Sales		100,000		35,000
Interest and other revenues		12,000		2,000
Cost of goods sold and related expenses	80,000		32,000	
Interest expense	6,000		6,000	
	$399,200	$399,200	$100,000	$100,000

The following information suggests consolidation working paper adjustments that must be made before the individual financial statements can be summed and consolidated statements prepared (dollar amounts in thousands):

(1) X Co. owns 60 percent of the common stock of Y Co. It acquired its interest in Y Co. on January 1, 1997. The difference between what it paid for its interest ($30,000) and the book value of its interest ($27,000) can be attributed entirely to land owned by Y Co., which

was worth more than its recorded value. (Be sure to eliminate the entire investment in Y Co. against capital assets and the two owners' equity accounts of Y Co. Also, reclassify the equity of Y Co.'s minority shareholders as "minority interest in subsidiary.")

(2) In 1997 X Co. made $10,000 of sales to Y Co. None of the goods purchased by Y Co. remains in its inventory. Hence, from a consolidated perspective, sales and cost of goods sold are overstated by $10,000.

(3) Y Co. still owes X Co. $4,000 for the merchandise purchased.

(4) In the course of the year, X Co. made loans to Y Co. X Co. charged Y Co. $2,000 of interest on the loans. Although there was no outstanding balance on the principal of the loans at year end, Y Co. was still indebted to X Co. for $1,000 of interest. Both companies have properly accrued the interest revenue or expense.

(5) During the year, X Co. sold land to Y Co. Selling price was $8,000. The land had originally cost X Co. $4,000. X Co. included the gain on the sale of land in "interest and other revenues."

(6) In preparing a consolidated balance sheet from the adjusted trial balance, it is important to remember that the balance in X Co.'s "retained earnings" does not reflect earnings for 1997. Correspondingly, the balance in "minority interest in subsidiary" (an account established by your journal entries) does not include the interests of the minority shareholders in the earnings of the subsidiary in 1997. It will be necessary, therefore, to add to the balance sheet account, "minority interest in subsidiary," the minority share of 1997 earnings and to add to "retained earnings" consolidated net income of 1997.

a. Make all adjustments necessary to prepare consolidated financial statements.

b. Prepare a consolidated income statement and balance sheet. Be sure to include minority share of subsidiary earnings as a deduction from consolidated income. You will probably find it useful to prepare a worksheet in which you establish columns for original balances, adjustments, and consolidated balances.

12. *This problem requires the preparation of a consolidated income statement and balance sheet.*

On January 1, 1997, Britain, Inc., acquired 90 percent of the outstanding stock of London, Inc., a manufacturer of scientific instruments. The balance sheet and income statement of the two companies are shown below. Britain, Inc., made no entries to reflect its share of London's 1997 earnings.

The primary reason why Britain, Inc., paid more than the book value for its acquisition of London was that London, Inc., had developed patents for technologically advanced equipment. In keeping with generally accepted accounting principles, London had assigned only nominal value to the patents. The remaining economic lives of the patents is 8 years.

During 1997 Britain made sales of $190 million to its new subsidiary.

It also made several loans to London, the year-end balance on which was $60 million. It charged London $12 million in interest.

Britain sold a parcel of land to its subsidiary for $40 million. It was its only sale of land during the year.

Balance Sheets
December 31, 1997
(in millions of dollars)

	Britain, Inc.	London, Inc.
Assets		
Cash	$ 46	$ 15
Accounts receivable	270	60
Notes receivable	300	100
Property, plant, and equipment (net of amortization)	1,200	380
Investment in London, Inc.	400	
Total assets	$2,216	$555
Liabilities and shareholders' equity		
Accounts and notes payable	$440	$130
Common stock	1,000	250
Retained earnings	776	175
Total liabilities and equities	$2,216	$555

Income Statements
1997
(in millions of dollars)

	Britain, Inc.	London, Inc.
Sales	$2,190	$270
Interest revenue	35	17
Gain on sale of land	24	0
Total revenues	$2,249	$287
Cost of goods sold	1,400	197
Interest expense	45	15
Other expenses	450	50
Total expenses	$1,895	$262
Net income	$ 354	$ 25

Prepare a consolidated statement of income and a consolidated balance sheet. You will probably find it helpful to make consolidating adjusting and elimination entries and to prepare a worksheet. Remember to take into account the interests of the minority shareholders. Remember also that the balances in retained earnings shown in the balance sheets are at year end 1997, not at date of acquisition. Assume that neither company declared dividends during the year.

13. *If management were not required to amortize goodwill, it could avoid "income statement responsibility" for amounts paid to acquire assets.*

Shortly after the Accounting Principles Board (APB) in the United States imposed the requirement that goodwill be amortized over a period of not longer than 40 years, International Telephone & Telegraph

Corporation (ITT) indicated in a footnote to its financial statements that it disagreed with the position of the board because, it asserted, the value of goodwill does not necessarily diminish over time.

a. If an asset, such as goodwill or land, does not diminish in value over time, do you think that it should be amortized?

b. Suppose that a company such as ITT wishes to acquire a manufacturing facility that makes solar energy cells. Solar Energy, Inc., offers to sell the company such a facility, its only asset, for $200 million. The remaining useful life of the facility is 40 years. Its value on the books of Solar Energy, Inc., is $40 million.

Alternatively, the owners of Solar Energy, Inc., offer to sell their *stock* (not the facility) to ITT for $200 million.

(1) Assume that ITT acquires the *facility* for $200 million. How much amortization would it charge each year?

(2) Assume instead that ITT acquires the *stock* for $200 million. Based on the "judgment" of management it allocates the entire excess of cost of its investment in Solar Energy, Inc., over its book value of $40 million to goodwill. If the company were not required to amortize goodwill, how much amortization would it charge each year on the facility? If, instead, it were required to amortize goodwill over a period of 40 years, what would be the combined amortization charge for goodwill and the facility?

(3) Why do you suppose the rule-making authorities decided that goodwill must be amortized?

14. *A merger or acquisition, particularly if accounted for as a pooling, may provide "instant earnings" to the firm whose shares remain outstanding.*

The following information pertains to the Cambridge Co. and the Leeds Co. as at December 31.

	Cambridge Co.	Leeds Co.
Number of shares of common stock outstanding	1,000,000	500,000
Net assets	$15,000,000	$5,000,000
Latest annual income	$ 1,000,000	$ 500,000
Recent market price of common stock (per share)	$40	$20
Earnings per share	$2	$2

The Cambridge Co. and the Leeds Co. have agreed to a business combination. Cambridge Co. will acquire 100 percent of the common stock of Leeds Co. at the recent market price of $20 per share.

a. Suppose that Cambridge Co. were to purchase all 500,000 shares of Leeds Co. for $20 per share in cash. Cambridge Co. would borrow the required funds at an interest rate (after taxes) of 5 percent per year. The combination would be accounted for as a purchase, and the excess of purchase price over book value would be amortized over a period of 20 years. Determine anticipated annual consolidated earnings per share of Cambridge Co. after the acquisition, assuming no substantive changes in the earnings of either company.

b. Suppose alternatively that Cambridge Co. were to acquire all 500,000 shares of Leeds Co. in an exchange of stock. The number of shares to be issued would be based on relative market values, and the combination would be accounted for as a pooling of interests. Determine the anticipated annual consolidated earnings per share of Cambridge Co. subsequent to the combination.

15. *Alternative means of merging may have differing impacts upon reported assets and equities.*

Indicated as follows are condensed balance sheets of the MNO Co. and PQR Co:

	MNO Co.	PQR Co.
Net assets	$5,000,000	$2,000,000
Common stock, no-par value	$2,500,000	$1,150,000
Retained earnings	2,500,000	850,000
Total shareholders' equity	$5,000,000	$2,000,000

Prepare balance sheets of the MNO Co. (consolidated as appropriate) to reflect the acquisition of the PQR Co. by the MNO Co. under each of the following conditions:
a. The MNO Co. purchases the net assets of the PQR Co. at a price of $3.0 million cash. To raise the necessary cash, MNO Co. issues 50,000 shares of common stock at $60 per share.
b. The MNO Co. purchases 100 percent of the outstanding stock of the PQR Co. at a total price of $3.0 million cash. To raise the necessary cash, MNO Co. issues 50,000 shares of common stock at $60 per share.
c. The MNO Co. issues 50,000 shares of its own common stock in exchange for 100 percent of the outstanding shares of the PQR Co. The market price of the MNO Co. stock at the time of the exchange is $60 per share. The transaction is to be accounted for as a pooling of interests.

16. *Alternative means of accounting for excess of purchase price over book value can have substantially different effects on reported earnings.*

At the beginning of 1996, the Federal Products Company acquired 100 percent control of Provincial Industries, Inc., for $400 million in common stock. At the time of the acquisition the net assets (assets less liabilities) of Provincial Industries were recorded on its books at $240 million. In 1996, Federal Products had earnings of $180 million, exclusive of earnings of Provincial Industries, Inc., which had earnings of $40 million. There were no material intercompany transactions during the year. Determine the consolidated earnings of Federal Products Company and its subsidiary under the following alternative assumptions:
a. The combination is accounted for as a purchase, and the excess of acquisition cost over book value is allocated to various fixed assets that have an average remaining useful life of 10 years.
b. The combination is accounted for as a purchase, and the excess of acquisition cost over book value is allocated entirely to "goodwill." The

14

Statement of Changes in Financial Position

The final three chapters of the text move away from the examination of specific balance sheet and income statement categories. This chapter returns to the third primary financial statement, the statement of changes in financial position. The purpose of this statement was explained in Chapter 2. In this chapter we examine in depth the information content of, and the mechanics of preparing, the statement of changes in financial position.

After studying this chapter, you will be able to:

- Understand the relationship of the statement of changes in financial position to the balance sheet and income statement
- Define cash and understand its importance to investors and managers
- Classify cash flows as to operating, investing, or financing activities
- Distinguish between the direct and indirect methods of presenting the statement of changes in financial position
- Prepare a statement of changes in financial position
- Understand the distinction between the cash and working capital definition of funds

The statement of changes in financial position is equal in status to the income statement and the balance sheet by way of official pronouncement, although not by tradition. The statement of changes in financial position is required to be presented for each period, unless it would not provide useful additional information. In some very simple operations the changes in financial position of a company fo a certain period may be obvious from the other financial statements. Prior to 1985, the statement of changes in financial position reported on changes in "funds," with considerable flexibility allowed in selecting the definition of funds. Many firms interpreted funds to mean working capital— that is, current assets less current liabilities. An increasing number, however— and by 1985 a majority—construed funds as cash or near-cash.

Exhibit 14-1 shows the consolidated statements of changes in financial position of Sun Ice Limited and its subsidiaries for the years ending January 31, 1994 and 1993.

EXHIBIT 14-1

Consolidated Statements of Changes in Financial Position
Sun Ice Limited

	(Dollars in thousands)	
Years Ended January 31	1994	1993
Cash provided (used) by		
Operating Activities		
Operations		
Net income (loss) for the year	$ 310	$ (304)
Items not involving cash		
Amortization	705	630
Deferred income taxes	(85)	(20)
Gain on disposal of capital assets	(1)	(243)
	929	63
Changes in noncash working capital balances		
Accounts receivable	(563)	(227)
Income taxes refundable	247	453
Inventory	(1,873)	2,859
Prepaid expenses and deposits	(196)	83
Accounts payable	718	(291)
Cash provided (used) by operating activities	(738)	2,940
Financing Activities		
Repayment of long-term debt, net	(286)	(752)
Share capital to be issued	791	—
Cash provided (used) by financing activities	505	(752)
Investing Activities		
Additions to capital assets	(120)	(12)
Increase in other assets	(450)	—
Proceeds on disposal of capital assets	176	1,343
Cash provided (used) by investing activities	(394)	1,331
Increase (Decrease) in cash and equivalents	(627)	3,519
Cash and equivalents, beginning of year	6,766	3,247
Cash and equivalents, end of year	$ 6,139	$ 6,766

In 1985 the CICA affirmed the trend toward reporting funds as cash rather than working capital. In revised Section 1540, "Statement of Changes in Financial Position," the CICA stipulated that the statement of changes in financial position should report the changes in cash and cash equivalents during the period.

In the United States, to emphasize the focus on cash, the FASB, in 1987, changed the name of the statement from *statement of changes in financial position* to *statement of cash flows*. The CICA allows the use of titles such as *cash flow statement,* and many companies in Canada do use a title emphasizing the cash nature of the statement. Since the majority of Canadian companies still use the title, statement of changes in financial position, this is the wording that will be used in this text.

OBJECTIVES OF THE STATEMENT OF CHANGES IN FINANCIAL POSITION

The statement of changes in financial position reconciles cash at the beginning of the year with that at the end. Its objective is to provide information about an enterprise's cash receipts and disbursements. As repeatedly emphasized throughout this text, cash is the premier of assets. Cash is what is needed by a business to satisfy its obligations as they come due, to meet day-to-day operating expenses, and to pay interest and dividends. Cash is the medium of exchange in our economy, and shareholders contribute cash to a business with the ultimate objective of receiving more cash than they have given up. As discussed in previous chapters, the value of individual assets and liabilities, as well as that of a firm as a whole, is determined by anticipated flows of cash. Investors and managers need to know why cash has increased or decreased in the past. It helps them to predict the cash that the firm will generate in the future, the cash that it will require to satisfy its commitments to outsiders, and the cash that it will have available for distributions to shareholders. The CICA, in Section 1000 of the *CICA Handbook,* "Financial Statement Concepts," stressed the importance of information about cash receipts and disbursements in assessing an entity's ability to generate cash flows in the future to meet its obligations and to provide a return to the shareholder. Section 1540 sets forth the objectives of a statement of changes in financial position. Those objectives are

1. To provide information about the operating, financing, and investing activities of the enterprise and the effect of those activities on cash resources

2. To assist financial statement users in evaluating the liquidity and solvency of an enterprise

3. To assist financial statement users in assessing the enterprise's ability to generate cash from internal sources, to repay debt obligations, to reinvest, and to make distributions to owners[1]

THE STATEMENT OF CHANGES IN FINANCIAL POSITION AS A COMPLEMENT TO THE STATEMENT OF INCOME

The statement of changes in financial position complements the income statement. A central theme of this text has been that *income* is superior to cash flow as a measure of overall organizational performance. Income, unlike

[1] "Statement of Changes in Financial Position," Section 1540.01, *CICA Handbook,* 1991.

cash flow, registers changes in the overall level of economic resources, not just selected assets.

Income, however, is a relatively subjective indicator. It is determined on an accrual basis. Revenues and expenses may be recognized before or after corresponding cash receipts and disbursements. The timing of recognition depends both upon guidelines established by rule-making authorities and upon the judgment of management. Moreover, income is constructed upon a framework of estimates, assumptions, and allocations. Amortization requires that asset life and salvage value be estimated. Cost of goods sold necessitates an assumption as to flows of costs (LIFO, FIFO, etc.).

Cash flow, by contrast, is objective. It focuses exclusively upon changes in cash. It is uncontaminated by estimates, allocations, and assumptions. Cash presents few problems of definition and measurement. The net change in cash for a period can be determined simply by subtracting the ending cash balance from the beginning.

The statement of changes in financial position also reports on activities that would not be shown on the income statement. Financing and investing activities, for example, do not increase or decrease the overall level of a firm's resources. Therefore they are not categorized as either revenues or expenses. When a corporation issues bonds or common stock, only balance sheet accounts are affected. No income is generated. Yet the transaction may be critical to the fiscal well-being of the enterprise.

WHAT IS CASH?

The balance sheet classification "cash" typically encompasses currency on hand as well as deposits in banks. There are valid reasons, however, to expand the focus of the statement of changes in financial position to include other assets as well. No well-managed enterprise maintains a significant balance in currency or in non-interest-bearing chequing accounts. Instead, it places its funds in short-term investments such as Government of Canada Treasury Bills, commercial paper, and money-market funds. These temporary investments are easily interchangeable with cash. Indeed, many companies transfer funds between cash and temporary investments on a daily basis. Because they are the virtual equivalent of cash, these "near-cash" assets must be incorporated into any meaningful definition of cash.

The question arises, however, as to how broad the definition of cash should be. Should it encompass marketable securities, such as stocks and bonds, which are also held as temporary investments and can be easily sold for cash? Should it include accounts receivable, which can be expected to be transformed into cash in a short time? Should it be reduced by accounts payable, which will soon necessitate cash payments? As the definition of cash is expanded, the statement of changes in financial position becomes less affected by arbitrary management decisions (e.g., whether to purchase or sell investments or to delay payments to suppliers). Correspondingly, however, it becomes less focused on cash itself, which is, after all, the asset of ultimate concern.

The CICA, in Section 1540, opted for a narrow definition of cash. It requires that the statement of changes in financial position focus only on *cash and cash equivalents.* Cash equivalents include short-term borrowings (a reduction of cash) and temporary investments. Although this would seem to suggest that marketable securities (investments in stocks and bonds) would be considered to be cash equivalents, firms generally only include as cash equivalents those temporary investments that can be readily converted to a known amount of cash. Examples are Government of Canada Treasury Bills and shares in money-market funds. Investments in marketable securities such as stocks and bonds, even if they are publicly traded and can be easily sold, are generally excluded.

CLASSIFICATION OF CASH FLOWS

Cash flows in the statement of changes in financial position are classified according to three primary categories of activities:

1. Operating activities

2. Investing activities

3. Financing activities

The objective of this classification is to enable the user of the financial statements to assess the impact of the three activities on the cash resources and financial position of the firm and to evaluate the relationships among the three activities.

Operating Activities

Operating activities include buying inputs for, producing, and selling the firm's goods and services and performing its administrative functions. In fact, operating activities encompass all transactions that are not categorized as investing and financing activities.

The operating classification includes both interest and dividends received and interest disbursed. Many accountants believe that interest paid should be shown as a financing activity and interest and dividends received as an investing activity. Interest is paid as a result of having borrowed financial resources; both interest and dividends are received as returns on investments in debt or equity securities. The specification that interest and dividends received and interest paid be classified as operating activities is consistent with the classification of these items in the computation of operating income. Almost all companies take in dividends received as well as interest both paid and received as part of operating income.

The payment of dividends, on the other hand, may be viewed as either a financing activity (i.e., a return to the financing source) or as part of normal operating activities. Either classification of dividends paid is acceptable.

The main cash *inflows* from operating activities are

1. Cash receipts from the sale of goods or services, including the collection of accounts and notes receivable arising from sales

2. Interest and dividends from loans and investments

3. All receipts not included among financing and investment activities, including proceeds of settlements of lawsuits, proceeds of insurance settlements, and refunds from suppliers

The main cash *outflows* from operating activities are

1. Payments for inventory and other goods and services

2. Payments for wages and salaries

3. Payments for taxes

4. Interest paid to lenders and other creditors

5. All payments not included among financing and investment activities, including payments to settle lawsuits, contributions to charities, and cash refunds to customers

Investing Activities

Investing activities include outlays for acquisition and proceeds on disposal of capital assets; making and collecting loans; and purchasing and selling the equity securities (stock) of other companies.

The main cash *inflows* from investment activities are

1. Receipts from the collection of loans made by the company or from the sales of notes and bonds (excluding interest, which is classified as an operating activity)

2. Receipts from the sale of the stock of other companies

3. Receipts from the sale of property, plant, and equipment.

The main cash *outflows* are

1. Amounts loaned to others, including the purchase of bonds and notes

2. Payments to acquire the stock of other companies

3. Payments made to acquire property, plant, and equipment and other long-lived assets

Only payments made at the time of purchase or shortly thereafter are included in the third category. Those made afterward are considered to be repayments of loans and included among financing outflows.

Financing Activities

Financing activities result in changes to the size and composition of the capital structure of the firm (both debt and equity) and include borrowing and repaying loans and issuing and redeeming stock.

The main cash *inflows* from financing activities are

1. Proceeds from issuing stock

2. Proceeds from issuing bonds, notes, and other instruments of debt

The main cash *outflows* are

1. Payments of dividends

2. Payments to redeem stock

3. Repayments of amounts borrowed

Effect of Changes in Foreign Currency Exchange Rates

A company that has cash flows in foreign currencies must combine them with the flows in Canadian dollars. The foreign flows would be translated using the exchange rate in effect at the time of the flows. If the beginning-of-year balance in foreign currency (translated at beginning-of-year exchange rates) is to reconcile with the end-of-year balance (translated at end-of-year exchange rates), an adjustment must be made for the changes in the exchange rates. This adjustment is reported on a single line in the statement of changes in financial position. It is captioned, "effect of exchange rate changes on cash."

REPORTING NONCASH FINANCING AND INVESTING ACTIVITIES

One of the principal ways in which the statement of changes in financial position supplements the income statement is by reporting on the investing and financing transactions indicated in the previous section. These transactions do not affect income in the period in which they take place and therefore would not be reported on the income statement. There are still other financing and investing transactions that do not involve cash receipts or disbursements. Therefore they would not naturally be reported on either the income statement or the statement of changes in financial position. The following are examples:

- A firm acquires property, plant, and equipment in exchange for a long-term note.
- A firm acquires the assets of another company in exchange for shares of its own stock.
- A firm redeems bonds payable by issuing common stock.
- A firm trades in one asset for another.
- A firm acquires property by entering into a capital lease.

These transactions can be thought of as an inflow of cash (e.g., cash proceeds on issue of long-term note) followed immediately by a cash outflow (e.g., payment for purchase of property, plant, and equipment), or vice versa. To make the statement of changes in financial position a complete report on investing and financing activities, the CICA recommended that such transactions should be disclosed. For example, in the acquisition of capital assets in exchange for a long-term note, the acquisition of the asset would be shown as a cash outflow under investing activities, and the issue of the long-term note would be shown as a cash inflow under financing activities. Obviously, the net of the two items would have a nil effect on net cash flow. Some transactions are part cash and part noncash. For example, a firm might acquire new equipment in exchange for both cash and used equipment. By recording both the acquisition and disposal in the investing section, the net cash flow from the transaction would automatically be disclosed in the statement.

DIRECT VERSUS INDIRECT PRESENTATIONS

Cash flows may be presented in either of two ways: the *direct* method or the *indirect* method. The difference in the two methods relates only to the manner in which *operating* cash flows are presented; the presentation of investing and financing activities is the same under both methods.

The Direct Method

The direct method reports all components of cash from operations. The payments are subtracted from the receipts. The operating activities section of a statement of changes in financial position might appear as follows:

Cash flows from operating activities	
Cash received from customers	$47,000
Cash paid to suppliers	(21,000)
Cash paid to employees	(12,000)
Cash provided by operating activities	$14,000

The Indirect Method

The indirect method reconciles reported income to cash flow from operating activities. The indirect method starts with net income as a cash flow. It then adjusts income for revenues and expenses that do not provide or use cash. Amortization, for example, is a noncash expense. The sales revenue of a firm may be greater or less than cash collected from customers. The amounts paid to purchase merchandise inventory may be greater or less than cost of goods sold.

Suppose the income statement for the same company as illustrated under the direct method is as follows:

Sales revenue		$50,000
Less: Cost of goods sold	$25,000	
Wages and salaries expense	10,000	
Amortization expense	5,000	40,000
Net income		$10,000

Assume further that

1. The firm collected only $47,000 of the sales revenue. (The $3,000 difference between sales and collections was added to accounts receivable.)

(d)

Amortization expense	....	$51
Accumulated amortization	....	$51

To record amortization

The only time that long-lived assets impact on the cash flow of an enterprise is when the asset is paid for and when any proceeds are received on disposition. The periodic amortization entries made between the date of purchase and disposal have no impact on cash, as can easily be seen by examining the amortization entry.

Interest Expense

In this example, we can assume that the interest payments for the year were equal to the interest expense. If they were not, then there would have been an increase or a decrease in (1) either a prepaid interest or an interest payable account or (2) either a bond premium or a bond discount account. The balance sheet in Exhibit 14-2 contains neither a prepaid interest nor an interest payable account. It does, however, contain a bond premium account. But the increase of $3 can be explained fully by the issuance of new bonds (see entry *n* below). Therefore the following entry would summarize both the cash payments and the interest expense:

(e)

Interest expense	....	$11
Interest payment (OA)	....	$11

To record interest

Income Tax Expense

Income tax expense, per the income statement, was $30. As indicated in the supplementary information, however, the actual income tax payment was only $23. As emphasized in Chapter 10, the reported income tax expense is based upon reported income rather than taxable income as calculated under the provisions of the Income Tax Act. The difference between the income tax that is payable for the current year and that recognized as income tax expense is added to, or subtracted from, the deferred income taxes account. Thus

(f)

Income tax expense	....	$30
Deferred income taxes	....	$ 7
Payment of taxes (OA)	....	23

To record income tax expense

Other Expenses

Other expenses required the disbursement of cash. We know this because, as with interest, there are no asset or liability accounts related to the expenses. Hence the expenses were equal to the cash payments:

(g)

Other expenses	....	$4
Payment of other expenses (OA)	....	$4

To record other expenses

Collections from Customers

Neither the financial statements nor the supplementary data reveal the collections from customers. The collections can be derived, however, from the related balance sheet (accounts receivable) and income statement (sales) accounts.

The balance in the accounts receivable general ledger account at the end of 1997 is the following:

> Accounts receivable, 31/12/96
> + 1997 Sales
> − 1997 Collections
> ─────────────────
> = Accounts receivable, 31/12/97

Therefore, by rearrangement, it is possible to determine the 1997 collections from customers:

> 1997 Sales
> + Accounts receivable, 31/12/96
> − Accounts receivable, 31/12/97
> ─────────────────
> = 1997 Collections

Therefore, 1997 Collections = $1,045 + $80 − $76 = $1,049

The following entry summarizes the collections:

(h)

Collections from customers (OA) $1,049
    Accounts receivable $1,049
To record collections from customers

Payments to Suppliers

Payments to suppliers are also not reported in the income statement, balance sheet, or supplementary data. They too must be derived. Payments to suppliers relate, first, to the amount of goods purchased and, second, to the amount of goods paid for. Unlike collections from customers, they must be derived from two, rather than one, balance sheet accounts—inventory and accounts payable.

Goods purchased can be calculated from the beginning and ending balances in inventory and from cost of goods sold.

The balance in the inventory general ledger account at the end of 1997 is the following:

> Inventory, 31/12/96
> + 1997 Purchases
> − 1997 Cost of goods sold
> ─────────────────
> = Inventory, 31/12/97

Therefore, by rearrangement, it is possible to determine the 1997 purchases from suppliers:

> 1997 Cost of goods sold
> + Inventory, 31/12/97
> − Inventory, 31/12/96
> ─────────────────
> = 1997 Purchases

Therefore, 1997 Purchases = $895 + $60 − $62 = $893

The purchase of inventory increases accounts payable; it has no impact on cash:

(i)

Inventory $893
    Accounts payable $893
To record purchases of inventory

Once the purchases are known, the actual cash payments can be derived by analyzing accounts payable.

The balance in the accounts payable general ledger account at the end of 1997 is the following:

Accounts payable, 31/12/96
+ 1997 Purchases
− 1997 Payments
_____
= Accounts payable, 31/12/97

Therefore, by rearrangement, it is possible to determine the 1997 payments to suppliers:

1997 Purchases
+ Accounts payable, 31/12/96
− Accounts payable, 31/12/97
_____
= 1997 Payments

Therefore, 1997 Payments = $893 + $56 − $62 = $887

The entry to reflect the payments would be:

(j)

Accounts payable $887
    Payments to suppliers (OA) $887
To record payments to suppliers

Many companies keep track of both collections from customers and payments to suppliers. Therefore they do not have to resort to the analysis just illustrated. The analysis is presented here to demonstrate that companies need not forsake the direct for the indirect presentation simply because their accounting systems do not keep track of collections from customers and payments to suppliers. These amounts can be derived from the income statement and the beginning - and end-of-year balance sheets. Indeed, the cash flows associated with any revenue and expense can be calculated by adding to it the net change in the related balance sheet account.

Purchase of Marketable Securities

The company purchased marketable securities for $110. Purchases of securities are classified as investing activities:

(k)

Marketable securities $110
    Purchase of marketable securities (IA) $110
To record the purchase of marketable securities

Purchase of Equipment

The company purchased equipment for $112. Purchases of property, plant, and equipment are categorized as investing activities:

(l)

Buildings and equipment	$112	
Purchase of equipment (IA)		$112
To record purchase of equipment		

Purchase of Land — A Noncash Acquisition

The company acquired land in exchange for 1 million newly issued shares of its own common stock. Since the stock had a fair market value of $6 per share, the purchase of the land would have been recorded at $6 million:

(m)

Land	$6	
Issue of shares for land (FA)	6	
Acquisition of land for shares (IA)		$6
Common stock		6
To record acquisition of land in exchange for shares		

The acquisition of the land is an investing activity and the issue of shares is a financing activity. Both will be included in the cash flows, but will net to zero.

Issuance of Bonds

The firm received $120 in cash by issuing bonds. The bonds had a face value of $117. The difference between the two amounts would have been credited to a bond premium account. The issuance of bonds is classified as a financing activity:

(n)

Issuance of bonds (FA)	$120	
Bonds payable		$117
Bond premium		3
To record issuance of bonds		

Payment of Dividends

The company paid $22 in dividends. Dividends are generally charged to "dividends," an account that has the characteristics of an expense account but is not incorporated into the calculation of income. The dividends account is "closed" into retained earnings at year end. The entry that follows gives effect to the payment of dividends. Dividends paid are classified as a financing activity:

(o)

Retained earnings	$22	
Payment of dividends (FA)		$22
To record payment of dividends		

Completing the Worksheet

After the entries that have been made so far have been posted to the worksheet, it is apparent that, with the exception of two accounts, all changes in the balance sheet during the year have been accounted for. That is, beginning balance, plus or minus adjustments, equals ending balance. The two accounts that do not yet reconcile are retained earnings and cash.

Retained earnings is decreased during the year when dividends are declared and increased at year end when revenue and expense accounts are closed out, thereby transferring net income to retained earnings. To this point, an entry has been made to recognize the declaration of dividends but none has been made to transfer the net income. This omission can be remedied with the following entry:

(p)

Net income	$60	
Retained earnings		$60
To transfer net income to retained earnings		

There is no additional cash flow related to this entry. All the cash flows from operating activities have already been accounted for.

The difference between beginning- and end-of-year cash balance ($10) has been accounted for by the entries to the cash flows section of the worksheet. The last entry completes the worksheet and serves as a check on our analysis:

(q)

Cash	$10	
Net increase in cash		$10
To reconcile cash		

If no errors have been made, then the $10 increase in cash will be equal to the difference between the cash receipts and payments that have previously been identified.

Preparing the Statement

The main body of the statement of changes in financial position can be prepared directly from the section of the worksheet indicating the cash flows. Exhibit 14-4 contains the same information as the worksheet with only minor rearrangement of some of the items. Exhibit 14-4 presents the completed statement.

EXHIBIT 14-4
Statement of Changes in Financial Position
Using the Direct Method

Taconic Corp.
Statement of Changes in Financial Position
Year Ended December 31, 1997
(all amounts in millions)

Increase (Decrease) in Cash

Operating Activities	
Collections from customers	$1,049
Payments to suppliers	(887)
Payments of interest	(11)
Payments of taxes	(23)
Payments of other expenses	(4)
Cash provided by operating activities	$ 124

EXHIBIT 14-4 (continued)

Investing Activities	
Proceeds from sale of equipment	$ 10
Purchases of equipment	(112)
Acquisition of land in exchange for shares	(6)
Cash used in investing activities	$ (108)
Financing Activities	
Proceeds from issuing bonds	$ 120
Purchases of marketable securities	(110)
Payment of dividends	(22)
Issue of shares in exchange for land	6
Cash used in financing activities	$ (6)
Increase in cash	$ 10

PREPARATION OF THE STATEMENT OF CHANGES IN FINANCIAL POSITION USING THE INDIRECT METHOD

The procedures for preparing the statement of changes in financial position using the indirect method are very similar to those for preparing the statement using the direct method. The worksheet for preparing the statement of changes in financial position using the indirect method is shown in Exhibit 14-5. The main difference is in the worksheet entries affecting cash from operating activities. The entries reconstructing the various revenue and expense accounts (entries **(a)** to **(j)** under the direct method) would be replaced with a single entry:

(a)

Net income (OA) $60
     Retained earnings $60
    To report net income as a cash flow

Thereafter entries would be made to adjust net income for each of the items required to reconcile net income to cash from operating activities. These adjustments are as follows:

Change in Accounts Receivable

Cash collections from customers exceeded sales by $4. Sales are associated with increases in accounts receivable, cash collections with decreases. Hence accounts receivable decreased during the year. The $4 *decrease in accounts receivable* (i.e., the amount by which collections exceeded sales) must be added to net income if net income is to be considered a source of cash from operations. This would be recorded on the worksheet as follows:

(b)

Decrease in accounts receivable (OA) $4
     Accounts receivable $4
    To adjust net income for the decrease in accounts receivable

Changes in Inventory and Accounts Payable

Cost of goods sold exceeded payments to suppliers by $8. This is because (1) the company used $2 more goods than it purchased, thereby reducing inventory by $2; and (2) it purchased $6 more goods than it paid for, thereby increasing accounts payable by $6.

EXHIBIT 14-5
**Worksheet for Preparing Statement of
Changes in Financial Position—Indirect Method**

		Year Ended December 31 Reconstructed Entries		
	1996	Debits	Credits	1997
Balance Sheet				
Cash	30	10 (m)		40
Accounts receivable	80		4 (b)	76
Marketable securities	50	110 (h)		160
Inventory	62		2 (c)	60
Building and equipment	328	112 (i)	37 (f)	403
Accumulated amortization	(72)	33 (f)	51 (e)	(90)
Land	67	6 (j)		73
Accounts payable	(56)		6 (d)	(62)
Deferred income taxes	(62)		7 (g)	(69)
Bonds payable	(261)		117 (k)	(378)
Bond premium			3 (k)	(3)
Common stock (no-par value)	(134)		6 (j)	(140)
Retained earnings	(32)	22 (l)	60 (a)	(70)
Total (check)	0			0

		Year Ended December 31 Reconstructed Entries		
	1996	Debits	Credits	1997
Cash Flows				
From operating activities				
Net income		60 (a)		
Decrease in accounts receivable		4 (b)		
Decrease in inventory		2 (c)		
Increase in accounts payable		6 (d)		
Amortization expense		51 (e)		
Gain on sale of equipment			6 (f)	
Increase in deferred income taxes		7 (g)		
From investing activities				
Sale of equipment		10 (f)		
Purchase of equipment			112 (i)	
Acquisition of land in exchange for shares			6 (j)	
From financing activities				
Purchase of marketable securities			110 (h)	
Issuance of bonds		120 (k)		
Payment of dividends			22 (l)	
Issue of shares in exchange for land		6 (j)		
Net increase in cash			10 (m)	
Total (check)		559	559	

The $2 *decrease in inventory* and the $6 *increase in accounts payable* must be added to net income to show the cash provided by income-producing activities:

(c)

> Decrease in inventory(OA) $2
>   Inventory $2
> **To adjust net income for the decrease in inventory**

(d)

> Increase in accounts payable (OA) $6
>   Accounts payable $6
> **To adjust net income for the increase in accounts payable**

Amortization Expense

Amortization is an expense that did not require an outflow of cash. Hence to reconcile income with cash from operations, it must be added to income:

(e)

Amortization expense (OA)	$51	
Accumulated amortization		$51

To adjust net income for amortization, a noncash expense

Gain on Sale of Equipment

Gain on sale of equipment is a noncash revenue. The entry to record the sale of the equipment was

Cash	$10	
Accumulated amortization	33	
Gain on sale of equipment		$6
Buildings and equipment		37

The sale of the equipment was a source of $10 in cash. It would be reported as cash from investing activities. But included in reported income would be the $6 gain on the sale. If income, including the gain of $6, is to be shown as a source of cash, and so also is the $10, then total sources of cash would be overstated by $6; the gain would be counted twice. If income is to be presented as a source of cash, any reported gains must be deducted. Similarly, any losses must be added to income. The losses, like the gains, would have had no impact on cash. Therefore they must be restored to income:

(f)

Proceeds on sale of equipment (IA)	$10	
Accumulated amortization	33	
Gain on sale of equipment (OA)		$ 6
Buildings and equipment		37

To adjust net income for the gain on sale of equipment

Increase in Deferred Income Taxes

Income taxes charged as an expense exceeded those actually paid. The difference of $7 was added to deferred income taxes. The *increase in deferred income taxes* must be added to income:

(g)

Increase in deferred income taxes(OA)	$7	
Deferred income taxes		$7

To adjust net income for the increase in deferred income taxes, a noncash expense

In the worksheet (and subsequently in the statement of changes in financial position), the difference between a revenue or expense and the cash received or paid is typically expressed as a change in the related asset or liability (e.g., "increase in accounts receivable"). There is no reason, however, why the change could not be described so as to indicate the reason behind it (e.g., "amount by which sales exceeded collections from customers").

The balance sheet reconstructing entries are identical to those used for preparing the statement using the direct method (entries (**k**) to (**o**) and (**q**)). These entries are repeated below (with new letters):

Purchase of Marketable Securities

The company purchased marketable securities for $110. Purchases of securities are classified as investing activities:

(h)

Marketable securities	$110	
Purchase of marketable securities (IA)		$110
To record the purchase of marketable securities		

Purchase of Equipment

The company purchased equipment for $112. Purchases of property, plant, and equipment are categorized as investing activities:

(i)

Buildings and equipment	$112	
Purchase of equipment (IA)		$112
To record the purchase of equipment		

Purchase of Land — A Noncash Acquisition

The company acquired land in exchange for one million newly issued shares of its own common stock. Since the stock had a fair market value of $6 per share, the purchase of the land would have been recorded at $6 million:

(j)

Land	$6	
Issue of shares for land (FA)	$6	
Acquisition of land for shares (IA)		$6
Common stock		6
To record acquisition of land in exchange for shares		

The acquisition of the land is an investing activity and the issue of shares is a financing activity. Both will be included in the cash flows, but will net to zero.

Issuance of Bonds

The firm received $120 in cash by issuing bonds. The bonds had a face value of $117. The difference between the two amounts would have been credited to a bond premium account. The issuance of the bonds is classified as a financing activity:

(k)

Issuance of bonds (FA)	$120	
Bonds payable		$117
Bond premium		3
To record issuance of bonds		

Payment of Dividends

The company paid $22 in dividends. Dividends are generally charged to "dividends," an account that has the characteristics of an expense account but is not incorporated into the calculation of income. The dividends account is "closed" into retained earnings at year end. The entry that follows gives effect to the payment of dividends. Dividends paid are classified as a financing activity:

(l)

Retained earnings	$22	
Payment of dividends (FA)		$22
To record payment of dividends		

Completing the Worksheet

After the entries that have been made so far have been posted to the worksheet, it is apparent that, with the exception of one account, all changes in the balance sheet during the year have been accounted for. That is, beginning balance, plus or minus adjustments, equals ending balance. The one account that does not reconcile yet is cash. Remember that when the worksheet was prepared under the direct method the retained earnings account also did not reconcile at this point. It does reconcile, however, under the indirect method because we used the net income for the year ($60) as our starting source of cash (see entry (a)).

The difference between beginning- and end-of-year cash balance ($10) has been accounted for by the entries to the cash flows section of the worksheet. The last entry completes the worksheet and serves as a check on our analysis:

(m)

Cash	$10	
Net increase in cash		$10
To reconcile cash		

If no errors have been made, then the $10 increase in cash will be equal to the difference between the cash receipts and payments that have previously been identified.

If the statement of changes in financial position is presented using the indirect method, then the cash flows relating to individual revenues and expenses are not reported. Exhibit 14-6 illustrates the presentation using the indirect method. Note that there is no difference in the statement of changes in financial position prepared on the indirect basis compared with the direct basis, except in the operating activities section. The investing and financing activities sections are exactly the same under both presentations.

WORKING CAPITAL

Changes in Working Capital as Changes in Nonworking Capital Accounts

Revised Section 1540 of the *CICA Handbook* directed that all firms issue a statement of changes in financial position on the cash basis, rather than the working capital basis that had been previously recommended. Working capital has long been used by financial managers, investors, and creditors as a measure of *liquidity*. Revised Section 1540 obviously diminished its accounting significance in that it will no longer be specifically reported upon in a separate financial statement. But Section 1540 is unlikely to reduce the emphasis that financial analysts and managers place on working capital. Many regard working capital as a fundamental indicator of a firm's ability to meet its short-term obligations as they come due.

Working capital is generally defined as current assets less current liabilities. It comprises the cash and other assets that will be transformed into cash, sold, or consumed within the normal operating cycle of a business. From these assets are subtracted the obligations that will have to be satisfied out of those assets.

EXHIBIT 14-6

Statement of Changes in Financial Position Using the Indirect Method

Taconic Corp.
Statement of Changes in Financial Position
Year Ended December 31, 1997
(all amounts in millions)

Increase (Decrease) in Cash

Operating Activities		
Net income		$ 60
Adjustments to reconcile net income to cash provided by operating activities		
Amortization	$ 51	
Gain on sale of equipment	(6)	
Decrease in accounts receivable	4	
Decrease in inventory	2	
Increase in accounts payable	6	
Increase in deferred income taxes	7	$ 64
Cash provided by operating activities		$ 124
Investing Activities		
Proceeds from sale of equipment	$ 10	
Purchases of equipment	(112)	
Acquisition of land in exchange for shares	(6)	
Cash used in investing activities		(108)
Financing Activities		
Proceeds from issuing bonds	$ 120	
Purchases of marketable securities	(110)	
Payment of dividends	(22)	
Issue of shares in exchange for land	6	
Cash used in financing activities		(6)
Increase in cash		$ 10

Current assets includes cash, marketable securities, accounts receivable, and inventories. *Current liabilities* includes accounts payable, wages and salaries payable, notes payable, and other short-term obligations. *Working capital*—the difference between the current assets and the current liabilities—is the margin of safety between a firm's liquid resources and the demands upon them.

Just as changes in cash are associated with changes in all noncash accounts, changes in working capital are associated with changes in all non-working capital accounts. The basic accounting equation provides that current assets *(CA)* plus other assets *(OA)* are equal to current liabilities *(CL)* plus other liabilities *(OL)* plus shareholders' equity *(SE)*. That is,

$$CA + OA = CL + OL + SE$$

When the terms in the equation are rearranged, it is clear that working capital (current assets minus current liabilities) must equal other liabilities plus shareholders' equity minus other assets:

$$\frac{\text{Working Capital}}{CA - CL} = \frac{\text{All Other Accounts}}{OL + SE - OA}$$

Increases in working capital result from *increases* in noncurrent liabilities or shareholders' equity and from *decreases* in noncurrent assets. *Decreases* in working capital result from *decreases* in noncurrent liabilities or shareholders' equity or *increases* in noncurrent assets. Thus

Sources of Working Capital (Events Associated with Increases in Working Capital)	Uses of Working Capital (Events Associated with Decreases in Working Capital)
Increases in noncurrent liabilities Issuance of notes or bonds *Increases in shareholders' equity* Periodic income Issuance of stock *Decreases in noncurrent assets* Sale of capital assets	*Decreases in noncurrent liabilities* Repayment of notes or bonds *Decreases in shareholders' equity* Periodic losses Redemption of stock Declaration of dividends *Increases in noncurrent assets* Purchases of capital assets

For most companies, the main source of working capital is income-producing activities. To reconcile income with working capital from operating activities requires far fewer adjustments than to reconcile income with cash from operating activities. Sales, for example, increase working capital regardless of how much cash is actually collected (since both cash and accounts receivable are components of working capital). Similarly, cost of goods sold is associated with an equivalent decrease in working capital, regardless of how much merchandise is purchased and how much is paid for (since inventory, cash, and accounts payable are all elements of working capital).

Exhibit 14-7 compares the impact of several common transactions on both cash and working capital.

A Caveat

Working capital, unlike cash, is not directly comparable among firms. Working capital includes both accounts receivable and inventories. Accounts receivable may be influenced by accounting policies as to revenue recognition, bad debt expense, and write-offs of uncollectable accounts. Inventories are affected by choice of inventory costing method and policies as to inventory write-downs.

Moreover, an increase in working capital can be as much a sign of fiscal weakness as of fiscal strength. It is not uncommon for a firm undergoing fiscal stress to experience increases in both accounts receivable and inventory—and therefore working capital. Accounts receivable increases as customers become slow in paying; inventory increases as merchandise which is difficult to sell builds up.

Summary

The statement of changes in financial position is the third of the three main statements that compose an annual financial report. Cash is the asset that is of primary concern to a business and its constituents. Cash is required to pay obligations as they come due, to meet daily operating costs, and to pay dividends and interest. Cash is the medium of exchange in our society, and it is the objective of a business to return more cash to its owners than they contribute.

EXHIBIT 14-7

Comparison of Impact of Selected Transactions on Cash and Working Capital

Transaction	Working Capital	Cash
Sales on account (Dr. accounts receivable; Cr. sales)	Increase	No effect
Recognition of cost of goods sold (Dr. cost of goods sold; Cr. inventory)	Decrease	No effect
Collection of accounts receivable (Dr. cash; Cr. accounts receivable)	No effect	Increase
Purchase of inventory on account (Dr. inventory; Cr. accounts payable)	No effect	No effect
Payment to suppliers (Dr. accounts payable; Cr. cash)	No effect	Decrease
Purchase of inventory for cash (Dr. inventory; Cr. cash)	No effect	Decrease
Declaration of a cash dividend (Dr. dividends; Cr. dividends payable)	Decrease	No effect
Payment of the cash dividend (Dr. dividends payable; Cr. cash)	No effect	Decrease
Purchase of equipment for cash (Dr. equipment; Cr. cash)	Decrease	Decrease
Recognition of amortization (Dr. amortization expense; Cr. accumulated amortization)	No effect	No effect
Sale of equipment at a loss (Dr. accumulated amortization, loss on sale, cash; Cr. equipment)	Increase	Increase
Recognition of bad debt expense (Dr. bad debt expense; Cr. allowance for doubtful accounts)	Decrease	No effect
Write-off of an uncollectable account (Dr. allowance for doubtful accounts; Cr. accounts receivable)	No effect	No effect
Purchase of shares of a subsidiary in exchange for bonds (Dr. investment in subsidiary; Cr. bonds payable)	No effect	No effect

The statement of changes in financial position is conceptually straightforward. It is a listing of cash receipts and disbursements classified into several categories. The three main groupings are cash from operating activities, cash from financing activities, and cash from investing activities.

The statement of changes in financial position can be prepared by analyzing a firm's cash receipts and disbursements journals. The journals of most firms, however, are not set up to provide the required data; time-consuming analysis of individual transactions would be required. However, the change in cash during the year is equal to the sum of the changes in all other balance sheet accounts. It is generally more convenient to prepare the statement by identifying the changes in all the other accounts.

Both the *direct* method and the *indirect* method of preparing the statement of changes in financial position are acceptable. The difference between the two is in the way cash from operating activities is shown. The direct method itemizes each of the cash flows associated with income. The indirect method, by contrast, shows net income as a single source of cash. Income is then adjusted for the non-cash components of the revenues and expenses. Most firms have elected to report using the indirect method.

The statement of changes in financial position is no less important to managers, investors, and creditors than the balance sheet or income statement. It not only completes the picture of financial status and performance painted by the other two, but adds another dimension.

A firm's condensed balance sheets for the years ending December 31, 1997 and 1996, and statement of income for 1997 are shown in the table below (all amounts in millions).

1. By how much did cash increase during 1997?

2. a. By how much did sales increase the accounts receivable, assuming all sales were "on account"?
   b. How much cash was collected from customers?

		1997		1996
Balance Sheet				
Assets				
Cash (and equivalents)		$100		$ 90
Accounts receivable		150		92
Inventory		39		18
Equipment	$245		$250	
Less: Accumulated amortization	(36)	209	(30)	220
Total assets		$498		$420
Liabilities and shareholders' equity				
Accounts payable		$100		$ 60
Deferred income taxes		11		4
Bonds payable	$200		$200	
Less: Bond discount	(4)	196	(5)	195
Contributed capital		15		15
Retained earnings		176		146
Total liabilities and shareholders' equity		$498		$420
Statement of Income				
Sales revenue			$278	
Cost of goods sold		$200		
Amortization expense		10		
Loss on sale of equipment		2		
Interest expense		17		
Income taxes		19	248	
Net income			$ 30	

3. a. By how much did cost of goods sold *decrease* inventory?
   b. How much inventory was purchased?
   c. By how much did purchases increase the accounts payable, assuming all purchases are on account and all accounts payable are to suppliers?
   d. How much cash was paid to suppliers?

4. a. How much did amortization expense add to accumulated amortization?
   b. By how much was accumulated amortization reduced when equipment was sold?
   c. Assume that the equipment that was sold had been acquired for $12. For how much cash was the equipment sold?
   d. How much cash was paid to acquire new equipment?

5. a. By how much did deferred income taxes increase?
   b. How much cash was paid in income taxes?

6. a. By how much did the bond discount decrease?
   b. What journal entry was made to record interest expense?
   c. How much cash was paid in interest?

7. a. By how much did retained earnings increase? Why?
   b. Have all changes in balance sheet accounts now been accounted for?
   c. Summarize all cash receipts and disbursements. Do they account for the change in cash?

Questions for Review and Discussion

1. A statement of changes in financial position is more objective than an income statement. Why?

2. Why is cash of greater concern to investors, creditors, and managers than are other assets?

3. When negotiating with its union, management argued that even though reported earnings were at record highs, the company was unable to afford even a small increase in wages. By contrast, a union in negotiating with its management asserted that even though earnings were at record lows, the company could well afford even a large increase in wages. What is likely to be the common basis for both contentions?

4. What are the primary objectives of the statement of changes in financial position?

5. Why does the statement of changes in financial position focus on temporary investments such as Treasury bills and commercial paper as well as on cash? Why does it not focus upon other temporary investments such as stocks and bonds?

6. What are the three main classifications of cash flows required by the CICA? Why did the CICA switch from the traditional definition of funds being working capital to cash?

7. Under which cash flow classification would interest be reported? Why?

8. What is the main advantage of the *direct* presentation over the *indirect*? Why is the indirect method permitted? Why do most firms choose to use the indirect method?

9. Why are some transactions reported on the statement of changes in financial position even though they result in neither an increase nor a decrease in cash? Provide examples of such transactions.

10. What warnings would you give an analyst who wants to compare the working capital position of one company with that of another?

11. The president of Presidential Realty Corporation, a firm whose shares are traded on the American Stock Exchange, made the following comment in a letter to shareholders:

In our opinion, however, conventionally computed "operating income" has never adequately measured the performance of real-estate development and investment companies such as ours. We believe that the best measure of our performance is the "Sum" of the operating income, the noncash charges against such income (consisting of rental property depreciation, write-off of mortgage origination costs, and deferred federal income taxes), and the funds generated from net gains from capital transactions. It is this "Sum" that is available for all corporate purposes, such as payment of mortgage debt, reinvestment in property replacements and new properties and enterprises, and distributions to shareholders.

The president of the company is, in essence, advocating a cash basis of reporting. Why, in light of his comments, has the accounting profession insisted that financial statements be prepared on the accrual basis and that noncash as well as cash charges be deducted from revenues in determining income? Do you believe that a better measure of performance is obtained if noncash expenses are added back to income? Can you think of any special characteristics of the real estate industry that may have influenced the president?

Problems

1. *"Missing" information on cash receipts and disbursements may be deduced by analyzing the changes in accounts other than cash.*

    The following account balances appeared on the financial statements of the Rackham Corp.:

	1997	1996
Buildings and equipment	$475,000	$400,000
Accumulated amortization	125,000	100,000
Amortization expense	40,000	35,000
Loss on sale of equipment	12,000	57,000

    During 1997 the Rackham Corp. purchased $134,000 in new equipment.
    a. Compute the increase in cash attributable to the *sale* of equipment in 1997 (*Hint:* Analyze the changes in the buildings and equipment and related accumulated amortization accounts, giving consideration to the types of events that cause their balances to increase or decrease.)
    b. Indicate any additions to, or deductions from, 1997 income that would be required if the statement of changes in financial position were to be prepared using the indirect method.

2. *Careful analysis of shareholders' equity accounts can provide considerable information on cash from financing as well as other activities.*

    The shareholders' equity section of the Driscoe Corp. balance sheet as at December 31, 1997 and 1996, contained the following balances:

	1997	1996
Common stock (no-par value, issued and outstanding 10,500 and 10,000 shares respectively)	$160,000	$140,000
Retained earnings	256,000	244,000

At the start of 1997, the company declared and paid a cash dividend of $1 per share and a 4 percent (400 shares) stock dividend. Reported 1997 earnings of the firm included a loss of $20,000 attributable to a fire at a company plant, amortization of $10,000, and a loss of $2,000 on the retirement of outstanding bonds.

The company issued for cash 100 shares of common stock.

Based on this information, determine, as best you can, the increase in cash associated with changes in the shareholders' equity accounts.

3. *A statement of changes in financial position, using the direct or the indirect method, can be prepared by analyzing all accounts other than cash.*

Comparative income statements and the balance sheets for the Whistler Sales Corp. for the years ended December 31, 1997 and 1996, are as follows:

Whistler Sales Corp. Balance Sheet as at December 31, 1997 and 1996

	1997	1996
Assets		
Cash	$ 40,000	$ 19,000
Accounts receivable	48,000	50,000
Inventories	28,000	20,000
Capital assets (net of accumulated amortization)	107,000	112,000
	$223,000	$201,000
Equities		
Accounts payable	$ 85,000	$ 82,000
Common stock	100,000	100,000
Retained earnings	38,000	19,000
Total equities	$223,000	$201,000

Income Statement for Years Ending December 31, 1997 and 1996

	1997	1996
Sales	$120,000	$85,000
Cost of goods sold	$ 90,000	$50,000
Amortization	5,000	5,000
Other expenses	6,000	8,000
Total expenses	$101,000	$63,000
Net income	$ 19,000	$22,000

a. All sales were made on account. By analyzing "accounts receivable," determine the amount of cash collected in 1997.

b. All "other expenses" were paid directly in cash. Indicate the amount of cash applied in 1997 to the payment of "other expenses."

c. Determine the amount of inventory purchased during 1997. Then, by analyzing "accounts payable," determine the amount of cash payments to suppliers made during the year.

d. Indicate any other expenses not requiring an outlay of cash.

e. Prepare two statements of changes in financial position. In the first, indicate directly all cash receipts and disbursements. In the second, start with net income as a source of cash and indicate any required adjustments (e.g., for changes in inventories and accounts receivable).

4. *For some decisions information on changes in cash may be more relevant than that in income.*

The Yukon Mining Co. was organized to remove ore from a specific tract of land over a period of five years. In its second year of operations the company incurred a loss of $400,000, determined as follows:

Sales of ore		$2,000,000
Less: Depletion of ore	$1,000,000	
Amortization on equipment	200,000	
Wages and salaries	600,000	
Other operating costs	600,000	2,400,000
Net loss		$ 400,000

In spite of the loss, the president of the company recommended to the board of directors that it declare a dividend of $300,000. One member of the board declared the recommendation to be nonsense. "How can we justify declaring a dividend in a year when we took a financial beating?"

a. How, in fact, might the board justify the declaration of a dividend?

b. Why would a statement of changes in financial position provide a better indication of the ability of the company to declare dividends than would a statement of income?

c. Suppose that the company had to acquire $400,000 of equipment during the year. Prepare a schedule that would support the position of the president that the company could "afford" to declare a dividend despite the required outlay for the equipment.

5. *In some industries changes in cash may provide a better measure of corporate performance than income.*

In January 1996 Real Estate Investors Corp. purchased an apartment building for $1 million. The company paid $100,000 in cash and gave a 10-year note for the balance. The company was required to pay only interest on the note for the first five years. In years 6 through 10 it was required to make principal payments of $180,000 per year.

In 1997 (the second year after the purchase of the property) the income statement of the company appeared as follows:

Revenues from rents		$200,000
Less: Amortization	$90,000	
Interest	54,000	
Other expenses	60,000	204,000
Net loss		$ 4,000

Amortization was based on the double declining balance method with an estimated useful life of 20 years.

a. Determine net cash inflow during 1997.

b. Compute return on investment on a cash basis (cash inflow divided by company investment in the apartment building).

c. Comment on why some real-estate experts believe that the statement of changes in financial position provides a better indication of corporate performance in the real-estate industry than does the income statement.

Consider the fact that many properties are sold long before the end of their useful (amortizable) lives.

6. *After only one year of a firm's operations it is relatively easy to identify the sources of cash and the uses to which it was put.*

The Earl Company began operations in 1997. Its income statement and balance sheet for its first year of operations follow (all amounts are in thousands):

Earl Company Statement of Income Year Ended December 31, 1997		
Sales		$188,000
Less: Cost of goods sold	$96,000	
Amortization	6,000	
Amortization of organization costs	4,000	
Income taxes	14,000	
Interest*	2,000	
Other expenses	40,000	162,000
Net income		$ 26,000

* The reported interest expense of $2,000 represents, in its entirety, amortization of discount on the note payable.

Balance Sheet As at December 31, 1997		
Assets		
Cash		$ 34,000
Accounts receivable		24,000
Inventories		16,000
Plant and equipment	$106,000	
Less: Accumulated amortization	6,000	100,000
Land		40,000
Organization costs	$ 20,000	
Less: Accumulated amortization	4,000	16,000
Total assets		$230,000
Equities		
Accounts payable		$ 38,000
Income taxes deferred until future years		4,000
Note payable	$80,000	
Less: Discount	12,000	68,000
Common stock		100,000
Retained earnings		20,000
Total liabilities and shareholders' equity		$230,000

Reconstruct as necessary the transactions of the year and prepare a statement of changes in financial position. (*Hint:* Be sure to account for the change in each noncash account. Make assumptions that are consistent with the information presented and with standard accounting practice. For example, income was $26,000, but the ending balance in "retained earnings" is only $20,000; thus it may be assumed that dividends of $6,000 were declared. It is also logical to assume that the declared dividends were paid, since there is no dividends payable balance.)

---

7. *It is possible to derive a statement of changes in financial position entirely from comparative balance sheets and a statement of income.*

Comparative income statements and balance sheets of the Hassel Corp. are as follows:

Hassel Corp.
Statement of Income
Years Ended December 31
(in thousands)

	1997	1996
Sales	$320,000	$292,000
Gain on sale of land sold	16,000	
	$336,000	$292,000
Less: Cost of goods sold	$216,000	$172,000
Amortization	20,000	18,000
Other expenses	40,000	20,000
Income taxes	16,000	22,000
	$292,000	$232,000
Net income	$ 44,000	$ 60,000

Balance Sheet
As at December 31

	1997	1996
Assets		
Cash	$ 60,000	$ 40,000
Accounts receivable	40,000	38,000
Inventory	20,000	16,000
Total current assets	$120,000	$ 94,000
Equipment	$300,000	$240,000
Less: Accumulated amortization	(80,000)	(60,000)
	$220,000	$180,000
Land	70,000	100,000
Total assets	$410,000	$374,000
Liabilities and shareholders' equity		
Trade accounts payable	$ 40,000	$ 62,000
Income taxes deferred until future years	18,000	14,000
Notes payable	60,000	50,000
Common stock	200,000	200,000
Retained earnings	92,000	48,000
Total liabilities and shareholders' equity	$410,000	$374,000

a. Determine the net change in cash.
b. Analyze each of the noncash accounts. Determine the most likely reason for the change in each of the accounts and reconstruct the journal entries that affected each account. Identify the entries associated with receipts or disbursements of cash.
c. Prepare a statement of changes in financial position.

11. *An income statement and an end-of-year balance sheet can be derived from a statement of changes in financial position and a beginning-of-year balance sheet.*

Quebec Co.'s 1997 statement of changes in financial position and January 1, 1997, balance sheet are presented below (all dollar amounts are in millions).

a. Prepare an income statement for 1997.

b. Prepare a balance sheet as at December 31, 1997.

Quebec Co. Statement of Changes in Financial Position Year Ended December 31, 1997	
Operating Activities	
Net income	$ 90
Adjustments to income	
Increase in accounts receivable	(75)
Increase in inventory	(60)
Increase in accounts payable	18
Increase in deferred income taxes	21
Amortization	30
Amortization of bond discount	3
Gain on sale of equipment	(6)
Cash provided by operating activities	$ 21
Investing Activities	
Sale of equipment	$ 9
Increase in cash	$ 30

Notes:
(1) The equipment sold during the year had been purchased for $15.
(2) Interest payments were $48.
(3) Income tax payments were $36.
(4) Payments made for the purchase of merchandise were $642.
(5) Revenue consisted entirely of sales and the gain on the sale of equipment.

Balance Sheet As at January 1, 1997		
Assets		
Current assets		
Cash		$ 180
Accounts receivable		285
Inventories		111
		576
Building and equipment	750	
Accumulated amortization	(90)	660
Total assets		$1,236
Liabilities and shareholders' equity		
Accounts payable		$ 156
Deferred income taxes		12
Bonds payable		600
Discount on bonds payable		(15)
		753
Contributed capital		45
Retained earnings		438
Total liabilities and shareholders' equity		$1,236

12. *This problem illustrates the practical problems of converting from the indirect to the direct method as well as of reconciling related amounts reported on the statement of changes in financial position to those on the balance sheet and income statement.*

The 1993 financial statements of Stelco Inc. (slightly modified) are presented below. All dollar amounts are in millions. The statement of changes in financial position is prepared using the indirect method.

Stelco Inc.
Consolidated Balance Sheets
December 31

	1993	1992
Assets		
Current assets		
Cash and short-term investments	$ 111	$ 68
Accounts receivable	396	343
Inventories	407	449
Prepaid expenses	13	7
	927	867
Other assets		
Capital assets, at cost	3,373	3,354
Less: Accumulated amortization	(2,179)	(2,045)
	1,194	1,309
Long-term investments	193	193
Deferred foreign exchange losses	4	7
Unamortized long-term debt issue expense	9	10
Deferred pension cost	37	37
Total Assets	$2,364	$2,423
Liabilities and Shareholders' Equity		
Current liabilities		
Bank indebtedness	$ 176	$ 190
Accounts payable and accrued liabilities	368	352
Income and other taxes payable	32	20
Cash dividends payable	4	—
Long-term debt due within one year	48	26
	628	588
Other liabilities		
Provision for blast furnace relines — beyond one year	87	74
Long-term debt	695	767
Deferred income taxes	25	27
Total Liabilities	1,435	1,456
Shareholders' Equity		
Preferred stock	178	178
Common stock	671	669
Contributed surplus	13	13
Retained earnings	67	107
	929	967
Total Liabilities and Shareholders' Equity	$2,364	$2,423

Stelco Inc.
Consolidated Statement of Income
Year Ended December 31, 1993

Revenue		
Sales		$2,491
Equity income		9
		2,500
Expenses		
Cost of sales, exclusive of the following	2,166	
Amortization	122	
Corporate services	32	
Payments to governments other than income taxes	125	2,445
Income from Operations		55
Interest on long-term debt		(78)
Other interest		(7)
Loss before Taxes		(30)
Income taxes		(6)
Net Loss		$ 36

Stelco Inc.
Consolidated Statement of Cash Flow
Year Ended December 31, 1993

Cash Provided by (Used for)	
Operating Activities	
Net loss	$ (36)
Noncash items:	
Amortization	122
Deferred income taxes	(1)
Provision for blast furnace relines	13
Equity income, net of dividends	6
Increase in accounts receivable	(53)
Decrease in inventories	42
Increase in prepaid expenses	(6)
Increase in accounts payable and accrued liabilities	16
Increase in income and other taxes payable	12
Other	10
Cash provided by operating activities	125
Investing Activities	
Expenditures for capital assets	(8)
Long-term investments (net)	(10)
Cash used in investing activities	(18)
Financing Activities	
Net proceeds from sale of common stock	2
Reduction of long-term debt	(52)
Cash used in financing activities	(50)
Net increase in cash	57
Cash, beginning of year	(122)
Cash, end of year	$ (65)*

* Cash is defined as cash and short-term investments less bank indebtedness.

a. Determine, as best you can, the amounts that follow. If you believe that necessary data are lacking, indicate the information you would need.
   (1) 1993 collections from customers
   (2) 1993 payments to suppliers
   (3) 1993 payments to employees
   (4) 1993 payments of interest

b. Can you reconcile the opening balance of capital assets with the December 31, 1993, balance? Were there any disposals of capital assets in 1993? Are you able to account for all transactions affecting accumulated amortization?

c. Can you account for all activity in the "long-term debt" account?

13. *This problem requires that a beginning balance sheet be constructed from an ending balance sheet and a statement of changes in financial position.*

   Methanex Corporation, based in Vancouver, is the world leader in the production and marketing of methanol. Methanol is used as an additive to gasoline to reduce harmful emissions. Shown below are a balance sheet as at December 31, 1993, and a statement of changes in financial position for the year ending December 31, 1993. All dollar amounts are in thousands.

   Reconstruct, as the data permit, Methanex's balance sheet as at December 31, 1992.

Methanex Corporation Balance Sheet December 31, 1993		
Assets		
Current assets		
Cash and cash equivalents		$ 86,222
Accounts receivable		84,825
Inventories		39,242
Prepaid expenses and deposits		12,054
		222,343
Capital assets, at cost	1,122,052	
Less: Accumulated amortization	(423,605)	698,447
Other assets		49,911
Total Assets		$970,701
Liabilities and Shareholders' Equity		
Current liabilities		
Bank indebtedness		$ 916
Accounts payable and accrued liabilities		87,987
Current maturities on long-term debt		32,269
		121,172
Long-term debt		409,069
Deferred income taxes		10,496
Total Liabilities		540,737
Shareholders' Equity		
Common stock		565,763
Deficit		(135,799)
		429,964
Total Liabilities and Shareholders' Equity		$970,701

Methanex Corporation
Statement of Changes in Financial Position
Year Ended December 31, 1993

Cash Provided by (Used in)

Operations

Net income	$10,726
Add (deduct)	
Amortization	57,793
Deferred income taxes	3,328
Other	(340)
Accounts receivable	(34,243)
Inventories	(9,620)
Prepaid expenses and deposits	(1,726)
Accounts payable and accrued liabilities	(17,433)
Cash Provided by Operations	8,485
Financing	
Proceeds on issue of long-term debt	431,270
Repayment of long-term debt	(377,902)
Issue of shares	7,500
Cash Provided by Financing	60,868
Investing	
Purchase of property, plant, and equipment	(69,095)
Purchase of other assets	(9,830)
Cash Used in Investing	(78,925)
Decrease in cash in year	(9,572)
Cash position, beginning of year	94,878
Cash position, end of year	$85,306

14. *Although Canadian firms no longer prepare a statement of changes in financial position on a working capital basis, many non-Canadian firms do. Hence it is useful to be able to convert from the working capital definition of funds to the cash definition of funds.*

The statement of changes in financial position presented below was taken (with minor modifications) from an annual report of Binney and Smith, Inc., the manufacturers of crayons and toys. (All dollar amounts are in thousands.)

Recast the statement, as best the data permit, into a statement of changes in financial position using the cash definition of funds. Use the indirect method, as sufficient data are not available for the direct method.

Sources of Working Capital	
Current operations	
Net earnings before extraordinary charge	$ 9,107
Charges not affecting working capital	
Amortization	2,291
Provision for deferred income taxes	138
Treasury stock provided to employees and charged to compensation expense	280
Working capital provided from operations	$11,816
Working capital used for extraordinary charge	(350)
Increase in long-term debt	111
Property, plant, and equipment sold	276
Proceeds from exercise of stock options	404
Other (net)	288
Total sources of working capital	$12,545

Applications of Working Capital	
Additions to property, plant, and equipment	$ 4,627
Cash dividends on common stock	3,341
Reduction of long-term debt	726
Changes in exchange rates	240
Increase in investment in unconsolidated subsidiary	81
Total uses of working capital	$ 9,015
Increase in working capital	$ 3,530
Changes in Components of Working Capital	
Increase (decrease) in current assets	
Cash	$ 6,131
Accounts receivable	1,959
Inventories	1,558
Prepaid taxes	(148)
Prepaid expenses and other current assets	61
	$ 9,561
Increase (decrease) in current liabilities	
Bank loans	(265)
Payables and accrued expenses	2,586
Accrued income taxes	3,695
Current portion of long-term debt	15
	$ 6,031
Increase in working capital	$ 3,530

15. *The reason for a change in working capital is more important than the magnitude of the change.*

Crown Industries is contemplating acquiring Omega Co. Although Omega reported a loss in 1997, management of Crown is impressed with its increase in working capital.

Comparative balance sheets and income statements of Omega are shown below.

a. By how much did working capital increase during 1997?

b. What were the sources of the increase?

c. Comment on whether the increase in working capital is more likely indicative of financial strength or weakness.

   (1) Compute and compare accounts receivable turnover for 1997 and 1996 (based on year-end accounts receivable balances).

   (2) Compute and compare inventory turnover for 1997 and 1996 (based on year-end inventory balances).

   (3) What is a possible reason for the increases in accounts receivable and inventory?

	1997	1996
Balance Sheet (millions)		
Assets		
Cash	$ 2	$ 4
Accounts receivable	24	12
Inventory	28	16
Long-lived assets	100	100
Accumulated amortization	(34)	(20)
Total assets	$120	$112

Equities		
Accounts payable	$ 24	$ 20
Long-term debt	50	42
Shareholders' equity	46	50
Total equities	$120	$112

Income Statement (millions)

Sales	$160	$140
Cost of goods sold (including amortization)	124	100
Gross margin	$ 36	$ 40
Other expenses	40	36
Net income (loss)	($ 4)	$ 4

16. *Seemingly similar types of transactions may have very different effects on working capital and cash.*

Indicate whether each of the following transactions would increase (I), decrease (D), or have no effect on (NE) the working capital and cash of a company.
a. Declaration of a $150,000 stock dividend
b. Declaration of a $150,000 cash dividend
c. Payment of the previously declared $150,000 cash dividend
d. Purchase of marketable securities for $12,000 cash
e. Sale, for $15,000 cash, of marketable securities that had initially cost $12,000
f. Declaration of $8,000 in dividends by a firm in which the company has a 5 percent interest
g. Declaration of $8,000 in dividends by a firm in which the company has a 40 percent interest
h. Write-off of an uncollectable account of $3,000 against the allowance for doubtful accounts
i. Acquisition of the shares of another company in exchange for $1 million in long-term notes
j. Repurchase of company's own common stock for $4,500 cash
k. Sale for $600 cash of merchandise that had cost $400

17. *Transactions that affect working capital may not affect cash; those that affect cash may not affect working capital.*

The following describes several transactions in which the Ramara Corp. engaged.
(1) Sold merchandise, on account, for $12,000. Cost of the goods sold was $10,000
(2) Collected $3,200 of the amount owed by customers
(3) Purchased additional inventory for $1,700 (on account)
(4) Paid $1,500 of the amount owed to suppliers
(5) Purchased marketable securities for $700 cash
(6) Sold the marketable securities for $900 cash
(7) Recorded one month's interest on notes payable, $50
(8) Paid one month's interest on the notes payable, $50
(9) Recorded one month's rent due from tenant, $200
(10) Received payment of one month's rent from tenant

a. Indicate whether the transactions would increase (I), decrease (D), or have no effect on (NE) the working capital of the corporation.
b. Indicate whether the transactions would increase (I), decrease (D), or have no effect on (NE) the cash balance of the corporation.

Solutions to Exercise for Review and Self-Testing

1. Cash increased by $10.

2. a. Sales increased accounts receivable by $278.
   b. By analysis of accounts receivable, collections from customers were $220:

   $$\text{Beginning balance + Sales − Collections = Ending balance}$$

   $$\text{Collections = Beginning balance − Ending balance + Sales}$$

   $$= \$92 − \$150 + \$278$$

   $$= \$220$$

3. a. Cost of goods sold *decreased* inventory by $200.
   b. By analysis of inventory, purchases were $221:

   $$\text{Beginning balance + Purchases − Cost of goods sold = Ending balance}$$

   $$\text{Purchases = Ending balance − Beginning balance + Cost of goods sold}$$

   $$= \$39 − \$18 + \$200$$

   $$= \$221$$

   c. Purchases increased accounts payable by $221.
   d. By analysis of accounts payable, payments to suppliers were $181:

   $$\text{Beginning balance + Purchases − Payments = Ending balance}$$

   $$\text{Payments = Beginning balance − Ending balance + Purchases}$$

   $$= \$60 − \$100 + \$221$$

   $$= \$181$$

4. a. Amortization expense added $10 to accumulated amortization.
   b. By analysis of accumulated amortization, equipment on which amortization of $4 had been accumulated was sold during the year:

   $$\text{Beginning balance + Amortization expense − Accumulated}$$
   $$\text{amortization on equipment sold = Ending balance}$$

   Accumulated amortization on equipment sold

   $$= \text{Beginning balance − Ending balance + Amortization expense}$$

   $$= \$30 − \$36 + \$10$$

   $$= \$4$$

   c. The equipment had a book value of $8 (cost of $12 less accumulated amortization of $4). It was sold at a loss of $2, per the statement of income. Therefore it was sold for $6.

d. By analysis of the equipment account, purchases of equipment were $7:

$$\text{Beginning balance} + \text{Purchases} - \text{Sales} = \text{Ending balance}$$

$$\text{Purchases} = \text{Ending balance} - \text{Beginning balance} + \text{Sales}$$

$$= \$245 - \$250 + \$12$$

$$= \$7$$

5. a. Deferred income taxes increased by $7.
   b. By analysis of the deferred income tax account, tax payments were $12:

$$\text{Beginning balance} + \text{Tax expense} - \text{Tax payments} = \text{Ending balance}$$

$$\text{Tax payments} = \text{Beginning balance} - \text{Ending balance} + \text{Tax expense}$$

$$= \$4 - \$11 + \$19$$

$$= \$12$$

6. a. Bond discount decreased by $1.
   b. Interest expense would have been recorded as follows:

Interest expense		$17
Bond discount		$ 1
Cash		16

   c. The cash interest payment was $16.

7. a. Retained earnings increased by $30. The entire increase is attributable to earnings.
   b. All changes in balance sheet accounts have been accounted for by the analysis above.
   c. Summary of cash receipts and disbursements:

Collections from customers	$220
Payments to suppliers	(181)
Payments of interest	(16)
Payments of taxes	(12)
Sale of equipment	6
Purchase of equipment	(7)
Net increase in cash	$ 10

This summary accounts for the net change in the cash balance.

15

Accounting for Changes in Prices

The limitations of historic cost-based financial statements have been referred to in previous chapters. In the chapters on marketable securities, inventories, and long-lived assets we examined how the effects of changes in prices might be incorporated into the accounting for those items. In this chapter we illustrate a full set of statements that reflect not only changes in the prices of specific resources but also the effects of general inflation. A related area, the conversion of financial measurements from one currency to another, is also introduced.

After studying this chapter, you will be able to

- Understand the difference between changes in specific prices and changes in the general price level
- Describe four possible accounting models that distinguish between changes in specific prices and changes in the general price level
- Prepare current cost/nominal dollar financial statements
- Prepare current cost/constant dollar financial statements
- Calculate purchasing power gains and losses from holding monetary items
- Understand the difference between integrated foreign operations and self-sustaining foreign operations for purposes of translating foreign currency financial statements

In the first major section of this chapter, we present a *current cost/constant dollar* model of accounting. This model is not today an integral part of generally accepted accounting principles (GAAP) in Canada. It is therefore not widely used by corporations in their reports to the public.

Why should students in an introductory financial accounting course be concerned with accounting practices that are not used today and may thereby seem to be of no more than academic interest? For at least two reasons: First, by understanding the alternative practices, one will obtain greater insight into the accepted practices. The discussion to follow highlights the limitations of historical cost-based statements. The rationale for the presentation is not that current cost/constant dollar accounting is necessarily preferable to historical cost accounting. Instead, it is that each model has positive and negative features. The historical cost model is the one that is generally accepted today. Nevertheless, both managers and investors (to the extent they can obtain the necessary data) should be able to convert to a current cost model when the information provided is better suited to the specific decisions at hand.

Second, it is widely recognized that the accounting profession has not yet dealt adequately with the issues of changing prices. As discussed in Chapter 8, in 1982 the CICA issued Section 4510 of the *CICA Handbook*, "Reporting the Effects of Changing Prices," recommending that certain large, public companies present current cost data in the notes that supplement their financial statements. In 1992, in the face of evidence that the information was not widely used, Section 4510 was removed from the *CICA Handbook*. In fact, for a number of years prior to its removal, most companies covered by Section 4510 were not providing the recommended supplementary disclosure. As an alternative to Section 4510, the CICA is currently considering the publication of a booklet summarizing the history of reporting the effects of changing prices, along with guidance to management on how to incorporate the effects of changing prices into their discussion and analysis of their financial results.

During the early and mid-1990s, the rate of inflation has been relatively low in Canada and most other industrialized countries. Hence the absence of concern on the part of both statement users and rule-making authorities is understandable. Nevertheless, there are inevitably "carry-over" effects from years when price changes were substantial to years when they were small. For example, current cost amortization would continue to be considerably greater than historical cost amortization. Should the rate of price increases accelerate in the future, there is sure to be renewed attention to the issues of current value accounting. Accountants, investors, and managers are certain to be affected by any new accounting remedies that will then be proposed.

THE ISSUES IN PERSPECTIVE

The central issues underlying almost all accounting problems turn on *recognition* and *measurement*. *When* does a firm recognize the *existence of or changes in the values of assets or liabilities? How* does a firm *measure* what it wishes to recognize? Or (inasmuch as the balance sheet must *articulate with* the income statement), when and how should *revenues* and *expenses* resulting from the value changes be measured and recognized?

The earliest—and indeed simplest—accounting systems recognized changes in values (and hence revenues and expenses) only on the basis of formal *exchanges,* most typically transactions involving cash. As discussed in Chapter 3, however, cash-based accounting fails to capture significant economic events in the period in which they have their primary impact. For example, rent would be reported as revenue when received under a cash-based accounting system rather than when earned.

Modern-day accounting systems are accrual-based and thereby reflect economic events in addition to those involving transactions. They thereby better meet the criteria that accounting information be both *relevant* and *reliable.*

A Matter of Timing

The issue of whether to recognize changes in the value of assets and liabilities due to changes in prices is simply an extension of revenue and expense recognition problems as applied to normal accruals. Should a firm record changes in values consequent upon changes in prices even though no transaction *by the firm* has taken place? Should accountants try to incorporate the impact of price changes into the basic accounts? These are questions which have split accountants over the years. Some have asserted that the verifiability of financial statements will suffer if changing prices are acounted for as they occur; others insist that the *relevance* and *representational faithfulness* of statements will be diminished if changing prices are *not* accounted for.

Consider the Schaefer Corporation example of Chapter 2. Suppose that corporate management elected to locate a store in the centre of town rather than in a suburban shopping mall. They chose the in-town site anticipating that the city would undertake an economic revitalization plan for the area surrounding the store. Having forecast correctly, they saw the value of their property increase by over 25 percent immediately upon the decision of the city council to undertake its improvement program.

The bookstore will reap the benefits (cash flows) of the revitalization either through *use* of the property and enhanced sales over its years of operation or through the *sale* of its property. The accounting issue is one of timing—when to recognize the gain. Current value advocates would say that it should be recognized when there is measurable evidence that the property has increased in value. In that way the gain would be assigned to a period within the tenure of the management team that made the correct location decision. It was in that period, after all, that there was an increase in the value of the company's assets (resources that are expected to yield future economic benefits). Countering objections that the property values might subsequently fall, they would contend that a loss should be recognized when the values decline. Thus income should not be smoothed by offsetting gains of one period with potential losses of another.

Changes in Specific Prices versus Changes in the General Price Level

Prices of goods and services increase or decrease for at least two reasons. First, there might be a change in either the demand for or supply of a specific product. A change in either would affect market value. Second, the purchasing power of the monetary unit (e.g., the dollar) may change. On average, taking into account all goods and services bought and sold in the economy, the monetary unit might buy more or less today than in a previous period. Although the number of monetary units required to buy a product might change, the price relationship between the product and that of other goods or services will remain the same. Increases in the number of monetary units required to purchase a typical *basket* of consumer goods is referred to as *inflation*.

Example

Suppose that in December 1996 a company acquired land at a cost of $100,000 and sold it in December 1997 for $125,000—an apparent gain of $25,000 dollars. Assume further, however, that during the year, the general level of prices increased by 15 percent. That is, a basket of typical consumer items that could have been purchased in December 1996 for $1,000 would have cost $1,150 in December 1997. In terms of goods and services—the only terms in which a dollar has meaning—it can be said that 1.00 1996 dollar was the equivalent of 1.15 1997 dollars:

$$\$^{96} 1.00 = \$^{97} 1.15$$

Most often the general price level is stated as an index value. One widely cited index is the *Consumer Price Index (CPI)*, maintained by Statistics Canada. The CPI expresses prices of various years as percentages of prices of a selected base year. The base year is assigned a value of 100. If, for example, 1996 is the base year, then the price level of 1997, in which prices are 15 percent higher, would be 115.

Thus the land acquired for $100,000 nominal (unadjusted) 1996 dollars must be thought of as having been acquired for $115,000 *1997 dollars*. The $115,000 was derived by multiplying the acquisition cost by the ratio of the 1997 price index value to that of the 1996 value:

$$\$100,000 \times 115/100 = \$115,000$$

The gain on sale, expressed in *constant* dollars—in this case, dollars of December 1997—is therefore only $10,000, rather than $25,000 in *nominal* (unadjusted) dollars:

Sales price, 1997 dollars	$125,000
Acquisition cost, 1997 dollars	115,000
Gain on sale, 1997 dollars	$ 10,000

FOUR POSSIBLE ACCOUNTING MODELS

The distinction between changes in *specific prices* (or values) and changes in the *general price level* suggests that accounting models can take at least four forms:

1. *Historical costs/nominal dollars.* This is the traditional accounting model, with resources stated at historical costs, without adjustment for changes in price levels.

2. *Historical costs/constant dollars.* In this model, resources are stated at their historical costs, expressed in dollars of the balance sheet (current) date rather than dollars of acquisition date.

3. *Current costs/nominal dollars.* In this model, resources are adjusted to take into account changes in market values, but no recognition is given to changes in the purchasing power of the dollar.

4. *Current costs/constant dollars.* Under this structure, resources are stated at market values, adjusted for changes in the purchasing power of the dollar.

Example

A company purchased land for $100,000 in December 1996. The land rose in value to $125,000 by December 1997. Retaining the land for another year, the firm then sold it on December 31, 1998, for $130,000. The price level was 100 when the company acquired the land. It was 115 on December 31, 1997; it was 127 on December 31, 1998.

EXHIBIT 15-1
Comparison of Four Accounting Models

Acquisition cost of land	$100,000
Market value of land, December 31, 1997	$125,000
Market value of land, December 31, 1998	$130,000
Constant dollars are those of December 31, 1998	
Consumer Price Index, December 31, 1996	100
Consumer Price Index, December 31, 1997	115
Consumer Price Index, December 31, 1998	127

	Historical Costs/Nominal Dollars	Historical Costs/Constant (1998) Dollars	Current Costs/Nominal Dollars	Current Costs/Constant (1998) Dollars
Acquisition cost of land, December 31, 1996	$100,000	$127,000[1]	$100,000[2]	$127,000[1]
Book value of land, December 31, 1997	100,000	127,000[1]	125,000[3]	138,043[4]
Gain on land, 1997	0	0	25,000	11,043
Sale price of land, December 31, 1998	130,000	130,000	130,000	130,000
Gain on land, 1998[5]	30,000	3,000	5,000	(8,043)

[1] $100,000 × 1.27/1.00.

[2] Market value of land on December 31, 1996.

[3] Market value of land on December 31, 1997.

[4] Market value of $125,000 × 1.27/1.15—the ratio of the purchasing power of the dollar on December 31, 1998 (1.27) to that of December 31, 1997 (1.15).

[5] Sale price of land less book value of land on December 31, 1997.

Exhibit 15-1 compares the book value of the land under each of the four models. It also shows the reported income (gain on land) for 1997 and 1998 using each model. Total income is the difference between the selling price of the land on December 31, 1998, and its acquisition cost on December 31, 1996. Notice that under the two nominal-dollar models, the firm earned income for the two years combined of $30,000, whereas under the two constant-dollar models it had income of only $3,000 (expressed in the monetary unit of 1998). Thus, in actual purchasing power, the firm gained only $3,000. Further, the *division* of the total gains (both nominal and real) between the two years differs sharply by model. Under the current cost models a portion of the income is assigned to 1997, whereas under the historical cost models, the entire income is allocated to 1998. Under the historical cost models the management team of 1997 would have received no credit for the increase in value that occurred during that year.

DOES IT MAKE A DIFFERENCE?

The *CICA Handbook,* Section 4510, required what was, in essence, *current cost/constant dollar* information. Exhibit 15-2 illustrates the disclosures of Inco Limited for the year ended June 30, 1983. Current cost *operating* loss for 1983 was $259 million as compared to historical cost loss of $235 million—a difference of 10 percent! Net current cost assets were $2,748 million compared with historical cost assets of $1,027 million—a variation of 167 percent!

EXHIBIT 15-2
Inco Limited and Subsidiaries

Consolidated Statement of Income from Continuing Operations Adjusted for Changing Prices		
	Dollars in Millions	
Year Ended June 30, 1983	As Reported in the Primary Statements (historical/ nominal dollars)	Adjusted for Changes in Specific Prices (current costs)
Net sales and other income	$1,195	$1,195
Cost of goods sold (excluding depreciation and depletion expenses)	$1,132	$1,071
Depreciation and depletion expense	126	259
Selling, general and administrative expenses (excluding depreciation expense)	102	106
Interest expense—net	112	112
Research and development expense	29	34
Exploration expenses	20	20
Provision for mining and income taxes	(91)	(91)
Loss from continuing operations	(235)	(316)
Gain from decline in purchasing power of net amounts owed		57
Total	$ (235)	$ (259)

Increase in current cost of inventories and property, plant, and equipment held during the year*	$ 66	
Effect of increase in general price level	173	
Excess of increase in general price level over specific prices	$ 107	

* At December 31, 1983, current cost of inventories was $773 million and current cost of property, plant, and equipment, net of accumulated depreciation, was $3,723 million.

Five-Year Comparison of Selected Supplementary Financial Data Adjusted for Effects of Changing Prices*

	Dollars in Millions (except per share data)				
Year Ended December 31	1983	1982	1981	1980	1979
Net sales and other income					
Constant dollar	$ 1,195	$ 1,318	$ 2,094	$2,644	$ 2,255
Historical	1,195	1,277	1,912	2,187	1,643
Income (loss) from continuing operations					
Current cost	$ (316)	$ (324)	$ (255)	$ (24)	$ (78)
Historical	(235)	(203)	20	262	142
Income from continuing operations per common share					
Current cost	$ (3.54)	$ (4.29)	$ (3.75)	$(0.74)	$ (1.47)
Historical	(2.69)	(2.81)	(0.10)	3.12	1.58
Gain from decline in purchasing power of net amounts owed	$ 57	$ 65	$ 151	$ 212	$254
Net assets at year end					
Current cost	$ 2,748	$ 3,052	$ 3,466	$4,139	$ 3,944
Historical	1,027	1,216	1,333	1,859	1,688
Excess of general inflation over (under) increase in specific prices of inventories and property, plant, and equipment	$107	$245	$ (35)	$ 79	$ 182
Dividends declared per common share					
Constant dollar	$ 0.20	$ 0.21	$ 0.65	$ 0.83	$ 0.69
Historical	0.20	0.20	0.59	0.69	0.50
Market price per common share at year end					
Constant dollar	$ 14.38	$ 12.13	$ 15.61	$24.64	$ 32.60
Historical	14.63	11.75	14.25	20.38	23.75
Average consumer price index (1967 = 100)	298.4	289.1	272.4	246.8	217.4

*All constant dollar and current cost amounts are stated in average fiscal year 1983 dollars.

As with most companies, a substantial portion of the difference in income results from the greater depreciation (note the use of the word depreciation here; prior to 1990, the term depreciation was used rather than amortization) charged under the current cost/constant dollar model. The additional depreciation is attributable to the restated value of long-lived plant assets, which had been acquired many years earlier. However, in Inco's case, the effect of the high inflation of the early 1980s is evident. The increase in the current cost of inventories, plant, and equipment of $66 million is net of a $173 million increase due to the increase in the general price level. This means that the specific costs of inventories and plant and equipment actually decreased in nominal dollars during 1983.

The reason for not using more recent financial statements (than Inco 1983) to illustrate the Section 4510 disclosure is the fact that most Canadian companies that were required to provide the supplementary disclosure never did. The few that did provide the information gradually stopped providing it by the mid- to late 1980s. Inco's disclosure, until 1983, was quite comprehensive due to the fact that it is listed on the New York Stock Exchange and was providing current cost information under U.S. GAAP as well as under Section 4510.

The extent of differences between traditional statements and current cost statements are not the same for all firms. They are affected by the average asset age, rate of turnover, and proportion of assets and liabilities that are monetary (having a specified dollar amount, such as accounts receivables and payables) rather than nonmonetary.

ADJUSTING HISTORICAL COST STATEMENTS FOR CHANGES IN SPECIFIC PRICES

In this section we demonstrate a general approach to adjusting historical cost accounts for changes in *specific* prices. Thus we illustrate a model based on *current costs/nominal dollars*. In a following section we extend the model to encompass changes in the overall level of prices (inflation), thereby transforming it into a *current cost/constant dollar* model. *Current cost* is used to mean an *input value*—the amount that it would cost to *replace* an asset.[1]

Historical cost statements of Daniel Gee, Inc., are presented in Exhibits 15-3 through 15-5. Exhibit 15-6 contains additional information relating to the firm. The company was incorporated on December 31, 1996, and all assets and liabilities are stated at their current costs as at that

EXHIBIT 15-3

Daniel Gee, Inc. Balance Sheets as at December 31, 1997 and 1996				
		1997		1996
Assets				
Cash		$ 46,000		$180,000
Accounts receivable		300,000		0
Merchandise inventory		260,000		100,000
Land		60,000		60,000
Building	$400,000		$400,000	
Less: Accumulated amortization	20,000	380,000	0	400,000
Equipment	250,000		250,000	
Less: Accumulated amortization	50,000	200,000	0	250,000
Total assets		$1,246,000		$990,000

[1] In a variation of the model presented, current cost could be defined as an *exit* value—the amount for which an asset could be sold. See Phillip W. Bell, *CVA, CCA and CoCoA: How Fundamental Are the Differences?* Australian Accounting Research Foundation, Melbourne, 1982, pp. 35–36, for a discussion of the two approaches.

Liabilities and shareholders' equity		
Accounts payable	$ 160,000	$ 0
Bonds payable	400,000	400,000
Common stock	590,000	590,000
Retained earnings	96,000	0
Total liabilities and shareholders' equity	$1,246,000	$990,000

EXHIBIT 15-4

Daniel Gee, Inc.
Statement of Income
and Changes in Retained Earnings
Year Ended December 31, 1997

Sales revenue		$1,890,000
Less expenses		
Cost of goods sold	$1,400,000	
Amortization, building	20,000	
Amortization, equipment	50,000	
Interest	64,000	
Selling and administrative	90,000	1,624,000
Net income		$ 266,000
Dividends		170,000
Increase in retained earnings		$ 96,000

EXHIBIT 15-5

Daniel Gee, Inc.
Statement of Changes in Financial Position
Year Ended December 31, 1997

Operating Activities	
Collections from customers	$ 1,590,000
Payments to suppliers	(1,400,000)
Payment of selling and administrative costs	(90,000)
Payment of interest	(64,000)
Cash provided by operating activities	$ 36,000
Financing Activities	
Payment of dividends	$ (170,000)
Change in cash	$ (134,000)

EXHIBIT 15-6
Additional Information Relating to Daniel Gee, Inc.

Analysis of Inventory, 1997 (FIFO Basis)	
Beginning inventory (5,000 units @ $20)	$ 100,000
+ Purchases (65,000 units @ an average price of $24)	1,560,000
= Goods available for sale (70,000 units)	1,660,000
− Ending inventory (10,000 units @ $26)	(260,000)
= Cost of goods sold (60,000 units)	$1,400,000

Building and Equipment, Useful Life and Amortization
Building: 20 years; $20,000 per year ($400,000/20 years)
Equipment: 5 years; $50,000 per year ($250,000/5 years)

Bonds
On December 31, 1996, the company issued $400,000 10-year, 16 percent bonds at par.
Required interest payments are $32,000 every six months.

Year-End Current Cost Information
Inventory: During the year 65,000 units were purchased at an average price of $24. Year-end price lists indicate that the market value of the 10,000 units in ending inventory is $27 per unit—$270,000.

Land: Records of area transactions indicate that during 1997 the market value of land increased by 30 percent from $60,000 to $78,000.

Building: Government-prepared indices of construction costs suggest that the replacement cost of the firm's building increased from $400,000 at acquisition date to $460,000. The building has an economic life of 40 years.

Equipment: Price lists of used equipment indicate the following replacements costs as at December 31, 1996 and 1997:

EXHIBIT 15-6 **(continued)**

	1997	1996
New equipment	$280,000	250,000
One-year-old equipment	210,000	250,000

Bonds: Interest rates on comparable bonds declined from 16 percent to 12 percent. The decline took place at midyear, after the first interest payment had been made. The decline caused the market value of the bonds to increase to $489,263. On December 31, 1997, after the second payment of interest, the bonds had a market value of $486,619.

Values of the Consumer Price Index
December 31, 1996	100
June 30, 1997	105
December 31, 1997	110

date. The fashioning of current cost/nominal dollar statements, shown as an end product in Exhibits 15-7 and 15-8, proceeds as illustrated in the section that follows.

The Current Cost/Nominal Dollar Balance Sheet

Under current cost/nominal dollar accounting, the balance sheet is conceptually straightforward. Both assets and liabilities are to be stated at their current values.

Cash, Accounts Receivable, and Accounts Payable

Cash, accounts receivable, and accounts payable are stated at the same value as on historical cost statements. Their current value is typically face value (less allowances for uncollectables or discounts for unearned interest).[2]

Other Nonamortizable Assets: Inventory and Land

Both merchandise inventory and land are recorded at current values. Thus for Daniel Gee, Inc., merchandise inventory would be stated at current replacement cost of $270,000 (10,000 units at $27) and land at $78,000.

Buildings and Equipment

Amortizable assets such as buildings and equipment are reported at current cost *less* an allowance for accumulated amortization. In our example, buildings will be accounted for slightly differently than equipment. For buildings, we are provided information on the amount required to *construct* a *new* building; there are no direct data available on what it would cost to *acquire* a comparable building of the same age and condition as the one owned.

The current cost of constructing the new building is $460,000. It is one year old and is being amortized over 20 years. Current cost accumulated amortization after one year must be 5 percent of its current cost new—$23,000.

---

[2] In some firms, such as banks and finance companies, accounts receivable are assets comparable to marketable securities. They are freely bought and sold. In those situations, the receivables should be stated at market value rather than adjusted face value.

For equipment we know not only the cost of *new* equipment, but also the market value of *used* equipment. The replacement cost of the new equipment is $280,000, that of one-year-old used equipment is $210,000. Thus on a current cost basis, the amortization for the first year of use, in terms of market value, is $70,000. The current cost balance sheet would show accumulated amortization as the difference between the current values of the new and the used equipment:

Equipment (current value, new)	$280,000
Less: Accumulated amortization	70,000
Equipment (current value, used)	$210,000

Bonds Payable

There is an active market for bonds and hence the issuer can retire its bonds by purchasing them in the open market. Daniel Gee, Inc., issued its $400,000 of bonds at face value. Therefore at issue date, the coupon rate of 16 percent was equal to prevailing interest rates. Six months later, however, interest rates dropped from 16 percent to 12 percent. Consequently, the market price increased to $489,263.[3] By December 31, 1997, the market price had fallen to $486,619. But this decline in value did not reflect a further change in interest rates. Instead, it resulted only from the passage of time which made the bonds one period closer to maturity.[4]

On the December 31, 1997, current cost balance sheet, the bonds would be shown at current market value of $486,619.

---

[3] The value of $400,000 in 16 percent coupon bonds (8 percent or $32,000 per period), with 19 periods remaining, sold to yield 12 percent (6 percent per period) would be

Present value of principal (per Table 2, present value of a single payment), 6%, 19 periods, $400,000 × .33051*	$132,204
Present value of interest (per Table 4, present value of an annuity), 6%, 19 periods, $32,000 × 11.15811*	357,059
Total present value	$489,263

*These present value factors are somewhat more precise than that found in Tables 2 and 4 since they are carried to five decimal places rather than only four. The reason for using the five-decimal-place factors is to avoid reconciliation problems due to rounding errors when calculating the realizable holding gain or loss on the bonds payable. The five-decimal-place present value factors will be used for all bonds payable market value calculations in this chapter.

[4] The value of $400,000 in 16 percent coupon bonds (8 percent or $32,000 per period), with 18 periods remaining, sold to yield 12 percent (6 percent per period) would be

Present value of principal (per Table 2, present value of a single payment), 6%, 18 periods, $400,000 × .35034	$140,136
Present value of interest (per Table 4, present value of an annuity), 6%, 18 periods, $32,000 × 10.82760	346,483
Total present value	$486,619

Shareholders' Equity

Shareholders' equity, because it is a residual, is reported as the difference between assets and liabilities. The paid-in portion is stated at historical cost amounts; the change in ownership equity, incorporating current cost adjustments, is made to retained earnings. The change in retained earnings is the net sum of the adjustments to the other accounts. The current cost balance sheet of Daniel Gee, Inc., is presented in Exhibit 15-7.

Current cost retained earnings must, of course, reconcile with current cost retained earnings of the previous period (i.e., be equal to beginning balance plus income less dividends). It is this reconciliation, which represents a fundamental check between the income statement and the comparative balance sheets, to which we turn our attention in the section that follows.

EXHIBIT 15-7

Daniel Gee, Inc. Current Cost Balance Sheets as at December 31, 1997 and 1996		1997		1996
Assets				
Cash		$ 46,000		$180,000
Accounts receivable		300,000		0
Merchandise inventory		270,000		100,000
Land		78,000		60,000
Building	$460,000		$400,000	
Less: Accumulated amortization	23,000	437,000	0	400,000
Equipment	280,000		250,000	
Less: Accumulated amortization	70,000	210,000	0	250,000
Total assets		$1,341,000		$990,000
Liabilities and shareholders' equity				
Accounts payable		$ 160,000		$ 0
Bonds payable	$400,000		$400,000	
Plus: Current cost adjustment	86,619	486,619	0	400,000
Common stock		590,000		590,000
Retained earnings		104,381		0
Total liabilities and shareholders' equity		$1,341,000		$990,000

The Income Statement

Two main types of adjustments are required to convert a historical cost income statement to a current cost income statement. First, *realizable* holding gains or losses must be recorded for each asset and liability that has been adjusted. Second, expenses must be amended to express the sale or consumption of resources based on their current, rather than their historical, costs.

A *realizable* holding gain is the total gain on assets or liabilities that takes place during the year on resources that both remain on hand at year end and were sold or consumed during the year. It is based exclusively on changes in prices that took place during the current year. As the assets which increased in value are "used up" through consumption or are sold, a portion of the realizable holding gain is realized. The portion realized through use is the amount by which the asset-related expense based on current costs exceeds the expense based on historical costs. Realizable gains on amortizable assets are realized by way of additional amortization expense; realizable gains on merchandise inventory are realized through additions to cost of goods sold.

To digress briefly from the Daniel Gee, Inc., case, suppose, for example, that in 1997 a firm acquired 1,000 units of merchandise at $100 per unit. At the beginning of the year the current value of the goods suddenly increased to $120 per unit. The realizable holding gain for 1997 would be $20 per unit—$20,000, in total. If the firm now sells the merchandise, current cost of goods sold would be $120 per unit—$20 more than historical cost of goods sold—and the realizable gain would thereby be realized. If the firm sold 750 units in 1997, it would realize $15,000 of the realizable gain—$20 times 750. If it sold the remaining 250 units in 1998, it would then realize the remaining $5,000 of the realizable gain—$20 times 250. The table that follows shows how the realizable holding gain affects income both at the time it takes place and in the periods in which it is realized. The table incorporates the further assumption that the selling price of the goods was $150 per unit.

	Current Cost		Historical Cost	
	1998	1997	1998	1997
Sales revenue (250 and 750 units sold @ $150)	$37,500	$112,500	$37,500	$112,500
Realizable holding gain	0	20,000	—	—
Total revenue	37,500	132,500	37,500	112,500
Cost of goods sold:				
Historical ($100 per unit)	25,000	75,000	25,000	75,000
Realized holding gain ($20 per unit)	5,000	15,000	—	—
Total cost of goods sold	30,000	90,000	25,000	75,000
Net income	$ 7,500	$ 42,500	$12,500	$ 37,500

Total income over the two years under each of the two models is the same. The realizable gain under the current cost model is offset by its subsequent realization. In essence, if the current cost of an asset increases, more expense will ultimately be incurred as the asset is charged to expense over the life of the asset.

In the income statement of Daniel Gee, Inc., realizable gains and losses are reported in a separate section of the income statement. The realized portions are included in their related expenses (e.g., cost of gods sold, amortization, interest).

Realizable Holding Gain on Inventory and Current Cost of Goods Sold

As illustrated in Chapter 8, the *realizable holding gain* can be determined by subtracting the period's *inputs* into the trading process (beginning inventory plus purchases), computed at current cost, from the period's *outputs* (ending inventory plus costs of goods sold), also computed at current cost. The formula for the realizable holding gain is based on the traditional equation for cost of goods sold:

$$
\begin{array}{ll}
& \text{Beginning inventory} \\
+ & \text{Purchases} \\
- & \underline{\text{Ending inventory}} \\
= & \text{Cost of goods sold}
\end{array}
$$

When the realizable holding gain is added:

$$
\begin{array}{ll}
& \text{Beginning inventory} \\
+ & \text{Purchases} \\
+ & \text{Realizable holding gains} \\
- & \underline{\text{Ending inventory}} \\
= & \text{Cost of goods sold}
\end{array}
$$

The terms have been rearranged and expressed in current costs:

$$
\begin{array}{ll}
& \text{Ending inventory at current cost} \\
+ & \text{Current cost of goods sold} \\
- & \text{Beginning inventory at current cost} \\
- & \underline{\text{Purchases}} \\
= & \text{Realizable holding gain}
\end{array}
$$

For Daniel Gee, Inc., then, we have

Outputs		
Ending inventory at current cost	$ 270,000	
Current cost of goods sold	1,440,000	$1,710,000
Less: Inputs		
Beginning inventory at current cost	100,000	
Purchases	1,560,000	1,660,000
Realizable holding gain on inventory		$ 50,000

The realizable holding gain is the *cost saving* achieved by company management by purchasing goods prior to a price increase.

Ending inventory of $270,000 is the amount reported in the current cost balance sheet in Exhibit 15-7. The current cost of goods sold of $1,440,000 is the 60,000 units sold times the average 1997 purchase price of $24. Because the company began operations in December 1996, the current cost ($100,000) of beginning inventory is the same as historical cost. Similarly, the current cost of 1997 purchases ($1,560,000) is also the same as historical cost.[5]

---

[5] The adjustments required to convert the historical inventory and related accounts to a current cost basis can be made by journal entries:

Merchandise inventory, current cost increment $50,000
    Realizable holding gain $50,000
To recognize the realizable holding gain

Cost of goods sold, current cost increment $40,000
    Merchandise inventory, current cost increment $40,000
To recognize the using up (i.e., the realization) of the holding gain

The $10,000 balance in "merchandise inventory, current cost increment" is carried over as a balance sheet debit to be added to the historical cost inventory balance of $260,000. This yields the $270,000 appearing in the current cost balance sheet in Exhibit 15-7.

Realizable Holding Gain on Land

Land increased in value by $18,000 during the year. This amount is the realizable holding gain. No land was consumed through either sale or amortization during the year. Hence no portion of the holding gain was *realized* during the year. It will be realized only when the land is sold.

Realizable Holding Gain on Assets Subject to Amortization and Current Cost Amortization

The current cost of the building new is $460,000; its historical cost is $400,000. The realizable holding gain is therefore $60,000.

The realizable holding gain for the building, like that for the inventory, is equal to the current year's outputs minus inputs. For assets subject to amortization, *outputs* are the current value of the building (net of amortization) at the end of the year and the portion of the building consumed during the year (i.e., current cost amortization). *Inputs* are the current value of the building at the beginning of the period plus additions during the year. Thus

$$\begin{array}{rl} & \text{Ending balance (net) at current cost} \\ + & \text{Current cost amortization} \\ - & \text{Beginning balance (net) at current cost} \\ - & \text{Additions} \\ \hline = & \text{Realizable holding gain} \end{array}$$

For Daniel Gee, Inc., then, we have

Outputs		
Ending balance (net) at current cost	$437,000	
Current cost amortization	23,000	$460,000
Less: inputs		
Beginning balance (net) at current cost	400,000	
Additions	0	400,000
Realizable holding gain on building		$ 60,000[6]

Annual *current cost* amortization charges for the building, which has an expected useful life of 20 years, would be $23,000—current cost of $460,000 divided by 20 years. This compares to historical cost amortization of $20,000. Hence $3,000 of the realizable holding gain would be realized each year.

The current value of the equipment new is $280,000. Beginning balance at market (which in this example is the same as historical cost) is $250,000. The realizable holding gain is therefore $30,000:

---

[6] These calculations, for both current cost amortization and realizable holding gain, are based on the assumption that prices "jumped" at the start of the year. If we were to make the more realistic assumption that prices rose gradually throughout the year (or jumped by the full amount *after* a half-year's amortization was charged, which has the same effect) then current cost amortization would be only $21,500 ($10,000 for the first half-year based on an asset value of $400,000, and $11,500 for the second based on an asset value of $460,000). The realizable holding gain would be only $58,500. In effect, a half-year-old asset, valued at $390,000 (net of amortization), is assumed to rise in price at midyear by 15 percent to $448,500 (net of amortization).

Outputs		
Ending balance (net) at current cost	$210,000	
Current cost amortization	70,000	$280,000
Less: Inputs		
Beginning balance (net) at current cost	250,000	
Additions	0	250,000
Realizable holding gain on equipment		$ 30,000

As pointed out in the section which addressed the balance sheet valuation of the equipment, current cost accumulated amortization at year end is the $70,000 difference between the current cost of new equipment and the current cost of one-year-old equipment. We assume that viable markets exist for both new and used equipment and quotes of current prices are readily available.

Inasmuch as this is the first year of operations, the accumulated amortization account had a zero balance at the start of the year. Therefore the entire $70,000 must be added to accumulated amortization and correspondingly charged as amortization expense. Historical cost amortization would be only $50,000. The $20,000 difference is the portion of the realizable holding gain that is realized in the current year.[7]

Realizable Holding Loss on Bonds Payable and Current Cost Interest Expense

Interest rates dropped gradually over the period from 16 percent to 12 percent. This is equivalent to assuming a sudden drop in rates at midyear (after the payment of interest for the first six-month period). Thus it can be assumed that the bonds increased in value from $400,000 to $489,263 at midyear. This increase resulted in a realizable holding *loss* of $89,263, the added amount that the company would now have to pay to retire the bonds by purchasing them in the open market.

Current cost interest expense must be based on the current value of the bonds and the prevailing rates of interest. Under these assumptions, current cost interest for the first half of the year prior to the change in interest rates would be 8 percent of $400,000 (thus $32,000), while current cost interest for the second half of the year would be 6 percent of $489,263 (thus $29,356). Total current cost interest would therefore be $61,356.

Historical cost interest expense would be the same in both periods— $32,000 ($64,000 for the year). The $2,644 difference between current cost and historical cost interest is the portion of the realizable holding loss that is *realized* in the current period because the firm is using money that has been borrowed at more than the current rate of interest.

From a more general perspective, realizable holding losses or gains on bonds, like those on assets, can be determined by comparing outputs and inputs. In this example, for instance, we have

---

[7] In this example, $20,000 of the total realizable gain of $30,000 will be realized in the current year, even though the anticipated useful life of the equipment is five years. The disproportionately large charge in the current year can be attributed to the relationship between the prices for new and used equipment. One-year-old equipment is selling for only 75 percent of the price of new equipment. By contrast, historical cost accounting would assign a net book value to the equipment after one year of 80 percent of initial cost.

Comparable computations would be made for the holding gains or losses on the building, equipment, and bonds payable:

	Unadjusted Amounts	Conversion Factor	Adjusted Amounts (31/12/97 dollars)
Building			
Outputs			
Ending balance at current cost	$437,000	110/110	$437,000
Current cost amortization	23,000	110/105	24,096
	$460,000		$461,096
Less: Inputs			
Beginning balance at current cost	400,000	110/100	440,000
Additions	0		0
	400,000		440,000
Realizable holding gain on building	$ 60,000		$ 21,096
Equipment			
Outputs			
Ending balance at current cost	$210,000	110/110	$210,000
Current cost amortization	70,000	110/105	73,333
	$280,000		$283,333
Less: Inputs			
Beginning balance at current cost	250,000	110/100	275,000
Additions	0		0
	250,000		275,000
Realizable holding gain on equipment	$ 30,000		$ 8,333
Bonds Payable			
Outputs			
Ending balance at current cost	$486,619	110/110	$486,619
Cash paid in interest	64,000	110/105	67,048
Cash paid for bond retirements or additions	0		0
	550,619		553,667
Inputs			
Beginning balance at current cost	400,000	110/100	440,000
Current cost of bond interest	61,356	110/105	64,278
	461,356		504,278
Realizable holding loss (gain) on bonds payable	$ 89,263		$ 49,389

Purchasing Power Gains and Losses from Holding Monetary Items

Third, the purchasing power gain or loss from holding monetary items must be computed. This is one of the most significant measures derived by adjusting the financial statements for changes in the general level of prices. If a company holds monetary assets during a period of rising prices, it incurs a monetary (purchasing power) loss. Its monetary assets are worth less, in terms of what they can purchase, at the end of the period than at the beginning. If it holds monetary liabilities (i.e., is indebted to others), it realizes a monetary (purchasing power) gain. It can satisfy its obligations in dollars that are worth less than when the debts were initially assumed.

To digress once again from Daniel Gee, Inc., suppose that throughout a year a firm held $100,000 in cash and accounts receivable. At the beginning of the year, a price index was at 200; at the end of the year it was at 240. Had it held assets that could have been transformed into year-end dollars, the firm would have been able to exchange the assets (assuming no change in intrinsic values) for $100,000 times 240/200, or $120,000. It would thereby have retained the same purchasing power. Instead, however, at year end it had only $100,000 in purchasing power, when $120,000 was needed to acquire the same goods and services. In terms of year-end dollars, it incurred a purchasing power loss of $20,000.

The overall gain or loss in purchasing power resulting from holding monetary items can be determined by subtracting the face amount of the items at the end of the period from the amount of current dollars that would be required to achieve the same purchasing power if there had been no decline in the value of the dollar. However, insofar as the monetary items are acquired in the middle of a period, then the purchasing power gain or loss must be measured from the date the item was acquired to the end of the year. If monetary items are disposed of during the year, then the gain or loss must be determined from the start of the year to the date of disposal.

For Daniel Gee, Inc., we will assume (to simplify the calculations) that all increases and decreases in monetary items occurred evenly throughout the year, with the exception of the decrease in cash associated with dividends. Dividends were paid at the end of the year.

The beginning balance of monetary assets will be converted using the price index as at December 31, 1996. The cash flows that took place during the year will be converted using the price index as at midyear. The dividends will be converted using the price index as at December 31, 1997.

The loss from holding monetary items (cash and accounts receivable less accounts payable) would be calculated as follows:

	Unadjusted Amounts	Conversion Factor	Adjusted Amounts (31/12/97 dollars)
Balance in net monetary assets, December 31, 1996	$ 180,000	110/100	$ 198,000
Add: Sales	1,890,000	110/105	1,980,000
	2,070,000		2,178,000
Deduct:			
Merchandise purchases	1,560,000	110/105	1,634,285
Selling and administrative costs	90,000	110/105	94,286
Interest payments	64,000	110/105	67,048
Dividends	170,000	110/110	170,000
	1,884,000		1,965,619
Net monetary assets necessary to be as well off on December 31, 1997, as on December 31, 1996			212,381
Less: Actual net monetary assets, December 31, 1997 (unadjusted)	$ 186,000		186,000
Difference: Loss (gain) in purchasing power			$ 26,381

The complete current cost/constant dollar income statement is presented in Exhibit 15-10.

EXHIBIT 15-10

Daniel Gee, Inc.
Current Cost Real Statement of Income and
Changes in Retained Earnings
Year Ended December 31, 1997
(current costs/constant dollars)

Sales revenue		$1,980,000
Less: Current cost expenses		
Cost of goods sold	$1,508,571	
Amortization, building	24,095	
Amortization, equipment	73,333	
Interest	64,278	
Selling and administrative costs	94,286	1,764,563
Current operating income		215,437
Plus realizable holding gains and loss on		
Inventories	$ 34,285	
Land	12,000	
Building	21,096	
Equipment	8,333	
Bonds payable	(49,389)	26,325
Comprehensive current income before loss in purchasing power from holding monetary items		241,762
Loss in purchasing power from holding monetary items		(26,381)
Comprehensive current income		215,381
Dividends		(170,000)
Increase in real retained earnings		$ 45,381

ASSESSMENT OF CURRENT COSTS AND CONSTANT DOLLARS

There are numerous characteristics of the current cost/constant dollar financial statements that make them useful for both managers and investors:

- The income statement separates earnings into three components: revenues and expenses from ongoing operations; currently accruing holding gains and losses from changes in the market value of assets and liabilities; gains and losses caused by inflation. Current operating income serves as a long-run benchmark from which to project future earnings assuming that prices will remain stable. This projection can then be adjusted to incorporate separate forecasts of changes in both specific prices and the general price level.
- Revenues and expenses of a current period are uncontaminated by gains and losses that may have occurred in prior periods. They reflect flows of resources based on current values. Income is therefore a more useful measure of current performance, particularly in comparing one firm in different years or several firms in a single year.

- Price-level adjustments increase the internal consistency of the statements. They assure that all amounts are stated in dollars of the same value rather than a hodgepodge of values from different years.
- Assets and liabilities are stated at current values, which are more likely than historical values to indicate an enterprise's earning potential. Moreover, they may even be less subjective than historical costs, which may be based upon estimates of useful life and salvage value and arbitrarily selected cost allocation formulas (e.g., FIFO versus LIFO; straight-line versus accelerated amortization).

The model, however, is not without its limitations:

- The values assigned to resources may be highly subjective. In an era of rapid technological change, it is exceedingly difficult to determine the "current" values of assets for which no viable used-asset market exists and hence that may not be replaceable in their current form.
- In a period of rising prices, current operating income may lead to overly conservative projections of future earnings. In many firms, increases in the prices at which it sells its output may lag increases in the replacement costs of its input. Current operating income may reflect increases in replacement costs of the input immediately (through amortization and cost of goods sold) but capture related changes in output selling prices only belatedly as they take place.
- The cost of the additional information may be greater than the benefits. Information is not a free good. The evidence, while at best clouded, suggests that the data that would be presented in general-purpose reports might not be sufficiently used to justify their cost.

The controversy as to whether supplementary current cost statements should be included in general-purpose financial reports is certain to continue for years to come. What is beyond debate, however, is that current cost data are essential for many specific decisions that both managers and investors are required to make.

ACCOUNTING FOR TRANSACTIONS IN FOREIGN CURRENCY

Overview of Issues

Similar to the issue of accounting for assets and liabilities stated in dollars of different years is that of accounting for assets and liabilities expressed in currencies different from the Canadian dollar. Both issues centre around changing units of measurement. Today, most major Canadian corporations have interests in other countries, and in recent years the value of the dollar has been subject to wide fluctuations against other major currencies. The problem of accounting for transactions in foreign currencies can be illustrated by way of an example (with dollars, and deutsche marks expressed in thousands).

Suppose that a Canadian firm invested $13,090 and formed a subsidiary company in Germany. At the time the new firm was organized, one Canadian dollar was equivalent in value to 1.29 German deutsche marks (DMs).

Conversely, 1 DM was the equivalent of 77 cents. Immediately after the new company was organized, its balance sheet, expressed in deutsche marks and translated into dollars, appeared as follows:

	DMs	Translation Factor	$Cdn
Assets			
Cash	DM 1,000	.77	$ 770
Accounts receivable	3,000	.77	2,310
Plant and equipment	15,000	.77	11,550
	DM 19,000		$14,630
Equities			
Accounts payable	DM 2,000	.77	$ 1,540
Shareholders' equity	17,000	.77	13,090
	DM 19,000		$14,630

Shortly after the company was formed, the value of the deutsche mark increased against the dollar. Whereas previously one deutsche mark could be acquired for 77 cents, it would now cost 88 cents.

The Canadian parent company clearly has benefited from the increase in the value of deutsche marks. It holds in cash DM 1,000. In addition, it holds accounts receivable for DM 3,000. The receivables are stated in deutsche marks, not dollars. The company will receive payments in deutsche marks, which can be converted into a greater number of dollars than when the receivables were first recorded. By contrast, the advantage of holding DM 4,000 in cash and accounts receivable is offset in part by the obligation to make payment of DM 2,000—deutsche marks that are more costly in terms of dollars than when the obligation was established.

Thus the company holds net assets of DM 2,000 (cash of DM 1,000 plus receivables of DM 3,000 less payables of DM 2,000) that can be said to be *denominated* in deutsche marks. Assets and liabilities that are denominated in a foreign currency are very much like monetary assets and liabilities as described in the section on price-level adjustments. They are contractually fixed; the number of monetary units to be received or paid will remain the same regardless of whether the value of these units increases or decreases. Inasmuch as the company holds DM 2,000 in net monetary assets and the value of each deutsche mark increased by 11 cents (88 less 77 cents), the company is $220 (DM 2,000 times 11 cents) better off as a result of the change in the rate of exchange.

The company also holds plant and equipment, which is recorded on its balance sheet at DM 15,000. Unlike that of cash or accounts receivable, the value of plant and equipment is not contractually fixed. The firm cannot automatically sell the plant and equipment for an established number of either deutsche marks or dollars. The plant and equipment have an intrinsic value apart from that of any particular currency. As the value of the deutsche mark, relative to the dollar, increases, the number of deutsche marks for which the plant and equipment can be sold may remain the same—thereby increasing their value in terms of dollars—or may decline in proportion to the increase—thereby causing their value in terms of dollars to remain the same. (Note that the magnitude of any price change will depend on a wide array of international economic factors.) Thus it cannot be said with assurance that the firm has benefited from the change in exchange rates because of its ownership of plant and equipment.

The key accounting issues as to assets and liabilities in foreign currencies relate to the rates of exchange at which they should be translated into dollars and to the timing of gains or losses associated with the adjustments in their balance sheet values. Should balance sheet accounts be translated at the current rate of exchange or the rate of exchange that existed when assets were first acquired and liabilities first incurred? Should a distinction be made between assets and liabilities that are denominated in a foreign currency and those that are not? Should gains or losses on currency fluctuations be recognized in the periods in which the exchange rates increase or decrease, or only as assets and liabilities are actually liquidated?

CICA Position

In 1978 the CICA issued Section 1650 of the *CICA Handbook*, which set forth specific rules for translating foreign currency transactions. In essence, Section 1650 stated that *monetary* assets and liabilities must be translated at the current rate of exchange; other assets and liabilities must be translated at the rate in existence when the asset or liability was first acquired or incurred. Thus cash, payables, and receivables should generally be translated at the current exchange rate; inventory and capital assets should be translated at the rate in effect when the assets were first acquired. Gains or losses arising from the "revaluation" of the monetary assets and liabilities should be reported in the income of the period of the change in the rate of exchange.

According to the recommendations of Section 1650, as it then existed, if a balance sheet of the illustrative company were prepared immediately after the rate of exchange changed from 77 cents to 88 cents per each deutsche mark, it would be translated as follows:

	DMs	Conversion Factor	$Cdn.
Assets			
Cash	DM 1,000	.88	$ 880
Accounts receivable	3,000	.88	2,640
Plant and equipment	15,000	.77	11,550
Total assets	DM 19,000		$15,070
Equities			
Accounts payable	DM 2,000	.88	$ 1,760
Shareholders' equity	17,000	(residual)	13,310
Total equities	DM 19,000		$15,070

Cash, accounts receivable, and accounts payable would be translated at the current rate of exchange. Plant and equipment would be translated at the "historical" rate of exchange—that which was applicable when the assets were acquired. Shareholders' equity is a residual; it reflects the original shareholders' equity of $13,090 plus the gain of $220 from holding the net monetary assets. The gain of $220 would be reported on the income statement as a currency translation gain.

Modifications to CICA Position

The recommendations of Section 1650 proved to be so controversial that the Section was withdrawn from the *Handbook* in March 1979. Most objectionable to many corporations was the requirement that a firm continually recognize gains or losses from holding net assets denominated in foreign currencies as the rate of exchange fluctuates, even if it had no intention of actually selling those assets or converting them into dollars. Many firms pointed out that their foreign subsidiaries require a stock of assets and liabilities denominated in foreign currencies to carry out normal operations. Changes in the exchange rate have no immediate effect on the ability of the parent companies to withdraw funds from their foreign subsidiaries and thus to benefit or suffer from the changes in the exchange rates. The firm's holdings in foreign currencies are, in essence, they said, long-term investments, not significantly different from those in plant and equipment. There would be no gain or loss until there was an actual exchange of currencies. Fluctuations in prices of foreign currency, they argued, should no more be recognized as they occur than should those in the prices of capital assets.

Realizing that reported earnings may be distorted by currency fluctuations, particularly when they are volatile, the CICA, in 1983, issued a revised Section 1650. The basis of revised Section 1650 is that the translation of the financial statements of the foreign operation should be that which best reflects the reporting enterprise's exposure to fluctuations in exchange rates as determined by the economic facts and circumstances.

Under this approach, it is recognized that different types of foreign subsidiaries may have different types of exposure to exchange rate fluctuation. In particular, Section 1650 defines two types of foreign operations:

(a) Integrated Foreign Operation—A foreign operation which is financially or operationally interdependent with the reporting enterprise such that the exposure to exchange rate changes is similar to the exposure which would exist had the transactions and activities of the foreign operation been undertaken by the reporting enterprise.

(b) Self-sustaining Foreign Operation—A foreign operation which is financially and operationally independent of the reporting enterprise such that the exposure to exchange rate changes is limited to the reporting enterprise's net investment in the foreign operation.[8]

Essentially, an integrated foreign operation is merely an extension of the Canadian parent company and the exposure to foreign exchange fluctuations is no different from what it would have been if the parent company engaged in the transactions directly. For example, if a Canadian company maintains a U.S. sales subsidiary that sells in the United States products made in Canada, it is likely to be considered an integrated foreign operation. A self-sustaining foreign operation, on the other hand, is one that operates largely independent of the parent company and where there are few day-to-day transactions between the two. If a Canadian company owns a British subsidiary that manufactures and sells its products primarily within the U.K., then the subsidiary is likely to be considered a self-sustaining foreign operation.

---

[8] "Foreign Currency Translation," *CICA Handbook*, Section 1650, 1983.

Under revised Section 1650, the reporting enterprise must first identify its foreign operations as either integrated or self-sustaining. The financial statements of the integrated foreign operations will be translated into Canadian dollars using the temporal method. The temporal method is the same method that was used in the original Section 1650. Monetary items are translated using the rate of exchange in effect at the balance sheet date, and nonmonetary items are translated using the rate that was in existence when the nonmonetary items were first acquired or incurred. Any gains or losses on the translation of the financial statements of the integrated operation would be taken to income immediately. The rationale for the gains or losses being recognized immediately in income is the fact that there will be exchanges of currencies between the parent and the subsidiary, resulting in real economic gains or losses to the parent company. The financial statements of the self-sustaining operations will be translated into Canadian dollars using the current rate method. Under the current rate method, all assets and liabilities will be translated using the rate of exchange in effect at the balance sheet date. In addition, any gains or losses on the translation will not go immediately to income. The gains or losses will be deferred and reported in a separate component of shareholders' equity. This is consistent with the fact that there will not normally be exchanges of currency between the parent and the foreign operation. Therefore, there will be no real gains or losses to the parent company until there are exchanges of currency. The separate component of shareholders' equity will be reduced by a transfer to income in a period in which there is a reduction in the net investment in the subsidiary (i.e., an exchange of currency).

Suppose that a Canadian firm invested in the German subsidiary described previously. As before, assume that immediately upon acquisition, the deutsche mark strengthened against the dollar, increasing from 1 DM = 77 cents to 1 DM = 88 cents. This time, however, assume that under *CICA Handbook* Section 1650, the German subsidiary satisfies the criteria to be classified as a self-sustaining foreign operation. The balance sheet of the subsidiary would now be translated using the current exchange rate of 88 cents for all assets and liabilities (not only those assets and liabilities denominated in deutsche marks, as was done previously). Thus

	DMs	Translation Factor	$Cdn.
Assets			
Cash	DM 1,000	.88	$ 880
Accounts receivable	3,000	.88	2,640
Plant and equipment	15,000	.88	13,200
Total assets	DM 19,000		$16,720
Equities			
Accounts payable	DM 2,000	.88	$ 1,760
Shareholders' equity	17,000	.77*	13,090
Equity adjustment from translation			1,870
Total equities	DM 19,000		$16,720

* Section 1650 is silent as to the exchange rate that should be used to translate shareholders' equity accounts. However, if the statements of the subsidiary are to be consolidated with those of the parent, it is necessary to use historical rather than current rates. Otherwise, the consolidating entry in which the subsidiary's shareholders' equity accounts and the parent's investment in subsidiary are eliminated could not be made without additional adjustments.

The equity adjustment from translation ($1,870) represents the net gain from translating the assets and liabilities at the current exchange rate (88 cents) rather than that in effect at the time the assets were acquired and the liabilities incurred (77 cents). In this example, it was derived simply by multiplying net assets by the change in the exchange rate (11 cents). The equity adjustment would be reported only on the balance sheet. It would *not* flow through to the income statement. This is in contrast to the way in which the currency translation gain would have been accounted for under the original Section 1650 and the way in which it would still be accounted for under the current Section 1650 if the subsidiary was considered to be an integrated foreign operation rather than a self-sustaining foreign operation. As indicated in the discussion pertaining to the previous illustration, the translation gain (then $220) would be reported on the income statement and reflected on the balance sheet as part of retained earnings.

Summary

Our economic world is one of changing tastes, resources, and technology. This inevitably means an environment of changing prices. In a market economy the intrinsic worth of goods or services is governed by forces of supply and demand. Prices, however, may change as a consequence not only of increases or decreases in intrinsic worth; they may also be affected by instability in the economy which results in changes in the purchasing power of the monetary unit. The accounting issues presented by these changes are variations of issues addressed throughout the text. Should these changes be recognized? If so, when and how?

In the first part of this chapter we presented an accounting model in which changes in specific prices are recognized as they take place—even if the changes are not authenticated by transactions in which the firm itself has engaged. In this model, assets and liabilities are stated at their current values, and gains and losses from holding the assets and liabilities are included in income in the period in which they occur. Correspondingly, revenues and expenses are measured by the current values of the resources received or consumed.

In the second part of the chapter, we extended the model to adjust for changes in the general price level. All transactions are thereby expressed in a common monetary unit—dollars of the balance sheet date. The result is financial statements that are internally consistent. An added benefit, however, is that the gain or loss from holding monetary assets and liabilities is specifically identified and reported.

In the third part of the chapter, we addressed the issue of accounting for changes in the monetary unit from a different, although related, perspective. We considered the accounting problems that arise when financial statements in one currency must be translated into those of another. Changes in the relationships between currencies affect the well-being of the reporting entity. The accounting issues of whether, when, and how to recognize these changes by the reporting entity are similar to those involving changes in the value of a single currency.

This chapter has emphasized general concepts rather than specific rules of practice. The accounting policies for changes in prices, values, and foreign currencies are certain to remain controversial for many years to come.

J. Bear, Inc., a retail store, is established on December 31, 1995. Common stock and bonds are issued on that date.

Comparative balance sheets for December 31, 1996 and 1995, as well as an income statement for 1996, are presented in Exhibit 15-11. The company needs to convert the 1996 statements to both a current cost/nominal dollar basis and a current cost/constant dollar basis.

Part I. Preparing Statements in Current Costs/Nominal Dollars

1. What value should be placed upon cash, accounts receivable, and accounts payable, assuming that there is no active market for the firm's accounts receivable and payable? At what amount should sales revenue and selling and administrative expenses be reported, assuming that their recorded amounts are indicative of their current values at the time of the underlying transactions?

EXHIBIT 15-11

J. Bear, Inc.
Balance Sheets as at December 31, 1996 and 1995

		1996	1995
Assets			
Cash		$270,000	$580,000
Accounts receivable		300,000	0
Merchandise inventory		180,000	0
Furniture and fixtures	$250,000		
Less: Accumulated amortization	50,000	200,000	0
Total assets		$950,000	$580,000
Liabilities and shareholders' equity			
Accounts payable		$100,000	$ 0
Bonds payable		250,000	250,000
Common stock		330,000	330,000
Retained earnings		270,000	0
Total liabilities and shareholders' equity		$950,000	$580,000

J. Bear, Inc.
Income Statement for Year Ended December 31, 1996

Sales revenue		$900,000
Less expenses		
Cost of goods sold	$500,000	
Amortization	50,000	
Selling and administrative	60,000	
Interest	20,000	630,000
Net Income		$270,000

2. Prices on the goods carried by the firm increased throughout the year. The average *current cost* of the merchandise sold was the same as its average purchase cost—$520,000. This compares with the historical cost of $500,000. At year end the current cost of merchandise held in inventory was $240,000 (versus historical cost of $180,000).

a. At what amount should inventory be reported? At what amount should cost of goods sold be reported?

b. Based on a comparison of outputs (ending inventory at current costs plus current cost of goods sold) and inputs (beginning inventory at current cost plus purchases), what was the *realizable* holding gain for the year? Of this amount, how much was *realized* (i.e., incorporated into cost of goods sold)? How much remains on the balance sheet as an addition to inventory? (Note that this example involves a company that has just begun operations. In a continuing company, realized holding gains for a particular year could exceed realizable gains for that year. That is because the realized gains can relate to gains that were realizable in previous years. For example, realizable gains on inventory would be recognized in the period of a price increase. The realized gain on those goods would be reported when the goods are sold.)

c. Of what use might the figures for current cost of goods sold and ending inventory be to managers and investors? (*Hint:* Refer back to the discussion of current costs toward the end of Chapter 8.)

3. The estimated useful life of the furniture and fixtures is five years, with no residual value. They were acquired on January 1, 1996. The current cost (new) of these items on December 31, 1996, was ascertained from suppliers to be $325,000 (compared with the historical cost of $250,000). It was also determined that identical items one year old could be purchased for $260,000.

a. At what amount should the furniture and fixtures be reported? What should be reported as current cost accumulated amortization?

b. Assume (for simplicity, as in the text) that the entire 30 percent increase in the current cost of the furniture and fixtures occurred at the start of 1996. What amount should be reported on the income statement as amortization expense?

c. Based on a comparison of outputs (ending balance at current cost plus current cost amortization) with inputs (beginning balance at current cost plus additions), what was the realizable holding gain for the year? Note that, in this example, beginning balance at current cost is the same as historical cost.

d. What portion of the realizable holding gain was realized (through use) during 1996, the first year of the useful life of the furniture and fixtures?

e. Of what use to managers and investors are the data on current cost amortization and realizable holding gains (which could also be called cost savings)?

4. The bonds payable were issued at par on December 31, 1995. They paid interest at a rate of 8 percent (4 percent per period) and were to mature in 10 years. During 1996, interest rates on comparable securities rose steadily and by year end were at 10 percent. As a consequence, on December 31, 1996, the company's bonds were being quoted at a price of $220,776.

a. At what amount should the bonds be reported? Verify that this value is consistent with the yield rate of 10 percent (5 percent per period) and the remaining maturity of 18 periods.

b. What is the amount that should be reported as current cost interest? [*Note:* The uniform increase in interest rates and the corresponding decline in market value are the equivalent to a one-time increase in interest rate and decline in market value at midyear. Hence interest charges can be computed in two parts: The first would be based on market values and the interest rate for the first half of the year (which in this case are the same as historical values and rates); the second would be based on the market value and the interest rate for the second half of the year. The market value of the bonds at midyear, immediately after the increase in interest rates, would have been $219,787. This represents the present value of $250,000 in 8 percent coupon bonds (4 percent per period) with *19* periods until maturity sold to yield the 10 percent (5 percent per period) market rate of interest.]

c. Based on a comparison of outputs (ending balance at current cost plus cash paid in interest plus any cash paid to retire bonds) and inputs (beginning balance at current cost plus current cost of interest charges), what was the realizable holding gain for the year on the bonds? (Note that although the outputs are less than the inputs, the company realized a gain; it could retire its debt at year end for less than it could at the start of the year. Moreover, it gained because it had the foresight to borrow at rates lower than those which subsequently prevailed.)

d. How much of the realizable gain was realized during the year?

e. Of what use to managers and investors are the data on the market values of the bonds, current cost interest, and realizable holding gains?

5. Prepare a current cost/nominal dollar financial statements. Since 1996 is the first year of operations, be sure that ending retained earnings equals income.

Part II. Adjusting the Current Cost/Nominal Dollar Statements to Reflect Current Costs/Constant Dollars

Relevant values of a general price index were as follows:

December 31, 1995	100
Average for 1996	110
December 31, 1996	121

The firm's revenues were generated and expenses incurred evenly throughout the year.

1. At what amounts should the firm's monetary items (cash, accounts receivable, and accounts payable) be stated on the December 31, 1996, balance sheet? Is any adjustment required. At what amounts should they be reported on the comparative December 31, 1995, balance sheet? (Be sure they are reported at an amount reflective of their purchasing power expressed in dollars of December 31, 1996).

2. At what amount should the other assets and liabilities be expressed on the December 31, 1996, balance sheet? Inasmuch as they are already stated at current costs, which are automatically expressed in dollars of December 31, 1996, are any adjustments necessary?

3. At what amount should the other assets and liabilities be expressed on the comparative December 31, 1995, balance sheet? These items must be shown at their current costs of December 31, 1995 (which in this example is the same as historical cost), expressed in dollars of December 31, 1996.

4. What adjustment is required to state common stock (an item which was reported at historical cost because it has no meaningful current costs) in dollars of December 31, 1996?

5. What adjustments are required to express each of the revenues and expenses (all of which were generated or incurred evenly throughout the year) in dollars of December 31, 1996?

6. Recompute the realizable holding gains for inventories, furniture and fixtures, and bonds payable by "dating" each of the elements that entered into the previous calculation of these gains. That is, multiply each of the elements by the ratio of the price index on December 31, 1996, to that on the date of the underlying transaction or balance.

7. Determine the purchasing power gain or loss from holding net monetary items (cash plus accounts receivable, less accounts payable).
   a. Prepare a schedule in which you reconcile the beginning balance in net monetary assets with the ending balance.
   b. Adjust each of the elements in the reconciliation by multiplying it by the ratio of the price index on December 31, 1996, to that on the date of the underlying transaction or balance. The resultant balance will indicate the net monetary items that the company should have had on hand to have avoided a loss in purchasing power.
   c. Subtract the net unadjusted monetary items (the amounts actually on hand) from the net adjusted monetary items (the amounts required to keep pace with inflation).

8. Prepare current cost/constant dollar financial statements. Be sure that retained earnings equals income.

Questions for Review and Discussion

1. It has been suggested that any move away from historical cost to current cost accounting will inevitably compromise "objectivity." Is current cost accounting necessarily less objective than historical cost accounting? How objective, in fact, is historical cost accounting? To what extent, for example, do "subjective rules objectively applied" govern the accounting for both inventory and plant and equipment?

2. "If prices rose substantially over the life of a business, then historical cost/nominal dollar financial statements would understate reported income relative to current cost/nominal dollar statements." Do you agree? Explain.

3. The manager of a gasoline distribution business anticipates a significant rise in wholesale prices and acquires a substantial amount of inventory

prior to the price increase. Under historical cost accounting models, when would the manager's foresight be reflected in the firm's reported income? Under current cost accounting, when would it be reflected?

4. "Price-level adjustments in no way undermine the historical transaction-based underpinning of financial accounting. Constant dollar statements must be distinguished from current cost statements because the former may be based on historical costs while the latter are not." Comment.

5. "Current cost accounting makes sense, if at all, only in times of inflation. Once a protracted period of price increases ends there is no longer any reason to account for price changes." Discuss, commenting specifically on the statement's implication that *past* price changes have no effect on *present* accounting reports.

6. What is meant by a *realizable* holding gain? How, in general terms, is it computed? How is a realizable holding gain on the following assets and liabilities "realized"?

    a. Buildings and equipment
    b. Merchandise inventory
    c. Bonds payable

7. It has been suggested that holding gains distort income. Income, after all, is a measure of how much better off a firm is at the end of a period than at the beginning. How can increases in the prices of inventories or other resources, which will have to be replaced at these higher prices, enhance the well-being of a firm? Comment.

8. "The realizable holding gains on assets in current cost/constant dollar accounting may be both misleading and irrelevant if a company has no intention of selling its assets prior to the conclusion of their economic lives. Further, a realizable holding gain or loss on bonds payable may be illusory if the firm plans not to pay off its debt until maturity." Discuss, considering the merits, if any, of having a framework for assessing managerial performance that attributes gains and losses to the periods in which they are "earned."

9. What is the difference between monetary and nonmonetary items? Why is it generally unnecessary to convert monetary items into constant dollars?

10. In converting the current cost/nominal dollar balance sheet into a current cost/constant dollar balance sheet at the end of a period, neither monetary nor nonmonetary assets and liabilities must be adjusted. Why?

11. What are purchasing power gains and losses? How are they computed?

12. Bonds payable, like accounts payable, have a "face value," which is indicative of the amount for which the obligation can be satisfied. Yet in our illustrations, bonds were accounted for as if they were nonmonetary rather than monetary items. Why?

13. What are the primary advantages and disadvantages of the current cost/constant dollar model over the historical cost/nominal dollar model? Over the historical cost/constant dollar model?

14. Suppose that a Canadian company owns a subsidiary located in a foreign country. Why will currency fluctuations have a different impact on assets and liabilities of the subsidiary denominated in the foreign currency than on other assets?

15. What were the primary criticisms directed at the original Section 1650? How were they addressed by the 1983 revision of Section 1650?

Problems

1. *Increases in prices must be distinguished from increases in value.*

    In 1993 a certain grade of lumber sold for $115 per 1,000 board feet. In 1997 the same grade of lumber sold for $165 per 1,000 board feet. In 1993, the Consumer Price Index was at 125; in 1997 it was at 188. By how much did the cost of lumber actually increase, after taking into account the decline in the overall value of the dollar? Express your answer in terms of 1997 dollars.

2. *In adjusting for changes in the general price level, monetary items must be distinguished from nonmonetary items.*

    Indicate whether each of the following items should be considered a monetary (M) or a nonmonetary (N) item:
    a. Cash on hand
    b. Cash in bank
    c. Marketable securities (e.g., common stocks)
    d. Accounts and notes receivable
    e. Inventories
    f. Refundable deposits
    g. Property, plant, and equipment
    h. Accumulated amortization
    i. Goodwill
    j. Patents, trademarks, licenses
    k. Accounts and notes payable
    l. Dividends payable
    m. Bonds payable
    n. Common stock
    o. Retained earnings

3. *"Earnings" from marketable securities may, in fact, be more than offset by losses in purchasing power.*

    At the beginning of 1996, an investor had $400,000 in cash. On the first day of the year she purchased a certificate of deposit for $200,000 and 4,000 shares of common stock (a nonmonetary asset) of a well-known company for $50 per share.

    In the course of the year, the investor earned interest of $12,000 on the money placed in the certificate of deposit. She earned dividends of $6,000 on the common stock which she held. At year end, she sold the 4,000 shares of common stock at a price of $52 per share.

A general-purpose price index at the start of 1996 was at a level of 149. On average during the year it was at 160, and at year end it was at 168.

  a. Determine income for the year on a conventional basis.
  b. Determine the gain or loss in purchasing power for the year. Be sure to take into account (and translate using appropriate price-index ratios) each of the receipts and disbursements of cash.
  c. Determine the gain or loss, on a price-level-adjusted (constant dollar) basis, from the sale of the common stock.
  d. Determine price-level adjusted earnings for the year, including the gains or losses in purchasing power and from the sale of the common stock.
  e. Reconcile, on a price-level-adjusted basis, the equity of the investor at the start of the year with that at the end. (Express beginning-of-year equity in terms of end-of-year dollars.)

4. *Current cost inventory and cost of goods sold data can help in decision making.*

The Monzi newspaper chain is considering investing in one of two major paper mills to ensure its raw materials supply. Both mills produce the same product using machinery of the same type and vintage. Mill B is about 50 percent larger than Mill A. Mill B can be bought for $60 million, Mill A for $40 million. The income statements for the last year for the two mills are shown below (in millions of dollars). The revenues and expenses seem to reflect reasonably well the relative performances of previous years.

		Mill A			Mill B
Revenue			$200		$300
Expenses					
Cost of goods sold					
Pulp	$150			$195	
Wages	30			50	
Other	15	$195		30	$275
Selling and administration		5	200		10	285
Net income			$ 0		$ 15

On the face of it, Mill B would appear to be the more efficient operation. It is earning a 25 percent profit on the value of its ownership equity, while Mill A's rate of return is 0 percent. The primary reason for Mill B's better performance would appear to be its more efficient use of pulp.

Mill A reports cost of goods sold on a FIFO periodic inventory basis, while Mill B uses a LIFO periodic inventory method. Monzi's analysts decide to put both income statements on a current cost basis so far as cost of goods sold is concerned, using the following (historical cost) facts provided by the two mills (units, hence values, in millions):

	Mill A	Mill B
Sales, paper	10 units @ $20.00 = $200.00	15 units @ $20.00 = $300.00
Purchases, pulp	15 units @ $10.00 = $150.00	21 units @ $10.00 = $210.00
Beginning inventory	1 unit @ $15.00 = $ 15.00	1 unit @ $ 7.50 = $ 7.50
Ending inventory	2 units @ $ 7.50 = $ 15.00	1 unit @ $ 7.50
		+1 unit @ $15.00 = $ 22.50

a. Assuming the average purchase price of $10 is the current cost of pulp for the year, put Mill A's and Mill B's income statements into current cost/nominal dollar terms so far as the cost of goods sold is concerned.

b. Which mill do you think is the better investment for the Monzi newspaper chain, all things other than profitability being equal? Why?

5. *Current cost/constant dollar adjustments have varying effects upon firms in different industries.*

Two companies, A and B, are in different industries. Both, however, are of the same size and do the same volume of business. The 1997 income statements and balance sheets for the two are as follows (in thousands):

Income Statements
Year Ended December 31, 1997

	Firm A	Firm B
Sales	$2,000	$2,000
Cost of goods sold	1,400	1,700
Amortization expense	400	100
Total expenses	1,800	1,800
Net income	$ 200	$ 200

Balance Sheets as at December 31, 1997

	Firm A	Firm B
Inventory	$ 400	$1,600
Capital assets	2,400	600
Less: Accumulated amortization	800	200
Net capital assets	1,600	400
Total assets	$2,000	$2,000
Shareholders' equity	$2,000	$2,000

The capital assets have a useful life of six years; they were acquired in January 1996. The prices of capital assets have increased by 10 percent in each of the two years since they were acquired. Hence fair market values (new) as of year ends were as follows:

	Firm A	Firm B
December 31, 1996	$2,640	$660
December 31, 1997	$2,904	$726

The inventory of both firms turns over rapidly. Their historical values are approximately the same as their market values.

a. Determine for both firms:
   (1) Current cost amortization expense for 1996 and 1997
   (2) Current cost of the capital assets (net of accumulated amortization) as at both December 31, 1996 and 1997
   (3) Realizable holding gain on capital assets for 1997

b. Prepare current cost/constant dollar income statements for 1997. (Assume that no general price-level adjustments are required.)

c. Comment on why the two companies differ in current cost/constant dollar earnings even though their historical cost earnings are the same and their capital assets increased in market value by the same percentage.

6. *In some industries current cost statements may be especially useful.*

LJG Associates is a real-estate firm whose only major assets are downtown office buildings. Historical cost financial statements (in millions) are presented in the accompanying tables.

The firm's buildings have a useful economic life of 20 years (no residual value). As at year end 1996 they had a current value (new) of $700 million. By year end 1997 their current value (new) had increased to $800 million.

The current values of the firm's other assets and liabilities were the same as their historical values.

a. Convert the 1997 income statement and *both* the December 31, 1997 and 1996, balance sheets to a current cost basis. Be sure to adjust retained earnings for both years.

  (1) Be certain that amortization expense for 1997 and accumulated amortization for both years reflect the year-end current costs of the building.

  (2) Determine the realizable holding gain for 1997 by comparing outputs with inputs (with both being valued at *current costs*).

  (3) Verify your adjustments by making certain that retained earnings of December 31, 1996, reconciles with that of December 31, 1997.

b. Suppose, as is typical in the real-estate industry, that the firm does *not* intend to hold its properties until the expiration of their economic lives. Which income statement, the historical or the current cost, provides the more useful and complete measure of performance? Explain.

LJG Associates Historical Cost Balance Sheets as at December 31				
		1997		1996
Assets				
Cash		$ 69		$ 30
Accounts receivable		12		10
Buildings	$400		$400	
Less: Accumulated amortization	120	280	100	300
Total assets		$361		$340
Liabilities and shareholders' equity				
Bonds payable		$200		$200
Contributed capital		50		50
Retained earnings		111		90
Total liabilities and shareholders' equity		$361		$340

Income Statement for Year Ended December 31, 1997		
Rent revenue		$80
Less expenses		
Amortization	$20	
Interest	24	
Other expenses	15	59
Net income		$21

7. *Current cost financial statements can easily be converted into current cost/constant dollar statements. (This problem shows how to reconcile the beginning- and end-of-year balances in retained earnings.)*

The current cost financial statements (in millions) of WXY Associates are presented below. The Consumer Price Index was at the following levels:

December 31, 1996	190
Average, 1997	200
December 31, 1997	220

a. Recast the December 31, 1997, current cost balance sheet into a "real" (i.e., constant dollar) balance sheet. Assume that the firm's common stock (reported as contributed capital) was issued on December 31, 1996. In adjusting the statements, remember that the firm's assets and liabilities, both monetary and nonmonetary, are already stated in dollars of December 31, 1997, and therefore need not be adjusted. Retained earnings can be adjusted as a "plug."

b. Recast the 1997 current cost income statement into a real income statement. Assume that all revenues and expenses, other than amortization, were recorded evenly throughout the year. Therefore they must be translated using the average index value for the year. Amortization was recorded at year end and based on the year-end current value of the building. Therefore it need not be translated.

   (1) Determine the purchasing power gain or loss from holding *monetary* assets and liabilities during the year.

   (2) Recalculate the realizable holding gain on the building (net of amortization). In comparing outputs with inputs, be sure to express the net current value of the building at the beginning of the year in constant (December 31, 1997) dollars. (That is, multiply the net *current* value by the ratio of the price index of December 31, 1997, to that of December 31, 1996.)

   (3) Translate other revenues and expenses into December 31, 1997, dollars.

c. Verify your income statement and balance sheet computations by reconciling December 31, 1996 and 1997, constant dollar retained earnings.

   (1) Recast the December 31, 1996, current cost balance sheet into dollars of December 31, 1997, by adjusting all amounts by the ratio of the value of the December 31, 1997, price index to that of the December 31, 1996, index.

   (2) Make certain that retained earnings at December 31, 1996, plus income equals retained earnings at December 31, 1997.

WXY Associates
Current Cost Balance Sheets as at December 31

		1997		1996
Assets				
Cash		$ 69		$ 30
Accounts receivable		12		10
Buildings	$800		$700	
Less: Accumulated amortization	240	560	175	525
Total assets		$641		$565
Liabilities and shareholders' equity				
Bonds payable		$200		$200
Contributed capital		50		50
Retained earnings		391		315
Total liabilities and shareholders' equity		$641		$565

Current Cost Income Statement
Year Ended December 31, 1997

Rent revenue		$80
Less expenses		
Amortization	$40	
Interest	24	
Other Expenses	15	79
Net operating income		1
Realizable holding gain		75
Net income		$76

8. *The next two problems are intended to provide perspective on the relationship between realizable holding gains and amortization. In the first, information as to value of used assets is not available; in the second, it is.*

On January 1, 1996, a company acquires equipment at a cost of $180,000. It has a three-year useful life with no anticipated residual value. Over the three-year period the cost to replace the equipment (new) is as follows:

December 31, 1996	$192,000
December 31, 1997	204,000
December 31, 1998	222,000

a. Prepare a table in which you indicate for each year:
   (1) The current value (i.e., replacement cost) of the equipment at year end
   (2) Amortization expense, based on year-end current value
   (3) Current cost accumulated amortization at year end
   (4) Net current value (i.e., current value less accumulated amortization) at year end
   (5) Realizable holding gain (i.e., end-of-year net current value plus amortization less beginning-of-year net current value)
   (6) Net cost of using the equipment during the year (i.e., current cost amortization expense less realizable holding gain)

b. Compare the net cost of using the equipment over the three-year period with what would be reported in a historical cost model. Is total cost the same? Comment on the reason for differences in the pattern of charges.

9. A company acquires the equipment described in the previous problem. The replacement cost of the equipment (new) is as indicated in the previous problem. Now, however, there is also an active market for used equipment. The fair market values of the used equipment is as follows:

December 31, 1996 (one-year-old equipment)	$100,000
December 31, 1997 (two-year-old equipment)	$ 40,000
December 31, 1998 (three-year-old equipment)	$ 0

Complete the requirements of the previous problem. (You might find it helpful, however, to compute year-end accumulated amortization before you calculate amortization expense. Amortization expense can then be calculated as the difference between beginning- and end-of-year accumulated amortization.)

10. *This problem shows the impact of changes in both specific prices and the general level of prices on the income statement and balance sheet. It also indicates how beginning balances are tied to ending balances.*

On January 1, 1996, Greenlawn, Inc., a lawn service company, had $160,000 in working capital (all monetary items) and vehicles and equipment that had cost, in total, $1,200,000. Book value of the vehicles and equipment, after taking into account accumulated amortization, was $300,000.

The following table indicates the replacement value of the vehicles and equipment, both new and used, as of the start and the end of 1996:

	January 1	December 31
New	$2,000,000	$2,200,000
Used	600,000	640,000

During 1996 the firm reported cash sales of $1,400,000 and incurred cash expenses of $1,100,000. In addition, it charged amortization expense of $120,000. Hence historical cost income was $180,000. The sales and expenses, including amortization, were recognized evenly throughout the year.

The Consumer Price Index for the year was as follows:

January 1	140
Average for the year	150
December 31	160

In its current cost/constant dollar balance sheet the firm states vehicles and equipment so that the gross value is the current cost of the assets new and the net value is the current cost of the assets used. The difference is accumulated amortization. On its current cost/constant dollar income statement, "annual amortization charges" is the difference between beginning and ending accumulated amortization (adjusted for any asset retirements).

a. What would reported accumulated amortization be at both January 1 and December 31? What would current cost amortization expense be for the year (i.e., the difference between the two amounts)?

b. What would be the realizable holding gain for the year, expressed in *real* terms? (*Hint:* Compute the realizable holding gain using "dated" dollars. That is, adjust each of the components by the appropriate price index ratio. For example, current cost amortization would be multiplied by 160/150, beginning balance by 160/140.)

c. Compute the gain or loss from holding monetary items during the year (i.e., the purchasing power gain or loss).

d. Prepare a current cost/constant dollar income statement. Be sure to adjust current cost amortization as well as the other revenues and expenses by the appropriate price index ratio.

e. Prepare a current cost/constant dollar balance sheet as at December 31. Remember, neither monetary items nor assets that are already stated in current values need be adjusted. Assume that the firm started the year with contributed capital (based on historical costs) of $200,000.

f. Verify your computations by reconciling beginning and ending retained earnings. To do this, you must prepare a current cost/constant dollar balance sheet as at January 1. In this balance sheet, *both* the monetary items and the vehicles and equipment must be expressed in constant (i.e., December 31) dollars. Multiply both assets and contributed captial by the ratio of 160/140. Consider retained earnings at January 1 to be a plug.

11. *Use of LIFO may compensate, in part, for failure to adjust for changes in current costs.*

Three companies, the LIFO Company, the FIFO Company, and the Current Cost Company, engage in identical operations. Each maintains its inventory on the basis indicated by its name.

At the start of 1996, each firm had 5,000 units of inventory on hand, stated on its books as follows:

LIFO	5,000 @ $34	$170,000
FIFO	5,000 @ $48	$240,000
Current Cost	5,000 @ $50	$250,000

During 1996 each company purchased 24,000 units as follows:

12,000 @ $52	$ 624,000
12,000 @ $56	$ 672,000
	$1,296,000

The purchases were made evenly throughout the year and the average price was $54. The final purchase of the year was made on December 31, at a price of $56. During the year each company sold 21,000 units.

a. Compute cost of goods sold for each of the three companies as well as the realizable holding gain for the Current Cost Company.

b. Comment on the extent to which LIFO is a reasonable substitute for current cost accounting.

12. *The separation of holding gains into realized and unrealized portions facilitates an understanding of the relationship between income statement and balance sheet accounts.*

A firm began operations on January 1, 1996. On that date it had $500,000 in cash and a corresponding amount of paid-in capital. At the start of the year the firm acquired capital assets at a cost of $200,000. The assets have an estimated useful life of four years, with no salvage value. Amortization is recorded at year's end. Throughout the year the firm made purchases of inventory for $450,000.

The historical cost income statement of the firm for its first year of operations indicates the following:

Income Statement (historical costs)		
Sales revenue		$600,000
Cost of goods sold	$350,000	
Amortization	50,000	
Other expenses	50,000	450,000
Net income		$150,000

By December 31, 1996, the replacement cost of the capital assets acquired at the start of the year had increased by 15 percent, to $230,000. The replacement cost of inventory on hand at year end had increased by 5 percent, from $100,000 to $105,000. The replacement costs of the $350,000 in goods that were sold were, at the times of sales, $367,500. All sales and purchases of goods and services were for cash. There was no general inflation during the year; hence all holding gains were "real."

Assume that the firm will prepare current cost financial statements.

a. What was the total holding gain related to inventory and cost of sales during the year? Of this amount, how much was realized (reflected in cost of goods sold) and how much unrealized (reflected in ending inventory)?

b. What was the total holding gain related to capital assets? Of this amount, how much was realized (reflected in amortization) and how much unrealized (reflected in year-end capital assets)?

c. Prepare a current cost statement of income.

d. Prepare a current cost balance sheet.

13. *Current cost adjustments may alter return on investment and, as a consequence, utility rates.*

A provincial public utilities board establishes rates so that utilities within its jurisdiction are permitted to earn a return of 10 percent on total invested capital. A condensed balance sheet and an income statement of Atlantic Gas and Electric Co. for the year ended December 31, 1996, appear as follows:

Atlantic Gas and Electric Co.
Balance Sheet as at December 31, 1996
(in millions)

Assets		
Cash and accounts receivable		$ 250
Inventories and supplies		16
Plant and equipment	$1,200	
Less: Accumulated amortization	300	900
Total assets		$1,166
Equities		
Current liabilities		$ 100
Long-term debt		500
Shareholders' equity		566
Total equities		$1,166

Statement of Income
Year Ended December 31, 1996

Revenues		$417
Operating expenses and taxes	$240	
Amortization	60	
Interest	35	335
Net income		$ 82

Return on investment is defined as net income before interest divided by total assets. Thus $82 million in income plus interest of $35 million is approximately 10 percent of $1,166 million in total assets.

At December 31, 1995, the plant and equipment had a market value new of $1,520 million. Accumulated amortization based on current costs was $304. At December 31, 1996, market value new had increased to $1,600 million. There was no viable market for used plant and equipment. The average useful life of the plant and equipment was 20 years.

The market value of supplies and inventories is approximately the same as their book value. There were no changes in inventory quantity or value during the year. The market value of long-term debt was also was equal to its book value both at the beginning and the end of the year.

Revenues and expenditures, with the exception of amortization, were reflective of current costs at the time they were recognized.

a. Prepare a current cost balance sheet and income statement for 1996. Be sure to take into account the holding gains on the plant and equipment.

b. Determine the rate of return on the basis of current costs. What would be the impact on utility charges if the board were to base rates on current costs, assuming no change on allowable percentage return?

14. *Adjustments for changes in prices may alter assessments of corporate efficiency as measured by financial ratios.*

Shown below are the disclosures of Rolland Inc., a leading manufacturer and distributor of fine papers, as required originally by the *CICA*

Handbook, Section 4510. (These disclosures are no longer required since Section 4510 has been withdrawn from the *Handbook.*)

a. For each of the two "models" for which data are presented, compute (1) inventory turnover and (2) plant and equipment turnover. Since data are presented for one year only, use year-end rather than average values in the denominator of the ratios. Comment on which model makes the company appear most efficient.

b. Have the values, as opposed to merely the nominal prices, of the the fixed assets of the company increased? How can you tell?

c. The reported value of fixed assets is greater under current cost accounting than under historical cost accounting. Does this seem inconsistent with your response to part (b)? If so, what is a possible explanation?

Rolland Inc. Consolidated Statements of Earnings and Selected Balance Sheet Data Adjusted for Changing Prices (in thousands)	As Reported in the Primary Statements	Adjusted for Changes in Specific Prices (current costs)
Net sales	$300,748	$300,748
Costs and expenses		
Cost of goods sold	$254,876	$252,617
Depreciation and amortization	4,243	5,644
Selling and administrative expenses	33,113	33,113
Interest expense	2,278	2,278
Other income	(1,787)	(1,787)
Income taxes	2,825	2,825
	$295,548	$294,690
Net earnings	$ 5,200	$ 6,058
Inventories	$ 35,634	$ 35,634
Fixed assets—net	$ 33,187	$ 45,698
Effect of increase in general price level on cost of inventories and fixed assets		$ 2,791
Decrease in specific prices (current costs)		(1,277)
Excess of increase in general price level over decrease in specific prices		$ 4,068

15. *Forest product firms have special problems of determining current cost.*

The table on the following page is an excerpt from the supplementary inflation accounting information in an annual report of Champion International Corporation, a producer of paper, building materials, and other forest-related products. (Amounts are in millions of dollars.)

a. Has the cost of the products sold increased in value (as opposed to price) since the products were acquired? Explain.

b. Did the firm, on average, hold net monetary assets, or was it obligated for net monetary liabilities during the year? Explain.

c. Did the current cost adjustments pertaining to inventories and property, plant, and equipment increase or decrease income (after taking into account real holding gains) relative to historical cost income?

d. A substantial portion of the firm's assets are in standing timber (i.e., trees). Many of the trees are too young for sale. How would you propose that the firm determine the current cost of its standing timber?

Champion International Corporation			
	As Reported in the Historical Dollar Statements	Adjusted for General Inflation	Adjusted for Changes in Specific Prices
Net sales	$3,753	$3,753	$3,753
Cost of products sold (excluding depreciation and cost of timber harvested)	2,985	3,032	3,011
Depreciation and cost of timber harvested	148	218	230
Selling, general, and administrative expenses (excluding depreciation)	369	369	369
Interest and debt expense	58	58	58
Other (income) expense, net	(31)	(31)	(31)
	3,529	3,646	3,637
Income before income taxes	224	107	116
Income taxes	42	42	42
Income from continuing operations	$ 182	$ 65	$ 74
Gain from decline in purchasing power of net amounts owed		$ 127	$ 127
Increase in specific prices (current cost) of inventories; property, plant, and equipment; and timber and timberlands held during the year			$ 446
Effect of increase in general price level (constant dollar)			478
Excess of increase in general price level over increase in specific prices			$ 32

16. *The main reason for controversy over foreign currency translation is uncertainty as to when a company will actually reap the benefits from, or incur the costs of, changes in exchange rates.*

Exports, Inc., a Canadian company, purchased for 10 million baht (B) the entire outstanding common stock of a firm in Thailand. At the time of acquisition, $1 = 21 B. The balance sheet of the subsidiary, in baht, appeared as follows (in thousands):

Assets	
Cash	8,600 B
Accounts receivable	11,200
Inventory	4,500
Plant and equipment	25,700
Total assets	50,000 B

Equities	
Accounts payable	4,900 B
Notes payable	35,100
Common stock	10,000
Total equities	50,000 B

Shortly after the acquisition, the Thai government devalued the baht so that the exchange rate was now $1 = 30 B.

a. What do you think was the value of the inventory, plant, and equipment, expressed in dollars, prior to the devaluation (assume that book values are representative of market values)? What do you think will be the value of the same assets subsequent to the devaluation? Explain.

b. What do you think was the value of the net liabilities denominated in baht (cash and receivables less accounts and notes payable), expressed in dollars, prior to the devaluation? What do you think will be their value subsequent to the devaluation? Explain.

c. Do you think that Exports, Inc. (the parent company), has benefited from the devaluation? Discuss, making alternative assumptions as to the relationship between the parent and the subsidiary and the nature of the business carried out by the subsidiary. Under what circumstances do you think that the consolidated entity should report a gain or loss from the change in the exchange rate?

d. Assume that the subsidiary is classified as a self-sustaining foreign operation under the criteria of Section 1650. Convert the balance sheet of the subsidiary to dollars. Justify the conversion factors used and the manner in which you accounted for any gains or losses.

17. *The nature of the foreign unit determines the way in which its currency is converted.*

Canada, Inc., established a New Zealand subsidiary, Rotorua Industries Ltd. Shortly after the new firm was organized, it prepared the following balance sheet (in thousands of New Zealand dollars):

Rotorua Industries Ltd.
Balance Sheet as at January 1, 1996
(New Zealand dollars, in thousands)

Assets	
Cash	$ 7,000
Notes receivable	9,000
Inventory	12,000
Property, plant, and equipment	26,000
Total assets	$54,000
Equities	
Accounts payable	$10,000
Bonds payable	15,000
Contributed capital	29,000
Total equities	$54,000

At the time the subsidiary was formed, the rate of exchange was $NZ 1 = $Canadian .65. Shortly after the company was organized, the Canadian dollar weakened against the New Zealand dollar to $NZ 1 = $Canadian .75.

Rotorua Industries Ltd. is a manufacturing and sales subsidiary and conducts business entirely in New Zealand.

a. Convert the balance sheet of Rotorua Industries Ltd. to Canadian dollars so that it can be consolidated into the financial statements of its parent. What would be the effect of the conversion on income of the parent?

b. Assume instead that Rotorua Industries Ltd. is merely a sales agent for the parent and that many of its transactions are conducted in Canadian dollars. Convert the balance sheet to Canadian dollars and indicate the effect of the conversion on income of the parent.

c. How can you justify the differences in conversion rates used for parts (a) and (b)?

Solutions to Exercise for Review and Self-Testing

Part 1. Current Costs/Nominal Dollars

1. None of these items have to be adjusted. Their historical values are also their current values.

2. a. Inventory should be reported at $240,000, its current cost at year end. Cost of goods sold should be reported at $520,000, the current cost of the goods sold at time of sale.

   b.

Outputs		
Ending inventory at current cost	$240,000	
Current cost of goods sold	520,000	$760,000
Inputs		
Beginning inventory at current cost	$ 0	
Purchases	680,000	680,000
Realizable holding gain on inventory		$ 80,000

   Realized holding gains of a period are the excess of the current cost of inputs consumed in a period over their historical cost. Thus, in this example, the realized gain is the $520,000 current cost of goods sold less the $500,000 historical cost—$20,000. $60,000 remains on the balance sheet as an addition to inventory.

   c. In Chapter 8 it was noted that managers and investors can be misled by traditional historical cost inventory procedures such as FIFO and LIFO. We presented an example in which sales declined and inventory prices increased. Under FIFO the company reported an increase in income. Under LIFO it reported a decline in income that far exceeded the decline in sales. The reason for the anomaly is that both LIFO and FIFO inventory costs do not reflect all events of the present period but do reflect events of prior periods. The current cost framework captures *all* events of the present period and *only* events of the present period.

3. a. Furniture and fixtures should be reported gross, at $325,000, the current cost of new assets. They should be reported net at $260,000, the

current cost of one-year-old assets. The difference of $65,000 should be reported as current cost accumulated amortization.

b. Inasmuch as 1996 was the first year of operations, amortization expense would also be $65,000.

c.

Outputs		
Ending balance (net) at current cost	$260,000	
Current cost amortization	65,000	$325,000
Inputs		
Beginning balance (net) at current cost	$ 0	
Additions	250,000	250,000
Realizable holding gain on furniture and fixtures		$ 75,000

d. The realized portion of the realizable gain is the difference between current cost amortization of $65,000 and historical cost amortization of $50,000—thus $15,000. As with inventory, this represents the excess of the current cost of inputs consumed in the period over their historical cost.

e. Managers should be held accountable (by investors and other managers) for the efficiency and effectiveness with which they control and consume resources each period. The value of the resources on hand, as well as the portion consumed, can most meaningfully be determined with reference to current market prices, not historical costs. Historical costs incorporate into income decisions and events of the past. At the same time, managers should also be assessed on their purchase decisions. They should be rewarded for having the foresight to acquire and hold assets prior to increases in prices. The cost savings from wise early purchases will be reflected in realizable holding gains.

4. a. The bonds should be reported at their current market value of $220,776.

Present value of principal (per Table 2, present value of a single payment) 5%, 18 periods, $250,000 × .41552*	$103,880
Present value of interest (per Table 4, present value of an annuity) 5%, 18 periods, $10,000 × 11.68960*	116,896
Present value of payments	$220,776

*As noted in the chapter, five-decimal-place present value factors are used to avoid rounding errors in the calculation of the realizable holding gain or loss on bonds payable.

b.

Beginning-of-year market value of $250,000 × .04	$10,000
Midyear market value of $219,787 × .05	10,989
Total current cost interest	$20,989

c.

Outputs		
Ending balance at current cost	$220,776	
Cash paid in interest	20,000	
Cash paid to retire bonds	0	$240,776
Inputs		
Beginning balance at current cost	$250,000	
Current cost of interest on bonds	20,989	270,989
Realizable holding loss (gain) on bonds payable		($ 30,213)

d. Of this amount $989 was realized. This is the difference between current interest cost of $20,989 and historical interest cost of $20,000.

e. Managers should be held accountable for financing a firm's assets as well as for using them. Current cost data on market values of bonds and rates of interest as well as realizable holding gains provide information as to whether the company effected cost savings by borrowing on favourable terms when interest rates were low and market prices high. Such data are extremely useful in evaluating and controlling a firm's borrowing activities. As has sometimes been pointed out, "one manages what one measures; one does not and cannot manage what one does not measure."

5. The current cost/nominal dollar statements are shown in Exhibit 15-12.

EXHIBIT 15-12

J. Bear, Inc.
Current Cost Balance Sheets as at December 31
(current costs/nominal dollars)

		1996	1995
Assets			
Cash		$ 270,000	$580,000
Accounts receivable		300,000	0
Merchandise inventory		240,000	0
Furniture and fixtures	$325,000		
Less: Accumulated amortization	65,000	260,000	0
Total assets		$1,070,000	$580,000
Liabilities and shareholders' equity			
Accounts payable		$ 100,000	$ 0
Bonds payable		220,776	250,000
Common stock		330,000	330,000
Retained earnings		419,224	0
Total liabilities and shareholders' equity		$1,070,000	$580,000

J. Bear, Inc.
Current Cost Income Statement for Year Ended December 31, 1996
(current costs/nominal dollars)

Sales revenue		$900,000
Less expenses		
Cost of goods sold	$520,000	
Amortization	65,000	
Selling and administrative	60,000	
Interest	20,989	665,989

Current operating income		234,011
Plus realizable holding gains		
Inventory	80,000	
Furniture and fixtures	75,000	
Bonds payable	30,213	185,213
Comprehensive current income		$419,224

Part 2. Current Costs/Constant Dollars

1. On the December 31, 1996, balance sheet the firm's monetary assets and liabilities should be shown at face value; they need not be adjusted. They are already expressed in dollars of 1996. Hence

Cash	$270,000
Accounts receivable	300,000
Accounts payable	100,000

By contrast, the monetary assets and liabilities of December 31, 1995, which are expressed in dollars of that date, must be adjusted so that they are in dollars of December 31, 1996. The index on December 31, 1996, was 121; that on December 31, 1995, was 100. The only monetary item on hand at December 31, 1995, was cash of $580,000. Thus

$$\text{Cash} = \$580,000 \times 121/100 = \$701,800$$

2. Other assets and liabilities need not be adjusted. Their current costs are based on dollars of December 31, 1996. Thus

Inventory		$240,000
Furniture and fixtures	$325,000	
Less: Accumulated amortization	65,000	260,000
Bonds payable		220,776

3. The other assets and liabilities of December 31, 1995, must be adjusted so that they are expressed in dollars of December 31, 1996. In this example, there are no other assets, only bonds payable. Thus for bonds payable December 31, 1995,

$$\$250,000 \times 121/100 = \$302,500$$

4. Common stock was issued on December 31, 1995. The required adjustment to express common stock in dollars of December 31, 1996, is the same for both the December 31, 1995 and 1996, balance sheets:

Common stock	$330,000 × 121/100 = $399,300

5. Revenues and expenses would be adjusted by the ratio of the price index at December 31, 1996 (121), to that of when the revenues were generated or expenses incurred (110). Hence

Sales revenue	$900,000 × 121/110 = $990,000
Cost of goods sold	520,000 × 121/110 = 572,000
Amortization	65,000 × 121/110 = 71,500
Selling and administrative	60,000 × 121/110 = 66,000
Interest	20,989 × 121/110 = 23,088

6. The realizable gains would be recomputed as follows:

	Unadjusted Amounts	Conversion Factor	Adjusted Amounts (31/12/96 dollars)
Inventories			
Outputs			
Ending inventory at current cost	$240,000	121/121	$240,000
Current cost of goods sold	520,000	121/110	572,000
	760,000		812,000
Inputs			
Beginning inventory at current cost	0	121/100	0
Purchases	680,000	121/110	748,000
	680,000		748,000
Realizable holding gain on inventories	$ 80,000		$ 64,000
Furniture and Fixtures			
Outputs			
Ending balance (net) at current cost	$260,000	121/121	$260,000
Current cost amortization	65,000	121/110	71,500
	325,000		331,500
Inputs			
Beginning balance (net) at current cost	0	121/100	0
Purchases	250,000	121/100	302,500
	250,000		302,500
Realizable holding gain on furniture and fixtures	$ 75,000		$ 29,000
Bonds Payable			
Outputs			
Ending balance at current cost	$220,776	121/121	$220,776
Cash paid in interest	20,000	121/110	22,000
Cash paid to retire bonds	0		0
	240,776		242,776
Inputs			
Beginning balance at current cost	250,000	121/100	302,500
Current cost of interest on bonds	20,989	121/110	23,088
	270,989		325,588
Realizable holding loss (gain) on bonds payable	($ 30,213)		($ 82,812)

7. The purchasing power loss would be calculated as follows:

	Unadjusted Amounts	Conversion Factor	Adjusted Amounts (31/12/96 dollars)
Balance in net monetary assets, December 31, 1995	$ 580,000	121/100	$ 701,800
Add: Sales	900,000	121/110	990,000
	$1,480,000		$1,691,800
Deduct:			
Purchase of furniture and fixtures	250,000	121/100	302,500
Merchandise purchases	680,000	121/110	748,000
Selling and administrative costs	60,000	121/110	66,000
Interest payments	20,000	121/110	22,000
	$1,010,000		$1,138,500
Net monetary assets, necessary to be as well off on December 31, 1996, as on December 31, 1995			553,300
Less: Actual net monetary assets, December 31, 1996 (unadjusted)	$ 470,000		470,000
Difference: Loss (gain) in purchasing power			$ 83,300

8. The current cost/constant dollar statements are shown in Exhibit 15-13.

EXHIBIT 15-13

J. Bear Inc.
Current Cost Real Balance Sheets as at December 31
(current costs/constant dollars)

		1996	1995
Assets			
Cash		$ 270,000	$701,800
Accounts receivable		300,000	0
Merchandise inventory		240,000	0
Furniture and fixtures	$325,000		
Less: Accumulated amortization	65,000	260,000	0
Total assets		$1,070,000	$701,800
Liabilities and shareholders' equity			
Accounts payable		$ 100,000	$0
Bonds payable		220,776	302,500
Common stock		399,300	399,300
Retained earnings		349,924	0
Total liabilities and shareholders' equity		$1,070,000	$701,800

EXHIBIT 15-13 **(continued)**

J. Bear, Inc.
Current Cost Real Income Statement for Year Ended December 31, 1996
(current costs/constant dollars)

Sales revenue		$990,000
Less expenses		
Cost of goods sold	$572,000	
Amortization	71,500	
Selling and administrative	66,000	
Interest	23,088	732,588
Current operating income		257,412
Plus realizable holding gains		
Inventory	64,000	
Furniture and fixtures	29,000	
Bonds payable	82,812	175,812
Loss in purchasing power from		
holding monetary items		(83,300)
Comprehensive current real income		$349,924

16

Financial Reporting and Analysis in Perspective

This final chapter puts into perspective the issue of financial reporting and analysis. The previous chapters have indicated the accounting and financial presentation for numerous categories of assets, liabilities, and owners' equity. Yet the resultant financial reports are useful only if they provide relevant information to various groups of users. Because of the nature of our generally accepted accounting model, the information in financial reports must be interpreted carefully. The users must be made aware of the assumptions and estimates that are inherent in the financial statement numbers. In addition, this chapter introduces return on investment as a measurement of performance.

After studying this chapter, you will be able to

- Understand the objectives of financial reporting
- Understand how reported earnings may be influenced by use of the accrual accounting model
- Describe required supplementary disclosures that alleviate some of the limitations to the reported financial statement numbers
- Understand that financial statements are only one source of information to be used in assessing the future prospects of an entity
- Calculate and understand the three return on investment measurements of corporate profitability and efficiency

The principal work in identifying the objectives of financial reporting has been undertaken by the FASB in the United States. In 1978 the FASB published a statement of objectives of financial reporting by business enterprises. This statement was the first part of their "conceptual framework" project, and the objectives were intended as the foundation on which a logical and orderly set of accounting standards could be constructed.

According to the FASB, financial reports should be directed primarily to potential investors and creditors. They should provide information that is useful in making investment, credit, and similar decisions. By implication, financial reports should not be specifically directed to managers and parties internal to the organization. Managers and other internal parties, unlike *investors* and *creditors,* have the authority to prescribe the information they want and can obtain it from sources other than general-purpose financial reports.

The FASB stated that financial reports should provide information that will help users to assess the amounts, timing, and uncertainty of *cash* that they will receive from an enterprise. Investors and creditors contribute cash to a business in the expectation of receiving more cash than they give up. Their cash returns will be in the form of dividends, interest payments, and proceeds from the sale, redemption, or maturity of securities and loans. Obviously, the prospects of investors and creditors receiving cash are dependent upon the ability of the enterprise itself to generate cash through its income-producing activities. Thus financial reporting must facilitate predictions of enterprise cash flows.

In addition, financial reporting should help investors, creditors, and others to assess an enterprise's financial performance during a period. It should serve as a basis for evaluating how well management has carried out its stewardship responsibilities to the owners of the business.

The CICA has not taken as detailed an approach to formalizing the objectives of financial reporting. In Section 1000 of the *CICA Handbook,* the objectives of financial statements are laid out. This is a narrower focus than the FASB's objectives of financial reporting, since the objectives apply to the financial statements only, and not to other aspects of financial reporting such as the additional information contained in the annual report. Section 1000 states that the objective of financial statements is to provide information to investors, creditors, and other users that is useful in making their resource allocation decisions and their assessments of management. To achieve this objective, the financial statements should provide information about a firm's economic resources, obligations, and equity; changes in those items over a period of time; and the economic performance of the firm. There is reference to the prediction of cash flows but it is not emphasized as much as it is by the FASB. The CICA objectives are not inconsistent with those of the FASB and, since the FASB has invested such significant resources into the determination of objectives of financial reporting, we will refer to the FASB objectives in the discussion that follows.

Although a key objective of financial reporting is to assist investors and creditors to predict the *cash* that an enterprise will generate, financial statements that reported merely changes in cash balances would inadequately satisfy that objective. The amount of cash to be generated depends mainly on the economic resources available to the firm. The resources include the complete array of assets controlled by the firm—tangible as well as intangible. Moreover, the performance of an organization over a specified period of time must be measured by the changes in those resources. *Accrual accounting* captures the changes in many more of a firm's resources than does cash accounting. Financial events are recorded when they have their substantive economic impact, not only when cash is received or disbursed. Accrual accounting, for example, records an increase in level of resources when a firm makes a sale, regardless of whether the proceeds are received before or after the date of sale. It records a decline in resources when equipment is consumed over time, not when it is acquired and not necessarily when it is paid for. Accrual accounting is generally seen as providing more useful information than cash accounting for both predicting cash flows and assessing the periodic performance of the firm and its managers.

CONSEQUENCES OF ACCRUAL ACCOUNTING

Complexity

Because accrual accounting reports upon changes in the full scope of a firm's resources and not just cash, it is necessarily more complex than cash accounting. Cash accounting involves little more than the identification, classification, and summarization of cash inflows and outflows—something that could be accomplished by an analysis of a firm's chequebook. Comparability of practices among firms could be achieved by merely establishing reasonable categories for classifying cash receipts and disbursements. There would be no issues of asset valuation; the only asset to be valued would be cash. There would be no questions of revenue or expense recognition; revenues or expenses would be concurrent with receipts or disbursements of cash.

Accrual accounting, by contrast, is concerned with *income*, not cash flows. The process of resource enhancement in a firm takes place over time and involves a series of related activities. In a manufacturing enterprise, for example, it includes the purchase of plant and equipment, the acquisition of raw materials, the manufacture and sale of the product, and the collection of cash. Accrual accounting requires a firm to determine (or make assumptions about) how much each particular activity contributes to increases in the firm's well-being—what the firm's resources are at any particular time and how much they have changed between two times.

If accounting reports are to be comparable, guidelines of income measurement must be established. But the commercial activities in which firms engage are both diverse and complicated. Financial arrangements that are similar in substance may differ considerably in form. It has proved impossible to issue a set of simple accounting principles that captures the economic essence of all transactions in which firms engage.

As recently as 25 years ago, however, guidelines of accrual accounting were few in number and broad in scope. Individual firms had considerable freedom in reporting upon their activities. The resultant diversity of practice decreased the comparability of reports and allowed for some clear-cut instances of intentional deception. In the last quarter century, the rule-making authorities of the accounting profession have narrowed the range of reporting options. But they have also made the set of rules to which firms must adhere more detailed and cumbersome. Greater comparability of reports has been achieved at the cost of greater complexity.

The trade-off between greater comparability and less complexity has proved especially difficult to avoid because *uniformity* of practice does not necessarily ensure comparability. The value of a firm's resources—the extent to which they will generate cash in the future—depends upon circumstances that are unique to each firm. The benefits to be derived from a capital asset in the control of one company may differ considerably from those from an identical asset in the control of another. Accounting rules that were to require identical useful lives and patterns of amortization may make the financial reports of the two firms uniform, but certainly not comparable.

Opportunities to Influence Reported Earnings

Despite the strides in recent years toward greater uniformity of practice, individual firms still have opportunities to influence *reported* (as opposed to substantive economic) earnings. These opportunities exist because of the inherent characteristics of accrual accounting. Over time the opportunities may be reduced in number, but they will likely never be eliminated. It is essential that managers and investors be cognizant of them, not only so they can spot blatant attempts at income manipulation, but more importantly, so that they can compensate for differences in reporting policies among firms.

In 1988 the Macdonald Commission determined that one of the major weaknesses in financial reporting in Canada was the availability of alternative acceptable accounting practices for the same circumstances. The Commission recommended that the profession move to eliminate alternative accounting methods that are not justified by significant differences in circumstances.[1] The CICA has been attempting to follow this recommendation in recent revisions, and additions, to the *CICA Handbook*.

The section that follows summarizes the ways in which management can influence reported earnings. Although the emphasis is on earnings, it must be remembered that any actions that affect *earnings* must necessarily affect assets, liabilities, or owners' equity.

There are three primary ways in which management can have an impact on reported earnings:

1. By choosing judiciously among acceptable accounting methods

2. By making biased estimates

[1] "Report of the Commission to Study the Public's Expectations of Audits," CICA, 1988.

3. By timing transactions so that changes in value that have occurred over time are given accounting recognition in the most opportune periods

Choosing among Available Accounting Methods

In the preceding chapters a number of areas were discussed in which alternative accounting methods may be used. Among them are

1. *Revenue recognition.* Although most businesses recognize revenue at time of sale, they may do so at other times as well. For example, revenue on a long-term project may be recognized as work is carried out (a percentage of completion basis), when the project is completed, or when cash is collected.

2. *Cost of goods sold.* Cost of goods sold and inventory values may be established by a number of costing methods, the most popular of which are FIFO and LIFO.

3. *Amortization.* Firms may select among straight-line and various patterns of accelerated amortization.

4. *Matching of costs to revenues.* Costs should be charged as expenses in the periods in which the revenues that they generate are recognized. Management, however, has considerable latitude in determining whether a cost should be considered a period cost to be charged as an expense as it is incurred, a product cost to be inventoried and charged as an expense as part of cost of goods sold, or a capitalizable cost to be amortized over several accounting periods. For example, the cost of drilling unsuccessful oil wells may be written off as incurred (the successful-efforts method) or capitalized as part of the cost of the successful wells (the full-cost method).

Some accountants and analysts characterize earnings in terms of their *quality.* The more conservative the accounting methods on which earnings are based, the higher the quality of earnings. Conservative accounting methods are those that recognize revenues later and expenses earlier.

Making Estimates

Accrual accounting requires that numerous management estimates be incorporated into the financial reports. Among them are

1. *Useful lives.* Management must determine the number of years over which to amortize the cost of capital assets and intangibles, including goodwill.

2. *Losses on bad debts.* Management must estimate the percentage of sales or accounts receivable that will be uncollectable, and credit such amount to an allowance for doubtful accounts account.

3. *Warranties.* Expenses must be matched with revenues. Therefore management must estimate repair and replacement costs that will be incurred subsequent to the period in which revenue is recognized, and it must charge such amounts to expense in the period in which the related revenue is recognized.

Selecting the Period to Recognize Gains and Losses

Gains or losses from changes in the value of assets or liabilities are ordinarily recognized when the assets or liabilities are sold or liquidated, not in the periods in which the changes take place. This is a result of our transaction-based accounting model. Thus a firm that owns assets that have appreciated or declined in value or owes liabilities that have appreciated or declined has a "reserve" of earnings (losses) that it can draw upon at its discretion. It can engage in the following types of transactions to realize the earnings (losses) in the reserve:

1. It can sell appreciated assets (such as marketable securities). The gain would be recognized entirely in period of sale, regardless of when the increase in value actually took place.

2. It can retire long-term bonds that have declined in value. Bonds would be traded at a price less than book value if interest rates have increased since the bonds were issued. The firm could purchase, and then retire, the bonds at an amount less than that at which they are recorded, and thereby recognize a gain in the period of retirement.

3. It can sell assets that have declined in value (such as long-term investments). The loss would be recognized entirely in the period of sale, regardless of when the decline in value actually took place. However, as noted in the chapter on long-term investments, if the decline in value had been considered to be permanent, then a write-down to reflect the loss in value would be required in the period it is determined that the decline in value is permanent. Therefore, there is less discretion in selecting the period in which to recognize losses than there is for gains.

These types of transactions may be economically insubstantial because the assets surrendered by the firm (such as the marketable securities and long-term investments or the cash used to repay the debt) may be replaceable without loss of economic utility. The assets may be repurchased at the price for which they were sold; the cash may be reborrowed at a rate of interest reflective of the price at which the debt was retired.

Limitations for Managers

Financial statements based on the principles of accrual accounting are designed for investors and creditors, not managers. Managers are responsible for planning and controlling the activities of an enterprise. Seldom do they focus on predicting cash flows or evaluating the performance of the firm as a whole. Instead, they are concerned with the cash flows that can be generated by *specific* projects, activities, and assets; they evaluate the performance of *individual* managers or corporate segments.

Managers need information that is tailor-made for the decisions at hand. Reports intended for investors and creditors are often inappropriate because they fail to isolate the changes in the resources that will be affected by the decision. Revenues and expenses as reported in the income statement, for example, are usually poor predictors of the cash consequences of any particular management action. They are "contaminated" by the estimates, allocations, and choices of accounting principles required by accrual accounting. Suppose that a manager must decide whether to increase production volume. The expense, "cost of goods sold," would provide little guidance as to the additional manufacturing costs that would be incurred. "Cost of goods sold" includes allocations of fixed costs (such as those for plant maintenance) that will be unchanged by the increase in volume. Moreover, it is influenced by estimates (such as that of the useful life of existing plant and equipment) and choice of inventory method (such as that between LIFO or FIFO) that will affect reported expense, but not actual manufacturing costs. Management would require a report that focuses directly upon the incremental cash flows attributable to the increase in production volume.

Similarly, when managers review the accomplishments of departments or divisions of the firm, they must focus attention exclusively on the components of performance over which the unit has control. Earnings, as computed in accordance with accepted principles of accrual accounting, incorporate elements that are likely to be beyond the influence of the managers of a specific unit. Amortization expense, for example, reflects decisions of the past. It is based on the amount paid to acquire an asset—an asset that may have been purchased in a period prior to that in which present managers took charge. Over time, of course, present managers can decide to dispose of old assets and buy new ones. But in the short run they are saddled with amortization charges which they can do little or nothing to reduce, and which are not relevant to any economic decision making.

Correspondingly, units may be credited with revenues or charged with expenses that are established "arbitrarily" at corporate headquarters. The revenues of a production unit may represent intracompany "sales" to a marketing division. The sales price (in actuality a *transfer* price since it represents the price at which goods are transferred from one unit of the firm to another) would be determined by the company itself. Its expenses may include allocations of common corporate costs (such as administrative and financing costs), also decided upon by company executives. Insofar as the unit lacks control over one or more key components of income, income cannot be used as a valid indicator of performance.

It would be incorrect to infer that financial reports based on accrual accounting are useless to managers and completely adequate for investors and creditors. Managers are themselves investors or creditors when they acquire securities of, or make loans to, other firms. And investors and creditors must make analyses similar to those of management when they decide whether to provide financial support for proposed corporate projects. On balance, however, accrual accounting is considered the preferred means of communicating financial information to investors and creditors. Reports that are specifically designed for the decisions at hand are required by managers. As indicated in Chapter 1, financial (accrual-based) accounting focuses on providing information to parties external to the firm—principally, investors and creditors. As such, financial accounting is subject to many rules to ensure comparability of reporting among firms. Management accounting is directed at insiders and can be in any format, and use any information, that is relevant to the particular management issue that is being evaluated.

The three basic financial statements are not a completely satisfactory means of conveying financial data to *all* investors and creditors. Users differ in their information requirements and preferences. The accounting and reporting practices that underlie the statements are the product of compromises and arbitrary decisions by rule-making authorities, the firm's managers, and its independent auditors. Moreover, the quantitative, tabular form of accounting statements can never fully capture all the events and circumstances that bear upon a firm's financial health. They must be supplemented by verbal reports and explanations.

In recent years there has been a sharp increase in the amount of information contained in notes that accompany the three basic statements. These notes form an integral part of the financial report and are intended, in large measure, to reduce the inherent deficiencies of the three basic statements themselves. The information contained in the supplementary notes varies from company to company. The following, however, are among the more significant types of disclosures and an indication of the deficiencies that they are intended to reduce:

1. *A summary of significant accounting policies.* The flexibility allowed firms in selecting accounting methods diminishes the objectivity and comparability of financial statements. The importance of the methods chosen is reduced, however, when the firm describes the methods used and provides the particulars of the transactions reported on. The user of the report is then able to adjust the statements to reflect his or her own preferred methods. The accounting policies a firm must describe in the supplementary notes are those over which a firm has discretion (i.e., where a selection has been made from alternative acceptable methods). They include those relating to inventories and cost of goods sold, amortization, income taxes, revenue recognition, and intercorporate investments. Presently, firms are not required to provide sufficient details of most types of transactions to permit accurate adjustments. But the information on accounting policies facilitates at least estimates of what the adjustments would be.

2. *Details of transactions.* The three primary statements may not reveal all important aspects of transactions in which a firm engages. For example, if a firm "defers" a portion of its income taxes, then the income statement would not indicate the amount of taxes actually paid. Similarly, if a firm capitalizes its lease obligations, then the reported lease (or interest) expense would differ from the actual cash paid. Typical of transactions about which additional information should be provided in supplementary notes are those involving income taxes, leases, research and development costs, and employee stock options.

3. *Breakdown of reported amounts.* The main body of each statement summarizes groups of accounts into single figures. But there is no optimum level of data aggregation. What is necessary detail to one user may be information overload to another. A firm can best satisfy

differing preferences of users by indicating summary balances on the face of the statements and supporting amounts in supplementary notes. In this way, the firm is able to present the necessary data both clearly and completely. Among the accounts for which supporting detail is often provided are long-term debt, interest expense, capital assets, and shareholders' equity.

4. *Outstanding commitments.* Accepted accounting principles do not require that all commitments be recorded in the financial statements. Yet some commitments may have a material impact on a firm's financial well-being and should therefore be disclosed. Examples are obligations for rent payments under noncancelable leases, commitments to make capital expenditures that are abnormal in relation to the normal business operations of the firm, promises to redeem preferred stock, and pledges to issue stock under employee stock options.

5. *Contingent losses.* Contingent losses are potential losses. They would be transformed into actual losses only if certain unfavourable events were to occur. They frequently result from pending litigation, threats of expropriation, and guarantees of the indebtedness of others. Contingent losses are reported on the income statement only if it is likely that the future unfavourable event, on which the loss is dependent, will occur and the amount of the loss can be reasonably estimated. But the consequences of an unfavourable event may overwhelm the information contained in the main body of the financial statements. If, for example, an unfavourable product liability ruling were to cause the firm to declare bankruptcy, then reported asset values (based on the concept of the going concern) would have little meaning. Firms are required (by *CICA Handbook,* Section 3290) to explain the nature of a contingency and to give an estimate of the possible range of loss, or state that such an estimate is not possible, even if the criteria for income statement recognition are not met.

6. *A 5- or 10-year summary of operations.* The body of a financial statement generally covers the fiscal year just ended plus only one (and sometimes two) preceding periods. Evaluations of past performance, as well as prediction of future results, require analysis of trends over time. Consequently, although not specifically required by the CICA, many firms summarize the financial statements of the past 5 to 10 years. Among the key figures the summaries indicate are sales, net income, earnings per share, working capital, and shareholders' equity. Obviously, if this summary information is not provided, it can easily be obtained by the financial statement user by referring to the financial statements of all of the years in question.

7. *Information on operations by industry and geographic area.* Many firms are engaged in a number of different types of business endeavours. Some companies are *conglomerates:* they are composed of divisions in a number of unrelated industries, often located in different parts of the world. Their consolidated financial statements

combine the financial position and results of operations of all their activities. They indicate neither corporate resources devoted to any particular industry nor the profits derived from them, nor the location of assets and sources of profit. Yet financial analysis is meaningful only when one firm is compared with others in the same industry. Also, the risks associated with doing business in different parts of the world is dependent on the political and economic climate that exists where the businesses are located. If the financial statements fail to provide data by industry and location, then comparisons are impossible.

Firms have been reluctant to disclose financial information for individual lines of business. They cite the inherent difficulties of allocating common expenditures, such as headquarters' costs, to the separate businesses and of classifying all products into lines of business. They have also feared that the additional data on product lines might aid their competitors. Nonetheless, the CICA now requires that public companies report revenues, income, and assets for each major industry segment and for each major geographic segment.

8. *Particulars of employee pension and post-retirement health benefits.* These must include information on accounting and funding policies as well as the assumptions underlying any estimates of future costs.

9. *Management explanations and interpretations.* The numbers in the primary financial statements describe quantitatively a firm's results of operations and financial position. But they fail to explain and interpret them. Managers can be expected to have insights into the firm's financial history and prospects that extend beyond the reported data. Although not required by the CICA, the Ontario Securities Commission requires public companies under its jurisdiction to include a Management Discussion and Analysis (MD&A) in the annual report. The MD&A is to provide management's explanations and interpretations of the financial performance of the year of the financial statements, the current financial position, and the prospects for future performance. Among the matters that management should address in the MD&A are favourable and unfavourable trends, changes in product mix, the acquisition and disposal of major assets or lines of business, and unusual gains and losses.

FINANCIAL ANALYSIS: AN OVERVIEW

Financial reports assist investors, creditors, and other users in predicting cash flows of the future and assessing enterprise performance of the past. They do not, however, include actual forecasts or evaluations. Investors, creditors, and other users must do their own forecasting and evaluating.

Two contradictory assessments can be made as to the role that financial reports play in facilitating forecasts and evaluations. The first is that financial statements provide an abundance of information about the company whose financial affairs they describe. The financial statements of a company enable an analyst to gain an insight into its economic well-being with a clarity that cannot be matched by any other documents or sources of information. A measure of expertise, however, may be required to discern the true nature of the firm's financial situation.

Financial statements are comparable to aerial photographs. An untrained observer may not only learn considerably less from an examination of the photographs than a skilled analyst, but the conclusions that he or she draws from them may be erroneous. A layperson, for example, may see in a series of aerial photographs nothing more than a pastoral landscape of rolling hills and farms dotted with residential homes and barns. An environmental expert, however, by carefully focusing on changes over time and relationships among the various types of vegetation, may detect a serious pollution problem lurking beneath the surface. Similarly, a casual observer may see in a set of financial statements a seemingly stable, financially sound corporation. A skilled manager or analyst, however, by studying trends over time and relationships among accounts, may discern the existence of financial factors that point to fiscal turbulence.

The second assessment is that the importance of financial statements can be easily overemphasized. For any decisions in which the financial prospects of a company must be taken into account, an analysis of the data contained in the financial statements is unquestionably necessary. But it is hardly sufficient.

Financial statements do not explicitly provide information on a number of factors that are likely to have an effect on the future success of a company. Financial statements, for example, do not generally report upon scientific or technological breakthroughs. And they are generally silent about changes in the economic or social environment in which the firm operates. Changes in the real income or in the tastes of the consumers served by the firm could have a major impact on its profitablility, but even a detailed examination of financial reports may not provide a hint of such changes.

Expertise in accounting must be recognized as being of limited utility. It enables one to prepare and interpret financial statements. But financial statements are only one source (albeit a crucial source) of information among many that must be taken into account in deciding whether to invest in a corporation. For every millionaire whose investment success can be attributed to a keen ability to interpret financial statements, there is undoubtedly another who cannot distinguish an asset from a liability.

Financial analysis is founded upon ratios and similar measures. No accounting numbers, including net income, have meaning in and of themselves. Therefore ratios are necessary to extricate information of significance from financial reports. Measures have been developed to describe quantitatively a firm's solvency and liquidity, its profitability, and its effectiveness in employing all, or selected categories of, the resources within its control. The financial measures discussed throughout this text are summarized in Exhibit 16-1.

RETURN ON INVESTMENT

Return on investment is the single most important measure of corporate profitability and efficiency. It encompasses all revenues and expenses as well as all assets and liabilities, and it is widely used as an evaluative criterion by managers as well as

EXHIBIT 16-1
Summary of Selected Financial Measures

Name	Formula	Objective
I. Profitability and activity measures		
A. Return on investment (all capital); see Chapter 16	$$\frac{\text{Net income} + \text{Interest after taxes}}{\text{Average assets}}$$	To indicate the efficiency of a business in employing *all* resources within its command
B. Return on investment (shareholders' equity); see Chapter 16	$$\frac{\text{Net income}}{\text{Average shareholders' equity}}$$	To indicate the efficiency of a business in employing capital provided by shareholders
C. Return on equity of common shareholders; see Chapter 16	$$\frac{\text{Net income} - \text{Preferred stock dividends}}{\text{Average equity of common shareholders}}$$	To indicate the efficiency of a business in employing capital provided by common shareholders
D. Price/earnings ratio; see Chapter 4	$$\frac{\text{Market price per share}}{\text{Earnings per share}}$$	To measure the return on the market value of common stock
E. Inventory turnover; see Chapter 8	$$\frac{\text{Cost of goods sold}}{\text{Average inventory}}$$	To measure the efficiency of inventory management
F. Accounts receivable turnover; see Chapter 7	$$\frac{\text{Sales}}{\text{Average accounts receivable}}$$	To measure the efficiency of accounts receivable management
G. Number of days' sales in accounts receivable; see Chapter 7	$$\frac{\text{Accounts receivable}}{\text{Average sales per day}}$$	To determine the average number of days accounts receivable are outstanding
H. Plant and equipment turnover; see Chapter 9	$$\frac{\text{Sales}}{\text{Average plant and equipment}}$$	To measure the efficiency of the utilization of plant and equipment
II. Liquidity ratios		
A. Current ratio; see Chapter 4	$$\frac{\text{Current assets}}{\text{Current liabilities}}$$	To measure a firm's ability to meet current obligations as they come due
B. Quick ratio; see Chapter 7	$$\frac{\text{Cash} + \text{Marketable securities} + \text{Accounts receivable}}{\text{Current liabilities}}$$	To measure, by a more severe test, a firm's ability to meet current obligations as they come due
III. Financing measures		
A. Debt-to-equity ratio; see Chapter 11	$$\frac{\text{Total debt}}{\text{Total shareholders' equity}}$$	To indicate the proportion of capital provided by creditors rather than by owners
B. Times interest earned; see Chapter 10	$$\frac{\text{Net income} + \text{Interest} + \text{Income taxes}}{\text{Interest}}$$	To measure a firm's ability to meet fixed interest charges

investors and creditors. Return on investment was discussed briefly in Chapter 4. In this section we shall expand upon its significance and indicate its limitations.

First, return on investment may be calculated so as to indicate enterprise profitability without regard to how it has been financed. Income, excluding a deduction for interest, is related to total capital employed in the business. Interest is excluded because, like dividends, it is a distribution to the parties which provided the capital. Total capital may be represented by either total assets (the left-hand side of the accounting equation) or total liabilities plus total shareholders' equity (the right-hand side).

Second, return on investment may be computed so as to signify profitability from the perspective of all the shareholders, both common and preferred. Net income (with interest included along with all other operating expenses) is related to the equity of the shareholders.

Third, return on investment may be determined so as to denote profitability to the common shareholders alone. Net income, less the dividends to the preferred shareholders, is related to the equity of the common shareholders (that is, capital contributed by the common shareholders plus retained earnings).

Return on Investment (All Capital)

During 1994 TransCanada PipeLines Limited, one of North America's major distributors of natural gas (see Exhibit 16-2), employed on *average* $9,620 million in capital. This was determined by summing the *total assets* at the end of 1994 and 1993 and dividing by 2. It is preferable to base the computation on the average capital rather than that at a single date to avoid distortions that would result if

EXHIBIT 16-2

Selected Data from the Financial Statements of TransCanada PipeLines Limited

	December 31	
	1994	1993
	(in millions of dollars)	
Total assets (or total liabilities and shareholders' equity)	$9,926	$9,313
Total liabilities	$6,777	$6,416
Shareholders' equity:		
Preferred stock	$ 810	$ 780
Common stock	947	864
Contributed surplus	267	267
Retained earnings	1,090	965
Foreign exchange adjustment	35	21
Total common shareholders' equity	2,339	2,117
Total shareholders' equity	$3,149	$2,897
Interest expense	$ 474	$ 464
Income before taxes	474	441
Income taxes	116	86
Net income after taxes	358	355
Preferred stock dividends	47	47

capital had been acquired or returned to investors during the year. Since the firm would not have had use of such capital for an entire year, it should not be expected to have earned a return on it for a full year.

In 1994 TransCanada PipeLines had earnings *after taxes* of $358 million. Deducted from revenues in the calculation of net income was interest expense of $474 million. This amount had been paid to the parties that supplied debt capital. The interest must be added back to net income if total income available to suppliers of capital is to be related to total capital employed by the company.

Interest, however, is a tax-deductible expense. The cost to the company of the interest paid was not the amount charged as interest expense; it was the interest expense less the tax saving. Notes to the statements indicate that TransCanada PipeLines paid taxes at a rate of 39 percent. Its after-tax interest cost was $474 million less 39 percent of $474 million—a net of $289 million.

TransCanada PipeLines in 1994 had a return on investment (all capital) of 6.7 percent:

$$\text{Return on investment (all capital)} = \frac{\text{Net income} + \text{Interest after taxes}}{\text{Average assets}}$$

$$= \frac{\$358 + \$289}{\$9,620} = 6.7\%$$

Return on Investment (Shareholders' Equity)

The firm's entire 1994 net income (after interest and tax expenses) of $358 million will accrue to its owners, the common and preferred shareholders. The average equity of the shareholders during 1994 (calculated by averaging *total* shareholders' equity for year ends 1994 and 1993) was $3,023 million. Return on investment (shareholders' equity) was therefore 11.8 percent:

$$\text{Return on investment (shareholders' equity)} = \frac{\text{Net income}}{\text{Average shareholders' equity}}$$

$$= \frac{\$358}{\$3,023} = 11.8\%$$

Return on Equity of Common Shareholders

Earnings applicable to common shareholders represent net income less dividends declared to preferred shareholders. The equity of common shareholders includes common shares, contributed surplus, foreign exchange adjustment, and retained earnings—that is, total shareholders' equity less preferred stock.

TransCanada PipeLines declared preferred stock dividends in 1994 of $47 million. Average equity of common shareholders (based on the average of 1994 and 1993) was $2,228 million. The return to common shareholders was therefore 13.9 percent:

Return on equity of common shareholders

$$= \frac{\text{Net income} - \text{Preferred stock dividends}}{\text{Average equity of common shareholders}}$$

$$= \frac{\$358 - \$47}{\$2,228} = 13.9\%$$

Return on Investment as an Indicator of the Successful Use of Leverage

As discussed in Chapter 10 in the section pertaining to junk bonds, the extent to which common shareholders use capital supplied by lenders and preferred shareholders is known as *leverage*. Common shareholders benefit whenever the firm earns a return on funds acquired from outsiders that is greater than their cost. Interest and preferred stock dividends are fixed in amount; any earnings in excess of the stipulated payments accrue entirely to the common shareholders.

TransCanada PipeLines made successful use of leverage. This is evident by comparing the return on investment (all capital) with return on equity of common shareholders. Return on investment (all capital) was only 6.7 percent; return on equity of common shareholders was 13.9 percent. The company earned more on the funds from bondhonders and preferred shareholders than it had to pay in interest and preferred dividends.

Success in employing leverage can be measured by the ratio of return on equity of common shareholders to return on investment (all capital). The higher the ratio, the more effective the use of leverage. However, as long as the ratio is greater than 1 to 1, the leverage is positive and has been used effectively. The ratio for TransCanada PipeLines is

$$\text{Leverage effectiveness ratio} = \frac{\text{ROI (common shareholders' equity)}}{\text{ROI (all capital)}}$$

$$= \frac{13.9\%}{6.7\%} = 2.07 \text{ to } 1$$

It is important to remember that increased use of leverage increases the level of risk associated with the firm. The risk increases because the fixed interest charges on the money borrowed must be repaid, whether the enterprise is operating profitably or not.

Pitfalls of Return on Investment as an Evaluative Criterion

Return on investment is a comprehensive measure of performance. But, taken by itself, it is not an adequate measure, since it is based upon accrual accounting and thereby has all of its limitations. What is more, it may not always reflect the interests of *existing* corporate owners.

Has Same Deficiencies as Accrual Accounting

Return on investment, in that it relates earnings to resources, is appropriate as an evaluative criterion only to the extent that the accounting measures of earnings and resources are appropriate. As indicated previously in this chapter, earnings—particularly over a short period of time—may not be a valid indicator of either management or enterprise accomplishments. Both reported earnings and resources may be subjective in that they are dependent upon arbitrary choices among accounting principles; they can readily be manipulated by nonsubstantive management actions; they may be influenced by unreliable or biased estimates; and they may be reflective of decisions that were made prior to the period under review. Moreover, because assets are generally stated at historical costs, the denominator of the ratio is likely to be an unsatisfactory indicator of the economic value of the resources which are committed to the enterprise.

May Lead to Dysfunctional Management Decisions

Management decisions taken with a view toward maximizing return on investment can lead to a *reduction* in the earnings per share of common shareholders. Actions taken to increase return on investment may therefore be counter to the interests of existing owners. By way of illustration, assume that a firm has the opportunity to acquire a parcel of land that it would lease to outsiders. It would finance the acquisition by issuing 50,000 shares of common stock. The following data are relevant to the proposed acquisition:

Cost of land	$1,000,000
Expected rent revenue per year (after taxes)	$ 120,000
Number of shares of common stock that the firm would issue to acquire necessary capital ($20 per share issue price)	50,000

Other factors that affect return on investment and earnings per share are as follows:

Present assets	$10,000,000
Present liabilities	$ 4,000,000
Present shareholders' equity	$ 6,000,000
Expected income (after taxes), prior to taking into account rent revenue from proposed acquisition	$ 1,100,000
Interest (after taxes) on outstanding debt (10% of $4 million)	$ 400,000
Present number of shares of common stock outstanding	1,000,000 shares

If the firm decided *not* to acquire the land, then return on investment (all capital) would be

$$\frac{\text{Net income} + \text{Interest after taxes}}{\text{Assets}} = \frac{\$1,100,000 + \$400,000}{\$10,000,000}$$

$$= 15\%$$

Return on investment (shareholders' equity) would be

$$\frac{\text{Net income}}{\text{Shareholders' equity}} = \frac{\$1,100,000}{\$6,000,000} = 18.3\%$$

Earnings per share of common stock would be

$$\frac{\text{Net income}}{\text{Number of shares outstanding}} = \frac{\$1,100,000}{1,000,000}$$

$$= \$1.10$$

If the firm elected to acquire the land and finance the purchase by issuing 50,000 shares of common stock at the market price of $20 per share, then income would increase by $120,000 and shareholders' equity by $1 million. Return on investment (all capital) would decline:

$$\frac{\$1,100,000 + \$400,000 + \$120,000}{\$10,000,000 + 1,000,000} = \frac{\$1,620,000}{\$11,000,000} = 14.7\%$$

So too would return on investment (shareholders' equity):

$$\frac{\$1,100,000 + \$120,000}{\$6,000,000 + \$1,000,000} = \frac{\$1,220,000}{\$7,000,000} = 17.4\%$$

Yet earnings per share of common stock would *increase*:

$$\frac{\$1,100,000 + \$120,000}{1,000,000 + 50,000} = \frac{\$1,220,000}{1,050,000} = \$1.162$$

Were the firm to use return on investment, regardless of whether all capital or shareholders' equity, it would turn down the proposed land acquisition. But by doing so, it would be passing up an opportunity to increase the dollar return to existing shareholders. The anomaly occurs because the percentage return on the additional investment of $1 million would be less than the *average* return that the firm was earning on previously invested capital. Nevertheless, the additional return of $120,000 would be greater than the cost of the additional capital. The cost of the additional capital would be $58,100—the dollars of earnings assigned to the newly issued shares (50,000 shares times income per share of $1.162). Thus the existing shareholders would be better off by $61,900 ($120,000 – $58,100).

Residual Income as a Means of Avoiding Dysfunctional Decisions

The danger that corporations will inadvertently maximize return on investment at the expense of returns to existing shareholders is especially pronounced in divisionalized firms. Corporations commonly permit their divisions broad discretion in making investment decisions. The divisions receive capital from the corporation and are charged interest for it; they have no control over how the capital is obtained. Their performance is evaluated on the basis of return on investment. Therefore there are decided risks that the divisions will reject any projects that do not increase their returns on investment, even if acceptance would work to the benefit of existing shareholders.

One means of avoiding this danger is to substitute residual income for return on investment as an evaluative criterion. *Residual income* is defined as net income (excluding any actual interest costs) *less an imputed cost of capital.* The imputed cost of capital would be determined by multiplying total assets by the minimum rate of return that top corporate managers or owners demand on invested capital.

Assume that in the previous illustration the company demands a minimum return of 11 percent on invested capital. If it did not acquire the land, the company would have $10 million in invested capital. It would therefore be charged $1.1 million in imputed capital costs (11 percent of $10 million). Its residual income would be $400,000, determined as follows:

Net income (given)	$1,100,000	
Plus: Interest after taxes (given)	400,000	$1,500,000
Less: Imputed cost of capital (11% of $10,000,000)		1,100,000
Residual income		$ 400,000

Were the firm to acquire the land, then it would earn an additional $120,000 in revenue. It would be charged with an additional $110,000 in capital costs (11 percent of $1 million). Residual income would increase by $10,000. Aware that its performance is being evaluated on the basis of residual income, management would elect to acquire the land—a decision consistent with the interests of the shareholders.

Measures of Performance That Supplement Return on Investments

In light of the limitations of return on investment—or any other individual income-based measure—it is necessary for firms to develop supplementary criteria of performance. These criteria can be tailored to the specific objectives of the firm. Among criteria that are widely used are *profit margin* (net income as a percent of revenues), *gross margin* [1 minus (cost of goods sold as a percentage of revenues)], *share of market, innovations in product and manufacturing processes, productivity of labour,* and *rate of growth.* Although these measures cannot be summed to provide an overall performance "score," and may be even more subjective than return on investment, taken together they may provide a fairly complete accounting of firm or divisional accomplishment.

RATIOS IN FINANCIAL ANALYSIS

Until the 1960s, financial analysis was generally not carried beyond the calculation of ratios. Today, however, ratios serve as the starting point of financial analysis. The following are merely suggestive of the ways in which ratios are used:

- Ratios are incorporated into statistical models that are intended to predict financial distress.

- They are used in making forecasts of earnings and cash flows.
- They are integral elements in investment models of asset valuation.
- They are used in assessing the risk of individual securities and portfolios of securities.
- They serve as the basis of comparing one firm with others in the same industry. Statistical tests have been developed to assess the significance of deviations from industry norms.

Financial statement analysis has become a specialized area within the disciplines of both accounting and finance. There is an abundant body of literature on the topic in textbooks, scholarly journals, and practice-oriented magazines.

Summary

Financial reporting is directed primarily to investors and creditors. It should enable them to assess future net cash receipts and to evaluate the fiscal performance of firms in which they have an interest. Accrual accounting, in that it captures the periodic changes in the full range of a firm's resources, better serves the objectives of financial reporting than does cash accounting, a far simpler and more objective form of accounting. But accrual accounting requires the development of an elaborate set of principles and rules and affords firms considerable leeway to influence the earnings that they report, which they do in selecting among acceptable principles, in making required estimates, and in timing planned transactions. Moreover, because reported amounts are based upon allocations, estimates, and choices among accounting principles, they may be inappropriate for many types of decisions required of managers. Managers usually need reports specially tailored to the decisions at hand—reports that focus upon cash flows associated with proposed projects and assets or upon activities under the control of specific organizational units.

Because of inherent constraints, the three primary statements can never fully report upon all events and circumstances relevant to a firm's fiscal well-being. They must be supplemented by notes that explain accounting policies and give details of balances and transactions, indicate commitments and contingencies, and interpret the numerical data.

Financial analysis begins with the calculation of ratios. Return on investment is the most encompassing of the ratios discussed in this text. But it incorporates all of the weaknesses of the underlying accounting numbers. Although the performance of corporations and their divisions is often evaluated using return on investment as a criterion, efforts on the part of managers to maximize return on investment can run counter to the interests of shareholders.

The following are balance sheets and income statements of Maple Leaf Foods Inc. (as at December 31, 1993), and Schneider Corporation (as at October 30, 1993), two of Canada's largest food products companies. They have been recast slightly to make them comparable. All amounts, except earnings per share, are in millions.

Balance Sheets		
	Maple Leaf Foods	Schneider
Assets		
Current assets		
Cash	$ 204.9	$ —
Accounts receivable (net of allowance for doubtful accounts)	230.7	39.6
Inventories	208.4	48.9
Prepaid expenses	10.2	—
Other current assets	—	3.5
Total current assets	$ 654.2	$ 92.0
Investment in associated companies	49.3	—
Property, plant, and equipment (net of accumulated amortization)	562.4	103.4
Goodwill	185.5	—
Other assets	49.1	18.7
Total noncurrent assets	$ 846.3	$122.1
Total assets	$1,500.5	$214.1
Liabilities and Shareholders' Equity		
Current liabilities		
Bank advances	$ —	$ 11.2
Accounts payable and accrued liabilities	347.7	42.7
Income taxes payable	21.5	0.4
Current portion of long-term debt	4.6	7.5
Total current liabilities	$ 373.8	$ 61.8
Other liabilities and deferred charges		
Long-term debt	47.5	59.5
Deferred income taxes	42.8	3.6
Other deferred charges	—	1.5
Minority interest	50.6	5.0
Total other liabilities and deferred charges	$ 140.9	$ 69.6
Total liabilities	$ 514.7	$131.4
Shareholders' equity		
Common stock	840.6	16.0
Retained earnings	145.2	66.7
Total shareholders' equity	$ 985.8	$ 82.7
Total liabilities and shareholders' equity	$1,500.5	$214.1

Income Statements		
	Maple Leaf Foods	Schneider
Net sales	$3,054.0	$727.5
Cost of goods sold	2,633.5	635.7
Selling and administrative costs	240.8	58.2
Amortization	54.1	13.6
Interest expense	2.6	7.1
Total expenses	$2,931.0	$714.6
Income before taxes	$ 123.0	$ 12.9
Income taxes	45.6	4.5
Income after taxes	77.4	8.4
Minority interest	7.2	0.7
Net income	$ 70.2	$ 7.7
Earnings per share	$ 0.87	$ 1.31

1. Which of the two firms had greater earnings, prior to taking into account the cost of capital, in relation to all the resources within its command? That is, which provided the greater return on investment (all capital)? Base your response to this and the following questions on year-end (rather than average) values. Assume, in calculating interest after taxes, that each firm paid taxes at an incremental rate of 42 percent.

2. Which of the firms provided the greater return to common shareholders as measured by income available to them as a percentage of their equity?

3. Which of the two firms was the more highly leveraged as measured by the ratio of total debt to total shareholders' equity?

4. Which of the two firms made more effective use of leverage?

5. Which of the firms appeared to be better able to meet its fixed interest obligations; that is, which firm "covered" interest the greater number of times with earnings?

6. Which of the firms was more likely to be able to meet its current obligations as they came due as indicated by the current ratio?

Questions for Review and Discussion

1. Per the objectives of the CICA and FASB, to which main groups of potential users should financial reports be directed? What two main functions should financial reports facilitate?

2. Why is accrual accounting more consistent with the objectives of financial reporting than is cash accounting?

3. Why is accrual accounting necessarily more complex than cash accounting?

4. What are three ways in which the management of a firm can exercise discretion over reported earnings?

5. Financial statements report the financial history of an organization. Managers as well as investors and creditors are concerned with what the organization has accomplished in the past. If accounting is to be objective, how can there be justification for presenting the history differently to investors and creditors than to managers?

6. What is meant by a *transfer price?* Why do transfer prices introduce additional elements of subjectivity into the determination of earnings of a corporate division?

7. Supplementary notes reduce some of the deficiencies of the basic financial statements. Provide illustrations of several types of disclosures made in supplementary notes and indicate the deficiencies that they reduce.

8. "The manner in which a ratio is determined should depend on the specific decision at hand." Illustrate this statement by comparing return on investment using total investment with that computed using shareholders' equity.

9. What is meant by *residual income?* In what way does it overcome a deficiency of return on investment?

10. The *Wall Street Journal,* in a story about Federated Department Stores, Inc., reported that the newly appointed chief executive officer said that Federated would continue to keep an eye on the bottom line. He noted, however, that the company was also making a concerted effort, particularly at the divisional level, to stress such other yardsticks as return on investment, share of market, and gross profit margin. Why is the "bottom line" (net income), by itself, an inadequate indicator of corporate or divisional performance?

Problems

1. *A forward-looking management should understand the impact of its actions upon widely used financial ratios.*

   What effect would each of the following transactions have on a firm's (1) current ratio, (2) quick ratio, (3) debt-to-equity ratio? Indicate whether each transaction would cause the ratio to increase (I), decrease (D), or have no effect (NE). Assume that any transactions involving revenues or expenses have an immediate impact upon retained earnings. Assume that all ratios are initially *greater* than 1:1.
   a. The firm sells goods on account. It maintains its inventory records on a perpetual basis, and the price at which the goods are sold is greater than their initial cost.
   b. The firm collects the amount receivable from the customer to whom it made the sale.
   c. It issues long-term bonds.
   d. It issues preferred stock in exchange for cash.
   e. It declares, but does not pay, a cash dividend on common stock.
   f. It pays the previously declared cash dividend.
   g. It purchases merchandise inventory on account.

h. It pays for the merchandise previously purchased.
i. It purchases equipment, giving the seller a three-year note for the entire amount payable.
j. It recognizes depreciation for the first year.
k. It writes off an uncollectable account receivable against the allowance for doubtful accounts.
l. It writes off inventory as obsolete.

2. *The factors that affect return on investment may be depicted graphically.*

   Return on investment may be computed several ways. One way, often associated with the Du Pont Company, is illustrated in the accompanying diagram. The diagram is intended to direct the attention of management to the various elements that have an impact upon return on investment.

   a. Refer to the 1993 financial statements of The Molson Companies Limited in Problem 4. Determine return on investment (all capital). Base your computations on year-end rather than average values and assume a tax rate of 40 percent.
   b. Determine return on investment (all capital) by filling in each of the boxes in the diagram and carrying out the required operations. "Other expenses excluding interest" should include income taxes. However, to income taxes must be added the tax "saving" on the excluded interest.

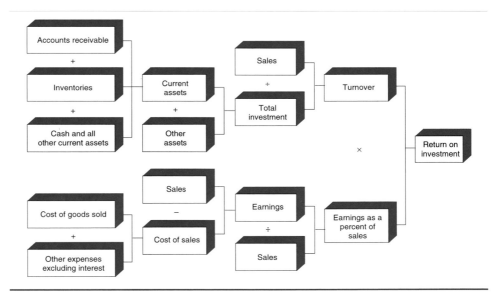

3. *Financial ratios incorporate all of the deficiencies of the underlying accounting data.*

   A friend, who is president of Statistical Software, Inc., invites you to acquire an interest in his company. In explaining to you the advantages of such an investment, he points to the firm's profitability as evidenced by a high rate of return on shareholders' equity and the security of the investment as measured by *times interest earned.*

   The firm develops and sells customized computer programs to industrial firms. The programs are intended to enable a firm to generate statistical information about its operations.

The president provides you with the company's 1996 financial statements. The statement of changes in financial position and the income statement are as follows:

Statistical Software, Inc. Statement of Changes in Financial Position Year Ended December 31, 1996			
Operating Activities			
Net income			$ 2,400,000
Adjustments to income to reconcile net income to cash provided by operating activities			
Amortization		$1,200,000	
Gain on sale of land		(3,200,000)	
Increase in accounts receivable		(3,400,000)	
Increase in advertising and promotion costs expected to benefit future periods		(600,000)	
Increase in program development costs applicable to software to be delivered in the future		(2,400,000)	(8,400,000)
Cash (used in) operating activities			$(6,000,000)
Investing Activities			
Sale of land			4,400,000
Increase (decrease) in cash			$(1,600,000)
Cash balance, beginning of year			8,200,000
Cash balance, end of year			$ 6,600,000

Statistical Software, Inc. Statement of Income Year Ended December 31, 1996		
Sales	$10,800,000	
Other revenues	5,200,000	$16,000,000
Cost of programs developed	$10,600,000	
Other expenses	1,800,000	
Interest	400,000	
Income taxes	800,000	13,600,000
Net income		$ 2,400,000

The balance sheet reveals that average shareholders' equity during the year was $12 million.

a. Determine the rate of return on shareholders' equity and the times interest earned measure of coverage of fixed charges.

b. Review carefully the two statements presented. Recognizing that no investment decisions can be made on the basis of statements for a single year, what questions would you raise (or what reservations would you have) pertaining to the firm's quality of earnings?

4. *The three problems that follow require that you compare and evaluate the performance of two national breweries.*

The income statement and balance sheet of The Molson Companies Limited, a leading brewery, are presented below and on the next page. In addition to its brewery business, these consolidated financial statements include the results of operations and financial position of Molson subsidiaries operating in a number of different businesses. These subsidiaries operate in such diverse businesses as commercial cleaning and water management (Diversy Corporation), hardware supplies (Beaver Lumber Company and Aikenhead's Home Improvement Warehouse), and sports (Montreal Canadiens hockey club). (All amounts, except per share data, are in millions.)

a. Compare the company's 1993 and 1992 financial performance in regard to the measures that follow. Use year-end, rather than average, balance sheet values.

(1) Return on investment (all capital) (Assume a tax rate of 40 percent.)
(2) Return on investment (common shareholders' equity)
(3) Debt-to-equity ratio
(4) Inventory turnover
(5) Current ratio
(6) Number of days' sales in accounts receivable

b. Explain, as best you can from the limited information contained in the financial statements, why net earnings increased in 1993.

The Molson Companies Limited Consolidated Statements of Earnings For the Year Ended March 31		
	1993	1992
Net sales	$ 3,094	$2,917
Cost of sales, selling, and administrative costs	2,405	2,240
Amortization of capital assets	97	82
Interest expense	56	69
Brewing excise and sales taxes	362	340
Total expenses, excluding income taxes	2,920	2,731
Income before taxes	174	186
Income taxes	10	61
Net earnings	$ 164	$ 125
Earnings per share	$ 2.76	$ 2.25

5. *The income statement and balance sheet of John Labatt Limited, another leading brewery, are presented bone pages 737–38. In addition to its brewery business, these consolidated financial statements include the results of operations and financial position of Labatt's subsidiaries operating in a number of different businesses. These subsidiaries operate in such diverse businesses as broadcasting (TSN television network) and sports (Toronto Blue Jays baseball club). (All amounts, except per share data, are in millions.)*

a. Compare the company's 1993 and 1992 financial performance using the measures that follow. Calculate the ratios with year-end rather than average balance sheet values. (Note: In the following financial statements there are numerous references to *discontinued operations*. During

The Molson Companies Limited
Consolidated Balance Sheets
As at March 31

	1993	1992
Assets		
Current assets		
Cash and temporary investments	$ 209	$ 98
Accounts receivable (net of allowance for doubtful accounts)	358	369
Inventories	336	383
Other current assets	228	32
Total current assets	1,131	882
Property, plant, and equipment (net of accumulated amortization)	783	784
Investments and other assets	803	701
Total noncurrent assets	1,586	1,485
Total assets	$2,717	$2,367
Liabilities and Shareholders' Equity		
Current liabilities		
Short-term debt	$ 275	$ 139
Accounts payable	417	427
Other	209	111
Total current liabilities	901	677
Other liabilities and deferred charges		
Deferred income taxes	—	32
Long-term debt	412	484
Other	229	244
Non-controlling interest	4	7
Total other liabilities and deferred charges	645	767
Total liabilities	1,546	1,444
Common shareholders' equity		
Common stock	449	327
Retained earnings	722	596
Total common shareholders' equity	1,171	923
Total liabilities and shareholders' equity	$2,717	$2,367

1992, Labatt recorded the sale of its nondairy food businesses (JL Foods, Everfresh, and Ogilvie Mills). In 1993, Labatt recorded the sale of its Canadian and U.S. dairy operations. Since both of these sales actually took place after the respective year ends, it is necessary to separate, in the financial statements, those amounts that relate to continuing operations from those that relate to discontinued operations. For example, at April 30, 1993, $340 million of current assets relate to discontinued operations. These are the current assets of the Canadian and U.S. dairy operations that were sold subsequent to April 30, 1993. In calculating the required ratios, you should use the numbers that relate to continuing operations.)

(1) Return on investment (all capital) (Assume a tax rate of 40 percent.)

(2) Return on investment (common shareholders' equity)

(3) Debt-to-equity ratio
(4) Inventory turnover
(5) Current ratio
(6) Number of days' sales in accounts receivable

b. Explain as best you can, from the limited information contained in the financial statements, why income declined in 1993.

John Labatt Limited
Consolidated Balance Sheets
As at April 30

	1993	1992
Assets		
Current assets		
Cash and securities	$ 276	$ 740
Accounts receivable (net of allowance		
for doubtful accounts)	286	246
Inventories	192	195
Other	93	82
Discontinued operations	**340**	**473**
Total current assets	1,187	1,736
Capital assets, net of accumulated amortization	784	684
Other assets	597	319
Discontinued operations	**452**	**649**
Total noncurrent assets	1,833	1,652
Total assets	$3,020	$3,388
Liabilities and Shareholders' Equity		
Current liabilities		
Bank advances and short-term notes	$ 88	$ —
Accounts payable	532	484
Taxes payable	—	33
Long-term debt due within one year	14	41
Discontinued operations	**298**	**346**
Total current liabilities	932	904
Other liabilities and deferred charges		
Long-term debt	630	646
Deferred income taxes	141	90
Total other liabilities and deferred charges	771	736
Total liabilities	1,703	1,640
Shareholders' equity		
Preferred stock	300	300
Common stock	597	592
Retained earnings	420	856
Total shareholders' equity	1,317	1,748
Total liabilities and shareholders' equity	$3,020	$3,388

6. *Compare the 1993 financial statements of The Molson Companies Limited and John Labatt Limited contained in the two preceding problems. In your comparison, be sure to calculate the John Labatt Limited ratios on its results from continuing operations only.*
   a. Which of the two firms would you characterize as more "conservative" based on capital structure (i.e., relationship of debt to equity)?
   b. Which of the firms successfully took advantage of leverage? Explain.

John Labatt Limited
Consolidated Statements of Earnings
Year Ended April 30

	1993	1992
Net sales	$2,780	$2,294
Cost of sales, selling, and administration expenses	1,781	1,420
Amortization expense	89	75
Interest expense	26	11
Brewing excise and sales taxes	645	567
	2,541	2,073
Earnings before the undernoted	239	221
Restructuring charges	45	101
Earnings before income taxes	194	120
Income taxes	61	39
Earnings from continuing operations*	133	81
Earnings (loss) from discontinued operations	**(203)**	**20**
Net earnings (loss)	$ (70)	$ 101
Earnings per share from continuing operations	$ 1.43	$ 0.78

* The company declared preferred stock dividends of $19 million in 1993 and $21 million in 1992.

  c. Which of the firms more efficiently employed its
    (1) Inventory?
    (2) Accounts receivable?
  d. As at April 30, 1993, the market price per share of The Molson Companies Limited was $25.00; that of John Labatt Limited was $18.00. Which of the two had the higher price/earnings ratio? Based on the ratios that you computed in the preceding problems, which firm do you think is fiscally more sound?

7. *Differences in return on investment may be more apparent than real.*

Rent-a-Truck, Inc., was founded in January 1996. The company issued 300,000 shares of no-par value common stock at $20 per share.

The company acquired trucks at a cost of $6 million. The useful lives of the trucks were estimated to be five years, with zero salvage value.

During its first year of operations, the revenues of the firm, less all expenses other than amortization and income taxes, were $2.6 million.

The applicable income tax rate is 40 percent. The company *defers* its tax expense; that is, *reported* tax expense is based on reported income; it is not indicative of the required current tax payment.

  a. Determine the first year's return on investment (shareholders' equity) under each of the following assumptions;
    (1) The firm uses double declining balance amortization for both book purposes and tax purposes.
    (2) The firm uses straight-line amortization for book purposes and double declining balance amortization for tax purposes.
    Base your computation on year-end shareholders' equity instead of average shareholders' equity.
  b. Comment on any substantive (that is, "real" economic) differences in rate of return under each of the two methods.

8. *Use of return on investment as a criterion of corporate performance may lead to dysfunctional management decisions.*

The president of Burnside, Inc., is faced with the decision as to whether to expand the corporation by acquiring a new plant. The cost of the new plant would be $500 million. The necessary capital could be acquired by issuing bonds which would provide a return to lenders of 12 percent per year. The new plant would increase corporate pretax earnings by $70 million prior to taking into account required interest payments of $60 million.

In recent years, Burnside, Inc., has had annual pretax income, after deducting $50 million in interest expense, of $250 million. As at year end, the firm had outstanding debts of $500 million and shareholders' equity of $1.5 billion.

The financial vice-president favours acquisition of the new plant, arguing that corporate earnings would be increased by $10 million. The corporate controller opposes acquisition, maintaining that it would result in reduction of the firm's return on invested capital.

a. Determine return on investment (all capital) if (1) the plant is not acquired and (2) the plant is acquired. Assume that earnings on the old facilities will be the same in the future as they were in the past. Disregard income taxes (i.e., add back to income the full amount of interest costs). Base your computations on year-end instead of average values. Assume also that all earnings are distributed as dividends.

b. Calculate earnings per share under the two alternatives. The company has 10 million shares of common stock outstanding.

c. Suppose instead that the company could acquire the necessary $500 million in capital by issuing 2 million shares of common stock. Compute return on investment (shareholders' equity) and earnings per share, assuming first that the company did not expand and then that it did.

d. Do you think the company should acquire the plant? Explain.

e. Comment on the potential dangers of using return on investment as a criterion for making investment decisions.

f. What criterion might be preferable to return on investment?

9. *The advantages of debt as opposed to equity financing may be illusory.*

The Dement Corporation has $30 million in total assets. It has $10 million in current liabilities outstanding and $20 million in shareholders' equity. There are presently 200,000 shares of common stock outstanding. After-tax earnings over the past several years have averaged $2.1 million per year.

The company has decided to expand its operations by constructing a new plant. The new plant will cost $6 million, and it is estimated that it will increase earnings by $360,000 after taxes, not taking into account costs of financing.

The company has two options available to it to finance the plant. First, it can issue additional shares of stock. The additional shares could be sold for $200 per share.

Alternatively, it can raise the required $6 million by issuing bonds. The bonds would be sold to yield purchasers 10 percent per year. The interest costs would be tax-deductible to the company. The applicable tax rate is 40 percent. The company "pays out" 100 percent of earnings as dividends.

a. Assume that the company will construct the new plant. For each of the alternatives, determine anticipated (1) return on investment (all capital), (2) return on investment (shareholders' equity), and (3) earnings per share.

b. After reviewing the figures just computed, the president of the company stated, "It is obvious that we are better off financing expansion with debt rather than equity. In the future, let's finance all additions by issuing bonds rather than stock." Comment on the president's logic.

10. *A balance sheet and an income statement can be derived from selected financial ratios.*

The Ventnor Company had net earnings in a particular year of $50,000.

a. Its return on investment based on shareholders' equity as of year end was 10 percent. Determine year-end shareholders' equity.

b. The firm's debt-to-equity ratio was 0.4:1. Determine year-end debt.

c. Ventnor Company's return on investment (all capital) was 7.6571 percent based on year-end capital. It paid taxes at an incremental rate of 40 percent. Determine interest expense for the year.

d. Its *times interest earned* ratio was 13:1. Determine income taxes.

e. The company's net earnings as a percentage of sales was 5 percent. Determine sales.

f. Its gross margin was 40 percent. Determine cost of goods sold.

g. Its inventory turned over six times. Determine year-end inventory.

h. The firm's accounts receivable turned over 25 times. Determine year-end accounts receivable.

i. Its capital assets turned over two times. Determine year-end capital assets.

j. Its only remaining asset was cash. Determine year-end cash.

k. Its current ratio was 2:1. Determine year-end current liabilities.

l. All expenses not yet determined may be classified as "sales and administration." Reconstruct, as best you can, Ventnor Company's income statement and balance sheet.

11. *If financial statements fail to take into account current costs, so also do the financial ratios.*

The financial statements of the Yorkville Bottling Co. revealed the following data for a recent year.

Current assets	$ 420,000
Other assets (property, plant, and equipment)	$ 6,580,000
Current liabilities	$ 670,000
Other liabilities	$ 2,308,000
Sales	$11,500,000
Interest expense, net of taxes	$ 350,000
Net income	$ 1,400,000

a. Determine the following relationships (based on year-end balances):
   (1) Return on investment (all capital)
   (2) Current ratio
   (3) Debt-to-equity ratio
   (4) Plant and equipment turnover

b. Investigation reveals that included in current assets are marketable securities that are recorded at a cost of $100,000. Their current market value is $450,000. Moreover, the company's plant is located on land that had originally cost $500,000. The land currently has a fair market value of $1 million. Recompute the foregoing relationships to take into account the additional information. Which set of relationships do you think is more relevant to most decisions required of both managers and investors?

c. Comment on how the revised ratios may affect the analyst's view of both financial position and operating performance.

12. *Ratio analysis may assist an investor in predicting whether a firm will "turn around" or run into serious financial difficulty.*

 The financial statements presented here were adapted from those of Repap Enterprises Inc., a fully integrated North American forest products company. Its primary products include coated paper (glossy paper for magazines), softwood kraft pulp for printing and writing papers, kraft paper for heavy packaging, and lumber.

a. Explain as best you can the reason for the decline in earnings in year 2.

b. Compare the liquidity of the company in year 2 with that of year 1.

c. Compare the debt-to-equity ratio of year 2 with that of year 1. For purposes of calculating the debt-to-equity ratio, consider the "Capital sources" to be a component of shareholders' equity.

d. Comment on the firm's ability to meet fixed interest charges.

e. Comment on the critical problems facing the firm in the following year. Do you see any bright spots? Do you believe that the ability of the firm to survive is in question?

Repap Enterprises Inc. Consolidated Statements of Income for Year Ended December 31 (in millions)		
	Year 2	Year 1
Net sales	$1,102.3	$1,104.6
Other revenues	15.6	7.7
Total revenues	$1,117.9	$1,112.3
Cost of goods sold	$ 876.9	796.2
Selling, administrative and other expenses	52.8	45.7
Interest	86.4	36.2
Depreciation and amortization	74.9	57.8
Income tax expense	13.6	72.9
Total expenses	$1,104.6	$1,008.8
Net income	$ 13.3	$ 103.5

13. *Analysis of financial data is necessary, but is it sufficient?*

 The table that follows on page 743 contains selected financial data of a leading Canadian airline for a period of four years. The data were taken from the firm's annual reports.

a. Evaluate the performance of the airline during the four-year period. Based on the information provided, indicate whether the outlook for

Repap Enterprises Inc.
Consolidated Balance Sheets as at December 31
(in millions)

	Year 2	Year 1
Assets		
Current		
Cash and equivalents	$ 23.1	$ 45.9
Accounts receivable (net)	152.4	148.3
Inventories	236.5	190.1
Total current assets	$ 412.0	$ 384.3
Noncurrent		
Property and equipment (net)*	$2,545.1	$2,266.8
Investments	30.8	43.0
Other assets	97.6	92.2
Total noncurrent assets	$2,673.5	$2,402.0
Total assets	$3,085.5	$2,786.3
Liabilities and shareholders' equity		
Current		
Short-term borrowings	$ 24.0	$ 39.2
Accounts payable	216.6	153.4
Current maturity of long-term debt	36.2	63.3
Total current liabilities	$ 276.8	$ 255.9
Noncurrent		
Grants	$ 84.6	$ 77.0
Revolving credit facilities	209.3	124.1
Long-term debt	1,334.6	1,143.6
Total noncurrent liabilities	$1,628.5	$1,344.7
Capital sources		
Minority interest	$ 102.4	$ 102.0
Deferred income taxes	20.0	28.7
Investment tax credits	341.9	330.8
Convertible debentures	75.0	75.0
Total capital sources	$ 539.3	$ 536.5
Shareholders' equity		
Preferred shares	$ 137.6	$ 137.6
Common shares	173.9	175.0
Retained earnings	353.6	361.0
Cumulative translation adjustment	(24.2)	(24.4)
Total shareholders' equity	$ 640.9	$ 649.2
Total liabilities, capital sources, and shareholders' equity	$3,085.5	$2,786.3

*Included in property and equipment (net) is $1,042.9 (Year 2–$1,200.8) of "Construction in Progress."

the company appears favourable. Compute whatever financial ratios you think would provide insight into the firm's results of the past and prospects for the future. Assume an income tax rate of 42 percent.

b. Despite the apparently unfavourable trends, are there any bright spots, drawn from the data, that you might offer to a prospective investor or creditor of the company?

14. One of these two airlines filed for bankruptcy within seven years.

The financial statements of two actual airlines, given the fictitious

	Year 4	Year 3	Year 2	Year 1
Operating revenues				
Passenger	$2,095.2	$1,988.1	$1,722.7	$1,438.6
Cargo and mail	221.8	209.8	189.1	158.4
Charter and tour	327.9	332.0	270.1	232.7
Contract services and other	100.7	118.8	101.7	100.8
	$2,745.6	$2,648.7	$2,283.6	$1,930.5
Operating expenses				
Salaries, wages, and benefits	$ 801.7	$ 746.9	$ 629.1	$ 528.5
Fuel	451.7	399.2	352.8	317.6
Marketing, sales, and passenger service	661.7	644.9	559.8	393.8
Amortization	81.5	95.7	67.5	63.8
Other	760.7	772.4	596.6	462.5
	$2,757.3	$2,659.1	$2,205.8	$1,766.2
Operating income (loss)	(11.7)	(10.4)	77.8	164.3
Interest expense	104.4	76.2	50.4	63.7
Other nonoperating (income) and expenses, net	(79.3)	37.2	(17.1)	35.2
Provision for income taxes (reduction)	(22.2)	(67.8)	14.2	37.0
Net income	$ (14.6)	$ (56.0)	$ 30.3	$ 28.4
Earnings per share	$ (0.60)	$ (2.18)	$ 1.25	$ 1.22
Current assets	$ 678.8	$ 436.5	$ 625.3	$ 368.4
Current liabilities	$ 913.6	$ 846.6	$ 572.9	$ 558.5
Total assets	$2,964.4	$2,911.6	$2,125.0	$1,989.2
Total liabilities	$2,109.2	$2,040.0	$1,379.9	$1,267.9
Total shareholders' equity	$ 855.2	$ 871.6	$ 745.1	$ 721.3

names Northern and Southern, are presented on page 744. Answer the following questions, providing support with appropriate ratios.

a. Which of the two companies used the total resources within its command more efficiently? Assume a marginal tax rate of 48 percent.

b. Which provided the greater return to shareholders?

c. Which was more highly leveraged? Which made the more effective use of leverage?

d. Which appeared to be the better able to meet its fixed interest obligations?

e. Which was better able to meet its current obligations with available current resources?

f. Based on the very limited information presented (i.e., financial data for one year only), which of the two do you think went bankrupt in seven years?

15. *The following news report highlights the deficiencies of accounting information as a basis for investor decisions.*

Depending on who was doing the analysis, the *Wall Street Journal* reported, the value of American Financial Corporation's common stock was somewhere between $5 and $70 a share. It was not surprising, therefore, that some shareholders did not find the company's proposed repurchase offer of $28 very enticing.

Balance Sheet
(in thousands)

	Northern	Southern
Assets		
Current		
Cash	$ 21,512	$ 45,549
Short-term investments, at cost	149,100	—
Accounts receivable (net of allowance for doubtful accounts)	332,979	318,506
Materials and supplies	180,803	47,493
Prepaid expenses and other current assets	28,407	76,650
Total current assets	$ 712,801	$ 488,198
Noncurrent		
Property, plant, and equipment	$3,839,212	$3,535,416
Allowance for depreciation	(1,537,198)	(1,590,955)
	$2,302,014	$1,944,461
Advance payments for new equipment	116,958	197,596
Other assets	93,114	27,625
Total noncurrent assets	$2,512,086	$2,169,682
Total assets	$3,224,887	$2,657,880
Liabilities and owners' equity		
Current		
Accounts payable	$459,426	$231,999
Notes payable	156,300	279,283
Other	232,712	232,711
Total current liabilities	$ 848,438	$ 743,993
Noncurrent		
Long-term debt (including obligations for leases)	$1,910,897	$ 362,774
Deferred tax credits and other liabilities	70,727	527,462
Total noncurrent liabilities	$1,981,624	$ 890,236
Preferred stock	$ 139,551	—
Common stock (par value and additional contributed capital)	$ 358,024	$ 199,371
Retained earnings (deficit)	(102,750)	824,280
Equity of common shareholders	$ 255,274	$1,023,651
Total liabilities and owners' equity	$3,224,887	$2,657,880

Income Statement
(in thousands)

	Northern	Southern
Operating revenues	$3,769,237	$3,617,523
Operating expenses	3,788,017	3,625,679
Operating profit (loss)	(18,780)	$ (8,156)
Nonoperating revenues (expenses)		
Interest expense	$ (178,274)	$ (60,438)
Gain on disposal of aircraft	32,735	1,570
Other (net)	79,063	51,819
Total nonoperating revenues (expenses)	$ (66,476)	$ (7,049)
Income (loss) before taxes	$ (85,256)	$ (15,205)
Provision for (reduction in) income taxes	(10,329)	(36,019)
Net income (loss)	$ (74,927)	$ 20,814

The *Journal* went on to relate that Carl Lindner, chairman, president, and founder of American Financial, who along with his family owns 45 percent of the firm's outstanding shares of common stock, was seeking to take over the company by acquiring the 55 percent of the stock held by parties other than the Lindner family.

Within days after Lindner offered to purchase the outstanding shares, minority shareholders filed suit, charging that the price of $28 was unfair and inadequate. One suit, the *Journal* indicated, charged that the offer did not consider future profits of American Financial and that it was less than the company's worth as a going concern. The latter assertion was backed by a financial analyst who estimated what American Financial would get for its assets if the firm were to be broken up and sold. Among the assets were insurance companies, convenience stores, savings and loan institutions, and investment positions in several companies. The analyst said that he based his estimates of the subsidiaries' values on the percentage amounts above or below book value that companies in their industries had recently received in the market. He valued American Financial's investment positions in other companies at current market prices. On the basis of these estimates, he calculated the company's worth at between $54 and $70 per share.

The *Journal* reported that American Financial belittled the estimate of the analyst. In fact, the company claimed its book value of $23.53 a share was deceptively high. The company believed tangible book value of its assets was more like $5 a share, in large part because the goodwill of its subsidiaries accounted for over half of the common stock's book value.

a. Comment on why book values cannot serve as the basis for establishing a fair value of the company, despite the assertion of the firm's auditors that the "financial statements present fairly" its financial position.

b. How would you assess the reliability of the procedure used by the financial analyst to estimate the values of the firm's subsidiaries?

c. Evaluate the explanation of American Financial as to why the book value of $23.53 was deceptively high.

16. *Leveraged buyouts do not always work out as intended.*

In 1986, to fend off the advances of a hostile corporate raider, the management of Fruehauf Corp. acquired the company in a leveraged buyout. The financial statements that follow are for 1987, the first full year of operations subsequent to the buyout, and 1986, the year of the buyout.

The statements are not directly comparable because the buyout was accompanied by a major reorganization and recapitalization. As is apparent from the statements, for example, the new company had significantly more long-term debt, and less shareholders' equity, than the old. Moreover, to finance its acquisition, management sold off key divisions.

Fruehauf manufactures trucks and auto parts. It is in an industry that is considered highly cyclical. That is, sales tend to increase when the economy is strong and decrease when it is weak.

By mid-1989, it was clear that the buyout was unsuccessful. Mangement was struggling to keep the company afloat by selling its most profitable divisions—those for which it could obtain the highest prices.

a. Compare the capital structures of the company before and after the buyout. Compute appropriate ratios.

Fruehauf Corporation
Balance Sheets

	1987	1986
Assets		
Current assets		
Cash and temporary investments	$ 75	$ 124
Accounts receivable (net of allowance for doubtful accounts)	201	343
Inventories	228	343
Other current assets	188	126
Total current assets	692	936
Land, buildings, and equipment (net of accumulated depreciation)	755	582
Investments	58	291
Equipment leased to customers (net of accumulated depreciation)	46	194
Other assets	187	0
Total noncurrent assets	1,046	1,067
Total assets	$1,738	$2,003
Liabilities and Shareholders' Equity		
Current liabilities		
Accounts payable	$ 196	$ 388
Taxes and other accrued liabilities	199	312
Total current liabilities	395	700
Other liabilities and deferred credits		
Deferred income taxes	183	77
Long-term debt and capital leases	780	206
Other liabilities	152	516
Total other liabilities and deferred credits	1,115	799
Total liabilities	1,510	1,499
Preferred stock	255	0
Common shareholders' equity		
Common stock, par value	1	23
Other paid-in capital	28	305
Retained earnings	(56)	275
Treasury stock	0	(99)
Total common shareholders' equity	(27)	504
Total liabilities and shareholders' equity	$1,738	$2,003

Fruehauf Corporation Income Statements

	1987	1986
Net sales	$1,854	$2,759
Cost of goods sold	1,539	2,271
Selling, general, administrative, and other costs	184	323
Interest expense	106	80
Depreciation	101	96
Total expenses, excluding income taxes	1,930	2,770
Income before taxes	(76)	(11)
Income taxes (tax benefit)	(34)	9
Income before extraordinary loss	(42)	(20)
Extraordinary loss (net of taxes)	—	(41)
Net income	$ (42)	$ (61)

b. What do you see as the major reason for the increase in losses (before the extraordinary item) in 1987? Compute appropriate ratios.

c. In 1987 the company declared $27 million in preferred stock dividends. From the perspective of the common shareholders, would you characterize these dividends as more like common stock dividends or interest payments?

d. Comment on the dangers of leveraged buyouts in cyclical industries.

17. *Are reported earnings a measure only of short-term, not long-term, well-being?*

The *Wall Street Journal* of April 14, 1981, described a proxy fight in which a group of dissident shareholders attempted to unseat the existing board of directors of American Bakeries Co. Although the firm was small, the effort to oust the directors raised an important issue, according to the *Journal*. The main problem was the extent to which managers of publicly held companies dared to sacrifice short-term profits and dividends for long-term growth. This is what Japanese companies often did.

The dissident shareholders cited several measures of what they considered the firm's dismal performance: a decline in net income to $2.1 million in 1980 from $5.8 million in 1977; omission of the past two quarterly cash dividends in 1980; uneven sales growth from 1976 to 1981; and a decline in profitability to 0.39 percent of sales in 1980 from 1.38 percent in 1975.

According to the *Journal*, the chairman of American Bakeries objected to the suggestion that declining financial results of the past five years reflected mismanagement. He said that the decline stemmed from the biggest capital spending program—$84 million—in their history; the program had spanned the five years that ended in 1980. He thought that effort critically important for competitiveness and growth prospects.

There was no question, the *Journal* said, that the depressed earnings over the past five years were a result of the company's big capital spending program. The American Bakeries' executives acknowledged that the company's annual depreciation expense rose nearly 40 percent during the period to more than $11 million in 1980 and that interest expenses increased to $6.1 million in 1980 from $2.1 million in 1976.

a. Reported earnings are supposed to be a measure of corporate well-being. Is it not a deficiency of financial reporting that if a firm takes actions such as increasing capital spending, which are admittedly in its long-run interests, it may have to report lower earnings?

b. Comment on the dangers of using reported earnings alone to evaluate management performance.

c. Would the firm be saddled with the lower reported earnings if it adhered faithfully to the *principle of matching*? Explain. What changes in accounting practices would enable a firm to avoid having to report lower earnings in periods prior to those in which the benefits of a capital spending program were realized?

1. Return on investment (all capital):

$$\frac{\text{Net income} + \text{Interest after taxes}}{\text{Assets}}$$

Interest after taxes = (1 – incremental tax rate) interest expense:

a. Maple Leaf Foods

$$\frac{\$70.2 + (1 - .42)\$2.6}{\$1,500.5} = 4.8\%$$

b. Schneider

$$\frac{\$7.7 + (1 - .42)\$7.1}{\$214.1} = 5.5\%$$

Schneider had the greater earnings relative to the resources within its command.

2. Return on investment (common shareholders' equity):

$$\frac{\text{Net income} - \text{Preferred stock dividends}}{\text{Equity of common shareholders}}$$

a. Maple Leaf Foods

$$\frac{\$70.2 - \$0}{\$985.8} = 7.1\%$$

b. Schneider

$$\frac{\$7.7 - \$0}{\$82.7} = 9.3\%$$

Schneider provided the greater return to common shareholders.

3. Debt-to-equity ratio:

$$\frac{\text{Total debt}}{\text{Total equity}}$$

a. Maple Leaf Foods

$$\frac{\$514.7}{\$985.8} = 0.52 \text{ to } 1$$

b. Schneider

$$\frac{\$131.4}{\$82.7} = 1.59 \text{ to } 1$$

Schneider was the more highly leveraged company.

4. Schneider made more effective use of leverage. It was able to increase the return to common shareholders 1.69 times that of the return to all capital (9.3% divided by 5.5%). Maple Leaf Foods, which also used leverage quite effectively, increased it 1.48 times (7.1% divided by 4.8%).

5. Times interest earned:

$$\frac{\text{Net income} + \text{Interest} + \text{Income taxes}}{\text{Interest}}$$

a. Maple Leaf Foods

$$\frac{\$70.2 + \$2.6 + \$45.6}{\$2.6} = \frac{\$118.4}{\$2.6} = 45.5 \text{ times}$$

b. Schneider

$$\frac{\$7.7 + \$7.1 + \$4.5}{\$7.1} = \frac{\$19.3}{\$7.1} = 2.7 \text{ times}$$

Maple Leaf Foods covered its interest costs by many more times than Schneider. However, Schneider's 2.7 times coverage is considered within the margin of safety.

6. Current ratio:

$$\frac{\text{Current assets}}{\text{Current liabilities}}$$

a. Maple Leaf Foods

$$\frac{\$654.2}{\$373.8} = 1.75 \text{ to } 1$$

b. Schneider

$$\frac{\$92.0}{\$61.8} = 1.49 \text{ to } 1$$

The current ratios of both firms are considered reasonably strong, with Maple Leaf Foods being slightly stronger.

Overall, the ratios that have been computed describe two firms that are generally healthy. Schneider is the more risky of the two as its capital structure contains relatively more debt. But, concurrent with the additional risk, Schneider is also considerably more profitable in terms of return to the common shareholder (9.3% versus 7.1%).

Appendix

TABLE 1

Future value (a) after n periods from investing a single sum (x)
(= \$1) at time 0 with interest i:

$$a_{\overline{n}|i} = x(1 + i)^n$$

No. of periods	2%	3%	4%	5%	6%	7%	8%
1	1.0200	1.0300	1.0400	1.0500	1.0600	1.0700	1.0800
2	1.0404	1.0609	1.0816	1.1025	1.1236	1.1449	1.1664
3	1.0612	1.0927	1.1249	1.1576	1.1910	1.2250	1.2597
4	1.0824	1.1255	1.1699	1.2155	1.2625	1.3108	1.3605
5	1.1041	1.1593	1.2167	1.2763	1.3382	1.4026	1.4693
6	1.1262	1.1941	1.2653	1.3401	1.4185	1.5007	1.5869
7	1.1487	1.2299	1.3159	1.4071	1.5036	1.6058	1.7138
8	1.1717	1.2668	1.3686	1.4775	1.5938	1.7182	1.8509
9	1.1951	1.3048	1.4233	1.5513	1.6895	1.8365	1.9990
10	1.2190	1.3439	1.4802	1.6289	1.7908	1.9672	2.1589
11	1.2434	1.3842	1.5395	1.7103	1.8983	2.1049	2.3316
12	1.2682	1.4258	1.6010	1.7959	2.0122	2.2522	2.5182
13	1.2936	1.4685	1.6651	1.8856	2.1329	2.4098	2.7196
14	1.3195	1.5126	1.7317	1.9799	2.2609	2.5785	2.9372
15	1.3459	1.5580	1.8009	2.0789	2.3966	2.7590	3.1722
16	1.3728	1.6047	1.8730	2.1829	2.5404	2.9522	3.4259
17	1.4002	1.6528	1.9479	2.2920	2.6928	3.1588	3.7000
18	1.4282	1.7024	2.0258	2.4066	2.8543	3.3799	3.9960
19	1.4568	1.7535	2.1068	2.5270	3.0256	3.6165	4.3157
20	1.4859	1.8061	2.1911	2.6533	3.2071	3.8697	4.6610
21	1.5157	1.8603	2.2788	2.7860	3.3996	4.1406	5.0338
22	1.5460	1.9161	2.3699	2.9253	3.6035	4.4304	5.4365
23	1.5769	1.9736	2.4647	3.0715	3.8197	4.7405	5.8715
24	1.6084	2.0328	2.5633	3.2251	4.0489	5.0724	6.3412
25	1.6406	2.0938	2.6658	3.3864	4.2919	5.4274	6.8485
26	1.6734	2.1566	2.7725	3.5557	4.4594	5.8074	7.3964
27	1.7069	2.2213	2.8834	3.7335	4.8223	6.2139	7.9881
28	1.7410	2.2879	2.9987	3.9201	5.1117	6.6488	8.6271
29	1.7758	2.3566	3.1187	4.1161	5.4184	7.1143	9.3173
30	1.8114	2.4273	3.2434	4.3219	5.7435	7.6123	10.0627
31	1.8476	2.5001	3.3731	4.5380	6.0881	8.1451	10.8677
32	1.8845	2.5751	3.5081	4.7649	6.4534	8.7153	11.7371
33	1.9222	2.6523	3.6484	5.0032	6.8406	9.3253	12.6760
34	1.9607	2.7319	3.7943	5.2533	7.2510	9.9781	13.6901
35	1.9999	2.8139	3.9461	5.5160	7.6861	10.6766	14.7853
36	2.0399	2.8983	4.1039	5.7918	8.1473	11.4239	15.9682
37	2.0807	2.9852	4.2681	6.0814	8.6361	12.2236	17.2456
38	2.1223	3.0748	4.4388	6.3855	9.1543	13.0793	18.6253
39	2.1647	3.1670	4.6164	6.7048	9.7035	13.9948	20.1153
40	2.2080	3.2620	4.8010	7.0400	10.2857	14.9745	21.7245
41	2.2522	3.3599	4.9931	7.3920	10.9029	16.0227	23.4625
42	2.2972	3.4607	5.1928	7.7616	11.5570	17.1443	25.3395
43	2.3432	3.5645	5.4005	8.1497	12.2505	18.3444	27.3666
44	2.3901	3.6715	5.6165	8.5572	12.9855	19.6285	29.5560
45	2.4379	3.7816	5.8412	8.9850	13.7646	21.0025	31.9204
46	2.4866	3.8950	6.0748	9.4343	14.5905	22.4726	34.4741
47	2.5363	4.0119	6.3178	9.9060	15.4659	24.0457	37.2320
48	2.5871	4.1323	6.5705	10.4013	16.3939	25.7289	40.2106
49	2.6388	4.2562	6.8333	10.9213	17.3775	27.5299	43.4274
50	2.6916	4.3839	7.1067	11.4674	18.4202	29.4570	46.9016

TABLE 1 Continued
Future value (a) after n periods from investing a single sum (x)
(= $1) at time 0 with interest i:

$$a_{\overline{n}|i} = x(1 + i)^n$$

9%	10%	11%	12%	13%	14%	15%
1.0900	1.1000	1.1100	1.1200	1.1300	1.1400	1.1500
1.1881	1.2100	1.2321	1.2544	1.2769	1.2996	1.3225
1.2950	1.3310	1.3676	1.4049	1.4429	1.4815	1.5209
1.4116	1.4641	1.5181	1.5735	1.6305	1.6890	1.7490
1.5386	1.6105	1.6851	1.7623	1.8424	1.9254	2.0114
1.6771	1.7716	1.8704	1.9738	2.0820	2.1950	2.3131
1.8280	1.9487	2.0762	2.2107	2.3526	2.5023	2.6600
1.9926	2.1436	2.3045	2.4760	2.6584	2.8526	3.0590
2.1719	2.3579	2.5580	2.7731	3.0040	3.2519	3.5179
2.3674	2.5937	2.8394	3.1058	3.3946	3.7072	4.0456
2.5804	2.8531	3.1518	3.4785	3.8359	4.2262	4.6524
2.8127	3.1384	3.4985	3.8960	4.3345	4.8179	5.3503
3.0658	3.4523	3.8833	4.3635	4.8980	5.4924	6.1528
3.3417	3.7975	4.3104	4.8871	5.5348	6.2613	7.0757
3.6425	4.1772	4.7846	5.4736	6.2543	7.1379	8.1371
3.9703	4.5950	5.3109	6.1304	7.0673	8.1372	9.3576
4.3276	5.0545	5.8951	6.8660	7.9861	9.2765	10.7613
4.7171	5.5599	6.5436	7.6900	9.0243	10.5752	12.3755
5.1417	6.1159	7.2633	8.6128	10.1974	12.0557	14.2318
5.6044	6.7275	8.0623	9.6463	11.5231	13.7435	16.3665
6.1088	7.4002	8.9492	10.8038	13.0211	15.6676	18.8215
6.6586	8.1403	9.9336	12.1003	14.7138	17.8610	21.6447
7.2579	8.9543	11.0263	13.5523	16.6266	20.3616	24.8915
7.9111	9.8497	12.2392	15.1786	18.7881	23.2122	28.6252
8.6231	10.8347	13.5855	17.0001	21.2305	26.4619	32.9190
9.3992	11.9182	15.0799	19.0401	23.9905	30.1666	37.8568
10.2451	13.1100	16.7386	21.3249	27.1093	34.3899	43.5353
11.1671	14.4210	18.5799	23.8839	30.6335	39.2045	50.0656
12.1722	15.8631	20.6237	26.7499	34.6158	44.6931	57.5755
13.2677	17.4494	22.8923	29.9599	39.1159	50.9502	66.2118
14.4618	19.1943	25.4104	33.5551	44.2010	58.0832	76.1435
15.7633	21.1138	28.2056	37.5817	49.9471	66.2148	87.5651
17.1820	23.2252	31.3082	42.0915	56.4402	75.4849	100.6998
18.7284	25.5477	34.7521	47.1425	63.7774	86.0528	115.8048
20.4140	28.1024	38.5749	52.7996	72.0685	98.1002	133.1755
22.2512	30.9127	42.8181	59.1356	81.4374	111.8342	153.1519
24.2538	34.0039	47.5281	66.2318	92.0243	127.4910	176.1246
26.4367	37.4043	52.7562	74.1797	103.9874	145.3397	202.5433
28.8160	41.1448	58.5593	83.0812	117.5058	165.6873	232.9248
31.4094	45.2593	65.0009	93.0510	132.7816	188.8835	267.8635
34.2363	49.7852	72.1510	104.2171	150.0432	215.3272	308.0431
37.3175	54.7637	80.0876	116.7231	169.5488	245.4730	354.2495
40.6761	60.2401	88.8972	130.7299	191.5901	279.8392	407.3870
44.3370	66.2641	98.6759	146.4175	216.4968	319.0167	468.4950
48.3273	72.8905	109.5302	163.9876	244.6414	363.6791	538.7693
52.6767	80.1795	121.5786	183.6661	276.4448	414.5941	619.5847
57.4176	88.1975	134.9522	205.7061	312.3826	472.6373	712.5224
62.5852	97.0172	149.7970	230.3908	352.9923	538.8065	819.4007
68.2179	106.7190	166.2746	258.0377	398.8813	614.2395	942.3108
74.3575	117.3909	184.5648	289.0022	450.7359	700.2330	1083.6574

TABLE 2
Present value (*p*) at time 0 of a single sum (*x*) (= $1) to be paid or received after *n* periods in the future with interest *i*:
$$p_{\overline{n}|i} = x/(1 + i)^n$$

No. of periods	2%	3%	4%	5%	6%	7%	8%
1	.9804	.9709	.9615	.9524	.9434	.9346	.9259
2	.9612	.9426	.9246	.9070	.8900	.8734	.8573
3	.9423	.9151	.8890	.8638	.8396	.8163	.7938
4	.9238	.8885	.8548	.8227	.7921	.7629	.7350
5	.9057	.8626	.8219	.7835	.7473	.7130	.6806
6	.8880	.8375	.7903	.7462	.7050	.6663	.6302
7	.8706	.8131	.7599	.7107	.6651	.6227	.5835
8	.8535	.7894	.7307	.6768	.6274	.5820	.5403
9	.8368	.7664	.7026	.6446	.5919	.5439	.5002
10	.8203	.7441	.6756	.6139	.5584	.5083	.4632
11	.8043	.7224	.6496	.5847	.5268	.4751	.4289
12	.7885	.7014	.6246	.5568	.4970	.4440	.3971
13	.7730	.6810	.6006	.5303	.4688	.4150	.3677
14	.7579	.6611	.5775	.5051	.4423	.3878	.3405
15	.7430	.6419	.5553	.4810	.4173	.3624	.3152
16	.7284	.6232	.5339	.4581	.3936	.3387	.2919
17	.7142	.6050	.5134	.4363	.3714	.3166	.2703
18	.7002	.5874	.4936	.4155	.3503	.2959	.2502
19	.6864	.5703	.4746	.3957	.3305	.2765	.2317
20	.6730	.5537	.4564	.3769	.3118	.2584	.2145
21	.6598	.5375	.4388	.3589	.2942	.2415	.1987
22	.6468	.5219	.4220	.3418	.2775	.2257	.1839
23	.6342	.5067	.4057	.3256	.2618	.2109	.1703
24	.6217	.4919	.3901	.3101	.2470	.1971	.1577
25	.6095	.4776	.3751	.2953	.2330	.1842	.1460
26	.5976	.4637	.3607	.2812	.2198	.1722	.1352
27	.5859	.4502	.3468	.2678	.2074	.1609	.1252
28	.5744	.4371	.3335	.2551	.1956	.1504	.1159
29	.5631	.4243	.3207	.2429	.1846	.1406	.1073
30	.5521	.4120	.3083	.2314	.1741	.1314	.0994
31	.5412	.4000	.2965	.2204	.1643	.1228	.0920
32	.5306	.3883	.2851	.2099	.1550	.1147	.0852
33	.5202	.3770	.2741	.1999	.1462	.1072	.0789
34	.5100	.3660	.2636	.1904	.1379	.1002	.0730
35	.5000	.3554	.2534	.1813	.1301	.0937	.0676
36	.4902	.3450	.2437	.1727	.1227	.0875	.0626
37	.4806	.3350	.2343	.1644	.1158	.0818	.0580
38	.4712	.3252	.2253	.1566	.1092	.0765	.0537
39	.4619	.3158	.2166	.1491	.1031	.0715	.0497
40	.4529	.3066	.2083	.1420	.0972	.0668	.0460
41	.4440	.2976	.2003	.1353	.0917	.0624	.0426
42	.4353	.2890	.1926	.1288	.0865	.0583	.0395
43	.4268	.2805	.1852	.1227	.0816	.0545	.0365
44	.4184	.2724	.1780	.1169	.0770	.0509	.0338
45	.4102	.2644	.1712	.1113	.0727	.0476	.0313
46	.4022	.2567	.1646	.1060	.0685	.0445	.0290
47	.3943	.2493	.1583	.1009	.0647	.0416	.0269
48	.3865	.2420	.1522	.0961	.0610	.0389	.0249
49	.3790	.2350	.1463	.0916	.0575	.0363	.0230
50	.3715	.2281	.1407	.0872	.0543	.0339	.0213

TABLE 2 Continued
**Present value (p) at time 0 of a single sum (x) (= \$1) to be paid
or received after n periods in the future with interest i:**

$$P_{\overline{n}|i} = x/(1 + i)^n$$

9%	10%	11%	12%	13%	14%	15%
.9174	.9091	.9009	.8929	.8850	.8772	.8696
.8417	.8264	.8116	.7972	.7831	.7695	.7561
.7722	.7513	.7312	.7118	.6931	.6750	.6575
.7084	.6830	.6587	.6355	.6133	.5921	.5718
.6499	.6209	.5935	.5674	.5428	.5194	.4972
.5963	.5645	.5346	.5066	.4803	.4556	.4323
.5470	.5132	.4817	.4523	.4251	.3996	.3759
.5019	.4665	.4339	.4039	.3762	.3506	.3269
.4604	.4241	.3909	.3606	.3329	.3075	.2843
.4224	.3855	.3522	.3220	.2946	.2697	.2472
.3875	.3505	.3173	.2875	.2607	.2366	.2149
.3555	.3186	.2858	.2567	.2307	.2076	.1869
.3262	.2897	.2575	.2292	.2042	.1821	.1625
.2992	.2633	.2320	.2046	.1807	.1597	.1413
.2745	.2394	.2090	.1827	.1599	.1401	.1229
.2519	.2176	.1883	.1631	.1415	.1229	.1069
.2311	.1978	.1696	.1456	.1252	.1078	.0929
.2120	.1799	.1528	.1300	.1108	.0946	.0808
.1945	.1635	.1377	.1161	.0981	.0829	.0703
.1784	.1486	.1240	.1037	.0868	.0728	.0611
.1637	.1351	.1117	.0926	.0768	.0638	.0531
.1502	.1228	.1007	.0826	.0680	.0560	.0462
.1378	.1117	.0907	.0738	.0601	.0491	.0402
.1264	.1015	.0817	.0659	.0532	.0431	.0349
.1160	.0923	.0736	.0588	.0471	.0378	.0304
.1064	.0839	.0663	.0525	.0417	.0331	.0264
.0976	.0763	.0597	.0469	.0369	.0291	.0230
.0895	.0693	.0538	.0419	.0326	.0255	.0200
.0822	.0630	.0485	.0374	.0289	.0224	.0714
.0754	.0573	.0437	.0334	.0256	.0196	.0151
.0691	.0521	.0394	.0298	.0226	.0172	.0131
.0634	.0474	.0355	.0266	.0200	.0151	.0114
.0582	.0431	.0319	.0238	.0177	.0132	.0099
.0534	.0391	.0288	.0212	.0157	.0116	.0086
.0490	.0356	.0259	.0189	.0139	.0102	.0075
.0449	.0323	.0234	.0169	.0123	.0089	.0065
.0412	.0294	.0210	.0151	.0109	.0078	.0057
.0378	.0267	.0190	.0135	.0096	.0069	.0049
.0347	.0243	.0171	.0120	.0085	.0060	.0043
.0318	.0221	.0154	.0107	.0075	.0053	.0037
.0292	.0201	.0139	.0096	.0067	.0046	.0032
.0268	.0183	.0125	.0086	.0059	.0041	.0028
.0246	.0166	.0112	.0076	.0052	.0036	.0025
.0226	.0151	.0101	.0068	.0046	.0031	.0021
.0207	.0137	.0091	.0061	.0041	.0027	.0019
.0190	.0125	.0082	.0054	.0036	.0024	.0016
.0174	.0113	.0074	.0049	.0032	.0021	.0014
.0160	.0103	.0067	.0043	.0028	.0019	.0012
.0147	.0094	.0060	.0039	.0025	.0016	.0011
.0134	.0085	.0054	.0035	.0022	.0014	.0009

TABLE 3
Future value (A) of an annuity (X) (= $1) paid or received at the end of every period for n periods

$$A_{\overline{n}|i} = X \cdot \frac{(1 + i)^n - 1}{i}$$

No. of periods	2%	3%	4%	5%	6%	7%	8%
1	1.0000	1.0000	1.0000	1.0000	1.0000	1.0000	1.0000
2	2.0200	2.0300	2.0400	2.0500	2.0600	2.0700	2.0800
3	3.0604	3.0909	3.1216	3.1525	3.1836	3.2149	3.2464
4	4.1216	4.1836	4.2465	4.3101	4.3746	4.4399	4.5061
5	5.2040	5.3091	5.4163	5.5256	5.6371	5.7507	5.8666
6	6.3081	6.4684	6.6330	6.8019	6.9753	7.1533	7.3359
7	7.4343	7.6625	7.8983	8.1420	8.3938	8.6540	8.9228
8	8.5830	8.8923	9.2142	9.5491	9.8975	10.2598	10.6366
9	9.7546	10.1591	10.5828	11.0266	11.4913	11.9780	12.4876
10	10.9497	11.4639	12.0061	12.5779	13.1808	13.8164	14.4866
11	12.1687	12.8078	13.4864	14.2068	14.9716	15.7836	16.6455
12	13.4121	14.1920	15.0258	15.9171	16.8699	17.8885	18.9771
13	14.6803	15.6178	16.6268	17.7130	18.8821	20.1406	21.4953
14	15.9739	17.0863	18.2919	19.5986	21.0151	22.5505	24.2149
15	17.2934	18.5989	20.0236	21.5786	23.2760	25.1290	27.1521
16	18.6393	20.1569	21.8245	23.6575	25.6725	27.8881	30.3243
17	20.0121	21.7616	23.6975	25.8404	28.2129	30.8402	33.7502
18	21.4123	23.4144	25.6454	28.1324	30.9057	33.9990	37.4502
19	22.8406	25.1169	27.6712	30.5390	33.7600	37.3790	41.4463
20	24.2974	26.8704	29.7781	33.0660	36.7856	40.9955	45.7620
21	25.7833	28.6765	31.9692	35.7193	39.9927	44.8652	50.4229
22	27.2990	30.5368	34.2480	38.5052	43.3923	49.0057	55.4568
23	28.8450	32.4529	36.6179	41.4305	46.9958	53.4361	60.8933
24	30.4219	34.4265	39.0826	44.5020	50.8156	58.1767	66.7648
25	32.0303	36.4593	41.6459	47.7271	54.8645	63.2490	73.1059
26	33.6709	38.5530	44.3117	51.1135	59.1564	68.6765	79.9544
27	35.3443	40.7096	47.0842	54.6691	63.7058	74.4838	87.3508
28	37.0512	42.9309	49.9676	58.4026	68.5281	80.6977	95.3388
29	38.7922	45.2189	52.9663	62.3227	73.6398	87.3465	103.9659
30	40.5681	47.5754	56.0849	66.4388	79.0582	94.4608	113.2832
31	42.3794	50.0027	59.3283	70.7608	84.8017	102.0730	123.3459
32	44.2270	52.5028	62.7015	75.2988	90.8898	110.2182	134.2135
33	46.1116	55.0778	66.2095	80.0638	97.3432	118.9334	145.9506
34	48.0338	57.7302	69.8579	85.0670	104.1838	128.2588	158.6267
35	49.9945	60.4621	73.6522	90.3203	111.4348	138.2369	172.3168
36	51.9944	63.2759	77.5983	95.8363	119.1209	148.9135	187.1021
37	54.0343	66.1742	81.7022	101.6281	127.2681	160.3374	203.0703
38	56.1149	69.1594	85.9703	107.7095	135.9042	172.5610	220.3159
39	58.2372	72.2342	90.4091	114.0950	145.0585	185.6403	238.9412
40	60.4020	75.4013	95.0255	120.7998	154.7620	199.6351	259.0565
41	62.6100	78.6633	99.8265	127.8398	165.0477	214.6096	280.7810
42	64.8622	82.0232	104.8196	135.2318	175.9505	230.6322	304.2435
43	67.1595	85.4839	110.0124	142.9933	187.5076	247.7765	329.5830
44	69.5027	89.0484	115.4129	151.1430	199.7580	266.1209	356.9496
45	71.8927	92.7199	121.0294	159.7002	212.7435	285.7493	386.5056
46	74.3306	96.5015	126.8706	168.6852	226.5081	306.7518	418.4261
47	76.8172	100.3965	132.9454	178.1194	241.0986	329.2244	452.9002
48	79.3535	104.4084	139.2632	188.0254	256.5645	353.2701	490.1322
49	81.9406	108.5406	145.8337	198.4267	272.9584	378.9990	530.3427
50	84.5794	112.7969	152.6671	209.3480	290.3359	406.5289	573.7702

TABLE 3 Continued
Future value (A) of an annuity (X) (= $1) paid or received at the
end of every period for n periods

$$A_{\overline{n}|i} = X \cdot \frac{(1 + i)^n - 1}{i}$$

9%	10%	11%	12%	13%	14%	15%
1.0000	1.0000	1.0000	1.0000	1.0000	1.0000	1.0000
2.0900	2.1000	2.1100	2.1200	2.1300	2.1400	2.1500
3.2781	3.3100	3.3421	3.3744	3.4069	3.4396	3.4725
4.5731	4.6410	4.7097	4.7793	4.8498	4.9211	4.9934
5.9847	6.1051	6.2278	6.3528	6.4803	6.6101	6.7424
7.5233	7.7156	7.9129	8.1152	8.3227	8.5355	8.7537
9.2004	9.4872	9.7833	10.0890	10.4047	10.7305	11.0668
11.0285	11.4359	11.8594	12.2997	12.7573	13.2328	13.7268
13.0210	13.5795	14.1640	14.7757	15.4157	16.0853	16.7858
15.1929	15.9374	16.7220	17.5487	18.4197	19.3373	20.3037
17.5603	18.5312	19.5614	20.6546	21.8143	23.0445	24.3493
20.1407	21.3843	22.7132	24.1331	25.6502	27.2707	29.0017
22.9534	24.5227	26.2116	28.0291	29.9847	32.0887	34.3519
26.0192	27.9750	30.0949	32.3926	34.8827	37.5811	40.5047
29.3609	31.7725	34.4054	37.2797	40.4175	43.8424	47.5804
33.0034	35.9497	39.1899	42.7533	46.6717	50.9804	55.7175
36.9737	40.5447	44.5008	48.8837	53.7391	59.1176	65.0751
41.3013	45.5992	50.3959	55.7497	61.7251	68.3941	75.8364
46.0185	51.1591	56.9395	63.4397	70.7494	78.9692	88.2118
51.1601	57.2750	64.2028	72.0524	80.9468	91.0249	102.4436
56.7645	64.0025	72.2651	81.6987	92.4699	104.7684	118.8101
62.8733	71.4027	81.2143	92.5026	105.4910	120.4360	137.6316
69.5319	79.5430	91.1479	104.6029	120.2048	138.2970	159.2764
76.7898	88.4973	102.1742	118.1552	136.8315	158.6586	184.1678
84.7009	98.3471	114.4133	133.3339	155.6196	181.8708	212.7930
93.3240	109.1818	127.9988	150.3339	176.8501	208.3327	245.7120
102.7231	121.0999	143.0786	169.3740	200.8406	238.4993	283.5688
112.9682	134.2099	159.8173	190.6989	227.9499	272.8892	327.1041
124.1354	148.6309	178.3972	214.5828	258.5834	312.0937	377.1697
136.3075	164.4940	199.0209	241.3327	293.1992	356.7868	434.7451
149.5752	181.9434	221.9132	271.2926	332.3151	407.7370	500.9569
164.0370	201.1378	247.3236	304.8477	376.5161	465.8202	577.1005
179.8003	222.2515	275.5292	342.4294	426.4632	532.0350	664.6655
196.9823	245.4767	306.8374	384.5210	482.9034	607.5199	765.3654
215.7108	271.0244	341.5896	431.6635	546.6808	693.5727	881.1702
236.1247	299.1268	380.1644	484.4631	618.7493	791.6729	1014.3457
258.3759	330.0395	422.9825	543.5987	700.1867	903.5071	1167.4975
282.6298	364.0434	470.5106	609.8305	792.2110	1030.9981	1343.6222
309.0665	401.4478	523.2667	684.0102	896.1984	1176.3378	1546.1655
337.8824	442.5926	581.8261	767.0914	1013.7042	1342.0251	1779.0903
369.2919	487.8518	646.8269	860.1424	1146.4858	1530.9086	2046.9539
403.5281	537.6370	718.9779	964.3595	1296.5289	1746.2358	2354.9969
440.8457	592.4007	799.0655	1081.0826	1466.0777	1991.7088	2709.2465
481.5218	652.6408	887.9627	1211.8125	1657.6678	2271.5481	3116.6334
525.8587	718.9048	986.6386	1358.2300	1874.1646	2590.5648	3585.1285
574.1860	791.7953	1096.1688	1522.2176	2118.8060	2954.2439	4123.8977
626.8628	871.9749	1217.7474	1705.8838	2395.2508	3368.8380	4743.4824
684.2804	960.1723	1352.6996	1911.5898	2707.6334	3841.4753	5456.0047
746.8656	1057.1896	1502.4965	2141.9806	3060.6258	4380.2819	6275.4055
815.0836	1163.9085	1668.7712	2400.0182	3459.5071	4994.5213	7217.7163

TABLE 4
Present value (P) of an annuity (X) (= $1) paid or received at the end of every period for n periods

$$P_{\overline{n}|i} = X \cdot \frac{1 - 1/(1 + i)^n}{i}$$

No. of periods	2%	3%	4%	5%	6%	7%	8%
1	.9804	.9709	.9615	.9524	.9434	.9346	.9259
2	1.9416	1.9135	1.8861	1.8594	1.8334	1.8080	1.7833
3	2.8839	2.8286	2.7751	2.7232	2.6730	2.6243	2.5771
4	3.8077	3.7171	3.6299	3.5460	3.4651	3.3872	3.3121
5	4.7135	4.5797	4.4518	4.3295	4.2124	4.1002	3.9927
6	5.6014	5.4172	5.2421	5.0757	4.9173	4.7665	4.6229
7	6.4720	6.2303	6.0021	5.7864	5.5824	5.3893	5.2064
8	7.3255	7.0197	6.7327	6.4632	6.2098	5.9713	5.7466
9	8.1622	7.7861	7.4353	7.1078	6.8017	6.5152	6.2469
10	8.9826	8.5302	8.1109	7.7217	7.3601	7.0236	6.7101
11	9.7868	9.2526	8.7605	8.3064	7.8869	7.4987	7.1390
12	10.5753	9.9540	9.3851	8.8633	8.3838	7.9427	7.5361
13	11.3484	10.6350	9.9856	9.3936	8.8527	8.3577	7.9038
14	12.1062	11.2961	10.5631	9.8986	9.2950	8.7455	8.2442
15	12.8493	11.9379	11.1184	10.3797	9.7122	9.1079	8.5595
16	13.5777	12.5611	11.6523	10.8378	10.1059	9.4466	8.8514
17	14.2919	13.1661	12.1657	11.2741	10.4773	9.7632	9.1216
18	14.9920	13.7535	12.6593	11.6896	10.8276	10.0591	9.3719
19	15.6785	14.3238	13.1339	12.0853	11.1581	10.3356	9.6036
20	16.3514	14.8775	13.5903	12.4622	11.4699	10.5940	9.8181
21	17.0112	15.4150	14.0292	12.8212	11.7641	10.8355	10.0168
22	17.6580	15.9369	14.4511	13.1630	12.0416	11.0612	10.2007
23	18.2922	16.4436	14.8568	13.4886	12.3034	11.2722	10.3711
24	18.9139	16.9355	15.2470	13.7986	12.5504	11.4693	10.5288
25	19.5235	17.4131	15.6221	14.0939	12.7834	11.6536	10.6748
26	20.1210	17.8768	15.9828	14.3752	13.0032	11.8258	10.8100
27	20.7069	18.3270	16.3296	14.6430	13.2105	11.9867	10.9352
28	21.2813	18.7641	16.6631	14.8981	13.4062	12.1371	11.0511
29	21.8444	19.1885	16.9837	15.1411	13.5907	12.2777	11.1584
30	22.3965	19.6004	17.2920	15.3725	13.7648	12.4090	11.2578
31	22.9377	20.0004	17.5885	15.5928	13.9291	12.5318	11.3498
32	23.4683	20.3888	17.8736	15.8027	14.0840	12.6466	11.4350
33	23.9886	20.7658	18.1476	16.0025	14.2302	12.7538	11.5139
34	24.4986	21.1318	18.4112	16.1929	14.3681	12.8540	11.5869
35	24.9986	21.4872	18.6646	16.3742	14.4982	12.9477	11.6546
36	25.4888	21.8323	18.9083	16.5469	14.6210	13.0352	11.7172
37	25.9695	22.1672	19.1426	16.7113	14.7368	13.1170	11.7752
38	26.4406	22.4925	19.3679	16.8679	14.8460	13.1935	11.8289
39	26.9026	22.8082	19.5845	17.0170	14.9491	13.2649	11.8786
40	27.3555	23.1148	19.7928	17.1591	15.0463	13.3317	11.9246
41	27.7995	23.4124	19.9931	17.2944	15.1380	13.3941	11.9672
42	28.2348	23.7014	20.1856	17.4232	15.2245	13.4524	12.0067
43	28.6616	23.9819	20.3708	17.5459	15.3062	13.5070	12.0432
44	29.0800	24.2543	20.5488	17.6628	15.3832	13.5579	12.0771
45	29.4902	24.5187	20.7200	17.7741	15.4558	13.6055	12.1084
46	29.8923	24.7754	20.8847	17.8801	15.5244	13.6500	12.1374
47	30.2866	25.0247	21.0429	17.9810	15.5890	13.6916	12.1643
48	30.6731	25.2667	21.1951	18.0772	15.6500	13.7305	12.1891
49	31.0521	25.5017	21.3415	18.1687	15.7076	13.7668	12.2122
50	31.4236	25.7298	21.4822	18.2559	15.7619	13.8007	12.2335

TABLE 4 Continued

Present value (P) of an annuity (X) (= $1) paid or received at the end of every period for n periods

$$P_{\overline{n}|i} = X \cdot \frac{1 - 1/(1 + i)^n}{i}$$

9%	10%	11%	12%	13%	14%	15%
.9174	.9091	.9009	.8929	.8850	.8772	.8696
1.7591	1.7355	1.7125	1.6901	1.6681	1.6467	1.6257
2.5313	2.4869	2.4437	2.4018	2.3612	2.3216	2.2832
3.2397	3.1699	3.1024	3.0373	2.9745	2.9137	2.8550
3.8897	3.7908	3.6959	3.6048	3.5172	3.4331	3.3522
4.4859	4.3553	4.2305	4.1114	3.9975	3.8887	3.7845
5.0330	4.8684	4.7122	4.5638	4.4226	4.2883	4.1604
5.5348	5.3349	5.1461	4.9676	4.7988	4.6389	4.4873
5.9952	5.7590	5.5370	5.3282	5.1317	4.9464	4.7716
6.4177	6.1446	5.8892	5.6502	5.4262	5.2161	5.0188
6.8052	6.4951	6.2065	5.9377	5.6869	5.4527	5.2337
7.1607	6.8137	6.4924	6.1944	5.9176	5.6603	5.4206
7.4869	7.1034	6.7499	6.4235	6.1218	5.8424	5.5831
7.7862	7.3667	6.9819	6.6282	6.3025	6.0021	5.7245
8.0607	7.6061	7.1909	6.8109	6.4624	6.1422	5.8474
8.3126	7.8237	7.3792	6.9740	6.6039	6.2651	5.9542
8.5436	8.0216	7.5488	7.1196	6.7291	6.3729	6.0472
8.7556	8.2014	7.7016	7.2497	6.8399	6.4674	6.1280
8.9501	8.3649	7.8393	7.3658	6.9380	6.5504	6.1982
9.1285	8.5136	7.9633	7.4694	7.0248	6.6231	6.2593
9.2922	8.6487	8.0751	7.5620	7.1016	6.6870	6.3125
9.4424	8.7715	8.1757	7.6446	7.1695	6.7429	6.3587
9.5802	8.8832	8.2664	7.7184	7.2297	6.7921	6.3988
9.7066	8.9847	8.3481	7.7843	7.2829	6.8351	6.4338
9.8226	9.0770	8.4217	7.8431	7.3300	6.8729	6.4641
9.9290	9.1609	8.4881	7.8957	7.3717	6.9061	6.4906
10.0266	9.2372	8.5478	7.9426	7.4086	6.9352	6.5135
10.1161	9.3066	8.6016	7.9844	7.4412	6.9607	6.5335
10.1983	9.3696	8.6501	8.0218	7.4701	6.9830	6.5509
10.2737	9.4269	8.6938	8.0552	7.4957	7.0027	6.5660
10.3428	9.4790	8.7331	8.0850	7.5183	7.0199	6.5791
10.4062	9.5264	8.7686	8.1116	7.5383	7.0350	6.5905
10.4644	9.5694	8.8005	8.1354	7.5560	7.0482	6.6005
10.5178	9.6086	8.8293	8.1566	7.5717	7.0599	6.6091
10.5668	9.6442	8.8552	8.1755	7.5856	7.0700	6.6166
10.6118	9.6765	8.8786	8.1924	7.5979	7.0790	6.6231
10.6530	9.7059	8.8996	8.2075	7.6087	7.0868	6.6288
10.6908	9.7327	8.9186	8.2210	7.6183	7.0937	6.6338
10.7255	9.7570	8.9357	8.2330	7.6268	7.0997	6.6380
10.7574	9.7791	8.9511	8.2438	7.6344	7.1050	6.6418
10.7866	9.7991	8.9649	8.2534	7.6410	7.1097	6.6450
10.8134	9.8174	8.9774	8.2619	7.6469	7.1138	6.6478
10.8380	9.8340	8.9886	8.2696	7.6522	7.1173	6.6503
10.8605	9.8491	8.9988	8.2764	7.6568	7.1205	6.6524
10.8812	9.8628	9.0079	8.2825	7.6609	7.1232	6.6543
10.9002	9.8753	9.0161	8.2880	7.6645	7.1256	6.6559
10.9176	9.8866	9.0235	8.2928	7.6677	7.1277	6.6573
10.9336	9.8969	9.0302	8.2972	7.6705	7.1296	6.6585
10.9482	9.9063	9.0362	8.3010	7.6730	7.1312	6.6596
10.9617	9.9148	9.0417	8.3045	7.6752	7.1327	6.6605

Glossary

Accounting Principles Board (APB) The standard-setting authority of the U.S. accounting profession from 1959 to 1973; the predecessor of the *Financial Accounting Standards Board*.

Accounting Standards Board (ASB) The authoritative body in Canada responsible for the development and continued evolution of generally accepted accounting principles for the private sector.

Accounts payable Amounts owed to suppliers for services, supplies, and raw materials purchased.

Accounts receivable Claims against debtors, usually resulting from the sale of goods, performance of services, or lending of funds.

Accrual basis of accounting A means of accounting whereby revenues are realized when there is evidence that a firm is economically better off because of its production and sales activities. Costs are charged as expenses in the same periods as the revenues to which they relate are recognized; distinguished from *cash basis*.

Accumulated amortization An allowance (contra account to a related capital asset) to reflect the "consumption" of an asset over time by wear and tear as well as by technological obsolescence; equal to the sum of the amortization charges over time on the related asset.

Accumulated depreciation This term means the same as accumulated amortization. The CICA has replaced the word depreciation with amortization, but the use of the term depreciation is still very common.

Accumulated obligation for pension benefits (pensions) The actuarial present value of all benefits that have been earned (not taking into account estimated future increases in wages and salaries).

Activity ratio A ratio which measures the efficiency of management in utilizing specific resources under its command; also referred to as a *turnover ratio*.

Actuarial cost method (pensions) A technique used by actuaries to determine the required contributions to a pension fund or amounts to be charged as pension expense.

Adjusting entries Entries, especially those at the end of an accounting period, to bring the accounts up to date and to correct known errors.

Aging of accounts receivable A means of classifying accounts receivable by the number of days they are past due; for example: current, up to 30 days, up to 60 days, etc.

AICPA See *American Institute of Certified Public Accountants*.

Allowance for amortization See *Accumulated amortization*.

Allowance for depreciation See *Accumulated depreciation*.

Allowance for doubtful accounts An estimate of the amounts owed to a company that will be uncollectable; usually reported "contra" to accounts receivable.

Allowance method (uncollectable accounts) A method of accounting for uncollectable accounts whereby a bad-debt expense is charged in the same period as the sales to which it relates; correspondingly, accounts receivable is reduced by adding to a contra account, "Allowance for doubtful accounts."

American Accounting Association (AAA) The leading association of accountants in the United States directed primarily to the interests of academic accountants.

American Institute of Certified Public Accountants (AICPA) The professional society of certified public accountants in the United States.

Amortization The process of allocating (amortizing) the cost of assets or a deferred charge over the accounting periods that it will benefit.

Annuity A series of equal payments at fixed intervals.

Annuity due An annuity in which the payments are made or received at the beginning of each period.

Annuity in arrears An annuity in which the payments are made or received at the end of each period.

Arm's-length transaction A transaction in which the buyer and seller are unrelated and independent, with both parties seeking to advance their own best economic interests.

ASB See *Accounting Standards Board*.

Assets Resources or rights incontestably controlled by an entity at the accounting date that are expected to yield future economic benefits to the entity.

Audit An examination of financial statements to determine whether they are presented fairly in accordance with generally accepted accounting principles; any systematic investigation or procedure to determine conformity with prescribed standards or guidelines.

Auditor's report   The report issued by an independent public accountant in which he or she expresses an opinion on whether the financial statements audited are in conformity with generally accepted accounting principles.

Authorized stock   The maximum number of shares, per its corporate charter, that a company is permitted to issue.

Bad debt   An uncollectable receivable.

Balance sheet   See *Statement of financial position*.

Betterments   Costs incurred to enhance an asset's service potential from what was anticipated when it was first purchased; distinguished from *repairs*.

Bond   A certificate of indebtedness in which the issuer promises to make one or more payments in repayment of the amount borrowed as well as provide interest payments.

Call premium (bonds)   An amount, in addition to the face value of a bond, that must be paid to the lender when a bond is redeemed (called) prior to its maturity.

Call provision (bonds)   A provision in a bond agreement which gives the borrower a right to redeem, at a fixed price, the bond prior to its maturity.

Canadian Academic Accounting Association (CAAA)   The leading association of accountants in Canada directed primarily to the interests of academic accountants.

Canadian Institute of Chartered Accountants (CICA)   The professional society of Chartered Accountants.

Capital assets   Identifiable assets held for use by the entity and not intended for sale in the ordinary course of business; includes both tangible and intangible assets. Tangible assets are commonly referred to as fixed assets.

Capital Cost Allowance (CCA)   The system specified in the Income Tax Act to write off the cost of capital assets for tax purposes. In the majority of cases the costs of capital assets are written off on a declining balance basis, with the maximum rate dependent on the category of asset.

Capital lease   A lease which in economic substance involves the purchase and sale of an asset in exchange for a promise to make a series of payments in the future; a lease which is recorded on the books of both the lessee and the lessor as if it were a purchase/borrow transaction.

Capital stock   The ownership shares of a corporation; see also *Common stock, Preferred stock*.

Capitalize   To record an expenditure as an asset and thereby defer its recognition as an expense until a later period.

Cash   Currency and demand deposits in banks.

Cash basis of accounting   A means of accounting whereby revenues and expenses are recognized if, and only if, there is a receipt or disbursement of ⌐ ⌐; distinguished from *accrual basis of accounting*.

Certified General Accountant (CGA)   The professional designation conferred by each of the provinces upon accountants who have satisfied specified educational and experience requirements and who have passed a uniform national examination administered by The Certified General Accountants' Association of Canada. CGAs are principally engaged in public accounting in Canada.

Certified General Accountants' Association of Canada (CGAAC)   The professional society of Certified General Accountants.

Certified Management Accountant (CMA)   The professional designation conferred by each of the provinces upon accountants who have satisfied specified educational and experience requirements and who have passed a uniform national examination administered by The Society of Management Accountants of Canada. CMAs are principally engaged in private, or internal, accounting in Canada.

Certified public accountant (CPA)   The professional designation conferred by each of the states upon accountants who have satisfied specified educational and experience requirements and who have passed a uniform examination administered by the American Institute of Certified Public Accountants.

CGAAC   See *Certified General Accountants' Association of Canada.*

Chartered Accountant (CA)   The professional designation conferred by each of the provinces upon accountants who have satisfied specified educational and experience requirements and who have passed a uniform national examination administered by The Canadian Institute of Chartered Accountants. CAs are principally engaged in public accounting in Canada.

CICA   See *Canadian Institute of Chartered Accountants.*

Close (accounts or books)   To transfer, at the end of an accounting period, the balances in each revenue, expense, and dividend account to retained earnings or a comparable owners' equity account.

Closely held corporation   A corporation owned by a comparatively few shareholders.

Common stock   Certificates of corporate ownership which typically give the holder the right to vote for members of the corporation's board of directors, as well as on numerous other corporate matters, and the rights to share in corporate profits whenever dividends are declared by the board of directors.

Compound interest   Interest resulting from applying a specified rate of interest to the sum of the original principal of an investment or loan plus any interest that has been earned on that principal from previous periods that has not yet been paid; interest accumulating on an investment of principal over a number of periods at a specified rate of interest.

Comprehensive income   The excess of revenues and other gains over and above expenses and losses of any entity. This difference represents the change in the entity's net assets (excluding the effect of transactions between the entity and its owners involving dividends and contributions of capital).

Comptroller   See *Controller.*

Conservatism   The accounting convention that it is generally preferable that any possible errors in measurement be in the direction of understatement rather than overstatement of net income and net assets; that in the absence of certainty, recognition of gains should be delayed, but that of losses should be accelerated.

Consolidated financial statements   Statements that report the financial positions and earnings of two or more corporations as if they were a single economic entity.

Constant dollars   Dollars of different dates adjusted so that they represent monetary units of equivalent purchasing power.

Consumer Price Index (CPI)   An index maintained by Statistics Canada which expresses prices of various years as percentages of prices of a selected base year.

Contingencies   Gains or losses that are uncertain as to both occurrence and amount.

Contingent liability   A potential liability, one that would have to be settled only if a specific event (e.g., loss of a lawsuit) occurred.

Contra account   An offset account in which the balance is always opposite, and reported directly beneath, that of the account with which it is associated (e.g., accumulated amortization, allowance for doubtful accounts, and bond discount).

Contributed surplus   See *Premium on capital stock.*

Control account   A general ledger account, the balance of which is equal to the sum of the individual balances in a subsidiary ledger. For example, a capital asset control account is equal to the total of the individual capital assets recorded in the capital asset subsidiary ledger.

Controller   The chief accountant of a company or other type of organization.

Convertible securities   Securities, usually bonds or preferred stock, that can be exchanged for shares of common stock.

Copyright   An exclusive right, granted by law, to publish, sell, reproduce, or otherwise control a literary, musical, or artistic work.

Corporation   A legal entity, separate and distinct from its shareholder-owners, that is authorized to operate by the federal or a provincial government.

Cost or market   See *Lower of cost or market rule.*

Cost method (intercorporate investments)   A method whereby a company records its investment in the shares of another company at the amount paid to acquire the shares and recognizes revenue from its investment only when the investee declares dividends; distinguished from *equity method.*

Cost of goods sold   An expense representing the cost to acquire or produce goods that have been sold.

Cost savings   See *Holding gain.*

Coupon rate (of interest on bonds)   The rate of interest specified in a bond indenture (agreement) that will be paid each period; distinguished from *yield rate.*

CPA   See *Certified public accountant.*

Credits   Entries in accounts (to the right-hand side of ledger accounts) that signify increases in liabilities and owners' equity (e.g., revenues) or decreases in assets; distinguished from *debits.*

Current assets   Assets that will either be transformed into cash or will be sold or consumed within one year (or sometimes within the normal operating cycle of the business if longer than one year); assets which are cash, are likely to be turned into cash within one year, or will obviate the need for cash in the coming year (e.g., prepaid expenses). Also included are marketable securities, accounts receivable, and inventory.

Current cost   The amount that would have to be paid to purchase an asset today (an *input* or *entry* value or purchase price); see also *Replacement cost.*

Current liabilities   Liabilities expected to be satisfied out of current assets (or through the creation of other current liabilities) within one year (or sometimes the normal operating cycle of the business if longer than one year); include wages payable, accounts payable, interest payable and taxes payable.

Current operating income   Revenue at current prices less expenses at current prices; the income computation that might be considered a long-run sustainable amount if present conditions do not change in the future.

Current ratio   A liquidity ratio that compares current assets to current liabilities.

Date of record (corporate stock)   The date as of which the list of shareholders and their holdings is established so as to determine dividend distributions.

Debentures   Unsecured bonds.

Debits   Entries in accounts (to the left-hand side of ledger accounts) that signify increases in assets or decreases in liabilities and owners' equity (e.g., expenses); distinguished from *credits.*

Debt-to-equity ratio   A financing ratio that compares claims of creditors (liabilities) with the equity of shareholders (shareholders' equity).

Declining balance (amortization)   A method of computing amortization whereby a greater proportion of asset cost is allocated to the earlier periods of use than to the later periods.

Deferred charge   A cost not recognized as an expense of the period in which incurred, but carried forward as an asset to be written off in future periods.

Deferred credits   Deferred revenue; increases in net assets not recognized as revenue in one period, but carried forward to be recognized in future periods.

Deferred income taxes   The excess of income taxes recognized for financial reporting purposes over that recognized for tax purposes when such excess is attributable to timing differences. Deferred income taxes are reported as liabilities which will be written off as the underlying timing difference is reversed.

Defined benefit plan (pensions)   A plan which requires an employer to provide employees with specified benefits upon their retirement; distinguished from a *defined contribution plan,* in which the contributions rather than the benefits are specified.

Defined contribution plan (pensions)   A plan which requires the employer to make specified contributions to a pension plan; distinguished from a *defined benefit plan,* in which the benefits rather than the required contributions are specified.

Depletion   The process of allocating the cost of using up natural resources over an anticipated recovery period.

Depreciation   See *Amortization.*

Direct cost   The cost of any product or service that is readily attributable to that product or service; distinguished from *indirect cost* or *overhead.*

Direct write-off method (uncollectable accounts receivable)   A method whereby an account receivable is written off and bad-debt expense is charged only when it is known to be uncollectable; distinguished from the *allowance method.*

Discount (bonds)   The excess of the face value of a bond over its issue price or other recorded value. Usually this difference results when the interest rate prevailing when a bond is issued or sold is greater than the coupon rate.

Discount note   A note in which face value may include not only the amount originally borrowed but also the applicable interest charges.

Discounted cash flow   The amount which if invested today at a specified rate of return would be the equivalent of a series of cash payments to be received in various times in the future.

Dividends   Distributions of the net assets of an enterprise to its owners; see also *Stock dividend.*

Double-entry record-keeping system   A method whereby each transaction is recorded in two or more accounts so as to affect the basic accounting equation, Assets = Liabilities + Owners' Equity.

Earned surplus   See *Retained earnings.*

Earnings   See *Income.*

Earnings per share   Net income less preferred stock dividends divided by the weighted average number of common shares outstanding during a period.

Entry value   The amount that would have to be paid to replace an asset; see also *Current cost.*

Equities   The claims against an enterprise, including liabilities and owners' equity.

Equity method (intercorporate investments)   A method by which a company records its investment in another company at cost, but periodically adjusts the carrying value of the investment to take into account its share of the investee's earnings and dividends subsequent to the date the investment was acquired; distinguished from *cost method.*

Executory contract   An agreement contingent upon the mutual performance of the two sides to the contract.

Exit value   The amount for which an asset can be sold; see also *Net realizable value.*

Expenses   Decreases in economic resources, either by way of outflows or reductions of assets or incurrences of liabilities, resulting from an entity's ordinary revenue generating or service delivery activities.

Extraordinary items   Gains and losses that are exceptional in nature, infrequent in occurence, and not at the discretion of management; unlikely to recur, including fires, natural disasters, and expropriations of property by foreign governments.

Fair market value   A value based on arm's-length transactions between buyers and sellers.

FASB   See *Financial Accounting Standards Board.*

FIFO (first in, first out)   A method of accounting for inventory in which the items acquired first are assumed to be sold or used first.

Financial accounting   The branch of accounting that is concerned with reporting to parties, such as investors and creditors, external to the organization; distinguished from *management* accounting.

Financial Accounting Standards Board   The authoritative body which is the generally accepted standard-setting organization for private-sector financial accounting and reporting in the United States.

Financing lease   See *Capital lease.*

Fixed assets   The old terminology for tangible capital assets. Now referred to as property, plant, and equipment. See *Capital assets.*

Foreign currency   A currency other than the functional currency of an entity.

Full cost method (oil drilling costs)   A method by which the costs associated with unsuccessful prospects (dry holes) are capitalized along with the costs associated with the successful properties; distinguished from the *successful efforts method.*

Funds   Variously defined as (1) cash; (2) cash plus selected current assets (such as cash, marketable securities, and accounts receivable) less current liabilities; (3) working capital (all current assets less all current liabilities).

Future value of an annuity   The amount to which a series of equal payments at fixed intervals will accumulate at a specified interest rate and in a specified number of periods.

GAAP See *Generally accepted accounting principles.*

Gains Increases in net assets resulting from transactions that are not typical of a firm's day-to-day operations.

General ledger A ledger in which all balance sheet and income statement accounts are maintained.

Generally accepted accounting principles (GAAP) Accounting practices that are either specially mandated by authoritative rule-making organizations or are considered acceptable because of widespread use, convention, or tradition.

Going-concern concept The assumption that the enterprise being reported upon will continue operating indefinitely into the future so that the firm will realize the benefits of all its assets and have to satisfy all its liabilities.

Goodwill The excess of an amount paid to acquire a company over the fair market value of the company's net assets; an asset that arises exclusively as the result of a business combination and can be thought to represent the value of certain intangible assets, such as reputation, location, and trademarks that cannot normally be specifically identified.

Gross margin Sales revenue minus cost of goods sold.

Historical cost The amount paid to acquire an asset, adjusted for subsequent amortization.

Holding gain A gain attributable to an increase in price since an asset was acquired; distinguished from *trading gain.*

IASC See *International Accounting Standards Committee.*

Imprest basis A means of accounting for petty cash whereby the general ledger account for petty cash will always indicate a specified balance. The actual petty cash on hand, plus receipts for payments made with petty cash, should always equal that balance.

Imputed interest Interest, at a rate approximately equal to prevailing rates, applied to a borrowing transaction to reflect economic substance, when the actual rate charged is considerably less than the prevailing rate.

Income The excess of revenues over expenses; in general, the change in equity (net assets) of an entity during a period from transactions (other than those with the entity's owners) and selected other events; see also *Comprehensive income.*

Income statement A report that summarizes the revenues (and other gains) and expenses (and any losses) of a period.

Indirect cost The cost of any product or service that cannot be readily attributable to that product or service; distinguished from *direct cost.*

Inflation An increase in the number of monetary units required to acquire a basket of typical goods and services.

Input value The amount required to replace an asset by purchase, manufacture, or construction; see *Replacement cost.*

Instalment basis (revenue recognition) A means of recognizing revenue based on cash collections.

Intangible asset An asset that lacks physical existence but is instead characterized by rights or other benefits. Examples include patents, trademarks, research and development costs, and goodwill.

Interest A service charge for the use of money, usually expressed as an annual percent of outstanding principal.

Interim financial report A report that covers less than a full year, usually a quarter or half year.

Internal auditor   An auditor who carries out his or her activities within a single organization and is employed by that organization.

International Accounting Standards Committee (IASC)   An organization with members from most of the leading accounting bodies in the world. Their objective is to develop a set of accounting standards that would be acceptable around the world.

Inventory   Goods held for sale to customers as well as raw materials, supplies, and parts to be used in the production or other activities of the entity.

Inventory turnover   A ratio that measures the number of times the annual cost of sales exceeds average inventory.

Investments   Property acquired to yield a return, such as the stock or bonds of another firm; may be either a current or non current asset.

Invoice   A document showing the terms of sale, including quantity, price, and discounts; a bill.

Journal   A book of original entry to record transactions. Transactions of similar types may be recorded in specialized journals, while the remainder are recorded in a general journal.

Journal entry   The written notation of a transaction in a journal, consisting of both debits and credits equal in amount.

Lease   A contract providing the right to use land, buildings, equipment, or other property for a specified period of time in return for rent or other compensation.

Ledger   A book which contains accounts; see *General ledger, Subsidiary ledger.*

Legal capital   Generally, an amount in owners' equity equivalent to the issue price of share capital. Normally, dividends cannot be declared which would reduce this legal capital.

Lessee   The party which leases property *from* another.

Lessor   The party which owns property and leases it *to* another.

Leverage   The issuance of debt or other securities having a fixed interest or dividend rate, rather than common stock, to finance asset acquisitions. This is done in the expectation that relatively small increases in net income will result in disproportionately large increases in return to existing common shareholders.

Liabilities   Obligations of an entity at the accounting date to make future transfers of assets or services (sometimes uncertain as to timing and amount) to other entities.

LIFO (last in, first out)   A method of accounting for inventory in which the items acquired most recently are assumed to be those sold or used first.

Liquidation value   The amount that could be realized if the firm were to be dissolved and its assets put up for sale.

Liquidity   The ability of a firm to convert its noncash assets to cash so as to satisfy its obligations as they mature.

Liquidity ratios   The ratios which show a company's ability to meet its short-term obligations; include current ratio and quick ratio.

Losses   Decreases in net assets resulting from transactions that are not typical of a firm's day-to-day operations.

Lower of cost or market rule   The principle of valuation which requires assets to be written down to market value whenever such value is less than historical cost.

Management accounting   The branch of accounting that is concerned with financial data as they are used within an organization; distinguished from *financial accounting*.

Management advisory services   The branch of the public accounting profession which provides consulting services to the management of corporations or other types of organizations.

Market value   The price at which an asset could be bought or sold.

Marketable securities   Securities, such as bonds, stock, and treasury bills, which are held by the reporting entity as short-term investments.

Matching principle   The principle which holds that costs should be recognized as expenses in the same accounting period as the revenues that they generate.

Minority interest   See *Non-controlling interest*.

Monetary items   Assets and liabilities which are contractually fixed or which are convertible into a fixed number of dollars, regardless of changes in prices.

Net realizable value   The amount for which an asset can be sold, less any costs that would normally be incurred to bring it to a salable condition; a current exit value or sale price, as contrasted to current cost, which is an entry value or purchase price.

Neutrality   The concept that economic activity should be reported as objectively as possible in a way not subject to any bias intended to influence users to a predetermined conclusion or in a particular direction.

Nominal dollars   Dollars that are not adjusted to take into account differences in purchasing power.

Noncontrolling interest   The equity of the nonmajority shareholders in the consolidated corporation.

Noncurrent assets   Assets that cannot expected to be sold or transformed into cash within one year (or sometimes the normal operating cycle of the business if longer than one year); include land, plant, and equipment; natural resources; and intangibles.

Noncurrent liabilities   Liabilities not expected to be liquidated within one year (or sometimes the normal operating cycle of the business if longer than one year); include bonds and other long-term obligations.

Normal operating cycle   The time it takes a business to purchase, provide, or manufacture goods or services, sell them to a customer, and collect the proceeds.

Note receivable   A written promise to pay a specified amount, together with interest at a stated rate.

NSF (nonsufficient funds) cheque   A cheque returned by a bank to a depositor because the party which wrote the cheque had insufficient funds in its account to cover the cheque.

Number of days' sales in accounts receivable   Accounts receivable as at a particular date, divided by average sales per day.

Objectivity   The characteristic of accounting information suggesting that it faithfully describes what it purports to represent and is verifiable and free from bias.

Obligation for pension benefits   The actuarial present value of all benefits that have been earned (taking into account estimated future increases in wages and salaries).

Operating cycle   See *Normal operating cycle.*

Operating lease   A contract that provides for the right to use property for a limited time in exchange for periodic rent payments; distinguished from *capital lease.*

Opportunity cost   The value of the sacrificed opportunity to employ an asset in its next-best use; the amount that might be earned if an asset were sold and the proceeds used in the best alternative fashion.

Organization costs   The costs incurred to organize a corporation. These include the legal fees required to draw up the documents of incorporation, filing fees, and clerical costs.

Other postemployment benefits   Benefits provided to retired employees in addition to pensions, the most common of which are life insurance and paid health care.

Output value   The amount for which an asset could be sold or exchanged.

Overhead   Any costs that cannot be directly ascribed to a product or service; distinguished from *direct cost.* See also *Indirect cost.*

Owners' equity   The residual interest in the assets of an entity that remains after deducting its liabilities; the interests of the owners in a business enterprise.

Par value   An arbitrary value, having some legal but little economic significance, which is assigned to a share of stock; similar to *stated value;* the minimum capital (i.e., net assets) that must be retained in an entity and thereby cannot be distributed to shareholders. No longer allowed in most jurisdictions in Canada.

Parent company   A company that owns an interest in, and controls, another company (known as a subsidiary). Control is typically indicated by ownership of at least 50 percent of the subsidiary's common stock.

Participating preferred stock   Preferred stock that entitles the holders to share in distributions in excess of the stipulated minimum dividend.

Partnership   A firm owned by two or more parties.

Patent   An exclusive right, granted by the federal government, to an inventor to produce and sell an invention.

Payable   A liability; see also *Accounts payable.*

Pension   A sum of money paid to a retired or disabled employee owing to his or her years of employment.

Percentage of completion method   A means of recognizing revenue, generally on long-term construction projects, whereby the amount of revenue recognized in each period is based on the percentage of the project completed in that period. The percentage completed in a period is determined by the ratio of costs incurred in that period to total anticipated costs.

Period costs   Costs that are recognized as expenses based strictly on time and assigned to particular periods regardless of productive output in that period; distinguished from *product costs.*

Periodic method   A means of accounting for inventory or other assets and liabilities, and their related revenues or expenses, whereby accounts are adjusted at the end of each period to bring them up to date. The adjustment is usually made on the basis of a physical count, or comparable measure, of the actual assets or liabilities. During the period, the account is debited or credited only for selected transactions and therefore may not be current. For example, when the periodic method is used to account for inventory, the inventory account may be debited during the period only for goods purchased. At year end a physical count of goods on hand is taken, and both the inventory balance and cost of goods sold are adjusted to reflect this count; distinguished from *perpetual method*.

Perpetual method A means of accounting for inventory or other assets and liabilities, and their related revenue or expenses, whereby the accounts are continually updated during a period as each transaction takes place; distinguished from *periodic method*.

Physical inventory A count to determine the actual amount of inventory on hand.

Pooling of interests (intercorporate investments) A method of consolidation whereby, for accounting purposes, two companies are joined together, with neither acquiring the other. The asset and liability values from the books of each of the companies are normally recorded at historical cost amounts and carried over to the consolidated statement without adjustment; distinguished from *purchase*.

Post-service cost (pensions) A component of pension expense arising from an employee's service in prior years.

Preemptive rights Rights granted by a corporation to existing shareholders to acquire newly issued shares of stock and thereby to preserve their proportionate interests in the company.

Preferred stock A class of stock with specified preferences and priorities, as well as limitations, as compared with common stock; often does not grant voting rights. The most common preference is a stipulated minimum dividend.

Premium (bonds) The amount in excess of face value received by a corporation on bonds. This additional payment is ordinarily made to equate the stipulated interest rate with lower prevailing market rates.

Premium on capital stock Amounts that a company receives when it issues stock for an amount in excess of the stock's par value. Also called contributed surplus.

Preopening costs Costs incurred prior to the commencement of a business's operations.

Prepaid expense An expenditure for benefits to be received or recognized in the future; see also *Deferred charge*.

Present value The value today of one or more future cash flows when these cash flows are discounted at a specified rate of interest.

Present value of an annuity The dollar equivalent today of a series of equal payments at fixed intervals, discounted at a specified interest rate and over a specified number of periods.

Price/earnings (P/E) ratio The ratio of the market price of a firm's common stock to its earnings per share for the year.

Price-level adjustments Adjustments to take account of the changing value of the monetary unit.

Principal The amount of a loan; distinguished from *interest*.

Product costs The costs, such as labour, materials, and overhead, that are assigned to a product; distinguished from *period costs*.

Profit See *Income*.

Promissory note See *Note receivable*.

Property, plant, and equipment   Capital assets that are tangible. Commonly referred to as fixed assets.

Proprietorship   A firm owned by a single individual.

Public Accountants   Accountants who make their services available to the public at large rather than to a single employer.

Public Sector Accounting and Auditing Committee (PSAAC)   A committee of the CICA responsible for establishing accounting, reporting, and auditing standards for the federal, provincial, territorial, and local governments.

Purchase (intercorporate investments)   A method of consolidation whereby the acquisition price of an investment is allocated to the net assets of the acquired company based on fair market value; distinguished from *pooling of interests*.

Purchasing power gains or losses   The gain or loss attributed to holding monetary assets and liabilities during a period in which the value of the monetary unit changes.

Quick ratio   A liquidity ratio that compares cash, marketable securities, and accounts receivable to current liabilities; a more rigorous test of ability to satisfy short-term obligations than the current ratio.

Realizable gain or loss (current cost accounting)   The total gain or loss on assets and liabilities that is earned during a period involving both resources and obligations that remain on hand at the end of a period and resources and obligations that were sold or consumed during the period.

Realize   To recognize a gain or loss upon the receipt of cash, receivables, or corresponding assets due to the sale or exchange of goods or services.

Receivable   A claim, usually stated in terms of a fixed number of dollars, arising from sale of goods, performance of services, lending of funds, or from some other type of transaction which establishes a relationship whereby one party is indebted to another.

Relevance   The characteristic of accounting information that makes it useful to a decision maker in that it will influence a decision.

Repairs   Costs incurred to restore an asset's service potential to what was anticipated when it was acquired; distinguished from *betterments*.

Replacement cost   The amount that would be required to purchase, manufacture, or construct a comparable asset (adjusted for age and use) at today's prevailing market prices; see also *Current cost*.

Reserve recognition accounting   A means of accounting for natural resources that requires that proven reserves be reported at the present value of the net cash flows that they are likely to generate.

Residual income   Net income (excluding any actual interest costs) less an imputed cost of capital.

Residual value   See *Salvage value*.

Retained earnings   The sum of the earnings of the accounting periods that the company has been in existence less the amounts declared as dividends to shareholders.

Return on investment (ROI)   Income as a percentage of invested capital; relates earnings of the enterprise to resources provided by its owners.

Revenues   Increases in economic resources, either by way of inflows or enhancements of assets or reductions of liabilities, resulting from the ordinary activities of an entity. Revenues of entities normally arise from the sale of goods, the rendering of services or the use by others of the entity resources yielding rent, interest, royalties or dividends.

Sale A business transaction involving the delivery of property or services in exchange for cash or other consideration.

Salvage value An estimate of the amount for which a fixed asset might be sold at the conclusion of its useful economic life as anticipated by its owner.

SEC See *Securities and Exchange Commission.*

Securities and Exchange Act of 1934 The act that grants the United States Securities and Exchange Commission (SEC) the statutory authority to control practices of financial reporting.

Securities and Exchange Commission (SEC) The federal regulatory agency created by the U.S. Congress in 1934 to administer the federal securities acts; powers include oversight of accounting procedures employed by all public corporations.

Shareholders' equity The residual interest in the assets of a *corporation* after deducting its liabilities; the interests of the shareholders in a corporation. See *Owners' equity.*

Sinking fund Cash or other assets set aside to repay debt, redeem stock, or achieve a similar objective.

SMA See *Society of Management Accountants of Canada.*

Society of Management Accountants of Canada (SMA) The professional society of Certified Management Accountants.

Sole proprietorship A firm owned by a single individual.

Spinoff A corporation's distribution to its own shareholders of its stock in a subsidiary as part of a plan to divest itself of the subsidiary.

Start-up costs Costs incurred prior to the point at which a venture is fully operational.

Stated capital The amount for which capital stock was actually issued or an amount designated (similar to par value) by the issuer which generally establishes a floor on the payment of dividends (i.e., a company cannot pay dividends that will reduce its shareholders' equity to less than its stated capital).

Stated value See *Par value.*

Statement of changes in financial position A report that reconciles cash at the beginning of the year with that at the end, the objective being to provide information about an enterprise's cash receipts and disbursements; one of the three primary financial statements, along with the income statement and balance sheet.

Statement of financial position A report indicating the financial position of an entity as at a specific point in time in terms of the entity's assets, liabilities, and owners' equity; commonly known as a *balance sheet.*

Statement of retained earnings A report that reconciles beginning- and end-of-year retained earnings; links the income statement and balance sheet, since beginning retained earnings plus income less dividends equals ending retained earnings.

Stock dividend A distribution by a corporation to its shareholders of additional shares of its own stock; a form of a stock split, but typically involving the issuance of a smaller number of new shares.

Stock option A right granted by a corporation to purchase shares of its own stock at a specified price.

Stock rights   See *Preemptive rights.*

Stock split   A distribution by a corporation to its shareholders of additional shares of its own stock in proportion to number of shares already owned; a form of stock dividend, but typically involving the distribution of a larger number of new shares.

Straight-line method (amortization)   A method of computing amortization whereby the cost of the asset (less anticipated salvage value) is allocated to the estimated periods of asset service in equal amounts.

Subsidiary company   A company owned or controlled by a parent corporation.

Subsidiary ledger   A supporting ledger which contains the individual accounts that compose a control account. For example, an accounts receivable subsidiary ledger would contain the individual customer accounts that support the accounts receivable control account.

Successful efforts method (oil drilling costs)   A method by which the costs associated with unsuccessful prospects (dry holes) are expensed as incurred rather than capitalized; distinguished from the *full cost method.*

Sum-of-the-year's digits (amortization)   A method of amortization whereby a varying fraction of asset cost (less salvage value) is allocated to each period of asset use. The denominator of the fraction, which remains constant over the life of the asset, is a sum of numbers starting with 1 and continuing to the total estimated useful life of the asset. The numerator, which changes from year to year, is the number of years remaining in the asset's useful life at the beginning of the year in question.

T account   A representation of a ledger account in the form of a T, with debits on the left side of the vertical line and credits on the right; used to demonstrate the effect of transactions on the accounts.

Tangible assets   Assets having physical form, such as land, buildings, equipment, vehicles, and furniture and fixtures.

Times interest earned ratio   A ratio that indicates the relationship between interest expense on the one hand and income before deducting both interest expense and income taxes on the other.

Trading gain   A gain arising out of the normal purchasing, manufacturing, and sales activities of a firm; distinguished from *holding gain.*

Treasurer   A senior fiscal officer of a company who is concerned primarily with the acquisition of capital, shareholder and bondholder relations, managing the firm's investments, and administration of insurance.

Treasury stock   Stock that is acquired and retained by the issuing corporation.

Trial balance   A listing of all accounts in a ledger, the purpose of which is to verify that the total debits equal the total credits.

Turnover   The number of times that specified resources, such as inventory, accounts receivable, and plant and equipment, are replaced during a period.

Turnover ratio   A measure of asset efficiency calculated by dividing sales (or cost of goods sold) by the balance in an asset account; also known as *activity ratio.*

Unrealized gain or loss   An increase in net assets that has not yet been incorporated into income.

Value   An assigned or calculated numerical quantity; the worth of something sold or exchanged; the worth of a thing in money or goods at a certain time; its fair market price; worth in usefulness or importance to its possessor; utility or merit.

Voucher An internal document authorizing a disbursement.

Warrants Certificates, usually issued in association with notes, bonds, or stock, that entitle the holder to purchase shares of stock at a specified price.

Warranty The promise of a seller to repair or compensate a buyer for any defects in the product sold.

Weighted-average method (inventory) The method of accounting for inventory whereby the costs assigned to each item that has either been sold or remains in inventory is the weighted average of the costs of all inventory items available for sale during a particular period.

Window dressing The practice of taking deliberate steps to inflate the current and quick ratios for financial reporting purposes.

Working capital The excess of current assets over current liabilities.

Worksheet A columnar collection of accounting data organized in a fashion that may help the user move through the accounting process from trial balance to completed statements.

Yield rate (of interest on bonds) The actual rate of interest to be paid on a bond, based on the coupon payments, the actual price for which the bond was issued, and the number of periods to maturity; distinguished from *coupon rate*.

Index

Accumulated amortization, 103, 140, 367–368
See also Property, plant, and equipment; capital assets
Accumulated depreciation; See Accumulated amortization
Activity ratios; *See* Ratios, activity measures
Actuarial valuation method (pensions), 452
Adjusting entries, 135-149
Adjustments for price changes; *See* price changes
Advances from customers, 133
Allied Stores Corp., 435
Allocation of costs; *See* Matching
Allowance for doubtful accounts; *See* Accounts receivable, uncollectables
Allstate Corp., 518
American Institute of Certified Public Accountants (AICPA), 16
See also Accounting Research Bulletin of the AICPA
Amortization:
    of bond discount and premium, 427-433
    of capital assets, 12, 37, 55, 140, 366-368, 374-386
        accumulated; *See* Accumulated amortization
        compound interest method, 381-382
        current (replacement) cost method, 384-386
        declining balance (including double declining balance) method, 377-378
        historical versus current cost method, 382-386
        not providing funds for replacement, 375-376
        straight-line method, 374-376
        sum-of-the-years' digits method, 376-377
        units-of-output method, 391-392
    of goodwill, 573-574, 585-586
Annuities:
    and future values, 242-244
    and present values, 244-247
    tables of, 756-759
Assets:
    classified, 35-36
    current, 36-37, 252
    defined, 34-35
    intangible, 36, 46
        See also Intangible assets
    liquid, 35
    monetary, 36, 672-673
    noncurrent, 35-39
    nonmonetary, 36
    tangible, 36
    valuation of, 36, 231-236
    See also Accounts receivable; Cash; Deferred charge; Goodwill; Inventories; Investments; Marketable securities; Notes payable and receivable; Prepayments and accrual accounting, prepaid expenses; Property, plant and equipment
Auditing, 19-21
    internal, 22
Auditor's report, 20
Average cost method of valuing inventories; *See* inventories

B

Bad debts:
    and Western Canada bank failures, 281-282
    See also Accounts receivable, uncollectables
Balance sheet, 4, 8-11, 34, 42, 46, 56, 101
"Big bath," 201
"Big Six," 20
Bonds payable, 423-437
    convertible, 494-498
    current cost adjustment for, 670-671
    discount or premium on, 424-433
    gains and losses on, 433-435
    interest on, 428-433
    nature of, 423-424
    par value of, 423
    realizable holding gain (loss) on, 670-671
    redemption, 433-435
    yield rate, 424, 428
    See also Junk bonds
Buildings and equipment; *See* Property, plant and equipment

C

Cable Television industry, 398
Campeau Corporation, 437
Canadian Academic Accounting Association, 16
Canadian Institute of Chartered Accountants, 16, 19
Canadian Institute of Public Real Estate Companies, 206n, 296
Capital assets;
    amortization of, 374-386
    definition of, 366
Capital cost allowance, 378
Capitalization of interest (financing constructed assets), 371-372
Capitalizing versus expensing of asset, 131
Career of accountancy, 1
Cash, 250-253
    classification of, 252
    petty, 251
    sinking fund, 252
Cash discounts, 285-287
Cash flow:
    deficiencies, 131
    distinguished from income, 59, 626-628
Certified general accountants, 19
Certified General Accountants' Association of Canada, 19
Certified management accountants (CMAs), 19

D

Debit and credit, 83-85
Decision-making, 2-3, 5, 6
Deferred charge, 37-38
    See also Prepayments, prepaid expenses
Depletion, 367
    units-of-production method, 391-392
Depreciation; *See* Amortization
Disclosure, 718-720
Discounts, cash, 285-287
Dividends:
    cash, 516-518
    date of payment, 516
    date of record, 516
    defined, 62
    nature of, 516
    stock, 520-522
Dividends in kind, 518-519
Double-entry accounting, 42
Doubtful accounts; *See* Accounts receivable,
    uncollectables

E

Earnings; *See* Income statement
Earning per share (EPS), 158, 529-533
    and convertible securities, 530-532
    and stock options, 532
    and stock rights, 530-531
    and stock warrants, 530-532
Economic consequences of accounting practices and
    regulations, 13-14, 18, 337, 585-586, 713-717
Efficient market hypothesis (EMH), 14-15
Elements of financial statements, 17
Employees, 3
Equity method; *See* Intercorporate investments
Errors and omissions, 148-149
Events (economic), 2, 8, 10, 41, 87-88
    actual versus description of, 13-14
    See also Transaction versus economic event
Executory contracts, 40
Expense:
    defined, 48
    See also Matching
Extraordinary items, 48, 528-529

F

Failure:
    audit, 23
    business, 23
Federated Department Stores Inc., 437
Financial accounting:
    defined, 3
    versus managerial accounting, 3

Financial Accounting Standards Board (FASB), 16-17
    See also Statements of Financial Accounting
        Standards(SFAS)
Financial analysis:
    overview, 720-721
    See also Ratios
Financial institutions and recognition problems, 210
Financial statements, elements of, 17
Foreign currency transactions:
    accounting for, 680-685
    issues and principles, 680-685
    See also CICA Handbook Section 1650
Franchise companies and valuation of receivables,
    297-298
Fundamental check between income statement and
    comparative balance sheet, 49-50
Future value:
    of an annuity, 242-244
    of a single sum, 237-239

G

Gains and losses, 48, 522-523
General purpose financial reports, 3, 4
Generally accepted accounting principles (GAAP), 3,
    4, 7, 10, 13
Going concern concept, 233
Goods sold, cost of; *See* Cost of goods sold
Goodwill 393, 568-569
    amortization of, 573-574
    and pooling, 581

H

Henry Birks and Sons Ltd., 437
Historical cost, 13, 232-234
Historical cost/constant dollar accounting, 659
Historical cost model versus current cost model, 5,
    339-345, 382-386, 659
Historical cost/nominal dollar accounting 659
Holding gain; *See* Realizable holding gain, Realized
    holding gain
Hudson's Bay Co., 518

I

IBM, 461
Inco Limited, 660-662
Income statement, 4, 8-10, 47-48, 56-57, 97-98, *See also*
    Extraordinary items
Income taxes, 421, 442-450
Instant earnings; *See* Consolidation
Insurance industry and recognition problems, 208-210
Intangible assets:
    amortization of, 56, 367

Public Sector Accounting and Auditing Committee, 23
Purchasing power, gains and losses 673, 677-679

Q

Quick ratio, 160, 302-303
Qualitative standards, characteristics of, 4, 17

R

Ratios as measures of financial performance and
        health, 157-161, 720-729
    activity (turnover) measures:
        accounts receivable turnover, 300-302
        inventory turnover, 345-346
        number of days' sales in accounts receivable,
            302
        plant and equipment turnover, 390-391
    financial measures:
        debt/equity ratio 161, 499
        leveraging effectiveness ratio, 725
        times interest earned, 435-436
    liquidity measures:
        current ratio 158, 160, 302-303
        quick ratio, 160, 302-303
    profitability measures:
        earnings per share, 158
        gross profit margin, 159
        net profit margin, 159
        pitfalls in return on investment measures, 725-
            727
        price/earnings ratio, 160
        return on investment:
            assets, 721-725
            owners' equity, 159
        supplements to profit and return measures, 728
Realizable holding gain:
    on bonds payable, 670
    defined, 666-667
    on inventories, 667-668
    on land, 669
    on property, plant and equipment, 669-670
Realizable real holding gain, 676
Realized holding gain, 667
Realization convention; *See* Recognition
Receivables, 274
    current versus noncurrent, 274
    definition, 274
    and franchise companies, 297-298
    net and gross method, 285-287
    and retail land sales companies, 295-296
    See also Accounts receivable; Notes payable and
        receivable
Recognition:
    issues, general, 41, 87-88, 656-657

realization convention, 127
    when right-of return exists, 284-285
    See also Contingencies; Gains and losses;
            Inventories and cost of goods sold; Leases;
            Liabilities; Notes payable and receivable;
            Pensions; Property, plant and equipment;
            Revenue recognition; Taxes, income;
            Warranty obligations
Relevance, 4-6, 657
Reliability, 5, 6, 196-197, 657
Replacement cost; *See* Market values
Representation faithfulness, 657
Research in accounting, 23-24
    capital markets, 23-24
    choice theory, 24
Research and development costs; *See* Intangible assets
Retail industry, 397-398
Retail land sales companies and notes receivable with
        implicit interest, 295-296
Retained earnings, 40, 51, 60-62, 516-518
    capitalization of (in case of stock split), 521-522
Revenue, defined, 48, 192
Revenue recognition, 5, 10, 191-210, 715
    on collection of cash (instalment basis), 199-200,
        206-207
    on completed production, 199, 203-204
    criteria, 196-197, 563
    on percentage of production completed, 198, 204-
        206
    and reliability, 196-197
    on sale, 199, 201-203
    selected industry problems, 207-210

S

Sales returns, 282-284
Sears Roebuck & Co., 518
Seagram Co. Ltd., 556
Securities and Exchange Act (1934), 17
Securities and Exchange Commission (SEC), 16
Securities markets (stock market) and accounting
        information, 14-15
    See also Research in accounting
Self-sustaining foreign operations, 683-684
Shareholders' equity, 486
Sinking fund; *See* Cash
Society of Management Accountants of Canada, 19
Spinoff, 518
Standard-setting, 15-18
Start-up costs, 397-398
Statement of changes in financial position; *See*
        Changes in financial position
Statement of financial position; *See* Balance sheet
Statements of financial accounting concepts (SFAC)
        of the FASB, 17

Statements of financial accounting standards (SFAS):
    No. 2 (research and development costs, 1974), 397
    No. 19 (oil and gas exploration costs, 1977), 395
    No. 48 (revenue recognition when right of return exists, 1981), 285n.
    No. 53 (revenue recognition in the motion picture industry, 1981), 208n
    No. 60 (revenue recognition in insurance, 1982), 209n
    No. 106 (accounting for postretirement benefits other than pensions, 1991), 460-461
Stock dividends: *See* Dividends
Stock options, 524-528, 531-532
Stock rights, 530
Stock splits, 519-520
Stock warrants, 530, 531-532
Stocks:
    versus flows in accounting, 49-50
    See also Common stock; Preferred stock; Treasury stock
Substance over form, 294-295
Surplus; *See* Retained earnings

T

"T-accounts," 83
    See also Ledgers
Taxable income versus reported income:
    allocation (inter-period)/deferral, 443-450
    temporary versus permanent differences, 442-443
Taxes, income, recognition issues, 421
Time value of money, 237-249
    tables, 751-759
    See also Future value; Present value
Transaction versus economic event 41, 87-88
Treasury stock, transactions in, 491-493
Trial balance:
    adjusted, 96
    post-closing, 96, 100
    pre-closing, 96, 97
    unadjusted, 96

U

Uncollectables: *See* Accounts receivable
Unearned revenue, 39
Usefulness of accounting information, 5, 232, 234
Users of accounting information, 2, 3
    See also Creditors; Employees; Investors; Managers

V

Value in accounting 232
    See also Accounts receivable; Assets; Current cost; Historical cost; Intangible assets; Liabilities; Market values; Marketable securities; Net realizable value or output value; Notes payable and receivable; Present value; Property, plant and equipment

W

Warranty obligations, 201-203
    recognition issues, 421, 715
Window dressing, 303
Working capital:
    defined, 630
    statement of:
        and fundamental equation, 631
        as substitute for statement of changes in financial position, 630-633
Worksheet for balance sheet and income statement, 143-145